# Free Trade and Sailors' Rights in the War of 1812

D1231103

PAUL A. GILJE
*University of Oklahoma*

Amigo Jap
"Free Trade and Sailors'
Rights!
Your Amigo
Paul A. Gilje
Pablo

CAMBRIDGE
UNIVERSITY PRESS

CAMBRIDGE UNIVERSITY PRESS
Cambridge, New York, Melbourne, Madrid, Cape Town,
Singapore, São Paulo, Delhi, Mexico City

Cambridge University Press
32 Avenue of the Americas, New York, NY 10013-2473, USA

www.cambridge.org
Information on this title: www.cambridge.org/9781107607828

First published 2013

Printed in the United States of America

*A catalog record for this publication is available from the British Library.*

*Library of Congress Cataloging in Publication Data*

Gilje, Paul A., 1951–
Free trade and sailors' rights in the war of 1812 / Paul A. Gilje.
    p.   cm.
Includes bibliographical references and index.
ISBN 978-1-107-02508-0 (hardback) – ISBN 978-1-107-60782-8 (pbk.)
1. Unites States – History – War of 1812.   2. United States – Foregin relations – 1783–1815.
3. United States – Commerce – History – 19th century.   4. Mottoes – United States –
History – 19th century.   5. Free trade – United States – History – 19th century.   6. Sailors –
United States – Social conditions – 19th century.   7. Impressment – History – 19th century.
I. Title.
E354.G464   2012
973.5′2–dc23        2012014474

ISBN 978-1-107-02508-0 Hardback
ISBN 978-1-107-60782-8 Paperback

# Free Trade and Sailors' Rights in the War of 1812

On July 2, 1812, Captain David Porter raised a banner on the USS *Essex* proclaiming "A free trade and sailors' rights," thus creating a political slogan that explained the War of 1812. Free trade demanded the protection of American commerce, while sailors' rights insisted that the British end the impressment of seamen from American ships. Repeated for decades in Congress and in taverns, the slogan reminds us today that our second war with Great Britain was not a mistake. It was a contest for the ideals of the American Revolution, bringing together the high culture of the Enlightenment to establish a new political economy and the low culture of the common folk to assert the equality of humankind. Understanding the War of 1812 and the motto that came to explain it – free trade and sailors' rights – allows us to better comprehend the origins of the American nation.

Paul A. Gilje is a George Lynn Cross Research Professor in the Department of History at the University of Oklahoma. He holds an M.A. and Ph.D. from Brown University and has held fellowships at Johns Hopkins University and Washington University in Saint Louis. Gilje is the author of *The Road to Mobocracy: Popular Disorder in New York City, 1763–1834*; *Riots in America*; *Liberty on the Waterfront: Society and Culture of the American Maritime World in the Age of Revolution, 1750–1850*; and *The Making of the American Republic, 1763–1815*. *Liberty on the Waterfront* received the 2004 Society for Historians of the Early American Republic Best Book Prize and the 2004 North American Society for Oceanic History John Lyman Book Award in the category of United States Maritime History. Professor Gilje has organized an adult civics program in the state of Oklahoma, consulted for museums, edited several books, and lectured widely in Europe and America. Throughout his career he has sustained an interest in how common people have been affected by the larger events of history.

*To Gordon S. Wood*
*Friend and Mentor*

# Contents

# Acknowledgments

As I have indicated in the Introduction, this book emerged while I was working on another book at the C. V. Starr Center for the Study of the American Experience, Chestertown, Maryland, in November 2008. For this opportunity to spend a month on the Maryland eastern shore I thank Adam Goodheart; Hodson Trust-Griswold, director of the center; Jill Ogline Titus, associate director; Michael Buckley, program director; and Jenifer Emiley, center coordinator. I owe also a special thanks to President Baird Tipton of Washington College and the crew of the *Sultana*, a re-created schooner from the eighteenth century, for a daylong cruise aboard the *Sultana* on the Chester River. I thank, too, Adam and Jill and the crew of the *Pride of Baltimore II* for a second sail on the Chester River on a tall ship built on the model of a War of 1812 privateer.

The long essay I wrote that November became the basis of my presidential address for the Society for Historians of the Early American Republic, which, thanks to Illinois State Historian Thomas F. Schwartz and SHEAR Conference coordinator Craig Friend, I delivered from the podium in the Old State House in Springfield, Illinois, on July 19, 2009. The thrill of speaking from the same platform used by Abraham Lincoln for his house-divided speech was matched by the enthusiastic response of my many friends and supporters within SHEAR. If I had any doubts about my decision to write this book, they quickly evaporated amid the encouragement I received that evening and the subsequent chants of "Free Trade and Sailors' Rights" at the banquet later that night. Indeed, that rowdy response, and the many notes I have received since with the phrase or versions of the phrase as a tag line, has further convinced me that there was something peculiarly catchy in Porter's motto that helps to explain its popularity during the War of 1812 and in the decades that followed.

The fall of 2010 brought me under the shadow of Adam Smith with a semester of teaching at the University of Glasgow. I thank Simon Newman for organizing this visit to Scotland and helping me arrange a series of lectures in the United Kingdom and France where I could share my ideas on the War of 1812. That fall I presented papers at the American Studies Seminar at the University of Glasgow (hosted by Marina Moscowitz); the Early American History Seminar at the University of Edinburgh (hosted by Frank Cogliano); the Rothermere American Institute, Oxford University (hosted by Peter Tuck); the Centre d'Etudes Nord-Américaines, L'ecole des Hautes Etude en Sciences Sociales, University of Paris (hosted by Pierre Gervais); and the Institut Charles-V, Paris Université Diderot-Paris (hosted by Allan Potofsky). I also delivered the Carolyn Robbins Lecture in Eighteenth-Century History at the Institute for the Study of America, University of London (hosted by Iwan Morgan). In each instance I was graciously received and enjoyed the challenge of questions from non-American audiences. More recently I presented some of my ideas on free trade and the origins of the War of 1812 on the American side of the Atlantic at the Boston Area Seminar on Early American History at the Massachusetts Historical Society, where my commentator was Drew McCoy and where I was hosted by Conrad Wright and Alan Rogers.

I owe a great professional debt to the many historians who have written on the early republic before me. The more I learned about the complexities of early American diplomacy, the more dependent on the work of others I became. My notes only begin to account for that debt. My editor at Cambridge, Lewis Bateman, has been especially supportive. When I first discussed this book with him and suggested that I would like to put off another book project until I had completed this work, without batting an eye he said that Cambridge would publish this book as well as the book I had signed on to write. Of course, the final manuscript still had to go through the normal peer review process, and I therefore thank the two anonymous readers who supported its publication. Also of assistance in preparing this book for publication at Cambridge University Press were Anne Lovering Rounds and Shaun T. Vigil. I thank, too, the copy editor of the book, Russell Hahn, for his keen eye and able pencil in correcting my prose.

In the final stages of completing the book I began rounding up the illustrations. Several individuals were helpful in this process. Nicholas West graciously offered the rights to his wonderful painting, John Archibald Woodside's *We Owe Allegiance to No Crown*, for the cover of the book and provided some additional assistance with the illustrations. I also thank Kristin Smith of the National Portrait Gallery; Bonnie Lilienfeld of the National Museum of American History; Paul J. O'Pecko of G. W. Blunt White Library, Mystic Seaport; Irene Axelrod and Christine Bertoni of the Peabody Essex Museum; Melanie Correia of the New Bedford Whaling Museum; and Frank Arre and Caitlin Schettino of the Naval Historical Foundation. I also owe a special thanks to Sherwin Tobayan for assistance with some of the photography.

The dedication of this book is to Gordon S. Wood, my mentor from graduate school. Gordon did not read a word of the book before it was published, and I am not sure whether he would approve of everything I write, yet his influence is on every page. Although part of that influence is reflected in the interpretation presented here, it is mostly reflected in my effort to think boldly and across great sweeps of time. Whether I have succeeded in this I will allow the reader to judge. Regardless of that success, I offer the dedication as testimony to my great respect for Gordon and the model of scholarship he has established.

This book represents an important bridge between teaching and research. In 2002 I began to teach in a master's program in international affairs offered by the University of Oklahoma on military bases overseas. This has been a wonderful experience, providing multiple trips to Europe and introducing me to many exceptional individuals in the American armed forces. I want to thank these students not only for serving their country, but also for responding so positively to the course I was offering. They nurtured in me an interest in the origins of American foreign policy that I took to the classroom in Norman, where, encouraged by my undergraduate students in Oklahoma, I probed more and more deeply into the subject until I felt compelled to write this book. I also want to thank the Glaswegian students who enrolled in my class on the early republic in Scotland. Taken together, these graduate and undergraduate students, now numbering in the hundreds, have contributed significantly to what I have written.

It has been my great fortune to work in the History Department at the University of Oklahoma for more than thirty years. The university is blessed with a great administration, including President David Boren, Provost Nancy Mergler, and Dean of the College of Arts and Sciences Paul Bell, who expect their faculty to be good teachers while also supporting innovative research. Within the History Department, Rob Griswold has not only been a superb chair, but has also been my good friend with whom I have shared so much in the years since we both arrived on campus in 1980. Several colleagues have heard me rant and rave over this project in the last few years, but I would especially like to single out Cathy Kelly, Josh Piker, and Fay Yarbrough, who have probably heard more about free trade and sailors' rights than they had ever expected. I have also been lucky enough to have had several able graduate assistants who have aided me in my research. These include Robert Barnett, Patrick Bottiger, Dan Flaherty, and Billy Smith. Robyn McMillin, who completed her dissertation under my direction a few years ago, has aided me in a number of ways. I will also mention three university colleagues, none of whom studies anything remotely close to history, who have heard me talk of this project on our noontime runs. Thanks, then, to Fred Carr of the School of Meteorology and David Sabatini and Randy Kolar, both of the School of Civil Engineering and Environmental Science, for being such good friends for so many miles.

The center of my life remains my family. As I get older, I think of how important my brother and sister, Stephen Gilje and Kathleen Gilje, are in my life even though they live far away. Words cannot express how excited I am about what wonderful adults my children, Erik and Karin, have become. I owe my greatest debt, always, to my wife and life partner, Ann. Thank you, Ann, for being there.

# Introduction

On July 2, 1812, Captain David Porter sailed the United States Frigate *Essex* out of New York harbor. From the "foretopgallant mast was hoisted a white flag, with these words 'A free trade and sailors rights.'" Porter's cruise was short and incredibly successful. In seventy days he captured ten prizes, including the outgunned HMS *Alert* – the first British warship to surrender to an American vessel during the War of 1812. This achievement was the beginning of a series of spectacular victories won by the American navy during the opening years of the conflict. When Porter returned to the United States, he was greeted with praise as his sailors poured into Philadelphia's taverns with pockets bulging with prize money. The British, on the other hand, were irate. Porter had disguised the *Essex* as a merchantman and lured the inferior twenty-gun *Alert* into range. He had then opened the frigate's gun ports and unleashed a devastating broadside. The uneven battle lasted about eight minutes and, along with the deception, made Porter appear ungentlemanly from the British perspective.[1] As a result, Sir James Yeo of the *Southampton*, which was a frigate of equal strength to the *Essex*, publicly issued a challenge. During the bravado that accompanied the exchange, Yeo requested a passenger from a captured brig "to present his compliments to Captain PORTER," declaring that he "would be glad to have a *tete a tete* anywhere between the Capes of Delaware and the Havanna, where he would have the pleasure to break his own sword over his DAMNED HEAD and put him down forward in irons." Porter, who like other American naval commanders believed in the punctilio of the *code duelo*, responded by returning his compliments to Sir James Yeo, and with tongue in cheek accepted "with pleasure his polite invitation." Asking to meet nearer the Delaware Capes, Porter pledged "his honor to Sir James that no other vessel shall interrupt their *tete a tete*." Porter, in an effort to make it plain that he would not disguise the

ILLUSTRATION 1. Frigate *Essex* by Joseph Howard. Sleek and fast, the frigate *Essex* began its career in the U.S. Navy as a subscription ship during the Quasi War. It was the first American naval vessel to enter the Indian Ocean and served in the Mediterranean during the Barbary Wars. At the beginning of the War of 1812, its commander, Captain David Porter, ran up a banner proclaiming "Free Trade and Sailors' Rights." Under that standard, the *Essex* wreaked havoc on the Pacific whaling fleet in 1813, and on March 28, 1814, the British captured the frigate in a desperate battle off the coast of Valparaiso, Chile. Photo courtesy of the Peabody Essex Museum, Salem, Massachusetts.

*Essex* this time, declared that his frigate "may be known by a Flag bearing the motto – *Free Trade and Sailors Rights*."[2]

This simple banner with which Porter sought to identify his ship created an important political slogan that encapsulated for many Americans the very meaning of the War of 1812. Other mottos from the era have had greater staying power in our history textbooks – phrases like Captain James Lawrence's "Don't give up the ship" and Commodore Oliver Hazard Perry's "We have met the enemy, and they are ours." These mottos may have resonated as battle cries or as a way of trumpeting military heroics for later jingoistic generations. But they did not carry the political potency of "Free Trade and Sailors' Rights" at the time.[3] Porter's first voyage and the exchange with Yeo were played out before a national audience, since they were reported in newspapers across the nation. For the remainder of the War of 1812 the phrase "Free Trade and Sailors' Rights" helped to define the aims of the Madison administration.

More importantly, common people – especially common people attached to the sea – embraced the motto as their own, and the slogan would appear and reappear for decades in many different circumstances and with a variety of different meanings.

Why, then, did "Free Trade and Sailors' Rights" have such resonance for the American people? The answer lay in how each of the two elements within the phrase – "Free Trade" and "Sailors' Rights" – represented important aspects of the Revolutionary heritage from the eighteenth century and reflected the melding of both high and low cultures in a unique way that rejected the traditional order of the Old World. In short, by joining these two different strains in one phrase Americans demonstrated the success of their revolution. Herein lies the true meaning of Porter's response to Yeo. On the surface Yeo's challenge was the more offensive and demonstrated an abrasiveness not immediately apparent in Porter's response. After all, Yeo promised not only to defeat Porter, but also "to break his own sword over his DAMNED HEAD and put him down forward in irons." Such treatment would have denied Porter the honors of war owed to an officer and a gentleman. Porter replied with more decorum – at least on the surface – by merely stating that he accepted the challenge and promised that no other ships would interfere. But he also declared that he would have that banner with "Free Trade and Sailors' Rights" emblazoned upon his masthead. Porter thereby declared his intention to defend his honor, the honor of his sailors, and the honor of his nation. More importantly, the *Essex* would be fighting for the Revolutionary ideals that reflected both those on the top and those on the bottom of society. To leave no doubt about his intentions to defend the American Revolution, Porter ended his response with the statement that if he was forced to surrender to Yeo, then he would "deserve the treatment promised by Sir James."

This book explores the full cultural meaning of the phrase "Free Trade and Sailors' Rights" in an effort to understand the central role of the War of 1812 in American history. Or, as one of my colleagues so pithily remarked as I explained the project, I am providing "meaning to a meaningless war." Too often the second war between the United States and Great Britain has been portrayed as an accident and merely a footnote to the longer narrative of our nation's history. At best it has been considered a second war for independence. More often, as Don Hickey's examination of the conflict explained, it has been viewed as a forgotten war, known more for catapulting Andrew Jackson to national prominence than for any tangible result.[4] In fact, the war has held a much greater significance for Canadians, who view it as their war for independence from a would-be conquering behemoth to the south. Perhaps, as the spate of new books on the War of 1812 appear in time for a commemoration of its bicentennial, we will come to a greater appreciation of its importance. More likely, our interest will be piqued for a few years only to lapse as we focus on the next anniversary. If Americans in the twentieth and twenty-first centuries forget the war, relegating it to a few short pages in college textbooks, Americans living in the first half of the nineteenth century saw it differently. Before the Civil War, the War of 1812 loomed large as a moment when the nation stood steadfast in the defense of ideals inherited from their revolution.

I began this book almost accidently in an eighteenth-century customs house overlooking the Chester River on the Maryland eastern shore.[5] History and the historian combined in an odd twist of irony. Sitting at a desk in the library in a building that is a relic of the British North American empire, I started to write about a slogan that included the phrase "Free Trade." I was also pulled toward the Chester River, which I could see from the windows of the library. I was fortunate enough to combine my interest in history and my attraction to sailing by going on two cruises of the river aboard historic replica tall ships. However limited and vicarious these experiences were – I briefly took the tiller of one vessel, and helped haul in the sails along with the other tourists on the other – they left a lasting impression and provided a waterside view of the river and the Custom House. Both vessels were schooners that were constructed for speed and maneuverability. One was on the *Sultana*, based on the design of a vessel built in 1767. The original *Sultana* had been used by the British to enforce the customs regulations that helped to trigger the American Revolution. The other was on the *Pride of Baltimore II*, a larger vessel and a topsail schooner modeled after the privateers for which its namesake city was famous – or infamous, from the British perspective – during the War of 1812.[6] Although most of the crews of the Baltimore privateers signed aboard for the loot available in this legalized form of piracy, these ships contributed to the fight for free trade and sailors' rights. I did not recognize the historical irony of these two sailing ventures until later, when I realized that these two ships reflected a great sea change in the history of American commerce: the one vessel was a defender of the mercantile system; the other sought to overthrow it.

I also experienced another odd intersection between history and the historian when I spent the fall of 2010, in the midst of writing this book, at the University of Glasgow. That semester I presented aspects of my work at both my host institution and the University of Edinburgh – in the very shadow of Adam Smith. I did not see his ghost, and I couldn't even find his grave – I looked one evening in Edinburgh, but gave up the search as an early twilight was shading into night. I did feel something of his presence, and it was a thrill to think I was talking about free trade at the same institutions at which Smith had taught over two hundred years ago. I also gave papers at several other British and French institutions, which, along with teaching British students about the early American republic and the War of 1812, allowed me to test my ideas on audiences very different from the ones I have encountered in the United States.

From a longer perspective, this book also reflects my own personal odyssey as a historian. I began my career studying riots and writing on the social history of the revolutionary and early national eras. I continued this focus on the common man with a social and cultural portrait of maritime workers. But I also extended my interests, both in the classroom and in print, by examining the relationship between the American Revolution and the rise of capitalism in the United States. In addition, in 2002 I started to teach a short course on the origins of American foreign policy in a masters degree program conducted by the University of Oklahoma overseas. The more I taught this course, the more my interest was piqued by diplomatic history and the importance of the great white men of the Revolution – a turn of events that bordered on sacrilege for a scholar who came of age in the early 1970s and believed in studying history from the bottom up. I found the subject so fascinating that I added an undergraduate course on early diplomatic history to my regular repertoire of offerings. When I wrote a survey of the early republic I decided to integrate these varied interests and to include some aspects of the history of the Founding Fathers in future works even though my focus was further down in society. Thus, I had planned to include an examination of the interaction between the mainstream and maritime cultures in a discussion of the phrase "free trade and sailors' rights" in a chapter in a book on the language of common sailors. I had become intrigued with how seamen used "free trade and sailors' rights" in many different ways during and after the War of 1812 and had hoped that the chapter would allow me to explore how the language of politicians and common seamen intersected. But as I began writing at the Starr Center in Chestertown, Maryland, the manuscript started to get away from me. Perhaps it was the Custom House and the surrounding memorabilia of George Washington. Perhaps it was the view of the Chester River from my windows, or my brief stint sailing on the river. Perhaps it was my growing interest in the rise of capitalism and diplomatic history, spawned in the classroom. For whatever reason, I soon had too many pages for a chapter, and with plenty more to say, I decided that I would write this book on free trade and sailors' rights, combining my long-standing concern with common folk and my newfound interest in the Founding Fathers.

I begin in the first section of this book by examining the ideological origins of the first of two elements embedded in the slogan – the idea behind "Free Trade." Although the phrase "Free Trade" could be used in a variety of ways, it harked back to a new vision of diplomacy that emerged out of the Enlightenment – a vision that promised to end war and conflict between nations and to increase the well-being of all the people in the world. This utopian ideal would be impossible to fulfill, but it reflected the hopes of many revolutionary leaders as they sought to release themselves from the shackles of the colonial system. Free trade also carried a special meaning for the common sailors aboard Porter's ship. They may not have heard of Adam Smith or the rarified ideas about a new diplomacy, but they understood that trade unfettered by restrictions meant jobs and higher wages. Any banner with the words "free trade" thus rallied those from the top as well as those on the bottom of society.

If the first section centers around the highbrow ideas of the Enlightenment and expressions of the Founding Fathers, as well as the personal interests of the common seaman, the second section shifts the focus to issues even more crucial to those further down in society, where a new conception of citizenship included men often thought to be on the margins of society – sailors. Many of their landlubber cousins looked askance at the men who went to sea, viewing them as only tangentially connected to a shore-based community. Sailors were generally poor and frequently misbehaved ashore. Yet they were crucial to the development of commerce and became central in the defense of the nation – both for the Anglo-American empire before independence, and for Great Britain and the United States as separate countries after independence. The assertion of sailors' rights, then, came to represent not only American opposition to British impressment, but also a broadened and more democratic definition of citizenship. That definition, however, was not the exclusive concern of sailors, or even of the common folk. As the political leadership struggled to define the meaning of the American Revolution, issues of citizenship – of who should be protected by the flag of the United States – became important to everyone in society. By raising a banner proclaiming "Free Trade and Sailors' Rights" Porter sent a potent message that his crew and all Americans understood. "Free trade" heralded a crucial value embedded in the American Revolution and insured continued maritime employment in times of peace, while "sailors' rights" informed the crew that the war was to protect them as Americans, and asserted a broad definition of citizenship that spread its guardian wings aboard ships as well as within the nation.

After tracing the two elements of the slogan separately, the third section looks to the causes of the War of 1812. The origins of the war were complex and entailed more than the slogan "Free Trade and Sailors' Rights" waving from Porter's masthead. Indeed, in many ways the roots of the war lay in a sordid expansionism that coveted not only Canada to the north and Florida (which belonged to neutral Spain) to the south, but also the Native American lands in between. For large numbers of Americans the war also had to be fought to sustain the honor of the republic that was being tested by an aggressive, arrogant, and oppressive Great Britain (and maybe France). Whatever the origins of the conflict, the rhetoric during the war emphasized the ideals encapsulated in Porter's motto.

The fourth section examines how the phrase became a key component of the wartime rhetoric. Words matter. There is no question that ideas are important, but in politics the way in which those ideas are packaged can often overshadow the ideas themselves. "Free trade and sailors' rights" was a phrase that carried the right punch, a phrase that simplified while at the same time it explained, a phrase that called upon an important legacy, and a phrase that caught the public's imagination. When he sent his message to Congress outlining his rationale for a declaration of war, James Madison gave several reasons for entering the War of 1812, but he emphasized the repeated British impositions on trade and impressment. Madison proclaimed that "[u]nder pretended blockades, without the presence of an adequate force and sometimes without the practicability of applying one, our commerce has been plundered in every sea, the great staples of our country have been cut off from their legitimate markets, and a destructive blow aimed at our agricultural and maritime interests." And, perhaps with even greater vehemence, he called attention to the thousands of American sailors pressed into the British navy. Madison declared that not only had the British navy committed a "crying enormity" by pressing British subjects from American ships, but also "under the pretext of searching for these, thousands of American citizens, under the safeguard of public law and of their national flag, have been torn from their country and from everything dear to them; have been dragged on board ships of war of a foreign nation and exposed, under the severities of their discipline, to be exiled to the most distant and deadly climes, to risk their lives in the battles of their oppressors, and to be the melancholy instruments of taking away those of their own brethren."[7] However intense and impassioned these words may sound, they are not pithy. But once those same ideas became encapsulated in Porter's motto "Free Trade and Sailors' Rights," the issues of unimpeded commerce and freedom from impressment became the accepted reason for the War of 1812. Echoed from the halls of Congress to the damp, dismal prisoner-of-war compound at Dartmoor in southwestern England, "Free Trade and Sailors' Rights" was both a powerful clarion and an assertion of American national identity. The Federalist Party leaders challenged this rhetoric, declaring that there was no need to fight Great Britain over its commercial policy. They also questioned the audacity of the Jeffersonians' claiming to protect the common sailor when for over a decade they had done little to come to a serious settlement on the issue of impressment. Even if the Federalists were right, and the war did not have to be fought, few people remembered that fact after 1815, when the Federalist opposition to the war at the Hartford Convention hinted at secession and appeared unpatriotic. The pathetic inability of the United States to fight the war effectively – a burned capital, failed invasions to the north, an army and militia that repeatedly lost on the battlefield, a national government barely able to sustain its military in the field, near national bankruptcy, and a breakdown of the banking system – all evaporated in the aura of a peace that settled nothing and a battlefield victory in New Orleans that was fought after a treaty had been signed.

Slogans can often have a life of their own. "Free trade and sailors' rights" became deeply imbedded in both the American maritime and mainstream cultures. What counted was how Americans remembered the war, not what actually happened. And here memory as something constructed and sustained becomes important. Americans remembered Porter's motto as a symbol of how the United States had faced a powerful enemy, survived, and thereby defined a burgeoning sense of nationhood. The fifth section of the book therefore examines how a few words of political rhetoric could be freighted with many and varied meanings after the War of 1812. Scholars have examined the importance of the memory of the American Revolution in the nineteenth century and the memory of the Civil War for generations of Americans, but have overlooked the War of 1812.[8] In the immediate aftermath of the war James Madison and the Republicans denied reality and asserted a victory that became embedded in the collective memory of the nation. Americans believed this fiction even if the Treaty of Ghent ignored free trade and sailors' rights. If a sense of relief at having survived the conflict and the triumph of the Battle of New Orleans, combined with a rising sense of American nationalism, explains much of the success of this effort to claim victory, another reason for this historical amnesia concerning the disastrous nature of the war can be found in the diplomatic efforts after the war to secure Americans from impressment and the continued importance of free trade on both the diplomatic and the domestic scene. In other words, the dream of revolutionary foreign policy persisted and was in many ways fulfilled as American diplomats sought to defend neutral rights, assert free trade by limiting mercantilist restrictions, and protect sailors aboard American ships.

During the 1820s and 1830s the memory of the War of 1812 merged with the memory of the Revolutionary War to provide a powerful argument for the democratization of society and politics in the United States. Although Americans continued to lionize the great leaders of both conflicts, they also trumpeted the heroism of the foot soldier and ordinary sailor. For the generation of the 1830s and 1840s, George Washington and the Continental soldiers at Valley Forge, as well as Andrew Jackson and his Tennessee Volunteers, were remembered for their sacrifices in war. So, too, John Paul Jones, Stephen Decatur, and their crews were viewed as a part of the pantheon of American heroes. Within this context a slogan that declared that the War of 1812 had been fought for principles linked to the American Revolution retained a resonance that lasted into the 1840s. For common folk, although at times they could use "free trade and sailors' rights" in self-mocking humor, the phrase continued to be significant after the War of 1812. But within a decade the original meaning weakened as Porter's motto appeared in many contexts, from change bills to advertisements. Politicians of all stripes could push and pull the slogan in all kinds of directions, including, in an amazing contradiction of terms, using it in defense of tariffs. However stretched and however misused, even in the 1840s the phrase retained some resonance and meaning as an assertion of something that Americans should strive for – the idea that commerce should be unrestricted and, perhaps more importantly, that all men had rights that needed to be protected. Without fully understanding free trade and sailors' rights, we cannot understand the War of 1812 or the legacy of the American Revolution.

# PART ONE

# FREE TRADE

W hy was free trade important to Captain David Porter and his crew? And why did the phrase become a part of both a rallying cry and an explanation for the War of 1812? To answer these questions we need to take a careful look at the concept of free trade in the fifty years before the opening of the nineteenth century. The ideals of the Enlightenment informed a more open revolutionary diplomacy attached to the principle of free trade. That free trade had multiple definitions ranging from commerce without restrictions to a belief in neutral rights. Americans rallied to the call of free trade in its varied and overlapping definitions during the Revolutionary War. As the first American diplomats began to reach out to other nations they hoped to create a new era in international relations by pursuing free trade in terms of both limiting restrictions on trade and pursuing neutral rights. Free trade even underpinned the relations among the individual states and became a vital component of the union in both the Articles of Confederation and the United States Constitution. Despite the sometimes twisted path of American diplomacy, during the 1790s opening commerce with "all the world" on an equitable basis and protecting neutral rights while other nations were at war remained the driving force in the foreign policy of the United States. By the beginning of the nineteenth century enlightened diplomacy and free trade had become embedded into American national identity and reflected patrician ideals of the revolutionary role of the United States on the world stage. For Porter and his crew, as well as for Americans rallying in support of the War of 1812, free trade represented an essential element in the heritage of the American Revolution.

I

# The Enlightenment and Defining Free Trade

In the late eighteenth century, free trade emerged as a crucial concept in political economy and the relationship between nations. Notions of free trade had been discussed for centuries, but the emphasis on reason in the Enlightenment provided a rationale and a new context that enhanced and strengthened the appeal of free trade. The Enlightenment also encouraged a new vision for diplomacy whereby nations would deal equitably and peacefully with one another and free and open commerce might even lead to the elimination of war. The key to this new world order would be free trade. These words, however, as they were used in the years before the American Revolution, had at least five different definitions. First, commentators frequently applied "free trade" to describe the ability to trade freely in any market. Second, and more important to the pre-1776 context, other authors used the phrase to describe opening trade between nations or colonies beyond imperial or governmental restrictions. Third, free trade came to be seen as setting up a reciprocal agreement whereby foreign merchants paid only the customs duties charged to the nation's own merchants. Fourth, pushed to its most extreme form, free trade meant, just as it does today, the absence of trade barriers. Finally, in a not wholly unrelated context, free trade also became associated with neutral rights and the idea that "free vessels make free goods," which meant that during a war no belligerent could interfere with the trade of a neutral power even if that trade was with an enemy nation. Although a modern observer can disentangle these different meanings of free trade, in the eighteenth century writers often used the term with less precision, intermingling, overlapping, and confusing the various definitions of free trade.[1]

Before exploring the meanings of free trade further, we need to understand the intellectual context in which they emerged. Thinkers during the Enlightenment held that everything should be organized along natural principles

discovered through reason. Beginning in the seventeenth century with Isaac
Newton in England and René Descartes in France, enlightened intellectuals
studied nature and applied reason in order to understand the fundamental laws
governing how the world worked. Thus Descartes emphasized observation and
the scientific method in his philosophy, and Newton relied upon mathematics
to develop calculus and study laws of physics such as gravity. The so-called
*philosophes* (philosophers of Enlightenment thought) applied the same principles to a variety of subjects. John Locke wrote about education and man's
ability to learn through his sensations. He also believed in the perfectabil-
ity of humankind and emphasized the importance of natural rights and the
social contract. Writers like Voltaire and Jean-Jacques Rousseau criticized the
old regime in France and argued for a society and government stripped of
anachronisms and based on reason and natural law. Denis Diderot compiled his
*Encyclopédie* to "exhibit ... the Order, Succession, and Connection of all the
Parts of human Knowledge" and to contain "the general Principles, or Funda-
mentals, of every Science, and every Art" and thereby to "assemble knowledge
scattered across the earth, to reveal its overall structure to our contemporaries
and to pass it on to those who will come after us."[2] This compendium became
the touchstone of the Enlightenment search for truth. Thinkers like the Baron
Montesquieu, in the *Spirit of the Laws*, provided a detailed political analysis
comparing governments and legal systems. Laws based on nature and reason
were also thought to lie behind the historical process. Montesquieu and others
saw history as operating in cycles, with societies moving in a line of progres-
sion from hunting and gathering, to pasturage, to agriculture, to commerce and
manufacturing. Governments, too, followed a cycle: beginning as small civil
societies, moving on to become expansive republics, and eventually developing
into monarchical empires. Such cycles repeated themselves. Nations were vigorous and expansive in their youth, powerful and wise in their maturity, but
decrepit and dying in their old age. After a nation expired, new polities would
emerge and begin the process over again. This approach to history meant that
no nation was ever secure and that all must sooner or later decline and fall –
a story told all too well by Edward Gibbon in his history of the Roman Empire.[3]

The Enlightenment also had an impact on views of diplomacy. Traditional
ideas of foreign policy depended on a theory of a balance of power and faith
in what Adam Smith called the mercantile system. Beginning in the late seventeenth century, as Europe moved away from the horrors of religious wars
and civil strife, the ideal of the balance of power gained a certain attractiveness
as each nation-state strove to ensure its future and its sovereignty. Like other
components of the intellectual world in the eighteenth century, the balance-of-
power ideal had an appeal because of its supposed symmetry. If the *philosophes*
spoke of a balance in nature, some Enlightenment thinkers might argue that
there ought to be a balance between states and even empires. These ideas,

combined with the perspective of traditional international power politics, helped to convince European leaders to view trade as just another weapon of diplomacy to be wielded in an effort to gain advantage over competing nations. Tariffs became a stick with which to beat one's opponents and a carrot with which to reward one's allies. Moreover, following the mercantilist's belief in a fixed amount of wealth in the world, every ounce of gold your nation paid to another while engaged in trade diminished the wealth of your own nation. War became a means to tilt the balance of power one way or another, and trade was a way of pursuing war by more peaceful means. European nations thus erected trade barriers and sought colonies, restricting commerce so as to enhance the economic well-being of the metropolis. As Diderot explained, colonies added to the agricultural production of the nation, provided markets for manufactured goods, increased profits from trade, and produced goods for re-export.[4]

Although the notion of a balance of power reflected one strain of the Enlightenment, other *philosophes* saw traditional diplomacy as a part of the *ancien regime* that had best be discarded. For these thinkers, diplomacy had become an art of subterfuge that reflected the corruption of the old order. The balance of power as practiced by the sovereigns of Europe led to war and devastation. In his satire "Political Principle of Rulers," Diderot had a monarch explain his method of operation: "Make alliances... only to sow hatred.... Incite wars among my neighbors and try to keep it going.... Have no ambassadors... but spies...." Even being neutral in a conflict was not altruistic but intended "to profit from the difficulties of others in order to improve one's own situation." As far as Diderot was concerned, wars were caused by "the blind passions of the princes." In this Machiavellian world of monarchs plotting against each other, treaties and alliances became not a means toward peace but rather, in the words of Rousseau, "temporary armistices" and, according to the Abbé Guillaume Raynal, "preparations for treason."[5] Some writers associated these practices with monarchy and believed that republics operated differently. As Montesquieu explained, "The spirit of monarchy is war and expansion; the spirit of republics is peace and moderation."[6] These themes were taken up most famously in the United States during the Revolutionary War by Thomas Paine. In *Common Sense*, Paine lambasted all monarchs as evil. After using the Bible to demonstrate that God had shown in the Old Testament that he was against kings, Paine asserted that "monarchy and succession have laid (not this or that kingdom only) but the world in blood and ashes" and then declared "In England a k – hath little more to do than to make war and give away places; which in plain terms, is to impoverish the nation and set it together by the ears."[7] This critique of traditional monarchy and diplomacy encouraged many thinkers in the eighteenth century to advocate more honest relations among nations. Embedded in the Enlightenment was a faith in nature and reason that shifted the way intellectuals viewed states. For many eighteenth-century *philosophes*, states no longer were to be identified with a crown or a royal family. Instead, they were best seen as comprised of a people. And if the people were unconstrained by the whims of a sovereign, or so the optimistic *philosophes* believed, they would naturally and reasonably be peace-loving. In short, without the jealousies of monarchs, a new world would emerge – one without war.[8]

Central to this understanding of the relations between nations was the role of commerce. Prosperity flowed from commerce, which was "the science of the needs of others," and was based on communication. Through communication came understanding, which in turn would lead to a global fraternity. The French economist Victor de Riquetti, marquis de Mirabeau, wrote that commerce "would benefit, foreigners as well as fellow citizens" and declared that "[e]verything in the universe is commerce because by commerce one must understand all the natural and indispensable relationships of the entire species, which are, and will always be those between one man and another, between one family, one society, one nation and another."[9] The economist Isaac Gervaise took this idea a step further with words that reflected the balance prized by enlightened thinkers by declaring "[t]hat if Trade was not curbed by Laws, or disturbed by those Accidents that happen in long Wars...Time would bring all trading Nations of the World into that Equilibrium, which is proportioned, and belongs to the number of their Inhabitants."[10] Diderot thought that war between commercial nations was impossible, since it "is a fire that destroys them all." Commerce would become the most important arena for action among states: "The time is not far off when the sanctions of rulers will extend to the individual transactions between the subjects of different nations, and when bankruptcy, whose impact can be felt at such immense distances will become affairs of state... and the annals of all peoples will need to be written by commercial philosophers as they were once written by historical orators." Diderot's "universal society" existed "for the common interests and the reciprocal interests" of men. Communication increased their happiness, and commerce was an "exercise of this precious liberty, in which nature has called all men to place their happiness and even their virtue."[11]

Some intellectuals disagreed with the more optimistic view of the ameliorative effects of commerce on world peace and believed that through the jealousy of trade, commerce could lead to war. David Hume argued that "states which have made some advance in commerce" become suspicious of others, coming to consider "all trading states as their rival, and to suppose that it is impossible for any of them to flourish, but at their expence."[12] Adam Smith decried both monarchs and merchants as causes of war. While recognizing that commerce "ought naturally to be, among nations, as among individuals, a bond of union and friendship," Smith argued that it had "become the most fertile source of discord and animosity," because merchants had convinced each nation "to look with an invidious eye upon the prosperity of all the nations with which it trades, and to consider their gain as its own loss." Adam Smith believed that "[t]he capricious ambition of kings and ministers has not, during the present and preceding century, been more fatal to the repose of Europe, than the impertinent jealousy of merchants and manufacturers," whom he believed were driven by a "mean rapacity" and "monopolizing spirit."[13]

Putting aside the qualms of writers like Hume and Smith, those who espoused the positive vision of a new diplomacy argued that diplomats needed to avoid subterfuge and to emphasize honesty. Indeed, many Enlightenment thinkers believed that relations between all humans should be open and that a person's inner being should be reflected in his behavior. In the eighteenth century, when an individual was described as sentimental, the person was not considered emotional or nostalgic. Instead, to be sentimental was to be transparent – in a positive way – and to wear one's sentiments – the inner self – on one's sleeve. In the same manner, many Enlightenment writers argued for a more "frank and open" diplomacy. All alliances and treaties became suspect, since they were concerned with gaining an advantage. If nations followed the precept of "sentiment" and dealt with each other without stealth, everyone would benefit. Mirabeau wrote that the prince who is "the Friend of Mankind" is one who has his "actions and opinions . . . all plainly to be seen and whose policies are in full public view." Following an open diplomacy, there would be no secret provisions compelling one nation to go to war if its ally engaged in a conflict. In fact, there would be no secrets and no war.[14]

As Enlightenment thinkers asserted universal ideals that ran counter to the anachronistic barriers of the past, some even came to attack the barriers created by borders. The first step in this process was to combine an understanding of politics and economy – political economy – and to argue that tariffs were unnatural and unreasonable and made no sense in an enlightened world. By the mid eighteenth century Europe was abuzz with these ideas, which were pushed by a group of French writers known as physiocrats, who held that true wealth could be found only in land and that the state should remove all obstacles to agricultural production, including, in France, internal duties. Other writers began to extend the idea of limiting restrictions to international relations. From this perspective, commerce should not be a diplomatic wedge to drive nations apart; instead, commerce should be a universal cement binding nations together. In other words, merchants shared a common interest separate and distinct from the monarch's that transcended borders. As the French playwright Michel-Jean Sédaine explained in his *Le philosophe sans le savoir*, merchants did not serve any one nation; rather, they were citizens of the world and at the service of humanity. It is in this context that Adam Smith famously attacked the mercantile system and argued that the greatest good for all mankind would result from free and open trade between nations.[15]

The Enlightenment challenged the way most nations did their diplomatic business in the eighteenth century. Central to this challenge was the ideology of free trade. The concept of free trade, however, had important roots beyond and prior to the Enlightenment. In the seventeenth century, the Dutch writer Hugo Grotius published his *Mare Liberum*, the *Free Sea*, arguing that the oceans were international avenues for trade and should be opened to all nations in order to attack the supposed monopoly of trade in the East and West Indies by the Portuguese and Spanish.[16] Thus, even in the seventeenth century there were some people who called for "free trade" or "economic freedom." A few English commentators believed that the success of the Dutch in trade was a result of their "natural liberty." In fact, the English government passed restrictions on trade – the Navigation Acts – to stave off Dutch competition. Although most people in the English Atlantic world accepted the Navigation Acts and considered them an important protection for national commerce, in the second half of the seventeenth century some West Indies governors and some merchants in colonial North America used the example of the Dutch to argue for getting rid of restrictions. This position was especially prominent in New York, which had previously been the Dutch colony of New Netherlands. By 1700 the arguments were less centered on the Dutch example and more focused on the advantages to trade that would result from fewer restrictions. In New York, most of the calls for economic freedom came from the smaller merchants who had a more difficult time competing against larger merchants who could operate within the imperial system with greater ease. Several factors made free trade even more appealing after 1713. These included increased productivity and more exports as well as changes in the definition of neutral shipping that moved from an emphasis on the origins of the goods to the origins of the ship. There was also the sense that economic freedom was connected to the changing ideas about liberty following the Glorious Revolution.[17]

If there was some discussion of free trade before the Enlightenment, rooted in pragmatic concerns over trade and personal self-interest, the Age of Reason provided an intellectual rationale that covered these more base motives with a polished veneer, adding an ideological luster to the principle of free trade. Like any good laquer applied to a piece of wood, this veneer enhanced the natural grains of the argument and increased its attractiveness. Those grains, however, ran along several different lines, sometimes crossing and joining with one another, and at other times pursuing separate paths. Perhaps the best way to understand free trade in its varied meanings is to trace the individual grains – the different definitions of free trade – and examine how the phrase was used before American independence.

The generic meaning of free trade as any unregulated financial transaction – either domestic or foreign – surfaced a number of times before the

Revolutionary War. At the end of the Townshend Duties controversy, several authors used the term "free trade" to describe the resumption of normal commerce. Thus a popular meeting in Charleston, South Carolina, voted to resume "a free trade as usual" with Great Britain, and from the other side of the Atlantic in Portsmouth, England, a correspondent wrote, "We are assured, that in confidence of a free trade with the colonies, goods are now shipping for America by the merchants of this city."[18] In both cases free trade meant simply that trade between Great Britain and the North American colonies had been reopened and was no longer hindered by the non-importation movement organized by colonists resisting imperial regulation. Similarly, in 1774 Loyalist James Rivington published an essay in his *New York Gazetteer* opposing the resistance movement and calling for law and order, labeling the committeemen enforcing local non-importation rules as "ambitious spirits, who are fond of *any* opportunity of giving themselves consequences with the populous" and who had "made a notable stalking horse of the word LIBERTY," fooling "many well meaning persons" with their "specious colouring of their sinister zeal." Thereby "[t]he free trade of the King's subjects was obstructed, property was violated," by a group of "desperadoes" – the Sons of Liberty – who were preventing the free exchange of goods.[19] In short, free trade could mean an open trade between merchants and groups of people with no reference to tariffs and international agreements.

While this more general use of free trade as the freedom to trade in any market was important, more frequently free trade was used to describe foreign commerce outside governmental controls. In this context free trade challenged the mercantile system described by Adam Smith. During the eighteenth century there was a dramatic shift in the ideology of empire. In the fifteenth and sixteenth centuries the ideal empire had been built on the Spanish model of conquest in Mexico and Peru. Through the success of its conquistadores Spain tapped into vast resources of gold and silver and became the richest nation in Europe. By the end of the seventeenth century, however, Spanish power was on the wane, and empires of conquest were seen as hollow and were giving way to empires based on commerce. Commentators like Smith, Montesquieu, Mirabeau, and Hume viewed the idea of conquest and the focus on single extractive products like gold and silver as bad for both the nation and the colonies. Indeed, Smith argued that this situation made the metropolis overly dependent upon the colonies. As William Paterson, the first governor of the Bank of England, explained, the Indies "properly speaking...may be said to have conquered the Spaniards, rather than having been conquered by them."[20] Spain was thus associated with the culture of conquest, much to its ultimate loss, while the French and British saw themselves as having created expansive commercial empires based upon trade. As one English essayist commented in 1783, "The empire of conquest is superceded by that of manufactures, and navigation."[21] If commerce trumped conquest, that commerce, at least initially, had to be regulated. Starting in the mid seventeenth century the English government sought to guide that commerce through its Navigation Acts in order to ensure that its colonies would operate to the benefit of the metropolis. By listing some products as enumerated goods that could be shipped only to England, by insisting that ships trading with the colonies had English or colonial crews and were built within the empire, by channeling imports through England and controlling most aspects of trade – practices similar to those followed by other European powers – proponents of this mercantile system sought to strengthen the crown and enrich the nation.[22]

One threat to the mercantile system and its Navigation Acts came through illegal free trade – smuggling. Smugglers, of course, honed the evading of these restrictions to a fine art on both sides of the Atlantic. Even during wars, trading with the enemy and evading the Navigation Acts persisted. In the French and Indian War, American colonists used all kinds of trickery to sidestep regulations in order to trade with the French West Indies. Sometimes merchant vessels sailed to the French West Indies in complete disregard of the law; at other times, they would use a cartel license to exchange prisoners of war and obtain an illegal cargo while in port. Merchants could even argue that trading with the enemy was good for the country. In 1762 New Yorkers sent a petition to Lieutenant Governor Cadwallader Colden pointing out that trade with the French and Spanish "furnished opportunities of exporting large quantities of British manufactures, the invaluable staple of our Mother Country, and thus of profitably exchanging with our enemy, the luxuries of life, for sugars, a commodity of great and general demand throughout Europe."[23] In 1766 Benjamin Franklin detailed the importance to the Anglo-American economy of illegal trade before the House of Commons, stating that "our merchants compute the imports from Britain to be above 500,000 Pounds" and that only a small proportion of these imports were paid for with North American produce. Franklin then went on to describe an elaborate trade – whether it was legal or not – "to the West-Indies, and sold in our own islands, or to the French, Spaniards, Danes, and Dutch" as well as to the North American colonies and "to different parts of Europe, as Spain, Portugal and Italy." Based on this vast network of trade – which Franklin implicitly argued should be free – colonial merchants collected "either money, bills of exchange, or commodities that suit for remittance to Britain." Thus, "all the profits on the industry of our merchants and mariners, arising in those circuitous voyages, and the freights made by their ships, center finally in Britain."[24] Smuggling was so extensive in the colonies that a government survey in 1760 discovered that the customs agency in North America cost more money to operate than was being gained in revenue. It was in large measure in reaction to this illegal practice of free trade that the British government began to strengthen customs enforcement in the colonies by using more writs of assistance, establishing admiralty courts, empowering the royal navy to seize illicit traders, passing new customs regulations, and purchasing fast and maneuverable schooners like the original *Sultana* of 1767 – all of which contributed to the imperial crisis of the 1760s and 1770s.[25] However, the tradition of illegal trade stretched across the Atlantic, since Englishmen were also well-practiced smugglers. The English aristocracy always had access to French wines both during the many wars with France and in peace, regardless of prohibitions and high tariffs. Adam Smith saw smuggling as a direct outgrowth of commercial regulation that led to a loss of revenue. He wrote, "Those mutual restraints" on trade between France and Great Britain "have put an end to almost all fair commerce between the two nations, and the smugglers are now the principle importers, either of British goods in France, or of French goods into Great Britain."[26] The New York petitioners in 1762 noted that British and Irish merchants had an extensive trade with the Dutch West Indies and the Spanish port of Monte Cristi on the island of Hispaniola; the goods were then channeled to other ports to supply the enemy. Smuggling also occurred during the Revolutionary War, with English merchants stationed in the Dutch West Indies island of St. Eustatia carrying on a brisk trade in arms and supplies with the North American rebels.[27]

If smuggling challenged the mercantile system directly through the illicit action of merchants, in the eighteenth century several colonists called upon Parliament to legitimize the smugglers' commerce and loosen the system of imperial regulation by allowing some free trade. As early as 1726, the New Yorker Cadwallader Colden suggested that duties on goods imported into the colony be decreased, since "the less the Charge upon Trade, the greater the Profit of the Province." He continued: "When Trade is eas'd, the Merchant can carry the Produce of the Country to more Markets, and sell what he Imports for the Use of the People, at a cheaper Rate; by which the Province gains doubly."[28] In 1750, the pamphlet writer Archibald Kennedy attacked the limitations on trade imposed by the Navigation Acts. He declared that "Enumerating our Produce, and confining it to one single Market, is a Solicism in Trade, and the Bane of Industry."[29] Both Colden and Kennedy, however, did not push for a complete overhaul of the mercantile system; rather, they sought a realignment that would include lower duties in order to enhance trade. Fundamental to this approach was the belief that "*Self Interest* is the grand Principle of all Human Actions" and that "No Government therefore can be wise or good, unless the Interests of Individuals is made co-incident with the Interest of the Publick."[30]

Such arguments for encouraging free trade by loosening imperial regulations intensified during the imperial crisis of the 1760s and 1770s. In 1764, although he did not use the phrase "free trade," Stephen Hopkins argued for a lessening, if not a removal, of the high impost duties on French and Spanish sugar shipped into the colonies. He pointed out that the high duties were so prohibitive that they were not being collected and led to "illicit methods to cover the merchants" in continuing the trade, a practice that "the Customs-House Officers have made a very lucrative jobb of shutting their eyes" to the detriment of the king's revenue. Hopkins also indicated that without this illicit trade, colonial merchants would make less money and be unable to buy English products, a loss that "in the end" would "fall on the manufacturers and merchants of the Mother Country."[31] Boston merchants made similar arguments in 1769, pointing out how the fisheries, lumber and shipbuilding, and even their rum trade to Africa were all dependent upon open access to the West Indies, southern Mediterranean, Azores, and Canary Islands markets. They therefore called not only for a repeal of the Townshend Duties and recent customs regulations, but also for a return to the pre-1733 Molasses Act conditions and the "free importation of foreign sugars." The merchants claimed that they were not interested in importing goods that competed with British manufacturers, but that they needed to import wines, sugars, and exotic woods in order to allow their trade to thrive and enable them to pay for British goods. They concluded that "[u]pon the whole, the trade of America is really the trade of Great-Britain herself" and that "any measures that have any tendency to injure, obstruct and diminish the American trade and navigation, must have the same effect upon that of Great-Britain, and in all probability PROVE HER RUIN."[32]

Throughout the imperial debate colonial leaders also argued that previous compliance with the Navigation Acts had been a form of taxation and that if new taxes were to be raised for revenue, then colonial merchants should be allowed to trade with non-English markets. As early as 1765 the Stamp Act Congress had resolved "[t]hat as the Profits of the Trade of these Colonies ultimately center in *Great-Britain*, to pay for the Manufactures which they are obliged to take from thence, they eventually contribute very largely to all Supplies granted there to the Crown."[33] In 1766, the American physician John Morgan wrote in a prize-winning essay on the advantages of "a perpetual union between Great-Britain and her American colonies" that "the whole trade of America to all parts of the globe employs, one year or another, above two thousand sail of English ships, by which treasures of greater wealth are conveyed to Great Britain, than are derived from Mexico or Peru.... From the commodities of America, chiefly manufactured in England, and conveyed through innumerable channels of trade to every quarter of the globe, Great-Britain acquires immense wealth, keeps up a spirit of industry among her inhabitants, and is enabled to support mighty fleets, great in peace and formidable in war." Morgan encouraged Great Britain "to consider the interests of America her own" and to treat the colonists with "equal laws and a free and open commerce." He also suggested that the result would be a "ballance of trade" that would "return more clear money from the American colonies, than can be extorted from them either by armies, taxes or tribute."[34] The Philadelphian

William Hicks made a similar point in 1767 when he wrote that "in the course of our most successful commerce, *Great-Britain* receives nine-tenths of the profit, whilst we are humbly contended with being fed and clothed as the wages of our labour." Hicks also offered a veiled threat that "as men attentive to our own particular interests, we cannot but discover the many advantages which the colonists would necessarily have over their brethren of *Britain*, in the course of a *free uninterrupted commerce*," but assured his readers that "as men of reason and integrity, we do not indulge a wish to enjoy these advantages at the expence of our fellow subjects" and asserted that the colonists "shall ever readily subscribe to such commercial regulations as may enable the inhabitants of Great-Britain and Ireland, to meet us at all foreign markets upon an equal footing."[35]

In an irony that would be repeated in the diplomacy of the early republic, colonial Americans sought to loosen commercial regulations and gain free trade by advocating boycotts, non-importation, and trade restriction as they resisted British efforts to tax the colonies and impose imperial constraints on trade. In 1765 and 1766 merchants in New York, Philadelphia, Boston, and other ports established a non-importation movement intended to put pressure on British merchants in the hope of getting the Stamp Act overturned. Local committees, often supported by boisterous crowds, succeeded in ending most imports until the act was repealed. Resistance leaders met with more mixed results in opposition to the Townshend Duties of 1767. The effectiveness of the non-importation movement varied over time and across locations, and by 1770, just as Parliament repealed all of these new duties except the one on tea, the boycott was beginning to fall apart.[36] The Tea Act of 1773 brought more concerted action. Confronted with the repressive Coercive Acts of 1774, the First Continental Congress agreed that "to obtain redress of these grievances [created by the Coercive Acts], which threaten destruction to the lives, liberty, and property of his majesty's subjects, in North-America, we are of opinion, that a non-importation, non-consumption, and non-exportation agreement, faithfully adhered to, will prove the most speedy, effectual, and peaceable measure." The Congress therefore, "under the sacred ties of virtue, honour and love of our country," agreed to form the Continental Association arranging a timetable to limit trade. Despite, or perhaps because of, this building tradition of limiting commerce in order to put pressure on the British to change policy, the allure of free trade remained.[37]

By the early 1770s a few commentators began to be more explicit in discussing the possible importance of free trade – trade outside mercantilist restrictions – to an independent America. In January 1772 "AN AMERICAN" wrote an open letter addressed to the "good PEOPLE of England, Scotland and Ireland," arguing that the British should seek a union with the colonists and "repeal every unconstitutional law, remove every unreasonable burden, and compromise all matters of dispute." Otherwise the colonists would have to seek independence. Revealing an arrogant belief in the value of what the colonists had to offer, the author added that "[t]he Americans well know their weight and importance in the political scale; that their alliance and the privilege of a free trade with them, will be courted by all the powers in Europe; and will turn the balance in favour of any nation that enjoys it." Indeed, "AN AMERI-CAN" believed that the colonists' "situation is such, their natural advantages so great, and so immense will be their sources of wealth and power, that instead of being subject to any foreign power (as some have vainly imagined) they may soon become the arbiters among nations, and set bounds to kingdoms – be the patrons of universal liberty, and the guardians of the rights of mankind." This author turned to the commercial model of the Netherlands, stating that the Americans would probably "form a government of their own, similar to that of the United Provinces in Holland, and offer free trade to all nations in Europe. This plan will effectually secure the Americans from the invasion of foreign enemies, for it will be in the interest of European powers to prevent one nation from acquiring more interest in America than the rest."[38] Two weeks later these sentiments were repeated in an essay in the same newspaper, cautioning the British that "[t]he insults and oppressions the Americans have suffered has been a school of political wisdom, and have taught them many important lessons. They now see that by one stroke of policy, they can form an independent state, secure from invasion of enemies – this, they can do immediately if they please. 'Tis only by forming a *states-general*, chosen by the provinces, and offering free trade to all nations in Europe, and the thing is compleated. – Let the sons of Britain hear this with profound attention – let them NOW hearken to reason, and follow the dictates of WISDOM."[39]

When resistance to British regulation shaded into rebellion, this interest in free trade as cutting the bonds of imperial restrictions persisted. In 1774, Thomas Jefferson claimed that before passage of the Navigation Acts the colonists in Virginia had "free trade with all parts of the world" as a "natural right" that "no law of their own had taken away or abridged."[40] Even the Loyalist Joseph Galloway, as he argued against the impossibility of resisting the power of Great Britain, suggested that the best way to change British imperial policy was to "[s]how them our incapacity to pay the impositions which they have laid upon us, without more freedom of commerce."[41] After hostilities broke out in the Revolutionary War the Virginia Convention complained that Parliament not only had refused to compromise, but also did "not lay open to us a free trade with all the world."[42] In 1775 John Wilkes gave a speech in Parliament attacking the war against the Americans as unjust and, presuming to speak for the revolutionaries, declared: "if you confine all our trade to yourselves, say they; if you make a monopoly of our commerce; if you shut all other ports of the world against us, tax us not too: if you do, then give us a free trade, such as you enjoy yourselves; let us have equal advantage of commerce; all other ports open to us; then we can, and will cheerfully pay taxes."[43]

As Wilkes's comments imply, discussion of free trade as commerce outside the bounds of imperial restrictions did not necessarily mean doing away with import and export taxes. Thus free trade could also mean lowering imposts and commercial fees as much as possible. During the eighteenth century not only did all European nations have tariffs, many also prohibited foreign merchants from importing certain items, prevented the exportation of other commodities, and practiced discrimination in arranging their charges on shipping. These discriminatory fees often came in the form of tonnage duties that were levied against every ship that entered a port on a per ton basis. A ship's size was measured in tons, and the tonnage duty would thus reflect how much a given vessel could hold. A nation's own merchants would be charged a lower tonnage fee than foreign merchants, thus encouraging their business while making it more difficult for others. There was also discrimination concerning imposts, setting different rates for a nation's own merchants than for those from other countries. In fact, tonnage duties and impost duties became important bargaining chips during negotiations over commercial treaties, with some nations being granted better terms than others. Diplomats referred to the best terms available to foreigners in commercial treaties as "the most-favored nation" provision, which stated that the various trading fees would be the same as those granted to the nation having a commercial agreement with the lowest charges. Seldom, if ever, were those charges the same as those granted to a country's own merchants.

Most discussions of free trade accepted the idea that there would be some duties charged, especially since imposts and other duties on trade were an important component of government revenue. As ideas of free trade began to challenge the mercantile system, the concept of reciprocity started to have greater currency. Reciprocity of trade came to mean that a merchant from a foreign nation would pay the same duties as the nation's own merchants. Thus duties would still be collected and revenue generated, but those duties would be lower and no one would be given an advantage regardless of the country of origin. In a few instances, reciprocity was not just an abstract concept. The English made many efforts to build connections with Scotland before the two kingdoms were united in 1707. Beginning in the sixteenth century some writers, like the duke of Somerset in 1548, wanted to set up a form of reciprocity that would give Scots the right to trade with England "as liberally and frely, & with the same, & no other custome or paimentes therefore then Englishmen, & the Kynges subjectes." The purpose of these rights, which were not granted at the time, would be to integrate the Scots into the English economic world. The Scots themselves would push for these rights after James VI ascended to the English

throne in 1603 (as James I of England) and continued to do so throughout the
seventeenth century. The Act of Union of 1707 granted the Scots this right and
access to colonial trade, establishing reciprocity within the kingdom of Great
Britain.[44] Adam Smith, who was a Scot, suggested that the British government
create a similar policy for the colonies and Ireland and wanted both to be
brought under the same laws and regulations as Great Britain. "The extension
of the custom-house laws of Great Britain to Ireland and the plantations,
provided it was accompanied, as in justice it ought to be, with an extension of
the freedom of trade, would be in the highest degree advantageous to both."[45]
The American Revolution made it impossible to implement this suggestion for
the North American colonies, but created an opening for Ireland. The Irish, who
remained in a subordinate kingdom under the British crown until 1800, sought
to escape commercial restrictions imposed by the British Parliament. In an effort
to mollify the Irish during the American Revolutionary War, in December 1779
the British government granted "free trade" to Ireland, removing restrictions
on exports of woolens and glass and allowing Irish merchants most of the
same commercial access as British merchants.[46] Wilkes and Smith, in essence,
had called for reciprocity between the colonies and Great Britain. Reciprocity,
however, remained an ideal brooded about, and would not be written into any
commercial treaties between foreign nations (as opposed to the related nations
of England, Scotland, and Ireland) until the nineteenth century.

Beyond reciprocity, in the best of all possible worlds, each country could ship
its goods without customs duties and for the benefit of mankind. Although free
trade has long been associated with Adam Smith, ideas concerning free trade
were swirling about Europe before the publication of *The Wealth of Nations*. In
1720 Isaac Gervaise anticipated some of Smith's arguments in his exploration
of world commerce by writing that "[t]rade is never in a better condition, then
when it's natural and free" and that "forcing it either by Laws, or Taxes" is
dangerous. It was therefore best to allow the channels of commerce to follow
their natural paths, since "Man naturally seeks, and finds, the most easy and
natural Means of attaining his Ends, and cannot be diverted from those Means,
but by Force, and against his Will."[47] Baron Montesquieu, in the *Spirit of the
Laws*, questioned national competition in commerce and government market
regulation. For Montesquieu, foreign trade established peaceful relations
among nations: "Two nations who traffic with each other become reciprocally
dependent for if one has an interest in buying, the other has an interest in
selling; and thus their union is founded on their mutual necessities."[48] The
physiocrats took this idea even further by ignoring the distinction between
foreign trade and colonial commerce and by advocating free markets, especially
grain markets. In his essays "Of Commerce," "Of the Balance of Trade,"
and "Of the Jealousy of Trade," David Hume attacked imposts generally as

ILLUSTRATION 2. The author of *The Wealth of Nations*. Although the idea of free trade had been discussed for over a century, we most associate the idea with Adam Smith and his *Wealth of Nations*, which was first published in 1776. Library of Congress, Washington, D.C.

obstructions and argued that the advantage was "proportionable to the art and industry of each nation."[49] In short, by the 1750s and 1760s several French and British writers had begun to question mercantilism and argue for complete free trade.[50]

Adam Smith's *Wealth of Nations* thus reflected a set of ideas that were already in circulation when the book was first published in 1776. Whatever the currency of the idea of free trade by the 1760s and 1770s, the policy has been associated with Smith and *The Wealth of Nations*. Like many Enlightenment figures, Smith sought ways to ensure the greatest good for the greatest number of people and based his analysis in nature and reason. The more he examined the mercantile system, with its complex of tariffs, restraints on trade, drawbacks, bounties, and other artificial barriers to commerce, the more he came to believe that free trade without such impositions would lead to cheaper goods, greater wealth, and prosperity for all. He argued that "[t]he interests of a nation in its commercial relations to foreign nations is, like that of a merchant with regard to the different people with whom he deals, to buy as cheap and to sell as dear as possible." He believed that a nation was "most likely to buy cheap, when by the most perfect freedom of trade it encourages all nations to bring to it the goods which it has occasion to purchase; and, for the same reason, it will be most likely to sell dear, when its markets are thus filled with the greatest number of buyers." In the process he challenged the mercantilist assumption that there was a fixed amount of wealth in the world and that in the aggregate there were winners and losers in commerce, just as there were winners and losers in wars. Smith dismissed the notion that the balance of trade was important: "Nothing, however, could be more absurd than this whole doctrine of the balance of trade, upon which, not only these restraints, but almost all the other regulations of commerce are founded." For Smith, free trade would create wealth, channel it along natural paths, and thereby benefit everyone. "Without any intervention of law, therefore, the private interests and passions of men naturally lead them to divide and distribute the stock of every society, among all the different employments carried on it, as nearly as possible in the proportion which is most agreeable to the interests of the whole society."[51]

Smith, however, was also a realist. Today free traders trace their intellectual heritage back to Smith and argue for unfettered trade. Smith himself was less absolute and believed that private interests were "too strong to allow the restoration of freedom of trade." He wrote: "To expect, indeed, that the freedom of trade should ever be entirely restored in Great Britain, is as absurd as to expect that an Oceana or Utopia should ever be established in it. Not only the prejudices of the public, but what is much more unconquerable, the private interests of many individuals, irresistibly oppose it."[52] As the scholar John E. Crowley points out, Smith "viewed free trade as a direction, not a condition, in which 'statesmen and legislators,' not 'politicians,' could lead their countries, and he recognized that the political process itself made arrival impossible." In other words, free trade was an ideal that should be strived for, but one that might never match reality. Recognizing these limitations, Smith accepted the proposition that reciprocity was the best policy, since he thought that "the goods of different nations" should be "subject . . . to the same duties."[53]

The idea of free trade could be used in yet another context; in the eighteenth century free trade could be defined as the right of neutrals to trade with belligerents during wartime. While not the free trade espoused by Adam Smith or embedded in the idea of reciprocity, the notion that "free vessels, make free goods" had a long history. As early as the thirteenth century the policy of *consolato del mare* – the idea that neutral property on enemy ships was safe from seizure, but that enemy property on neutral ships was not – had become widespread among the Mediterranean maritime states. *Consolato del mare* was a step toward recognizing neutral rights during wartime, but was not as sweeping as the idea that "free vessels make free goods," which provided protection even for enemy goods on neutral shipping. By the mid seventeenth century, Great Britain had adopted *consolato del mare*, while the French followed a more severe policy of seizing all cargo, whether enemy or neutral, when found on an enemy ship. Through hard-nosed bargaining, both the British and the French abandoned the traditional *consolato del mare* and established a new policy based on "free vessels, made free goods" in the Treaty of Westminster in 1655 and the Treaty of St. Germaine-en Laye in 1677. By accepting the idea that free ships make free goods, the French were retreating from their harsher policy, but the British had to concede something as well. The British agreed – at least implicitly – to the idea that enemy ships make enemy goods, meaning that any property owned by neutrals aboard an enemy ship was liable to seizure. During the same period, in treaties in 1654 (Portugal), 1674 and 1686 (the Netherlands), the British accepted the right of the Portuguese and Dutch to trade between enemy ports. At the beginning of the eighteenth century, both Great Britain and France recommitted themselves to the protection of neutral trade in the Peace of Utrecht in 1713, declaring in unmistakable terms "that free ships shall also give a freedom to goods."[54]

Regardless of the level of acceptance or tolerance of neutral trade, nearly all nations believed that contraband was liable to seizure during wartime. The question remained, however, what constituted contraband? Implements of war were, of course, contraband. But what about naval supplies, or even food that was going to be used to supply an army? Nations argued over this question, sometimes spelling out answers in treaties. In the commercial agreement between France and Great Britain signed at Utrecht in 1713, the two nations agreed not to include food, clothing, or even naval stores "either for building or repairing ships" as contraband.[55]

Although the origins of the idea may have been in the power diplomacy of the seventeenth century, neutral rights as expressed in the language of the Treaty of Utrecht, "that free ships shall also give a freedom to goods," also reflected the spirit of the Enlightenment's emphasis on nature and reason. Thus, when the Swiss theorist Emer de Vattel spelled out what he saw as the law of nations, he included a provision for protecting neutral commerce: Vattel wrote that "each nation should be left in the peaceable enjoyment of that liberty which she inherits from nature."[56] If a nation was to have the "peaceable enjoyment" of this liberty, its merchants and ships had to be protected from the depredations of nations at war regardless of destination.

For much of the eighteenth century Vattel's ideals were inoperable in the face of complex alliances that brought nearly every major nation in Europe into every conflict one way or another. Regardless of Enlightenment principles, nations tended to pursue whatever policy suited their needs best in the realpolitik of hard-nosed diplomacy and war. By the mid eighteenth century, Great Britain had shifted its position and rejected the idea that free ships make free goods. Recognizing the role of commerce in maintaining the British empire, the journalist William Horsely explained in 1748 that the "[t]wo great points to be considered" in war "are the preservation of our Trade, and Ruin of that of the Enemy." Few British commentators saw anything wrong with the British navy and privateers engaging in extensive search and seizure of enemy ships and goods, and even of neutrals. During the 1740s and 1750s there was virtually no questioning in Great Britain of the "dubious wartime practice of searching neutral ships for enemy goods."[57] Anglo-Dutch treaties in the seventeenth century may have upheld the free movement of Dutch ships as neutral traders, but to prevent the French from using Dutch shipping during the Seven Years' War the British government issued the Rule of 1756, which stated that any trade prohibited in peacetime should be prohibited during war.[58] The French might complain about the British dictating the terms of international trade, but they were just as willing as the British to impose their own restrictions. Although eager to use Dutch shipping in time of war, in the summer of 1756 the French government issued a *Mémoire Instructif*, informing the Dutch that "[e]very power at war is naturally attentive to prevent its enemies from carrying on a free trade under the protection of neutral colors," and that since "Hollanders are neutral in the present war it is their interest to conform to the regulations of France."[59] During the Revolutionary War, the British again wanted to expand the definition of contraband – goods that could be used to sustain a war – beyond military arms to cover ship's stores such as timber, masts, sailcloth, pitch, tar, hemp, and cordage. As one pamphleteer explained: "We are, of any nation, the best situated for trade; we are the best-provided with good harbours; and we have all the conveniences necessary to become the general mart of the world, and to prescribe laws upon the ocean; whereon, did we only exert our power, we are capable of giving maritime laws upon the ocean to the world."[60]

Ideas of free trade could thus take many forms as Americans began their revolution. Free trade could refer to the opening of any market, ending colonial restrictions, establishing reciprocal agreements, eliminating tariffs, or protecting neutral commerce. Many of these ideas concerning free trade had an ancient lineage, but the ideas of the Enlightenment, especially the belief in a new and open diplomacy, strengthened the appeal of free trade by portraying the concept as essential to the rational and natural world of commerce. However important free trade may have appeared in Enlightenment circles before 1776, by declaring independence and establishing their own government, American revolutionaries created a new political and economic laboratory that would allow them to experiment with free trade and challenge the old diplomatic order by putting theory into practice.

# 2

# The Revolutionary Experience

Revolutionary Americans seized upon the enlightened concept of free trade in its varied and overlapping meanings and the new approach to diplomacy to make them their own. The different uses of free trade spiraling around the Atlantic world before 1775 continued to swirl and interact in the minds of many Americans after the war broke out and during the opening years of the early republic. This interest in free trade arose despite a resistance movement that had advocated boycotts to oppose British imperial regulation and the debate over market controls during the resistance movement and the war. If anything, support for free trade became more intense as Americans discussed how to organize a domestic market economy within the new states, and proclaimed the benefits of free and open commerce for a republican and revolutionary order in international relations. In the minds of most Americans, free trade and enlightened diplomacy became identified with their Revolution.

Use of the phrase "free trade" as an unregulated transaction in a free market appeared in debates over price regulations during the Revolutionary War. Faced with inflation and skyrocketing prices, the Continental Congress waffled on the issue of a free market. Sometimes Congress endorsed price regulation; at other times Congress reversed itself. On April 8, 1778, Congress encouraged the states to set prices, but it then abandoned this position in June, determining that such efforts "are not only ineffectual," but also "productive of very evil Consequences to the great Detriment of the public Service and greivous Oppression of Individuals."[1] There were also a number of regional conventions of states that sought to stem inflation and set prices, and several states passed harsh legislation to enforce price scales, threatening legal action against violators. Increased demands for supplies by the military of all belligerents – American farmers fed the Continental, French, and British armies – and the failure of every state to establish price controls doomed these efforts. For example, when

Connecticut passed draconian price regulation, neighboring Massachusetts did not, compelling Connecticut to repeal its law.[2]

The resolutions of the Continental Congress, regional conventions, and state action led to debates over the role of a free versus a regulated market throughout the United States. Jonathan Trumbull, the conservative governor of Connecticut, warned that without a free market and the high prices it brought, there would be no incentive to produce a surplus, and "the farmer will cease to till the ground for more than is necessary for his own subsistence – and the merchant to risque his fortune on a small and precarious prospect of gain."[3] Both the president of Princeton and a congressman, John Witherspoon believed that "[f]ixing Prices by Law never had nor ever will have any Effect but stopping Commerce and making Things scarce and dear." Supporters of price controls disagreed. Congressman John Armstrong argued that "the Hacknied Maxim that Trade Must alwais Regulate itself, Is in our situation as impolitick as it is arrogant and absurd." Many common folk believed that a free market only lined the pockets of the rich at the expense of the poor. One writer in rural Needham, Massachusetts, declared that New England merchants had decided to "get what you can, no matter how, or who is oppressed and distressed thereby."[4]

The debate over free trade as a free market also triggered violent popular disorder that only intensified the contest. There were at least thirty food riots during the war, where men and (especially) women registered their concern over profiteering caused by an inflationary currency combined with high demand for foodstuffs and wartime shortages. These crowds often claimed that the engrossers of items like bread, tea, coffee, sugar, meat, and salt were Tories, whose behavior they likened to the oppression of British imperial regulations. Crowds therefore physically abused individuals who charged too much for goods and sometimes drove them from the community. Rioters claimed to speak on behalf of the revolutionary cause. One crowd in rural Massachusetts accused a merchant of selling goods at "extravagant prices," a practice that led to inflation and was "very detrimental to the Liberties of America," while women rioters in Fishkill, New York, charged another merchant with making "a prey of the friends of the United States by asking a most exorbitant price" for tea. Other revolutionaries, frequently led by merchants, opposed the price control rioters. Some Bostonians saw efforts to regulate prices as "directly opposite the idea of Liberty," and a town meeting in Providence, Rhode Island, resolved that measures to limit prices "render a Man's House and Store liable to be opened and searched in a Manner most ignominious and unworthy in Freemen." That crowds were willing to use coercion to oppose prices set in a free market only made such efforts an even greater affront to liberty. As New York's provincial congress explained after a price control riot in New Windsor, "In a free country no man ought to be divested of his property, but by his own consent to the laws of the land."[5]

The issue of government control over prices became particularly heated in Philadelphia in 1779, when crowds attacked shopkeepers and radicals created a Committee of Trade to set prices. Neither side in the debate seemed to have a monopoly on the rhetoric of the Revolution. Many merchants opposed these price limits, explaining that "[f]reedom of trade, or unrestrained liberty of the subject to *hold or dispose of* his property as he pleases, is absolutely necessary to the prosperity of every community and to the happiness of all individuals who compose it." Pelatiah Webster declared, "Let *trade be as free as air*. Let every man make the most of his goods and in his own way, and then he will be satisfied. Let every man taste and enjoy the sweets of that liberty of person and property, which was highly expected under an independent government." He asserted that restrictions on trade were "a sad omen to find among the first effects of independence" and reflected "greater restraints and abridgements of natural liberty, than ever we felt under the government we have lately renounced and shaken off."[6] Although the radicals rejected this argument, they felt compelled to offer their own definition of free trade: "The frequent declarations and reasonings" of those "in favour of a *free trade*, are in our opinion delusively applied to cases they have no concern with, unless it can be proved that a right to extort and a power to enforce that extortion is one of the descriptive principles of a free trade, which we deny." Free trade – trading freely – had to be fair trade. "A *free trade* consists in the right of every one to partake of it, and to deal to the best advantage he can, on just and equitable principles, subordinate to the common good; and as soon as this line is encroached on, either by the one extorting more for an article than it is worth, or the other demanding it for less than its value, the *freedom* is equally invaded, and requires to be regulated."[7] According to the radicals in Philadelphia the merchants wanted "freedom to extort," not "freedom of trade." The issue of free trade as trade within unrestricted markets was so explosive that it erupted into a gun battle between radical militia who supported price controls and advocates of free markets defending the house of the merchant James Wilson on October 4, 1779. Several men were killed in the fighting, and mounted troops sympathetic to the merchants had to be used to rout the radicals.[8]

Whatever the debates over unregulated markets during the Revolutionary War, Americans came increasingly to espouse free market ideas and associated this meaning of "free trade" with the heritage of the Revolution. So pervasive was the notion of free trade that even the Philadelphia radicals had to cast their support for price regulation by declaring that free trade was fine as long as it was fair and took into account the common good. This position suggests that many of those who had wanted price controls viewed their actions as temporary expedients dictated by the exigencies of war. After the Fort Wilson riot, price controls lost some of their attraction. By 1780 the Continental Congress had turned its back on price regulation and seemed to embrace the free market.

Many state governments followed suit, at least in regard to domestic commerce. In 1791 "A FARMER" addressed the "Yeomanry of Pennsylvania," conflating free trade in the domestic and international arenas. The essay proclaimed, in the high tones of the Enlightenment worthy of Adam Smith, that "[t]here is a law anterior to civil laws, the support of which ought to be the only object of government. It is the sacred law of PROPERTY: By this, every man has a right to the free disposition of his person, and of goods acquired by his industry as far as he does not injure the rights of others. This principle so simple in itself constitutes the foundation and basis of civil law." The author believed that upon the right to dispose of one's own property "is founded his right to a free, unlimited commerce, or exchange of such property. This liberty is necessary to accomplish the mutual exchange of property amongst men, to satisfy their reciprocal wants. This exchange is a contract purely natural, where the command of property should be free in its most extensive sense. Civil law may intervene to compel the execution of a contract; but it ought not to regulate the conditions or limit the price." The end of this natural right was "[a] perfect free trade" that "will always ensure to the farmer the highest price for his produce, by bringing purchasers of every denomination to his very doors: and by creating a competition between the purchasers, that price will always afford the most just criterion of the real value of property." To try to influence the natural price was an unnatural act that "instead of being an amicable exchange of property, becomes the theatre of little, low, cunning and deception." The supposed farmer then extended his discussion of the domestic economy to the larger issue of free trade on the international scene by lamenting "that the commercial regulations and laws of all the nations in Europe, are founded in error and injustice."[9] Although there were debates over the role of the government in the economy in the 1790s and early 1800s, few commentators would have discussed seriously restricting the free market within the United States by means of price controls, and, as several scholars have demonstrated, the new American republic became increasingly committed to a market economy.[10]

Given the currency and frequency of the use of the language of free trade, and its association with the American Revolution, it should not be surprising to see, on a more prosaic level, the usage of "free trade" as a descriptive term for trading freely in any market in a variety of contexts in the 1780s and 1790s. At the end of the war, the inhabitants of Albany held a public meeting and "unanimously resolved in favour of free trade," which allowed ships arriving from British-occupied New York City "to expose their goods for sale," assuring the Loyalist merchants "protection both in person and property."[11] Similarly, during the 1790s there were several newspaper reports that described the British commercial access to Native Americans living in territory claimed by the United States as having "a free trade with the Indians."[12]

However it might be used within the domestic sphere, free trade retained its greatest resonance on the international front. Recognizing that independence would shatter imperial restrictions, many revolutionaries combined the ideal of free trade with the enlightened vision of diplomacy. This combination and usage helped to cement the developing bonds among revolutionary ideology, the enlightened diplomacy, and free trade. In 1776 Thomas Paine agreed with many of the European *philosophes* and saw Europe as hopelessly committed to the old way of doing things. As he explained in *Common Sense*, "Europe is too thickly planted with kingdoms to be long at peace." Americans therefore had to declare their independence, since "whenever a war breaks out between England and any foreign power, the trade of America goes to ruin, *because of her connection with Britain.*"[13] As republicans, independent Americans could avoid these problems. European thinkers had long associated commerce with republics. Only in republics could the networks of trust essential for free trade be formed, and only in republics did people understand that commerce should be for the benefit of all.[14] Moreover, North America had bountiful resources desired by the rest of the world. A republican government and attractive natural resources in agricultural products, timber, fish, and even iron made for a winning combination. Thus, a new nation without a monarch could move in a different direction based on trade. As Paine explained, "Our plan is commerce, and that, well attended to, will secure us the peace and friendship of all Europe; because, it is the interest of all Europe to have America a *free port.* Her trade will always be a protection, and her barrenness of gold and silver secure her from invaders." Without a king, Americans could simply pursue commerce and be at peace with the world.[15]

This sentiment, which pulled the United States toward a new revolutionary and enlightened diplomacy, was shared by other Americans. In 1775, the Congregational minister Moses Mather argued for opening America's ports. He wrote that "since parliament will have our trade only on terms incompatible with our liberty," the colonies should "welcome all nations to our ports and to a participation of our trade." Like Paine, Mather believed that the united colonies should not enter into any alliances with foreign countries, so that "we may enjoy the commerce of all, without being concerned in the quarrels of any."[16] A few years later, David Ramsay, a South Carolina politician and doctor, explained in a Fourth of July oration that the Revolution opened new prospects for trade: "Our change of government smiles upon our commerce with an aspect peculiarly benign and favourable" because "the wealth of Europe, Asia, and Africa, will flow upon America." With American trade no longer "confined by the selfish regulations of an avaritious stepdame," the United States would "now have a free trade with all the world" and Americans would "obtain a more generous price" for their produce while gaining "foreign goods on easier terms" than was possible when they "were subject to a British monopoly."[17]

The Continental Congress pursued a policy of free trade even before the Declaration of Independence by voting on April 6, 1776, to open American ports to foreign vessels. Although the revolutionaries were unsure what the future might bring, and even hoped that their actions might coerce Great Britain into returning to previous mercantile regulations, by opening the North American ports to all comers, Congress not only took an important step toward independence, but also began to articulate the policy of free trade that came to be identified with the American Revolution.[18] In the summer of 1776, as the new United States contemplated diplomatic relations with the rest of the world, John Adams drafted a model treaty to be sent with Benjamin Franklin on his mission to France. Adams, ever the careful student of history, took note that at the Peace of Utrecht England and France had written a commercial agreement distinct from the treaty that ended Queen Anne's War.[19] Congress supported the idea of separating the issues of war and commerce, believing that if the Americans signed a military alliance with France, they would merely be substituting one European master for another and would continue to be sucked into whatever military conflagrations broke out an ocean away. Combining the practice of distinguishing commercial and military pacts with the Enlightenment ideal that free trade would benefit all and ensure peace and prosperity, Adams proposed to ask France, and then the rest of Europe, for commercial treaties based on reciprocity. The document – sometimes referred to as the Plan of Treaties – sought to have the French pay the same duties in the United States as Americans did, and to have Americans pay the same duties in France as the French did, creating in practice reciprocal free trade. The treaty opened by stating that the people of each country "shall enjoy all other the Rights, Liberties, Priviledges, Immunities, and Exemptions in Trade, Navigation and Commerce in passing from one Part thereof to another, and in going to and from the same, from and to any Part of the World" as those of the other country. On one level, this approach appears incredibly naive. Revolutionary Americans seemed sincerely to believe that the European powers would reject their time-tested diplomacy of advantage in order to gain the benefits of trade with the United States. On another level, the approach is exhilarating in scope in imagining a new international world order.[20]

Of course, reality came crashing down on these utopian hopes. The revolutionary leaders knew that they needed to get tangible assistance from European nations if they had any hope of defeating the British. In its instructions to its delegation to France, the Continental Congress was willing to concede some ground on trade, but revolutionary leaders did not accept the idea that they needed a military alliance until well into the fall of 1776, when the situation on

ILLUSTRATION 3. Franklin in Paris, 1776. When Benjamin Franklin arrived in Paris in December 1776 to represent the United States, he donned simple clothes and, even though he was probably one of the most famous men of his time, posed as a humble American from the land of nature and reason – North America. As the "Quaker" from "Pennsylvania" (Franklin was not a Quaker and had been born in Boston), the lightning tamer appeared the epitome of enlightened diplomacy. Library of Congress, Washington, D.C.

the ground deteriorated and the Continental Army all but disappeared. At that point, Congress revised its instructions and told its representatives in France to obtain military aid. Even with this concession, the American government remained cautious about having any French troops sent to North America. It was more than a year before the French came to a formal agreement with the United States. With at least a nod to the revolutionary diplomatic ideals, the American delegation in France – Benjamin Franklin, Silas Deane, and Arthur Lee – signed two treaties in February 1778. One was a defensive military alliance that all but guaranteed that France would join the war on the side of the United States and assured the French of future cooperation to protect their American possessions. The other was a commercial treaty that did not include reciprocity. The French, however, were not immune to the appeal of Enlightenment values and saw their concessions in the treaty – the most-favored nation clause and the qualified opening up of the French West Indies to American merchants – as a step toward a new type of commercial relationship and the creation of a new civil society among nations.[21]

At the end of the Revolutionary War, American diplomats surprisingly hoped to gain reciprocity with Great Britain during the negotiations for a peace treaty in 1782 and 1783. John Jay included a provision for reciprocity in his preliminary draft of the treaty. Although the British insisted on removing the clause, the earl of Shelburne, who headed the British government at the beginning of negotiations, believed in free trade. He therefore introduced into Parliament an American Intercourse Act that would have opened commerce in both the West Indies and Great Britain to American merchants paying the same duties as their British counterparts. The bill failed, and Shelburne's administration collapsed after being blamed for being too lenient on the Americans. The new British government turned its back on free trade and followed the advice of Lord Sheffield, who argued that "[b]y asserting their independence, the Americans have renounced the privileges, as well as the duties, of British subjects" and should be glad that they were allowed to trade at all. To grant the Americans reciprocity would mean that all nations with most-favored nation status would have to be granted the same conditions and would ruin British commerce. Furthermore, Sheffield claimed, no special privileges need be granted in order to gain American trade. He argued that once the peace was signed, historic patterns of commerce, based largely on the connections between merchants and the credit provided the Americans by the British, would resume without any special agreement. As a result of this shift in policy, a British order in council of July 2, 1783, closed the British West Indies to the United States, while another order on December 26, 1783, allowed American merchants to ship nonmanufactured goods – except whale oil – to Great Britain "on the same terms as from a British colony" and permitted exports to the United States.[22]

Although Americans had to retreat from the ideal of free trade and the reciprocal arrangements of the model treaty, and were unable to obtain reciprocity with Great Britain in 1783, they were successful in establishing a more complete free trade in one important and often overlooked area – the compact that bound the United States together. Today, Americans assume that the United States has always represented a single entity and one nation. The situation was not so clear for revolutionary Americans. Confronted with the outbreak of hostilities after the battles at Lexington and Concord on April 19, 1775, the Continental Congress gradually shifted its role from that of a deliberative body expressing colonial grievances and organizing resistance to British imperial regulations to become a quasi-government fighting a war. The exact nature of that quasi-government remained ad hoc and ill-defined. As Congress turned its attention to the armed conflict, each colony underwent a transformation by ending royal government and developing an independent state government. At that point no one knew what the final result of this process would be. Most revolutionaries assumed that the states would form some sort of confederation, but whether it would merely be a military alliance among independent states or something stronger and more binding remained to be determined. In 1776, it must be remembered, the vast majority of revolutionaries believed that a republic could be sustained only within smaller geographical boundaries. A large single continental state would create too much power in a central government and was therefore out of the question. With these concerns in mind, a committee of Congress drafted the Articles of Confederation, which protected the integrity of each state while conceding some power to a larger entity called the United States – although even the plural "states" in the name of that entity suggests the ambiguous nature of the national government. The second article of the Articles of Confederation asserted that each state retained "its sovereignty, freedom, and independence" and granted to the states "every Power, Jurisdiction, and right, which is not by this confederation expressly delegated to the United States, in Congress assembled." The independent nature of each state within the United States was also implied in the third article, which seemed to describe a military alliance rather than a granting of authority to a national government: "The said States hereby severally enter into a firm league of friendship with each other, for their common defense, the security of their Liberties, and their mutual and general welfare, binding themselves to assist each other, against all force offered to, or attacks made upon them, or any of them, on account of religion, sovereignty, trade, or any other pretense whatever." If the second and third articles seemed to treat the states as independent entities, the fourth article organized a customs union that did away with any potential trade barriers and granted reciprocal trading rights by stipulating that "[t]he better to secure and perpetuate mutual friendship and intercourse among the people of the different states in this union, the free inhabitants of each of these states . . . shall be entitled to all privileges and immunities of free citizens in the several states." This arrangement allowed that "the people of each state shall have free ingress and regress to and from any other state" and granted them "all the privileges of trade and commerce, subject to the same duties, impositions, and restrictions as the inhabitants thereof respectively." Moving beyond reciprocity, the Articles established free trade among the states by asserting that any restrictions passed by one state would "not extend so far as to prevent the removal of property imported into any state, to any other state, of which the Owner is an inhabitant; provided also, that no imposition, duties or restriction shall be laid by any state, on the property of the united states, or either of them."[23]

The Articles of Confederation may have established a free trade agreement between the states rebelling against King George III, but that agreement had some problems concerning commerce that became increasingly evident in the 1780s. Embedded within the Articles was a contradiction regarding international affairs. The Articles granted Congress "the sole and exclusive right and power of determining on peace and war," while conceding to the states the power to regulate commerce, including the right to establish imposts except in violation of proposed treaties with France and Spain.[24] Any commercial agreement with another nation drawn up under the authority of the Confederation to write treaties might conflict with the impost duties passed by an individual state. This problem had the potential to wreak havoc on international negotiations and the free trade among states as each state set its own imposts on imports from other countries. Technically, a merchant from one state, since he had "free ingress and regress to and from any other state" and could bring his property across state lines without restrictions, could sidestep the higher import duties in his state by first importing the goods into another state. The difficulties associated with this contradiction became acute during the 1780s, when several states passed legislation creating higher impost duties and tonnage fees for British goods in the hope of coercing Great Britain into granting more favorable trading rights to their merchants. What followed was a patchwork quilt of regulations – a state like Massachusetts passed prohibitory duties on British merchants, while Connecticut, for example, did not. But even without this special legislation there were problems with customs differentials between the states. As George Washington explained after the Constitutional Convention, one state passed "a prohibitory law respecting some article," while another opened "wide an avenue for its admission." As far as Washington was concerned, "One assembly makes a system, another assembly unmakes it," and it was useless "to think of making commercial regulations on our part" until the national government had the power to regulate commerce.[25]

As the timing of Washington's comments suggests, the United States Constitution was written to correct this problem. The Constitution prevented states from laying "any Imposts or Duties on Imports or Exports" or tonnage duties without the approval of Congress and lodged all diplomacy within the national government. It further stipulated that Congress regulated "Commerce with foreign Nations, and among the several States" and empowered the president, "with the Advice and Consent of the Senate, to make Treaties" and appoint ministers and consuls in foreign countries.[26] In the process, the American union of states was strengthened in its dealings with other nations. Moreover, the free trade agreement among the states was not only confirmed, but also enhanced to the point of obliterating the independent commercial identity of each state. In short, out of a loose confederation of states bound by a military alliance and a free trade agreement under the Articles, there emerged under the Constitution a single national entity with no internal trade barriers either in law or in practice. Thus, the very identity of the United States was bound to the idea of free trade.

Even before the writing and ratification of the United States Constitution, American diplomats achieved some success in sustaining their enlightened ideals in another area of free trade by gaining limited recognition of free trade as neutral rights. American leaders in 1776 were fully aware of the issue of neutral rights that European powers had debated throughout the eighteenth century, and Adams's Plan of Treaties included a provision that borrowed much of its wording from the Treaty of Utrecht and declared, "And it is hereby Stipulated that free Ships shall also give a freedom to Goods, and that every thing shall be deemed to be free and exempt, which shall be found on board the Ships, belonging to the Subjects of either of the Confederates." In 1778 this language was incorporated into the commercial treaty with France almost verbatim. Identical provisions were written into the commercial agreements with the Netherlands (1782) and Sweden (1783).[27]

Americans considered this acceptance of free trade as protecting neutral rights as a provision to be stipulated by treaty. However, when several European nations joined in the League of Armed Neutrality to defend this policy (as much for political as for idealistic reasons), American diplomats came to see the idea that free ships make free goods as an established principle. During the Revolutionary War, Great Britain found itself increasingly isolated diplomatically and had no major allies in Europe. France, Spain, and the Netherlands eventually went to war against Great Britain, although only France agreed to an official alliance with the United States. All other major powers stayed out of the conflict, but as neutrals, Austria and Russia sought to act as mediators to end the war in Europe with little regard for American interests. The British defeat at Yorktown in 1781 stifled these efforts. In the meantime several European nations moved toward protecting neutral trade from all belligerents. In 1778, the Scandinavian countries approached Russia about using their combined navies to protect neutral shipping. Although the Russians at first did not respond to these overtures, Catherine the Great, in an effort to assume a leadership role among the nations of Europe, changed her mind and decided to organize the League of Armed Neutrality with a proclamation on February 28, 1780. Over the course of the next three years several other nations joined the league: Denmark (July 9, 1780), Sweden (August 1, 1780), Prussia

(May 19, 1781), Austria (October 9, 1781), Portugal (July 24, 1782), and Naples (February 21, 1783). The four key provisions of the League stated: that neutral ships could navigate freely between ports of nations at war; that goods belonging to belligerents on board a neutral ship were protected from seizure; that there was a limited definition of contraband that excluded naval stores; and that blockading ships had to be sufficiently near to the port "as to render access thereto clearly dangerous."[28]

Whatever the power politics behind Catherine's decision to create the League, it was defended using the high ideals of the Enlightenment. In the spring of 1780 Prince Dmitri Alekseevich Golitsyn, Russia's special envoy at the Hague, issued a memorial defining "free trade" based upon "notions most simple, most clear, and most determined by the natural right."[29] On June 28, 1780, a League convention agreed that "the general principles of natural right" included "the liberty of commerce and navigation, as well as the rights of neutral nations," and resolved that those rights would not "any longer depend on the arbitrary interpretation suggested by independent and momentary interests." From the perspective of diplomats like John Adams and Benjamin Franklin, what had previously been a provision for specific treaties now assumed the aura of natural law agreed to by most civilized nations.[30]

Although technically the League was geared toward protecting neutral trade from depredations by all belligerents, its policies hurt Great Britain, which had the strongest navy and most extensive merchant shipping of its own, more than France, Spain, and the United States, which were more dependent upon neutrals for shipping. As early as July 1778, the French had declared that they were willing to abide by "free ships make free goods" if the neutral powers could convince the British to accept the idea as well. In the same spirit, Spain claimed that any of its seizures of neutral shipping had only been in reaction to the British refusal to respect the neutral flag, and then asserted that Spanish ships would respect neutrals until it was clear what the British response would be. Faced by the opposition of the League of Armed Neutrality, the British did not change their minds, or their attitude, on the issue of neutral trade and contraband. In an effort to dodge the issue the king said that the British had followed the law of nations and had paid particular respect to the Russian merchant ships. In private, however, the British rejected the idea that neutral ships make free goods as inconsistent with international law. As one Foreign Office memo explained, "We cannot, and shall not, subscribe to such doctrine."[31] The British navy continued to enforce its more restricted understanding of neutral trade and contraband, although the admiralty courts often granted neutrals damages after seizures, thus compensating the neutral owners while denying Britain's enemies the benefits of trade. To minimize the impact of the League, the British used the opportunity of the capture of the American envoy Henry Laurens on the high seas in 1780, along with the recovery of some papers that wrongly implicated the Dutch as supporting independence for the United States, to declare war on the Netherlands before it could join the League. This action kept the largest neutral trader out of the League and made Dutch merchant ships and colonies fair game for the British.[32] Regardless of the actual effectiveness of the League in protecting neutral trade, reports of the League's defense of free trade appeared in American newspapers as early as the spring of 1779, when the *Pennsylvania Packet* printed a letter indicating that the Danes and Swedes were signifying "their intention of supporting a free trade with France, America, and all the world" by organizing the League. In 1781, an article in the *Massachusetts Spy* described how several nations had joined the League and declared "[a] free trade for all the world with the new States of America, to be the end and basis of the whole plan!"[33]

Many Americans believed that the efforts to protect neutrality and assert free trade promised to fulfill the enlightened hopes for a new diplomatic order. One Boston paper printed a letter written by "a Gentleman of good intelligence in Europe" that gushed over the possibilities and linked free trade as neutral trade with free trade as opening international markets. "The spirit of commerce seems to pervade the nations of Europe, and to form a complexion of the present age," wrote the correspondent, and "[h]appily for mankind, this spirit, by opening a friendly intercourse between distant nations, and rendering them reciprocally dependent, enlarges and polishes the human mind; checks ferocity; abates bigotry; softens the rage of war; makes us citizens of the world, and surprizingly changes that self interest from which it springs into the means of promoting the benevolent affections, and the pleasures of human society." For this author "[t]he powers that formed the armed neutrality" believed "that trade has been loaded with too many restrictions, and that in a time of war it has suffered more than it ought to have done." Therefore, the European nations wanted to embrace some free trade – or at least freer trade – "and are supposed to be desirous of making it part of the basis of a new general system." For its part, "America, without doubt, wishes to trade with all the world upon the most liberal and extensive plan, and every nation would be glad to have as large a share as may be in the trade of America."[34] This optimism concerning the importance of free trade both as protecting neutral trade and as lifting mercantilistic trade barriers only enhanced the relationship between free trade and the American Revolution.

By the end of the 1780s, free trade had become imbedded in American national identity. Although Americans debated price controls during the Revolutionary War, both supporters and opponents of regulations claimed to speak for a free market. Ultimately free markets triumphed on the domestic scene. Internationally, Americans rallied to free trade in order to open commerce "with all the world," end mercantilist restrictions, establish reciprocal treaties, and protect neutral rights. Americans had limited success in pushing this revolutionary agenda with other countries, but managed to create a "continental" – to use a word adopted by the revolutionaries – free trade zone in the Articles of Confederation and the United States Constitution.

# 3

# The New Diplomacy

In the wake of independence, most Americans shared a vision for a new diplomacy based on free trade. James Wade gave a "[s]alutatory oration in Latin on the advantages which the United States may expect to derive from a free trade with the whole world" at his graduation from the University of Pennsylvania in 1781.[1] Several merchants named their ships *Free Trade* in the 1780s.[2] The phrase "free trade" also appeared repeatedly in toasts offered on the Fourth of July and other celebrations. After the reading of the Declaration of Independence in East Greenwich, Rhode Island, thirteen toasts were drunk, including "Free trade with all the world."[3] A Sons of St. Tammany celebration on May 1, 1784, had as one of its thirteen toasts a statement that summarized the Enlightenment ideal for diplomacy by proclaiming "*Free trade* in American bottoms, and peace with all the world."[4] A year later the New York Chamber of Commerce not only toasted "A free trade with all the world," but also declared, "May the commerce of the United States, under the guidance of our foederal Council, be as prosperous as her arms have been victorious."[5] In 1790 the Society of Cincinnati reiterated these principles with the toast "Peace and free trade with all the world."[6] By the 1790s, regardless of party and principles – the toasts quoted here represented various social and economic groups – free trade, enlightened ideas concerning diplomacy, and the belief that a republic should thrive by pursuing open commerce and peace with all nations had become a part of the American national consciousness.[7]

Fulfilling the vision of a new world order based on free trade and mutually beneficial international relations was not going to be easy. Indeed, American foreign policy after 1783 was marked by an effort to apply the new diplomacy in a hostile international environment. Fortunately for the United States, its diplomats, while sometimes expressing high ideals, were often willing to compromise and engage in hard-nosed bargaining. But whatever the realistic

AMERICA TRIUMPHANT and BRITANNIA in DISTRESS

EXPLANATION.

I America fitting on that quarter of the globe with the Flag of the United States diſplayed over her head, holding in one hand the Olive branch, inviting the ſhips of all nations to partake of her commerce, and in the other hand ſupporting the Cap of Liberty.

II Fame proclaiming the joyful news to all the world,

III Britannia weeping at the loſs of the trade of America, attended with an evil genius.

IV The Britiſh flag ſtruck, on her ſtrong Fortreſſes.

V French, Spaniſh, Dutch, &c ſhipping in the harbours of America.

VIA view of New York, wherein is exhibited the Traitor Arnold, taken with remorſe for ſelling his ... and Judas like hanging himſelf.

ILLUSTRATION 4. "America Triumphant and Britannia in Distress." This allegorical print from 1782 represents the anticipated prosperity from a free trade with all the world for the United States at the end of the Revolutionary War. America, the Minerva figure under the flag on the right, holds out an olive branch to the French, Spanish, and Dutch ships in New York, while Britannia on the left weeps at her loss. Library of Congress, Washington, D.C.

streak of the diplomats, they still hoped to establish a new revolutionary regime in foreign affairs based on free trade. During the 1780s American diplomats sought recognition for the United States, reduction of commercial restrictions, an end to mercantilist practices, and a guarantee that "free ships make free goods." Free trade as neutral rights became even more important after Great Britain and France went to war in 1793. That conflict dramatically increased American commerce, but left the nation lurching from one crisis to another as Great Britain, France, and even Algiers sought to impose on the trade of the United States. Free trade may not have been at the core of every diplomatic controversy – at times boundaries, debt, Native Americans, and other issues took precedence – but it remained an unrelenting presence in early American foreign policy; sometimes it emerged to the forefront, and sometimes it receded into the background; sometimes it came into greater focus with one meaning, and sometimes with another. Often the phrase had multiple meanings simultaneously. However imprecisely Americans might define free trade, they persisted in their commitment to it as an ideal despite opposition from other nations.

The "Gentleman of good intelligence in Europe" understood the difficulties of pursuing enlightened ideals and free trade in the harsh world of European diplomacy. The "Gentleman" recognized that the independence of the United States had created a new situation. But the path toward free trade before the United States was full of obstacles: "a plan for an extensive enlargement of the freedom of trade is . . . attended with more real difficulties" than you can imagine. "If some special indulgences are proposed for America, from any nation, the other European powers in commercial alliance with that nation, immediately expect similar indulgences for themselves and their independencies abroad." In other words, the intricacies of European foreign relations interceded, and most-favored-nation clauses meant that free trade for one country would lead to free trade with all most-favored nations. This problem contributed to the disruption of a potential commercial agreement with the British. As the "Gentleman" explained, when Great Britain signed a preliminary peace with the United States, it seemed as if the negotiators were ready "to grant the United States the most liberal terms of commerce, and a trade to the British islands with every former privilege of freight, &c."[8] Objections in Parliament that similar privileges would have to be granted to all most-favored nations, and the belief that Americans would have to trade with the British on British terms anyhow, killed the proposal. Likewise, efforts at obtaining free trade with France had difficulties. The French were afraid that loosening trade restrictions would hurt their own commerce.[9] "The merchants of France stand ready to evidence that a free trade from America to those islands [the French West Indies] would not only essentially injure their own private interests, but greatly diminish in various ways this importation of money [the excess of profits to France]." Moreover, the French shared the British concerns about the implications of granting the United States open access to their ports, since "according to the treaties which France has entered into with other nations, an admission of the Americans to such a free trade, would necessitate her to grant the same admission to those nations" with which she had most-favored-nation treaties. The "Gentleman of good intelligence in Europe" thus put his hands on the horns of the dilemma faced by the United States: how to make good on the promise implicit in the Revolution of establishing "a free trade with all the world" when that world was full of monarchies jockeying for position and power.[10]

The solution to this problem was compromise. As the war was winding down to the final peace in 1783, the Continental Congress decided to appoint Thomas Jefferson to join John Adams and Benjamin Franklin in Europe as a commission to establish commercial treaties with other powers. The commissioners were instructed to contact a total of sixteen European nations and the Barbary States (Great Britain, Hamburg, Saxony, Prussia, Denmark, Russia, Austria, Venice, Rome, Naples, Tuscany, Sardinia, Genoa, Spain, Portugal, Turkey, Algiers, Tripoli, Tunis, and Morocco). The idea was not only to have a commercial agreement based on the best possible terms, but also to gain acknowledgment of the independence of the United States and to have the new republic received into "the fraternity of other nations." The commission had only limited success.[11]

Before heading for Europe as a diplomat, Thomas Jefferson wrote the congressional instructions for the commission that were to become the basis for a new model treaty. Jefferson had intended that this plan of treaties be applied to negotiations with Denmark, and then to the other nations. Instead, they became the basis of the Prussian treaty of 1785.[12] Jefferson believed in complete reciprocity. If Jefferson had had his way, he would have extended reciprocity to full rights of citizenship for foreign nationals, as he suggested in a secret letter to Adams.[13] Jefferson recognized, however, that such openness was unrealistic and did not push this idea in his model treaty. As Jefferson explained to James Monroe in 1785, imposts for European nations "are fixed upon them, they are interwoven with the body of their laws and the organisation of their government, and they make a great part of their revenue; and they cannot then get rid of them."[14] Jefferson's model treaty, unlike Adams's 1776 Plan of Treaty, therefore did not include a provision for reciprocity in trade and called only for most-favored-nation status, more typical of European statecraft.[15]

Jefferson may not have pushed for free trade through reciprocity, but his model treaty, as had the plan drawn up by Adams, sought to establish another crucial tenant of enlightened ideas concerning free trade – that "free vessels make free goods." Like the earlier plan, this treaty would protect neutral rights if either nation went to war: "If one of the contracting parties should be engaged in war with any other power, the free intercourse and commerce of the subjects or citizens of the party remaining neuter with the belligerent powers shall not be interrupted. On the contrary in that case as in full peace the vessels of the neutral party may navigate freely to and from the ports and on the coasts of the belligerent parties, free vessels making free goods." Jefferson explained further that "all things shall be adjudged free which shall be on board any vessel belonging to the neutral party," even if the property was owned by "an enemy of the other." This "same freedom shall be extended to persons who shall be on board a free vessel," again including those who were "enemies to the other party: unless they be souldiers in actual service of such enemy." The Adams treaty had contained similar provisions, but Jefferson took the idea of neutral shipping even further. The protection of "free vessels" extended to merchant ships captured by an enemy of one power and then recaptured by one of the signatories of the treaty. In that case the recaptured ship "shall be brought into some port of one of the parties and delivered into the custody of the officers of that port in order to be restored entire to the true proprietor as soon as due proof shall be made concerning the property thereof." This procedure deviated from the usual rules of war, according to which a seized ship was a legal prize. Jefferson believed that even war materials should not automatically be considered contraband; instead, if a nation at war searched a neutral ship with armaments it could simply "stop such vessels and articles and detain them for such a length of time as the captors may think necessary to prevent the inconvenience or damage that might ensue from their proceeding," as long as the captor compensated the owner of the neutral ship for the time lost by the delay. Jefferson also suggested that in order to simplify things the captor could buy the war material for his own use. Under the regular rules of contraband such materials were liable to seizure and confiscation.[16]

Jefferson's concern for free trade even extended to protecting merchants if war were to break out between the two countries signing the treaty. Article 23 would permit merchants to continue to do business and settle their affairs for up to nine months after a declaration of war, rather than have their property made liable to confiscation and any debts made uncollectible. Jefferson viewed these provisions as part of the "humanizing" process of the "Law of Nations," an improvement that extended protection to civilians. In fact, as Jefferson explained, there were several categories of men who "should be undisturbed, have the protection of both sides, and be permitted to follow their employments in surety." These included "cultivators of the earth" and fishermen, "because they labour for the subsistence of mankind," merchants and traders in unarmed ships, because they "accommodate different Nations by communicating and exchanging the necessaries of life," and "Artists Mechanics inhabiting and working in open towns."[17] These provisions were all incorporated, with slight changes in wording, into the 1785 commercial treaty with Prussia.[18] Jefferson saw these protections as leading to "the total emancipation of commerce." John Adams, who had included some of these provisions in his own ideal treaty and who conducted the negotiations with Prussia, wrote Frederick the Great that he was "charmed to find the King" honoring the United States by agreeing "to the Platonic Philosophy of some of our Articles, which are at least a good Lesson to Mankind, and will derive more Influence from a Treaty ratified by the King of Prussia, than from the writings of Plato."[19]

Unfortunately for the United States, it was a lesson that the rest of humanity – other nations – had little interest in following. Only Prussia signed the new agreement, but to little avail, since its trade with the United States remained minimal. The hoped-for Danish treaty never materialized. Tuscany considered and then rejected any negotiations, while Portugal flirted with lowering its duties but did not do so. The rest of Europe had a studied indifference to the United States. As Jefferson explained in his autobiography: "They [the nations of Europe] seemed, in fact, to know little about us, but as rebels, who had been successful in throwing off the yoke of the mother country. They were ignorant of our commerce, which had always been monopolized by England, and of the exchange of articles it might offer advantageously to both parties."[20] The most important trading partners with the United States – France, Spain, and Great Britain – did not accept the idealistic proposals of the commission. The French already had the 1778 agreement, which included a free ships, free goods clause but not reciprocity. The Spanish were reluctant to sign a formal treaty without major concessions from the Americans until 1795. And while the Treaty of Paris of 1783 with Great Britain granted generous terms to the United States – an extended boundary to the Mississippi River, fishing rights to the Grand Banks, and recognition of independence – it excluded the hoped-for commercial arrangements.[21]

The new government under the Constitution of the United States, at least from the perspective of James Madison and Thomas Jefferson, provided the diplomatic tools needed to pry open markets and convince other nations to accept the revolutionary diplomacy of the Enlightenment centered on free trade. Madison and Jefferson argued for discrimination against Great Britain in customs duties and tonnage fees, hoping to compel the British to sign a commercial treaty that allowed American vessels to trade with the British West Indies colonies. During the debates over the impost in 1789 Madison declared that he was for free trade, but that "[i]f America was to leave her ports perfectly free" and treat merchants from other nations the same as merchants from the United States, while other nations did not reciprocate, "it is obvious that such a policy would go to exclude American shipping altogether from foreign ports" to the detriment of American interests.[22] Madison maintained that the way to gain "a reciprocity in commerce" was through "discrimination" and that "if we were disposed to hazard the experiment of interdicting the intercourse between us and Powers not in alliance [nations without a trade agreement], we should have overtures of the most advantageous kind tendered by those nations."[23] Madison wrote in 1789 that the refusal of Great Britain to sign a commercial treaty had "bound us in commercial manacles, and very nearly defeated the object of our independence," and he demanded additional imposts and tonnage duties to compel the British to open their ports.[24] As secretary of state, Thomas Jefferson agreed with Madison. "Instead of embarrassing Commerce under piles of regulating Laws, Duties, and Prohibitions" he explained, all nations should remove their "shackles" on trade and "every Country be employed in producing that which Nature has best fitted it to produce, and each be free to exchange with others mutual surplusses, for mutual Wants." If such an ideal commerce could be reached, Jefferson noted, using language that echoed with Enlightenment principles, "the greatest mass possible would be then produced of those Things which contribute to human life and human happiness; the numbers of mankind would be increased and their condition bettered." Jefferson believed that the United States should sign an agreement with any nation willing to open its trade. However, in the meantime, "should any Nation" (read here Great Britain), "contrary to our wishes, suppose it may better find it's advantage by continuing it's System of Prohibitions, Duties and Regulations, it behoves us to protect our Citizens, their Commerce and Navigation, by Counter-Prohibitions, Duties and Regulations, also." He concluded, "Free commerce and navigation are not to be given in exchange for Restrictions and Vexations; nor are they likely to produce a relaxation of them."[25] Despite their pleas, and despite his own support for the idea in *Federalist* Number 11, Treasury Secretary Alexander Hamilton opposed discrimination and successfully blocked its passage.

The French Revolution that began in 1789 brought new opportunities and challenges for American free trade. Some Americans hoped that a French republic might be more open to the new diplomacy. Most merchants, however, were mainly interested in what the French Revolution might mean for American trade with the French West Indies. An article published in several newspapers in the spring of 1790 suggested that "[i]f the government of the French West-India islands should be really free, and formed on the principles and declarations made by their National Assembly, concerning the rights of men, a very beneficial commerce to those islands and these States must follow." The expenses of sugar plantations in colonies that had "a free trade with this country, may be so reduced, that it would be impossible for a neighboring island to flourish" without similar benefits.[26] The French Revolution, however, led to the outbreak of the Anglo-French Wars in 1793. These conflicts tested American diplomatic idealism. As long as the United States could sustain its neutrality, and somehow get warring nations to accept that "free vessels make free goods," huge profits could be made and the revolutionary ideals of diplomacy maintained. Between 1790 and 1800 exports from the United States grew from $20 million to over $70 million and the re-export trade – shipping goods from the British, French, and Spanish West Indies colonies to the belligerent nations in Europe after bringing the cargo to the United States – went from virtually nonexistent in 1790 to almost $50 million by 1800.[27] The profits that accompanied this trade were huge. But so were the dangers.

In 1794 there was a crisis in relations with the British centered on the definition of free trade as neutral commerce. President George Washington had sought to avoid confrontation with all belligerents by issuing his neutrality proclamation on April 22, 1793, which asserted that the United States would not aid any nation at war. Although the proclamation did not mention free trade, or overtly state that "free ships make free goods," it did warn American merchants against carrying "those articles which are deemed contraband by the *modern* usage of nations." The proclamation did not define "*modern* usage," but given the previous broad definition used by American diplomats and the Enlightenment-inspired understanding of neutrality, "*modern* usage" meant that the United States should be allowed to engage in the re-export trade and to continue to carry agricultural produce as well as ship's stores even if these items were used to support armies and navies.[28] The proclamation satisfied neither France nor Britain: it sidestepped the French alliance, and its "*modern* usage" definition ran counter to British ideas of neutrality. The British government issued an order in council on June 8, 1793, stating that any ship bringing flour to France was liable to seizure. This measure was followed by a secret order in council on November 6, 1793, declaring that "all ships laden with goods the produce of any colony belonging to France, or carrying provisions or other supplies of any such colony" could be captured. The British quickly seized 250 American ships. This action, coupled with repeated American defeats at the hands of the Indians in the Ohio country and the bellicose statements of the governor of Canada encouraging those Indians, made war between the United States and Great Britain appear almost inevitable. By the spring of 1794 the crisis began to subside. The United States established a temporary embargo on March 26, 1794, which limited the sailing of American vessels, and hence their capture. In the meantime the British had issued a new order in council on January 8, 1794, which eased tensions by allowing the United States to engage in the re-export trade so long as the goods were not contraband. With the situation quieting down, Washington sent John Jay to England to seek a settlement.[29]

The negotiations between Jay and Lord Grenville, the British foreign minister, lasted until November and ensured that there would be no war between the two countries. The United States had few bargaining chips in the discussions. In March, Sweden and Denmark organized an armed neutrality pact similar to the accord of 1780, and sought to get the United States to join them. But Washington was determined not to tie American peace prospects to other countries even if they supported the ideal that "free ships make free goods." With almost no armed forces and no real allies, Jay accepted a treaty that allowed the British to dictate the terms of neutral trade. The final agreement, however, dealt with several outstanding issues between the two countries: it provided for the withdrawal of troops from frontier forts occupied by the British since the end of the Revolutionary War; it established commissions to settle questions concerning debts owed to British merchants, British seizures of American ships, and boundary disputes; it regularized commercial relations between the two countries on the basis of most-favored-nation status; it opened up the East Indies to trade with Americans; and it allowed vessels from the United States under seventy tons to trade with the British West Indies colonies. (The Senate considered this last provision an affront to national pride and deleted it from the final treaty, leaving the British West Indies technically closed to American ships for decades to come.) The treaty also marked a significant retreat from the free trade ideal. There was no guarantee that neutral ships made neutral goods. The British insisted on a broad definition of contraband that included military equipment as well as "Timber for Shipbuilding, Tar or Rozin, Copper in Sheets, Sails, Hemp, and Cordage, and generally whatever may serve directly to the equipment of Vessels, unwrought Iron and Fir planks only excepted." "Provisions and other articles" could also be considered as contraband, but these items were not subject to seizure. Instead, they were to be purchased by the power that had captured the goods, paying "the full value of all such Articles, with a reasonable mercantile Profit thereon, together with the Freight, and also the Demurrage incident to such Detention." If the British decided that food was contraband, the goods would be purchased by Great Britain in order to compensate the owners.[30]

Republicans vehemently opposed the Jay Treaty. A Boston meeting at Faneuil Hall on July 13, 1795, resolved that the treaty was "highly injurious to the commercial Interests of the United States, derogatory to their national Honor and Independence, and may be dangerous to the Peace and happiness of their Citizens." Although the meeting's resolutions attacked almost every provision in the treaty, much of the argument centered on trade, including the complaint that the treaty "prevents the United States from imposing any further restrictions on British trade *alone*" – discrimination – and "surrenders all or most of the benefits of a commercial nature, which we had a right to expect from our neutrality in the present war." In other words, by granting most-favored-nation status to Great Britain the treaty denied the possibility of using discrimination to open the British West Indies completely, ending any hope for a truly free trade outside the old mercantilist restrictions. Moreover, by accepting a limited definition of neutral rights, including a broad definition of war contraband, the Washington administration appeared to be turning its back on the ideals of the revolution and the concept of free trade and the rights of neutrals.[31]

However, as we have already seen, the concept of free trade was broad and had many definitions. Indeed, during the Jay Treaty debate of 1795–96 Federalist Party leaders proclaimed that the treaty did allow free trade, since it permitted commerce with some parts of the British Empire in Europe and the East Indies while opening up the possibility of trade with other parts, including the West Indies and Canada. One correspondent declared that the provision allowing American trade with India should "be written in Letters of Gold," since "a free trade is voluntarily given to the British settlements in the East-Indies," adding that the trade with Europe would not be impeded and that "it is highly probable that ultimately free commerce will be granted to all the British West-India Islands."[32] Another commentator put a similar spin on Article III concerning Canadian trade. Although the article prohibited

American ships from entering Canadian ports, it allowed complete freedom of trade over land and on rivers and lakes based on reciprocity, with "Goods and Merchandize ... subject to no higher or other Duties than payable" by the subjects and citizens of each country. As one treaty defender argued, "This free intercourse will be highly advantageous to our citizens on the frontier" involved in the fur trade and would provide farmers a market for their produce. Thus "just in proportion to the number of people in the United States, who are to carry on and partake in that free trade, will be the benefits of this article of the treaty."[33] The same essayist also pointed out, using a different meaning of "free trade," that the fourteenth article of the treaty "admits Americans to a free trade" – as in opening up trade – "to the British dominions in Europe, and British subjects to the same free trade in the United States" by establishing most-favored-nation status between the two countries.[34]

The Federalist Party did not have a monopoly on the language of free trade during the war crisis with Great Britain. In January 1794 Madison led another effort in Congress to pass discriminatory duties against Great Britain. During these debates, Madison reiterated his support for free trade and again advocated the use of commercial regulations to get the British to open their markets. "It might," Madison said, "be a question, how far it is proper for a government of any country to intermeddle in the management of its commerce. Perhaps it might be for the universal benefit of mankind, to establish a free trade in every quarter of the world, and at once knock down all the barriers which had been erected by prejudice, by avarice and despotism. This might perhaps be proper, but even to this theory of commerce there were some strong exceptions." One such exception was the British system of navigation laws that had channeled British trade into British ships. Madison went on to ask: "What would be the consequence to America ... if her trade were left by government to regulate itself? The sequel would be, that other nations would regulate our trade for us. This would destroy all the resources of our natural maritime strength, and leave us defenceless [sic] in the event of a rupture with any foreign nation." Madison also argued that the regulation of commerce was one of the principle reasons for the Constitution, one without which, the Constitution might never have been written. For Madison, the only way to gain a proper balance of trade with the British was to force them to accept American trade on equal terms by passing discrimination.[35] Another Republican used the ideals of free trade to attack the British. The author wrote that "[l]iberty and free trade, wherever they appear, are the objects of her [Great Britain] fear, her hatred, and her vengeance," whereas "the fixed principles of liberty and free trade" were essential to the United States. The essayist went on to say that the British had given Americans just cause to declare war, but as a republic the United States had a better option than war – "we have other means more rational and effectual, to redress ourselves, and check injustice. I allude to our consumption of her manufactures, which we may, if necessary and advisable, either restrain or prohibit." The author believed that political liberty produces "those enlarged ideas of a free trade."[36] A Philadelphia Republican celebration of the French Revolution and the Fourth of July in 1795 demonstrated the commitment to free trade, liberty, and the enlightened ideals of diplomacy with a series of toasts: the twelfth toast was "Free trade and commerce with all the world, unshackled by treaties"; the thirteenth was "The waters of the globe; may they be for an high way to all nations, without let or interruption, with free access to every port"; the fourteenth was "An universal umpire, or general congress, where the disputes of nations shall be settled, as those of individuals, by reference, that war may cease forever"; and the fifteenth was "The republics of France, Holland, and America; may the principles of their union in the cause of liberty be to the nations of the world as the centre of gravity to the material system."[37]

Almost simultaneous with the British war scare was a crisis with Algiers that threatened American trade with southern Europe in both the Atlantic Ocean and the Mediterranean Sea. Once again free trade became a diplomatic issue. The British and Algerian difficulties were not unrelated. In 1785 the British encouraged the Algerians to capture some American ships, hoping to control American trade with southern Europe. The Algerians seized two vessels and twenty-one seamen before Portugal went to war with Algiers, blockaded the Straits of Gibraltar, and prevented Algerian cruisers from entering the Atlantic. With a weak national government and no navy, the United States could do little to help the captives who languished as slaves in Algiers. After 1785 Americans either used false papers or had trouble sailing in the Mediterranean. However, American merchants could trade with both Portugal and Spain's Atlantic ports unmolested by Barbary raiders. In 1793 the British convinced the Portuguese to sign a peace with Algiers, opening up the Straits of Gibraltar to the Algerians, who quickly captured 11 American ships and over 100 seamen. Although Portugal soon resumed its war with Algiers, closing off the Atlantic to the Algerians, the American public became irate over the seizures and the threat to American trade. Congress authorized the building of a navy to confront the Algerians, but before any of the new frigates could be completed, a settlement was negotiated that eventually cost one million dollars. The issue here is not the final treaty or the treatment of captives. It is that the Algerians posed another threat to American free trade. As one correspondent explained before the treaty was completed, the problem with the Barbary states left "our prospects of a free trade up the Mediterranean . . . clouded" and made it "extremely imprudent to risk the citizens of the United States . . . [or] their property within the Straits [of Gibraltar]."[38]

Free trade was also an issue in the treaty with Spain signed in 1795. During the 1780s the Spanish refused to agree to a commercial treaty with the United

States unless the Americans ceded their right to navigate the Mississippi River, which the Spanish controlled. John Jay had been willing to accept this condition in his negotiations with Don Diego de Gardoqui, who promised to open Spanish ports and "[t]hat all Commercial regulations affecting each other shall be founded in perfect reciprocity."[39] Despite the promise of free trade with Spain, only seven states voted to cede the right of navigation of the Mississippi for a set number of years, and negotiations ended without any agreement. The wars of the French Revolution had altered the situation by 1795, and Spain agreed to a Florida boundary favorable to the United States, allowed free navigation of the Mississippi and the right of deposit – a privilege that permitted citizens of the United States to store goods in New Orleans before shipping without paying customs duties. Although the treaty did not establish most-favored-nation status, the right of deposit and free navigation of the Mississippi was as free as international trade could get. The treaty included a "Free Ships shall also give freedom to goods" provision and offered a limited definition of contraband that excluded clothing and naval stores.[40]

After peaceful settlements with Spain, Algiers, and Great Britain, problems emerged with France concerning the Jay Treaty. As far as both the Americans and the French were concerned, free trade lay at the very core of the controversy, since the 1778 treaties had committed both France and the United States to the ideal that free ships make free goods. The Jay Treaty compelled the French to rethink their relationship with the United States. From the French perspective the Jay Treaty had repudiated the American treaties with France and, in the words of one French journalist, the United States had "concluded with our most implacable enemies a treaty wholly inimical to our interests."[41] The French argued that without a "free ships make free goods" clause and with a broad definition of contraband, the Jay Treaty placed them at a distinct disadvantage. The French had other grievances, reaching back to the American delay in paying off the debt from the Revolutionary War, the appointment of Gouverneur Morris as the American minister in Paris, and the recall of his republican and sympathetic replacement, James Monroe. But the limits on neutral trade included in the Jay Treaty lay at the center of the controversy.[42] French privateers began seizing American ships in the West Indies in 1796. Then, on March 2, 1797, the French government issued a decree that denied the principle that free ships make free goods by ordering "that merchandise belonging to the enemy shall be declared good and lawful prizes, and be confiscated to the profit of the captors."[43] With each nation believing the other had turned its back on enlightened principles of free trade, mutual grievances started to mount. Between October 1, 1796, and June 22, 1797, the French captured over 300 American merchant ships. In the March decree, the French declared that any American serving in the British navy would be treated as a pirate and that any American ship that did not have a *rôle d'équipage* – a list of passengers and crew acceptable to the French – could be considered a lawful prize. The French also refused to receive a new American minister, Charles Cotesworth Pinckney.[44]

Responding to these actions, President John Adams called for a special session of Congress. Adams gave a bellicose speech before Congress on May 16, 1797, in which he claimed that the French fostered divisions within the United States by trying to persuade the American people "that they have different affections, principles, and interests from those of their fellow citizens whom they have chosen to manage their common concerns." Although Adams did not mention free trade directly in the speech, he discussed the importance of commerce to the nation's economy and the need to protect the rights of the United States as an independent and neutral nation. He also cautioned against becoming involved in the "political system of Europe," while he asserted the importance of demonstrating to "the maritime and commercial powers of the world" that "the United States of America" formed "a weight in that balance of power in Europe which never can be forgotten or neglected." Ultimately, however, Adams hoped that an agreement could be worked out by a special commission he appointed to negotiate with the French.[45]

The commission, comprised of Pinckney, John Marshall, and Elbridge Gerry, had no success, even though the negotiators seemed ready to compromise on principles. Instructed to obtain a new treaty that would supersede the current treaties, the commissioners were told that the United States would provide no aid to France in its current war against Great Britain and other powers, and that there could be no challenge to the Jay Treaty. In obtaining a new French treaty the negotiators were to get rid of the American military guarantee of French territory in the West Indies. However, in a concession to the realpolitik of the era, the commissioners were willing to accept limits on the idea that free ships make free goods similar to the stipulations in the Jay Treaty. This concession did not reflect a total abandonment of free trade. As John Marshall explained in a note he submitted to the French in January 1798, which represented a shift in the American position since the Revolutionary War, the principle that neutral ships make neutral goods was not set in the law of nations, but was established through treaties. Consequently, the fact that the Jay Treaty excluded this provision did not represent a violation of the law of nations. Having conceded that the Jay Treaty fell short of the ideal, Marshall also asserted that the United States remained committed to free trade. He wrote: "The desire of establishing universally the principle that neutral bottoms make neutral goods, is, perhaps, felt by no nation on earth more strongly than by the United States. Perhaps no nation is more deeply interested in its establishment." But, he stipulated "the wish to establish a principle is essentially different from a determination that it is already established." Marshall made a similar point about the definition of contraband in the Jay Treaty, asserting that "[i]t is true that the United States, desirous of liberating commerce, have invariably seized every opportunity which presented itself to diminish or remove the shackles imposed on that of neutrals," but that this effort and concern did not make international law. Thus, while the United States remained dedicated to free trade and a liberal understanding of contraband, in the Jay Treaty the noninclusion of a "free ships make free goods" provision and the broad definition of contraband were perfectly legitimate.[46]

The French were unresponsive to this parsing of international law. As preconditions for negotiations the French demanded an apology for John Adams's comments concerning French efforts to divide the American people, a loan of about $10 million, and a bribe of $250,000 for the French foreign minister, Charles Maurice Tallyrand-Périgord (Tallyrand). The French also wanted the United States to repudiate the Jay Treaty. Although the commissioners considered paying the bribe, the other demands violated their instructions, and after months of fruitless informal contacts Pinckney and Marshall headed back to the United States, while Gerry decided to wait in Paris on the chance that an agreement could somehow be reached.[47]

The apparent affront to American national honor escalated the crisis. The envoys reported the French demands to President Adams, who initially did not relay them to Congress. However, the Republicans in Congress, believing Adams was hiding information favorable to France, insisted on seeing the dispatches. After the release of these diplomatic documents in early April 1798, with the names of the four anonymous French agents indicated by the letters W, X, Y, and Z, the public became outraged, and Congress took retaliatory action. As in the past, the United States resorted to limiting trade in order to obtain a more free trade: Congress voted an embargo on all commerce to France and its colonies to go into effect on July 1, 1798, and a week later all treaties with France were abrogated.[48]

The XYZ affair (most references to the incident use only the last three letters of the alphabet) highlighted the American commitment to the diplomatic language of the Enlightenment. The new world of enlightened and sentimental diplomacy – or so it was portrayed – was confronted by the corrupt Old World diplomacy of bribery and treachery. Although some Republicans, like Benjamin Franklin Bache, reminded readers that the United States did not scruple to pay Algiers for a peace treaty, for most Americans the notion of offering a bribe was unthinkable. In public meetings across the nation, supporters of the administration professed their loyalty to the United States and their outrage at French behavior. Deluged with addresses from these meetings, President John Adams basked in a newfound popularity and wrote a response to each meeting, often contrasting the corruption of Europe with the virtue of America. For Adams, Europe was the scene of "old republics... crumbling into dust, and others forming, whose destinies are dubious," while in the United States the "spirit of patriotism and independence" was "rising into active exertion, in opposition to seduction, domination, and rapine." The United States remained "untainted with the principles and manners which are now producing desolation in so many parts of the world" and continued "sincere, and incapable of insidious and impious policy." Adams called the French behavior in refusing to negotiate "circumstances of indecency, insolence, and tyranny" and advised that "[t]he best 'diplomatic skill' is *honesty*, and whenever the nation we complain of [France] shall have recourse to *that*, she may depend upon an opportunity to boast of her address – till then, she will employ her *finesse* in vain." Adams believed "it is impossible to be at peace with *injustice* and *cruelty*, with *fraud* and *violence*, with *despotism*, *anarchy*, and *impiety*. A *purchased* peace could continue no longer than you continue to pay; and the field of battle at once, is infinitely preferable to a course of perpetual and unlimited contribution."[49] As one toast at a banquet held for John Marshall on his return to the United States summarized, in a phrase that quickly became a political slogan for the Federalist Party, "Millions for Defense, but not a Cent for tribute."[50]

In the spring and summer of 1798 the United States prepared for a war to defend free trade by expanding the navy and army and allowing merchant ships to arm and defend themselves against the French. Both private individuals and the government participated in this effort. A group of Baltimore merchants, "sensible of the great national advantage of a free trade, and alarmed at the piratical depredations constantly made on American property," collected almost $100,000 to build and equip ships of war to defend American commerce.[51] Salem merchants funded a subscription frigate, the *Essex*, that would gain fame in the War of 1812. President Adams in the meantime dispatched an enlarged navy to the West Indies. Although there were several naval engagements between French and American ships in the so-called Quasi War, Adams hesitated to pursue all-out hostilities. He did not authorize attacks on French merchant ships, nor did he push the expansion of the army as rapidly as the more ardent Federalists wanted. Asserting that in his Plan of Treaties of 1776, as well as in his negotiations in Paris in 1782, he had subscribed to the "rule to admit nothing which could compromise the United States in any future wars of Europe," Adams opposed enmeshing the nation in an entangling alliance with the British.[52] He also feared the military ambitions of Alexander Hamilton. The aging George Washington, who had agreed to lead the army, had insisted on Hamilton as his second in command. This turn of events meant that for all intents and purposes Hamilton ran the army. Lurking behind Adams's concerns was faith in enlightened diplomacy and a belief in the importance of commerce and free trade. Instead of pursuing war, upon receiving reports that France was willing to negotiate, Adams decided to send a new delegation to work out a settlement. This policy did not endear him to the more strident Federalists.

Nor did it win over the Republicans, who remained convinced that Great Britain was the real enemy of the United States and the ideal of free trade. As one newspaper editor explained, any differences between the United States and France were temporary, while England was the "only permanent adversary we have upon the ocean." Injuries to American commerce committed "by the predatory violence of the French corsairs" were "the result of accident," whereas the seizures by the British navy were "the necessary effect of a deep laid system of national aggrandizement." The affinity between France and the United States was based in both interest and ideology, since "[i]t was always in the interest of France; that Neutrals should have a free Trade in time of war." For this Republican author, free trade and the American Revolutionary tradition went hand in hand. During the Revolutionary War the French had supported the League of Armed Neutrality, while the British opposed it. Great Britain "of course would never permit enemies goods to be secure in neutral bottoms: while the French have considered a Free trade as the ultimate object of their policy." The author concluded that "[i]t is only by supporting the declining power of the French marine that we can expect a free Trade with the rest of the world" and thereby "reestablish those just principles of political Œconomy to which we are indebted for our late happy Revolution."[53]

In the midst of this crisis concerning free trade as neutral trade, some Americans continued to press the idea of free trade as breaking mercantilist restrictions. This notion of free trade appeared in the effort to open up the rebellious French colony of St. Domingue (modern Haiti) to American commerce despite the conflict with France. St. Domingue had been an incredibly profitable colony for the French. But beginning in 1791, it became engulfed in a complicated series of wars, rebellions, and interventions by the British and Spanish that often erupted into nasty racial conflict. By 1798 much of St. Domingue was under the political control of Toussaint Louverture, a black ex-slave, who claimed to remain loyal to revolutionary France while operating almost like an independent head of state. In November, desperately needing supplies from the United States, Louverture sent a letter to John Adams expressing his sorrow that American ships were not trading with St. Domingue, and promising to open the colony to American shipping and to prevent privateers from using its ports. Adams dispatched Edward Stevens as his agent to St. Domingue in May 1799. Stevens brokered a deal with Louverture based on the November letter (Louverture came to a similar understanding with the British). The American navy even aided Louverture in putting down a rebellion by another Haitian leader.[54]

This arrangement should not have come as a surprise. As early as July 1798 one Federalist correspondent reported that if the United States went to war with France, then St. Domingue "will declare itself independent, and seek an alliance with the United States." This writer thought that defending

St. Domingue from the French would be well worth whatever it might cost, since "a free trade to that island for only a few years, is worth ten times more than we should probably expend to obtain it for ever." Moreover, an independent St. Domingue "would enrich the farmer, the merchant, the mariner, and the government, and break up nests of pirates who will be continually committing depredations on our commerce."[55] By early 1799, American merchants were salivating at the possibility of an independent St. Domingue. As one newspaper reported, "The probable independence of St. Domingo [St. Domingue], is an object highly interesting to us" and would be "incalculably beneficial to the United States, in a Commercial view." The prospect of "a free trade with so valuable an Island, would open mines of wealth to the active and enterprising." It would afford a market for American products and offer an abundant supply of "West-India produce" that would give "a spring to our Commerce."[56] During the congressional debate to permit the president to issue a decree suspending non-intercourse with St. Domingue, both Federalists and Republicans used the term "free trade" interchangeably with "commercial intercourse."[57]

However, with the threat of war hanging over the nation, the United States was also willing to retreat somewhat from its commitment to the "free ships make free goods" principles. This shift in policy appeared not only in the preliminaries to the XYZ affair, but also in the negotiations for a new commercial treaty with Prussia in 1797. As Secretary of State Timothy Pickering explained to his envoy in Berlin, John Quincy Adams, the United States hoped that the principle of "free ships make free goods" would become universal and had included it in all of the treaties made by the country, except the Jay Treaty with Great Britain. Since the British were the strongest naval power on the high seas, the principle was impossible to enforce. Moreover, Pickering noted, France, regardless of some assertions otherwise, was also violating the principle. The result was that if war were to break out, the policy would injure the United States, and it would "be extremely impolitic to confine the enterprises and exertions of our armed vessels within narrower limits than the law of nations prescribes," since France would shelter her commerce "under neutral flags; while ours would remain exposed, as at present, to the havoc of her numerous cruisers." Following Pickering's pragmatic advice, the younger Adams therefore made sure that Article 12, concerning neutral trade, was written to preclude "free ships make free goods." But he also made it clear in the treaty that the change resulted from the fact that the provision had not been respected in recent wars and declared that once peace was established, both nations, as well as any other maritime power who might be interested, would make "such arrangements and such permanent principles as may serve to consolidate the liberty and safety of the neutral navigation and commerce in future wars."[58]

The United States took a similar position concerning "free ships, free goods" in its negotiations with France that began in 1800, although the final agreement between the two countries included a reiteration of their earlier rhetorical commitments to the principle. The instructions to the American commissioners – Oliver Ellsworth, William Davie, and William Vans Murray – accepted some limitation of free trade by allowing for the capture of a vessel for "having on board property belonging to the enemy" of the capturing nation and by indicating a willingness to accept a most-favored-nation status for commerce between the two nations. But the instructions also stipulated that France should open all of its ports, including those of its colonies, to American ships. Moreover, the instructions offered a limited definition of contraband and allowed for the seizure of a ship carrying that contraband or enemy property.[59] The final agreement, however, included an article declaring that "free ships shall give a freedom to goods." The French supported this provision for neutral rights for their own geopolitical reasons, since they hoped to use it to isolate the British diplomatically and maneuver the United States into joining a new European armed neutrality. The Russians, under the leadership of Czar Paul I, invited Sweden and Denmark to join a league of armed neutrality on August 27, 1800, based on the "free ships make free goods" ideal, which was formally agreed upon on December 16, 1800. Although Prussia soon joined the league, the British opposed it, and retaliated by placing an embargo on Danish, Swedish, and Russian ships in British ports. The league fell apart after Paul died in 1801 and the British attacked the Danish fleet in Copenhagen. Ignoring the French hopes, the United States refused even to consider joining the short-lived league for fear of becoming entangled in a European alliance.[60]

By the end of 1801, although battered and torn by the diplomatic crosswinds of a world at war, the United States remained committed to free trade, neutral commerce, and enlightened diplomacy. After some additional haggling, peace was established between France and the United States. Both powers agreed to the initial convention – the document was not called a treaty – on September 30, 1800. However, ratification of the peace agreement between France and the United States was delayed until December 21, 1801, because the two sides dickered over ending the alliance and the payment of reparations for seized shipping. In the end, the United States gained peace and the termination of its entangling alliance with France in exchange for no payment of reparations and mutual most-favored trading nation status. If there was no push for reciprocal free trade or a more wide open Smithian free trade, Americans could at least continue to participate in the carrying trade as a neutral and could have access to French colonies. Moreover, the *Polly* decision in the British admiralty court, followed by a written opinion by the King's Advocate, established "that the landing the goods and paying the Duties in the Neutral Country breaks the continuing of the voyage, and is such an importation as legalizes the trade, although the goods be re-shipped in the same Vessel, and on account of the same Neutral Proprietors, and to be forwarded for sale to the Mother Country."[61] For the time being, at least, American merchants were able to navigate the treacherous waters between the Scylla and Charybdis of French and British regulations and retained a commitment to free trade.

# 4

# Legacy

In a letter he wrote in 1780, John Adams directly connected free trade to the meaning of the American Revolution. Adams argued that the Americans were not fighting the revolution out of enmity toward the British or anyone else; instead, they were "animated by higher Principles and Better and Stronger Motives than Hatred and Aversion." Even before he discussed the importance of "the purest principles of Liberty civil and religious," Adams pointed out that the revolutionaries "universally aspire after a free Trade with all the commercial World, instead of that mean Monopoly, in which they were shackled by great Britain." Adams believed that "God and Nature intended, that So great a Magazine of Productions the Raw Materials of Manufactures, So great a source of Commerce, and so rich a Nursery of Seamen as America is should be open."[1]

If Adams identified free trade with the American Revolution, the phrase retained for all Americans in the eighteenth century a certain ambiguity and had multiple meanings. These meanings often shaded into one another and came into clearer focus at one time or another depending upon specific circumstances. The issue of free trade as free markets emerged occasionally in the colonial period, came into sharp relief during the price regulation debates of the Revolutionary War, and developed into an accepted doctrine during the early republic. In his first inaugural, Thomas Jefferson proclaimed faith in the free market at home by declaring that "a wise and frugal Government, which shall restrain men from injuring one another, shall leave them otherwise free to regulate their own pursuits of industry and improvement, and shall not take from the mouth of labor the bread it has earned."[2] During the colonial period and into the revolutionary crisis, the idea of free trade as a release from mercantile restrictions appeared most prevalent and was reflected in Adams's 1780 letter. But this notion did not disappear after the Revolutionary War.

Newspapers published Adams's letter at least twice – in 1789 and 1796 – and Americans seized the opportunity offered by the Anglo-French wars that began in 1793 to challenge colonial mercantile barriers in the West Indies and even put aside racial prejudice to trade with the regime of Toussaint Louverture in St. Domingue in 1799 and 1800.³ Although the issue of reciprocity was not prevalent before independence, inspired by the ideals of the Enlightenment it became a central tenet of American diplomacy. Written into the model treaty of 1776, during the early years of the American republic diplomats did not successfully gain reciprocity agreements with European powers despite the hope that the British might grant it to the United States during the peace negotiations of 1782–83, and despite the willingness of some Americans to use the coercive and pragmatic policy of discrimination to obtain reciprocity as an idealistic end. The revolutionaries, however, not only established reciprocity in the Articles of Confederation, and later in the United States Constitution, but also tied what could have been simply a group of allied independent and sovereign states into a free trade pact that did away with all commercial barriers in the spirit of the Enlightenment and the works of Adam Smith. Free trade as protection of neutral trade, an idea that had antecedents in the seventeenth century but that came into its own during the Enlightenment of the eighteenth century, also became a crucial principle imbedded in American revolutionary diplomacy and written into the commercial treaties with France (1778), the Netherlands (1782), Sweden (1783), and Prussia (1785). The notion that free ships make free goods, however, came under severe strain after France and Great Britain went to war in 1793. The United States retreated from the principle in the Jay Treaty and, in a concession to practicality, was willing to abandon the ideal temporarily in 1797–99 and 1800 in negotiations with Prussia and France. Although excluded from the Prussian treaty of 1799, a "free ships make free goods" provision, largely at the insistence of the French, was included in the Convention of 1800 that ended the Quasi War. In an odd turn of events, this agreement, combined with the *Polly* decision in British courts, allowed the United States to retain its commitment to free trade as neutral trade at the opening of the nineteenth century.

However pushed and pulled, however varied in its meaning, free trade thus remained central to American foreign policy and connected to the high ideals of the Enlightenment. John Adams had demonstrated his commitment to enlightened diplomacy by trumpeting American honesty and forthright diplomacy in contrast to the corruption and duplicity of France during the XYZ affair. Although Thomas Jefferson reflected a different political philosophy, he shared many of the same values rooted in the Age of Reason. As Jefferson looked across the Atlantic in 1801, he was relieved that the United States had been "separated by nature and a wide ocean from the exterminating havoc of one quarter of the globe" and that the nation was "too high-minded to endure the degradations of the others." That high-mindedness led him to view commerce as the "handmaid" of agriculture and to proclaim his support for the new republican diplomacy by emphasizing the relationship between "peace, commerce, and honest friendship with all nations, entangling alliances with none." Republics sustained peace through commerce and an open diplomacy. His declaration of "friendship with all nations" implied that Americans had a right to trade freely outside the traditional mercantilist bonds and "entangling alliances." Without using the phrase "free trade" – after decades as a central theme in American diplomacy it hardly needed to be mentioned – Jefferson's words suggest how deeply embedded the idea of free trade had become in the American consciousness.[4]

# PART TWO

# SAILORS' RIGHTS

The "free trade" portion of the slogan "Free Trade and Sailors' Rights" was only the first half of Porter's intended affront at the beginning of the War of 1812. If the ideal of free trade traced its roots to the high culture of the Enlightenment, to the rarified writings of the *philosophes* and the ruminations of Adam Smith, the declaration for sailors' rights expressed a different strain of the revolutionary heritage tied more directly to the politics of the streets – and of the waterfront – that reflected the democratic nature of the American Revolution. Not only was this low culture message meant to rile aristocratic captains like Sir James Yeo, it was also a not-too-subtle form of subversion intended to appeal to the common seamen who manned the *Southampton*. Any banner that included the phrase "Sailors' Rights" proclaimed to the impressed seamen of the British navy that the *Essex* was fighting for the rights of American seamen and, by extension, the rights of all seamen. Such a statement had revolutionary implications that had deep roots in the history of Anglo-American relations.

Like the patrician appeal of "free trade," the more plebeian "sailors' rights" traced its antecedents to the colonial period. The idea of sailors' rights spoke directly to the ability of individual seamen to control their own lives and labor. Impressment – the forced recruitment of men into the navy – threatened this right. Colonial Americans rioted against impressment, and the issue was an important backdrop to the participation of waterfront crowds during the resistance movement. That experience, coupled with the sacrifices sailors made during the Revolutionary War and the early republic, helped to incorporate maritime workers into an expanding definition of citizenship by the opening of the nineteenth century.[1]

# 5

## Anglo-American Traditions

Anglo-American traditions of opposition to impressment are crucial to understanding the later reaction to the forced recruitment of sailors from American ships and the development of the idea that sailors had rights in the early republic. In England, impressing men into the military reached back at least to the Middle Ages, but it had occurred only sporadically until after 1660, when it became a more regular feature of naval recruitment. Throughout the eighteenth century and into the beginning of the nineteenth century, impressing grew in intensity and in the public consciousness. As the British navy relied on the press with increasing frequency, a debate emerged in England. On the one side was the government and the navy, which tended to view the press as necessary to protect the nation. On the other was a public that at times accepted the press as a reality of life for the lower orders, but that also objected to the practice because of its threat to the lives and livelihood of common people. By the mid eighteenth century there emerged a group of writers who supported this opposition and decried the impress as a violation of the liberty of Englishmen. This tradition of opposition reached across the Atlantic and included Britons in North America and the West Indies. In fact, parliamentary legislation in the early eighteenth century prohibiting impressing in the colonies raised even more legal ambiguities about the right to press in North America than existed within the British Isles. As the American colonies were further integrated into the British Empire in the mid eighteenth century, the practice of the impress expanded, and, so did colonial resistance to press gangs. Violence at sea, as well as riots in port cities, strengthened American determination to oppose forced recruitment into the British navy and enhanced the colonial experience with collective action against unpopular parliamentary measures.

To fully comprehend the role of impressing in its Anglo-American context, we need to look first at the origin of the word "impress" as it related to forced recruitment into the military. The word itself had a dual etymology. As a noun and as a verb, the word "impress" was an extension of the word "press," which was often used interchangeably with "impress" and derived from the Latin *premure* (to press) and French *empressor* (to press), meaning to apply pressure and compel. A similar word, "imprest," was used as an adjective, as in the phrase "imprest money" (also referred to as the king's shilling), which was to describe the bounty given pressed men and which represented their acceptance of their new status in the military. "Imprest" derived from the Latin *imprestare* (to advance). The word "impress" thus reflected the joining of "press" and "imprest," with both words revolving around the idea of compelling men into the military and paying them a symbolic advance on their wages. The *Oxford English Dictionary* cites the earliest use of the word "impress" in Shakespearean plays; at that time it could be applied to forced recruitment into both the army and the navy.[1] The more formal-sounding word "impressment" was an extension of the word "impress" and emerged in the United States in the mid 1790s.

For most of the eighteenth century the word "impress" was usually applied to the taking of seamen from the merchant marine and making them serve on naval ships. As Great Britain fought a series of wars with France and other European powers, the navy needed hordes of men to sustain the blue water policy of extending the overseas empire while protecting the island of Great Britain from invasion. In the second half of the eighteenth century the demand for sailors was mind-boggling: during the Seven Years' War the navy peaked at around 85,000 men; during the Revolutionary War at 105,500 men; and during the French Revolutionary and Napoleonic Wars at 140,000 men. Since during peacetime the British merchant marine ranged around 75,000 men, and the colonies in 1775 had only about 10,000 seamen, in times of war the British admiralty confronted an almost constant crisis in manning the navy.[2] The navy therefore sought men wherever it could. Although the navy offered bounties to sailors, landsmen, and foreign seamen, ultimately it had to use the impress to gain more manpower. The navy also needed to be careful not to strip the merchant marine of all its labor, since the whole purpose of an overseas empire was to increase trade and make a profit. Therefore, the navy often limited its use of the impress. Most impressing took place at sea, usually as a merchant vessel was approaching its destination. As a general rule – violated in times of high demand for seamen – the pressing officer would take only one in five seamen from a merchant vessel in order to ensure its safe arrival in port. Outbound vessels were ordinarily immune from the impress, since removing sailors from a ship at the beginning of a voyage put the commercial enterprise in jeopardy. To augment the crews of merchant ships during wartime, the government relaxed the Navigation Laws limiting the number of non-British subjects aboard non-naval ships. This policy had an additional benefit: any foreigner who served for two years under the British flag aboard a merchant ship became liable to the impress as a new British subject. The impress, however, was not limited to the sea; press gangs would also go ashore, search the waterfront, and compel any sailors they found to join the navy.

Although government officials generally defended the eighteenth-century impress as necessary to ensure the protection of the nation, the practice, especially the activities of the press gang, was often condemned by the public. Indeed, by the mid eighteenth century pamphlets and newspaper articles appeared that decried the impress as hypocritical and a reproach to English liberty. As early as 1728 the author of an anonymous pamphlet called the "The Sailors Advocate" argued that "the pressing of Seamen," was "a proceeding authorized by nothing but forced Constructions of laws, or Unwarrantable violence." The author believed the impress was a violation of the Magna Carta, an injury "to Liberty," and even "tends to the destruction of Government itself." "The Sailors Advocate" wondered "[h]ow can it be expected that a man should fight for the Liberty of others, whilst he himself feels the pangs of Slavery." Considering sailors "so very useful a part of his Majesty's subjects," the author was outraged that "[t]he prest person is assaulted and seized on the King's highway, hurried into a floating prison, without being allowed time to speak or write his friends."[3] One London paper in 1757 declared that the forced recruitment of sailors was "so oppressive and arbitrary a Thing, and attended with such a numerous Train of Evils, as makes it the Reproach of a free Liberty we boast of." In 1770 another critic used similar terms and wanted to know if "a people, who boast their liberty as a birthright" could "tamely sit down contented under a measure, the most arbitrary that human understanding can suggest?" The philosopher David Hume was also outraged by the impress and saw it as violence against liberty committed by the crown.[4] The engraving "The Press Gang or English Liberty Display'd," which appeared in the *Oxford Magazine*, was one of many popular illustrations portraying the impress as an evil institution and a violation of liberty. In the print, a press gang of sailors armed with clubs and directed by an officer drags its victim to the seaside, where a longboat waits to take the man to a warship in the harbor. The man is not "used to the sea" as his clothes denote a landsman: his long coat, vest, and britches are in stark contrast to the waist jackets, pantaloons, and scarves of the sailors. His wife is on her knees nearby, begging for the release of her husband as she explains that "he maintains his Father, Mother, Sister & Wife." The officer, unmoved, callously retorts, "let them starve & be damnd. the King wants Men. haul him on Board you dogs." The illustration played to the emotional and popular view of the press gang as targeting landsmen, although more often than not the navy was really just interested in men who had experience at sea. The engraving also suggested that the only landsmen who should be taken were criminals and the poor. The pressed man, using language denoting

ILLUSTRATION 5. Press gang from *Oxford Magazine*. The engraving "The Press Gang or English Liberty Display'd" appeared in the *Oxford Magazine* and portrayed the impress as an evil institution and a violation of liberty. The illustration played to the emotional and popular view of the press gang as targeting landsmen, although more often than not the navy was really just interested in men who had experience at sea. Yale University Library, New Haven, Connecticut.

he is not from the lowest strata of society, declares, "For Gods sake Gentlemen don't drag me like a Thief." Popular literature reinforced this negative image of the impress, as can be seen in Tobias Smollett's *Roderick Random*, where the main character is whisked from shore to a series of life-threatening ordeals at sea.[5]

But there was also a certain ambiguity, reflecting mixed feelings among many Englishmen, in Smollett's portrayal of Random, since Random actually experienced some social mobility by going to sea. Throughout the eighteenth century, despite the negative image of the impress, many people accepted it, so

ATTIC MISCELLANY.

MANNING THE NAVY.

ILLUSTRATION 6. Manning the navy. This British depiction of the impress elicits much less sympathy than "The Press Gang or English Liberty Display'd," with both the press gang and its victim sketched in caricature. Here the victims of the press gang almost appear deserving of their fate. National Maritime Museum, Greenwich, UK.

long as the right "recruits" were taken. As Henry Fielding explained in *Tom Jones*, a vagabond was "as proper as any fellow in the streets to be pressed into the service." It was even possible to portray the press gang as upholding the social order. The musical comedy *Plymouth in an Uproar* (1779) had the press gang disperse a mob and, by implication, recruit the lower orders into the navy. The 1790 print "Manning the Navy" elicits much less sympathy than "The Press Gang or English Liberty Display'd," with both the press gang and its victim sketched in caricature. The victim's tattered clothes indicate that he is impoverished, making him an appropriate subject for the press. Moreover, his exact status as a landsman is unclear. Although his clothes are different from those of the sailor who has hold of his scarf and wields a club, the "recruit's" coat is not quite as long as the officer's or the victim's in the previous print, and not that different from the coats worn by some of the sailors in the crowd behind him. The woman in the background does not protest vehemently and is more the passive observer than beseeching participant. Eighteenth-century Anglo-American culture frequently portrayed sailors as a breed apart, with different speech, values, and concerns. Viewing sailors as a different set of people made it easier to accept their exploitation and vulnerability to the impress. On the English popular stage, dramatists featured sailors in many plays and portrayed them as men who belonged to the sea. The impress thus became merely a brief episode in a longer set of adventures in defending the nation. English autobiographies of sailors tended to jump over impressment and concentrate on other aspects of their experience at sea, even when life aboard ship was portrayed as a struggle. Many newspaper articles, especially in the first half of the eighteenth century, did not dwell on the unfairness of the impress. Instead, they might report a "hot press" or examples of the impress without comment, and sometimes even repeated stories of evading the press in an almost comical style.[6]

Despite the acceptance of the impress as a practical necessity to protect the British nation, many people agreed with the pamphlets and statements decrying the practice as a violation of English liberty. Enhancing the impact of such expressions of opposition was the realization that conditions for common seamen in the British navy were abysmal. The men lived in crowded ships, ate wretched food, were poorly paid, and sometimes served for years, even decades, without returning home. Although actual combat could be terrible, the daily grind was often worse. Seamen were liable to horrendous punishments for the slightest offense, and death from disease, especially in the far-flung stations in the West Indies, East Indies, and off the coast of Africa, killed far more men than battle.[7]

Because of the fear of this hard life and the deprivation of liberty, opposition to the impress in Great Britain could turn violent. As ships approached port, sailors sometimes banded together and fought the impress in battles to protect their freedom. In 1744 the crew of the *Tarleton* beat back sailors from the HMS *Winchelsea* in the Mercey River near Liverpool, proclaiming that "they would fire upon the King's Boats before they would be impressed." The two sides exchanged shots as the crew landed at a dock and quickly dispersed into the city streets before they could be grabbed by the navy. Such resistance was risky, since a naval vessel, especially further out in the open sea, might use its superior fire power to guarantee the success of its press efforts.[8] On land, the impress could also break out in violence, as crowds rallied in the streets to save their own from the clutches of the British navy. Nicholas Rogers has counted 602 affrays between press gangs and crowds from 1738 to 1805 in Great Britain, including 246 before 1776. The largest percentage of these disturbances occurred in and around London, but every part of Great Britain and Ireland was susceptible to outbreaks of rioting in reaction to the impress. In 1755 hundreds of whalers attacked a press gang at Greenland dock in London and freed its captured seamen. Anti-impress crowds could also include individuals who were not sailors and who sought to protect their friends, neighbors, and relatives. In many cases women would join the crowd. Unlike other eighteenth-century Anglo-American riots, disturbances against the impress, with lives as well as livelihoods so much at stake, could lead to extreme physical violence and even fatalities. Rogers estimates that one in four anti-impress affrays ended in serious injury or death. These casualties were not limited to the riotous crowd; in 10 percent of the affrays members of the press gang were killed.[9]

One of the reasons for violence against press gangs was that the law was unclear concerning the right to resist the impress. Two major eighteenth-century legal cases reflect this ambiguity. In *Rex v. Broadfoot*, in 1743, the judge in a local Bristol court upheld the legality of the impress, declaring that "the Right of Impressing Mariners for the publick Service is a Prerogative inherent in the Crown, *grounded upon Common-Law, and recognized by many acts of Parliament.*" He also admitted that the "impress is a restraint upon the Natural Liberty of those who are liable to it," but felt that it was not a violation of the Magna Carta, since it was consistent with "*Civil* Liberty" and "appeareth to be necessary to the Good and Welfare of the Whole, and to be warranted by Statute-Law, as well as immemorial Usage." Despite detailing the bona fide nature of the impress, the judge charged the jury not to convict the sailor (Alexander Broadfoot), who had shot and killed one of the press gang, of murder and instructed it to find him guilty of the lesser charge of manslaughter because the attempted impress had been carried out without an officer present, as required by the impress warrant. As the judge explained, everything the press gang "did was to be looked upon as an Attempt upon the Liberty of the Persons concerned, without any Legal Warrant" because the actual warrant had not been followed to the letter of the law. This ruling seemed to encourage resistance, since in the hubbub of a press gang confronting a boisterous crowd it might be difficult to establish whether the navy had a proper warrant and was acting legally. Without seeing a warrant, a crowd could believe it had the law on its side.[10]

Similar confusion concerning the right to impress can be seen in the *Rex v. Tubbs* ruling by Lord Mansfield, chief justice of the Court of King's Bench, in 1776. Once again the court agreed that the press was legal, insisting that "[t]he power of pressing is found upon immemorial usage, allowed for the ages" and was "vindicated or justified" by "the safety of the state." But Mansfield also openly sympathized with the impressed by stating that "[i]n every case of pressing, every man must be very sorry for the act, and for the necessity which gives rise to it." Because of this sympathy Mansfield warned the navy to act "with the greatest moderation, and only upon the most cogent necessity" and

cautioned impress officers not to abuse their position.[11] The Bristol judge had
limited his ruling to "Mariners, Persons who have freely chosen a Seafaring
life, Persons whose Education and Employment have fitted them for the Service,
and inured them to it" and purposefully had not considered "Whether People
may be taken from their Lawful Occupations at Home, and sent against their
Wills into a remote and dangerous Service; into a Service they are utterly
unacquainted with, and possibly unfit for."[12] Mansfield, however, addressed
the issue of landsmen more directly and wrote into his ruling a stipulation that
had been the general practice of the impress, but which now would have the
sanction of the highest authority of the King's Bench behind it, by declaring that
"Persons liable" to the impress "must come purely *within the description* of
seamen, sea-faring men, &c." and that whoever "is not within the description,
does not come within the usage." In short, a landsman could believe he was
legally justified in resisting the impress.[13]

Colonial Americans shared in this cultural heritage concerning the impress.[14]
Before the 1740s most references to the impress in colonial newspapers reflected
a matter-of-fact attitude that appeared in descriptions of incidents of impressing in Great Britain and the colonies. For example, in the summer of 1734
several newspapers reported an impress in London that "cleaned the River of
upwards of 15,000 Men, besides a great Number out of Gin-shops, and several remote Places in divers Parts of the Town."[15] In 1738 the Philadelphia
*American Weekly Mercury* reprinted an account from London that "Most of
the Homeward bound Ships had their Men taken from them, at Dartmouth,
Falmouth, &c. by virtue of Impress Warrants," and a year later the *Boston
Gazette* informed its readers that in June "there was a great Impress for Seamen on the River Thames, when above 2000 Men were taken."[16] Colonial
impressment occurred on a less extensive scale. A newspaper article in 1739
mentioned that a British warship was stationed off Sandy Hook outside of
New York harbor to impress men on arriving ships, but the incident made it
into the news largely because the press gang had discovered smuggled Dutch
gunpowder from St. Eustatia after boarding a Bermuda sloop. The British navy
seized the vessel, worth £1,000, for violating the Navigation Acts and earned
its crew an unexpected reward.[17] In some instances, colonial Americans could
even welcome the press. In August 1740 a Cambridge, Massachusetts, court
failed to convict "an eminent Horse–stealer" who was acquitted for want of
evidence. No sooner had the reputed thief been released than "to his great
Mortification" a press gang seized him and took him aboard the HMS *Africa*
bound for Jamaica. The British captain "promis'd he would take particular
Care of him," assuring that "all Gentlemen Farmers, who keep good Horses,
need not break their Rest for the future" for fear of this thief.[18]

Of course, colonial Americans were also aware of the resistance to the
impress in Great Britain. In 1742 a Boston newspaper reprinted an article

describing in mocking tones "a sharp Engagement between a press-Gang and a Mobb, near the May-Pole in St. Oglives, Southwark." As the press gang entered a public house in search for "skulking Seamen" they were "oppos'd and insulted by the Company that were drinking there." Angered by this greeting, the press gang "began to exercise their oaken Towels" – wooden clubs often used by the press – while "the People in return had recourse to Paring-Shovels, Broomsticks, Pokers, Tongs, or any other thing they could lay hold of." Although the outcome was in doubt for awhile, with several injuries on both sides, the press gang emerged victorious, driving "the Enemy from the Field of Battle" and carrying "off five Prisoners, sorely wounded, on board their Tender."[19] Regardless of the comic conceit of the article, which no doubt reflected the class bias of both the original author in England and the editor in Boston who reprinted the piece, this type of report suggested that the press did not go uncontested in the Anglo-American world.

Colonial Americans might accept the impress as a fact of life (especially in England), cheer the pressing of a criminal who might otherwise have gotten off scot-free, and even chuckle at the humorous description of a fight between a motley crew in an English public house and a press gang. But they also recognized that the impress was serious business and posed a special threat to their society. In the colonial world the boundary between life at sea and life ashore was even more fluid than it was in Great Britain. Many men went to sea more as a stage of life than as a permanent means to make a living. Before 1750 most settlements in colonial America were within fifty miles of salt water, and young men would often spend a few years as sailors before settling down as farmers or tradesmen. Moreover, colonial American employers had a desperate need for labor of all sorts. Grabbing sailors on a return voyage thus posed a special threat in North America, since it stripped the colonies of strong young men necessary to sustain economic development. The importance of protecting this labor pool became especially acute during war, since the colonies had a more than thousand-mile frontier vulnerable to attack from Native American, French, and Spanish enemies.[20]

The British government acknowledged the special need for labor in North America by passing laws either restricting or banning the impress. However, this legislation was not always clear-cut or fully enforced. When combined with the English court decisions creating ambiguity over the right to resist a press gang, there was even a more muddled legal legacy concerning the impress for the colonies than existed in Great Britain. Before 1696 there were no explicit restrictions on the impress, but an order in council in that year granted colonial governors the sole power to issue impress warrants. In 1708 Parliament passed the most important impress legislation for the colonies, "An Act for the Encouragement of Trade to America." Popularly referred to as the Sixth of Anne (British laws are named in relation to the year of the reign of the ruler at the time), the law prohibited any impressing in colonial America except in an effort to recover deserting sailors. For many colonial Americans the Sixth of Anne settled the issue: the impress was banned in North America and the West Indies. However, it was not clear if the legislation was meant to be a wartime measure that would end with the peace, which took place in 1713, or if it was to continue in perpetuity. If colonial Americans believed they were protected after 1713, the navy often acted as if colonial sailors were not, and on occasion would press men in North American waters. In 1746 the situation became even more bewildering when Parliament passed a new law that prohibited impressing in the West Indies unless the local governor issued a press warrant. Many North American colonists assumed the law covered them as well. Compounding this confusion were assurances issued by British naval officers that they would not press local seamen for fear of disrupting supplies being brought into colonial ports.[21]

It is against this background that the impress became an increasingly important issue as North America became more fully integrated into the British Empire in the mid eighteenth century. Trade between the North American colonies, Great Britain, and the West Indies expanded rapidly after 1700. In 1700 British overseas exports and imports to the Americas represented about 10 percent of the total value of trade; by 1774 it comprised well over a third of all trade. During the same period the economy in colonial America grew at an astounding 3.5 percent per year, while the British economy expanded at only 0.5 percent.[22] With the increasing trade there was a need for more sailors in colonial America and a need for a greater naval presence to protect that trade. At the same time British officials began to pay more attention to the North American colonies as a theater of imperial competition and warfare. By the opening of the French and Indian War (the Seven Years' War in Europe) North America had become the center of attention of the British overseas empire. These interrelated developments intensified demands for manpower in the merchant marine and the navy. Both sides in this contest for labor turned to the best means at their disposal to obtain the men they needed. Merchants raised wages and enticed sailors to desert the navy. As one British officer complained, "their Men [were] inveigled, and seduc'd from them," and even Governor William Shirley of Massachusetts had to admit that "an unaccountable humour frequently prevails among Sailors to quit his Majesty's Service, without leave." The navy reacted to this "unaccountable humour" by using the impress to force men back into the navy.[23]

Aggravating the situation were the losses experienced in the West Indies due to disease. Any ship that sailed to the Caribbean was bound to lose men to yellow fever, malaria, and other tropical ailments. The death of a sailor or two on a merchant vessel with a crew of ten to fourteen might be tolerable even if it affected the sailing efficiency on the voyage. The loss of more men could leave a merchant vessel in desperate straits. Aboard a naval ship the spread of a contagious disease could be even more devastating. On a ship packed with humanity – a frigate could have a crew of 250 and a ship-of-the-line (a vessel with at least 64 guns) might have two or even three times that many – an outbreak of yellow fever could sweep through a crew, killing scores and even hundreds. A depleted crew might leave a warship unable to defend itself thousands of miles from its home port in Great Britain. What happened in the West Indies had a direct impact on the North American colonies. Many colonial ships sailed to the Caribbean loaded with supplies and returned with sugar, molasses, coffee, cotton, and other tropical products. Moreover, given the prevailing sailing patterns, most ships using wind and current would sail from Great Britain to the West Indies before following the Gulf Stream to the North American coast. In addition, ships from the Caribbean would sail back to Britain by passing near North America. In the process naval ships would often stop in a port to refit, obtain victuals, and recruit seamen – including the use of the impress – before their transatlantic voyage.[24]

Like their British cousins, colonial Americans resisted the impress, using both legal and extralegal means. Colonial American complaints about the impress appeared by 1691, and there was some resistance to the impress in the early eighteenth century.[25] This activity increased in the 1740s and 1750s during the British wars for empire against the French. Because of its central role as the staging ground for attacks on Canada in the 1740s, Boston became the first hotbed of opposition to the impress in the colonies. After fifty men deserted a British warship in June 1741, the British captain began to impress men from coasting and fishing vessels for replacements. A crowd of about 300 formed on the night of June 8, and threatened the captain. The following spring the same captain returned and began impressing more local seamen. This time provincial officials interceded: the Massachusetts legislature complained to Governor William Shirley that the captain had committed "the intolerable Violence and Injury . . . to the Liberty of his Majesty's Subject of this Province their Trade and Business, and his cold Contempt of his Majesty his Crown and Dignity."[26] Avoiding further violence, Shirley negotiated the release of the impressed seamen and lodged a complaint with Admiral Edward Vernon. Boston's opposition became more intense when a press gang misbehaved in 1745. After Lieutenant Governor Spencer Phips issued a warrant to Captain Forest of the HMS *Wager* to impress fifteen men, a press gang stormed ashore and forced their way into one house, "where they curs'd and swore, and behaved like Fiends of Hell," threatening "Death and Destruction to all that should oppose them." Seizing five sailors from this location, they went to another, where they were met with a group of seamen armed with a gun and determined to oppose this "Gang of Ruffians." As members of the recent expedition to Louisbourg, the sailors had been promised protection from the impress. Once the captain from their previous cruise explained this to the press gang, the situation appeared to be defused. But after the captain left, one of the press gang called out a signal and turned out the lights, and the gang fell upon the now unarmed men "with their Cutlasses, and stab'd and hacked two of them in so terrible and inhuman a Manner" that they later died from their wounds.[27]

The largest colonial riot against the impress occurred in 1747 in Boston in reaction to the practices of Commodore Charles Knowles, who had a long history of problems with enforcing the impress in the West Indies. Usually the British navy pressed only men from inbound vessels and would not take sailors from the area.[28] In Boston, Knowles violated local sensibilities by pressing men from outbound vessels, and, as in the controversies of 1741, 1742, and 1745, he took Massachusetts men. The riot not only reflected the accumulating tensions in the colonial port between the navy and the Boston community, but also was an important precursor to the popular disorder that accompanied the resistance to British imperial regulation in the 1760s and 1770s in both form and substance. The ritualized behavior of the crowd can be seen in the way the rioters briefly held a naval officer hostage, but centered most of their rage on symbols of government authority by beating an undersheriff and then placing him in stocks, by occupying the townhouse, and by burning a longboat in a public bonfire (the crowd believed the boat would convey pressed seamen to the naval vessels). All of these actions may have presaged the ritualized activity of the pre-revolutionary crowd, but the main thrust of the anti-Knowles agitation had nothing to do with challenging the imperial relationship and centered instead on defending the local labor force and expressing a sense of plebeian justice.[29]

The impress continued to be a problem for colonial sailors both in North American waters and beyond. During the French and Indian War the British navy used the press in several colonial ports. Perhaps the largest single colonial operation to impress sailors occurred in New York in 1757 and was coordinated by the army, which sent 3,000 troops sweeping through the city's taverns and brothels during the early morning hours of May 20. The soldiers took about 800 men into custody, but released over half as not being "of the sea," netting a total of about 400 men for the navy.[30] More typical was the searching of inbound ships, gaining only a handful of seamen at a time. In June 1757 the navy pressed two men from an inbound Rhode Island sloop, and in 1761 stationed ships off Sandy Hook to search incoming vessels for additional men. The lure of merchant vessels and even privateers left British captains little choice but to use the impress. In early 1761 the HMS *Fowey* lost about a dozen sailors to desertion in New York. The ship then pressed men from the ships in the harbor as replacements. When the *Fowey* left port in May, it sailed to Nantucket first and boarded a privateer and took an additional twenty-eight men. To counter these efforts, seamen often left their ships on the Long Island shore or the Lower New York Bay before coming to port.[31] Local officials also sought to protect maritime labor. In 1758 so few coasters were bringing supplies into Boston for fear that their crews would be pressed that Captain Charles Hardy wrote to the colony's governor assuring him that local seamen would be "*protected from all Impress*" and had Hardy's "utmost Countenance and Protection."[32] At about the same time New York's Lieutenant Governor James De Lancey issued a similar proclamation for "Persons employed on Board Vessels laden with Provisions" for New York. However, he also warned that "the Desertion of Seamen ... when there is so great a Demand for their Service" would not be tolerated and that anyone "who shall harbour or conceal any Seamen, or other Deserter, belonging to any of his Majesty's Ships ... shall be prosecuted with the utmost Rigour of the Law."[33] In 1760 the New York mayor obtained a promise from the British navy not to "impress any Boatman, Landsman, or Marketman, out of any Boats going to, or returning from" the city.[34]

Threatened with the impress, sailors and their supporters, as they had done before, also turned to violence. After the pressing of a local sailor in December 1757, a crowd of several hundred in Portsmouth, New Hampshire, seized a naval longboat and dragged it through town in an action similar to the Knowles riots in Boston a decade earlier.[35] Colonial seamen resisted the impress in England as well as in the West Indies. When the crew of a Virginia tobacco ship opposed a press gang boarding their vessel outside Bristol, England, in September 1756, the press gang fired shots into the Virginia ship, killing the cook and wounding others. Within a few days the tobacco ship sank – perhaps, so the report suggested, from a shot that struck between wind and water.[36] The most violent resistance to the impress during the French and Indian War occurred in New York, where four instances led to fatalities. Two separate deaths occurred on the same day in the spring of 1758. The first occurred when Captain Jasper Farmer and a party of militia boarded the *Charming Jenny* at New Dock. They pressed several seamen easily enough, but four sailors retreated to the roundhouse. Even though Farmer promised the men that they would be used in the transport service and not the regular navy, the four sailors refused to surrender and fired a blunderbuss at the press gang, killing Farmer. It took a detachment of regulars to subdue the men, who were later tried for murder. On the same morning another party of militia searched the outskirts of town for sailors. At one house they found nine Dutchmen hiding in the garret. When they refused to come down, the militia officer ordered his men to fire, killing one and wounding another. Neither those being pressed nor the press gang were immune from harm in such confrontations.[37] Just how dangerous the impress could be can be seen in two incidents in 1760. On August 5, 1760, a British naval longboat approached the ship *Minehead*, eight weeks out of

Lisbon and headed for New York loaded with salt. The merchant crew locked up the captain and officers, seized the ship's small arms, and began to fire on the press gang. Responding to a signal for support, three other longboats approached, and a gun battle ensued in which one sailor was killed and another wounded.[38] A few weeks later a similar and more deadly incident occurred as the British navy attempted to press some of the crew of the *Sampson* from Bristol. Again the navy sent a small boat to search the ship, and again the crew locked up the captain and officers – or so the officers claimed – and secured small arms to defend themselves. Despite several shots fired from the HMS *Winchester*, at least one of which struck the *Sampson*, the vessel made its escape. In the process the crew began shooting at the small boat, killing three men and injuring another. After the *Sampson* reached the docks in New York City, the crew continued its resistance and refused to be boarded by the local authorities. When a naval warship approached, most of the crew jumped into the ship's boats and made their escape to Long Island or up the East River.[39]

The colonial experience with the impress before 1763 carried several meanings that could not be missed by any of the participants. First, colonial Americans shared many of the ideas about the legality of the impress that were held in Great Britain. Although there was some acceptance of the impress as a necessity to protect the empire, many believed they had a right to oppose the impress and questioned whether it was a legal practice consistent with English liberty. Second, sailors demonstrated that they would act to protect themselves from the press gang, sometimes by running from the press, sometimes by seeking legal protections, and by sometimes turning to violent resistance. Third, sailors were an important part of the community and often gained support from that community in opposing the press gang. Fourth, popular resistance to the impress contributed to the development of a tradition of collective action that would have an important impact on the rioting of the resistance movement and the American Revolution. Finally, the concern with the impress was the beginning of the idea that sailors had rights that needed to be protected.[40]

# 6

# The Rise of Jack Tar

The American Revolution and the importance of commerce in the new republic led to the rise of Jack Tar in American popular consciousness. The revolutionary experience strengthened the idea that sailors had rights by bringing together the interest in protecting sailors from the impress and the crowd action against imperial regulation. Beginning with the Stamp Act riots of the 1760s, the "Sons of Neptune" – waterfront workers – became the shock troops of the Revolution. Sailors and those tied to the maritime trades had a direct interest in liberating colonial America from restrictions on trade that limited their employment opportunities, and they sought to protect themselves from impressment. The conjoining of these two issues enhanced the popular mobilization of the waterfront crowd and strengthened a growing egalitarianism that fed the democratic impulse of the American Revolution. The importance of the waterfront went beyond crowd action and opposition to the impress. The fact that so many Americans fought on the high seas, and that the British captured many of these men, who then suffered as prisoners of war, furthered the sense that mariners played a special role in the creation of the United States. In the decades immediately after the war, the involvement of sailors both in commerce and as protectors of the United States only enhanced Jack Tar's visibility. By 1800, few Americans doubted that sailors were a part of the political nation.

During the 1760s, even after the end of the war with France, the British navy continued the impress in North American waters. By all rights, the British navy should have had little reason to press men in the colonies after the Treaty of Paris of 1763. Ordinarily peace meant demobilization and a shrinking of the navy. Periods immediately following wars often led to economic recession, a decline in shipping, and with it a decline in the demand for labor on the waterfront and aboard ships. The years after the British-American triumph in Canada were no different as men returned from the army, left their privateers, and ran into difficulties finding employment.[1] But even a depressed job market in North America offered wages that were enticing to experienced seamen serving in his majesty's ships. Desertions continued. In 1765 Captain Archibald Kennedy explained to the Admiralty back in Great Britain that "it is not in the power of Man . . . to prevent Seamen from running away," since the merchants offered higher wages "and other inducements." If the navy impressed seamen from the merchant service it was no real loss to the merchants, because whenever they needed men "they inveigle the seamen from the Men of War." Peace also did not make the West Indies any healthier for men in the navy. Yellow fever, malaria, and other tropical ailments took no note of treaties. Any ship sailing through the Caribbean lost men who needed to be replaced. Moreover, the decision to reform the British Empire with new imperial regulations, and the further integration of North America into the British-Atlantic economy, meant an enlarged presence of the British navy in order to enforce customs regulations as well as to protect commerce in the event of renewed war. The British navy, therefore, had to use the impress, although it often strove to conduct these activities "with Diligence and Descretion."[2]

Even if the British acted "with Diligence and Descretion," colonial American seamen did whatever they could to avoid the press. Sailors continued to slip ashore before their vessels reached port if a press gang was in the offing. Upon returning from a voyage from Georgia to Sandwich on Cape Cod aboard the sloop *Remembergrace* in 1766, Thomas Nicolson noted that the pilot they spoke to at Gay Head on Martha's Vineyard told them that "their [there] was a Tender in at holms hole" looking to press men. The captain swung into action to protect his crew, and "we hove out our Boat and too [two] of the people went a Shore in her for fear of Being pressed. At half past one in the afternoon we Came to an anchor in holmes hole the tenders people Came on board of us. but found Nothing that was Seasable [seizable]."[3]

If the navy had a difficult time finding sailors on inbound ships, they had an even more difficult time sending press gangs ashore. There were impressment riots in several cities and towns in the 1760s, often occurring in close proximity to the opposition by British Americans to imperial regulations. On July 9, 1764, a crowd threw stones at a boat's crew sent to retrieve a deserter in Newport, Rhode Island. The British sailors had to beat a hasty retreat without the man they had hoped to bring with them. The violence escalated as Newporters fired several shots at a British ship in an effort to gain the return of a local pilot who had been impressed. The conflict ended abruptly when the British navy threatened to return the fire.[4] Two days later an anti-impress disturbance broke out in New York City, protesting the seizure of some local fishermen. When the captain of the British vessel came to the city on the morning of July 11, 1764, a mob "suddenly assembled" and seized his boat. The captain wisely agreed to release the fishermen. In the meanwhile the crowd dragged his boat to the green, and in an action reminiscent of the Knowles riot, burnt it in a public bonfire.[5] A similar riot occurred in Newport in June 1765, triggered by "an extravagant height of imprudence and insolence" by the British navy and, as in New York, the pressing of local fishermen. The rioters in Newport also burned a naval boat as an act of public defiance against the impress.[6] A month later a New York crowd "pretty roughly treated" an officer from the HMS *Hawke*, which had been pressing men from every inbound ship and even some of the smaller coastal vessels.[7] In 1767 Captain Jeremiah Morgan determined to retrieve deserters and press any other seamen he found in "either a Publick House or Bawdy House" in Norfolk, Virginia.[8] The press gang, however, may have been less discriminating than these orders suggested, since they knocked on every door in the part of town inhabited by seamen and with "oaths and threats" swept through "the houses like so many tigers and wolves, seizing every man they met with." Rallied by the cry that there was "*A riot by man of war's men, with Capt.* Morgan *at their head*," a crowd quickly formed that drove Morgan and his press gang back to their ship.[9]

These actions did not occur in isolation. Beginning in the summer of 1765, and continuing thereafter, sailors and other denizens of the waterfront reacted to new imperial measures like the Stamp Act (1765) and Townshend Duties (1767) by participating in scores of riots. As in the case of the anti-impress riots, the crowd was concerned with threats to their livelihood, since any new tax, and more effective customs enforcement, would make it more difficult for sailors and those in the maritime trades to earn a living. In these disturbances the people in the street relied on their previous experience with popular disorder in anti-impress demonstrations and in other urban crowd rituals like Pope Day processions. Repeatedly colonial Americans had burned boats belonging to customs officials or the navy while demonstrating against the impress. Revolutionary crowds also publicly burned things. These crowds may have used different objects to represent their concerns, such as effigies of unpopular officials (an idea borrowed from the Pope Day processions), but the final result was the same: a bonfire surrounded by a jeering host, celebrating the triumph of their community over an enemy viewed as an imperious outsider. Whether the fuel for the fire was a boat or an effigy, with their silhouettes etched against the raging conflagration the people in the street formed a communal bond and pledged to defend their liberty in both a personal and a principled manner. Although at sea sailors could turn violent and even kill when protecting themselves from the impress, colonial anti-impress rioters on land seldom went to such extremes. Instead, they would harass an individual, break windows, shout, threaten, and even toss a few stones. Seldom did rioters maim or seriously injure. The revolutionary crowd usually followed a similar pattern when acting against stamp agents, violators of non-importation, and supporters of the crown before 1775. For anti-impress and revolutionary crowds the idea was to intimidate, not to punish. Even when revolutionary crowds developed tarring and feathering in 1767 – a complex ritual that owed much to waterfront traditions – the object was to humiliate and inflict some physical torment, not to murder the victim. The importance of this waterfront ritual cannot be underestimated – the participation of the people of the waterfront in the riots of the 1760s and 1770s politicized the participants and democratized the resistance movement.[10]

The intermixture of the resistance movement and concern with the impress can be seen in Boston during the *Liberty* riot, perhaps the most important anti-customs disturbance of the 1760s. On June 10, 1768, customs officials seized the sloop *Liberty*, owned by John Hancock, for smuggling wine. A dockside crowd attempted to block the seizure, but sailors from the HMS *Romney* cut the sloop's ropes and brought the *Liberty* under the guns of their warship. This action only angered the crowd further, since the *Romney* had recently impressed several seamen in the harbor, and a crowd had harassed a press gang the day before. As many as 2,000 people collected and, after roughing up some customs officials and breaking a few windows, the crowd followed what was by then a well-worn tradition in colonial protest: they dragged a pleasure boat belonging to one of the customs agents and burned it on Boston Common. In the immediate wake of the *Liberty* riot, Boston's radical leadership, including Hancock, Samuel Adams, and James Otis, orchestrated a series of town meetings. In a petition to the governor they professed their belief that "the British constitution" was "the basis of their safety and happiness" and asserted that that constitution established the idea that "[n]o man shall be governed by laws, nor taxed but by himself or representative, legally and fairly chosen." The Boston leaders reiterated these points after they had received a response from Governor Francis Bernard by observing with "mortification" how Parliament had passed one act after another "for the express purpose of raising a revenue from us" and complained about seeing "our money continually collecting from us without our consent." The Bostonians also decried "[a] multitude of placemen and pensioners, and an enormous train of underlings and dependents" – the customs officials – whose "imperious tempers" and "rash inconsiderate and weak behavior" were well known. They pointed to the *Romney*, a mere cable's length from the docks, moored "with design to overawe and terrify the inhabitants of this town, into base compliances and unlimited submission." Amid this principled argument for the protection of the property of rich merchants like Hancock, and the complaint about the threatening cannon on the gundecks of the *Romney*, the Sons of Liberty did not forget the concerns of the common seamen who made up so much of of the crowd. The leaders sought "to endeavour, that impresses of all kinds... be prevented," quoted at length the Sixth of Anne law against the impress in the colonies, and concluded "that any impresses of any mariner from any vessel whatsoever, appears to be in direct violation of an act of parliament."[11] In the twisted interplay between constitutional and popular issues, Parliament could simultaneously be blamed for violating liberty by usurping property and cited as a guardian of liberty for protecting the common seamen.

The long-term implications of the *Liberty* riot were profound, but it also had a more direct impact on the waterfront laborers and seamen in the crowd. In the larger story of the resistance movement, the threatening tumult in the city convinced the customs officials to escape Boston and seek refuge first on the *Romney* and then on Castle Island in Boston harbor. To protect those officials the British government ordered troops to Boston, setting off the spiral of confrontations that eventually broke out in the Boston Massacre on March 5, 1770. Whatever the effect of these actions on the narrative of the American Revolution, the one immediate tangible result for the people in the street was an assurance from the captain of the *Romney*, perhaps understanding the surest way to defuse the crowd, that "he would not impress any belonging to, or married in this Province [Massachusetts], nor any employed in the Trade along Shore, or to the neighboring Colonies."[12]

Despite these promises, Massachusetts experienced more pressing of its sailors in 1769, leading to a violent confrontation off Cape Ann and a controversial legal case that helped to convince the British navy to avoid future conflict and limit the impress in North American waters. Although the HMS *Rose* had already pressed two men from the brig the *Pitt Packet*, Lieutenant Panton led another boarding party to the ship to take some more men. Four of the crew "secured themselves in the Fore-Peak" and determined to defend themselves "against any illegal Attack on their Liberty." The lieutenant remonstrated with the men, but found his entreaties ineffective. In the confusion a midshipman fired a pistol, wounding at least one of the sailors. Despite this injury the men remained adamant, declaring that "they preferred Death to such a Life as they deemed slavery" aboard a man-of-war. The sailors threatened to kill any man who would try to take them and wounded one of the press gang. The violence did not end there. Panton, who assumed that his status as an officer could intimidate the obstreperous sailors, advanced. As he approached, one of the resisting mariners – Michael Corbet – threw a harpoon, striking Panton in the jugular vein. The lieutenant expired in a pool of his own blood. The sailors continued to defend themselves even though a body of marines boarded the vessel. The standoff ended as the sailors, probably recognizing the hopelessness of their situation, began drinking alcohol and became so intoxicated that they could easily be captured. Officials brought Corbet and the three other sailors to Boston to try them for piracy and murder on the high seas. The incident put Boston into an uproar. As one newspaper reported, "The inhabitants were not a little alarmed to learn that those [the British navy personnel] who were the Aggressors, and acted in Defiance of an Act of Parliament [the Sixth of

Anne], are left at Liberty, while the Men who only stood upon their Defence against an illegal attempt upon their Liberty are confined in Irons" and were to be tried for their life. John Adams served as one of the counsels defending Corbet and his shipmates, and he prepared a massive legal argument based largely on the Sixth of Anne. After the court began hearing the case, the judges interceded and, without a full legal explanation, decided for the defendants, declaring that the murder of Panton was in self-defense. All of Boston rejoiced at this outcome, although Adams later recounted his own frustration at not getting to make his arguments and complained that the court had been arbitrary in dealing with the case. Thomas Hutchinson, who was one of the judges at the time, later claimed that the case had been dismissed because there was no press warrant issued to the captain of the *Rose*, and the impress was therefore illegal.[13] Whatever the reason, the impress receded as a divisive issue between the colonies and Great Britain in the early 1770s.

Although the impress was not much of an issue after 1769, the long experience with opposition to the impress, and its role in politicizing the waterfront and in defining the rights of Englishmen, continued to influence the resistance movement and the crowd in the street. Riots are complex affairs, and there are as many reasons for any single riot as there are rioters. Although some participants joined in the affrays simply in the spirit of mischief, there is no disguising the larger meaning of these disturbances. Anti-impressment riots defended the liberty of the seamen just as resistance leaders proclaimed they were defending the liberty of the colonies. The conjunction between popular issues for the common folk of the waterfront and the constitutional issues of the leaders evident in the *Liberty* riot and other disturbances enhanced the meaning of the tumult both for the crowd and for those who organized resistance to the imperial measures. Anti-impressment riots helped to teach the people of the North American port cities the efficacy of crowd action. These lessons were learned all too well. The waterfront remained the locus of much of the resistance movement, including the act of defiance of throwing tea into the Boston harbor that brought Parliamentary retribution in the form of the Coercive Acts and began the final movement toward revolution and independence.[14]

As the British government reacted to the passage of the Continental Association in 1774, which promised to end trade with Great Britain unless Parliament relented, Lord North's administration passed two additional laws limiting colonial American maritime activity that affected the impress in North American waters. Parliament passed the first of these measures on November 29, 1774. Called "An Act for the Encouragement of the Fisheries Carried on from Great Britain," the law shifted the locus of fishing off the Newfoundland coast from New England to Great Britain, insisting on largely British crews and British-built, not colonial-built ships. Echoing the concerns of the navy, the statute even prohibited British fishing vessels from visiting the mainland

North American colonies to prevent the desertion of seamen. This fisheries act also officially repealed the Sixth of Anne law against the impress in North America, because it had "proved an Encouragement to Mariners . . . to desert in Time of War . . . to the *British* Plantation on the said Continent of *America*." No longer could John Adams, the people in the street, or anyone else claim that colonials had a legal exemption from the impress.[15] The other measure was the New England Restraining Act, passed on March 30, 1775, and extended to the other colonies (except New York, Delaware, North Carolina, and Georgia) in April 1775. This law banned New Englanders from the fishing grounds off Newfoundland and Nova Scotia and prohibited all trade with other nations except Great Britain and some of its West Indies colonies. Any ship caught in violation of this law, even if that trade had previously been legal, and any New England fishing vessel working the fertile waters off Canada, was liable to seizure.[16]

Often overlooked – although not by the men who lived through the war – was that after the passage of the New England Restraining Act and the outbreak of hostilities that soon followed, many of the sailors captured aboard American merchantmen, as well as a large number of seamen taken aboard privateers or naval vessels, were pressed into the British navy against their will. Thomas Jefferson in the Declaration of Independence recognized this development in his list of grievances by complaining that the king "has constrained our fellow Citizens taken Captive on the high Seas, to bear Arms against their Country, to become the executioners of their friends and Brethren, or to fall themselves by their Hands." As with most of the so-called grievances listed in the Declaration, the iconic document did not relate the full story. Many sailors were impressed during the war. Others, after varying degrees of coercion, "volunteered" for British service. American seamen could switch sides a number of times, sometimes because they had little choice, and sometimes because they sought whatever opportunity they could find to earn a living. Joseph Bartlett was captured at least twelve times aboard American, British, and French ships, often changing sides in the process. In other words, the plot to usurp liberty by constraining "our fellow Citizens" was neither as nefarious nor as concerted as Jefferson stated. For much of the Revolutionary War the British were uncertain about the exact status of prisoners of war captured on American ships. Initially, as rebels against their king, the British government considered men taken on privateers and naval ships as pirates headed for the hangman. This threat, however, was never carried out, and eventually most Americans captured on warships were sent to internment as prisoners of war. Men found on merchantmen were seldom sent to prison; the British navy simply swallowed them up in its great hunger for manpower. But even men on revolutionary warships might be immediately pressed into the British navy. When the British captured the privateer *Ranger*, some of the crew were sent to prison, while others – like William Lamb, who had previously been found by the Americans on a British ship – were pressed into the service of the king.[17]

Whatever the shifting loyalties of individual seamen, the inclusion of the concern for the impressed seamen in the Declaration of Independence, as well as the entire experience of the Revolutionary War, only strengthened the growing faith that sailors had rights. Modern popular stories of the War for Independence dwell on the few thousand men at Valley Forge and the trials and tribulations of the Continental Army. For the first few generations of Americans in the United States, the memory of combat at sea and the ordeal of imprisonment loomed almost as large. Although land-based military activity was crucial to the conflict, as many as 200,000 men fought the British in some capacity as privateersmen or in the revolutionary navies – several states had their own navies, and there was a navy supported by the Continental Congress. Thousands of these men were captured by the British. The image of this sacrifice, especially aboard the death traps of the prison ships in New York harbor, was seared into the collective American memory. Indeed, for generations of Americans the mere mention of the prison ship *Jersey* conjured up images of hardship and British brutality. Anti-impressment riots, participation in the mobs of the port cities, sailing in defense of the nation, and the suffering of hellish imprisonment during the Revolutionary War convinced many Americans that sailors had rights.[18]

The importance of seamen and trade to the early republic only enhanced this faith in sailors' rights. This interest in Jack Tar built upon a British background that celebrated the role of maritime workers in Great Britain, reflected the experience of men at sea during the Revolutionary War, and was strengthened by the significance of commerce to the economy of the young United States in the 1780s and 1790s. Threats to trade that jeopardized the well-being and lives of American sailors by the Barbary states as well as by the French and the British after 1793 furthered these developments.

During the eighteenth century the British nation identified with overseas trade, which became, as Daniel Defoe explained, "the life of the nation, the soul of its felicity, the spring of its wealth, the support of its greatness, and the staff on which both the king and parliament must lean." Without it, "the whole fabric must fall, the body politic would sicken and languish, its power decline, and the figure it makes in the world grow by degrees contemptibly mean."[19] By the same token, commerce became the driving force in the British Empire, guaranteeing a liberty absent in empires of conquest. As the historian David Armitage argues, "Empire could only be compatible with liberty if it were redefined as maritime and commercial, rather than territorial and military." Thus liberty would lead to commerce, which would lead to greatness, which would lead to a redefined empire without threatening liberty.[20] This equation connecting liberty, commerce, and empire was best expressed in the most popular tune of the eighteenth century, a song that to this day is identified with being British. Written in 1740, "Rule Britannia" had as its refrain a phrase that declared that Britannia ruled the waves and that "Britons never will be slaves." The lyrics not only proclaimed that Britons would forever oppose tyrants, but also heralded commerce and insisted that there were "manly hearts" – sailors – "to guard the fair." During the 1750s a "blue-water" policy, implicit in the words of "Rule Britannia," became increasingly popular in Great Britain, which depended upon the navy and the water barrier surrounding the British Isles as the main line of defense from the rest of Europe.[21] In fact, at the end of the 1750s the British navy would be lionized and obtain its own anthem in the popular song "Heart of Oak," which included the refrain:

> Heart of oak are our ships, jolly tars are our men,
> We always are ready; Steady, boys, steady!
> We'll fight and we'll conquer again and again

Often portrayed in comical strains, the sailor ultimately became an important trope on the British stage – both "Rule Britannia" and "Heart of Oak" first appeared in theaters. Whether he served in the merchant marine or in the navy, the "jolly tar" had a vital function in carrying commerce during peace and in defending the nation in war.[22] As John Adams reported from England in 1785, "The words 'Ship and Sailor' still turn the Heads of this People. They grudge to every other People, a single ship and a single seamen" and were jealous of American navigation.[23]

Although the revolutionaries denied the identification of the British Empire with commerce and liberty, Americans adopted British attitudes toward sailors and retained a belief in the close relationship between freedom and trade. During the Revolutionary War sailors fought on American ships for a variety of reasons, ranging from the prosaic and practical concern of making money to the patriotic defense of their rights, and thus combined interest in commercial enterprise with ideals about liberty. One revolutionary ballad about naval Captain John Manly was addressed "to the JOLLY Tars, who are fighting for the RIGHTS and LIBERTIES of AMERICA," but recruiters emphasized the profits to be made by privateers and the navy.[24] Perhaps as important as the actual reasons for fighting were the remembered reasons for supporting the Revolution in the years after the war. Thomas Andros admitted to being attracted to the possible prize money he might earn when in the 1830s he wrote his memoir of his experience as a sailor in the Revolution, but he also claimed that as a seventeen-year-old boy he had signed aboard a Connecticut privateer with the "full conviction... that the Revolutionary cause was just."[25] In an even clearer statement about the importance of seamen to the Revolution and their political and personal ties to the United States, seaman John Foss referred to the Jack Tar captured by the Algerians in 1793 as "the humane benevolent man; the respectable citizen, and affectionate parent" who had "vindicated the sacred cause of liberty, and adorned society by inflexible honor" during the Revolutionary War.[26]

Not only was Jack Tar significant to the American republic in defending the nation, he was also valued for carrying goods to market. After the Treaty of Paris in 1783, trade, which had been so crucial during the colonial period, remained a central element of the economy of the new nation. Even politicians like Jefferson, better known for extolling the virtues of the yeoman farmer, recognized that without sailors there would be no way to export agricultural surplus safely. Jefferson viewed sailors as the second most useful group within society, next to his beloved farmers, and considered them "valuable citizens." Jefferson studied maritime enterprise, writing an insightful pamphlet on whaling in the 1780s when he was minister to France, and producing well-researched state papers on the fisheries and commerce as secretary of state in the 1790s. Jefferson knew the tonnage of vessels and the sizes of the crews. He even studied the various types of whales and the oil they produced. Moreover, throughout much of his public career Jefferson had to think about sailors while seeking to protect them from capture by the Barbary states and dealing with the issue of impressment into the British navy. Based on his intensive study and experience, Jefferson had three reasons for thinking positively about Jack Tar. First, he admired the skill and expertise of mariners who brought manufactured goods from Europe and allowed the export of commodities that enabled his favored farmers to be independent. If commerce was a necessary evil, required to sustain agriculture and free the United States from manufacturing – which Jefferson saw as a bane to the republic, since it created dependent men – then the honest tars responsible for that commerce were a blessing that needed to be encouraged. As Jefferson explained: "The loss of seamen, unnoticed, would be followed by other losses in a long train. If we have no seamen, our ships will be useless, consequently our Ship timber, Iron, and hemp: our Ship building will be at an end, ship carpenters go over to other nations, our young men have no call to the Sea, our produce, carried in foreign bottoms." Ultimately the United States would become dependent and be dragged into foreign wars. In addition, having ships from other nations carry American goods would mean the loss of "the carriage for belligerent powers, which the neutrality of our flag would render an incalculable source of profit" during European wars. Without American shipping the nation would "have ruined or banished whole classes of useful and industrious Citizens." Second, fishing and whaling reaped the harvest of the seas. This activity was thus closely akin to agriculture. The people of Nantucket, Jefferson believed, turned to whaling because "[t]heir country, from it's barrenness, yielding no subsistence, they were obliged to seek it in the sea which surrounded them." These hardy yeoman farmers of the sea "instead of wages, had a share in what was taken." This practice "induced them to fish with fewer hands, so that each had a greater dividend in the profit. It made them vigilant in seeking their game, bolder in pursuing it, and parsimonious in all their expenses." Finally, sailors were the first line of defense of the nation. Merchant shipping and fishing would be the nurseries of mariners who could man the privateers and navy that would help counter the power of any European king who made war on the United States.[27]

This same interest in sailors as the purveyors and protectors of trade appeared throughout American society during the early republic. A refrain from "The American Tar" by Susannah Rowson explained in 1800:

> For commerce whilst the sail we spread
> To cross the foaming waves boys....
> Boldly assert each sacred right
> Be Independent, Brave & Free....
> Then Huzza, Huzza, Huzza for America

In 1794 Rowson made the same point in her celebration of the mariner's itinerant life in one of her most popular tunes, which had in each refrain the sailors toast, "To America, commerce, and freedom!"[28] Rowson's theatrical work and poetry were only a small part of a veritable explosion of concern with sailors during the 1790s, celebrating their role in commerce and the navy.

Although stridently patriotic and nationalistic, in many ways this interest built upon the British precedent that had developed over the previous century and that was reaching new heights during the French Revolutionary and Napoleonic Wars. The American stage featured British productions like Thomas Arne's *Thomas and Sally: Or the Sailor's Return*, which originally opened in London in 1760.[29] This saccharine story portrayed a young milkmaid, Sally, waiting for her sailor fiancé, Thomas, to return from a voyage. She struggles to fend off the advances of the local squire, who is about to have his way with the maid when Thomas appears and, with language that reflects his nautical occupation, sends the squire packing. Thomas and Sally marry, but in the end Thomas goes to sea again because King George needs him to fight against the French navy. The musical thus had the common sailor triumphing over the menacing squire. Centered on a romance, the production had great fun with the character of the "jolly tar" and emphasized the sailor's role in defending the nation. Although written within the context of a developing British nationalism, American audiences greeted the show with enthusiasm. It was so popular that Americans produced their own versions of the story, including a song written by Susannah Rowson. Moreover, the images of the "Sailor's Goodbye" and the "Sailor's Return" became stock illustrations in both British and American iconography well into the nineteenth century. Beyond this popular production of a British musical, during the 1790s and early 1800s American publishers produced several compendiums of sailor and sea songs that helped to define an emerging American nationalism, even though the songs themselves were often borrowed from British counterparts. These books – with titles like *The Festival of Mirth and American Tars Delight*; *Patriotic Medley: Being a Choice Collection of Patriotic, Sentimental, Hunting, and Sea Songs...*; *The Sailor's Medley: A Collection of the Most Admired Sea and Other Songs*; *The Syren*; *A Choice Collection of Sea, Hunting, and Other Songs*; and *Songs in the Purse; or, Benevolent Tar...* – included a wide range of songs. Many were versions of the Sally and Thomas story, but other tunes were more recent and reflected American maritime and naval experiences.[30]

Those experiences could at times be wrenching for individual sailors, but they also helped to further catapult Jack Tar into the national consciousness and strengthened the case that he was a citizen who had rights that needed to be protected. When Algerian cruisers captured two American merchant ships in 1785, there was little the United States could do but fulminate and let the imprisoned common seamen rot in Algiers. In 1793, however, after the Algerians seized 11 American ships and enslaved over 100 seamen, Americans reacted with indignation. Suddenly the idea that free men could be enslaved at the whim of a dark-skinned North African potentate became a violation of American national identity. One captive, Captain William Penrose, wrote a letter that was published in many newspapers complaining of the failure to redeem or even provide clothing for the captives and declared that this inaction "will remain a stigma on the American character." Highlighting his own patriotism and the revolutionary sacrifices of his fellow imprisoned sailors, Penrose lamented that America, "the freest country upon earth," had ignored its citizens "who had fought and bled to establish that liberty."[31] Newspapers in the United States filled with protests. The Barbary conflict became part of the American public spectacle: wax museums exhibited Barbary scenes; circuses held benefit performances to ransom captives; the "machinery in transparency" – an early form of American film – projected Barbary displays.[32] On the stage, Susannah Rowson's *Slaves in Algiers* portrayed the autocratic Dey of Algiers as the worst of despots and the antithesis of any liberty-loving American. Mathew Carey, an author and book publisher, reminded his readers of the dependence of "the people of the United States" upon trade and that Americans "cannot be unconcerned at knowing the fate of those of their countrymen who, by being exposed to the severe and perilous duties of the sea" suffered "the hard conditions of slaves, to the most ferocious enemies to humanity."[33] David Humphreys, the diplomat most responsible for dealing with the Algerians, wrote to the secretary of state: "*If we mean to have a commerce*, we must have a *naval force* (to a certain extent) to defend it."[34] In response to this Algerian crisis and the threat to the nation's seamen and their right to freedom, the United States created a navy and paid one million dollars to purchase peace with Algiers and to liberate the imprisoned American sailors.[35]

The Barbary States, however, represented a limited threat to American commerce and the sailors who served in the American merchant marine. Far more serious were the depredations committed by the British and the French: together they seized over 500 American ships and their crews in the decade after their war began on February 1, 1793. As Jefferson had earlier predicted, "the carriage for belligerent powers" became "an incalculable source of profit" so long as the United States could maintain "the neutrality of our flag." But sustaining that neutrality was not easy. As the American merchant marine expanded, both the opportunities and the dangers for merchants and sailors increased. One problem became immediately apparent in 1793: preventing Americans from joining in the warring navies. George Washington's neutrality proclamation had explicitly warned against "citizens of the United States . . . committing, aiding, or abetting hostilities" between the belligerent powers, and his administration promptly prosecuted some seamen who signed on with the French.[36] Another issue was the treatment of sailors aboard American ships seized during the Anglo-American crisis of 1794–95. As Fulwar Skipwith, the American consul in Martinique, explained, the crews of the American ships captured in the West Indies were "stripped . . . of the little resources they had possessed." A representative of the American government, Skipwith chartered ships in order to return to the United States these "honest tars" who could not be "diverted from hastening to the arms of their much injured country." This effort to guard "our seamen" was not entirely successful, since several American sailors who had been left penniless and in desperate straits "entered into foreign service."[37] In 1795 one Republican essayist complained, with some exaggeration, "that thousands [of American sailors] have lost their lives in anxious prisons, while their vessels were carried into British ports for legal adjudication."[38] No sooner had this crisis subsided with passage of the Jay Treaty than France began to capture American shipping in retaliation for the Anglo-American agreement. Again, the treatment of American sailors aboard the condemned vessels became a point of contention. Secretary of State Timothy Pickering reported in 1797 that seamen, "our citizens," had been "beaten, insulted, and cruelly imprisoned" when their ships were taken by the French. Moreover, the French decree of March 2, 1797, which allowed the seizure of any ship carrying British goods, also declared that any American serving in the British navy would be treated as a pirate and thus become liable to execution.[39]

The crisis with France led to a limited naval conflict in the Quasi War of 1798–1800. Although Congress had created a navy in 1794, it was not until the confrontation with France that the navy became a separate department of the government and that its vessels were put into service. Led by Secretary of the Navy Benjamin Stoddart, the navy grew to thirty-three ships, including six super frigates. The navy quickly drove French privateers from North American waters and began to challenge the French in the West Indies.

In the process the United States experienced some spectacular successes, especially the victory of the super frigate *Constellation* in defeating the French
forty-gun *L'Insurgente* on February 9, 1799, and fighting to a draw the larger
fifty-four-gun *La Vengeance* on February 1, 1800. These triumphs swelled
American pride in their country's maritime prowess and brought adulation
to officers like Captain Thomas Truxton and praise for the common seamen.
Susannah Rowson's "Truxton's Victory," listed as a "Naval Patriotic Song,"
begins with a paean to both the captain and his men:

> When freedom, fair freedom her banner displayed,
> Defying each foe whom her rights would invade
> Columbia's brave sons swore those rights to maintain
> And O'er ocean and earth to establish her reign
> United they cry
> While the standard shall fly
> Resolv'd firm and steady
> We always are ready
> To fight and to conquer; to conquer or die.

In the same vein was the final refrain of the "New York Patriotic Song":

> A free navigation, commerce and trade:
> We'll seek for no foe[,] of no foe be afraid:
> Our frigate's shall ride
> Our defence and our pride;
> Our tars guard our coast,
> And huzza to our toast,
> The *Federal Constitution, Trade, and Commerce,*
> Boys forever.

Dozens of similar songs appeared, promising that "valiant Tars" and "brave
yankee Boys" would defend American liberty and commerce.[40]

Jack Tar thus gained national visibility because of his role in a commerce
wedded to the concept of liberty. The experience of the Revolutionary War,
the significance of trade during the 1780s and 1790s, the ordeal of Algerian
captivity, and the threats posed by the British and French enhanced the idea
that the sailors who ploughed the sea were important to the United States.
Naval conflict in the Quasi War with France strengthened the profile of the
sailor as the defender of national honor. The brave American tar emerged as a
symbol for the nation. As such, he became a citizen who had a legitimate claim
to the right to define the terms of his labor.[41]

# 7

# Impressment

Nothing threatened the common American sailor more than being compelled to serve in the British navy. Impressment challenged the rights of American citizens at sea and therefore challenged the American national identity. Throughout the 1780s and early 1790s, the issue of the forced recruitment of American sailors percolated beneath the surface of British and American relations until it burst onto the American political stage in the debate over the Jay Treaty. At that point Republican newspapers became consumed with reporting incidents of the pressing of American sailors, and Republican politicians used this arbitrary practice as an example of British barbarity and perfidy. As Republicans decried the cruelty and "the flagrant violations" of the rights of American citizens, a new word came into use – impressment.[1] This more formal-sounding noun was mentioned in diplomatic correspondence in 1794, but in 1796, during the Jay Treaty debates, it appeared with greater frequency. Indeed, the word was so potent and useful that scholars have seized upon impressment ever since and have applied it to the years before 1796. Impressment implied a policy; the impress or the press – the nouns previously used – reflected more a practice. And as a policy, opposition to or acceptance of impressment during the early republic could be applied as an acid test of patriotism: Americans who might acquiesce in the policy were portrayed as "avaricious tools of a corrupt and corrupting foreign faction."[2] In the process it became possible to ask, "Is not a Seamen also a Citizen?" and then answer that "the Mariner has an equal claim upon his country with a legislator."[3]

In many ways the idea of pressing North Americans was merely an extension of colonial practices and, as American politicians came to realize, reflected a denial of the independent status of the United States. In supporting John Jay's first draft of the Treaty of Paris of 1783, British negotiators believed that granting extensive commercial privileges to the United States (an idea

ILLUSTRATION 7. Impressment of an American sailor in the early 1800s. After the War of 1812 Americans romanticized the issue of impressment, as shown in this nineteenth-century illustration. The manly American tar stands defiantly before the aristocratic British officer as he is about to be taken into the British navy. This image differs dramatically from the two British illustrations and reflects the violation of American rights and the depiction of Jack Tar as a citizen sailor. Almay Pictures.

quickly abandoned) and permitting Americans to fish off the Grand Banks (a provision included in the final treaty) would not really hurt British interests. In fact, they argued that these provisions would encourage Americans to become seafarers and that these seamen could then become a pool of sailors who might be impressed or recruited into the British navy during wartime, since they already spoke English and would have little to distinguish them from British sailors.[4]

Periodically before 1793 the British navy appeared to act upon this idea. There were a few American seamen pressed throughout the 1780s and early 1790s, but in times of crisis or threats of war, the number of Americans pressed into the British navy increased. During a war scare in the fall of 1787 several American captains asked John Adams, who was serving as the first minister to the Court of St. James from the United States, for assistance in returning sailors pressed from their ships in British ports. Adams did what he could to help the seamen and lodged a formal protest, writing that "this practice" had become "too common" and was particularly "aggravating," since British press gangs went "on board American vessels, which ought to be protected by the flag of their sovereign."[5] But with no war in the offing, the problem subsided, only to reappear in 1790 during a "hot press" when Great Britain threatened to go to war with Spain over the Pacific Northwest in the Nootka Sound controversy. During this crisis British press gangs seized scores of Americans. Without an American minister or consul in London at the time, there were no formal channels for redress. John B. Cutting, a private citizen, spent $7,642.19 to aid impressed American seamen.[6] Gouverneur Morris, who was in England as the personal representative of President George Washington and was attempting to open negotiations with Great Britain, did lodge complaints on behalf of the United States despite his quasi-official status as a diplomat. Morris, with a wry flair at which he excelled, noted to British officials that press gangs "had entered American vessels with as little ceremony as those belonging to Britain," commenting that impressing American seamen was "the only instance in which we are not treated as aliens." Morris also suggested that the best way to deal with the problem was for the admiralty courts in America to issue certificates of citizenship. William Pitt agreed that this might be a good idea, but thought that the process would allow too many British seamen to obtain protection illicitly. Morris, who was always quick with a verbal riposte, replied that it was best "for the commercial interest of Britain rather to wink at such abuse," since if there was a war with Spain or France, "our commerce with Britain must be in American bottoms," and "no wages would induce our seamen to come within the British dominions if they were thereby liable to be impressed."[7]

The issue of impressing American seamen remained an irritant in relations between the United States and Great Britain, but it was not a major point of contention. Occasionally the impress was mentioned in American newspapers.

In 1791 one article compared the autocracy in pre-Revolutionary France to the absolutism of the press gang, "by whom men are seized in the streets, and cuffed, tumbled into the hold of a tender, forced upon a boisterous element ... penned up in a floating coop, to be shot at, and exposed at once to the rage of the elements, the fire of the enemy, and the pestilential disorder of their ships." Such treatment, the author suggested, was worse than being sent to the Bastille.[8] The possibility of impressing American sailors also rankled American officials. When George Washington appointed Thomas Pinckney as the new minister to Great Britain in 1792, there had been no official representative at the Court of St. James since John Adams's departure in 1788. Secretary of State Thomas Jefferson instructed Pinckney that his most important charge was "the patronage of our commerce." But he also wanted Pinckney to aid any American seamen who were exposed "to peculiar oppressions and vexations" by being forced into the British navy, following the "peculiar custom in England of impressing seamen on every appearance of war." Jefferson hoped that Pinckney would come to "some arrangement for the protection of our seamen on those occasions." However, Jefferson rejected Morris's earlier suggestion that "our seamen should always carry about them certificates of their citizenship," since no other nation had to submit to this indignity and since it would be ceding to the British the right to impress any seaman, regardless of citizenship, who did not have such a certificate. This requirement, Jefferson thought, would be extremely hard for many sailors to fulfill because they would seldom have the "precaution to comply" and because "the casualties of their calling ... expose them to the constant destruction or loss of this paper evidence." Instead, Jefferson believed that "the simplest rule will be that the vessel being American, shall be evidence that the seamen on board her are such." Jefferson recognized that this carte blanche policy might create a problem for the British, who feared that "our vessels might thus become asylums for the fugitives of their own nation from impress-gangs." Jefferson was therefore willing to compromise and stipulate that the number of men protected on an American ship be pegged to the tonnage of the vessel, with any additional men beyond the appropriate tonnage-to-manpower ratio liable to a press conducted civilly by British officers. Both Jefferson and Pinckney hoped to settle the question before the British entered any new war, because, as Pinckney explained "it would be most advantageous to discuss such a subject while no immediate interest gives an unfavorable bias to either party."[9]

The clock, however, ran out on conducting these negotiations during a time of peace. On February 1, 1793, Great Britain and France went to war, and the British began to impress seamen with abandon, including Americans. Pinckney did what he could to aid the pressed Americans, and if he provided documentation that they were indeed American citizens, he occasionally managed to gain their release. Diplomatic discussions over the issue continued, but led to no resolution. Lord George Grenville, the British foreign secretary, rejected Jefferson's ideas and wanted to have the British consuls in the United States issue protections to ensure that adequate proof of citizenship was provided. This procedure, which denied the sovereign right of the United States to identify its own citizens, was unacceptable to Pinckney.[10] He insisted on reciprocity, with British sailors providing proof of their being subjects of King George when they entered American ports. These discussions proved fruitless, and the impressing of American seamen continued. As the war between Great Britain and France intensified, Pinckney found it more difficult to negotiate the release of American seamen from the British navy. Before returning to the United States in 1796, he once again brought up the issue, this time focusing on the pressing of American seamen on ships at sea. Grenville defended the practice, saying that Great Britain had "the right to take its own subjects found on board of a foreign vessel on the high seas." He pushed the argument even further and said that the British navy had searched American ships with discretion. He did admit that occasionally an American might be taken, but he insisted that his government had returned such men when proof of citizenship had been provided. He also said that he was willing to come to an agreement by "mutual concurrence" to identify the "native citizens" of the United States if the American government were willing to do so. Such an agreement would have denied the process of making seamen naturalized citizens – a practice, as Pinckney pointed out, followed by Great Britain since 1740 and by the United States since 1790 (and by the individual states even earlier). All Pinckney could do was to declare that no "Maxim of the law of Nations" or any treaty permitted such searches, and echoed the position Jefferson had taken in his instructions: "I own I cannot foresee the principles on which it will be contended that a man shall be liable to be taken from on board an American vessel on the high seas merely because he may not have with him the proofs of his being an American, while no testimony is offered of his being a British subject."[11]

During the crisis in Anglo-American relations in 1794, press gangs were the least of the nation's problems. When Washington sent John Jay to London to seek an agreement over trade, his instructions did not even mention the impress.[12] In one of the first uses of the new noun, Jay complained about "impressment" in his written exchanges with Grenville, and acknowledged the seriousness of the question by writing of "the *injuries* done to the unfortunate individuals," those sailors who were impressed, and "the *emotions* which they must naturally excite, either in the breast of the nation to whom they belong, or of the just and humane of every country." But he used diplomatic subtlety to downplay the question by stating that he relied on "the justice and benevolence of His Majesty" to issue orders so "that Americans so circumstanced, be immediately liberated" and that the navy would "in future, abstain from similar violence." Grenville also responded with diplomatic finesse, indicating that he wished to sidestep the issue. He assured Jay "that if, in any instance, American seamen have been impressed into the King's service, it has been *contrary* to the King's desire." Although he admitted that some such cases had occurred, arising "from the difficulty of discriminating between British and American seamen, especially where there so often exists an interest and intention to deceive," he sustained the diplomatic dance around the question by telling Jay that whenever a complaint had come to his attention, he had begun an inquiry and ordered the release of the pressed seamen "if the facts appeared to be satisfactorily established." Out of this exchange, with neither side wishing to derail negotiations over the pressing of some common seamen, a rough understanding was worked out that the British would try not to be too blatant about impressing Americans. As a result, despite this unofficial compromise, the final Jay Treaty contained not a word on the impress. This omission was a political mistake.[13]

Opponents of the Jay Treaty assailed the agreement on multiple fronts as an insult to American honor and a surrender to the naval power of the British. The failure to mention impressing only added to the potency of these attacks. One essayist asked, "Could not the principle of reciprocity," as it related to the mutual assurance of hospitality for the ships of war of each nation, "as well as humanity, suggest to Mr. Jay, that some provision should be made to protect our citizen sailors from the fangs of British press gangs in England?"[14] Another writer lambasted the treaty for allowing the impress and worried that there would soon not be enough seamen left to man American merchant ships because of "the infinite loss of those of our Seafaring citizens who are carried into the islands, and compelled to serve on board ships of war in this unhealthy station." This author believed that American commerce was "upon a much worse footing than it was before Mr. Jay went to England."[15] It was in the midst of this assault on the Jay Treaty that Republicans began to use the word "impressment" – a neologism that might have been created by Jay himself during his negotiations – to portray the forced recruitment of American sailors by the British as more formidable and nefarious. The Republican mouthpiece, the *Aurora*, first used the word on June 4, 1796, in an article pointing out that "[t]he impressment of American seamen by the British" was so notorious that even the Federalist newspapers could no longer deny it.[16]

Efforts by the Federalist Party to defend the Jay Treaty and its failure to include an impressment provision were met with sarcasm and derision. After Alexander Hamilton suggested that Americans should rely on "the good faith" of the British in his *Camillus* essays, Republicans responded by questioning that good faith when the British were impressing "a most valuable classes of our citizens" in the West Indies and even in "the very port of London, notwithstanding the reclamations of our consul."[17] When a group of merchants held a meeting early in 1796 and reported that the seamen they hired did not complain of the impress and were not discouraged from going to sea for fear of the press, Republicans retorted that this statement should not be a surprise given that these same men had declared the Jay Treaty good and "[a]fter this prostitution of sentiment" were capable of saying anything. Republicans argued that sailors complained to both the American and British governments about being pressed and that "every American . . . *who has not sold himself to a British faction*" should "be loud in their complaints on the subject." Besides, the Republican author noted, if seamen were so willing to sign on ships, why had wages increased so much?[18] A few Federalist partisans agreed that wages had increased, and that this was good for seamen who were not impressed. Republicans found this proposition contemptible, responding that "the honest bosom of the hardy seamen" refused "to assist despotism in her endeavours to overthrow liberty, for a paltry addition to his wages" and that only those who were corrupted by the British would think that a sailor would want higher wages at the expense of his suffering shipmates exposed to "British tyranny and brutality."[19] Republicans believed that any suggestion that it might be acceptable for the British to impress a naturalized citizen was wrongheaded, since even pressing a British seaman from an American ship was a violation of American sovereignty: "Our ships are as much neutral ground as our cities." This same patriotic author, with tongue in cheek, thought it might be all right for the British to come on shore and press those Americans who supported Great Britain and the Jay Treaty.[20]

Aggravating the situation was the fact that the British continued to impress American seamen even after the Jay Treaty in apparent disregard for the supposed understanding between Jay and Grenville. Republican newspapers in the mid-1790s were filled with reports of Americans being taken by the British navy. One correspondent reported that thirty-five of the eighty-seven-man crew on a British sloop of war off Jamaica were Americans. The officers of this ship knew they impressed Americans, explaining they "wanted men, and would have them, let the consequences be what they may."[21] Under the heading of "BRITISH CRUELTY" one newspaper printed a letter from St. Domingue by Captain Benjamin Moody detailing two cases of impressment. The first was that of a ship's apprentice who was taken by the British despite Moody swearing an oath that the young man was an American. The second impressment was by Captain Hugh Pigot on the HMS *Success*. Pigot, who already was developing a notorious reputation as an autocratic disciplinarian, took every sailor aboard Moody's ship except the cabin boy and a slave. Fortunately for Moody's crew, Pigot later released any sailor who had documentation to prove he had been born in the United States. Pigot kept the naturalized citizens, even though, as Moody explained, "they fought for America in the war."[22] Most cases of impressment occurred in the West Indies. Occasionally, a British captain pressed sailors in American waters. After he had already antagonized the Newport community with threats and bluster, Captain Rodham Home of the HMS *Africa* took three men from a merchant vessel off the coast of Rhode Island at the end of August 1795. This violation of national sovereignty led to a formal protest by the American government.²³ Newspapers carried notices of single men being pressed, often in terms that tugged at the heart-strings of the reader. The *Salem Gazette* reported that William Atkinson, a seventeen-year-old who was the sole support of an aged female relative who had raised him, had been impressed, noting, "Thus does British power and barbarity daily rend asunder those who are connected by the tenderest ties of nature and affection."²⁴ At other times the newspapers highlighted more mas-sive instances of impressing where the sheer numbers were shocking. On July 4, 1795, the commander of the frigate *Hermione* – a ship that Pigot would later make infamous – took between sixty and seventy men from several American ships, leaving only the captains and mates. All but two of the seamen were American-born, and the two non-native Americans were naturalized citizens originally from Denmark.²⁵

Just as had occurred in the colonial period, American sailors sometimes took their fate into their own hands and forcefully resisted the impress. On the night of January 22, 1796, a press gang grabbed an American on the Liverpool waterfront. About 250 American seamen stormed the rendezvous house and liberated the pressed sailor. They also forced the recruiting captain and his men into the center of the room and "compelled them to give three cheers to the United States of America." Another incident occurred in Liverpool on the night of January 27. This time the Americans assaulted the press gang, throwing two men off the dock, with one of them drowning in the frigid waters. The exact role of the American captains during these riots remains unclear. But when the officers were hauled in front of the local magistrates and told to control their men and prevent them from insulting the press gang or face the consequences of the law, the captains were defiant, proclaiming "[t]hat they were citizens of an independent nation, and would receive no insults with impunity from the subjects of any nation – and that attempts to impress their men was an outrage and insult that the English government did not justify – and that if they would not trouble the Americans, they would conduct themselves with propriety, and not trouble them." The Liverpool press gangs left the Americans alone thereafter. This action met with public approval in the United States. As one commentator explained, the sailors' "conduct was such as justified the title of freemen, and they supported the honour of the nation to which they belonged."²⁶ Conflict also erupted in the West Indies. On February 9, 1796, a British naval officer, who had been a Loyalist during the Revolutionary War, impressed several seamen in the port of Jérémie in St. Domingue. When some American captains protested, the British officer threatened that "[b]y God he would strip the whole of the American vessels that night of their men." This effrontery was too much for the American captains, who combined their forces on board a Baltimore schooner and twice beat off British boarding parties, with the loss of one American and three English sailors. Among the Americans opposing the press gang was a young David Porter, the future captain of the *Essex*. On hearing that the British were to try to board for a third time, augmented by a detachment of soldiers, the Americans left the schooner unmanned and retreated to another ship. The British boarded the empty vessel and ransacked it, but got no men that night. The next day the American captains went to the British commander on shore, who, probably because he needed the supplies on the American ships, told them that he "would not permit an insult to the American flag" and that "he would prevent any British naval officer from impressing any American Citizen."[27]

The conflict over impressment, as it had during the colonial period, reflected the fact that both the American merchant marine and the British navy were in need of men. After the outbreak of war between Great Britain and France, Gouverneur Morris's prediction came true: more and more trade between Great Britain and the United States, as well as trade between the United States and the rest of Europe, was carried "in American bottoms." The American merchant marine expanded by leaps and bounds. Crews aboard these ships were minimal. A full-sized three-masted ship might have a crew of eight or ten. Merchant seamen would be divided into two work groups, called watches. Each watch would work four hours on and four hours off, with an overlap dogwatch in the evening to ensure that the time of day worked by each watch would be constantly changing. In each watch of four or five men it might be acceptable to have one or two inexperienced hands, but it was also absolutely essential to have one or two expert seamen who had to literally know the ropes and be able to hand, reef, and steer. To attract such seamen American merchants paid high wages – higher than could be earned aboard ships from another country, and much higher than could be earned in the British navy. Every time a British ship came to a North American port, or even within hailing distance of an American ship in any port, some sailors were bound to desert for the high wages and better treatment in the American merchant marine. Given the growth of American commerce and the thousands of ships sailing under the American flag by the late 1790s, skilled seamen from the British navy became an essential part of the American maritime workforce. Jefferson's solution to the problem – setting a tonnage-to-manpower ratio for American ships – may have appeared simple enough on the surface. But it was also self-serving. It guaranteed that however much the American merchant marine grew, it would always have its crews protected, even if some members of those crews were British subjects or British deserters.[28]

From the British perspective such a solution was unacceptable. As Phineas Bond, who had served as the British consul in Philadelphia, explained to Lord

Grenville, "such a compact would operate most beneficially in favor of the navigation of that country and most fatally to the navigation of this [Great Britain]." Bond pointed out that "if a scrutiny were to be made into the description of their crews at this time, it would be found they were indebted to us for a considerable portion of their seamen." Jefferson's plan meant that "[e]very British seaman who chuses to avoid the dangers of war would betake himself to America and under the flag of the United States enjoy the security which national neutrality would afford him."²⁹ For the British, this situation was much like the situation during the colonial period: the American merchant marine seemed to have plenty of men, many of whom had been born in Great Britain, and many of these had deserted from the British navy. Losses from desertion, compounded by deaths due to battle and disease, convinced British captains to simply take what men they needed. One British frigate had buried fifty-five men in three weeks due to disease, and, after sailing into Port-au-Prince in St. Domingue, "impressed every seaman ... without respect to quality or country."³⁰

Both the British and the Americans commented on how difficult it was to distinguish nationality based on language alone. Today there are clear differences between American English and the English spoken in the United Kingdom. But the language in both countries has gone through many changes since the eighteenth century. In the 1790s, the differences were not as great. In fact, there were probably larger differences among dialects within England than between England and the United States, since immigrants from various parts of Great Britain had populated the United States, creating a more uniform pattern of speech. Moreover, the number of immigrants who came to North America in the 1760s and 1770s, as well as the increasing wave of immigrants arriving in the 1780s and 1790s (there was little immigration during the years of the Revolutionary War), only strengthened the similarity between the English spoken in Great Britain and North America. The Englishman Nicholas Creswell in 1777 thought that even "[t]hough the inhabitants of this Country are composed of different Nations and different languages ... they in general speak better English than the English do." Sailors also had their own argot and manner of speaking, and this nautical language was shared by English-speaking sailors on both sides of the Atlantic. Thus, it was almost impossible for British officers to hear a language difference between American and British seamen.³¹

Attitude also mattered. British officers still had difficulty in accepting the outcome of the Revolutionary War. The British officer in the confrontation in Jérémie reportedly called the Americans resisting his efforts "*You damned Yankees!*" and "*You damned rebellious rascals.*"³² When an American captain protested the impressment of one of his seamen, he asserted that his own word was as good as the British naval captain's, declaring, "I conceive myself your equal any where, except on board your ship." This egalitarian response, claiming the same status as a British naval officer, was not met with kindly, and the American was quickly ordered "out of the ship, and shewed the gangway." It seems that few British naval officers, and few British officials, took the independence of the United States seriously. Nor did they hide their feelings. Americans recognized the haughtiness, even the imperiousness, of the British. After reporting the impressing of sixty Americans by the *Hermione* at Jérémie, one newspaper editor sarcastically pondered, "Was ever a nation treated with similar indignity? Were we worse off when British colonies? We had surely better return to our allegiance to king George, if we are so weak as not to be able to maintain an hounourable independence." And to hammer this point home, the editor commented, "We, like froward children, chose to leave our mother country, and she now, out of extreme kindness, chastises some by the arm of the others."[33] Although the demand for men by both countries, the similarity of language, and the attitude of the British officers all contributed to the controversy concerning impressment, much of the debate over the issue ultimately hinged on what it meant to be a subject of the king of Great Britain or a citizen of the United States.

# 8

# Citizenship

The public discussion of impressment during the Jay Treaty debates, as well as the trumpeting of Jack Tar as the purveyor of commerce and defender of the nation, helped to define sailors as citizens at a time when the idea of citizenship was undergoing rapid change. Regardless of this change, during the 1790s sailors became not just citizens, but "most valuable citizens." By the end of the decade, the United States government had passed legislation to protect American sailors and pledged the might of the American navy in defense of sailors' rights.

There was a shift during the American Revolution from viewing everyone as the subject of a king to seeing each individual as a citizen of the nation. The transition from subject to citizen, however, was neither smooth nor linear. During the 1760s and 1770s, revolutionary leaders had called upon crowds, many of whose members were waterfront workers and sailors, to express themselves politically. Although local committees might bring the common folk into the political process under the rubric "inhabitants," ultimately this action awakened a civic consciousness among the people, including sailors and propertyless males as well as some women, minors, and African Americans. Whether the leadership of the revolution liked it or not, more and more individuals came to think of themselves as citizens. Once independence had been won, the exact nature of the political nation remained in dispute. Eventually, women and most African Americans were excluded from the political process, if not from their claim to citizenship. Adult European-American propertyless males, on the other hand, were increasingly awarded the right to vote and included in the political nation.

Even as more and more people crowded under the spreading umbrella of the concept of citizen, defining citizenship remained difficult, especially when it came to granting naturalization to immigrants. During the 1780s each state established its own procedures for making immigrants citizens, with some states spelling out the process in their constitutions and others relying on regular legislation. The result was that there was no uniform policy. In Pennsylvania an immigrant became a "free denizen" after only a year of residency; in neighboring Maryland there was a seven-year wait before an immigrant could gain the same rights as a "natural born subject of this state." Under the United States Constitution, Congress created a national system for naturalization in 1790 that established a two-year residency for citizenship. Naturalization, especially as it related to foreign-born seamen, soon became politicized. Leaders of the Federalist Party tended to follow British thinking concerning nationality – and hence citizenship. They believed that a person's place of birth should determine citizenship and advocated laws that made it more difficult for immigrants to become citizens by extending the residency requirement to five years in 1795 and to fourteen years in 1798. The Republicans saw nationality and citizenship as determined by allegiance and residence. After Republicans came to power in 1801 they returned the residency requirement to five years in 1802.[1]

The language of citizenship was also important. Confusion over what to call people who owed allegiance to a state, as opposed to a king, appeared in the state regulations for naturalization: Maryland legislators used the older royal "subject," while Pennsylvanians opted for the more neutral-sounding "denizen." During the 1790s, as can be seen in the discussion concerning sailors and impressment, "citizen" became the word of choice. This development was a natural outgrowth of a democratic revolution. But it also reflected the influence of French revolutionaries, who used the word "citizen" to emphasize the equality of mankind. During the 1790s Republicans in the United States seized upon "citizen," and women even used "citizeness" as a symbol of their allegiance to the ideal of equality. The Republicans hoped to abandon all hint of hierarchy in addressing people. They replaced the generic "Mr." with "Citizen" for a while. Supporters of the Federalist Party decried this usage, but ultimately the word "citizen" became the accepted mode of identifying the relationship between the individual and the state.

Citizenship included the idea that each individual had specific rights that had to be protected by the government. This point was so important to the American revolutionaries that several states included a bill of rights in their first state constitutions. In the midst of a war with King George III over his supposed usurpation of these rights, the revolutionaries were determined to ensure that future rights – freedom of speech, the right to due process, and similar provisions – had a written guarantee. The failure of the Philadelphia Convention to include such a bill of rights in the United States Constitution became a major point of contention for the Anti-Federalists. So potent were the Anti-Federalist arguments for a bill of rights that the Federalists had to agree to adding amendments guaranteeing certain rights to help get the Constitution ratified (we call the first ten amendments the Bill of Rights). This public discussion of rights, and the inclusion of specific provisions for the protection of rights on both the state and national levels, enhanced public awareness of the importance of rights. When French revolutionaries issued their Declaration of Rights in 1789, they contributed an international dimension to this interest in rights. The very first of these rights, echoing the American Declaration of Independence, was that "Men are born and remain free and equal in rights." Thomas Paine's defense of the French Revolution, *The Rights of Man*, added further currency to the call for the rights of all. In short, proclaiming sailors to be citizens who had rights that needed to be protected was a political act that had profound implications within the context of the Age of Revolution.

That political act had special meaning. Although Jack Tar had become an important symbol for the new American nation as a defender and purveyor of commerce, many people within mainstream society looked askance on sailors, viewing them as occupying a lower stratum of society, having weak ties to the community and often dependent on merchants and captains for employment. As such, they did not appear to be a part of the normal political process. If they voted at all, they did so at the behest of others. Sailors also often misbehaved ashore, drinking and carousing. As James Madison once explained, a sailor's "virtue, at no time aided, is occasionally exposed to every scene that could poison it."[2] Compounding this negative image was the fact that many sailors in the 1790s were African Americans. Sailors were thus on the periphery of society. Yet, within the new egalitarian and democratic atmosphere of the United States, whether white or black, native-born or immigrant, sailors were now citizens who had rights.[3]

If sailors had rights, how could they be protected? The answer was to pass special legislation. Congress first considered such a bill in May 1794, but dismissed the idea after a brief nonpartisan debate. Another law was proposed in 1796, and after a longer debate, it passed. A handful of Federalists opposed the law, but even they believed, as expressed by Congressman Uriah Tracy, in "the propriety of extending the benefit of the laws to every class of citizens, and to none more than to American seamen." What they questioned was the efficacy of the provisions, as well as the constitutionality of a law that dictated that the executive appoint specific agents to deal with impressment. They wanted such appointments to be at the discretion of the executive. The debate over the measure occurred at a particularly contentious time in the House, as Republicans were demanding to see the executive's secret diplomatic correspondence concerning the Jay Treaty negotiations, and when they sought to nullify the treaty by blocking the funding for its implementation. Despite this partisan bickering over other issues, the final vote on "An Act for the Relief and Protection of American Seamen" was bipartisan and overwhelmingly in favor, with seventy-seven votes for it and thirteen against. The measure passed in a more strongly Federalist Senate without too much difficulty and was signed into law by President Washington.[4]

The statute had two major components. The first was to establish special government agents to investigate specific impressments and to work to gain the release of Americans who were impressed. Before passage of the law, government officials and private citizens had repeatedly expended both time and money to aid impressed Americans, with mixed results. Consuls, officials who resided in foreign ports, and whose main job was to facilitate trade were most active in these efforts, especially after the American Consuls Act of April 14, 1792, which charged consuls with protecting seamen overseas. Ordinarily, the idea was for consuls to find passage for sailors stranded in foreign ports after their ships were sold or if an illness prevented them from completing a voyage. But many consuls interpreted the law to mean that they were also to try to rescue impressed seamen. As unpaid government officials, consuls were often preoccupied with their own mercantile enterprise and had little time to deal with the British navy and its impressed Americans. Congress therefore created a minimum of two government-supported officials who would be stationed in England and other "foreign parts" – such as the West Indies – to monitor British impressment and to get American sailors released from the British navy. The bill's sponsor, Edward Livingston, optimistically hoped "that when the Government of Great Britain sees a step of this sort taken, she will give up the practice of seizing American seamen, and let them pass in quietness."[5] Others were less sanguine and thought that the law marked only a first step toward solving the problem and would encourage the recruitment of more native-born Americans into the merchant marine, as opposed to foreigners, who would not be protected. In addition, since the new agents were also to report to the government the cases of impressment they examined, a more accurate measure of impressment was possible.

Unfortunately for the sailors, Livingston's hopes went unfulfilled, and the British continued to impress Americans. Silas Talbot was the first agent for the West Indies and served from 1796 until 1798, when he became an officer in the American navy. Talbot had some success and even found a few of the British naval officers helpful. However, most British officers were less willing to allow the release of Americans. The agents appointed to serve in England had similar problems. The second agent sent to London was David Lennox. He had difficulty getting sailors released if they did not have proper identification. He wrote that these practices were "degrading to our citizens and insulting to our flag."[6]

The second component of the legislation was to regularize and nationalize the process of providing protection papers for seamen. There was a long history of issuing protections before the law. During the eighteenth century, the British Admiralty issued many protections for "reserved occupations" as a way

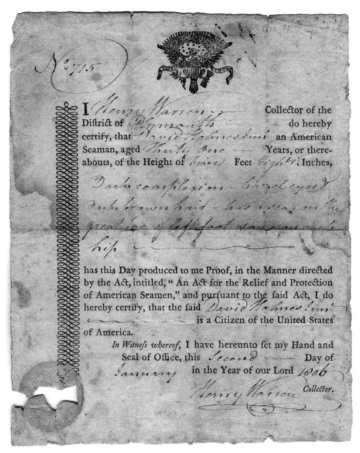

ILLUSTRATION 8. Impressment certificate. The United States issued protection certificates to idenitfy the individual sailor as an American. This certificate, for Henry Warren of Plymouth, Massachusetts, states that he was thirty-one years old when the certificate was issued and stood five feet eight inches tall. Additional information describes Warren as having a dark complexion, hazel eyes, and dark brown hair, with scars on his great toe and each hip. G. W. Blunt White Library, Mystic Seaport, Mystic, Connecticut.

to guarantee that merchants would have enough sailors to continue commerce during wartime. In the Seven Years' War the Admiralty issued as many as 50,000 such certificates a year.[7] The Sixth of Anne regulation and the assurances given by local naval captains during the colonial period had established something of a protection for North American colonists. After independence, there developed an ad hoc method of writing protections. Sometimes local officials in the United States issued documents attesting to the citizenship of a sailor, and sometimes consuls overseas issued them. Consuls wrote general protections that were supposed to cover an entire crew, but most of the time they were given to individual seamen. As Thomas Pinckney reported to Thomas Jefferson, "our consuls are allowed to give protections, where the master of the vessel and the mariner, swear, that the party is an American native and citizen, which protections, in general, are respected, though some irregularities occasionally take place." Pinckney failed to mention that often the affidavit was sworn not only before the consul, but also before a British magistrate or mayor.[8] The new law provided that the collectors of customs in each district in the United States register the names of seamen who had provided proof of their citizenship and issue them protection certificates. These certificates, popularly referred to as protections, were signed by the sailor, a witness, and the collector; the protection listed the sailor's name, identifying characteristics – height, complexion, tattoos, scars, and the like – and the location of his birth. Other forms of protection continued to be used, since the collector's register was not required. These other forms included protections issued by public notaries, justices of the peace, judges of local courts, mayors of cities, secretaries of the different states, secretaries of the United States, consuls, and governors, as well as by collectors. Although often ignored by the British navy because of the confused melange of certificates, the ease with which they were forged, and the fact that some sailors would even sell their own protections, the United States government took the documents seriously. Between 1796 and 1812 the total number of seamen registered at customs houses was 106,757.[9] As required by the law, beginning in 1797 the State Department also sent to Congress the name of every sailor impressed by the British navy who had reported his condition. These lists fill pages and pages of the *American State Papers* and offer a brief testament to the ordeal experienced by as many as ten thousand American seamen. The government of the United States did not remain indifferent to the impassioned pleas of pressed American seamen. American diplomats lodged official protests for thousands of individual cases and actually obtained the release of many, but not all, of the seamen in the records. Countless others, however, went unreported and remained imprisoned in his majesty's navy.[10]

Although the United States became embroiled in an armed conflict with France from 1798 to 1800, the issue of impressment by the British navy did not disappear. On several occasions diplomats from the United States sought to negotiate the issue with the British government, with little success. During the Quasi War two incidents between British and American warships captured the attention of Americans and reinforced the notion that the sovereignty and identity of the nation was wrapped into the issue of impressment and sailors' rights. On November 16, 1798, Captain Isaac Phillips of the twenty-gun *Baltimore* was escorting a small convoy of merchant ships into Havana when a squadron of British ships, including three ships of the line and two frigates, appeared. The

British commodore, Captain John Loring of the HMS *Carnatic*, seized several of the American merchant ships, claiming they were carrying contraband as defined in the Jay Treaty. When Phillips approached the *Carnatic* to discuss the matter with Loring, his problems began in earnest. Faced with overwhelming firepower – the five British ships combined carried over 300 cannon – and not anticipating any hostile action, Phillips found himself at the mercy of Loring, who demanded that Phillips surrender all of his seamen who did not have protections. Phillips protested that to do so "would deprive him of nearly all his men, as not even those who were really Americans, or at least very few of them, could shew protections, because it was always thought that our flag on board a Government ship was a sufficient protection." Loring ignored these protests, sent a lieutenant aboard the *Baltimore* and took fifty-five men. Loring then offered what he must have thought was a reasonable compromise; he would trade all of the Americans in his squadron for all of the British subjects on the *Baltimore*. Phillips, who thought he was defending the honor of his flag and the navy, refused this proposition, declaring that "he could not know any of his men as British subjects, nor could he, as Commander of a ship in the service of the United States, voluntarily give up any of his men." Perhaps recognizing that his ploy to exchange seamen had not worked, and after hearing the plea from Phillips that the loss of almost a third of the crew would make it impossible for him to defend his ship from the French, Loring returned all but five sailors to the *Baltimore* and sailed away with his captured prizes. This affront raised a howl of complaint in the United States. Congressman Josiah Parker called the action "the most flagrant and violent that could have been offered to the American flag."[11] Secretary of State Timothy Pickering lodged a formal protest, while President John Adams dismissed Phillips for mustering his men at the command of the British and allowing his nation to be humiliated. At the behest of the president, Secretary of Navy Benjamin Stoddert issued new orders that stated "that on no pretence whatsoever" were naval captains to allow their vessels "to be detained, or searched, nor any of the officers or men belonging to her to be taken from her, by the ships or vessels of any foreign nation, so long as you are in the capacity to repel such an outrage on the honour of the American flag." In short, American ships were "to resist that force to the utmost of your power, and when overpowered by superior force, you are to strike your flag, and thus yield your vessel."[12]

No sooner had the order been issued than a second incident in early January 1799 revealed how a spirited captain should react to an effort to impress men who were members of the American navy. The details of the incident remain unclear. Several accounts appeared in the newspapers, and some Federalist editors even proclaimed the story a fabrication.[13] The most extreme version of the story had Captain Thomas Tingey of the twenty-four-gun *Ganges* face down a British frigate by declaring his willingness to die before surrendering a single sailor. Upon hearing of this "determination," the British captain decided he would rather not "fight for dead men!"[14] Tingey's own version of the incident was more modest, but carried the same message: American naval vessels were protected by the flag of the United States. According to Tingey the British ship, the *Surprise*, had only thirty-two guns, and the request for British subjects was more civil. Despite this politeness, Tingey responded with firmness by declaring that he considered all of his crew as "Americans by birth or adoption" and "that there were no protection[s] on board to my knowledge – the only we carried in our public ships being our flag." That evening, Tingey called all hands and pledged to his crew "that not a man should be taken from me, by any force whatever, while I was able to stand at my quarters," to which the men gave a spirited three cheers. Regardless of the details of the story, Tingey's reported actions, which appeared in newspapers across the country, redeemed the honor of the nation and once again revealed a determination to protect seamen from impressment and ensure that sailors had rights.[15]

The interest in impressment demonstrated to all Americans that sailors really did have rights that the government intended to defend. As Congress considered passage of "An Act for the Relief and Protection of American Seamen," Republican papers directly linked the spirit of 1776 and the proposed law by declaring that "[t]he people who are attached to the principles and objects of the American Revolution, feel themselves deeply indebted to the spirited and patriotic conduct" of Edward Livingston, who had sponsored the bill.[16] By the opening decade of the nineteenth century impressment had become an important political issue that had tremendous popular appeal, since it had a direct impact on common folk – many Americans personally knew or had heard of someone who had been impressed or threatened with impressment. The notion that sailors had rights, which by 1800 had become so important in the United States, also reached into nearly every bay and inlet in the Atlantic basin.

# 9

# The *Hermione* and the Rights of Man

The experience of the American Revolution, the international call for the rights of man that came with the French Revolution, an English reform movement stifled by a reactionary British government, and the example of the new United States defending sailors' rights all had an impact on the British navy. In turn, what happened in the British navy had an effect on the United States and its commitment to sailors' rights. Aggravated by harsh treatment, meager rations, and poor pay, two great mutinies swept through the British navy in the spring of 1797. The sailors in the channel fleet at Spithead off Portsmouth mutinied on April 16, limiting their action to a petition of grievances while asserting loyalty to King George. Thanks to timely action by Admiral Richard Howe, who offered some concessions and a carte blanche pardon, the men resumed their duty on May 14. The British government was less lenient with the mutiny in the fleet stationed at the Nore, at the mouth of the Medway leading to the Thames River and protecting London. The sailors in these ships, who began their mutiny on May 12, espoused a more radical agenda by drawing up a revolutionary constitution, placing committees in command of their ships, threatening to blockade London, and even discussing joining the French. By mid-June this revolutionary movement began to fall apart as one ship after another returned to the control of its officers. By June 16 the mutiny was over. Authorities executed thirty-six of the ringleaders, including the president of the delegates of the fleet, Richard Parker.[1]

Americans quickly became aware of the great mutinies. Newspaper coverage of Spithead and Nore was mixed. Some accounts merely reproduced material found in British papers, which tended to see the mutinies as unprecedented and threatening to the British nation. A correspondent from Portsmouth in England described the Spithead mutiny as "the present alarming discontents, which threaten the pillars of empire," and another letter from England referred to one confrontation during the mutiny as "the most shocking business that ever happened."[2] Other editors, especially those allied with the Republican Party, expressed sympathy for Parker and his followers and emphasized the order and regularity observed aboard the ships controlled by the seamen. These newspapers summarized the sailors' grievances, including the desire for better pay and fair rations, and the request that sailors not "be punished for any trifle" offense. There were even reports that the seamen had their own regulations, including punishment for men who drank too much alcohol.[3] These descriptions of reasonable demands and orderly behavior suggest that many Americans understood the British sailors' grievances and wanted the mutiny to succeed. A few papers, led by the stridently Republican *Aurora*, expressed outright support for the mutineers, declaring that the British were only getting their just deserts for their poor treatment of sailors and their autocratic demeanor.[4]

As important as the fleet mutinies were as a call for reform in the Atlantic world, the mutiny that had its largest impact on the United States, and on the idea that American sailors had rights, was the bloody single-ship uprising in the West Indies on the frigate *Hermione*. On the night of September 21, 1797, the crew of HMS *Hermione*, a thirty-two-gun frigate, mutinied against Captain Hugh Pigot. The ship and the captain had already gained notoriety in the United States for impressing seamen.[5] At least four of the men aboard the ship during the mutiny were Americans. Pigot drove his men ruthlessly, often bellowing orders, curses, and threats, whereas most captains left the immediate handling of the ship to subordinate officers. He was arbitrary and seemed to take a sadistic pleasure in punishing sailors even for minor infractions of regulations. On one occasion he spotted an improperly tied knot in the rigging. He then chastised the experienced midshipman in charge of the work and, when the young man refused to beg the captain's pardon on his knees, Pigot had him derated of his commission and flogged with twelve lashes. In another instance of brutality, Pigot believed that the men on the mizzen-topsail-yard had not worked quickly enough in reefing a sail during a squall. When the sailors completed their task on the heaving ship, Pigot shouted to them that the last man down would be flogged. As the not-so-nimble tars scrambled down the rigging, three leaped to get ahead of the others, missed grabbing hold of the ropes, and fell dead to the deck. Pigot, with total contempt, ordered that the lifeless bodies immediately be heaved overboard. Incidents like these, along with the spread of republican ideas about the equality of man, convinced some of the crew to take matters into their own hands. Using cutlasses and hatchets, the mutineers overpowered the marine guard stationed at Pigot's door, hacked and mutilated the hated captain, and then, while he was still alive, tossed Pigot overboard. The mutineers killed several other officers, took command of the ship, and sailed it to La Guaira on the coast of South America, where they surrendered the ship to the Spanish. A few crew members declared themselves prisoners of war as a testimony to their opposition to the mutiny. The rest, knowing that even passive concurrence with the mutiny would bring a death sentence in a British court-martial, scattered.

The fate of the Hermiones – crews were called by the name of their ship – became a subject of deep interest to the British Admiralty, which determined to hunt down the mutineers and punish them as examples to the rest of the navy. The British even placed agents in several ports to identify any of the Hermiones who might appear along the waterfront as they sought maritime employment. It was only to be expected that some of the mutineers would find their way to the United States, where there were plenty of opportunities for employment in the American merchant marine and navy.

Over the next few years three cases were brought before American courts to decide what to do with Hermiones who had washed upon the shores of the United States. All three cases bear testimony to the extent that Americans believed that sailors had rights that needed to be protected. The first Hermione found in the United States was Simon Marcus, who was discovered aboard a merchant vessel in Wilmington, Delaware, on February 16, 1798. Frances Marten, the wife of the bosun who had been killed on the *Hermione* and who had moved to New York City, identified Marcus. Like the wives of many petty officers in the British navy, she had been on the *Hermione* and thus knew Marcus personally. However, since Marten did not provide testimony that Marcus had participated actively in the mutiny, he was released without being turned over to the British. This decision was made at the highest level, since it was Secretary of State Timothy Pickering, in consultation with President Adams, who ordered that Marcus not be extradited. No sooner had the Marcus case been settled than three other Hermiones – William Brigstock, John Evans, and Joannes Williams – were found in Perth Amboy, New Jersey, on March 10, 1798. All three were probably Americans. Once again the fate of the mutineers was discussed at the highest level, with Attorney General Charles Lee determining that the case should be tried in a United States federal district court. Frances Marten testified that the men had been aboard the ship during the mutiny and that Brigstock had been actively engaged in killing the officers. The jury, however, acquitted the men of piracy. No reason was given for this decision. In the case of Evans and Williams the verdict may have reflected the fact that they were Americans who were on the *Hermione* but were not mutineers. Brigstock, also an American, was identified as an active mutineer. Despite that testimony, he may have been acquitted because he was an impressed American citizen who was justified in his actions in a rightful effort to regain his liberty. Without any explanation for the court's decision, we cannot know the jury's thinking in this case. However, as is apparent in the third *Hermione* case, many Americans had come to believe that sailors not only had rights but also could act to protect those rights, even to the point of murder, when they were threatened with impressment into the British navy.[6]

That third case centered on Jonathan Robbins, alias Thomas Nash, who had been one of the ringleaders of the mutiny. Robbins/Nash was turned in by a shipmate who had overheard him brag to French privateersmen in St. Domingue about being on the *Hermione*. When their ship arrived in Charleston, South Carolina, the sailor, who apparently did not like Robbins/Nash, reported him to the authorities. This information created a problem for Judge Thomas Bee, who was unsure how to proceed and sought the approval of the president before handing Robbins/Nash over to the British. Adams was reluctant for the executive to tell the judicial branch what to do, but he advised that if Robbins/Nash was not an American, and if there was evidence to show that he was a mutineer, then he should be surrendered to the British. After the legal proceedings began in July 1799, Robbins/Nash, who was probably an Irishman, claimed to be an impressed seaman from Danbury, Connecticut. Robbins/ Nash had taken too long to make this claim, and with the judicial machinery already in motion, he was handed over to the British, tried in Jamaica, and hanged.[7]

The Robbins/Nash case did not end with this execution; it opened a maelstrom of political debate that included a call for a congressional censure of the president for violating the doctrine of the separation of powers (between executive and judicial authority) and for ignoring Robbins/Nash's claim to citizenship in violation of his rights. Republicans also used the controversy to once again assail the Jay Treaty, claiming that the twenty-seventh article, which stated that each country would extradite persons charged with murder, meant that "a citizen of the United States might be dragged from his country, his connexions, and his friends, and subjected to the judgement of an unrelenting military tribunal." The debate in the House of Representatives was long and acrimonious, but one thing was clear: both the Republicans and the Federalists claimed to be protecting the rights of sailors. Although no one in Congress believed that Robbins/Nash was innocent or really an American, several members from both sides of the aisle argued that his claim should at least have merited serious consideration. In an incredible statement about the importance of protecting American seamen and their rights, the Georgia Federalist James Jones declared that "he deemed it totally immaterial whether the man was . . . an Irishman or not; whether he was a Turk, a Hottentot, or a native-born American, if he claimed to be an American citizen, and produced a certificate in due form," he deserved to have his claim carefully considered. To do otherwise was to "put in jeopardy" all citizens. "This man was a citizen to all intents and purposes, so far as respects precedent, if he claimed that right and produced a voucher to testify it," and, as such, he "was entitled to all the privileges of a citizen until his claim and certificate had been formally proven to be false." In an extended and tightly reasoned legal argument, Congressmen John Marshall defended the president's action and the Jay Treaty. At the end of his speech, Marshall went on to make it clear that although the president was correct in surrendering Robbins/Nash to the British, American sailors as United States citizens retained the right to defend themselves against impressment. Marshall agreed with Republican congressman Albert Gallatin and insisted that the government "could never surrender an impressed American to the nation which, in making the impressment, had committed a national injury." He also stated that "[h]ad Thomas Nash been an impressed American, the homicide on board the *Hermione* would, most certainly, not have been murder." He explained: "The act of impressing an American is an act of lawless violence. The confinement on board a vessel is a continuation of the violence, and an additional outrage." Therefore, "Death committed within the United States, in resisting such violence, would not have been murder, and the person giving the wound could not have been treated as a murderer." Robbins/Nash could have been set free only if he were "an impressed American liberating himself by homicide."[8]

For the British, such words had a chilling effect. As one British visitor to the United States explained to Lord Grenville after his return to England, "it was Mr. Marshall, the present Secretary of State, a Virginian lawyer of considerable abilities, who in Congress maintained the argument . . . that American seamen had a *right* to do what had been done on board the *Hermione*." Marshall defended the president's surrender of Robbins/Nash to the British because Robbins/Nash was an Irishman, even though, the author continued sarcastically, Marshall "took the occasion at the same time to proclaim and enlarge on the very humane and liberal principle I have stated." Combined with popular support for the mutinies at Spithead and the Nore, which many in the United States "ascribed to the *brave* efforts of impressed American seamen," there was little doubt that the Americans had pushed the idea of sailors' rights too far for this British aristocrat.[9]

British and American tars might disagree with this conclusion. The mutinies at Spithead and the Nore, as well as the violence on the *Hermione*, had a deep resonance for common seamen on both sides of the Atlantic. On at least two occasions discontent American sailors cited the example of the Hermiones as they themselves challenged the authority of the quarterdeck. In 1800, aboard the very same *Essex* that Porter would later command, a sailor whose tongue had been loosened by liquor told his shipmates that they should attack the officers and treat them "as we did on board the Hermione and serve them right." Four years later a common seaman aboard the *President* wrote a letter to Commodore Samuel Barron complaining that "[t]he President is arrived to such a pitch as to exceed the Hermione." Neither incident led to a mutiny, and both sailors found themselves severely punished. How many other times sailors in the American and British navies may have muttered about the *Hermione* we can only conjecture. But when Porter raised his banner proclaiming "Free Trade and Sailors' Rights," he was offering a not-too-subtle reminder to the common seamen aboard his own ship, and the ships of the British enemy, that sailors had rights that were worth fighting for.[10]

The belief in sailors' rights had become an accepted axiom of the American creed long before Porter flew his standard. By 1800 the idea that sailors had rights had become firmly ingrained in the popular American imagination. Beginning with the Anglo-American background heralding the importance of sailors in a commerce crucial to English liberty and in defending an island nation, and accelerated by the experience of so many seamen in the Revolutionary War, Jack Tar became increasingly essential to the identity of colonial America and then of the new United States. These developments continued in the 1780s and 1790s as American commerce expanded and as that commerce was challenged by the Algerians, British, and French. Confronted by the threat of impressment, the United States government passed legislation offering to protect its sailor-citizens. Ultimately the growing democratic and egalitarian ideas pulsating throughout the Atlantic world, along with the threat of impressment, which challenged the sovereignty of the United States, convinced Americans of every political stripe that sailors not only had rights but also that those rights should be defended even if it meant mayhem, mutiny, and murder.

PART THREE

# ORIGINS

By the inauguration of Thomas Jefferson on March 4, 1801, the two elements of Porter's motto – free trade and sailors' rights – had become entrenched in American political and popular culture. Although they were sometimes mentioned in close proximity to each other, they had not yet become connected. If both ideas were important in American relations with Great Britain, France, and even the Barbary states, they remained distinct and different concepts. During the decade after Jefferson's revolution of 1800 they would gradually merge, although Jefferson and James Madison were often more concerned with the patrician free trade, especially as it related to neutral rights, while common folk, newspaper editors, and even many Republican politicians focused more on the plebeian sailors' rights. As the United States moved toward war with Great Britain, other issues also intruded, so that by the eve of the War of 1812 Americans had multiple reasons to fight the British. Not only were they concerned with neutral commerce and the question of impressment, they were also interested in expanding the republic and ending the Native American presence east of the Mississippi. To understand how and why free trade and sailors' rights were brought together and became the rhetorical explanation for the conflict, we need to examine those other reasons and then trace the story of free trade and sailors' rights individually from 1801 to the outbreak of the war. In the end, free trade and sailors' rights combined with each other and with the other causes of the War of 1812 to convince many Americans that they had to protect the honor of the nation in a world where monarchs competed for empire and scoffed at the idea that a government based on republicanism should be taken seriously.[1]

# 10

# Empire of Liberty

Many scholars who have examined the expansion of the United States assume that the Founding Fathers always had some grand vision of sweeping across the continent and establishing an empire of liberty. Fueled by the later success of the so-called manifest destiny, these scholars read the language of Thomas Jefferson, James Madison, and other Republicans in the 1790s and assume that their interest in expanding across space meant that they knew that yeoman farmers – God's chosen people, in Jefferson's memorable phrase – would pour over the Appalachians, fill the Ohio Valley in less than a generation, and then charge to the Pacific.[1] Such a view grants too much prescience to the Jeffersonians. Yes, it is true that even before the Declaration of Independence, some Americans sought to add Canada to their cause. And once the Treaty of Paris established the new nation's boundaries, others hoped to add Florida to the south. But there was no great master plan, no sense that the United States would march west. As late as 1790 Jefferson was willing to guarantee the Spanish control of Louisiana if they ceded Florida to the United States. During the early republic Americans only gradually came to see expansion as part of their destiny, and even then, there remained many who were skeptical of creating an overblown republic that might easily be torn apart or become imperial in ambition and unrepublican in spirit. After the United States accidentally added Louisiana in 1803, the push for Florida became more concerted, and territorial expansion became a more salient issue for increasing numbers of Americans. By the beginning of the War of 1812 many of the War Hawks hoped to use the opportunity of conflict with Great Britain to gain new territory. Although these crass bellicose ambitions might be expressed by politicians and newspaper editors, they could never become the main explanation for a republic going to war in 1812. Instead, the conflict was best explained by proclaiming principles and ideals like free trade and sailors' rights.

It is in this context that we need to understand that Jefferson, who has often been seen as the architect of American expansion, may have talked about an empire of liberty, but he did not necessarily envision a single transcendent nation. Rather, he imagined that there might be a host of sister republics, linked by their commitment to the ideal of liberty, that shared values and heritage. Shortly after he became president, Jefferson wrote enthusiastically to James Monroe that "it is impossible not to look forward to distant times, when our rapid multiplication will expand... & cover the whole Northen, if not the Southern continent with a people speaking the same language, governed in similar forms, & by similar laws."[2] He thought that the United States, as he explained in 1786, "must be viewed as the nest from which all America, North and South is to be peopled."[3] The metaphor was appropriate, since it implied that while the United States might nurture the development of new republics, eventually, like young birds, those republics had to leave the nest and become independent. Values, rather than a single government, would bind Jefferson's sister republics. As Julian P. Boyd wrote in 1943, Jefferson's empire of liberty centered "in the realm of the mind and spirit of man, freely and inexorably transcending political boundaries, incapable of being restrained, and holding imperial sway not by arms or political power but by the sheer majesty of ideas."[4] Madison, too, spoke about the importance of the West to the future of the republic and saw increased settlement as the best means to sustain the agrarian character of the nation and to stave off the corruption and decay that came with manufacturing and advanced stages of economic development. But his West in the 1790s was the huge tract of "unsettled" (Native Americans might disagree with the term) land between the Appalachians and the Mississippi.[5] Both men assumed it would take at least a generation before this vast expanse would be brought under the plough. Jefferson, with great hyperbole, proclaimed in his first inaugural address in 1801, before he ever imagined purchasing the Louisiana Territory, that the United States had "room enough for our descendants to the thousandth and thousandth generation."[6] Most Americans who considered expansion in the earliest years of the republic centered their interest on the trans-Appalachian West.[7]

Even so, there were Americans who looked to the frontier with fear and trepidation. Although the supporters of the United States Constitution had sought to dispel the belief that republics could not be sustained in a large state, most famously in Madison's essay *Federalist* Number 10, there were still plenty of Americans concerned with exactly how big a republic could be before it became too big, necessitating too much power and thereby threatening liberty. Anti-Federalists made this point repeatedly in their opposition to the Constitution, and its ratification did not automatically mean that everyone ignored what had been the best political science of the day, which stipulated that republics could not long exist in a large geographical area. These fears became all too real for members of the Federalist Party during the debates over the Louisiana Purchase. Although he supported the purchase, Alexander Hamilton believed "that should our own citizens, more enterprizing than wise," decide to settle the "wilderness" of the trans-Mississippi West, "it must not only be attended with all the injuries of a too widely dispersed population, but by adding to the great weight of the western part of our territory, must hasten the dismemberment of a large portion of our country, or a dissolution of the Government."[8] Most Federalists opposed the purchase, believing that adding "to the Union of a territory equal to the whole United States" would "overbalance the existing territory, and thereby the rights of the present citizens of the United States be swallowed up and lost."[9]

Other Americans were worried about the type of people who settled on the frontier. Jefferson looked on the farmer as the bastion of the republic, an individual whose independence and judgment would ensure the future. Some commentators, however, feared the primitive nature of the frontier and believed that society could regress. In 1786 Jefferson's friend Benjamin Rush described "the *first* settler in the woods" as "a man who has outlived his credit or fortune in the cultivated parts of the State." Living more like a Native American than a European American, he depended on hunting and fishing, raising only small crops of corn. These frontiersmen were a far cry from the industrious yeoman of Jefferson's imagination. The frontiersman loves "spirituous liquors," while "he eats, drinks and sleeps in dirt and rags in his little cabin." When civilization caught up to him, he grew discontent and did not seek improvement. "Above all, he revolts against the operation of laws," since "[h]e cannot bear to surrender up a single natural right for all the benefits of government." Rush hoped that with a more ordered settlement of the West, with men "of property and good character," this primitive stage could be avoided.[10] For many other Americans, the western frontier was packed with hardscrabble disorderly men who threatened the stability of the republic.

That these individuals might be enticed to the allegiance of a foreign power, or support some breakaway movement, only made the danger more real. The loyalty of the leaders in the West was often questionable. In 1793 Edmond Genêt, the French minister to the United States, recruited George Rogers Clark to lead an expedition against Spanish Louisiana for France. While a senator, William Blount became involved in a scheme in 1797 to conquer Louisiana for the British. Beginning in the 1780s, General James Wilkinson swore allegiance to the king of Spain and received a retainer for many years. And most notoriously, in 1806 Aaron Burr led a conspiracy that had as its goal some sort of expedition in the West, either to set up an independent nation or to attack the Spanish in Texas and Mexico. Common folk in the West could easily slip into the orbit of another power or strike out on their own. George Washington's comment in 1784 that "[t]he Western settlers . . . stand as it were upon a pivot;

the touch of a feather, would turn them any way" held true throughout the period.[11] In the late 1790s the Spanish distributed handbills in Kentucky enticing settlers to cross the Mississippi and settle. One Kentucky leader reported that "the poorer Class of people" were moving en masse and becoming subjects of the king of Spain. Daniel Boone, after the failure of his speculations in Kentucky, left the United States with much of his extended family and headed for Spanish territory in 1800, accepting appointment as an administrative officer.[12] The West was fraught with both dangers and possibilities that could tear apart the republic.

As suggested by the plots and conspiracies of men like Clark, Blount, and Wilkinson, the West was also contested by foreign powers. The Treaty of Paris had granted the United States a generous western boundary in ceding it the territory east of the Mississippi, north of Florida, and south of the Great Lakes. Gaining control of this trans-Appalachian region was not easy. Regardless of the treaty provisions, until passage of the Jay Treaty the British refused to evacuate a series of forts on what was technically United States soil. From these outposts the British continued to exert influence on the Indians of the Northwest and dominated the trade of the region. During the Nootka Sound controversy of 1790, when Great Britain and Spain almost went to war over claims in the Pacific Northwest, the United States would have been helpless to stop a British army from marching from those forts to attack the Spanish along the Mississippi. Perhaps even more irksome was the supposed influence exerted by the British in encouraging hostile Native Americans to resist the United States. The Jay Treaty, after some further delays, ended the direct British military presence in the United States. But the treaty also opened complete access for British traders into the United States (as well as access for American traders into Canada). British agents continued to be busy and were a presence in the Old Northwest until the opening of the War of 1812.

If anything, the situation faced by the United States in the Old Southwest during the 1780s and early 1790s was even more grave. By the end of the Revolutionary War, Spain controlled both sides of the Mississippi from the mouth of the river at least to the conjunction with the Ohio. The Spanish also gained Florida. Having conquered West Florida during the war, they obtained East Florida in compensation for not capturing Gibraltar. During the 1780s, whatever the peace treaty with Great Britain may have said, the Spanish extended the earlier British northern boundary of West Florida of 32°28', and insisted that Florida reached all the way to the Tennessee River. They backed up this claim with forts and treaties with the local Indians. Spanish control of the Mississippi presented real problems for the United States, since it meant that they occupied the natural outlet for the agricultural produce of the Ohio River Valley and much of the trans-Appalachian West. When John Jay, in negotiations with the Spanish minister Don Diego Gardoqui in 1786, appeared willing to cede the navigation of the Mississippi for twenty-five to thirty years in exchange for a commercial agreement to open Spanish ports to American ships, Congress became embroiled in a bitter debate that ended any hope for the treaty. Spain, in the meanwhile, sought to woo settlers in the West with promises of land and arrangements like the secret payments to Wilkinson. The situation in the Southwest remained stalemated, and the port of New Orleans was officially closed to Americans until 1795. At that point the Spanish, suffering from the upheaval of the French Revolution, and interested in placating the Americans after the Jay Treaty had ended the threat of war between the United States and Great Britain, ceded a generous boundary, setting a northern border of Florida at the thirty-first parallel. Although for over a year the Spanish delayed withdrawing from their forts in the ceded territory, this agreement opened new lands for European-American settlement. Just as importantly, the treaty allowed Americans the right of deposit – in essence, free trade – in New Orleans for three years. The Spanish renewed this provision thereafter until 1802, when they again closed the port to Americans.[13]

The Spanish closure of New Orleans had the potential to create a major diplomatic crisis. Since the Pinckney Treaty had guaranteed some open port when the Spanish closed New Orleans, Americans felt cheated and betrayed. Jefferson exclaimed that the closing of the river threw the "country into such a flame of hostile disposition as can scarcely be described."[14] Jefferson believed that Americans had a natural right to the port of New Orleans, and as early as 1792 had argued that "Spain holds so very small a tract of habitable land on either side below our boundary, that it [the Mississippi River] may in fact be considered as a streight of the sea" rather than a river. He also thought both the river and its shores should be open to American commerce.[15] Fearing a confrontation with the United States, and more concerned with its problems in Europe and other American colonies, Spain reopened New Orleans in early 1803. This action did not have any long-term implications because France was about to take possession of the Louisiana Territory. In 1786 Jefferson had written that Spain was "too feeble to hold on to" its North American colonies and was afraid that other nations might swallow them up before the American "population can be sufficiently advanced to gain it from them piece by piece."[16] The French action was exactly the type of territorial cession he had feared.

Instead of facing Napoleon's armies on the Mississippi, Jefferson stumbled into the Louisiana Purchase, which doubled the size of the nation. This good fortune came at the expense of the lives of thousands of French soldiers and Haitian revolutionaries on the island of Hispaniola. No sooner had Napoleon Bonaparte agreed to the Convention of 1800 ending the Quasi War, than he decided to build his own empire in the Western Hemisphere and send an army to the rebellious colony of St. Domingue. To supply what had once been the most profitable colony in the New World, Napoleon wanted to control

Louisiana, a great stretch of territory in the interior of North America that France had ceded to Spain in 1763. Since Napoleon was in a position to dictate terms to Spain, he had that country retrocede Louisiana to France in the Treaty of San Ildefonso on the day after he made peace with the United States. When Jefferson learned of this action, despite his French sympathies, he immediately recognized the danger to the United States and wanted Robert R. Livingston, the American minister to France, to begin negotiations to purchase the port of New Orleans and, if possible, Florida (which remained a Spanish possession, but which Jefferson thought – hoped? – was part of the French deal with the Spanish).[17] Jefferson also dispatched James Monroe to join in the negotiations. The idea behind gaining control of New Orleans and Florida was not so much to extend the empire of liberty as it was to provide outlets for the commerce of settlers in the trans-Appalachian United States, either down the Mississippi or through the numerous waterways draining into the Gulf of Mexico from what is now Georgia, Alabama, and Mississippi.

Napoleon's grand dreams of a Franco-American empire disintegrated amid the heat, disease, and bitter racial warfare of St. Domingue. The French sent over 30,000 troops to Hispaniola under the command of Napoleon's brother-in-law General Charles Victor Emmanuel LeClerc. Although the French experienced some initial success, they were worn down by tropical maladies. Victory slipped away after LeClerc arrested Toussaint Louverture and began massacring black troops who had agreed to join the French, triggering renewed resistance.[18] By 1803, with war again looming with Great Britain, and with the failure to control St. Domingue, Louisiana looked more like a military liability than a strategic asset. Short of cash, Napoleon offered to sell the entire territory to the United States for $15 million. Monroe and Livingston jumped at this opportunity, even though it exceeded the amount they had been authorized to spend. The subsequent purchase treaty also violated their instructions by granting citizenship to the current inhabitants of Louisiana. Regardless of these obstacles, some constitutional scruples on the part of Jefferson, and the opposition of members of the Federalist Party, the United States Senate ratified the treaty. Expanding the empire of liberty, then, was an accident that happened as Jefferson sought to protect American commerce by gaining control of New Orleans.[19]

If Jefferson obtained control of New Orleans and the Louisiana Territory, Florida remained in Spanish hands. Florida held special interest for Americans in the early nineteenth century. The peninsular area of Florida was unimportant, and no one really cared about the huge expanses of swamp that make up what is today south Florida. The coastal region of Florida along the Gulf of Mexico, and land immediately south of Georgia on the Atlantic Ocean to St. Augustine, was the Florida that Americans coveted. The Gulf Coast, stretching from the Mississippi River east, controlled the mouths of several rivers that were the natural outlets for the region that by the 1830s would become the heart of the cotton kingdom.

Florida was important for other reasons. The Spanish hold on Florida was tenuous. The colony had a small European-descendent population and, as a borderland, it created problems for the United States. Florida offered a safe haven to escaped slaves from the South. As long as this outlet remained open, the institution of slavery, which had become so central to the expansion of settlement in the Old Southwest, was in jeopardy. Florida also was a home for Native Americans hostile to the United States, who could strike into Georgia, Alabama, and Mississippi and retreat to Florida with impunity. Smugglers and illegal traders proliferated in the region, evading American customs laws and threatening the stability of the borderland by supplying Indians. Moreover, if the Spanish somehow lost the territory to the British or the French, then a potentially powerful and hostile presence would occupy the nation's southern boundary.

Control of Florida became one of the key objectives of American foreign policy from independence to the Adams-Onis Treaty of 1819, which ceded what remained of the territory to the United States. Interest in Florida lay behind the Pinckney Treaty of 1795. Florida, too, was one of the real aims behind the Louisiana Purchase. No sooner had the United States closed that deal than some Americans declared that Florida had been a part of the package, even though Spain had not ceded it to the French. In 1804 Congress passed the Mobile Act, which claimed as United States territory all navigable rivers that emptied into the Gulf of Mexico and set up a special customs district for the region. The Spanish protested this blatant land grab. Jefferson sidestepped the issue by explaining that customs would be collected only from within the boundaries of the United States. In 1805 Jefferson sought to obtain all of Florida through negotiations and even contemplated a military alliance with Great Britain in case these efforts failed.[20]

During the 1790s and early 1800s some people from the United States, often debtors and men on the run, crossed into Florida. Aaron Burr, for example, headed for Florida when his supposed conspiracy in the West imploded. Despite the marginal status of many of the Americans in Florida, this group was the nucleus of a pro-American movement that became more active in the years leading up to the War of 1812. On September 23, 1810, eighty of these rough characters seized Baton Rouge on the east bank of the Mississippi, issued a declaration of independence, and then petitioned to be brought into the United States. James Madison annexed the area by presidential decree on October 27, 1810, maintaining the legal fiction that West Florida "has at all times, as is well known, been considered and claimed" by the United States "as being within the Colony of Louisiana." Madison explained that the area had been under the temporary control of the Spanish through "the acquiescence of the

United States," and "by their [American] conciliatory views, and by a confidence in the justice of their cause." Madison continued by stating that he would be remiss in his duties if he did not take possession of the territory now that there was "a crisis" that was "subversive of the order of things" that endangered "the tranquility and security of our adjoining territories." He sent troops to Baton Rouge and then declared that the boundary between Spain and the United States was the Perdido River, stationing troops outside Mobile in West Florida, in 1811. When Louisiana became a state in 1812, it included a section of West Florida that jutted east under the current state of Mississippi.[21]

Madison endorsed a similar filibuster – the name applied to the American invasions into Spanish territory in the early nineteenth century – to seize portions of East Florida in 1812. American settlers from the area, joined by Georgians eager for new lands, crossed into Florida on March 12, 1812. They captured Amelia Island and the port of Fernandina, both of which had been smuggler hideouts for over a decade. These "Patriots," as they called themselves, declared independence and quickly elicited support from the American navy. They also marched on St. Augustine and were even joined by a detachment of the United States army. Although the "Patriots" had the tacit support of Madison, the Senate refused to condone the operation. Between Spanish attacks, which drove the Americans away from the walls of St. Augustine, and Seminole raids, the expedition failed to wrest Florida from the Spanish. A bitter guerilla war continued for over a year, with raid and counter-raid and each side looting the other. The biggest losers in the campaign were the Seminoles, who had supported the Spanish. An American army marched into their settlements in 1813 and drove them from their rich cattle lands and into the forest and swamps of Florida. The region, however, remained Spanish for the time being.[22]

Americans were involved in several other similar adventures to the south. In 1806 Francisco de Miranda recruited men and ships in New York to launch an invasion of his native Venezuela and liberate it from Spain. Miranda had fought in the Spanish army during its conquest of West Florida in the Revolutionary War, visited the United States in the 1790s, and had joined the French revolutionaries in Europe. He returned to the United States late in 1805. Although he met with both Jefferson and Madison, he did not gain any official sanction for the expedition he launched in 1806. Unfortunately for the 200 men who joined him, many of whom were Americans, Spanish forces repulsed Miranda's invasion. Most of his followers were captured by the Spanish, and those who were not executed were left to languish in Spanish prisons. For his part, Miranda escaped and later joined Simón Bolívar in his effort to liberate South America.[23] The revolution that started in Mexico in 1810 also brought other Americans into the fray. Several hundred Americans joined with Mexicans and Indians to cross into Texas in the summer of 1812. Although the Texas filibusters realized some successes, ultimately royalists supporting Spain beat back the invaders. Taken all together, the efforts to snatch Florida from the Spanish, the involvement in the Miranda fiasco, and the Texas incursion indicate that some Americans were looking south – not west – for areas into which the United States might expand the empire of liberty in terms of land acquisition, trade, and creating sister republics.[24]

Other Americans cast their glances to the north and coveted Canada. During the Revolutionary War, Americans launched an overly ambitious expedition into Canada that got as far as the gates of Quebec. The Continental Army proposed other invasions during the war, but nothing ever came of these plans. At the end of the war, the British were well entrenched in Canada, enhancing their position by offering a safe haven for Loyalists and Native Americans who had fought in defense of King George. During the 1790s thousands of other migrants from the United States began to enter Canada, attracted by the nearly free land and low taxes offered to settlers by the British crown. Referred to as the "late Loyalists," these individuals have often been portrayed as Loyalists who were escaping persecution and prejudice in an independent United States. However, they probably had more ambiguous allegiances and, like their cousins in the United States, were eager to capitalize on whatever opportunities the frontier offered.[25] Many of these people found the more autocratic government in Canada and its leniency toward French-speaking Catholics difficult. To placate these settlers, in 1791 the British split Canada into two provinces, Upper Canada (Ontario) and Lower Canada (Quebec), granting Upper Canada a more representative form of government reflecting the principles of the British constitution. Americans, however, believed that many of the English-speaking Canadians might support the more democratic United States in a conflict with Great Britain.

Canada was also a target of American interest because it was the staging ground for British trade with the Indians of the American Northwest and because it was from Canada that the British seemed to encourage Native American hostility toward the United States. These concerns increased by 1808. Convinced that the British were urging Native Americans to oppose the United States, Congressman W. A. Burwell of Virginia proclaimed in 1809 that "[t]he expulsion of the British from Canada has always been deemed an object of first importance to the peace of the United States." By 1811 and 1812 the saber rattling had become loud and persistent.[26] Felix Grundy of Tennessee, one of several in Congress known as War Hawks, summed up this approach when he declared, "We shall drive the British from our Continent – they will no longer have an opportunity of intriguing with our Indian neighbors, and setting on the ruthless savage to tomahawk our women and children." Once Canada could be joined to the American union, so Grundy and others argued, settlement south of the Great Lakes might proceed in a more peaceful manner.[27]

Although at times Thomas Jefferson wrote about the empire of liberty in relation to a set of ideas and sister republics, in the years immediately before the War of 1812 he began to discuss a more specific agenda. In 1809, shortly after he retired from the presidency, he wrote in an expansionist frame of mind to James Madison and sketched a plan of action, to reach across the continent not to the vacant West, but to the North and South. Jefferson wanted the United States to gain control of Canada, Florida, and even Cuba – there is no mention of the Rockies, the Pacific, or California. In a fit of hubris that grossly underestimated the difficulties of conquest, Jefferson wrote that the Floridas "are ours in the first moment of the first war" and then, a few lines later, that "we should then have only to include the North in our confederacy, which would be of course in the first war." These acquisitions, which were so easy to describe on paper, would be enough for Jefferson, after which he believed Americans "should have such an empire of liberty" as the world had never "surveyed since the creation."[28] In these years many Americans, like Jefferson, began to envision an expansionist United States, and this interest in territorial acquisition would help convince the nation to enter the War of 1812. But as a rallying cry, and as a reason for the war, the expansion of the empire of liberty paled in comparison to "Free Trade and Sailors' Rights."

# 11

# Indians in the Way

If much of the interest in expansion before 1812 centered on the trans-Appalachian West, then the biggest problem for the United States was that there were Indians in the way. These Indians were both diverse and dynamic. Between the Mississippi River and the region settled by European Americans, Native Americans spoke a wide variety of languages, usually lived in villages or towns, and practiced a mixed economy dependent on agriculture (work normally done by women), hunting (work normally done by men), and trade. Although European Americans identified specific tribes among the Indians, Native American political structure did not fit any neat proto-state categories, and authority within their communities was usually dispersed and diffuse. There were no chiefs who could dictate policy or speak for an entire people. The so-called Creek nation, for example, really represented a cluster of towns in what is now Georgia and Alabama divided into clans without any central authority. Moreover, as a result of migrations in the eighteenth century, many Indian towns included individuals from a variety of different groups. The Shawnee had five major divisions, and had settlements spread across much of the Ohio River Valley, yet many Shawnee also lived in towns with other Indian groups.[1]

In the mid eighteenth century the Native Americans in the interior, while challenged by the presence of European Americans, in many ways thrived in the spaces between the British, Spanish, and French North American empires. Eager to trade, these Native Americans played one European power off against the other. Most of these Indians – based around the Great Lakes, in the Ohio River Valley, and in the South living along rivers that drained into the Gulf of Mexico – sided with the French during the Seven Years' War. After that conflict, and the subsequent challenge to British control in Pontiac's War, the Indians in the Ohio Country and the Great Lakes region traded with the British and their American colonists, hoping to keep European-American settlers at bay. To the south, the Cherokee, Creek, Choctaw, and Chickasaw still had the presence of the Spanish in Louisiana as a counterweight to the British. During the Revolutionary War many of the trans-Appalachian Indians fought with the British against the revolutionaries, who had begun to clamor for land in the West. The campaigns along the frontier were nasty and brutal, with Indians raiding and destroying the crops and settlements of European Americans, and revolutionary forces entering Indian territory and doing the same. However, despite the exploits of George Rogers Clark in capturing Vincennes and some other outposts in the region, the United States did not conquer the West during the Revolution.[2] In fact, the Indians of the Northwest believed that they were winning the war after defeating a force from Kentucky at the Battle of Blue Licks (August 19, 1782) and an expedition from Pennsylvania and Virginia in the Battle of Sandusky (June 4–5, 1782). These Native Americans were completely surprised when they discovered that their territory had been ceded to the United States by the British in what they considered a base betrayal and "an Act of Cruelty and injustice that Christians only were capable of doing."[3] In the South, although the Cherokee had been hard pressed, the war had a less serious impact on the Creek, Choctaw, and Chickasaw. Much of the land occupied by these Indians was claimed by both Spain and the United States.[4]

Whatever the realities on the ground, the Continental Congress saw things differently and proclaimed that the Indians had been subdued and that the United States had complete sovereignty over the territory between the Appalachians and the Mississippi River. For Congress, the generous boundaries granted in the Treaty of Paris of 1783 stood as proof of the American victory. This fiction was important to Congress, since the sale of lands in the West, especially in the public domain north of the Ohio River already ceded by the states, had the potential to settle all of the government's financial problems and enable it to pay off the national debt. In 1783 a congressional committee, in part following the recommendations of Philip Schuyler and George Washington, insisted upon some Indian land cessions. The committee, with false generosity, also waived "the right of conquest" and offered "clemency," agreeing that the Indians could continue to live in peace on most of their lands west of the Appalachians. Congress's idea was to establish an orderly process whereby European Americans would occupy the ceded land and then, little by little, extend the limits of settled territory.[5] As Washington explained, "the gradual extension of our Settlements will as certainly cause the Savage as the Wolf to retire; both being beasts of prey tho' they differ in shape." Thus without the force of arms and without the "distresses which helpless Women and Children are made partakers" in Indian wars, the land could be obtained by peaceable means.[6] With this approach in mind, the United States forced a series of treaties, often without the full representation of the Indian tribes present, ceding the requisite land in modern Ohio.

Practical as well as ideological reasons led to a change of policy in the late 1780s. Pragmatically, the United States government had neither the money nor the military to enforce these cessions against Indians who did not accept the coerced treaties. As Henry Knox, head of the War Department during the confederation period and the first secretary of war under the United States Constitution, admitted in 1787, "in the present embarrassed state of public affairs and entire deficiency of funds an indian war of any considerable extent and duration would most exceedingly distress the United States."[7] Ideologically, the coercive nature of this policy began to bother some of the nation's leaders. The empires of the Old World might conquer nations in order to expand, but not republics. Men like Knox argued that the nation had to approach expansion with a greater sense of morality. Knox wrote in 1789, "a nation solicitous of establishing its character on the broad basis of justice, would not only hesitate at, but reject every proposition to benefit itself, by the injury of any neighboring community, however contemptible and weak it might be, either with respect to its manners or power." He continued, "The Indians being the prior occupants, possess the right of the soil. It cannot be taken from them unless by their free consent or by the right of conquest in case of a just war." Using the language of the Enlightenment, Knox declared, "To dispossess them on any other principle, would be a gross violation of the fundamental laws of nature, and that distributive justice which is the glory of a nation." Knox repeated these sentiments in a later report, asserting that the Indians had "the natural rights of man," including "the right to all their territory" not granted in fair treaties, and expressed concern about the image of America by noting that "[i]f our modes of population and War destroy the tribes the disinterested part of mankind and posterity will be apt to class the effects of our Conduct" with "that of the Spaniards in Mexico and Peru," long held in contempt in both Great Britain and America.[8] At the urging of Knox and others, and faced with the practical reality of the lack of funds, Congress decided to be more "politic and Just," to "treat with the Indians more on a footing of equality" and to seek to purchase lands rather than simply to demand them.[9] By the 1790s this new policy also included another component – urged by Knox and Washington, among others – intended to bring civilization to the Indians by convincing them to turn to the agricultural practices of the European Americans and accept the idea of private property. Whatever the larger philosophical underpinnings of the government's Indian policy, the same basic aim remained paramount: to obtain cessions of land and open new territory for European-American settlement.[10]

Some Indians were accommodating and sold land to the United States, whether they had a claim to the land or not. Others were not so easily coerced. European Americans may have streamed into Kentucky in the 1780s and early 1790s, but they could not so easily cross to the north shore of the Ohio, where the Miami, Shawnee, Delaware, and other tribes had joined in a loose confederation to defend their land in opposition to the claims of the United States. Refusing to accept land cessions by some members of their tribes in Ohio, this confederation defeated armies under Josiah Harmar in 1790 and Arthur St. Clair in 1791 and insisted on the Ohio River as the boundary between Indian country and land available to European Americans from the United States, even if the Northwest Ordinances had set up a system to establish such settlement. In 1793 the confederation refused to negotiate directly with the United States. The Indians were so confident in their position that they informed the commissioners sent to gain land cessions that "[m]oney, to us, is of no value" and would not induce them "to sell the lands on which we get sustenance for our women and children." Instead, the Indians suggested that the commissioners pay the same money to the poor white people to leave the Ohio country, since this would be cheaper than trying to buy land from Indians, and "they would most readily accept of it." This policy would also avoid "the great sums you must expend in raising and paying armies" to fight the Indians.[11] British forts in the Northwest, especially at Detroit, supported these Native Americans with trade and arms, and in 1794 the governor of Canada, Lord Dorchester, told a delegation of Indians that the United States had rejected efforts by the British to mediate a peace and establish an independent Native American state. He went so far as to say that the king and the Americans would soon be at war and that the Indians and British together could then draw the boundary as they pleased. With the British seeking to create a Native American buffer zone that they could dominate economically, and faced with concerted Native American opposition, the Washington administration increased taxes and organized a more formidable army that was fortunate enough to defeat the Indian confederation at the Battle of Fallen Timbers on August 20, 1794. In the meantime the international situation changed. The British government withdrew its support for the Indians and, in the Jay Treaty, promised to evacuate the forts in United States territory. Abandoned by the British and defeated on the battlefield, the Native Americans in the region ceded half of present-day Ohio to the United States in the Treaty of Greenville in 1795. Most of the rest of the Northwest Territory, for the time being, remained in the hands of the Indians.[12]

The situation south of Kentucky was also unstable. Because states like Georgia and North Carolina hesitated in renouncing their claims to western land and insisted on dealing with the Indians in the region on their own terms, the United States government had difficulty establishing itself as the nation's single voice in Native American diplomacy. In the 1780s and 1790s both the state and national governments intimidated, bribed, and tricked the Creek and Cherokee into ceding more of their lands, straining relations throughout the period. Here, too, international diplomacy played a part. The Treaty of San Lorenzo with Spain in 1795 left most of this territory undisputably under the jurisdiction of the United States. The Spanish remained along the coast of the Gulf of Mexico, and could still offer an outlet for some trade, but their ability to influence the region was greatly curtailed after their retreat in 1795.[13]

Congress passed several measures to control the interaction between European Americans and Native Americans on the frontier. The Act to Regulate Trade and Intercourse with the Indian Tribes (July 22, 1790), also known as Indian Trade and Intercourse Act, stipulated that only traders licensed by the federal government could enter Indian territory and had to operate under "such rules, regulations and restrictions" as were established by the government of the United States. Limited to two years, the license could be rescinded at any time. The law gave the United States sole authority to purchase Indian lands. Congress extended and strengthened the law a number of times in the 1790s, empowering the president to punish illegal settlers on Indian lands and authorizing the expenditure of money to provide the tools – looms, farming implements, and the like – to help the Indians on the path to civilization. In addition, a law passed in April 1796 established a factory system of government-run trading posts in Indian country to provide goods to Native Americans without fraud and to wean them from foreign suppliers like the British and the Spanish.[14]

Despite the best of intentions, European-American actions aggravated tensions with Native Americans and led to renewed conflict. The relentless pressure of frontiersmen heading west remained a problem. No sooner was a new line drawn between Indian territory and land open for European-American settlement than hardscrabble interlopers crossed the line to settle on Native American land, regardless of treaty stipulations or federal law. Occasionally the United States Army would be used to evict such squatters, but more often than not the frontiersmen remained, became an irritant to the Indians, and triggered additional bloodshed. Also, "Land Jobbers, Speculators, and Monoplisers," in George Washington's words, sought to engross frontier lands, creating conflicting land claims and antagonizing Native Americans with surveying parties as precursors of settlement. Traders, too, continued to travel through Indian country, plying their wares, selling liquor as well as other trade goods. Even the trading factories contributed to the problem. They became centers for new European-American settlements, and Indians would often run up debts that could be paid only by agreeing to new treaties and ceding more land to the United States.[15]

By the time Thomas Jefferson became president, the basic outlines of an Indian policy had been formed. The plan was to extend the settlement of European Americans (along with their African-American slaves in the South) little by little, putting pressure on Indians to make new treaties and cede more land. In turn, the United States would pay the Indians for the land, but never more than two cents an acre (for land the government would then sell for two dollars an acre). The Indians were expected to use the money earned from the sale of their lands to purchase agricultural implements and other accoutrements of civilization, and transform themselves into farmers like the European-American settlers. Jefferson and Madison continued this policy, pursuing it even more rigorously than their Federalist predecessors.[16] Between 1801 and 1812, Jefferson and Madison signed over 30 treaties with Indian tribes that gained over 220,000 square miles for the United States. After hearing the news of the French taking over Louisiana, Jefferson became almost obsessed with the need to secure the western flank of the nation and urged government officials to get Native Americans to cede lands on the east bank of the Mississippi. Once the United States purchased Louisiana, the immediate military need abated. Jefferson, however, continued to seek land cessions along the Mississippi and other major rivers in order to surround and isolate native territory, creating even more pressure from European-American settlements and an incentive for the Indians to make additional sales of land. The purchase of Louisiana also provided another possibility for those trans-Appalachian Indians reluctant to give up their traditional ways and live like European Americans: they could be removed farther west. Only a few Indians pursued this path before the War of 1812. But the door had been opened for the later Indian removal policy of the 1830s and 1840s. In the meantime, both Jefferson and Madison insisted that the Indians had complete control over their land. They also believed that the Indians should sell "empty" land so that they could adopt agriculture and domestic manufacturing and thereby take steps toward civilization. Jefferson, in particular, urged the Indians to become more like the white man. In his second inaugural address Jefferson declared "humanity enjoins us to teach them agriculture and the domestic arts; to encourage them to that industry which alone can enable them to maintain their place in existence and to prepare them in time for that state of society which to bodily comforts adds the improvement of the mind and morals."[17] In 1808 Jefferson paternalistically told a delegation of Miami, Potawatomi, Delaware, and Chippewa that "temperance, peace and agriculture will raise you up to be what your forefathers were, will prepare you to possess property, to wish to live under regular laws, to join us in our government, to mix with us in society, and your blood and ours united will spread again over the great island."[18] To ensure that Indians would learn how to be like white men, the government supplied tools and appointed agents to teach farming to men and weaving to women.[19]

Benevolent as this approach may have seemed to Jefferson, the relentless pressure to sell more land continued. The executive may have insisted that the Indians retained the right to say no to these treaties, but his commissioners and agents in the field pushed one treaty after another upon the Indians east of the Mississippi, bribing recalcitrant chiefs, plying negotiators with liquor, and doing whatever it took to gain concessions. The government built roads through Indian lands, supposedly for military purposes and to transport mail; in reality they also served as a wedge of settlement that was soon expanded. Jefferson even advocated the building of more trading posts, since they would provide goods to entice Indians to domesticate animals and engage in domestic manufacture. The Native Americans would therefore need less land to support themselves and could sell even more territory to the United States. Jefferson also understood that the trading posts would encourage purchases on credit and that the accumulated native debt could be converted into the surrender of more land. In a private letter to William Henry Harrison, Jefferson confided that he would "be glad to see the good and influential individuals among them [the Indians] run in debt, because we observe that when these debts get beyond what the individuals can pay, they become willing to lop them off by a cession of lands."[20] As a result of these policies, inviolable lines supposedly established for all time, like the cessions granted in the Treaty of Greenville, would be revised, changed, and extended only a few years later. In short, during the opening decade of the nineteenth century, the Indians of the trans-Appalachian region were besieged and pushed into a corner.

The Indian reaction to this pressure was mixed. Some became accommodationists, willing to accept bribes and take what money they could get. A few, especially among the Cherokee, Creek, Choctaw, and Chickasaw, bought into the "civilization" program and began to raise livestock and practice agriculture while their women left the fields to spin and weave in the household. These tribes, however, were often divided, with traditionalists insisting on maintaining their old way of life. Although Jefferson may have thought he was helping Indians to emerge from the Dark Ages and primitivism, his efforts to promote "civilization" meant a cultural transformation that many Indians were unwilling to accept. Most Native Americans east of the Mississippi already were agriculturalists, except that the farm work was done by women and not men. To insist that Indian men pick up a plow meant a complete shift in gender roles. To take women out of the field and move them into the household to engage in manufacturing, a shift some women eagerly accepted, altered the way Indians worked and lived. "Civilization" also meant owning private property, with permanent housing, fences, and even the use of locks. Among the Creek and Cherokee, civilization led to the purchase of African American slaves and the development of plantations for a select few. To protect that property, ideas about authority had to change. Both the Creek and Cherokee developed their own police forces in the closing years of the eighteenth century and centralized authority in elected councils. These innovations were not welcomed by all Indians. Among the Creek, in particular, there remained a core of traditionalists whose opposition to the rich and powerful leadership, many of whom had European-American blood, would erupt into a brutal civil war in 1813 and 1814 that merged into the fighting during the War of 1812.[21]

The traditionalists combating the accommodationist Creek Council and American troops during the Creek War referred to themselves as "red sticks" and were inspired in part by a prophetic religious movement. Other Indians joined similar movements, called by scholars "revitalization cults," which either reasserted the indigenous culture or combined elements of that culture with some attributes of European-American culture. Sometimes revitalization could be peaceful. The Seneca leader Handsome Lake had a series of visions in 1799 and 1800 in which he claimed to have seen a better way of life for Indians. He argued for a complete end to drinking alcohol and the adoption of European-American–style agriculture, while urging natives to withdraw into their own communities. He also wanted a certain number of Indians educated in European-American schools so that they could learn to read and write and thereby prevent whites from taking advantage of Indians. In other instances, like that of the red sticks, the revitalization movements were more warlike.[22]

Tenskwatawa, also known as the Shawnee Prophet, took the more bellicose track. Along with his brother, Tecumseh, he developed a pan-Indian movement that had the potential to stretch from the Great Lakes to Georgia – Tecumseh even visited the Creek before the outbreak of the civil war there. Tenskwatawa had visions in 1805 that were inspired by a combination of Christian and native theology. In his vision he had gone to the Master of Life, or Great Spirit, and seen the paradise of the spirit world where he had been told that the Indians had to return to a more traditional way of life. No longer could the Indians drink alcohol, eat non-Indian food, or follow any of the practices of European-American culture. Instead, Native Americans had to restrict contact with European Americans, especially those from the United States. This vision of a purer Indian society attracted large numbers of Native Americans, who gathered in a community called Prophetstown near modern-day Lafayette, Indiana. Tecumseh hoped to use his brother's spiritual guidance to unite Native Americans west of the Appalachians and secure Native American lands. Traditionally, Native Americans had believed that there was no such thing as private property and that people had the right to use the land only while living. Tecumseh asserted a communal Indian ownership of land when he proclaimed that "the Great Spirit intended" the land "to be the common property of all the tribes" so that it could not "be sold without the consent of all."[23] This view of Indian corporate ownership of land posed a serious problem for the United States, since it prevented the government from making any treaty with one specific tribe or subgroup of a tribe. Consequently, and this was Tecumseh's intention, no additional treaties ceding land in the Northwest could be made without leading to a conflict with Tecumseh and the prophet's followers. In a confrontation in August 1810, in which Tecumseh and William Henry Harrison almost came to blows, Tecumseh informed Harrison of his view on land ownership, admitted that he had organized a confederation to protect that land, and stated baldly that those chiefs who had recently signed the Treaty of Fort Wayne ceding more land would be executed. Although tensions eased briefly thereafter, in the fall of 1811 Harrison led an army to Prophetstown. At the Battle of Tippecanoe on November 7, 1811, Harrison was able to beat off a surprise attack on his camp outside the Indian community. Harrison then sacked Prophetstown. But he did not end either the influence of Tenskwatawa or the military power of the confederation forming under Tecumseh, who was absent from the battle. Both remained a threat to American settlers in the trans-Appalachian West at the outbreak of the War of 1812.[24]

In the years before Tippecanoe, Tecumseh had made several trips to Canada to meet with British officials. After the Jay Treaty, the British maintained some contact with the Indians of the Northwest through the fur trade, which was permitted by the treaty, but they did not provide much military support. In the wake of the *Chesapeake* Affair in 1807, the British sought to counter the image of British betrayal that had developed among Native Americans out of the experience in the Revolutionary War and the Jay Treaty, and sought to strengthen contacts with the Indians of the Northwest. Their hope was to use the Native Americans to help stave off an invasion of Canada. Treading a fine line, British officials like Sir James Craig, the governor general of Canada, espoused a policy whereby they publicly advocated peace while secretly working to prepare for war with the Indians. Local Indian agents, such as Matthew Elliott at Amherstburg, across the river from Detroit, pushed things further than more distant officials would have liked. Tecumseh went to Amherstburg after his meeting with Harrison and told Elliott that he now had most of the Indians of the Northwest behind him and that he was prepared to go to war with the Americans. He did not ask for direct military aid, stating "we think ourselves capable of defending our country," but he did want supplies from the British. Although the Indians were encouraged by Elliott, officially the British sought to avoid war, and in early 1811 Governor Craig actually warned the Americans of possible Indian hostilities and instructed his officers to prevent open conflict. This two-faced approach continued into the spring of 1812. The new Canadian governor, George Prevost, sought to prevent an Indian war, while Colonel Isaac Brock and the Indian Department worked to prepare and encourage the Indians to fight. If the British were hedging their bets in the hope of using the Indians to protect Canada, the Native Americans were also using the British for their own ends – to defend their land and their culture from the onslaught of the United States.[25]

The subtleties and vacillations of British Indian policy were missed by the Americans, who looked across the border to Canada and blamed the British for their own problems with the Native Americans. Felix Grundy of Tennessee cited several reasons for preparing for war with Great Britain in his speech before Congress on December 9, 1811, but ultimately he found his mind

ILLUSTRATION 9. Hair buyer. "A scene on the frontiers as practiced by the 'humane' British and their 'worthy' allies," by William Charles, appeared shortly after the outbreak of the War of 1812. A British officer hands money to an Indian in exchange for scalps on the left side, with another Indian removing the scalp of a dead soldier on the right. At the bottom are a few lines of verse encouraging Columbia's sons to arise and redress the country's wrongs and fight both the British and the Indians. Library of Congress, Washington, D.C.

"irresistibly drawn to the West" and proclaimed that the British had encouraged the Indians to attack American settlements and that "British gold . . . their baubles and trinkets, and the promise of support and a place of refuge if necessary, have had their effect."[26] The Kentuckian Joseph Desha, who had lost two brothers in Indian wars, centered his congressional speech on the issue of defending American honor, demanding the repeal of the orders in council and the ending of impressment. But Desha also advocated, in case war broke out, "a descent on their [British] North American possessions, by which we shall check their influence, particularly over the savages by cutting off all communication with those hostile barbarians on our borders."[27] William Findley, from Pennsylvania, pointed out that the British had encouraged Indians to make war on the United States in the 1790s and argued that they were doing so again.[28] This belief that British agents were encouraging the Indians on the frontier helps to explain the success of the print "A scene on the frontiers as practiced by the 'humane' British and their 'worthy' allies," by William Charles, that appeared soon after the outbreak of the war. The print depicts a British officer handing money to an Indian in exchange for scalps, on the left side, with another Indian removing the scalp of a dead soldier on the right. At the bottom are a few lines of verse encouraging Columbia's sons to arise, redress the country's wrongs, and fight both the British and the Indians.[29]

Given the expressions of several congressmen, and the effectiveness of the William Charles print in stirring up support for the war, there can be little doubt that concern with driving the Indians from the trans-Appalachian West was an important factor in starting the War of 1812. All along the Ohio River Valley, and throughout the European-American settlements in the South, frontiersmen looked to rid themselves of what they perceived as a menace and sought to gain access to the rich lands still occupied by Native Americans. And, when all was said and done, perhaps the only tangible military achievement of the war was to break the back of Indian power east of the Mississippi. North of the Ohio, Tecumseh died in the Battle of the Thames (October 5, 1813) in Canada, ending his efforts at creating a pan-Indian movement. South of the Ohio River, the defeat of the dissident Creek by a combination of American troops under Andrew Jackson and Indian allies, including many pro-American Creek, at the Battle of Horseshoe Bend (March 27, 1814) led to a huge cession of land in the Treaty of Fort Jackson and ended any hope for sustained Indian resistance above the Florida boundary. However real the banal motivation of wanting to kill Indians and take their land may have been, and however successful Americans were in pursing these ends, republicans had difficulty acknowledging their own dark nature. Instead, in the spirit of the Indian policy that had developed since the 1780s, they claimed to want to help the Indians move toward civilization. Republicans fought only in just wars to defend themselves from the savages and barbarians who refused to change. When it came to explaining the entry into the War of 1812, the Indian war was only of secondary importance. More important, as nearly every speech in Congress in 1811 and 1812 made clear, was the problem of commerce and the British practice of impressment.

# 12

# Contested Commerce

In the decade before the War of 1812 the contest over commerce appeared on both the international and domestic fronts. When Thomas Jefferson became president in 1801, many of the problems with France and Great Britain that had plagued the foreign policy of the 1790s had subsided. John Adams had settled the Quasi War with France; the British had accepted the American role as a neutral carrier in the *Polly* decision, which permitted the re-export trade; and Great Britain and France had agreed to the Peace of Amiens, temporarily ending their conflict. In 1803 the British and the French resumed hostilities and, operating from more traditional assumptions about diplomacy, used trade as a weapon of war. Caught in the middle between two belligerent nations, the United States struggled to find some means to sustain its commerce with both. Beginning in 1806, when the crisis intensified, the Republicans in Congress passed a series of measures to pressure both the French and the British to accept American trade without any restrictions. During the ensuing debates Republicans and Federalists called upon their shared revolutionary values to control the language and legacy of free trade. Although the Federalists emphasized open markets in opposition to government measures limiting trade, they merged the idea of free trade as unrestricted commerce with the concept of free trade as neutral rights. Republicans responded by asserting that they were the ones who were defending the ideal of free trade. They, too, mixed free trade as neutral rights with free trade as open commerce, but stressed the former over the latter. After the repeal of the Embargo Act of 1807, as the United States continued to seek a peaceful means to coerce Great Britain and France to ease or even end their commercial restrictions, free trade as an ideal and as a slogan became firmly entrenched in the political rhetoric of both parties, with each side using the multiple meanings and ambiguity of the term to its own advantage in an effort to seize the heritage of the American Revolution.

Oddly, in the years leading up to the War of 1812, which Republicans believed was fought for "Free Trade and Sailors' Rights," the Federalists often used the language of free trade more effectively than their Republican opponents. In the end, however much the Federalists declared their allegiance to free trade, the inability to solve the dilemma of sustaining American commerce in a world at war allowed the Republicans to proclaim free trade as a central reason for the War of 1812.

Although Americans often viewed British policy in the decade before the War of 1812 as a consistent violation of American maritime rights, the British actually vacillated, depending upon their own internal politics and upon the exigencies of war. The British Whigs were generally more sympathetic to the United States and were interested in sustaining the American market for British manufacturers. The Tories, on the other hand, encouraged by West Indies planters and British shipping interests, wanted to pursue a more mercantilist policy. With the Whigs in power under Henry Addington when the French war was renewed, there was no real concerted action against American commerce. But once William Pitt and the Tories came to office in May 1804, the British government moved to strip the United States of its trade. In 1804 Lord Sheffield, who had attacked American trade so vehemently in the 1780s, again wrote about the dangers of American competition in trade and argued for mercantilist policies. Other Tory writers agreed. In October 1805 James Stephens published a pamphlet, titled "War in Disguise: or, the Frauds of the Neutral Flags," in which he called for greater limits on neutral commerce. He saw the American carrying trade as benefiting Napoleon and hurting British maritime security. In such a conflict, "one party must give way, or war must be the issue" and since "[t]he neutral powers can subsist without this newly acquired commerce; but Great Britain cannot long exist as a nation, if bereft of her ancient means of offensive maritime war," Great Britain had to insist on the Rule of 1756 (which held that any trade prohibitions in peacetime could not be suspended during war) and limit neutral trade with enemy colonies. As harsh as this approach might have sounded, Stephens also hoped that the "equity of our cause will have a more direct and powerful influence" on the Americans, who shared "ties of a common extraction" and had similar "sympathies of religion, language, and manners." He pointed out that "the iron yoke of a military despotism is now rivetted on the neck of that powerful people [the French], which aspires to universal domination." Nor did he doubt that the Americans would see "that the subjugation of England, would be fatal to the last hope of liberty in Europe." The British government under the Tories did not think that the Americans would fight over commerce, but decided that even if they did, a war with the United States was better than continuing the current trade practices.[1]

It was in the spirit of this concern with American trade that the British Admiralty Court issued the *Essex* decision in 1805. The case centered on the transport of wine from Spain (at the time an ally of France) to Cuba. The judgment declared that since the reshipment of the wine from the United States had been intended to evade British restrictions, under the Rule of 1756 it was illegitimate and liable to seizure. In addition, the decision placed the burden of proof (i.e., of innocence of engaging in illegal trade) on the ship owner and not on the British naval officer searching the vessel. Armed with this precedent, British naval captains seized scores of American merchant ships within a few months.

The *Essex* decision may have demonstrated a lack of respect for the American flag, but it did not mark a decisive rift in Anglo-American diplomacy. The United States and Great Britain had been working to improve relations for several years before 1805. Until May 1803 Rufus King was the American minister in Great Britain. The British respected King, and he successfully negotiated a series of agreements while in London, including settlement of the outstanding debts owed by Americans to British merchants from the period before the Revolutionary War.[2] Trade, too, continued to grow. On July 1, 1804, James Monroe, who replaced King in London, wrote to Secretary of State James Madison that "our commerce never enjoyed in any war, as much freedom, and indeed favor from this govt. as it now does." Monroe believed that the British generally had a "friendly deportment" toward the United States, and even though their differences – Monroe used the phrase "little bickerings" – might not be settled in "a treaty which trenches on their antient usages & pretensions, or what they call their maritime rights," it was possible to gain "an accommodation precisely [to] the same in effect, by their own orders to the admiralty."[3] As late as 1805 relations were so benign that Thomas Jefferson could contemplate forming an alliance with the British against Spain so that he could acquire the Floridas. Moreover, despite the restrictions following the *Essex* decision, American merchants quickly figured out new ways to make their reshipment manifests appear more legitimate and continued the re-export trade almost unabated.[4]

If on one level Anglo-American relations did not seem to be in crisis by the end of 1805, on another level, especially for many Republicans, increased seizures by the British, and their insistence on at least paying lip service to the Rule of 1756, were a call for action. As early as July 1805, some Republicans used the language of free trade to argue that "[t]he United States certainly have it in their power . . . to command a free trade" by suspending "commercial intercourse" between the two countries. Such an action "would be less injurious to the U[nited] States, than to submit to the commercial regulations of any foreign power."[5] To make matters worse, the British government passed a series of regulations that permitted British merchants to engage in the re-export trade just as that same trade was being denied to American merchants. As President Thomas Jefferson explained to Congress on December 3, 1805: "New principles, too, have been interpolated into the law of nations, founded neither in justice nor the usage or acknowledgment of nations." According to these self-declared principles – Jefferson did not have to label them as explicitly British – "a belligerent takes to itself a commerce with its own enemy which it denies to a neutral on the ground of its aiding its" enemy. For Jefferson, "reason revolts at such inconsistency," and the "authority of reason" was "the only umpire between just nations." Jefferson called for "an effectual and determined opposition to a doctrine so injurious to the rights of peaceable nations."[6] Madison explained the administration's position in an extended pamphlet, really a small book, arguing that the Rule of 1756 had no basis in international law and had been initiated by the British in order to serve their own needs. In what amounted to a legal brief, Madison launched a multipronged attack on the British position, asserting that it ran counter to "the depositories and oracles of the law of nations,... the evidence of treaties,... the judgement of nations,... the conduct of Great Britain herself," and the very "reasoning employed in favor of the principle." Madison recited the history of British maritime policy, demonstrating its many shifts and contradictions, with one order in council repealing another, and with one judicial decision countermanding another. For Madison, the current British measures were "extravagantly preposterous and pernicious." They were merely a matter of expediency and self-interest intended "to transfer to herself as large a share as possible of the commercial advantages yielded by the colonies of her enemies," and these "unexampled and vexatious proceedings" had "in view *the entire obstruction* of colonial re-exports from the United States." In the final analysis, Madison claimed that the "true *foundation* of the principle*" of the Rule of 1756 was "*a mere superiority of force.*"[7]

Although Madison did not explicitly recommend a course of action, his ideas set the stage for legislation in defense of free trade as neutral rights. On January 29, 1806, Congressmen Andrew Gregg of Pennsylvania proposed a resolution for the complete prohibition of imports from Great Britain until the outstanding maritime issues, including commercial regulations and impressment, were settled.[8] Over the next couple of months Congress debated the issue of non-importation, finally settling on a more limited measure on April 18, 1806. This law proscribed some metal goods, cloth made of hemp or flax, certain expensive woolens, glass, finished clothing, beer, ale, and a few other items, but the most significant British products, such as, cottons, cheap woolens, iron, and steel, could still be imported. Jefferson supported this approach, which had precedents in the call for discrimination in the 1790s and the colonial resistance movement of the 1760s and 1770s, because he believed that it would provide enough pressure on the British to demonstrate that the United States could hurt the British economy if there were no abatement of trade restrictions on neutrals. To give the British some time to negotiate a new commercial agreement (the Jay Treaty had expired in 1803), the Non-Importation Act was not to go into effect until November 15, 1806.[9] The problem with the law was that it was so weak that it was hard for the British to take it seriously; they looked at it as a "foolish and teasing measure." The British could not imagine that Americans could do without British-produced consumer goods.[10] For a variety of political reasons, the implementation of non-importation was delayed even further and would not be instituted until late in 1807, when Anglo-American relations had deteriorated even further.[11]

While developments within the United States contributed to the emerging diplomatic rift between America and Great Britain, alterations in both the European geopolitical and the British internal political landscapes led to a further shift in British policy that only aggravated the situation. By the end of 1805 the war between France and Great Britain had become a stalemate. The British navy had triumphed at the Battle of Trafalgar (October 21, 1805), ensuring the safety of the British Isles from French armies and gaining a supremacy on the seas that could not be challenged. After Napoleon's victory at Austerlitz (December 2, 1805), French armies held sway over most of the continent of Europe. Confronted with a largely hostile Europe, a new coalition of Whigs and some Tories in Great Britain, called a government of "All the Talents," felt compelled to take a more forceful position concerning French trade while trying not to alienate the United States. This administration issued an order in council on May 16, 1806, which set up a paper blockade of Europe from the Elbe to Brest, but which permitted some trade except from the Ostend to the Seine. From the British perspective this measure allowed American merchants, in the words of Lord Grenville, "the carriage of Colonial Produce (whether the Enemy's or not, for after *actual* importation into the U.S. they are indistinguishable)."[12] The British also passed the American Intercourse Act on July 21, 1806, which permitted a significant amount of trade to the British West Indies. Although the law included some restrictions on the types of goods imported to the islands, it at least regularized what had hitherto been an illegal trade. Taken together, the two measures partially granted the United States two of its prime commercial goals: the re-export trade and the opening of the British West Indies.[13]

Examined from the perspective of later events, the May 16, 1806, orders in council have been considered as the first in a series of measures enacted by both the British and the French to limit American neutral trade, rather than as a sincere attempt by the British to deal with a crisis in Europe while seeking to be fair to the United States. This approach, written into American history books ever since the War of 1812, reflected the perspective of the many Americans who viewed the British actions not as concessions but as impositions. Already angry about British trade regulations at the beginning of the year, they saw anything short of a complete acceptance of neutral rights as onerous. Moreover, from this point of view, the May 16, 1806, order in council had set up a paper blockade that the British navy could not enforce. Americans also believed that the limited opening of the British West Indies would at best be temporary. Both measures would leave American shippers liable to abuse by British naval captains eager to find illegal goods on board American ships. Although the re-export trade grew to $60 million in 1806, the fact that the British navy captured somewhere between 300 and 400 American merchant ships in 1805–06 seemed to support this argument. The majority of these ships were subsequently released by British admiralty courts, but insurance rates quadrupled, and the cost of business increased.[14]

Against this background of swelling animosity toward the British, an incident occurred in American territorial waters off Sandy Hook, New Jersey, that antagonized the American public even further. Three British warships stationed themselves outside New York to search every vessel entering the harbor for contraband and illegal commerce (as defined by the British). When a cannonball from HMS *Leander*, firing a warning shot to get a vessel to stop so that it could be searched, accidently struck and killed seaman John Pierce on April 25, 1806, there was an immediate outcry. New Yorkers seized supplies destined for the British ship and distributed them to the poor. A massive public funeral was held for Pierce, and both Republican and Federalist politicians decried the incident. Republicans highlighted what they saw as British perfidy, pointing out that "[f]rom insult 'His Majesty's' Ships at the Hook, *within our very waters*, have proceeded to MURDER!" This action made a mockery of Federalist Party pretensions that Americans could rely on "[t]he British government – British theory – British practice – British justice – British magnanimity – and British valour."[15] The Federalists blamed Jeffersonian policies and weakness for the tragedy of Pierce's death. They chided Jefferson for spending money on purchasing Louisiana instead of building a navy to protect the United States. One editor urged his readers to weep over the grave of Pierce, since it was also the "GRAVE OF YOUR NATIONAL HONOR!!!" and proclaimed Americans were "tributaries to France" while the English butchered their "citizens with impunity."[16] Newspapers across the country of every stripe reported "*this atrocious Murder*," and Pierce became the subject of special odes and Fourth of July toasts as a common sailor whose life had been taken by the nefarious British, who had virtually blockaded an American port. There were even reports that the *Leander* had pressed American seamen. President Jefferson lodged a formal complaint concerning the event, demanded the captain's recall, and ordered the *Leander* and its accompanying vessels out of American waters.[17]

Despite the orders in council and the *Leander* incident, there was still hope for reconciliation. In many ways the situation in the spring of 1806 was similar to the situation in the spring of 1794, when relations with Great Britain had almost reached the point of going to war. In 1794 George Washington had sent John Jay to Great Britain to negotiate an agreement that would defuse the crisis. The subsequent treaty, although unpopular with many, had stabilized Anglo-American relations and contributed to a decade of expanding commerce. President Jefferson also sought a diplomatic way out of the 1806 crisis and sent William Pinkney, a Republican from Maryland with some diplomatic experience, to London to join Monroe. Madison's instructions, dated May 17, 1806, made three key demands of the British: to repudiate impressment, permit American trade with enemy colonies as it had existed before the *Essex* decision, and provide payment for seizures made under the *Essex* decision. Like Jay before them, Monroe and Pinkney could not obtain a treaty that met all of the stipulations in their official instructions, but they did manage a deal that was at least as good as the Jay Treaty and that could have avoided further conflict with Great Britain. Yet when they sent the Monroe-Pinkney Treaty back to the United States, Jefferson refused even to submit it to the Senate for consideration.[18]

Jefferson said that his major objection to the treaty was that it failed to include a provision concerning impressment, but he also listed a host of commercial issues that needed to be renegotiated, suggesting that ultimately he may not have wanted any binding agreement with Great Britain at all. As he commented to Madison, he had become "more & more convinced that our best course is to let the negociation take a friendly nap."[19] This approach should not be surprising. Jefferson, along with many of his Republican followers, had begun to wonder if commercial treaties were really worth the effort, especially if the treaties reflected a denial of free trade. In 1804, when discussion of renewal of the Jay Treaty was gaining momentum, a Republican writer openly queried: "why agree to any commercial treaty?" This Republican partisan continued by highlighting America's revolutionary heritage: "Why give up the rights we ought to enjoy, as the inheritance of a brave people, bound by no ties but those which our independence gave us?" A commercial treaty was nothing more than a web spun to entrap peaceful countries. "The belligerent nations" were "the spiders, and the neutrals are no other than the poor unfortunate flies, which get entangled in the snares of Admiralty Courts . . . where their wings are clipped, and if they escape adjudication it is more than what may be expected." As such, "a commercial treaty similar to Jay's . . . is totally inadmissable," since it defined contraband too broadly and abandoned "the right of free trade."[20] Other Republicans picked up the rhetoric of free trade to defend neutral commerce. "The Examiner" argued that "[i]t would be a benefit to both nations, if neutrals were at liberty to pursue a free trade." Combining the definition of free trade as neutral trade with free trade as commerce in unregulated markets, the author explained: "The demand in the respective markets would determine the port of entry; and if England gave a better price than France, or France a greater price than England, the cargoes would naturally be shipped to those who offered the greatest profit." The same essayist also attacked the Jay Treaty, writing that "the treaty has peremptorily forbid the United States from *ever exercising* those rights" – respecting the desire to trade with all the world – "which Mr. Madison and Mr. John Adams, and all other civilians considered as the palladium of American commerce."[21]

The similarity between the Monroe-Pinkney Treaty and the Jay Treaty may well have been the key to Jefferson's decision not to send it to the Senate. In the 1790s Jefferson and Madison had believed that the Jay Treaty was an insult to American nationhood that prevented the United States from using discrimination and trade restrictions to open markets. The Monroe-Pinkney Treaty would have had the same effect. Commerce might have prospered, and war might have been averted, but the United States would have abdicated its freedom of action in setting its own commercial policy. Consequently, the Monroe-Pinkney Treaty, like the Jay Treaty before it, would have made the United States a junior partner in its commercial arrangements with Great Britain. From Jefferson's perspective, this status was unacceptable. The British government had recently granted broader neutral rights to Russia, Denmark, and Sweden than they were offering to the United States. Perhaps more importantly, it was unclear when the Anglo-French war might end. Given the stalemate and Napoleon's continued triumphs on land – he drove the Prussians out of the war after the Battle of Jena (October 14, 1806) – the British and the French could come to terms at any moment. A peace might well have included generous commercial terms that would have left the United States high and dry. This point was discussed at a cabinet meeting on February 3, 1807, when Jefferson noted that a peace settlement in Europe would probably include "more latitude" concerning neutral rights and trade "than Gr. Br. would now yield them to us, & our treaty wd. place [us] on worse ground as to them than will be settled for Europe." In short, the Monroe-Pinkney Treaty abdicated all hope for the notion that free ships make free goods and ran counter to the ideal of free trade which was so central to the American Revolution.[22]

The Republicans could cling to their revolutionary principles and hold out for an agreement closer to the free trade ideal because they thought they retained a diplomatic trump card. Regardless of what happened in Europe in terms of potential peace, the United States could implement the Non-Importation Act and use the threat of further commercial discrimination to convince the British to change their minds. At least since the 1780s Jefferson and Madison had believed that Great Britain needed American produce and markets more than the United States needed British trade. As Madison reminded Monroe and Pinkney in his letter rejecting their treaty in 1807, "the necessaries of life and cultivation can be furnished" to the British West Indies "from no other source than the United States." Great Britain, too, depended upon America "as an auxiliary source for naval stores" and as "one of the granaries which supply the annual deficit of the British harvests." With Napoleon cutting off European sources of these items, American products only became more important. Thus, Madison believed non-importation and further discrimination alone should have been enough to change British minds. Yet, if the British persisted and declared war, he explained, the conflict would involve "a complete loss" not only "of the principal remaining market for her [British] manufactures," but also "of the principal, perhaps the sole, remaining source of supplies, without which all her faculties must wither."[23]

The British, however, had bigger problems than the United States. With Prussia out of the war and with Russia switching sides and becoming an ally of the French in the Treaty of Tilsit (July 7, 1807), the British stood against Napoleon almost alone. Unable to strike at the British Isles because of the protection afforded by the British navy, Napoleon retaliated for the May 16, 1806, order in council with the Berlin Decree of November 21, 1806, declaring a blockade of Great Britain. The British responded with a new order in council on January 7, 1807, prohibiting neutrals from carrying goods from port to port in a Europe dominated by the French. The British Whigs hoped that this regulation would not hurt the transatlantic trade of the United States. They were wrong, because most merchant ships called at several ports to sell their cargoes. Americans therefore considered the order another imposition intended to harm their commercial interests. The order in council was also ill-timed, since it was issued only days after the British government agreed to the Monroe-Pinkney Treaty. British Tories saw the new regulations as too soft, and after they regained control of the government in March 1807 they sought sterner measures. On November 1, 1807, the Tories issued the most restrictive orders in council to date, supplemented by additional orders on November 5, which prohibited trade with a Europe controlled by Napoleon, except with special licenses granted by Great Britain. Napoleon was not pleased with these actions and upped the ante further with the Milan Decree of December 17, 1807, which stated that any ship with such a license was to be seized by France and its allies. Americans viewed these increasingly confining and antagonistic regulations as aimed at the United States. In reality, Great Britain and France aimed their regulations at each other.[24] Unfortunately, as the French sought to strangle the British and the British sought to strangle the French, the United States was caught in the middle with little wiggle room at a time when relations with Great Britain had again reached a crisis stage.

On June 22, 1807, the American diplomatic position worsened when HMS *Leopard* attacked the USS *Chesapeake* and forced Commodore James Barron to surrender four deserters from the British navy. The battle, if the uneven contest could be called a battle, was a direct insult to the American flag. The *Chesapeake* had not cleared for action at the approach of the *Leopard*, which was a larger and more powerful ship. In fact, the *Chesapeake* had set sail for the Mediterranean in some disarray, with its decks cluttered with gear and provisions, and could not fight effectively. The result was that the *Leopard* fired three broadsides – after several warnings – into an almost helpless frigate, killing three men and wounding eighteen others before Barron hauled down his colors. The British were not interested in taking possession of the *Chesapeake* and simply seized the four men in question and left a humiliated *Chesapeake*, after a rejected offer of help, to limp back to Norfolk.[25]

The attack on the *Chesapeake* led to calls for a declaration of war against Great Britain. The popular outrage made the reaction to the murder of Pierce look mild. With British ships riding in Hampton Roads, the people of Norfolk believed they were on the front lines of a war that was about to start. A crowd destroyed 200 water casks belonging to the British navy. A public meeting on June 24, 1807, labeled the attack on the *Chesapeake* "unprovoked, piratical, savage and assassin like," and, in a move that mimicked the organizational activity of the American Revolution, formed a committee of correspondence to deal with the crisis.[26] For a few weeks the situation in Norfolk remained tense, with the British threatening to blockade the port unless the town reopened contact and sold supplies to their squadron. People throughout the United States declared a period of mourning for the men killed by the British, held public meetings, passed resolutions, and prepared for the worst. A bellicose meeting in Alexandria, Virginia, called the attack on the *Chesapeake* "odious among civilized nations." The Alexandrians wanted to show "that haughty nation [Great Britain] that the spirit of '76 yet reigns" in American hearts and tendered their services as "a Voluntary Corps" pledged "never to disgrace the American Flag." These volunteers were ready "at a moment's warning, to obey the call of honor, in defence of our national dignity."[27] The people of Petersburg, Virginia, considered the British attack on the *Chesapeake* "tantamount to a declaration of war on the part of Great Britain."[28] As one commentator pointed out, "No occurrence since the Revolutionary War so deeply interested and agitated the public mind, as the unexampled outrage of the British man of War, Leopard." This writer believed that "there appears to be but one sentiment in the heart of every American from Georgia to Maine – A spirit of just indignation and revenge is predominant – Party spirit has given place to patriotism."[29] Even a Federalist essayist had to admit that "[a]ccording to the laws of nature and nations, we are now in a state of war with Great Britain" and encouraged full preparations for continued hostilities.[30] Republicans were less temperate. One rural editor, citing both the murder of Pierce and the attack on the *Chesapeake*, wrote, "The dye is now cast. No alternative is now left us but to pursue with vigour a war which the most aggravated insults have forced us, or submit to still further degradation."[31]

Jefferson, however, found an alternative to war. Had Jefferson simply called a special session of Congress that summer, it would have supported a declaration of war. But the United States was hardly prepared for a military conflict.

Most of the navy was stationed in the Mediterranean to keep the Barbary states in check. The size of the army had been reduced as part of Jefferson's budget cuts. The militia remained the main defensive military force. Citizen soldiers might rally to the aid of Norfolk when that city expected an invasion from the British squadron in late June and early July, but it would be difficult to sustain such volunteers in the field over a longer period of time. Jefferson did take some action. On July 2, 1807, he issued a proclamation ordering British vessels out of American waters, while forbidding "all intercourse with them" and prohibiting "all supplies and aid from being furnished" to them.[32] That summer Jefferson made other preparations for war: he told the state governors to get ready to activate 100,000 men in the militia; he recalled the navy from the Mediterranean; he expanded the number of gunboats; he ordered coastal fortifications strengthened; and he had munitions stockpiled. These measures had limited effect. The British ignored Jefferson's directive and continued to sail in American waters throughout the crisis. Indeed, at one point a British tender chased a revenue cutter carrying Vice President George Clinton in the Chesapeake Bay.[33] It would take months before the small American navy could return from the Mediterranean, and although units of Virginia militia patrolled the shoreline near Norfolk, there was no mass call-up of men.[34]

Jefferson, in short, delayed. He still believed that war might be averted and wanted to give diplomatic channels a chance to solve the crisis. He hoped that the popular outrage within the United States would have an impact on the British. As he explained to his son-in-law, Thomas Mann Randolph, the United States had three concerns that dictated taking some time. First, the law of nations mandated that each nation should have the opportunity to explain itself and find a peaceful solution when there was a misunderstanding. Second, there was the pragmatic consideration that the United States had hundreds of merchant ships at sea carrying 40,000 seamen. Precipitous war would leave this vast wealth of property and manpower to be swept up into the coffers and prisons of the British. Finally, declaring war was not a prerogative of the president; it was instead within the powers of Congress.[35]

By the time Congress met, the air had been let out of the war balloon, and some other means of coercing the British had to be found. Despite the lack of progress on the diplomatic front, in October and November Congress did not move decisively. In December, at Jefferson's instigation, Congress finally acted. On December 14, 1807, Congress allowed the nonimportation act against the British to take effect. Four days later Jefferson requested "an inhibition of the departure of our vessels from the ports of the United States" because of the "great and increasing dangers with which our vessels, our seamen, and merchandise are threatened on the high seas and elsewhere from the belligerent powers of Europe." Within days of receiving this message, Congress passed the Embargo Act (December 22, 1807).[36]

The diplomatic logjam that had been building since France and Great Britain recommenced hostilities in 1803, and which was then aggravated by the British assault on the *Chesapeake*, had left the United States with three options: accept the humiliating conditions of British restrictions on American trade; declare war on Great Britain or France or both; or rely on commercial coercion. The Jeffersonians had already rejected an accommodation with the British by refusing to consider the Monroe-Pinkney Treaty. They were unprepared for armed conflict and ideologically opposed to resorting to the traditional realpolitik tools of war and diplomacy. War, after all, was the resort of "the irresponsible governments of the old world."[37] So Jefferson once again relied on the revolutionary idealism that had underpinned much of American diplomacy since 1776: the American Embargo of 1807 used trade not as a weapon of war or as an effort at playing power politics. Instead, it was meant as a peaceful way to convince the European powers to accept neutral trade without threatening war. Jefferson and Madison had at last turned to the ultimate form of discrimination and were testing the idea that an agrarian republic could use commerce instead of war to gain free trade.[38]

The test ended in failure. Jefferson had believed that republican farmers did not need to purchase imported goods from Europe and that the British and French depended upon the agricultural produce of the United States. However, the independent yeoman farmer was not independent of markets. Wheat dropped from two dollars to seventy-five cents a bushel, and southern growers of tobacco, cotton, and rice experienced an even greater decrease in prices. Farmers unable to repay loans taken to expand production went bankrupt and faced the auction block and sheriff sales. Exports fell from about $108 million to $22 million, imports from $144 million to $58 million, and the re-export trade from $60 million to $13 million.[39] Government revenues, relying on the impost and port duties, also withered. Sailors and the maritime tradesmen could find little work, and some American tars headed for Halifax to join the British merchant marine. Many would eventually be swept up by press gangs. Large demonstrations occurred in Baltimore, Philadelphia, and New York as unemployed seamen clamored for work. Farmers, whom Jefferson believed were the repositories of virtue, turned to illicit means to gain a living and, especially along the border, eagerly smuggled their produce. Congress had to pass several laws to strengthen enforcement of the Embargo, and Jefferson, who had been so reluctant to fight a war, declared Vermont to be in a virtual state of "insurrection" and had to dispatch the army and navy to try to stop the shipment of goods to Canada.[40]

There was also a political price to pay for the Embargo. The measure was so unpopular that it awakened a moribund Federalist Party to new life when its leaders attacked Jefferson's commercial policy as ineffective and harmful to the American economy. Federalist newspapers railed against the Embargo

ILLUSTRATION 10. "O grab me." Federalists jumbled the words for embargo and came up with "O grab me." This anti-Embargo print has an "ograbme" turtle biting the pants of a would-be smuggler before he can take a cask to an awaiting British ship. Granger pictures.

at every opportunity. Editors reversed the letters of the word "embargo" to become "o-grab-me" and published pictures of a turtle enforcing the law by grabbing a would-be offender in its mouth. "Ograbme laws" were impossible to enforce in some locations; custom houses operated under the "Ograbme principle"; stories about the Embargo became "Ograbme news"; and smugglers were "Ograbme evaders." By the same token, revenue vessels were labeled "Ograbme cutters," and officers enforcing the law were called "Gen. Ograbme."[41] Jumbling the word "embargo" further, Federalists came up with a poem that suggested that the Embargo would lead to greater social discord:

> Embargo read backwards, Ograbme appears,
> A scarey sound ever for big children's ears.
> The syllables transposed, Go bar em comes next
> A mandate to keep ye from harm says my text.
> Analyze miss Embargo, her letters I'll wage
> If not remov'd shortly will make a Mob Rage.[42]

It was also during the Embargo that the Federalist reliance on the rhetoric of free trade began. By focusing mostly on the idea that commerce should be without government restrictions and open to all nations and by using the words "free trade," the Federalists could appear to be defending the principles of the American Revolution. The fact that the phrase had multiple meanings only enhanced its appeal. In the Massachusetts state elections in the spring of 1808, Federalists rallied around their candidate for governor, Christopher Gore, under the slogan "GORE and FREE TRADE!" At the same time they associated the Republican candidate, James Sullivan, with the Embargo.[43] One Federalist newspaper printed an election handbill that declared the Federalist candidates "THE FRIENDS OF PEACE AND FREE TRADE; IN OPPOSITION TO *EMBARGOES and unnecessary War*."[44] Local candidates also picked up on the symbolic significance of free trade. One politician was described as "a gentleman of unquestionable probity, and political rectitude: the friend of peace and free trade; and an enemy of unnecessary wars and embargoes."[45] Similarly, the report of another local election marked the triumph of "the friends of *Impartial Justice*, and *Free Commerce* with all Nations" with the victory of "the *Free Trade*, or federal ticket over the *Embargo*, or democratic ticket."[46]

The free trade rhetoric spread. Federalists in Hartford, Connecticut, reported that the "friends to a free trade and to the prosperity of this city and the country, and opposers of a ruinous embargo, and an unnecessary war" had gained control of the municipal offices.[47] The Federalists repeated many times the contrast between their support of "free trade" and republican restrictions, preferring what they called "a bold FREE TRADE to a sneaking EMBARGO."[48] They even argued that the British were the ones willing to give American merchants a free trade and that they were concerned with neutral rights. Under the heading "A FEW PLAIN TRUTHS" Federalist newspapers declared that "Great Britain allows us a free trade to her ports both at home and abroad" while "France denies us that privilege."[49] The orders in council, Federalists argued, "do not proscribe Neutral Commerce, and of consequence we might have free and *profitable* trade, sufficient to take nearly all our produce."[50] Another writer pointed out that during "the years in which England has ruled the ocean" the United States had "grown rich beyond example," and that the "profits of a *free trade*," permitted by the British, had "built up our cities and improved the face of every hill and valley."[51]

Republicans contested the Federalist claim to the legacy of free trade. If the Federalists seemed to speak more about opening markets, Republicans emphasized neutral rights. But like their Federalist opponents, they did not confine themselves to only one definition of free trade, and connected it to the heritage of the American Revolution. Pacificus supported the Embargo, noting that both the British government and Napoleon "leave to neutrals no remaining claims to the freedom of the seas." Facing the no-win situation created by the British orders in council and the French decrees, Republicans believed not only that the Embargo was necessary, but also that it was the only way to avoid war. Supporting the Embargo "with firmness and patience" would lead the two belligerents to "relax from their present decrees, as to allow a free trade from the United States with each."[52] A Republican in South Carolina rejected the British system of granting licenses to trade with Napoleonic Europe, arguing that it would be paying a tax to King George and that it would "be said of us, being an independent nation, that we pay a tribute to purchase a free trade in 1808, when our fathers resisted the very principle of taxation in 1775."[53] As one Republican explained, "*Free trade*, in the *federal* vocabulary, means a trade carried on *under his Britannic Majesty's License*, on condition of paying *tribute* on each article shipped."[54] Republicans mocked their opponents as roaring out for "war and free trade" and wanting to sign an alliance with the British.[55] They also used the slogan themselves. At a Fourth of July celebration in Pittsfield, Massachusetts, in 1808, Republicans connected their cause to the American Revolution by saluting "The Day and its principle – Our fathers resisted British Taxation in '76; their decedents will not submit to it in 1808." For them the Embargo meant "A fair trade, a free trade, or no trade at all."[56]

As Republicans persisted in supporting the Embargo, and the American economy worsened, the Federalists seemed to be winning the argument, and their use of "free trade" gained greater acceptance. In September 1808 Republicans admitted that the British and the French had "annihilated the springs of commerce and free trade" and thereby "deprived us of the luxuries of life and the means of enterprize." Vainly declaring their agrarian values, and seeking to recapture the revolutionary heritage, they also asserted that the belligerents "cannot deprive us of the products of our fields and the fruits of honest industry" and wondered "[w]here has fled that spirit of *seventy-six* which prompted our fathers to forego every enjoyment of life, to offer their lives a sacrifice for the freedom of their country, if we are unable to suffer a minor inconvenience, the privation of gain?"[57] More than "privation of gain" was at stake, as Federalist petitioners in New Haven reminded Jefferson. They believed that "whatever may be at risk, we are persuaded that the losses incurred by a free trade, would be an incomparably less public evil, than a total prohibition of foreign commerce."[58] Jefferson's response to this petition reiterated his original argument for the Embargo without addressing its economic impact. By the fall of 1808 too many Americans had begun to wonder if Jefferson and the Republicans were wrong in their belief that submitting "our rightful commerce to prohibitions and tributary exactions from others" was surrendering "our independence." For the Federalists, Jefferson's reference to "*the protection of seamen and property*" seemed to be misinformed, "when every merchant knows that the embargo dissipates our seamen and destroys more property than we could possibly lose by a free trade." These critics of the administration thought that Jefferson had *"give[n] himself up to a party"* and did not understand the true situation of the nation. They therefore urged – strangely, for a party with an elitist outlook – *"that the PEOPLE should be THEIR own organs of communication,* and let the President know the real state of public opinion."[59]

By the beginning of 1809, whatever Jefferson may have thought, most Republicans came to see that the Embargo was a failure. The British had been insulated from the predicted economic impact on their exports, since they had opened up new markets with the Portuguese and Spanish colonies that were breaking away from the Napoleonic orbit. The Tory government was thus more than happy to maintain the status quo, since they believed the Embargo hurt the French more than it harmed the British. Moreover, because one of their main concerns had been the competition provided by Americans, the virtual elimination of shipping flying the flag of the United States gave their own merchants a huge advantage.[60] In an effort to drag out the crisis without pushing the United States past the brink of war, the British sent a special envoy to the United States early in 1808. His instructions were very limiting: he could offer reparations for the *Chesapeake* attack, but only if the United States first rescinded Jefferson's proclamation excluding British ships from American waters. He was also expected to get the Americans to apologize for recruiting British sailors into their navy, and could not address the general issue of impressment. These conditions were unacceptable to the United States, so the negotiations went nowhere.[61] The French also remained inflexible. In September 1807, they began to enforce the Berlin Decree against American shipping (until that time it had been unclear whether the French restrictions would apply to the United States) and retaliated against the British with the Milan Decree in mid-December.[62] On April 17, 1808, Napoleon issued the Bayonne Decree, which ordered the confiscation of all American ships in French-controlled ports, since, in a cynical reading of American law, these vessels either had to be trading illegally in violation of the Embargo, or were British ships in disguise.[63]

Confronted with no progress on the international front, a worsening economy, and Federalist political gains, Republicans in Congress passed the Non-Intercourse Act, to take effect on March 15, 1809, after the inauguration of President James Madison. Even when the Embargo had become an obvious failure and nearly ruined the American economy, the Republicans continued to have faith in economic coercion as a means to obtain free trade. The Non-Intercourse Act of 1809 opened trade with all nations except France and Great Britain. The law also explicitly prohibited the warships of either belligerent from entering American waters, except under duress. This measure wielded both a carrot and a stick, or at least so the Republicans thought. The stick was to outlaw all trade with the two belligerents. The carrot was to empower the president to suspend the act with the nation that revoked or modified its edicts and thereby ceased "to violate the neutral commerce of the United States," while maintaining non-intercourse against the other power.[64]

As meaningless as the Non-Intercourse Act may have been, it almost worked. David M. Erskine, the British minister to the United States, who had been appointed by the Whigs and allowed to keep his position by the Tories through the *Chesapeake* crisis, admired the United States and did everything he could to patch together an agreement. In April 1809 he exchanged a series of notes with Secretary of State Robert Smith that promised to end all discord between the two nations. First, Erskine wrote that because the Non-Intercourse Act had placed the two belligerents – Great Britain and France – on equal footing, his instructions permitted him to assure the United States that the king would offer "an honorable reparation for the aggression, committed by a British naval officer, in the attack on the United States' frigate Chesapeake." Having given this promise of settling the *Chesapeake* affair, Erskine then reported that he had been authorized to inform the United States – again because France and Great Britain were now on equal footing owing to the Non-Intercourse Act – that the king would send "an envoy extraordinary, invested with full powers to conclude a treaty on all points of the relations between the two countries." In the meantime, Erskine continued, "His Majesty would be willing to withdraw his orders in council of January and November 1807" if the president would issue a proclamation to open up trade with Great Britain, as called for in the Non-Intercourse Act. After a few more notes Erskine and Smith agreed to reestablish commerce between the two countries as of June 10, 1809. The problem with these developments was that Erskine had given an overly optimistic reading of his official instructions of January 23, 1809. Erskine's concessions also reflected a misunderstanding of a series of conversations he had had with several members of the Republican administration. When the British foreign secretary, George Canning, found out about the Erskine agreement, he repudiated it and recalled his minister back to Great Britain. In turn, Madison reinstated non-intercourse with the British on August 9, 1809.[65]

By early 1810, whatever their political rhetoric, it was clear to the Republicans that as a modification of the Embargo, the Non-Intercourse Act did not help American commerce very much, since Great Britain and France had been the most significant trading partners of the United States, and since much of Europe remained controlled by France. The American economy continued to stagger, and trade languished. Reflecting in part the temporary lifting of the trade ban against Great Britain during the peak sailing months of the summer, trade increased moderately: in 1809 exports more than doubled in value to about $52 million; re-exports increased to almost $21 million; and imports remained at the same level as in 1808. Overall, commerce in 1809 was far below the pre-embargo levels.[66] Stuck in a diplomatic quagmire and struggling with an anemic economy, the Republicans in Congress, still hoping to avoid war by using commerce as a wedge to pry open markets and gain free trade, readjusted their policy again. At the urging of Secretary of the Treasury Albert Gallatin to either return to the Embargo or get rid of all trade restrictions, Congress passed the so-called Macon's Bill Number 2 on May 1, 1810, repealing the Non-Intercourse Act and opening trade with both belligerents. The legislation also authorized the president to reinstate non-intercourse with one power if the other removed its trade restrictions.[67] At first, neither France nor Great Britain seemed interested. Tensions with both countries remained high. The French had seized millions of dollars worth of shipping in 1809, and had issued the Rambouillet Decree on March 23, 1810, declaring that any American ship in a French port since May 20, 1809, was to be confiscated. This measure led to even more seizures. On August 5, 1810, in an apparent reversal of policy, and recognizing that the American reopening of trade favored the British because of their control of the seas, Napoleon had his foreign minister, the duke of Cadore, inform John Armstrong (the United States minister in France) that the Berlin and Milan Decrees could be considered revoked as of November 1, 1810. Cadore made this statement conditional, dependent upon the United States resuming non-intercourse with the British.[68] The Tories in Great Britain were unmoved, believing that Madison was incompetent, pro-French, and anti-British. They considered Macon's Bill Number 2 an American surrender caused by their own steadfast persistence in a policy of trade restrictions. They also thought that the Cadore letter, as the French promise to revoke its trade restrictions came to be known, was a trick and that no one should trust Napoleon. Madison, however, took Napoleon at his word and saw the Cadore letter as a release from an embarrassing situation in which Americans appeared all bluster and no action. Despite the vagueness of the Cadore letter, Madison reinstituted non-intercourse with Great Britain beginning on November 1, 1810.[69] The French, however, never really rescinded their decrees. High tariffs, limits on imports, delays in releasing American ships in port, and the continued seizure of American vessels for a variety of so-called violations of mercantile regulations rendered the Cadore letter little more than a meaningless piece of paper.[70] Madison, however, persisted in maintaining the fiction that the change in French policy was real. In March 1811 a new non-intercourse bill became law, aimed only at Great Britain. As a law, it had loopholes big enough to sail a ship through, delaying the closure of all imports from Great Britain and permitting the export of some American products. These looser restrictions, however, were meant as a salve to American farmers and merchants and had little effect on the British. By the time the Twelfth Congress convened in the fall of 1811, war appeared inevitable.[71]

Throughout all of the diplomatic maneuvering and shifts in policy after the Embargo, the political debate continued. Recognizing the effectiveness of the language of free trade, both Federalists and Republicans strove to deploy the phrase "free trade" as they sought political advantage. In late 1808 and early in 1809, building on the unpopularity of the Embargo, the Federalists heralded their candidates as the friends of free trade. John Spayd, the Pennsylvania gubernatorial candidate, headed his ticket with the motto "Spayd and free trade, *Liberty and the Constitution.*"[72] In New Hampshire, Jeremiah Smith ran for governor as "the friend of commerce and free trade" who would "keep the military in due subordination to the civil authority" while the current Republican Governor John Langdon threatened "your rights & liberties" by enforcing the Embargo, seizing property, and searching private papers.[73] In Massachusetts, Christopher Gore was again heralded for "the American stand he made against the Embargo," which "intitled him to the gratitude and support of every friend to free trade."[74] A writer for the *American Eagle* described the era of the "federal administration" of George Washington and John Adams as "the proud days of American greatness; of national prosperity" when "[w]e had a free trade to every part of the world," whereas under the current administration, "Our vessels [were] dismantled and commerce annihilated."[75] In upstate New York, Federalists supported "Trial by Jury – Free Trade – Agriculture – Commerce – and Peace!" while they called the Republicans "Tories" who supported "Despotism – Embargoes – Non-Intercourse – Non-Importation – and War!"[76] The Federalists in New York City greeted news of the Erskine agreement in 1809 as a triumph of their policy and declared a special "day of rejoicing with the friends of peace and free trade with England" during which they displayed flags throughout the harbor, rang bells, and fired a special "federal salute" in the morning, at noon, and at sunset. They also reminded anyone who would listen that it was "the patriotic minority in Congress" who had fought "to remove this mill-stone [the Embargo] from around your necks, to restore your commerce, and to secure an unshackled and free trade with England and with the whole commercial world," while "Mr. Jefferson, the French Citizen, the friend of Bonaparte," forced an oppressive embargo on the American people.[77]

In 1809 Republicans, too, relied upon the rhetoric of free trade for political purposes. At a meeting on Long Island in New York early in the year, Republicans declared that had there not been so many "unprincipled smugglers," the Republican measures "would before this time have bro't us a free trade."[78] One orator, celebrating the inauguration of James Madison, admitted that "[s]ince the revolution our country has accumulated wealth with a progress rapid almost beyond belief: peace and a free trade have been the cause." He also warned that "too many ... golden voyages have made a shipwreck of their principles" and that trade at any cost, such as accepting British restrictions, was bad. Unable to avoid the diplomatic storms created by both the French and the British, the speaker argued that the administration was compelled to take action to restrict commerce.[79] Although it was difficult to oppose the Erskine agreement before it was rejected in England, Republicans still believed *"[t]hat a trade to Britain only, without a free trade to the continent of Europe, is ruin to both the grower of produce, and the merchant who exports it."*[80] Some Republicans thought that it was the Embargo itself that had compelled Erskine and Great Britain to relent and repeal the orders in council.[81] After the failure of the Erskine agreement, Republicans became increasingly aggressive in their attacks on the Federalist Party. One newspaper made fun of a Federalist election procession in Maine (then a part of Massachusetts) that had a float – "a beautiful Ship 'FREE TRADE'" – built by the order of "our most excellent Sovereign, Christopher I" (Christopher Gore).[82] Newspaper editors mocked Gore's political slogan of the year before. As one editor put it, "'*Gore and Free Trade!*' has been the hosanna of the Pickeroon federalists. It may now with propriety be called, *Gore and Fleece Trade*, as every arrival brings accounts of the depredations made on our commerce" by the British.[83] In a coincidence that did not elude his critics, Gore was lambasted both for his support of opening trade with the British and for his laissez-faire approach to banking regulations when the speculative schemes of Andrew Dexter, Jr., collapsed after March 1809. The *Independent Chronicle* reported "'GORE AND FREE TRADE!' was all the cry – whereas, since his election [as governor], our commercial intercourse is more exposed to the depredations of the British, by their perfidy, than before; and our citizens are more injured by *internal banking depredators*, than ever by the marauders of Europe."[84] One Republican wag joked, "'Gore and a Free Trade' is a ditty which cannot any longer be set to music."[85] In short, "*Gore and Free Trade* has lost its charm." In its place, urged the *Eastern Argus*, should be the slogan *"Madison and Free Trade!,"* which represented *"rights and privileges, religious & civil* – commerce free – national dignity – republican institutions."[86]

In 1810 and 1811 both Republicans and Federalists continued to use the rhetoric of free trade as they explained their own reading of the complicated series of events that had brought the nation to the brink of war. Republicans criticized the Federalists, who had "bellowed for a free trade, clogged with licenses and clouded with risk," before 1810 and then, after the opening of commerce under Macon's Bill No. 2, complained about having their ships seized by both the French and the British.[87] With trade so restricted by the belligerents, Republicans concluded that *"Peace and free trade,* are out of the question with America"[88] Elated by news of the Cadore letter, Republicans proclaimed that with the revocation of the French decrees, the British would probably be forced to repeal their orders in council, and there would be a "Restoration of free Trade and Preservation of Peace."[89] Federalists were not so convinced that the French were sincere. They claimed that the Madison administration wanted to "unite with the fortunes of France and her allies, in order that we might have a free trade" with the French only.[90] As reports arrived suggesting continued difficulties in trading with Napoleonic Europe, Federalists argued that reinstating non-intercourse with the British was premature, because "instead of a free trade being permitted, there is not the least hopes of any trade at all, with the countries under the controul of Bonaparte."[91]

This acrimony continued as the United States slipped into the final crisis that would lead to the War of 1812. In the spring of 1811 Massachusetts Federalists once again relied upon the motto "GORE AND FREE TRADE" and called themselves the "friends of Peace, Commerce and Free Trade."[92] The Federalists even tried to convince farmers – the bedrock of Jeffersonian support – "that *free trade* is twined" with their "dearest interests" because their "fortunes languish with the merchants" and their "farms will lie fallow for the want of a market" while their "laboring men will resort to Canada for employment, or lie down in idleness, dissipation and despair."[93] In June the Federalists mocked Republican Governor Elbridge Gerry when he referred to "Free trade & naval defence!"[94] Among the banners displayed in a Federalist Fourth of July parade in Boston was one emblazoned with the words "Free Trade."[95] Repeatedly pointing to the failure of the French to live up to the promise of the Cadore letter, Federalists claimed that Great Britain was the real friend of the United States, willing to support American free trade.[96] Some Federalists admitted that the British had not granted free trade, but held that if Jefferson had accepted the Monroe-Pinkney Treaty, "Americans in all probability might have had from that time to this, a free trade to Great Britain" and much of the rest of the world.[97] Others, more sympathetic to the British, noted that the British had little choice but to maintain their orders in council, because otherwise "[a]ll the nations of the continent," who were allied with the French, would "have a cheap and free trade for imports and exports, without risque," and the British might well lose the war.[98] By the end of 1811 some Federalists even argued that the United States would be better off going to war with France rather than Great Britain because "France has treated America with *unparalleled* injustice and insolence." Napoleon, "without a shadow of justice or the least pretext," had seized American ships in French ports, fixed prices of those few goods he had permitted American merchants to sell in France, insisted on his own licensing system, dictated terms to the American government while heaping "every epithet of reproach and scorn" upon both the administration and the American people, and violated "the express articles of a solemn treaty."[99]

The Republicans continued to contest the Federalist claim to free trade. They persisted in their attack on the slogan "Gore and Free Trade," called it a "sophistical and delusive" phrase, and asserted that the magic of these words had sent American ships "to *condemnation* in almost every port in Europe!"[100] Republicans reminded readers that Federalists, shouting "'Gore and free trade,' 'Gore and no Embargo,'" had used crowd action in 1808 to oppose the Embargo, "thus jacobinically establishing a *Mob Law*, and setting at defiance the Constitution and the Statutes of the land!"[101] Defining the idea of free trade loosely as "buying what we chose and selling what we had," Republicans continued to reject the idea that the English had granted the United States free trade.[102] The editor of the *Essex Register* argued that the British sought "to embroil us with their enemies" and "that they give us a free trade, when we are allowed to supply their wants, and to trade only in such parts of their dominion as is for their own profit, and dictated by their necessities." If peace were to come tomorrow, the British "would annihilate a commerce which they believed could not exist with safety to their own."[103] In early 1811, Republicans held that the opening of French ports would force the British to give up their orders in council and provide Americans with "[a] comparatively free trade."[104] By the summer of 1811, some Republicans began to admit that the situation vis-à-vis France was unclear and that trade was not as free as they had hoped. But they still thought that the British were not offering any real alternative and that they wanted to curtail and injure American commerce.[105] Once again the Jeffersonians argued that the United States might have to rely on republican virtue. As one essayist explained, "For if we cannot by negociations secure a free trade, it would be far better to have no trade abroad, than to sacrifice our independence on the altar of mercantile profit, or make a surrendry of our country's dearest rights and privileges, for the fineries and luxuries of other nations." After all, the author reminded, "The surplus produce of our country will always find a market somewhere," even if the purchasers had to come to the United States to buy them. This withdrawal from commerce should last until "the two infuriated powers of Europe shall return to an honorable observance of the law of nations, and Great Britain shall renounce her pretended right to the monopoly of the commerce of the world, and restore the freedom of the seas."[106] As this last quotation suggests, even agrarian isolationists were not ready to give up on the ideal of free trade.

During the decade leading up to the War of 1812, both political parties turned to the language and ideal of free trade in order to defend their positions on the international crises confronting the nation. The Federalists, especially after the Republicans began to use economic coercion against the British and the French, cried out against restrictions on commerce as a violation of free trade. This language, in part because of the importance of free trade to revolutionary ideology, and in part because the multiple meanings of "free trade" allowed the phrase to be stretched in a variety of ways while retaining its popular appeal, proved an effective political tool. Republicans, who long had spoken out for neutral rights, also used the rhetoric of free trade. They even mimicked their Federalist rivals, incorporated the phrase "free trade" into their own slogans, and declared that they were the true party of "*Commerce and free Trade*."[107] With a military conflict looming, late in 1811 the Committee on

Foreign Relations submitted a report to the House of Representatives that urged a military buildup and outlined reasons for fighting the British, centered on the idea of free trade. Dwelling mostly on the question of maritime rights, the report asserted that "the United States, as a sovereign and independent Power, claim the right to use the ocean, which is the common and acknowledged highway of nations, for the purposes of transporting, in their own vessels, the products of their own soil, and the acquisitions of their own industry, to a market in the ports of friendly nations."[108] In short, they were demanding a right to free trade. During the ensuing debates, interest in conquering new territories was mentioned, and there was some concern with fighting Indians in the trans-Appalachian West. But the most important reason to make preparations for what seemed to be the inevitable war was Britain's commercial restrictions. As Felix Grundy explained, echoing the words of the committee report, "The true question in the controversy . . . is the right of exporting the productions of our soil and industry to foreign markets."[109] This refrain was repeated throughout the debate. Both as an idea and as rhetoric, "free trade" lay at the core of the causes of the War of 1812, and, as was made clear in one Fourth of July toast, it could be associated with the rights of man.[110]

# 13

# The Ordeal of Jack Tar

The connection between free trade and the rights of man reflected the emerging connection between free trade and the rights of specific men – sailors. Before 1812 the phrase "sailors' rights" had not yet been reified into an icon in the same manner as "free trade," but as an idea it had an even greater popular appeal. As they did with free trade, Republicans and Federalists contested the idea of protecting sailors' rights, as both parties claimed to sympathize with the ordeal of Jack Tar. All Americans agreed that the sailor was a central symbol for the new nation. The experience of the war against Tripoli enhanced that significance, especially for the Republicans, when sailors defended the nation and, in the case of the crew of the *Philadelphia*, were victims of captivity. Any threat to the mariner's liberty – his freedom in both real and symbolic terms – became increasingly important to many Americans. British impressment of American sailors, which had subsided as a practice with the Peace of Amiens, emerged as the central issue in the discussion of sailors' rights after France and Great Britain renewed their war in 1803. Federalists at first minimized the threat of impressment, but still competed with the Republicans in claiming to represent the interests of seamen. That Federalist appeal grew during the controversy over the Embargo. President Thomas Jefferson and his secretary of state, James Madison, often defended sailors' rights, but by 1807 sought to sidestep the problem of impressment in negotiations with Great Britain, since they were more interested in free trade than in sailors' rights. Impressment, however, remained too big an issue for the Federalists to ignore entirely or for Jefferson and Madison to put on the back burner. Indeed, attacking impressment provided many Republicans an edge in claiming to speak in defense of sailors' rights. This interest in impressment created a popular momentum all its own, regardless of the position of the Federalist Party or the

Republican administration, and along with free trade the issue became the major explanation for the War of 1812.

The sailor remained crucial to the American society and economy during the opening decade of the nineteenth century. Although often seen as rough characters who might misbehave while ashore, seamen retained a special place in the hearts of many Americans. "Our hardy mariners" were "the pride of our country and vanguard of our waters."[1] As one newspaper editor proclaimed on the eve of the War of 1812, mariners were "the men who have enriched the country by industry, the greatest toils, and braving the greatest dangers in navigating our ships on perilous seas, and to unknown, inhospitable, and sickly regions." Americans owed their "principle comforts of life" to "the sweat and zeal of this class of the community." Indeed, "We riot on the fruits of their labor" and "reap the benefits of the industry of our seafaring brethren." Without maritime workers it would be impossible to export the agricultural produce of the nation or to import manufactured goods that added to the quality of everyone's life. These comments echoed the sentiments expressed by Thomas Jefferson and John Adams in the 1790s and stand as a stark testament to the overall importance of commerce to the fiber of American well-being, and to the role of the common sailor in that commerce.[2]

This interest in the sailor went deeper than simple economics and extended to military considerations. One newspaper, denying the negative view of sailors as peripheral beings, declared that common seamen were "not the '*sweepings of vessels holds.*'" Instead, "With the militia they form the whole defence of our nation."[3] The American experience in the war against Tripoli only reenforced the idea developed during the Quasi War that seamen were the first line of protection for the nation's interests and highlighted the sacrifices made by sailors. Although President Thomas Jefferson was fortunate that John Adams had settled the crisis with France before his own inauguration, he immediately confronted a problem with the Barbary states that prevented his complete dismantling of the deep sea navy. Instead, Jefferson had to dispatch a squadron to the far-off coast of North Africa in response to a declaration of war by the bashaw of Tripoli, Yusof Qaramanli. Initially, the American navy did not make much progress in the conflict, exposing the Republican administration to some ridicule for ineffectively waging a war. Then, on October 31, 1803, the situation went from bad to worse with the grounding of the frigate *Philadelphia* and its capture by the Tripolitans. The disaster surrendered over 300 American sailors to the bashaw. This adversity, however, enhanced the profile of the American sailor. On February 16, 1804, Stephen Decatur launched a nighttime raid in the harbor of Tripoli and burned the *Philadelphia*, thus snatching a symbolic victory from the jaws of defeat. The *Philadelphia*, which had briefly come to represent American naval ineptitude, suddenly reflected an intrepid and enterprising spirit that even garnered the admiration of Horatio Nelson. Republican

ILLUSTRATION 11. "Decatur's Conflict with the Algerine at Tripoli." This Alonzo Chapel engraving from 1858 of a common sailor stepping in to take a blow meant for Stephen Decatur demonstrates the intense hand-to-hand fighting that took place during the war with Tripoli and was a means of heralding the heroics of the officers and enlisted men in the American navy. Naval History Center, Washington, D.C.

newspapers seized upon the image of the dashing Decatur to counter Federalist criticism and to assert the Jeffersonian commitment to defend commerce. In the summer of 1804 the American navy fought a series of engagements against Tripoli, further demonstrating a martial spirit. During the fighting off Tripoli, Decatur again appeared on center stage when he beat back an attack from Tripolitan gunboats and then rashly, albeit heroically, returned to the fray after hearing that his brother had been killed on another ship. During the hand-to-hand melee that ensued, Decatur himself was about to be slain by a sword-wielding North African when a common seaman stepped in and took the blow in defense of his captain. This sailor, whose name has been variously reported as Daniel Frazier and Reuben James, became a hero, too, as the loyal and honest American tar willing to sacrifice himself for his nation.[4]

The war against Tripoli also dramatized the ordeal of Jack Tar. The 300 prisoners held by the Tripolitans became a symbol of the long-suffering seaman. Federalists might decry the debacle of the *Philadelphia* – at least until Decatur's famous escapade – and lament a conflict that had left so many Americans in the hands of the bashaw, but the captives also provided a reason to continue the war despite the difficulties faced by the navy. After the capture of the *Philadelphia*, Jefferson expanded the number of ships committed to the war and even raised taxes to pay for the conflict. When the final peace was concluded, the release of the captive tars (for which the negotiators agreed to pay a $60,000 ransom) was touted as an American triumph. The United States, which depended upon the common sailor for commerce and for defense, had responded to the ordeal of Jack Tar in captivity and secured his liberty. Upon their return, the released captives were feted and treated as heroes. The toasts at a dinner held for Captain William Bainbridge, who had lost the *Philadelphia*, and several of his officers in Richmond, Virginia included "*The officers and crew of the Philadelphia,*" heralding them as "Magnanimous in captivity," because "they supported the dignity of the American character, unsubdued by the gloom of a dungeon, unappalled by a sanguinary banditti." Another toast declared, "*The new principle in the Tripoline Treaty* – American *prisoners* no longer *slaves.*" In a similar spirit the Baltimore theater promised not only the performance of the standard maritime fare, but also a special dance to honor "THE SAILOR'S RETURN from TRIPOLI." A popular song celebrating the victory spoke directly to the crew of the *Philadelphia*: "Hail Captives no more! – You were born to be free! / And Hail lovely Peace, with divine Liberty!"[5]

It is against this image of the sailor-citizen as the purveyor of commerce and protector of the nation, and as a sufferer under Barbary captivity, that we need to examine the issue of renewed impressment by the British in 1803. The forced recruitment of American sailors into the British navy meant that the ordeal of Jack Tar was no longer limited to a few hundred men held in Tripoli. Between 1803 and 1812 at least ten thousand Americans were impressed. Every American who went to sea was vulnerable to the arbitrary actions of the British navy in its insatiable demand for manpower.[6] News of British impressment began to arrive in American ports soon after the renewal of war between France and Great Britain in 1803. The first notices discussed impressment only in general terms.[7] Soon enough, however, word arrived from England, the West Indies, and elsewhere that the press gangs were taking American as well as British sailors. Worse, some of the impressment occurred not in distant ports within the British Empire, but in sight of the American shore in the territorial waters of the United States. To compound the insult to national sovereignty, the protections issued by the American government often were not respected by the British.[8]

Republicans were outraged. By the summer of 1803 they were lamenting this "violation of the rights and liberty of our citizens." As one editor explained, in an early joining of the ideas of free trade and sailors' rights: "We have a right to free and unshackled trade with all the world, and our seamen ought not to be seized and detained."[9] Others also combined the issues. William Duane's *Aurora* attacked a British order in council of June 24, 1803, that mandated the seizure of ships carrying contraband goods – a move that was relatively mild compared to later orders – as a function of British "naval dictatorship" whereby the British were adding "new and unwarrantable principles of seizure to the old abuses of impressment, spoilation, and suspension of our commerce by new and overstretched blockades."[10] For Republicans the idea that the "brave and worthy sons of fathers who once fought and bled to support the independence of the United States" would be compelled to enter the service of foreign masters was intolerable and infringed upon "their personal and unalienable rights."[11] Pointing out that many in England believed that impressment was evil, and claiming that killing a member of a press gang while resisting impressment in England was not considered murder, another writer declared, "How, then, must the spirit of every American revolt at the knowledge" that citizens from their own country were being "taken from our own vessels by British press-gangs, and carried from their country, their homes, their friends and every thing that can be dear to man."[12] The same paper declared two years later that "There is no imposition at which the minds of American freemen revolt with more indignation than the impressment of their fellow-citizens."[13] Republican editors did not hesitate to use extreme rhetoric in attacking impressment, referring to impressment as "inexcusable and a barbarous oppression" and a severe, wanton, and "nefarious business." Several authors compared impressment to slavery and called the British behavior "an outrage." Some even drew connections to the Tripolitan captivity. "If there is any difference between the captivity of our men by the British and the Tripolitans, the conduct of the former is most unjustifiable and atrocious, for with one we are at peace and at war with the other," noted Duane's *Aurora*.[14] Republican editors also believed that the American flag should act as a shield for all sailors, whether they were born citizens, naturalized, or even new arrivals. Duane exclaimed that "[a] seaman on an *American* ship is to be presumed an *American*." Republicans even complained of the pressing of immigrant passengers from ships as they approached the United States.[15] Extremists in Congress, led by Samuel Smith in the Senate, introduced a bill that would have denied forever "the rights of hospitality in the ports, bays, and harbors of the United States" to any nation that pressed American sailors. This measure would have cut off the British navy from vital supplies that enabled them to maintain their posts on the North American station. Although Smith's more extreme law failed to garner enough votes at this time, the fact that it was debated in the halls of Congress suggests the interest that impressment generated as early as 1803.[16]

Federalists scrambled to defend the British. Few Federalists believed that the British had a right to impress Americans. Indeed, the British government never made such a claim and asserted that they had the right only to press British subjects from American ships. Sharing with the British an understanding of citizenship based on birth, most Federalists sympathized with the royal navy's position. As one writer explained, "A British subject" – who from both the British and Federalist perspective was anyone born in the British Isles, not in the United States at the time of independence – "when the safety of his country calls for it, is as much subject to impress on board a foreign vessel, as a British one."[17] Another Federalist wrote that "[i]f we detain her seamen, under *forged protections of citizenship*, England is the injured nation, and she is justified in seizing her own citizens." The problem was simple: "because we have engaged her seamen in our service, which she [Great Britain] has reclaimed," his majesty's navy was justified in removing their native-born sailors "when they meet them" on the high seas. The British, so the Federalists often admitted, could even legitimately ignore protection certificates, because "the fact is too *notorious* to be controverted, that *forged* protections are made use of without number." The Federalists often minimized British impressment and claimed that men with legitimate protections were released. Federalist Anglophiles charged that the Republicans were friends of Napoleon and the French, who had made themselves at least as culpable as the British by practicing their own form of impressment (conscription), seizing American shipping, and mistreating American seamen. Larger issues, too, came into play, since the Federalists argued that Great Britain was not only in a struggle for its very existence, but was also "making a noble, and solitary, stand for the *liberty of mankind*."[18] As the question of impressment festered without any resolution, some Federalists began to lambast Jefferson for inaction, charging that the money wasted on purchasing Louisiana could have been used to build a navy to protect American commerce and that sending the navy to fight the Tripolitans was also a misuse of resources. Federalists charged the Republicans with hypocrisy, noting that after claiming during the 1790s that the Washington and Adams administrations were impotent when confronted with impressment, Jefferson had done even less to help pressed seamen now that he was in power. In a year and a half, one Federalist editor wrote, "the British have impressed a greater number of American seamen than we recollect to have heard of during the whole of the last war [the Anglo-French war from 1793 to 1801], and this too when all the powers of government have fallen into the hands of those men who were to be the *special protectors* of their country's rights against *British aggressions*." Instead of action, such as increasing the size of the navy and preparing appropriate defenses, "our seamen are abandoned to the protection of democratic Newspapers and Mr. Jefferson's philosophical remonstrances."[19]

With impressment quickly becoming a hot-button political issue, Jefferson's administration hoped to obtain a diplomatic solution, at least before 1807. Rufus King believed he had almost come to an agreement with the British in 1803 before he left his job as the American minister to King George. The British told King that they were willing to forego impressing men from American ships on the high seas. But the negotiations foundered on the British refusal to give up the right to search neutral ships for British subjects on the "narrow seas" – the English Channel and water surrounding the British Isles. If anything, both nations hardened their positions thereafter. In the 1804 instructions to James Monroe, when he became the United States minister to Great Britain, Madison indicated a willingness to agree that the two nations would return deserters to each other, but he also informed Monroe that he could never accept the right of the British to search ships on the high or narrow seas.[20] Monroe therefore made no progress on the question. Diplomatic discussions in Washington also quickly reached an impasse when Anthony Merry, the British minister to the United States, told Madison that Great Britain would never "relinquish her practice of taking her own subjects out of neutral vessels," and Madison replied "that no administration would dare" accept a policy that surrendered "the rights of the American flag."[21] During the Anglo-American crisis of 1806, Madison insisted that impressment be included in the negotiations to replace the Jay Treaty and stipulated that an end to impressment was a precondition for the government to consider canceling the implementation of non-importation.[22]

Regardless of their instructions and the apparent obstinacy of their governments, left to their own devices the British and American negotiators in London were willing to find a middle ground whereby the British promised not to impress sailors from American ships and the Americans agreed to return deserters from the British navy. The British admiralty rejected this explicit settlement. Even so, the negotiators came to an informal agreement outlined in a note issued on November 6, 1806, whereby the British said that they would not surrender the right of searching for British subjects to impress, but that they would issue orders to use "the greatest caution in the impressing of British seamen; and that the strictest care shall be taken to preserve the citizens of the United States from any molestation or injury; and that immediate and prompt redress shall be afforded upon any representation of injury sustained by them." Monroe and Pinkney took this note, along with private assurances, as a British concession that enabled them to complete the rest of the negotiations.[23] Jefferson and Madison found this informal agreement unacceptable and used it as an excuse to reject the Monroe-Pinkney Treaty.[24]

There was more to the Republican administration's failure to settle the question of impressment than met the public eye. In the middle of considering the Monroe-Pinkney Treaty, Jefferson came to a cold calculation. Secretary of Treasury Albert Gallatin estimated the size of the merchant marine at 70,000 seamen. He also determined what proportion of these men were the most highly skilled and experienced sailors. Gallatin believed that there were 18,000 highly skilled seamen on American ships, half of whom were British subjects, even using American definitions of citizenship. As had been true in the 1790s, the high proportion of British skilled seamen aboard American ships provided a crucial component of the American maritime labor force. Gallatin explained that any equitable agreement, which would have had to include the return of British deserters to the royal navy, would cripple the American merchant marine: "an engagement on our part to employ no British sailors, would materially injure our navigation."[25] Jefferson and Madison agreed. Jefferson informed Gallatin: "Your estimate of the number of foreign seamen in our employ, renders it prudent, in my opinion, to drop the idea of any proposition not to employ them."[26] In other words, the British skilled seamen were worth more to American commerce than the American regular seamen lost to impressment. No doubt in a perfect world, the British should have respected the United States flag and not taken anyone – American or British – from the decks of American merchantmen. But the world was not perfect, and Jefferson and Madison understood that diplomacy was often a matter of compromise. Their rejection of the Monroe-Pinkney Treaty based on its failure to include a provision on impressment was disingenuous, and their insistence that any future treaty include such a provision ensured that no such treaty could be signed. It also guaranteed the continued employment of skilled British seamen vital to American commerce.[27]

However much Jefferson and Madison wanted to sidestep the issue of impressment in 1807, neither the Congress nor the public at large would let it go. As early as January 1805 Congressman Jacob Crowinshield from Salem, Massachusetts, had compared the condition of the impressed sailor to being "in a state of slavery."[28] A year later, Senator Robert Wright introduced a bill that made Smith's earlier proposal appear mild. Wright's bill declared impressment to be piracy and empowered a sailor to use lethal force to resist it. The bill also entitled any American sailor forced into the royal navy to compensation of $60 a month (a princely sum at the time) to be paid by the British. In addition, if any American sailor was corporally punished or executed while impressed, the law authorized the president to obtain "the most rigorous and exact retaliation on the subjects of that government." These last two measures would have meant American seizures of British property to obtain compensation and the arrest of British subjects to inflict corporal and even capital punishment in retribution for actions taken against Americans. During the subsequent debate, Wright referred to the "present degraded state of impressed American seamen," who were "compelled by whips and scourges, to work like galley slaves." The bill was tabled to await the results of the Monroe-Pinkney negotiations.[29]

Jefferson and Madison might have wanted to focus on free trade, but throughout the festering crisis with Great Britain, it became impossible for many Republican politicians to discuss the issue of neutral rights without also bringing up the problem of impressment.[30] In the spring of 1806, as the House of Representatives considered the non-importation bill, ostensibly in response to the *Essex* decision and British limits on American neutral trade, almost every speaker in Congress mentioned impressment in stark and dramatic terms. The Pennsylvanian John Smilie believed that impressment was worse than Algerine slavery and pointed out that "[y]our citizens are seized by the hand of violence, and if they refuse to fight the battles of those who thus lay violent hands on them, you see them hanging at the yard arm." Another speaker, Barnabas Bidwell, compared the effort to liberate the captives in Tripoli to the lack of action to prevent merchant seamen from impressment and declared, "They are our fellow-citizens, and have as fair a claim for public protection, as we ourselves have." Another congressman asserted that "They are men and citizens, they have friends, connexions, and a home, and are employed in an honest occupation" and have been thrown into "a state . . . worse than African slavery, on board those floating castles which spread terror through the world.[31] In a speech in Congress, Matthew Lyon asserted the principle that "free ships" make "free goods" and his belief that "impressments constitute slavery."[32]

Republican newspapers increasingly joined neutral rights in commerce with the issue of impressment. In March 1805, William Duane referred to "the British piracies upon our merchantmen" as well as the "impressment of our seamen." A month later he reported an impressment and quickly declared, "Outrages of this kind, and the rapacious seizure of American vessels, by foreign cruisers contrary to law and justice, merit the most serious notice of the people and the interference of congress."[33] A Charleston, South Carolina, paper began by reporting the large number of seizures by the British, but then noted, "The interruptions to our commerce would not be so alarming, where [sic] they unaccompanied by actions purely hostile" such as "[t]he impressment of our seamen," which is carried on "without regard . . . to the regular certificates of citizenship."[34] Early in 1806 the New Haven Chamber of Commerce decried "the depredations committed on our unprotected trade by lawless freebooters and the unwarrantable impressment of our Seamen" as violations of the "code of laws which the commercial nations of Europe have long held themselves bound to respect."[35] A Fourth of July toast in Salem in 1806 lumped the two issues together: "No more impressments, and no more captures of American vessels engaged in lawful commerce."[36] The murder of John Pierce by a stray cannonball from the *Leander*, which had a record of impressing American seamen, only added fuel to the fire. As an atrocity committed against an American seaman, the *Leander* incident would be mentioned repeatedly in the same breath as reports of continued impressment.[37]

The refusal of the Republican administration to negotiate impressment in good faith contributed to the tragedy of the *Chesapeake* affair. The confrontation on June 22, 1807, should never have happened. That spring, at least a dozen sailors had deserted a British squadron off the port of Norfolk. Officers in the British navy knew the identity of these men and knew that several of them had joined the American navy. Indeed, they had seen the deserters at a rendezvous house for recruitment for the USS *Chesapeake* and watched the men parade through the streets waving an American flag. In one instance, when an officer was about to persuade a man to return to his majesty's service, another deserter threatened to rip the more compliant tar's guts out and declared that he was in the "Land of Liberty; that he would do as he liked," and that the British officer "had no business with him." American navy recruiters were under orders not to accept deserters, but with plenty of berths available on merchant ships it was not easy to muster enough men. The American recruiting officer, desperate to fill the complement of the crew in order to sail on time, told the deserters to give a "second" name so that the rosters would not reveal their true identities. Commodore James Barron also promised the men that they would be protected by sailing in an American warship. The British, in the meantime, appealed to the recruiting officer and local officials but received no satisfactory answer. Further appeals were sent to Washington, D.C., where Madison said there was little he could do without a formal agreement or treaty between the two nations. Madison, however, asked Secretary of the Navy Robert Smith to look into the identity of the recruits. Smith referred the inquiry to Barron, who decided that the sailors in question may well have been deserters, but since the men had said that they were impressed Americans, the British had no real claim on them. Later testimony indicated that three of the four men were Americans, but those three, as well as the fourth, who was British, had all volunteered to serve in the British navy. In other words, if the Americans had simply refused to recruit British deserters into their navy, there would have been no attack on the *Chesapeake*. Or, as had been suggested during the Monroe-Pinkney negotiation, had the United States simply returned the British deserters, there would not have been a problem. On the other hand, had the British commander of the squadron, Vice Admiral Sir George Canfield Berkeley, not given explicit orders to intercept the *Chesapeake* once it reached international waters in order to make an example of a handful of men, a major diplomatic crisis could have been avoided.[38]

Regardless of whether or not the incident could have been prevented, it created a diplomatic imbroglio between the two nations and led to the Embargo of 1807. Although Jefferson and Madison focused on the issue of neutral rights almost to the exclusion of impressment, for many Americans the two issues remained intimately connected: "We consider the Embargo, at the present crisis, as a measure best calculated to preserve our property from plunder, and our Seamen from impressment and our nation from the horrors of war," proclaimed the Republicans of Essex County, Massachusetts, in a meeting on February 24, 1808.[39] A few months later another Republican made the same point in a letter dated from Washington, D.C., by reminding readers that their "independence" had been "wantonly invaded – your flag violated – your commerce destroyed – your seamen impressed and detained in British servitude."[40] During the summer of 1808, Republicans in St. Mary's County, Maryland, not only applauded "the embargo, and the principles under which it was enacted," but also "cheerfully" submitted "to its necessary privations" and "earnestly" desired "its continuance, so long as our seamen are subject to impressment and our commerce to plunder and devastation" by "a lawless band of kidnappers and highway robbers."[41] At the end of January in 1809, as the nation was about to repeal the Embargo, upstate New York Republicans expressed their belief that by keeping sailors ashore the measure had saved American citizens from impressment, "a service as severe as the slavery of Algiers." These Republicans believed that protecting American seamen was "the cause of humanity."[42]

For most Americans the *Chesapeake* affair was about impressment. "The main ground of dispute between the United States and Great Britain," proclaimed the *American Citizen* early in 1808, "is the right of searching for men."[43] One crude index of this increased interest in impressment can be derived from a search of the databank for America's historical newspapers. From 1803 to 1805 "impressment" appeared in anywhere from seventy-one to eighty-three articles each year. In 1806 and 1807 articles with the word "impressment" appeared about 250 times. In 1808, reflecting the interest in the subject spawned by the *Chesapeake* affair and the Embargo, the number jumped to 738. Over the next few years references to impressment ranged from 464 (1810) to 664 (1811). In 1812, as the nation entered the war, the total reached a startling 1,798 articles.[44]

The social position of the sailor, even his race, almost didn't matter. Jack Tar was a citizen as worthy of protection as any member of the elite. The federal government issued protections to sailors whether they were white or black. One of the sailors seized from the *Chesapeake* was described as a "colored man" from Massachusetts, and another was referred to as an "Indian looking man" from Maryland.[45] "Can any measure be more degrading to the American flag than to suffer our seaman to be exposed to such an outrage [impressment]?" asked one author. "The RIGHTS of SAILORS may be lightly estimated by some of our land lubbers, whose idol is their money . . . but let them reflect that while they allow the right of search under the pretence of deserters, the industrious, worthy, honest American SAILOR falls a sacrifice to a banditti, acting under the uncountrouled authority of his Majesty's Proclamation." The same writer went on to ask, "Suppose there were as many American lawyers, bank directors, merchants &c. unlawfully confined on board the British navy as there were sailors, what a hue and cry would there be! . . . How we should weep and mourn to find the fraternity of the bar in a ship's hold as deserters, or lashed to the gang way to receive the stripes of the cat-o-nine tails? . . . The order of sailor is as valuable in society as the order of lawyers; and we believe more people would mourn for the former, rather than the latter."[46]

As the author who placed sailors on the same level as "lawyers, bank directors, merchants &c." suggested, the surge in public outrage over impressment also reflected the resentment caused by the royal proclamation of October 16, 1807, that officially recalled all British seamen from foreign service and ordered naval officers to press any British subjects they found aboard neutral merchant vessels. In early 1809 John Adams wrote an extended essay against impressment, not only making a case for the illegality of the practice on the high seas and even in England, but also denouncing the king's proclamation in the strongest of terms, asserting "with confidence, that it furnished a sufficient ground for a *declaration of war.*" The retired president believed "not the murder of Pierce, nor all the murders, on board the Chesapeake, nor all the other injuries and insults we have received from foreign nations, atrocious as they have been, can be of such dangerous, lasting and pernicious consequence to this country, as this proclamation, if we have the servility enough to submit to it." For Adams, the king's assertion of the right to recall all of his subjects, and the order to have his naval officers take men from American ships, was a direct challenge to the independence and sovereignty of the United States.[47]

Just as it had been in the colonial era and during the 1790s, the common folk's interest in opposing impressment was also expressed in popular disorder. Not only did the good people of Norfolk destroy water casks belonging to the British navy after the attack on the *Chesapeake,* mobs continued to gather in cities to express their opposition to the autocratic practices of the British navy throughout these years of controversy. On September 5, 1807, during the height of the *Chesapeake* affair, a New York crowd quickly formed on the waterfront to protect deserting seamen when a British boat crew, ferrying an officer to shore, bolted and ran from his majesty's navy. Captain Isaac Chauncy had to rescue the hapless British lieutenant from possible rough treatment from the crowd. In early September 1810, crowds in Fell's Point, Baltimore's dockside neighborhood, intimidated British officers into surrendering an impressed seamen aboard a ship that had entered the harbor. Similar incidents occurred in other ports as Americans protected deserters or threatened British officials. Americans also misbehaved overseas. One young sailor noted in his journal how he had joined an anti-impressment riot in Liverpool in June 1809, claiming that he had a right to riot because the British navy had pressed one of his shipmates.[48]

Given this public interest, it should not be surprising that Jefferson and Madison continued to pay lip service to the issue of impressment. When Madison sent his instructions to Monroe in Great Britain about negotiating a settlement over the attack on the *Chesapeake*, he not only called for the return of the four seamen and payment of reparations, he also demanded that any agreement include a final settlement of impressment. This proviso stifled negotiations, especially since Monroe, not knowing Madison's wishes, had previously sent a letter to George Canning decrying impressment in general but noting that it would be improper to connect that issue with "the present more serious cause of complaint."[49] Likewise, when George Henry Rose, representing the British ministry, was sent to the United States to deal specifically with the *Chesapeake* affair, Madison's linkage of a settlement to impressment, as well as the British stipulation that Rose could not begin negotiations until the president rescinded his order excluding all British war vessels from American waters, doomed the mission.[50]

Oddly, although they may not have wanted a fair settlement to the question of impressment, and may not have even wanted a regular commercial agreement with Great Britain, Jefferson and Madison, by continuing to insist on settling the impressment issue before addressing other diplomatic questions, strengthened the connection between sailors' rights and free trade. Whatever Madison's real intentions as secretary of state or as president, Republicans took him at his word and joined impressment to commercial restrictions as causes of complaint against the British. The connection of the two questions persisted and built to a crescendo leading up to the War of 1812.[51]

This link became so compelling that, just as Federalists sought to compete with Republicans in supporting free trade, they also claimed to defend sailors' rights and even began to backpedal on the issue of impressment. For example, Federalists denied that the Embargo had "preserved and protected our Seamen" as Republicans claimed. Instead, it had driven sailors into British service, "having no other alternative, than to starve, or seek an honest livelihood from any nation who would employ them."[52] In May 1808 one Federalist newspaper reported that two hundred seamen had arrived in New Brunswick "in quest of employment" and concluded, "Thus it is the policy of Mr. Jefferson that drives our neglected mariners into a foreign land to procure a living."[53] To demonstrate the despair of so many American seamen, and to show their sympathy for the poor men who had been forced to desert their country by Jeffersonian policies, Federalists organized a street protest in Newburyport, Massachusetts, in late 1808 to commemorate the anniversary of the Embargo. "A procession of Sailors looking each of them a 'bloodless image of despair,'" marched with crepe armbands to muffled drums, escorting a large model of a dismantled ship with a flag proclaiming *"Death to Commerce"* and the words *"O grab me"* painted on the bows.[54] Sailors, too, especially in New England, supported collective action in opposing the Embargo restrictions. Maritime crowds in Newburyport, Providence, New Haven, and elsewhere intimidated customs officials in efforts to sidestep enforcement of the Embargo. During one incident in Castine, Maine, one man was killed, and a mob rescued several men who had been arrested.[55]

Accepting the idea that "[t]he impressment of our seamen, is the main point of dispute between the United States and G. Britain," some Federalists admitted that impressment represented a legitimate grievance. The Federalists charged that neither Jefferson nor Madison had seriously sought a settlement on impressment, believing that the informal accord worked out by Monroe and Pinkney was viable and that the Republican administration had ignored the issue in the short-lived Erskine Agreement and in subsequent negotiations.[56] Federalists also called for compromise and suggested that the best way to avoid conflict was to avoid using British sailors in either the merchant marine or navy.[57] They believed that "deserters like forgers and murderers, are offenders against human society" who "act *upon a principle* hostile to the *human* race." When *"pointed out and demanded,"* they "ought to be surrendered by all *nations.*"[58] Insisting that they did not want "to justify the conduct of the British on the subject of impressment," and noting that it was "a serious evil and ought not to be permitted," several Federalists asked that the "business" be "placed in a fair point of view" while mocking the extreme rhetoric used by Republicans like William Duane.[59] More conservative Federalists continued to claim that the number of sailors pressed was minimal and excused the British for occasionally taking an American because of the similarity of language, the inadequacies of the protection law, and the necessities of fighting a war to defend world liberty. They also believed that non-native sailors should not be protected by the American flag, since "[t]he foreign seamen are birds of passage."[60] But even these hard-liners gave ground, conceding that some Americans were being forced into the British navy and that this practice was "vexatious," "dreadful," and "a most wanton outrage on our sovereignty and personal rights."[61] As the crisis with Great Britain intensified, and in reaction to the duplicitous Cadore letter in which Napoleon gave false assurances of lifting his trade restrictions on the United States, the Federalists highlighted the poor treatment of American seamen by French authorities, calling it the equivalent or worse than British impressment.[62]

Federalists viewed the virulent Republican anti-impressment rhetoric and the Republican appeal to the maritime community as hypocritical and driven by politics. "Whatever may be the sufferings of our seafaring brethren," commented one New England Federalist, "so long as British impressments can be converted into electioneering materials, to promote the election of the leaders of democracy, so long the evil will be suffered to exist."[63] As a Rhode Island editor explained: "The horrours of impressment, is the standing chorus to the war song; the leaven of malignity, with which they raise and excite the inert mass to action."[64] Another Federalist editor wrote that Jefferson and Madison had purposefully not settled the impressment issue, using it "as a mere electioneering engine, while the impressed men were suffered to lie neglected and abandoned."[65] Yet another declared that "every new instance of impressment affords many a democrat a kind of savage joy, because he can vent his hatred and abuse upon those who differ from him in opinion." Worse, "Cases are fabricated and every colouring given to them to excite party purposes and many an aspiring demagogue has mounted to office by a dexterous use of hypocritical canting about injuries our neglected seamen suffer."[66] As one Federalist lamented, "The passions of men are so easily excited on this subject [impressment], that there is little chance for candour or argument to gain a hearing."[67]

Those passions became especially excited because the quality of the newspaper coverage intensified after 1809. Earlier discussions of impressment would occasionally suggest the personal cost of having Americans impressed by commenting on the "families left to suffer at home, in dependence and penury."[68] Such references elicited sympathy, but they did not fully personalize what it meant for the individual Jack Tar to be impressed. That changed with the appearance of the story of Ben Bunting. Although the character is likely fictional, his words reflected a reality easily imagined by many Americans. When confronted by the impressing officer, Bunting asked, "Know you not that I am the citizen of a country free, sovereign, and independent as your own?" and then asserted, like any true-blue American, "It is one of the privileges of my birth-right to use my limbs, and to seek my fortune at my discretion." These claims did not protect him from the British "floating Hell," and he was "cast like a dead dog, into the noisome hold of their ship of war, where I was thrown into the heaviest chains." Bunting exclaimed, "I was once a freeman – now a slave."[69] Over the next few years Republican editors continued to personalize the impressment experience by printing other stories about specific men pressed into the British navy and by using a saccharine prose style meant to elicit sympathy for the sailor and create anger at the British and any Federalist who dared to support them. After providing testimony describing the impressment of James Wheeden from Jamestown, Rhode Island, one Republican editor explained, "He was born among us, always lived with us; and if HE was not exempted from his fate, we know that every one of our citizens is exposed to it, who ventures as a seaman on the ocean." Not only did impressment cut Wheeden off from his "[h]ome, and its endearing attractions," he was also compelled "to associate with a crew of wretches who daily embitter his misery, and point its stings; to undergo toils beyond his strength, or suffer under the lash till he faints with the loss of blood; to waste his health in pestilential climes, and commit his life to the disastrous chances of battle." The editor asked, "Is the ruthless tyrant of the ocean to be tolerated in this tyranny over the persons of our fellow citizens?"[70] Similar articles painted vivid pictures that pulled at the heartstrings. Introducing the deposition of John Eaton, an impressed sailor, one editor labeled the British "thieves," "murderers," and "pirates." After describing corporal punishment aboard his majesty's ships, the editor asked, "Ye tender mothers, what would be your sensations, to see your beloved sons, whom you have nurtured at your breasts; whom you have embraced in the arms of maternal tenderness; whom you have beheld with ecstasies of delight; what would be your feelings to see these beloved sons mangled by the scourge of British butchers – to see their garments wet with their streaming blood – to hear their cries and groans, and to see them writhe in excruciating agonies?" Any toleration of impressment was unacceptable, and Federalist excuses were dismissed as Tory cant that should be rejected as efforts "to palliate the crimes of British murderers."[71]

Although opponents of impressment had long played the race card – explicitly by comparing forced recruitment into the British navy to slavery, and implicitly by decrying flogging – one of the most dramatic anti-impressment stories centered on a black sailor.[72] While the USS *Essex*, Porter's later ship, was in an English port in 1811, "a black seaman" from a British ship entered into American service. When the British demanded the return of the man, who could not produce any papers proving citizenship, Captain John Smith of the *Essex* "politely gave him up." As the sailor headed below to fetch his clothes, he "seized a hatchet, laid his left hand on a gun, *and chopped it off close to his wrist.*" The British officer left the black seaman on board the *Essex*. The sailor, according to a southern newspaper editor, had a "'complexion *incompatible with freedom*'" and had been pressed into the British navy. Despite the color of his skin, when faced with the alternative of either being "*enslaved or crippled,* he unhesitatingly chose the latter." The lesson of this "manly act" for a "*pusillanimous congress*" and the people of the United States was clear: "A nation of six millions of souls submits to British impressment; while 'a black seaman,' *maims himself* to break *his* yoke."[73]

In publishing these personal accounts Republicans could claim that Jack Tar was speaking for himself. In the political contest over who best represented the sailor, the Republicans gained the upper hand. Republicans understood the need to appeal to sailors. They often labeled the Federalists "the uniform advocates of British impressment of American seamen" and recited a litany of actions reaching back to the 1790s in which the Federalists had ignored the interests of the common seaman. One newspaper editor declared, "It was a federal negotiator [John Jay] that in forming a treaty with Great Britain, waved the claims of our seamen to protection against impressments." The same author also noted that it was "a federal Captain" [Isaac Phillips] who "tamely suffered the officers of a British frigate to take his men" and that John Adams had surrendered Jonathan Robbins to the British. The editor also attacked more recent Federalist comments against the Republican government and in support of British actions and then sarcastically concluded, "And yet these same federalists profess to be the exclusive friends of our seamen."[74] Another editor condemned the Federalists as disgraceful because they failed to commiserate with "the fate of thousands of our unhappy brethren who now experience the most abject slavery on board British ships" and had "scoffed at their miseries, applauded their tyrants, and thwarted the measures employed for their release."[75]

Republican congressmen took up the cause of impressment. During the debates over the repeal of the Embargo, Representative John G. Jackson of Virginia waxed eloquent in attacking impressment and defending sailors. Highlighting the special role of seamen as the protectors of the nation, Jackson asserted that the United States had an obligation to "the brave tars, whose lives are at their country's call, and who constitute its sole defence at sea," and that "never" could he deny "that correspondent protection, which is the promised equivalent for allegiance." For Jackson, "The rights of our citizens are the same at sea as on land, and their seizure by a foreign nation is inadmissable in the one case as the other." The issue was one of national pride: "Whilst we are a nation, and claim the attributes of independence, I for one will never consent that our flag shall wave unfurled over authorized disgrace." Jackson then pledged to "nail the flag to the main mast – make one last, mighty struggle – and if all will not avail, rather than survive our lost honor, go down to the bottom all together, amidst shouts of liberty or death!"[76]

Republican politicians took direct action to placate maritime workers and gain their support. To ease the unemployment created by the Embargo, and to keep maritime workers loyal to the Republican cause, officials in several ports – New York, Philadelphia, and Baltimore – started public works projects to create jobs and minimize economic stress. Republicans, like their Federalist counterparts, used street politics to appeal to sailors. In New York City, Republican politicians organized a memorial for the sailors who had died aboard prison ships during the Revolutionary War."[77] Ever since the British had evacuated the city in 1783, the proper burial of the bones of the ten thousand sailors who had died as prisoners during the war had festered unresolved. Republicans resuscitated the issue during the Embargo crisis as a means of garnering continued political support and "in commemoration of their [the sailors] heroic constancy and valor and their contempt of death." This effort helped the Republicans to rally common folk in the spring elections: artisans and sailors shouted "No Jersey Prison ships – no war – no Tories – no Federalists – our country forever" as they paraded to the polls. Republicans also highlighted the importance of mariners in a funeral procession for the burial of the bones of the dead prisoners of war on May 26, 1808, by giving the "brave Republicans of the Ocean" precedence even over the governor during the ceremonies.[78] In a similar spirit, to celebrate their electoral victory in the fall of 1808 Republicans in Baltimore held a parade prominently featuring maritime themes. The procession began in Fell's Point and included 300 Jack Tars carrying a banner emblazoned with "A Proof that all American Seamen are not gone to Halifax." These words countered Federalist claims that the Embargo had compelled American sailors to seek employment with the British. Like the Federalists in Newburyport, Baltimore Republicans used a scaled-down replica of a ship – "The elegant schooner 'Democratic Republican,'" – drawn through the streets as a float, manned by a sea captain accompanied by "other seamen, boatswain, etc."[79]

However important impressment became to many Americans on its own, by the eve of the War of 1812 the two issues of sailors' rights and free trade were becoming increasingly conjoined. The Embargo, according to Boston Republicans, protected property and prevented impressment.[80] After the British repudiation of the Erskine Agreement, "MARCELLUS" wrote, "Our commerce is again to be exposed to the rapacity of her cruisers, and our seamen to impressment and murder."[81] In the same spirit a Republican meeting in Waterville, Maine, lamented "the murder and impressment of our citizens" and defended "our commercial rights" against the "overbearing spirit of the British government."[82] As the crisis with Great Britain intensified in 1811, Republican rhetoric persisted with the same refrains. "Nothing in the annals of civilization," wrote one commentator, "can equal the daring villany of the British myrmidons infesting our coasts, in plundering American vessels of not only the property of our citizens, but even of the citizens themselves."[83] The Tammany Society in Philadelphia toasted both "The rights of American citizens" to be protected against impressment and "The freedom of the ocean."[84] Even those who lambasted both Great Britain and France for violating American commercial rights combined the two issues. "Great Britain...by her orders, and blockades, but above all her monstrous conduct in impressing native American seamen...[has] reduced us to the necessity of adopting rigorous measures towards her as well as France."[85] Like many of his fellow congressmen, John C. Calhoun, then a fire-breathing war hawk, saw commercial rights and impressment as one issue. Calhoun explained: "The question...is reduced to this single point – which shall we do, abandon or defend our own commercial and maritime rights, and the personal liberties of our citizens employed in exercising them?" Others shared Calhoun's sentiments. Richard M. Johnson, a congressman from Kentucky, demonstrated how intertwined the two issues had become when he exclaimed that "[b]efore we relinquish the conflict, I wish to see

Great Britain renounce the piratical system of paper blockade [free trade]; to liberate our captured seamen on board her ships of war [sailors' rights]; relinquish the practice of impressment on board our merchant vessels [sailors' rights]; to repeal her Orders in Council [free trade]; and cease in every other respect, to violate our neutral rights [free trade and sailors' rights]; to treat us as an independent people."[86] Amid the war debates in December 1811, one Republican editor labeled the British as bandits and assassins and concluded: "The American nation will resist *all* robbers – The British Orders in Council, which are no other than a system of *robbery* – and the British system of impressment, which is no better than *assassination*, must be given up – or WE MUST HAVE WAR."[87]

# 14

# Honor

The notion of honor helped to cement the bond between free trade and sailors' rights. Honor in the early republic was an important principle in politics and society. Honor combined integrity, self-possession, and bravery. Integrity meant that an individual was honest and sentimental in the eighteenth-century sense of the term – that is, the individual was open about his true self and sentiments. A person's word was sacred and reflected his sincere beliefs. This integrity was central not only to personal relations, but also in relations between nations. Self-possession meant that an individual exerted independent judgment and was in control of himself and his own destiny. Self-possession also reflected the means to sustain one's independence, both socially and economically, without interference from others. Again, this idea had an application to diplomacy, since it meant that a nation should operate on equal terms with other nations without being dictated to. Bravery indicated a willingness to confront one's enemies without flinching, even if it meant facing death. On the personal level this notion of bravery led to the *code duelo*, whereby on the "field of honor" one was willing to exchange pistol shots – or use other lethal weapons – with an equal who had given one offense (the code allowed other types of action if your traducer was an inferior). Bravery, too, had implications for foreign affairs, since a nation was expected to defend itself against insults with force of arms, if necessary.

Although honor had long been associated with aristocracy, it seemed to have a special meaning in the new democratic world created by the American Revolution. With the egalitarian leveling of society, it became more difficult for political and even military leaders to distinguish themselves from the common herd. Asserting a highly refined sense of honor became a means of doing so. During the Revolutionary War the *code duelo* swept through the officer corps with such force that the French minister, a true scion of the aristocracy, was shocked by the "rage of dueling" among Americans.[1] After the war, the military continued to be a hotbed of dueling, especially the navy. During the opening decade of the nineteenth century dueling became so common in the navy that it threatened the efficiency of operations. Politicians, too, were prone to fighting duels. The most famous duel of the early republic, between Alexander Hamilton and Aaron Burr, led to Hamilton's death, with severe ramifications for the Federalist Party. Honor and the *code duelo* were essential components of the culture of the early republic.[2]

American politicians had long viewed the ongoing diplomatic crisis with Great Britain in terms of honor. Much of the hoopla following the *Chesapeake* affair centered on the violation of American honor. The *Leopard*'s attack on the *Chesapeake* was a direct violation of American sovereignty and a military humiliation. In the summer of 1807 the citizens of Baltimore pledged their support to the Jefferson administration, confident that it would gain "satisfaction for an outrage so daring and injurious to the honor and dignity of our country," and were ready "with our lives and fortunes [to] support the government in all such measures as they may adopt."[3] Likewise, the impressment issue was often cast in terms of honor. A Kentucky editor proclaimed in 1808 that "[t]he impressment of our seamen is an insult to the nation, and degrading to humanity."[4] Two years later another Republican noted that "[w]e have forfeited our national honor irratrievably, if the menaces of the British faction [Federalists] prevent congress taking effectual measures both for recovering our seamen already in bondage, and for preventing their impressment in the future."[5] Calling impressment a dishonor, one writer believed that "[t]his violation [impressment] of American independence is, alone, sufficient to rouse government to a warlike attitude."[6] Another Republican declared that "[n]o nation, besides ourselves, would suffer its citizens to be kidnapped."[7] The issue cut to the core of American identity and independence. "Not to establish a perfect security for seamen sailing under our flag, is to abandon the most sacred of our rights and the sovereignty and independence of our country."[8]

Ultimately, however, the question of national honor involved impressment and the protection of commerce – sailors' rights and free trade. For many Republicans the issue of safeguarding both American property and persons at sea were intrinsically connected. One Republican in 1808 believed that they were directly joined to the purpose of government, although he saw the protection of trade as the responsibility of the national government while the protection of individuals was the responsibility of all levels of government. After stating that "[u]nder the pretence of taking their own men, the British have actually forced into their service many thousand of American citizens, who are now fighting their battles against nations with whom we are at peace," this writer asked, "Can an independent nation suffer a greater injury than this?" The answer, of course, was no, since "[t]he protection of commerce was the principle object of forming the constitution of the United States," while "the protection of the personal freedom of our citizens forms the basis ot [of] all our constitutions."⁹ Many Republicans talked of war at the height of the *Chesapeake* affair. Calls to defend honor continued to be voiced thereafter. A Republican wrote in 1809 that "[t]he concerns of America are rapidly approximating to that crisis which, at first view, admit no alternative but submission or war; war to defend those rights which are guaranteed by the laws of reason and of nations, or submission to the impressment of our seamen, and plunder of our property. If we remain passive while Britain enforces orders which not only impair our rights, but strike a death-blow at the vitals of our independence, what is it but submission, of the basest, of the most ignoble kind."¹⁰ As the New York *Public Advertiser* succinctly put it: "The United States can never abandon their commercial or maritime rights with *safety* or with *honor*."¹¹

In an essay signed "Wallace," another Republican compared the question of national honor to individual honor in terms that everyone in the early republic would recognize. From this perspective, the United States had not behaved honorably. "Such has been the punctilious nature of national honor, in ancient as well as modern times, (*with the exception of the United States of America*) that the least insult offered to the ensigns of national authority, or the slightest infringements on national privileges...has been deemed sufficient cause for war." Failure to act was a "[s]ubmission to insult" and led "to further indignity." Wallace compared the refusal of the United States to defend its honor militarily with the *code duelo* behavior of a gentleman in the early republic. "A gentleman will submit to no premeditated affront, of however trifling import, if reparation be denied, he is prepared to hazard his life in defence of his honor." Following the *code duelo*, the question "is not that the trifling insult offered him, makes an immediate serious impression on his interests." Rather, "it is the *principle* he objects to: – the consequences that will result, of which he is apprehensive." Small slights had to be guarded against, since they lead to larger insults, and those larger insults lead to a complete loss of honor. Wallace made the analogy explicit: "that a *Nation* claiming to be independent, should have for a series of years, its sovereignty vitally attacked; should behold its flag outraged; the property of its citizens depredated on; its citizens themselves forced into foreign allegiance and service: – *and still remain in a state of peace*; is one of these paradoxes, which bewilder the understanding."¹²

Events in the years immediately leading up to the War of 1812 brought the question of honor into sharper focus. Americans viewed the lack of progress on the diplomatic front as a sign that the British did not respect the United States and thereby dishonored the nation. As Congressmen Joseph Desha of Kentucky explained, "insult has been the result of all late attempts at negotiation."¹³ When Great Britain refused to ratify the Erskine agreement, Republicans cried foul and charged the British with duplicity (ignoring their own rejection of the Monroe-Pinkney Treaty in 1807). David Erskine's replacement as minister in Washington was Francis Jackson – known as "Copenhagen Jackson," he was the British diplomat who had delivered the ultimatum to Denmark demanding the surrender of its fleet in 1807. The appointment of a minister associated with the national humiliation of Denmark reflected the high-handed diplomacy Republicans had come to expect from the British. The negotiations between Secretary of State Robert Smith and Jackson only reenforced this idea. When Smith asked Jackson to explain the repudiation of the Erskine agreement, the British minister indicated that Erskine had not followed his written instructions, which limited his power to negotiate and make concessions. Smith considered the failure to provide a more detailed explanation as a violation of the law of nations and dishonorable behavior. He also believed that, since Jackson operated under the same instructions, any negotiations without the full power to settle differences was a denial of the equality of nations and disregarded "the self respect enjoined on the attention of the United States." To make matters worse, Jackson indicated that Smith and Madison had been aware of these limitations during the negotiations with Erskine, implying that they had acted in bad faith concerning the British government. Smith reacted with wounded pride to Jackson's comments, calling them a "gross insinuation." In order "to preclude opportunities which are thus abused," he decided to end all communication with Jackson, and demanded his recall. Aggravating this diplomatic impasse, the Smith-Jackson correspondence quickly appeared in American newspapers, leading Republicans to decry the affront to American dignity.[14] Jackson's replacement, Augustus John Foster, fared only a little better. Arriving in Washington in July 1811, like Jackson and Erskine before him Foster was constrained by instructions preventing him from negotiating on commercial issues or conceding anything on impressment. Instead, increasing tensions even further, he rigorously protested American incursions into Spanish Florida. Permitted by his instructions to settle the American complaint about the *Chesapeake* affair, he waited until November 1811 to inform the State Department that his government was willing to make amends on this question. By that time Congress was ready to debate preparations for war. The offer of reparations and the promise to return the two remaining men taken from the decks of the American frigate (one had been hanged and another had died) was too little too late. The concession, Madison wrote, in words that suggest the depth of the sense of violated honor, "takes one splinter out of our wounds" and had "the appearance of a mere anadyne to the excitements in Congress and the nation."[15]

Another splinter – or perhaps a larger shard of wood – had been removed from the American sense of injury a few months earlier in the violent encounter between the American frigate *President* and the smaller British ship *Little Belt*. When Captain John Rodgers and the *President* left Annapolis, Republican

papers were filled with news of the egregious impressment of John Diggio
from Maine. Many Americans mistakenly believed that Rodgers had orders to
recover the man from the British. Even without these orders, when Rodgers
spotted the *Little Belt* on May 16, 1811, he thought the vessel was the frigate
HMS *Guerrière* and, believing Diggio was on board, decided to see if he could
get the pressed sailor released. In the fading light of that evening the two
vessels closed and cleared for action (a standard procedure when approaching
an unidentified warship at sea). As they neared, each vessel demanded that the
other identify itself. Honor reared its ugly head in this tense situation, since
ordinarily the weaker ship was to identify itself first. But the British captain,
Arthur Bingham, was not ready to concede anything to the larger American
ship. And the captain of an American frigate was not about to humble himself
to a British sloop of war. The British and American accounts painted two
different pictures of what happened next, with each side claiming the other
fired first. The tenor of Rodgers' report, however, suggests the important role
of honor in the contest. Rodgers wrote that he had unleashed his more powerful
broadside only after the ships had exchanged one shot, followed by a larger
salvo from the British. Believing this "immediate repetition of the previous
unprovoked outrage" was "premeditated," he determined not to "suffer the
flag of my country to be insulted with impunity." Rodgers ordered his guns
to fire. It was an uneven battle, and the *Little Belt* was soon a near-wreck.
Bingham had thirteen men killed and nineteen wounded; Rodgers reported
only one boy slightly wounded. For Americans this action was redemption and
a defense of national honor. For the British, Rodgers was a bully who had
launched an unprovoked attack on a smaller vessel.[16]

American sensibilities were further agitated by an espionage controversy
that erupted early in 1812, when Madison's government spent the entire secret
service budget of $50,000 for a cache of papers from the British spy and would-
be agent provocateur John Henry. Irish by birth, Henry had arrived in Canada
in 1807, having first lived in the United States, where he developed connections
with the Federalist Party. Henry ingratiated himself with Canadian officials in
part by talking up American political differences and hinting that the United
States was on the point of disunion. After a business trip to New England
in 1808, Henry reported that the divisions had only deepened as a result of
the Embargo. Early in 1809 the Canadian governor sent Henry back to New
England, authorizing him to offer support to any disunionists he might find
among the Federalists. On this trip Henry wrote a series of letters indicating
extensive support for British intervention in New England, but he did not
identify specific individuals who would join the British. Most of what Henry
reported was gossip, dinner party conversations, and idle speculation at coffee
houses. Nothing tangible came from Henry's sojourn in New England other
than his writing the incriminating letters. In early 1812 Henry, always looking

out for the main chance, and encouraged by a charlatan Frenchman by the name of Paul-Emile Souriron, agreed to sell his papers to the United States. Their subsequent publication caused a stir. Republicans asserted that they were proof positive that the Federalists had flirted with secession. The Federalists argued that the letters had not revealed any treason and that Madison had wasted money in purchasing the Henry papers. For many Americans the issue was not whether or not Federalists had actually plotted disunion – the disreputable source of the letters and their failure to provide details made many question the authenticity of their content. Rather, the Henry correspondence demonstrated that the British had once again traduced American honor by hiring an agent to foment disunion.[17]

By the spring of 1812 the momentum for war appeared unstoppable. Americans had many reasons for going to war. For some, the war offered an opportunity to add Canada and even Florida to the American constellation of states. For others, the war would enable them to strike at "hostile" Indians who stood in the way of further expansion in the Ohio River Valley and in the lands farther to the south. As significant as these reasons may have been, for republicans they were too self-serving, too aggrandizing, or too embarrassing. Far better to portray America as a violated nation whose honor was at stake. For most Americans the war was tied to commerce. Challenges to that commerce threatened the honor of the United States, its identity as a nation, even its heritage of the revolution. Impressment and limitations on trade were as powerful a reason for war, so many Americans believed, as the British impositions that had led to the Revolutionary War. "Our Independence is *lost* if we submit," the Brooklyn *Long-Island Star* urged. "Let us *recover* it by resistance."[18] As explained in a Vermont newspaper, "If our rights are not worth fighting for, we should not thank our ancestors for their achievements in the revolution – but we know that without freedom, without liberty, any thing else is bitter – life is not worth possessing."[19]

Americans also believed that they were about to fight a war for reasons that reached beyond their own immediate interests. They were concerned with demonstrating that in a world packed full of monarchs who constantly sought advantage through the raw use of power, a republic, which had done all it could to avoid a war, was capable of waging war to defend itself. Congressman Hugh Nelson of Virginia explained to his constituents that European monarchies had begun to believe that the American republican government was too "inefficient and incompetent to exert the power and energy of the nation, and assume the attitude and posture of war." It was to "repel these unfounded imputations" that Nelson supported the war, and "to shew that our republican government was competent to assert its rights, to maintain the interests of the people, and to repel all foreign aggression."[20] The viability of the American republic – indeed, the very idea of a republic – was at stake.

Herein lies the beauty of Porter's motto. For the better part of a decade, Americans of every political stripe had seized upon the phrase "free trade" and trumpeted it for their own purposes. In doing so they had built upon the identification of that phrase, in its many varied meanings, with the American Revolution. At the same time both political parties had claimed to defend the interests of sailors as citizens. Although the parties differed in how they used free trade and which sailors were considered citizens, the constant repetition of the rhetoric of free trade and the persistent concern for the ordeal of Jack Tar left an indelible mark on all Americans. That free trade reflected a patrician strain of the revolutionary heritage and that sailors' rights represented a plebeian strain, only enhanced the potency of combining the two. The manner in which the two phrases were joined was also significant, since Captain David Porter used "free trade and sailors' rights" in an exchange that could only be described as a naval affair of honor. With Americans consumed with the idea of defending their national honor, Porter's exchange with Captain Yeo had a deeper meaning that went beyond a simple challenge for a ship-to-ship engagement. For Porter and the sailors aboard the frigate *Essex*, plastering the phrase "Free Trade and Sailors' Rights" upon a banner flying from a mast on their ship was an immediate insult to the honor of Sir James Yeo and the British navy. It also asserted American national honor and identity, summarized the main reasons why the United States entered the war, and proclaimed universal principles connected to revolutionary ideas about the nature of commerce and the equality of mankind.

# PART FOUR

# WAR

As we have seen, both high and low cultural threads came together and were woven into the pennant placed aboard the *Essex* as it headed to sea in 1812. From that point forward the political slogan gained a life of its own. The rest of the American navy quickly adopted the motto. A series of surprising American triumphs at sea only strengthened the appeal of free trade and sailors' rights. Porter and the *Essex* also added luster to the phrase by sailing to the Pacific and decimating the British whaling fleet. Even in defeat at the Battle of Valparaiso, Porter and his crew enhanced the appeal of the rallying cry. The war on land produced some language of combat that augmented Porter's motto, but did not replace it. Slogans like "Don't give up the ship" and "We have met the enemy and they are ours" have become a part of American folklore, and Francis Scott Key's poem "Defence of Fort McHenry" later became the lyrics of the national anthem under the title "The Star Spangled Banner." Yet for the generation who fought the War of 1812, free trade and sailors' rights retained its special appeal. Within months of the opening of the war politicians were using the phrase in speeches in the halls of Congress to summarize the war aims. And even when the exact words were not used, every time politicians had to explain the war they depended upon the basic concepts expressed by the phrase. Both Republicans and Federalists relied on its rhetoric to defend or attack the war. The ideals of free trade and sailors' rights fared less well in diplomacy. Although the British had ceded some ground on free trade by repealing the orders of council as the war commenced, American insistence on British concessions on the issue of impressment helped to prolong the war. Peace became attainable when diplomats abandoned both free trade and sailors' rights, but they did so only after the Anglo-French war was over and the issues had become less acute. Whatever the decisions of politicians and diplomats concerning free trade and sailors' rights, the words remained deeply ingrained with the American people. The experience of the sailor prisoners of war at Dartmoor, and popular reaction to the Dartmoor Massacre on April 6, 1815, demonstrated the continued adherence among Americans to both the words and ideas of free trade and sailors' rights.

# 15

## The Odyssey of the *Essex*

Captain David Porter was the ideal candidate to combine free trade and sailors' rights. As a young merchant sailor and as an officer in the American navy, Porter came to understand what each concept meant at first hand. Born into a maritime family, the teenage Porter sailed on several merchant ships commanded by his father on voyages to the West Indies. There, he experienced the impositions of both the British and the French that threatened sailors' rights and limited American trade. When only sixteen, Porter was on board his father's schooner, *Eliza*, and helped to beat back a British press gang in the confrontation at Jérémie, St. Domingue, on February 9, 1796. Men were killed and wounded on both sides in the affray. Porter may have faced British press gangs two other times in his early maritime career. Porter's own son wrote a biography detailing one occasion on which Porter hid in a ship as a press gang searched for men, and another time when Porter was actually pressed into British service, but managed to escape. Whatever the truth of these additional stories, the battle at Jérémie was real and must have left an indelible mark on the future captain of the *Essex*. The Porter family also faced French depredations. On his father's next voyage after the battle with the press gang – it is unclear whether Porter was with him – French privateers stopped and searched the ship. Although the privateers allowed the senior Porter to proceed, they looted the cargo and robbed the passengers. As the United States responded to such French outrages and entered the Quasi War, Porter garnered a midshipman's commission on April 16, 1798, and was aboard the *Constellation* when it fought *L'Insurgent*. Porter remained in the navy after the crisis with France had passed and was dispatched to the Mediterranean, where he served on several ships protecting American trade against the Barbary states. Unfortunately for Porter, he was on the *Philadelphia* when it grounded off Tripoli, and he suffered eighteen months of captivity, providing him further insight into the ordeal of Jack Tar.

After his release, Porter had command of his own ships on the Mediterranean station, and then the navy charged him with enforcing the Embargo in New Orleans. By the time he took command of the *Essex* in 1811, he was not only an experienced naval officer, but also a man who had both free trade and sailors' rights etched into his being.[1]

Porter's new ship, too, had a special relationship with free trade and sailors' rights. The *Essex* was built in Salem, Massachusetts, to protect free trade as a subscription ship (the money for construction was raised locally and lent to the United States) in response to the Quasi War. A fast-sailing small frigate, the *Essex* was almost half the tonnage of the American super frigates (the *Essex* was 850 tons, while the *Constitution* was 1,576 tons). Most frigates had more weaponry than their standard ratings indicated. Although rated at thirty-two guns, the *Essex* was originally armed with thirty-six long guns (twenty-six twelve-pounders and ten six-pounders). Shortly before Porter took command of the *Essex* the ship was refitted with forty thirty-two pound carronades and six eighteen-pound long guns, for a total of forty-six guns with much greater firepower. The carronades, however, were effective only at short range, a deficit that greatly disturbed Porter and that would create problems in the battle at Valparaiso.[2] Launched on September 30, 1799, the *Essex* departed two months later for the Indian Ocean and the East Indies, where it convoyed American shipping. After the Quasi War the navy sent the *Essex*, like Porter, to the Mediterranean, where it continued to protect American shipping in order to ensure free trade. The *Essex* was also the scene of one of the most dramatic impressment stories immediately before the outbreak of the War of 1812. While in an English port, a British deserter who had joined the crew of the American frigate chopped off his own hand rather than be dragged back to his majesty's service. Long before Porter raised his banner from the masthead, free trade and sailors' rights were already a part of the timbers of the ship.[3]

As an officer, Porter had a highly tuned sense of honor and his own dignity that, with his penchant for bravado, bordered on petulance. His actions often earned him praise and respect from his fellow officers and the American public, while sometimes garnering criticism from his superiors and gaining the enmity of the British. In August 1806 Porter commanded the schooner *Enterprise* and almost created a diplomatic crisis in Malta when he had a drunken British sailor dragged on board his ship and whipped for being insolent to one of his officers. Outraged at this behavior, local British officials ordered Porter not to leave the harbor until the matter had been investigated. Porter was not to be dictated to by anyone but his superior officers (if even then), and, ignoring the British threat to fire upon his ship, he defiantly sailed the *Enterprise* into the open sea.[4] Porter later added to his reputation among the British as a hothead who mistreated British common seamen – odd behavior for a man so committed to sailors' rights. On June 12, 1812, before he set sail on his first cruise in the War of 1812, he mustered the crew of the *Essex* and asked if there was anyone who would not swear an oath of allegiance to the United States. John Ervin said he was an Englishman and that he was unwilling to fight against his king. Porter dismissed Ervin and allowed him to go ashore, but not before some of the crew gave the self-professed Englishman a coat of tar and feathers. The incident did not end there. Secretary of Navy Paul Hamilton reprimanded Porter for allowing this mob action, while Augustus John Foster, the departing British minister, protested this breach of decorum. Both the whipping and the tarring and feathering were later brought up in British newspapers in a general assault on Porter's character. A few more recent scholars also attribute Yeo's animosity to Porter to his treatment of Ervin.[5]

The exchange of challenges between Porter and Yeo fits a pattern of behavior repeated several times in Porter's career. Like many young American officers, Porter was acutely sensitive to the *code duelo* and was involved in affairs of honor, but as far as we know he always served as a second rather than as the principal duelist in his early years. While he was captain of the *Essex*, one of his officers killed another in a duel at a time when Porter desperately needed the dead officer's navigational skills. Rather than punishing the survivor, Porter did not even mention the man's name in his journal; he merely noted that the navy had "received an irreparable injury . . . by a practice which disgraces human nature" and let the matter pass.[6] Whatever Porter's real attitude toward dueling on a one-to-one basis, he viewed a challenge between captains for ship-to-ship engagements as an intrinsic part of naval etiquette, as we have seen in his exchange with Yeo. While cruising the Atlantic in the summer of 1812, Porter intercepted a convoy of British merchant ships. He captured one, and then challenged the frigate escorting the convoy, HMS *Minerva*, to a single-ship action. The captain of the *Minerva* was not eager to abandon his duty to play the knight errant and refused the challenge. In like manner, Porter's pursuit of glory brought him to Valparaiso at the end of his Pacific cruise, where the *code duelo* and challenges came into play before his battle with the British.[7]

That voyage, which was long, arduous, and one of the greatest naval sagas of the war, needs to be placed in the context of the other developments in the naval contest between the United States and Great Britain. The American navy had a string of spectacular ship-to-ship victories that stunned both the British and the Americans. Congress had been reluctant to commit resources to an outmatched navy before the war. The comparisons were overwhelming, and the British Goliath looked poised to overwhelm the American David. At the beginning of the war the Americans had 17 vessels to the British 1,048; those American ships had a total of 15,300 tons to the British 860,990 tons; the Americans had 442 guns to the British 27,800 guns; and the American navy contained a mere 5,025 men to the British 151,572. Even with the British having the world to patrol and a war against Napoleonic France to fight, the odds were daunting. Moreover, the American navy did not contain any large ships of the line. No one gave the navy much of a chance against the British. In a fit of optimism soon after the outbreak of war, Thomas Jefferson wrote that no war had been "entered into under more favorable auspices" and that "[o]ur present enemy will have the seas to herself, while we shall be equally predominant at land, and shall strip her of all her possessions on this continent."[8] Jefferson's words were never to prove more wrong. In the early days of the war defeat followed defeat in Canada, and the British province was not to be conquered from the south. Meanwhile the puny American navy provided the only victories early in the war. Porter's own capture of the *Alert* was a mismatch that was important only because the *Alert* was the first British ship to surrender to the Americans. More significant was the *Constitution*'s defeat of the *Guerrière* on August 19, 1812. Both ships were frigates, although the *Constitution* was larger and had more guns and men. Still, the *Guerrière* was pounded into submission and was in such bad shape at the end of the battle that it had to be sunk. The record of the American super frigates continued when the *United States* captured the *Macedonian* on October 25, 1812, and the *Constitution* destroyed the *Java* in a fierce battle in the South Atlantic on December 29, 1812. Astounded by these defeats, the British admiralty ordered its captains to avoid single-ship actions and proclaimed that battles against the super frigates were not even contests. American triumphs, however, occurred with smaller ships as well. On October 18, 1812, the eighteen-gun sloop *Wasp* had the effrontery to attack a British convoy and then captured the twenty-two-gun *Frolic*. Unfortunately for the Americans, no sooner had the *Wasp* beaten the larger British vessel than a seventy-four-gun British ship appeared, forcing the hobbled *Wasp* – its rigging was in shambles from the battle – to surrender. The Americans scored another victory on February 24, 1813, when the brig *Hornet* met the *Peacock* off the coast of South America. The battle was short and brutal. Although the vessels were about the same size, the *Hornet* had more firepower, was better handled, and had more effective gunnery. In a matter of minutes the *Hornet* so overwhelmed the *Peacock* that it soon sank.[9]

As American armies stumbled their way into Canada only to face defeat and two massive surrenders, the naval victories proved an important tonic for the pride of the United States. The navy suddenly appeared to be the proper vehicle to defend free trade and sailors' rights. Congress began to commit money to the navy and an extensive program of building warships.[10] Like many developments during the War of 1812, the timing was all wrong. Despite the brief chimera of American invincibility at sea cast by the single-ship victories in the early months of the war, the British naval supremacy was real. Perhaps the fate of the ill-starred *Chesapeake* should have been seen as an omen. Captained by James Lawrence, who had won accolades for commanding the *Hornet* in its triumph over the *Peacock*, the *Chesapeake* headed out of Boston harbor on

ILLUSTRATION 12. Engagement of the *Chesapeake*. The British public was so excited by the victory of the *Shannon* over the *Chesapeake* that Thomas Whitcombe painted the battle scene, a painting that was published as a print in London on May 1, 1814. Despite the defeat, Americans viewed Captain James Lawrence as a hero who died defending national honor, even though the nation's interests would have been better served had Lawrence avoided the duel with the *Shannon* and escaped to raid British commerce. The painting includes a white banner flying from the foremast of the *Chesapeake* proclaiming "A free trade and sailors' rights." Courtesy of the Naval Historical Center, Washington, D.C., from the U.S. Naval Academy, Annapolis, Maryland, Beverly R. Robinson Collection.

June 1, 1813. From the masthead the Americans had raised a banner emblazoned with free trade and sailors' rights. Waiting for the *Chesapeake* was HMS *Shannon*, under Captain Philip Vere Broke, carrying one of the best-trained crews in the British navy. The *Chesapeake* was not a super frigate and had a green crew that was still getting its sea legs. Lawrence mishandled his ship and sailed passed the *Shannon*, only to luff (a maneuver to slow the ship down) and have his stern exposed to British broadsides. Wounded, Lawrence called to his men, "Don't give up the ship," a phrase that was soon to be immortalized. Lawrence's words had little effect on the battle; his ship, with its decks covered in blood, unable to defend itself, surrendered. The American spell of victories had been broken. Lawrence became a hero who had sacrificed himself for the American cause. Newspaper stories of the funeral of Lawrence and one of his lieutenants, after their bodies had been returned by the British, began with "MARTYRS IN THE CAUSE OF 'FREE TRADE & SAILOR'S RIGHTS,'" and the sailors who rowed Lawrence's body ashore for the funeral had blue ribbons on their hats with "*Free Trade and Sailors' Rights*" printed on them. Whatever spin Republicans put on the situation – and there would be occasional other sea battles that the United States would win – the British navy began to tighten its grip on the East Coast, and most of the American navy remained trapped in rivers and harbors.[11]

It is against this background of American naval triumphs, followed by American naval travails, that Porter's second cruise on the *Essex* must be viewed. When Porter responded to Yeo's insulting language with his own more subtle affronting challenge in the fall of 1812, he was also preparing the *Essex* to return to the sea. Fully aware of the first wave of naval victories, Porter was eager to prove his mettle. He had been ordered to sail in concert with the *Constitution* and the brig *Hornet* on a cruise to the South Atlantic. After leaving Philadelphia and failing to find any sign of Yeo off the Delaware capes, Porter headed for his rendezvous somewhere near Brazil. Although Porter made several captures in the first phase of the voyage, including one British ship loaded with $55,000 in specie, he never saw the rest of the squadron, nor did he meet with a comparable-sized enemy to fight and earn the honor and glory he so desperately sought. In the meantime both the *Constitution* and the *Hornet* gained victories and renown for their captains, and returned to the United States. With plenty of cash on hand and ready for some action, Porter turned his ship southward, made a tumultuous passage around Cape Horn, and entered the Pacific in search of the British whaling fleet.[12]

The *Essex*, which had been the first American naval vessel to enter the Indian Ocean, now claimed pride of place for the navy in the Pacific Ocean. Porter took this bold action just as the British had tightened their blockade so that most of the American navy was unable to get to sea. Months passed without any word from the *Essex*. As far as anyone in the United States knew, the ship could have been lost in a storm or captured by the British. In July 1813, news arrived that the *Essex* had entered the Pacific. Over the next several months other reports dribbled in, and then, in December, letters from Porter arrived detailing many of his captures. At a moment when the war seemed to drag on and the navy had been driven from the ocean, Americans discovered that one of their frigates was wreaking havoc in the Pacific. In American imaginations this feat was reminiscent of Columbus, Magellan, and Drake. Porter became, as newspapers crowed after another report in May 1814, "the *Admiral of the Great South Sea*," destroying the British whaling fleet while protecting

American whalers in the region. This "gallant" American captain was striking such a terrific blow against the British economy – and once again defending free trade and sailors' rights – that the British dispatched whole squadrons to hunt for a man whom they called a "buccaneer."[13]

The voyage of the *Essex* was a story for the ages. After stopping in Valparaiso to refit, the *Essex* sailed up the west coast of South America, liberating captured American whalemen and disarming a Peruvian privateer. Informed that most British whaling ships were centered on the Galapagos Islands, Porter sailed to that isolated archipelago, and cruised among the island chain from April 17 to June 8 and then from July 22 to October 3, 1813. In the process he swept the seas of British whalers, capturing thirteen prizes. The year at sea and all of those prizes stretched his crew thin and pushed his ship to its limits. The prizes needed to be manned and navigated (here the loss of a lieutenant to a duel was particularly harmful). Porter recruited men from among the Americans who had previously been captured by armed British whalers. He also allowed some of the British seamen, whether they claimed to be Americans or not, to join his forces. In October 1813, only a few months after the first news of his entry into the Pacific reached the United States, Porter took the *Essex* and a flotilla of his prizes to the Marquesas Islands in the middle of the Pacific. There they careened their ship, replenished their supplies, and engaged in the exotic pleasures offered by the South Sea islanders. Porter's journal described the nearly naked women who eagerly handed out their sexual favors: "Virtue among them...was unknown, and they attached no shame to a proceeding which they not only considered as natural, but as an innocent and harmless amusement." Lest his meaning be lost on his readers, Porter wrote that "[w]ith the common sailors and their girls, all was helter skelter, and promiscuous intercourse, every girl the wife of every man." Of course – or at least so Porter noted in his published journal – for "those of a superior class" – officers – "the connexions formed were respectable" and more permanent, despite occasional "little tricks of infidelity."[14] While the native girls may have fulfilled Jack Tar's sexual fantasies, all was not peaceful in paradise, and Porter found himself drawn into native warfare, taking the side of his hosts against two other Polynesian tribes. Porter claimed the island chain for the United States, an act that the government never affirmed. Leaving some of his prizes and a small party of men on the island of Nukahiva, Porter left the Marquesas on December 13, 1813. Sailing with him was a whaler converted to a warship, the *Essex Junior*. Porter could have turned east and attacked British shipping in the China seas or the Indian Ocean. Instead, he headed for the one place he was sure the British would look for him – Valparaiso, Chile.[15]

When Porter arrived in Valparaiso on February 3, 1814, he found his reception a little cooler than he had on his last visit. During Porter's first stop in Chile, the distant Spanish colony had been in the midst of rebellion and had

ILLUSTRATION 13. *Essex* in Nukahiva. This illustration in David Porter's account of his cruise into the Pacific during the War of 1812 depicts the refitting of the *Essex* on Nukahiva in the Marquesas Islands. The other ships in the picture appear more an armada of warships than the workhorse whalers he captured from the British. The illusion is intended to highlight Porter's triumph against the British. Also shown here is the American flag on a mast on a shoreside hill and the indigenous peoples of the island. David Porter, *Journal of a Cruise Made to the Pacific Ocean by Captain David Porter, in the United States Frigate Essex, in the Years 1812, 1813, and 1814...*, 2 vols. (Philadelphia Bradford and Inskeep, New-York Abraham H. Inskeep, and for sale by O. C. Greenleaf, Boston, 1815).

greeted the Americans with enthusiasm. By early 1814, the ardor for revolution in Chile had softened, since local officials understood that there were British ships allied with Spain in the area. The Chileans did not want Porter to sell any of his prizes in their territory, but still welcomed him and offered the protection of their neutrality. Two British ships appeared on February 8, 1814: the thirty-eight-gun *Phoebe*, which was a frigate and actually carried over fifty guns, including thirty long guns (twenty-six were eighteen-pounders and four were twelve-pounders) and sixteen carronades (fourteen were thirty-two-pounders and two were of lesser caliber); and the smaller *Cherub*, with twenty-eight guns, mostly carronades of varying size. Ship to ship the *Phoebe*'s long guns gave her an advantage over the *Essex* from a distance, while the more powerful weight of the carronades on the *Essex* might have given Porter an edge in an exchange of close-in broadsides. The *Cherub*, however, had a greater number of guns, a larger crew, and was more substantially built than the converted whaler *Essex Junior*, and therefore tilted the balance of firepower in favor of the British.[16]

The appearance of the British ships, however, did not lead to immediate mortal combat. Instead, there began a bizarre battle of words that, there on the far side of the world, gave meaning to the war between the United States and Great Britain.[17] The catalyst for this contest was the banner waving from the mast of the *Essex* declaring "Free Trade and Sailors' Rights." After the British ships sailed into Valparaiso harbor, with the *Phoebe* almost colliding into the *Essex* – or so Porter claimed – they anchored within earshot of the Americans. The crews often serenaded one another with their patriotic songs. The men aboard the *Essex* relied on different versions of "Yankee Doodle," while the British sailors retorted with songs of their own. The sailors embellished these tunes with "nautical sarcasms" in order to taunt each other. Although Porter and the British commodore, James Hillyar, knew one another and remained on cordial terms, tension built between the men and their ships. In response to Porter's banner, and understanding the subversive message implicit in the American slogan, Hillyar raised his own motto – "God and country; British sailors best rights; traitors offend both." For any British-born seamen serving on the *Essex*, the threat was palpable. British subjects were supposed to stand by their nation. Anyone who did not do so was a traitor and destined for the hangman. Porter was never a man to be outdone and supplied a new banner for his ship: "God, our country, and Liberty – tyrants offend them." He did not explain this new slogan. But by adding the word "liberty" to "God and country," Porter may well have been reminding the British sailors what the American Revolution was all about. And, if Hillyar's motto was an implicit threat to any ex-British sailors that they might be considered traitors, Porter was suggesting that tyrants – whether they be on the quarterdeck at sea or on a throne in England – were offensive to God and to the new United States ("our country") as well as to liberty. In the context of the French Revolution and the British threat to traitors, he might also have been suggesting that tyrants, too, would face execution. The sailors pushed this contest even further. American seamen issued their own challenge to the *Phoebe*, urging that the *Cherub* be sent away so that the two frigates could fight on almost equal terms. This challenge, like Porter's earlier challenge to Yeo, contained a more potent and subtle message suggesting that the British sailors would be better off if they lost the battle. Addressing themselves "to their oppressed brother tars," the Americans – "The sons of liberty and commerce, on board the saucy Essex, whose motto is 'Free Trade and Sailors' Rights'" – told their British counterparts that if the *Phoebe* were to win, the British seamen might have gained a victory for the king, but "for the service you render in a cause every brave and free man detests," upon their return the British sailors would either be sent to Greenwich hospital as wounded and worn out veterans or be forced to serve on another ship. In either case they would not have any true freedom. Whereas, if the Americans were to triumph, "we shall respect the rights of a sailor, hail you as a brethren whom we have liberated from slavery, and place you in future beyond the reach of a press gang." In short, by losing, the British sailors would gain their rights![18]

The British responded with poetry– although the Americans claimed the verse was written by a midshipman.

> Your proffered liberty cannot avail,
> For virtue is the sons of Albion's crest
> Our God, our king, our country, our laws,
> We proudly reverence like Britons true;

The poem continued with a direct response to the American offer of freedom:

> Your vile letter, which on board was brought,
> We scorn to answer, tho' with malice frought
> But if, by such means, you think to make
> Dissentions rise our loyalty to shake,
> Know then we are Britons all, both stout and true,
> We love our king, our country, captain too;

Over the passing weeks the British sent notes to the Americans encouraging them to desert, and the Americans responded in kind, each side hurling "insulting epithets" at the other. Porter suspected the hand of officers and maybe even Hillyar himself in these exchanges, but asserted that the American notes were "couched in the ordinary language of sailors."[19]

All of these exchanges, insults, and enticements highlight an important tension when it came to the lives of ordinary people in the British Empire and the American republic: at a time when both the British and the Americans were defining their nationhood, loyalties and allegiances remained ambiguous when examined on a local and individual level. This ambiguity was especially pronounced among the maritime community, even though that same community often served as the focus of the development of national identity. We do not know the nativity of the men who served under Porter and Hillyar. All American naval warships had British subjects as part of their crew. The *Essex* was no exception, as the case of John Ervin indicated. Ervin differed from the other British sailors on board by refusing to fight against the king. His coat of tar and feathers probably ensured that anyone else would think twice before using his birth as a means of escaping service on the *Essex*. Porter also recruited sailors in the Pacific who were aboard British and American whalers. Some of those men were from Nantucket – a place where loyalties remained in flux throughout the war and that served as a recruiting ground for whalemen sailing for the United States, Great Britain, France, and who knows where else. Others among the whalemen recruits were probably British. Others still might have been from any number of nations. Wherever they had been born, aboard the *Essex* they became Americans and would fight, and in many cases die, for the United States and what that nation stood for – in this instance, free trade and sailors' rights. Aboard the *Phoebe* there were probably American sailors. Some of those men had been impressed and might be attracted by the call to sailors' rights. Others could well have volunteered. Like American warships, British warships had polyglot crews, with men from all nations. Many of the sailors, however, were British. Although they, too, could be attracted to free trade and sailors' rights, we should not underestimate their loyalty to king and country. The Americans might view the British sailor as trapped aboard his ship, but that was not always the way the British sailors viewed it. On several occasions in the decade before the War of 1812, sailors had deserted the American navy to join the British navy. The letters encouraging the men aboard the *Essex* to desert were not necessarily futile missives. Given the difficult situation of the *Essex* in Valparaiso, deserting was a viable option that would bring prize money, ensure against being sent to a prison, and provide protection from execution. Back in the Marquesas, British whalemen led a successful mutiny, captured one of Porter's prizes, sailed it to New Zealand, and eventually returned to Great Britain. In the hazy atmosphere of conflicting loyalties, the songs, poems, letters, and even the pennants had a dual purpose. On the one hand, they reached out to brother tars to bring them over to your side; on the other, they helped to create bonds of solidarity and nationality within crews regardless of birth or previous allegiances.[20]

Against this background of lower-deck activity, Porter and Hillyar also engaged in verbal jousting. When one of Porter's prisoners made good his escape from the *Essex Junior*, Porter complained to Hillyar that his crew should not have intervened, fished the man out of the sea, and protected him from recapture. Hillyar responded by charging Porter with keeping British prisoners in irons, a mode of treatment that Hillyar declared to be "contrary" to normal procedure and "the usages of honourable warfare." Challenging Porter's honor, no doubt, made the American captain bristle. He retorted that he knew all about "honour and humanity" and that the men in irons had previously broken their "parole of honour" and "made a diabolical attempt to possess themselves of my prize by means of poison." Porter explained that of all the many prisoners he had taken since the beginning of the war – Porter assumed that Hillyar would know he had captured hundreds of British sailors on his two cruises – "none have been confined but for my own security; or otherwise punished but when they deserved it." The matter did not end there. The two captains met and discussed the prisoner-of-war issue in Valparaiso. Porter then sent a note offering to send all of his prisoners to England in one of his prizes, a proposition that Hillyar declined. In turn, the British captain asked Porter to liberate the men in Valparaiso, pledging that he would not permit the men "to serve on board any of his majesty's ships under my orders" and assuring Porter that an equal number of Americans would be freed by the British government. Promised that the prisoners would not be immediately pressed into the British navy, Porter released the men in the Chilean port. Throughout this entire controversy, Porter never demanded the return of the escaped prisoner, noting that he considered the precedent advantageous to him because British sailors were predisposed "to desert at every opportunity," and had Hillyar returned the escaped seamen, Porter might be honor-bound to return a deserting British sailor.[21]

However they might dicker over prisoners, banners, songs, notes, and the like, the real issue as far as Porter was concerned was whether Hillyar and the *Phoebe* were willing to face Porter and the *Essex* alone. Here, too, the captains engaged in a delicate verbal dance. Porter panted for the opportunity to match the *Essex* against the *Phoebe* in combat, but since his ship was smaller than Hillyar's, he could not issue the challenge. He was afraid his country would think him reckless. However, if Hillyar challenged him and sent the *Cherub* away, it would then be a point of national honor, and Porter "would have no hesitation in fighting him." Hillyar refused to accommodate Porter, telling him that since "naval actions were very uncertain," he would not "yield the advantage of superior force." The British commodore took his two vessels out to sea and cruised off the coast of Valparaiso, preventing the departure of the *Essex*. Still the taunting continued. On February 26, 1814, Porter decided that a grand gesture might elicit the hoped-for challenge and took one of his prizes out into the harbor and burned it in sight of the British ships. The American captain intended this wanton destruction of British property as an insult and on the next day seemed to have elicited "the desired effect." With the *Cherub* at some distance, Porter wrote in his journal, the *Phoebe* "shortened sail, fired a gun to windward, and hoisted the flag containing the motto intended as a response to" the American slogan. Believing that Hillyar was at last throwing down the gauntlet, Porter raised anchor, hoisted his banner proclaiming "Free Trade and Sailors' Rights," and sailed toward the *Phoebe*. Much to Porter's chagrin, the *Phoebe* did not close to engage and headed for its consort. Denied one-on-one battle, Porter returned to Valparaiso and soon told all the locals that he believed Hillyar had "acted in a cowardly manner, by running away from Essex, after challenging her." Hearing these reports, Hillyar sent an officer aboard the *Essex* to explain that the *Phoebe* had merely been sending signals to the *Cherub* and that Hillyar "was a religious man" who "did not approve of sending challenges."[22]

Finally understanding that he was not going to receive the desired challenge, and knowing that the British were soon to gain reinforcements, Porter decided that he had best use his superior speed to escape Valparaiso. If he could get ahead of the British ships, either both would chase him and he could outrun them, pulling the British away from Valparaiso to allow the *Essex Junior* to escape, or, if the *Cherub* remained behind to continue the blockade, then he could turn on his pursuer and have his ship-to-ship engagement and day of glory. On March 28, 1814, his ship accidently broke one of its cables and dragged the other out to sea. Seizing this opportunity, Porter made all sail, hoping to pass to the windward of the British. As he headed round a point of land, a huge gust of wind struck the ship, taking away the top of the mainmast and plunging two men into the sea. With the ship hobbled, Porter realized that he would not be able to outrun the British and decided to return to his anchorage. But the condition of the ship prevented him from taking that tack. Instead, he brought the *Essex* into a small cove close to shore, believing that he was still in neutral waters. Hillyar decided that since the *Essex* was no longer in Valparaiso harbor, it was fair game. He brought the *Phoebe* and the *Cherub* into range of their long guns and began firing into the *Essex* mercilessly. The battle was an uneven contest. The British broadsides faced the stern and the bow of the *Essex*, with only the six *Essex* long guns (and even those were available only some of the time) able to bear on them. After a fruitless effort to get under way and draw near enough to the *Phoebe* to board, the *Essex* was smashed into submission. The carnage aboard the *Essex* was frightful, in one of the bloodiest naval engagements of the war. Porter later reported that of his 255 men, 58 were killed, 66 wounded, and 31 missing (Hillyar gave slightly smaller numbers for Porter's casualties). Newspapers would later provide some details of how the American sailors demonstrated their "fearless and patriotic spirit" while combating "the tyrants of the seas." After losing a leg, John Ripley said, "'farewell boys, I can be of no use to you,' and hopped out of the bow port." Another sailor threw himself into the sea, saying he could never allow himself to be taken as a prisoner by the English. John Alvison had an eighteen-pound cannonball pass through his body. Amid the blood and gore and in the agony of death, he exclaimed, "'Never mind, ship mates: I die in defence of 'free trade and sailors' r-i-g-h-t-s,' and expired with the words *rights* quivering from his lips."[23]

Surrender did not end the controversy that always seemed to swirl around the prickly Porter. Although he "could never be reconciled to the manner of" Hillyar's "attack on the Essex," Porter thought the British captain's behavior to the American prisoners of war was gracious.[24] Still the men disagreed over the violation of neutrality, the length of the engagement, a delay in the recognition of surrender, and the total number of casualties. For his part, Hillyar was distressed to discover that Porter had given permission for his men to swim ashore to elude capture and thereby deprive him of some of his rightful laurels. (Porter does not mention his reason for this unusual action, but he may have been allowing British subjects an escape from what might have been a hangman's

ILLUSTRATION 14. Capture of the *Essex*. Porter's sketch of the Battle of Valparaiso emphasizes the uneven nature of the contest. The *Essex* is hobbled, with its mainmast broken from a sudden gust of wind that struck the ship as it attempted to escape the harbor. The British ships are positioned to rake the American vessel, while the *Essex*'s broadside is of little use. Both the *Phoebe* and the *Essex* have banners with their dueling mottos displayed. Because of perspective and positioning, the British ships look even larger than they were in relation to the *Essex*. Although outgunned and crippled, Porter demonstrates his ship's fighting spirit by the plumes of smoke from his forward guns and the holes shot in the sails of the British ships. David Porter, *Journal of a Cruise Made to the Pacific Ocean by Captain David Porter, in the United States Frigate Essex, in the Years 1812, 1813, and 1814 . . .*, 2 vols. (Philadelphia Bradford and Inskeep, New-York Abraham H. Inskeep, and for sale by O. C. Greenleaf, Boston, 1815).

noose.) Ultimately the two captains put aside their differences and agreed to turn the *Essex Junior* into a cartel ship, with a passport allowing the vessel, and the remainder of Porter's crew, to sail around Cape Horn and back to North America past the British blockade.²⁵ Once Porter arrived on the coast of the United States, new problems arose. Stopped by a British man-of-war, Porter was initially allowed to sail toward New York. The British captain then had second thoughts and decided to detain the Americans for a while, and ordered the *Essex Junior* to remain with the warship. Affronted by this delay, Porter declared himself a prisoner of war who was no longer obligated to respect his parole. As usual, Porter put the issue in terms of honor. He "was now satisfied, that most British officers were not only destitute of honour, but regardless of the honour of each other." He took a gig from the *Essex Junior*, leaving the ship and the rest of the crew in the charge of his first officer, and headed for the coast. Using the *Essex Junior* to shield his escape, he was almost out of the range of the British guns before he was discovered. The British pursued him, but he sailed into a fog bank and made his way to the Long Island shore.[26]

Porter returned to the United States to a hero's welcome. When he arrived in New York, "the people took the horses from his carriage, and amidst the shouts of the whole city, hauled him to his lodgings." After the British released the *Essex Junior* a few days later, the rest of his officers and crew were also greeted with acclaim and feted by the city. At the end of July, New York's Republicans hosted a dinner to celebrate the return of "the brave crew" of the *Essex* frigate, who assembled at the battery and then, accompanied by a naval band, marched to Tammany Hall. As they paraded through the city under banners emblazoned with the mottoes "*God, our Country, and Liberty – Tyrants offend them*" and "*Free Trade and Sailors' Rights,*" the streets were lined with citizens who burst into applause as "the noble defenders of their country's rights" passed. When they arrived at their destination, the main meeting room was "most elegantly decorated with trophies of our Naval Victories." There were also pictures depicting the major maritime triumphs during the war as well as a scale model of the *Essex*, with pennants flying and small operating guns to fire a salute. The first of the many patriotic toasts was offered by William Kingsbury, the boatswain of the *Essex*. "Our noble commander, Captain Porter, his Officers, and Crew" was followed by these lines:

> Free Trade and Sailors Rights
> Shalt ever be our boast
> When Johnny Bull those rights invade,
> Then Johnny Bull we'll roast.[27]

Newspapers poured encomiums on Porter and his men. Editors praised the captain of the *Essex* as "the matchless *Porter*" and "the noble and gallant Porter" who had gained a moral victory by his defeat in Valparaiso. Porter had "sustained the reputation of the immortal bond of naval heroes to which he belongs."[28] The *United States Gazette* declared that "though the country has lost a ship, it has lost nothing else." "The gallantry of the defence made by captain Porter and his brave crew" had increased rather than diminished the nation's glory. The battle had been "a test of the valor and hardihood of our seamen," and "our defeat in this instance may be put in competition with the most splendid of our victories."[29] Other Republicans echoed these sentiments. One New York editor reported, "We have lost another frigate – but our naval glory has not been tarnished." As far as he was concerned, "The American flag has been struck, but not a star upon it, has lost its lustre."[30] Another editor explained that he was unsure whether to offer the nation "our condolements or congratulations," since "we have *lost* a fine vessel and the valuable lives of a great part of her brave crew; but we have *gained* new glory to our gallant navy, new honour to the American name among all the nations of the earth."[31]

Porter's achievement – if the loss of his ship and most of his prizes can be called an achievement – went beyond his valor in defeat. The captain of the *Essex* was "the bravest among the brave, . . . who proudly carried his country's flag to earth's remotest parts, and flash'd its most resplendent glories in the eyes of nations to whom we were almost unknown as a people."³² "Oscar" commented that "Porter's cruise and combat will become as renowned in history as the battle of Leonidas. He is the Leonidas of naval annals – his men are the Spartans – for he singly has dared the overwhelming storm of English power, and they have sacrificed their lives resolutely opposing it." For Oscar, no "action since the commencement of our war" reflected "so much honor on the country."³³

The British, in turn, were vilified. When the London merchant exchange celebrated Hillyar's victory, "and the British parliament-house" resounded "with triumphant cheers" over the capture of the *Essex* by superior force, Americans believed "these demonstrations of the enemy's joy constitute the highest eulogium that can be pronounced upon the brave champions of SAILORS' RIGHTS AND FREE TRADE."³⁴ One Connecticut writer saw the *"British treachery and massacre"* that was "grossly displayed . . . in the attack on the Essex in a neutral port" as fitting a pattern of the violation of neutral rights that had led to the outbreak of the war. "Claiming the sovereignty of the ocean, like so many outlaws and bucaneers . . . they acknowledge no rule but their weight of metal, and allow no international rights to interfere with their designs and operations."³⁵ The editor of the New York *Columbian* facetiously referred to the "'magnanimity' and bravery of the 'lords of the ocean'" in the attack, and then declared, in case a careless reader had missed his sarcasm, that the behavior of Hillyar was "cruel and treacherous." Hezekiah Niles wrote, "The attack upon the *Essex* in a *neutral port*, by double her force, as well in men and guns, she being crippled, is of a piece with the total disregard for national law that has long marked the proceedings of our enemy." He declared it both *"unmanly"* and *"unlawful,"* while the editor of the *Virginia Argus* mocked Hillyar and the *Phoebe* as behaving like "old *Jack Falstaff"* by delaying the acknowledgment of the surrender of the *Essex* for fear that the dead on the ship might still have some fight left in them.³⁶

If Porter's thirst for honor and glory had first brought the phrase "free trade and sailors' rights" into public view at the beginning of the war, his losing battle at Valparaiso further entrenched its ideals in the American consciousness as the war wound down. The Philadelphia *Democratic Press* seized upon Porter's motto to memorialize the loss of the *Essex*. America, declared the editor, should be proud "of her brave sons, who in sanguinary combat with an overwhelming force . . . rent the air with shouts of 'Victory or Death' and whose latest wor[d]s were 'Free Trade and Sailor's Rights.'" These men had "nobly died! They have died as became brave men! Fighting against Impressment and Slavery."³⁷

# 16

# The Language of Combat

Free trade and sailors' rights remained a potent clarion during the war. The conflict created some new language of combat – words and phrases used to generate support for the American cause. Men declared that they would "CONQUER OR DIE" as they marched into Canada, while others looked to a call for vengeance as they charged into battle. This rhetoric, however, was often ephemeral. Some phrases, like "Don't give up the ship" and "We have met the enemy and they are ours," have been repeated in our histories of the war so often that they have become part of a national mythology. The language of combat also highlighted a few individuals; Andrew Jackson, for example, was the "Hero of New Orleans." And of course, after the Battle of Baltimore in 1814, Francis Scott Key wrote the poem "Defence of Fort McHenry," later to become known as "The Star Spangled Banner," which glorified the American flag. As important as all of this language became for Americans, for the generation of men and women who lived through the War of 1812, free trade and sailors' rights remained a source of inspiration and served as an explanation for the war that reflected national ideals. Americans clung to Porter's motto as tenaciously as John Alvison had as he expired on the deck of the *Essex* "with the words *rights* quivering from his lips."

Part of the reason for the continued resonance of Porter's motto lay in the dismal nature of the war itself, which made it difficult to sustain many of the other rallying cries. Despite the optimism of Jefferson and other Republicans, the war quickly became a disaster on land. With unbounded confidence, the Americans planned to invade Canada during the summer of 1812 along three separate fronts: in the West, across the Niagara River, and at the Lake Champlain corridor. All of these campaigns ended in failure. After six months of fighting, not only had the military not made any inroads against the British, but a large swath of United States territory had fallen into enemy hands. Over the next few years the arena of conflict spread to the South and along the Atlantic Coast. Americans managed a few successes, but the invasion of Canada was as elusive as ever. Defeats outnumbered victories. Whatever the claims of politicians, by the end of the war the nation was on the brink of falling apart.

In the summer of 1812 the biggest disaster was in the West. On July 17, the British seized the vital straits between Lakes Huron, Michigan, and Superior by capturing Fort Mackinac. With this distant outpost gone, the American commander in the West, General William Hull, ordered the evacuation of Fort Dearborn (modern Chicago) at the foot of Lake Michigan. Unfortunately for the defenders, on August 15, despite being granted safe passage, Indians attacked them on their march back to American-held territory. The resulting massacre, in which most of the garrison and its dependents were killed, sent a wave of panic across the frontier. In the meantime, Hull had advanced into Upper Canada across the Detroit River. His army of militia and regulars numbered over 2,000 men, although at least 200 Ohio militia had refused to enter Canada, claiming that they could serve only within the boundaries of the United States. Much of the rest of the army brimmed with determination, and many of the men placed labels in their caps proclaiming "CONQUER OR DIE." As it turned out, the army did neither. Hull hesitated in attacking his outnumbered foe at Fort Malden. Then he decided to pull back into a defensive position in Detroit to await supplies and reenforcements. His opponent, General Isaac Brock, pushed the advantage, crossed into Michigan, and began a siege of Detroit. By this time the elderly Hull (his military experience had been in the Revolutionary War) had lost the confidence of his men. Hull was also stricken with depression and melancholia. When Brock threatened that he would not be able to control his Indian allies if Hull did not surrender, the old general capitulated, and on August 16, 1812, he handed the British a huge cache of weapons and supplies as well as his entire army. The British paroled 1,600 militia men, but kept Hull and about 600 regulars as prisoners of war. Michigan Territory, for all intents and purposes, became part of Upper Canada, and the Ohio River Valley was open to Indian raids and possible invasion from the north. "CONQUER OR DIE" could do little to inspire under these circumstances.[1]

The situation along the Niagara River was not quite so catastrophic, but also ended in humiliation and defeat. As was true farther west, the American advantage in numbers and bravado could not make up for faulty leadership, poor organization, and ineptitude. The American command was divided between General Stephen Van Renssalear of the New York militia, pushing for a quick attack, and General Alexander Smyth of the regular army, who was more hesitant. Van Renssalear sent a portion of his troops across the Niagara River and seized control of Queenston Heights on October 13, 1812. Smyth would not come to his support, and many of Van Renssalear's militia refused to cross into

Canada, claiming that they, like some of the Ohio militia farther west, were only a defensive force. Boatloads of bloody wounded returning from the battlefield probably helped the militia come to this conclusion. Some reenforcements under Winfield Scott – Van Renssalear himself stayed on the New York side of the river – joined the Americans on the heights. But their numbers were not enough to beat back the British counterattack, led by Brock, who had recently arrived from his triumph at Detroit. Overwhelmed by Brock's men, and cut off from retreat across the Niagara by Indians whom he feared were bent on a massacre, Scott surrendered. In the fighting that day, the American lost about 90 dead, 100 wounded, and 1,000 captured; the British had 14 dead and 77 wounded. To the dismay of the British, Brock was among the fatalities. Smyth, revived from his lethargy, or perhaps no longer jealous of Van Rensalear, who resigned after the battle, tried to capture Fort Erie in Canada in November. This effort, too, failed. Despite the Americans outnumbering the enemy by at least three to one, the Niagara campaign ended in defeat and with no language of combat to trumpet support.[2]

The third invasion was largely a nonevent, although the troops in the Lake Champlain corridor could at least claim they were not beaten on the battlefield. Instead, they had a "miscarriage without even [the] heroism of disaster."[3] With an army of six to eight thousand men, General Henry Dearborn wound his way slowly from Albany to Lake Champlain. In November the army reached Canada, although again some militia units refused to cross the border. After a few skirmishes without any real success, and facing the rigors of winter, Dearborn withdrew his army.[4] Altogether, the campaign season had been an embarrassment. As Albert Gallatin explained, "The series of misfortunes . . . in our military land operations exceeds all anticipation made even by those who had least confidence in our inexperienced officers and undisciplined men." Proclaiming a "series of misfortunes" – a generous phrase to describe the army's disasters – would never rally any troops.[5]

The year 1813 was more of a mixed bag on the battlefield and in producing language which could inspire. Although 1813 began in the West with a disaster and another surrendered army, by the end of the year American fortunes had taken a dramatic turn in the region. In an attempt to erase the defeat at Detroit, William Henry Harrison sent General James Winchester to the rapids on the Maumee River in northern Ohio in the middle of the winter. Winchester got too far ahead of Harrison and the main army and drove a British garrison out of Frenchtown (modern-day Monroe, Michigan) on January 18, 1813. Four days later, Colonel Henry Proctor led 1,300 Native Americans, Canadian militia, and British regulars in a counterattack against Winchester's 934 men, who had spread out along the River Raisin. Surprised by the appearance of the enemy, the Americans fought bravely for a while before they began to withdraw. Fearing the retreat would turn into a rout followed by a massacre

by the Indians, Winchester surrendered his army. After Proctor returned to
Detroit with those American prisoners who could be moved easily, Indians
fell upon the wounded Americans left behind and killed thirty to sixty men.[6]
Word of this butchery, as many Americans viewed it, was soon reported in the
American newspapers, and "Remember the Raisin" became a rallying cry for
the troops in the Northwest. During the rest of the winter Harrison did little
more than seek to consolidate his position in Ohio and use the defeat at the
River Raisin as a rationale for demanding the commitment of even more men.
He built Fort Meigs on the south bank of the Maumee River to guard against
further British attacks and to serve as a forward base for later operations.
Proctor began a siege of the outpost on May 1 and was able to defeat an attack
by a relief column on May 5, inflicting heavy casualties: Harrison lost 135
killed, 188 wounded, and 630 captured in the fighting. Yet Proctor could not
drive the Americans from their fortifications and had to lift the siege when his
militia needed to return to Canada to plant crops. Proctor returned to attack
Fort Meigs in July, but again could not capture the post.[7]

Harrison was biding his time, awaiting the outcome of a naval engagement
on Lake Erie. Throughout the summer two energetic young naval commanders
– Oliver Hazard Perry for the Americans and Robert Heriot Barclay for the
British – led a furious effort on each side to build and man a fleet of ships to
see who would control the lake. Barclay initially had the advantage, but by
early September he had a smaller fleet with fewer men and resources. Unable
to convince his superiors to send him men and additional guns, he stripped
Fort Malden of its cannon for his squadron. Perry had meanwhile amassed a
fleet of ten ships to meet Barclay. As the British and Americans jockeyed for
position near Put'n Bay on the western end of Lake Erie, the fate of the entire
western campaign was at stake. In a hotly contested battle, the two squadrons
met on September 10, 1813. The fighting inflicted horrendous damage on both
ships and men. Perry's flagship, named after Captain James Lawrence, who
had died after losing the *Chesapeake* to the *Shannon*, used Lawrence's famous
words "Don't give up the ship" as a banner at its masthead. Perry, however,
had to give up the *Lawrence* after it was disabled, and transferred his flag
to the *Niagara*. If the *Lawrence* had been severely battered, the British ships
were in worse shape. Perry sailed the relatively unharmed *Niagara* straight into
the British line, captured the British flagship, and compelled the rest of the
British ships to surrender. Casualties were numerous. Each side had about 500
men at the beginning of the battle. By the time the British hauled down their
colors, Barclay had lost 134 killed and wounded (including a seriously injured
Barclay); Perry had 123 casualties. In a memorable use of combat rhetoric,
Perry sent a short message to Harrison – "We have met the enemy and they are
ours" – words quickly repeated in newspapers at the time and in history books
ever since.[8] This motto, however, did not replace Porter's slogan in importance

at the time. Reports of Perry's victory at the Battle of Lake Erie appeared under the heading "Free Trade and Sailor's Rights," and songs celebrating the victory included a paean to the motto.[9]

Control of the lake enabled Perry to ferry most of Harrison's 5,500-man army to Upper Canada and cut off the British at Detroit (although again there were a few militia units that refused to leave the country). Recognizing the hopelessness of his position, Proctor, who had fewer than 1,000 regulars and militia, abandoned Detroit and Fort Malden and headed east with his army and Indian allies. Proctor quickly demonstrated that leadership problems were not limited to the American side in the war. He was lackadaisical in his withdrawal and appeared more concerned with the safety of his family and baggage than with the condition of his troops. He failed to have key bridges destroyed and did not move fast enough. Harrison initially hesitated in his pursuit, but began to follow Proctor on October 2. Three days later, believing that he could no longer outrun the Americans, Proctor made a stand at the Thames River. With the Thames River on the left, the exhausted and demoralized British and Canadian troops drew up in a line, while their Indian allies waited in a large swamp on the right. At the recommendation of Congressman Richard M. Johnson, who headed the Kentucky mounted volunteers, Harrison used an unorthodox tactic. He allowed Johnson's men to charge the British on horseback, cross their defensive position, dismount, and attack from the rear. Shouting "Remember the Raisin," Johnson's men carried out this maneuver flawlessly and leveled a devastating fire from behind the British, who quickly capitulated. The Indians put up stouter resistance until Tecumseh was killed in the battle. (Johnson personally claimed credit for this act and would ride the resulting renown all the way to the vice presidency in 1836.) Proctor escaped with 250 men, while the rest of his army was either killed or captured. Although Fort Mackinac continued in British hands, and with it the control of the Upper Great Lakes, the victory crushed Native American power in the near Northwest, brought most of Michigan back into the United States, and secured the Ohio River Valley against both the British and the Indians.[10]

If the war in the West in 1813 began poorly and ended in victory, the fighting along the Niagara followed the opposite course: it began well and ended in defeat. On May 24 the Americans opened an artillery bombardment on Fort George at the mouth of the Niagara River on Lake Ontario and opposite Fort Niagara. When Colonel Winfield Scott, who had been captured the previous year and then exchanged, led an amphibious landing across the river three days later, he threatened the fort from the rear. A British counterattack failed. With a garrison of about 1,100 men, and facing 5,000 Americans, the British abandoned the fort. The Americans had expected naval support on Lake Ontario. Captain Isaac Chauncey, however, delayed his arrival because he was concerned with the possibility of meeting a British squadron under Sir

James Yeo – the same officer who had challenged the *Essex* to a ship-to-ship action in the Atlantic. That summer – indeed, for the rest of the war – Yeo and Chauncey did not fight in a winner-take-all battle as had occurred on Lake Erie. On a number of occasions their squadrons maneuvered for position, fired upon one another, and seemed poised to fight such a battle. But in each instance, one or the other pulled back, believing the other had an advantage.[11] This stalemate on the lake inhibited the action of the land forces on both sides. Without naval support, the Americans did not press their advantage after capturing Fort George and most of the west bank of the Niagara. Over the summer the American position on Canadian territory deteriorated. In July the British won several skirmishes and again began to move toward Fort George. In the fall, American troops were transferred from the Niagara front to the St. Lawrence River for an advance toward Montreal. With only a few hundred unhappy New York militia under his command, on December 10, 1813, General George McClure abandoned Fort George and burned the adjacent town of Newark. The Americans had a more severe setback on December 18, 1813, when the British surprised and captured the garrison at Fort Niagara on the American side of the river and then ransacked Buffalo and other Niagara towns in retaliation for the destruction of Newark. What had begun with so much promise, ended with the surrender of a fortress on American territory that for fifty years had served as one of the keys to the control of the North American continent.[12]

Perhaps this loss would have been worthwhile if the Americans could have gained control of Lake Ontario and the St. Lawrence River to the north. But that did not happen. Using Chauncey's fleet, the army had destroyed the British administrative center at York (later Toronto) in late April 1813. The British in turn raided Sacket's Harbor on May 29, 1813. They did not capture the town, although the Americans burned their own shipyard to prevent it from being sacked by the British. Perhaps the biggest disappointment on this front was the aborted advance on Montreal. Secretary of War John Armstrong advocated a two-pronged attack, with General James Wilkinson leading an army up the St. Lawrence and General Wade Hampton advancing from Lake Champlain. Neither general liked or trusted the other. Although the Americans began this move late in the season for a campaign on the northern New York–Canadian border, they outnumbered their enemy and, combined, represented a significant invasion threat. The troops, however, were poorly trained and were quickly handicapped by sickness and the weather. Hampton headed into Canada from Lake Champlain on October 21, 1813. Once again, in a familiar refrain, some militia refused to cross the border with Hampton. Undeterred, Hampton marched 4,000 men to the Châteauguay River. Reaching a log barrier defended by 1,700 Canadians and some Indians on October 25, Hampton sent a detachment under Colonel Robert Purdy across the river to outflank the main Canadian defensive line. Purdy's men got lost and were stopped the next morning by a smaller body of Canadians. Hampton then ordered the remainder of his troops, under George Izard, to assault the enemy line directly. Unable to dislodge the entrenched enemy, and believing that he was facing a large force, Hampton returned with his men to New York. In the meantime Wilkinson left Sackets Harbor on October 17, 1813, with an army of 7,000 men and headed down the St. Lawrence River in open boats. Many of the American troops disembarked near Crysler's Farm to get around some rapids. Lieutenant Colonel Joseph Morrison and about 1,200 British and Canadians, who had been following the Americans, threatened to attack. Poorly trained, sick, and cold, about 4,000 Americans launched a series of uncoordinated assaults on November 11, 1813. After three hours of fighting and with the loss of 400 killed, wounded, or captured, Wilkinson withdrew. Morrison had won a great battle for Canada, but lost a sixth of his men. Hampton and Wilkinson blamed each other for the failed invasion. Whoever was at fault, there was little in this campaign to brag about and no language that could be used to rally the troops.[13]

In 1813 there was a major expansion of the war into the South. The Americans, ignoring Spanish neutrality, had conducted some operations against Florida in 1812. A group of Georgians, later supported by a detachment of regular army troops, had invaded eastern Florida early in 1812 before the conflict with Great Britain broke out. Their failure to capture St. Augustine, and the refusal of the Senate to support the operation, meant that this incursion had devolved into a nasty border conflict that ultimately left the Spanish in control of the region.[14] Further west, on April 15, 1813, the Americans seized Mobile in West Florida from the Spanish in order to prevent the British from using it as a base of operations. The most important fighting in the South, however, broke out in the interior in the Creek War. The Creek nation was divided into two factions. The Lower Creek wanted to reach an accommodation with the United States, while the Upper Creek, known at this time as the Red Sticks and influenced by Tecumseh's "nativist" movement, defended their traditional culture and opposed concessions to the United States. These divisions broke out into a civil war in 1812. After American soldiers raided the Creek village of Burnt Corn on July 27, 1813, the Red Sticks retaliated by massacring 500 Americans and peaceful Creek at Fort Mims a month later on August 30, 1813. The Fort Mims massacre brought official American intervention into the Creek conflict. Armies invaded the Red Stick territory – in modern Alabama and Georgia – from the north, west, and east. A series of hard-fought battles followed, with heavy casualties on both sides. Because of short enlistments, the Americans had a difficult time maintaining their militia in the field, and late in the year the number of soldiers in Andrew Jackson's army of Tennessee volunteers decreased to only a few hundred. However, in early 1814 Jackson rebuilt his army to include about 4,000 troops and allied Indians

(500 Cherokee and 100 Lower Creek). Jackson attacked the Red Stick village of Tohopeka on March 27, 1814 (the Battle of Horseshoe Bend), ending the Creek War. He followed this triumph with a peace treaty that ceded twenty-three million acres of Upper and Lower Creek land to the United States.[15]

By the time of Jackson's victory, however, the war against the British looked as if it was going to take a turn for the worse. All attempts to invade Canada had ended in failure or had stalled. The British navy had increased its presence along the Atlantic Coast and demonstrated its ability to land raiding parties at will in the Chesapeake. The defeat of Napoleon in France meant that more troops and resources could be devoted to North America to punish the United States. It appeared that the war might become not a venue for glorious conquest and assertion of rights, but a struggle for survival. As the Maryland politician Joseph Nicholson explained, the conflict was now "not for free Trade and sailors rights[,] not for the Conquest of the Canadas, but for our national Existence."[16] Events in 1814 would almost destroy the republic. Realizing that the nation stood on the brink of disaster and might lose territory, break apart, or maybe even cease to exist – a realization that became especially evident in early October, when Madison released copies of British demands concerning land cessions and protections for Indians – even some Federalists joined the war camp. Despite continued military bungling, Americans demonstrated a strange resilience. The United States repeatedly cobbled together army after army – albeit often poorly equipped and trained. The same factors that made it so difficult for the United States to wage war – a weak central government, a large geographical area, and a heavy reliance on local militia – also made the nation almost impossible to conquer. This was a lesson the British had learned during the Revolutionary War, and would learn again in 1814. From the rubble of the near-disaster of the war in 1814 would emerge a strengthening nationalism, and out of the language of combat would appear the words that would become the national anthem.

In early 1814 Madison and his cabinet still hoped that an invasion of Canada would convince the British to end the war. Once again, however, the campaign season brought no real gains. Suspecting that his days were numbered as a commanding officer after the debacle of Crysler's Farm, James Wilkinson led an early spring offensive into Canada north of Plattsburgh. On March 30 he encountered about 600 men in a British garrison at La Colle Mill. Wilkinson took most of the day to get his troops into position to attack, and never brought up his big guns. The fighting began about 3:00 P.M. and lasted until dusk without the Americans dislodging the British. Wilkinson did not press the attack the next day and retreated to his base in the United States. The American army of 4,000 men sustained about 254 casualties in the futile assault; the British had about 60 men killed, wounded, or missing.[17] The Americans also sought to regain Fort Mackinac and control of the Upper Great Lakes. Despite having the advantage of men and ships, this expedition failed to capture the outpost and even lost two schooners to boarding parties from boats during the summer.[18]

As had been true throughout the war, the most intense fighting occurred along the Niagara. Except for Fort Niagara, the British had pulled back from the American side of the river after ransacking the region in December 1813. The Americans in the meantime had beefed up their military presence with additional regulars who at last were being molded into a respectable fighting force. On July 3, 1814, the Americans under General Jacob Brown seized Fort Erie and then marched north. The British sent reenforcements to the area and fought the Americans in two of the bloodiest battles of the war. In the Battle of Chippewa on July 5 the American regulars under Winfield Scott surprised the British by standing up to their withering fire. Because Scott's men wore grey jackets – there had not been enough material to make their uniforms with the standard blue of the regular army before the beginning of the campaign – the British had believed that they were facing militia who would run at the first sight of red coats. Witnessing the firmness with which Scott's men stood their ground, the British General Phineas Riall reportedly declared, "Why, these are regulars by God!" This language has become so deeply implanted in the lore of the United States Army that the dress uniforms of the cadets of West Point remain grey to honor Scott's regiment.[19] Whatever Riall might have said or not said during the battle, the result of the fighting was an American victory as the British withdrew from the field. The British lost about 200 dead and 360 wounded or captured from an army of about 2,000; Brown lost around 60 dead and 270 wounded of his 3,500 men.[20] On July 25 the two armies met again at the Battle of Lundy's Lane, near the great falls of the Niagara. Scott had advanced his men northward to probe the enemy lines. Believing the hill near Lundy's Lane was lightly defended, Scott pressed his men forward in the evening, only to discover that British reenforcements had arrived. In the fighting that followed Scott's regiment came under heavy fire and then held its position in the center. Both sides rushed more soldiers into the fight. General Brown ordered an attack on the British left and captured the enemy's artillery. The British counterattacked three times as the fighting continued after dark in a confusing and bloody melee that left heavy casualties. The British lost 81 killed and 562 wounded; the Americans had 171 killed and 573 wounded. Each side claimed victory. The Americans drove back the British, but could not carry away the captured artillery and withdrew that night. Eventually most of the Americans pulled back to the New York side of the river, although they held on to Fort Erie as a bridgehead into Canadian territory.

Fort Erie remained an irritant to the British after they believed they had defeated another American invasion. On August 13, 1814, the British began a bombardment of the fortress. Two days later General Gordon Drummond ordered an assault. Just as the British breached the defenses on the third wave of attack, a powder magazine exploded with devastating effect on the British. Drummond lost 1,000 men in this unsuccessful assault on the fort. General Brown reenforced the garrison, and on September 17 he ordered his men on a sortie to drive the British away. In the fighting that followed the British lost 600 and the Americans lost 500 men. After sustaining such heavy casualties the British gave up the siege. The Americans then decided that the fort was not worth defending; on November 5 they blew it up and withdrew to the United States. Another campaigning season was over along the Niagara, with no real gains for either side. This time the stalemate came at a frightening cost in lives.[21]

With men and equipment pouring into Canada, the British decided to invade the United States on two other fronts. They occupied most of eastern Maine almost unopposed in the late summer of 1814.[22] In early September the British also advanced into New York State along Lake Champlain with 10,000 men under General Sir George Prevost. Facing him were fewer than 5,000 regulars and militia under General Alexander Macomb. By September 5, Prevost had occupied Plattsburgh, and Macomb had pulled back to a defensive position south of the Saranac River. Prevost opened the battle on September 11 with an artillery barrage while ordering 7,000 men to a ford upstream that was defended by 2,500 Vermont militia. Although delayed, this flanking maneuver was on the verge of succeeding and sweeping the entire American army from the field when Prevost ordered a withdrawal because of the destruction of the British navy on Lake Champlain. As had occurred on Lake Erie in 1813, a naval engagement on fresh water had determined the fate of a campaign. While Prevost began his assault on the American army, two nearly equal squadrons fought on the lake. The American commander, Thomas Macdonough, had anchored his ships in Plattsburgh Bay with springs to allow the vessels to swirl around and use fresh broadsides when the guns on one side became disabled. At the beginning of the battle that morning the British had the initial advantage with their long guns, but as they closed, the pounding of the American carronades took their toll. When Macdonough's flagship, the *Saratoga*, swung around and brought its fresh guns into the fray, the British flagship, *Confiance*, attempted to mimic the maneuver. The British ship's rigging ran afoul. In the confusion it suffered such damage that the crew refused to fight, and the ship had to haul down its colors. Two other British ships surrendered in the battle. The American triumph was complete despite heavy losses: the British had at least 270 killed and wounded and about 200 captured; Macdonough lost 54 men killed and 57 wounded out of 800 men. With the Americans in control of the lake, Prevost could not continue his invasion and retreated back to Canada in an operation that became an embarrassment to Great Britain.[23]

If the British were humbled by the defeat on Lake Champlain and the retreat from Plattsburgh, the Americans were humiliated by the burning of Washington, D.C. During the summer of 1814 the British navy tightened its blockade of the Atlantic seaboard. In 1813 the British had established their dominance on the waters of the Chesapeake by seizing Tangier Island and raiding towns up and down the bay, capturing supplies and even destroying an iron foundry. They suffered only one reverse in a failed assault on Craney Island outside of Norfolk on June 22. The British continued to control the bay in the spring and summer of 1814. In August the British landed 4,500 men at Benedict, Maryland, and began marching toward Washington. On August 24, 1814, approximately 7,000 Americans, composed of 500 regulars, 400 sailors, and about 6,000 militia arranged in three lines on a hill above Bladensburg, prepared to meet this advance. The Americans, however, were in some confusion. The military commander was General William Winder, but Secretary of State James Monroe appeared and rearranged the troops, making it impossible for the third line to support the first. Although exhausted from marching all day in the summer heat and humidity, the British immediately attacked. The militia were not prepared to meet veteran soldiers with bayonets and began to pull back. A few units, including the sailors manning some artillery, held their ground, but the retreat quickly turned into a full-blown rout. The British later explained that the only reason they did not capture more prisoners was that the Americans ran too fast. After a battle lasting only three hours, the British lost 64 killed and 185 wounded; the United States had only 10 or 12 killed, 40 wounded, and about 100 captured. With the evaporation of all American resistance, the British marched into the American capital and burned the nation's public buildings.[24]

The Americans were mortified by the success of the British. In a degrading use of the language of combat, Madison and his cabinet's appearance at the battlefield and then withdrawal was soon derisively called the "Bladensburg Races."[25] However comical his political opponents thought Madison's escape from the British might seem, supporters of the war decried the destruction of Washington's buildings as barbaric, and the smoldering fires at the capital left the nation ashamed and severely handicapped. Several northern politicians urged moving the government to a city with a larger population to protect it from further depredations, but southerners voted this idea down. There was a run on most American banks, leading to a suspension of specie payments. More importantly, the nation almost came apart at the seams. Every local district became more interested in its own defense than in offensive operations. Efforts to raise support for the regular army were futile. Further invasions of Canada would be almost impossible as Congress was willing to support the recruiting of troops only if organized by the individual states. In many ways conditions were moving toward a situation similar to what had existed under the Articles of Confederation, when the United States operated more as a loose alliance than as a consolidating national government.[26]

As desperate as the situation appeared to Madison and his truncated cabinet – Secretary of War John Armstrong resigned and thereby took most of the blame for the disaster – the British did not enjoy their triumph for long. Attempting to replicate their achievement in Washington, the British landed 4,500 troops under General Robert Ross at North Point, 14 miles from Baltimore. The British hoped that they could punish this city of 40,000, which had been a haven for privateers throughout the war. However, as the third-largest city in the United States, and unlike Washington, which had only about 13,000 residents, Baltimore had a large body of manpower to fill the ranks of the militia. After suffering heavy casualties, including Ross, who was killed in the first phase of the battle, the British drove back about 3,200 militia under General John Stricker on September 12. The next day, as the British advanced on Baltimore, they discovered an even larger number of Americans entrenched in front of them. Concerned that a frontal assault would be too costly, and unable to draw the Americans into the open, in the late afternoon the British withdrew. In the meantime the British navy's efforts also foundered. Beginning on the morning of September 13 and lasting for twenty hours, the navy fired a spectacular bombardment of more than 1,500 shells and rockets at Fort McHenry guarding the entrance to Baltimore Harbor, to little effect. That night an attack with 1,200 men sent up the river in barges also failed. On September 14, the British gave up their attempt to capture the city.[27] The rain of explosives over Fort McHenry produced a language of combat that came to represent the epitome of American pride and national spirit. Aboard the British fleet shelling the fort was an American, Francis Scott Key, who had crossed British lines to negotiate the release of a prisoner of war. The British agreed to free both Key and the prisoner, but held them in custody until after the battle. From the decks of a British warship Key watched the "rockets red glare" and the "bombs bursting in air" throughout the night. In the morning, despite the thunderous uproar and spectacular fireworks, Fort McHenry remained under the tattered United States flag. Inspired by this sight, Key penned a poem, "Defence of Fort McHenry," which was published in papers throughout the nation and was soon put to the music of an eighteenth-century drinking song. Over a century later, in 1931, Congress made the renamed "Star Spangled Banner" the national anthem.[28]

Although the United States as a nation was on the brink of falling apart, the British began to wonder if it was worth the expense in men and resources, after more than twenty years of war in Europe, to push for complete victory in North America. The stalemate on the Niagara, the failure on Lake Champlain, and the repulse at Baltimore suggested that even a disintegrating United States might be difficult to defeat. If there were any doubts that peace was a wise course of action, the Battle of New Orleans settled the matter. As a part of the larger strategy for winning the war, the British began a southern offensive in the fall of 1814. They failed in their attempt to capture Mobile from the Americans on September 14 and 15, but then landed 8,000 men under General Edward Pakenham a few miles east of New Orleans in late December. Andrew Jackson had a hodge-podge army of 4,000 men comprised of hardened Kentucky and Tennessee volunteers, Native Americans, a regiment of the regular army, and pirates under Jean Laffitte. This eclectic force defended a trench on the grounds of Chalmette Plantation outside of New Orleans. On Jackson's right was the Mississippi River, and on the left was a swamp with allied Indians ready to stop any flanking maneuver. On January 8, Packenham, an experienced veteran of the Napoleonic wars, had his men advance in ranks straight at the Americans. The open field they marched across became a killing ground as Jackson's artillery and infantry mowed down the well-trained British. In a few hours, between 2,100 and 2,600 British were killed, wounded, or captured. Among the dead was Packenham. The Americans lost 55 killed and 278 wounded or missing.[29] In an odd twist of irony, once again the slow communication of the early nineteenth century took its toll. On December 24, 1814, negotiators in Ghent agreed to a treaty ending hostilities. In a war that had begun after the British repealed its orders in council, the last major land battle was fought after a peace treaty was written.

During the fighting, despite the many disasters, the language of combat produced several memorable phrases, some of which have echoed through the generations. Textbooks repeat Lawrence's determination not to give up the ship and Perry's succinct report of capturing the British squadron on Lake Erie. The "Defense of Fort McHenry," written by Key, has given a name to the nation's flag and serves as a patriotic testament of loyalty to the United States. At the time, however, free trade and sailors' rights persisted as the rhetoric of choice. In New York in August 1814, Porter used his motto to issue a call to his crew to march in defense of the capital. After the British withdrawal from Washington, a banner with "Free Trade and Sailors' Rights" flew in proud defiance on a battery protecting the burned ruins of the White House, and that summer intrepid sailors wrote the same words across "the star spangled banner" as they raided British commerce in the English Channel.[30]

# 17

## Politics of War

In 1812 Porter's motto quickly became central to the politics of the war. One of the appeals of free trade and sailors' rights was that it simplified the war aims in an explosive political environment – an environment that became so contentious that it made the war almost impossible to fight. Not only did the Madison administration face ardent opposition from the Federalist Party, it often confronted obstruction from dissidents and factions within the Republican Party. Amid the debates over funding the war, peace initiatives, even resolutions on minor points of information, Congress repeatedly revisited the origins of the war. These debates often hinged on the ideas and words embedded in Porter's motto. Beyond the halls of Congress, free trade and sailors' rights appeared as a powerful political slogan for Republicans. So potent was the phrase that Federalists even sought to use the rhetoric for their own purposes. When they failed, the Federalists turned to the slogan as a means of exposing the hypocrisy of the Republicans.

Historians often misrepresent politics in the years leading up to the War of 1812. Although it is possible, and at times useful, to discuss politicians as supporting either the Republicans or the Federalists, this two-party division fails to capture the intricate and fluid nature of the political divisions. Both parties were riven by factions that often relied on personal allegiances and connections as well as ideology. As the dominant political force, the Republicans were especially divided, forming multiple factions organized around both people and policy. There were Republicans, referred to as the "invisibles" or "malcontents," who rejected Madison's reliance on diplomacy and economic coercion after 1809 and wanted to move the nation toward war. This group included the Smith brothers – Senator Samuel Smith and Secretary of State Robert Smith – of Maryland, the Nicholas family in Virginia, William Duane and Michael Leib of Pennsylvania, as well as the Clintons (George and

DeWitt) in New York. Allied with the Clintons was John Armstrong, who had been ambassador to France and had accepted the Cadore letter. There was also a group of "Old Republicans," headed by James Monroe, who did not want tougher measures and who still hoped to find a negotiated settlement. The most extreme Republicans were led by the Virginian John Randolph of Roanoke, who opposed James Madison and wanted to withdraw from commerce entirely and avoid war by relying only on agriculture to maintain a world of republican simplicity.[1]

Caught in the middle of these conflicting currents of Republicanism was President Madison, who not only had to navigate through the hostile commercial impositions of both the French and the British, but also had to placate each of these factions as he prepared for his reelection in 1812. This task became increasingly difficult. A political crisis erupted in his cabinet early in 1811, when Robert Smith as secretary of state decided that the Cadore letter could not be relied upon and that French policy had not changed. Smith believed that it was useless to continue to pursue economic coercion and urged more forceful measures in opposition to both European powers. The situation came to a political boil in March 1811 after Secretary of the Treasury Albert Gallatin, who was a rival of Smith's and disturbed by growing opposition in Congress, offered his own resignation. Madison needed Gallatin in the cabinet and therefore forced Smith to leave the State Department. Madison replaced the bellicose Smith with James Monroe, whose hope for a peaceful settlement quickly evaporated when there was no change in the British Tory government.[2]

By the summer of 1811, the political and diplomatic situation had only worsened. In July, Robert Smith published his *Address to the People of the United States* attacking Madison for not wanting to prepare for war. Smith wrote that "if the honor and the interest of the United States did in fact imperiously call for War," then, rather than taking "half-way measures," the nation needed to demonstrate "a determination to take a manly stand." Smith also said he opposed Macon's Bill No. 2, which he claimed had been written under Madison's direction, and refused to believe the French had repealed the Berlin and Milan Decrees. In short, he questioned Madison's ability to lead the nation and called for a replacement who would be "a man of energetick mind, of enlarged and liberal views, of temperate and dignified deportment, of honorable and manly feelings, and as efficient in maintaining, as sagacious in discerning the rights of our much injured and insulted country."[3] Simultaneously, negotiations with Augustus John Foster, the British minister in Washington, got nowhere. Foster indicated that the British would repeal the orders in council only when the Americans could prove that the French had rescinded the Berlin and Milan Decrees. His comments also suggested that the British saw their commercial regulations as a customary maritime right that, even if they did withdraw the orders in council, they could reinstitute at any time. Faced with this hardening of the British position just as his Republican critics were turning up the pressure, the president felt compelled to act. Madison issued a call on July 24 for an early session of the Twelfth Congress to begin on November 4 to discuss war.[4]

That session of Congress only intensified the divisions within the Republican Party. The War Hawks debated not so much with the Federalists as with Randolph, who opposed them. Even when the Republicans agreed on the need to raise an army, they disagreed over its size and funding. Madison and the House of Representatives wanted only a 10,000-man army, believing that the government would not be able to recruit, train, and supply any more soldiers. The Senate insisted on a 25,000-man army. Congress also dithered over the control of the militia. Taxes, too, were a problem. On January 10, 1812, Gallatin asked for a tax package that would double import duties and pass direct and indirect taxes, including levies on salt, spirits, stills, sugar, auction sales, retail licenses, carriages, and stamped paper. Congress passed the higher impost duties and a bill providing loans to the government, but balked at the other taxes. In the first half of 1812, as war preparations stalled and Republicans continued to contend with each other, the Federalists became more obstructionist. Most Federalists had supported expanding the army and navy as a matter of principle, since a military buildup was consistent with their ideas concerning a stronger central government. When a British war began to look more likely in the spring of 1812, they started to vote against such measures. In June, an unlikely alliance between the Federalists, the malcontents, and some Republicans who wanted to delay until the nation was better prepared, almost defeated the declaration of war in the Senate. Taken together, the political divisions meant that the United States was to enter the war without the full army that had been legislated, and without enough tax revenue to prosecute the war effectively. During the campaigning of that summer, these inadequacies contributed to military failure.[5]

In the meantime, Madison barely squeaked out a victory in the presidential election. Supporting a war ensured his nomination by most of the Republican Party. Republican dissidents, however, led by the New York legislature, nominated DeWitt Clinton for president. Clinton was in the odd position of arguing not only that the war was foolish, but also that Madison's conduct of the war was inept. In a testimony to the fluid nature of party politics during the early republic, the Federalist Party did not nominate its own candidate for president; instead, most Federalists supported Clinton, who posed as antiwar in Federalist strongholds while supporting a more vigorous prosecution of the war elsewhere. The final tally was close. Had Clinton won Pennsylvania, he would have been elected president. After his reelection, Madison replaced the secretaries of war and the navy. He placed Armstrong, in part to build bridges to New York Republicans, in the War Department, and William Jones became head of the Navy Department.[6]

Congress remained contentious throughout the war. Despite the initial wave of naval victories, there were still many Republicans who were reluctant to see the government sink additional money into ships. In late December 1812, a minority of Republicans along with the Federalists passed a navy bill that provided $2.5 million for the navy. Republicans also divided over limitations on trade as a means of coercing the British. During the early months of the war, shipments of wheat continued to go out to the British army in Spain and elsewhere. Believing the war would be aborted once the Americans saw that the orders in council had been repealed, British merchants loaded their ships and sent them to the United States in the summer of 1812. Republicans disagreed over how to treat these goods. Gallatin wanted to seize the goods as illegal imports, but political pressure convinced him to impose hefty fines instead. However, even this compromise was unsustainable. A minority of Republicans joined with the Federalists to protect the merchants and passed a bill allowing the imports to be sold without restrictions and paying only the regular duties. Problems continued in 1813. Madison wanted to increase taxes, but found many in his own party in disagreement. Congress passed the new levies only after an acrimonious caucus during which each congressman sought to protect the interests of his own constituents. In the spring, attempts to establish an embargo to prevent the supplying of the British fleet off the coast of North America passed the House but failed in the Senate. Congress finally enacted an embargo in December 1813, only to repeal it four months later, hoping to open trade with neutral nations as the war in Europe was coming to an end. Needing a more reliable vehicle to lend the government money, Madison proposed the establishment of a new national bank in 1814. Republicans in Congress so mangled the legislation, creating a bank that was little more than a mechanism for paper money emission, that Madison vetoed it. By the end of 1814, the lack of unity among Republicans, along with Federalist opposition, had paralyzed the government and crippled the war effort.[7]

If Republicans nitpicked over how to pay for and fight the war, Federalists hammered away at its causes. All throughout the fall of 1812, the Federalists challenged the Republicans on the causes of the war every chance they could. When Madison requested more troops in early 1813, Federalists attacked the war as "both politically and morally wrong." They decried the invasion of Canada as "totally inconsistent with the spirit and genius of our Constitution" because "Republics ... ought never to be engaged in a foreign offensive war."[8] As soon as the next session of Congress began in June, Daniel Webster submitted a resolution requesting that the president provide details concerning when and how he had heard of the French St. Cloud Decree, which had supposedly repealed French impositions. The problem was that the decree was post-dated

April 28, 1811, although it did not become public knowledge until May 1812. The Federalists wondered why the measure had not been made public, since they believed official notification of the revoking of French impositions on trade would have led to an earlier repeal of the British orders in council. This supposedly simple request for information led to a fearsome attack on Madison in which the Federalists questioned the very basis of the war. Republicans scrambled to Madison's defense and reiterated the maritime roots of the hostilities.[9] And so it went, time and again; Federalists and Republicans debated the reasons for war while Madison sought the means to fight it.

However much they bemoaned this "war of conquest" and complained about "Mr. Madison's war," Federalists almost always identified two issues as the cause of the conflict: the orders in council (free trade) and impressment (sailors' rights). Since the British had suspended the orders in council two days before Madison signed the declaration of war without knowing of the change in British policy, Federalists believed that the only issue that separated the two nations was impressment. Repeating the arguments made before the war, Federalists held that the problem of British forced recruitment of American sailors was not as significant as Republicans made out. Elijah Brigham of Massachusetts asserted that previously Congress had viewed impressment as being "of minor importance and as a proper subject of negotiation between the two nations."[10] Federalists also rehearsed the history of diplomatic relations with Great Britain, noting that both Jefferson and Madison had rejected the informal arrangement concerning impressment in the Monroe-Pinkney accord, and that Madison had embraced the Erskine agreement, which did not mention the issue. In June 1813, as Federalists lambasted the administration for being duped by the Cadore letter and the post-dated documentation from France, William Gaston of North Carolina declared that the question of impressment "had slept" (words surprisingly close to Jefferson's in a letter to Madison) in the years since Monroe's dismissed treaty in 1806. After that failure, Gaston contended, the administration "could not have had the audacity or the guilt to plunge into a war about 'seamen's rights,' without an attempt to secure them by negotiation."[11] The New Yorker Thomas Jackson Oakely made the same point and told Congress that he did not believe "that the sober sense of this House, or of this people," would "have sanctioned a declaration of war on the ground alone of the British claim to impress their own seamen."[12] Thomas Peabody Grosvenor, another New York Federalist, expanded on these themes: "though always a subject of difference between the two nations," impressment "had never been by our Government for a moment considered as a sufficient cause of war." According to Grosvenor, only after the British had repealed the orders in council did "the subject of impressment" swell "into that hideous form it now wears" and become "'a dog of war'" that "was dragged forward . . . to justify the Administration for 'wading deeper and deeper in blood.'"[13] A few

Federalists even berated the very idea of free trade. Alexander Contee Hanson, whose strident language as a newspaper editor had provoked riots in Baltimore in the summer of 1812, assailed the Republicans by claiming neutral rights were a part of the "Napoleonic code" that "shall give to the neutral flag, a piece of striped bunting [the French tri-color], backed by quaker cannon [fake guns used to mislead would-be attackers], the magical effect of preserving inviolate all that sails under it." The emperor and the president shared similar sentiments "that 'the flag shall cover the merchandise and the crew' – that free ships shall make free goods."[14] Despite minimizing the importance of impressment, and at times even the idea of free trade as neutral commerce, the Federalists recognized the appeal of the issue of sailors' rights when combined with the call for free trade. Grosvenor unwittingly acknowledged the draw of Porter's motto even as he attacked it. The congressman dismissed "[t]he cant of 'free trade and sailors' rights'" as being "heard only in the woods of the West where no trade exists, and no sailors are to be found," and believed that it "could not have drowned out the voice of commerce, of agriculture, of justice, and of peace"[15]

Republicans countered this invective with their own political rhetoric. The response was twofold: Republicans contended that it would take more to reverse the British violation of American commercial rights than the repeal in June 1812 of the orders in council, and they held that impressment by itself was reason enough to fight the war. John Rhea, from "the woods of the West" in Tennessee, believed the "plain facts" were obvious. "England has for several years past, to enrich and aggrandize herself and to humble the United States, carried on war in disguise against them." Pushing this play on the words of a British pamphlet arguing for commercial impositions on the United States, Rhea offered an indictment of Great Britain: "she unjustly took the property of our citizens, impressed the seamen, and violated in many instances the sovereignty of the United States." As such, simply repealing the orders in council – a repeal "loaded with restrictions, limitations, and reserves" – did not demonstrate a willingness "to end the war and be at peace." In order to do so, the British needed to "restore American seamen" who had been impressed, "indemnify for all the spoliations," and make amends "for all violations of the sovereignty of this nation."[16] Another westerner, Felix Grundy, echoed these sentiments and concluded, "If both the property and liberty of American citizens on the ocean are subject to her [Great Britain's] disposal, you cease to possess the rights of a sovereign and independent nation."[17] George Michael Troup from Georgia noted "the gallantry and skill" of American sailors in combat and that "whatever be the description or character of the seaman fighting under the American flag, that seaman ought to be protected. Not a hair on his head should be touched by the enemy with impunity."[18] Republicans continued to question the significance of the repeal of the orders in council. Henry Clay, in one of his most memorable speeches during the war, refused to acknowledge "that had the Orders in Council been repealed . . . before the war was declared, the declaration would have been prevented," and he did not hesitate "in saying, that I have always considered the impressment of American seamen as much the most serious aggression." Clay even decried the use of protections, comparing them to "the passes which the master grants to his negro slave," because they denigrated American citizen sailors and implied "[t]hat Great Britain has a right to take all who are not provided with them." For Clay, "The colors that float from the mast-head should be the credentials of our seamen." He declared that "[i]t is impossible that this country should ever abandon the gallant tars who have won for us such splendid trophies." Pronouncing the government's responsibility to protect all citizens, Clay maintained that "[n]o matter what his vocation, whether he seeks subsistence amid the dangers of the deep, or draws it from the bowels of the earth, or from the humblest occupations of mechanic life, whenever the sacred rights of an American freeman are assaulted, all hearts ought to unite and every arm should be braced to vindicate his cause." Clay concluded his speech with a dramatic flourish: "In such a cause" – defending the rights of sailors and all American freemen – "with the aid of Providence, we must come out crowned with success; but if we fail, let us fail like men – lash ourselves to our gallant tars, and expire together in one common struggle, fighting for 'seamen's rights and free trade.'"[19]

Clay's use of these last words to end his speech, even as he reversed the order of Porter's motto, and the fact that both Federalists and Republicans centered their debate on the origins of the war on the ideas encapsulated by the slogan, testified to the constant appeal of free trade and sailors' rights. Other congressmen relied on the phrase (in the correct order) to give meaning to the war. As early as November 1812, David R. Williams of South Carolina defended the war and the attempted invasion of Canada by using the slogan and explicitly crediting Porter for creating it: "the war on both elements [land and sea] is for the same object; not as the gentleman [Josiah Quincy] says, to rob and plunder in Canada; but, according to the motto of the gallant Captain Porter, for 'free trade and sailor's rights!'"[20] In 1814, Congressmen Charles Jared Ingersoll used the phrase during a debate concerning an army bill, declaring that the real reason for the war was to protect maritime rights, which he viewed as "the lineal offspring of those precious birth rights for which are fore fathers invincibly contended." Ingersoll continued with rhetoric that is difficult to disentangle, conflating a standard bearing the motto "Free Trade and Sailors' Rights" with the American flag. Ingersoll proclaimed, "The American flag has not been struck. It never must be struck. It never will be removed from the mast, where it floats, the glorious banner of 'Free Trade and Sailors' Rights.'" Ingersoll's confused use of pronouns and shift from the Stars and Stripes to "Free Trade and Sailors' Rights" suggests that the slogan used by Porter had become associated with national identity. The phrase continued to reverberate in the halls of Congress. A few months after Ingersoll's speech, John C. Calhoun traced the origins of the war to, "as it had been emphatically and correctly stated, a war for Free Trade and Sailors' Rights."[21]

Beyond the nation's capital, Republicans repeated the phrase in order to generate public support. This use of Porter's motto in popular politics demonstrated the ubiquitous nature of the slogan. Even before Clay's oration, free trade and sailors' rights appeared in songs and in toasts at Republican meetings throughout the country. In "Sovereignty of the Ocean," a "new song" that celebrated the victory of the *Constitution* over the *Guerrière*, one stanza had Isaac Hull cry "free trade, seamen's rights, now let every shot tell."[22] On January 11, 1813, the Jeffersonians of Havre de Grace, Maryland, held a dinner to honor the victory of the *Wasp* over the British sloop *Frolic*, and included among their toasts: "The internal prosperity of the U. States, agriculture and the arts; their external glory, free trade and sailors' rights." Among the toasts given by Republicans in Wilmington, North Carolina, while commemorating George Washington's birthday in 1813 was "'Free Trade and Sailors Rights' – Courage to the heart, and verve to the arm of him who defends them."[23] Republicans in Charleston marched in a procession under a banner "on which was inscribed '*Free Trade and Sailors Rights*'" and toasted, "Sailors rights and free trade – May the war never cease until those two principles, so essential to the honor, dignity, and independence of the republic, be obtained." The celebrants followed this declaration with seventeen cheers – one for each state in the union – and the band playing "Yankee Doodle."[24] A cartoon that appeared in 1813 to commemorate the victory of the *Hornet* over HMS *Peacock* depicted a hornet about to sting a bull (representing John Bull) with peacock feathers, declaring "Free Trade and Sailors' Rights, you old rascal!" Soon those who supported the war were identified as the "friends of '*Free Trade and Sailors Rights*.'"[25] The Republicans of Salem, Massachusetts, called themselves "the supporters of the Rights of their country, the advocates of '*Free Trade and Sailors Rights*,' the real Republicans," as opposed to the Federalists, whom they labeled as "the advocates of British Tyranny."[26] In the spring of 1813, New York Republicans advertised political meetings in the fourth, fifth, sixth, seventh, and eighth wards and called all the friends of "*Union of the States, Free Trade and Sailors' Rights*" to attend.[27] A "GENERAL REPUBLICAN MEETING" at Tammany Hall in New York City agreed to form "an association to support their country in the present contest for "free trade and sailors rights."[28] Republican newspapers even put the phrase atop their endorsements for political tickets.[29]

Republican editors found other uses for the slogan, associating it with American independence, the determination to fight, national honor, and faith in the union. In the fall of 1812 one newspaper reported how Captain Isaac Hull's

ILLUSTRATION 15. "The *Hornet* and *Peacock*; Or, John Bull in Distress." One of several prints made during the War of 1812 to highlight American naval triumphs, Amos Doolittle produced this etching on March 27, 1813, only a little more than a month after Captain James Lawrence in the *Hornet* defeated the somewhat smaller *Peacock*. The two ships appear in the background, while a caricature in the foreground showing a hornet about to sting a creature that is half bull (John Bull represented Great Britain) and half peacock (for the name of the British ship and, because of the large plume occupying much of the top left of the illustration, implying that the British were like the show-off bird known more for strutting its feathers than for its bellicose attributes). While the half bull/half peacock cries "Boo-o-o-o-hee!!!" the hornet proclaims "Free Trade & Sailors Rights you old rascal." Yale University Library, New Haven, Connecticut.

"brilliant achievement...had an electrical effect" on Congress, convincing many members to expand the navy. For this editor, the British insistence on the "'right of impressment' from our merchant ships" was "a point which we cannot admit, without a surrender of our personal and national rights, which no nation that regards its independence can ever submit to." With Great Britain "resolved to fight us, rather than yield to the justice of our claim, let us nail our colors to the mast" – this phrase, which was also used by Clay and others, was a standard maritime expression indicating a determination never to surrender – "and our motto shall be, "*Free Trade and Sailors' Rights*," and "broadside and broadside our seamen shall argue the question at the cannon's mouth, till

---

*"Free Trade and Sailor's Rights."*

"DON'T GIVE UP THE SHIP."

*Never despair of the. Republic.*

*Bergen County*

REPUBLICAN TICKET.

*For Council—*Elias Brevoort.
*For Affembly—*John A. Weftervelt, Garret A.
Lydecker, John T. Banta.
*For Sheriff—*George Zabrifkie.
*For Coroners—*David I. Chriftie, Jofiah John-
fon, Peter Sipp.

ILLUSTRATION 16. Republicans used the phrase "Free Trade and Sailor's Rights" to rally support to their candidates, including this copy of a Republican ticket in Bergen County, New Jersey. Elizabethtown *New-Jersey Journal*, September 14, 1813.

England cease to violate the rights that God and nature gave, and suffer us to pass and repass the ocean without interruption."[30] The *Baltimore Patriot* used the motto to highlight "the noble" and honorable western and southern support for the war – a contest for "*Free Trade and Sailors' Rights*" – in contrast to New Englanders, whose maritime interests were most at stake. The descendants of "the heroes of Bunker Hill" were not living up to their revolutionary heritage as the "Cradle of Liberty" and were "ungrateful" and "degenerate" in opposing the war.[31] A Boston editor excitedly reported an increase in Republican voting in Massachusetts in the spring of 1813 by exclaiming, "Within a short space of five months, there has been an astonishing gain in favor of those who contend for *National Honor, Free Trade, and Sailors' Rights*."[32] Republicans not only nominated a slate of candidates for local and state offices, they also passed a series of resolutions, "approbating measures calculated to secure the rights of our fellow citizens, protecting commerce, and rendering inviolate the sacred union of the states."[33]

Republican newspapers often emphasized the nautical connections of the slogan. One essayist, in a call for unanimity in the nation, wrote that "[w]e are now engaged in a struggle . . . for one of humanity's dearest rights – we will protect our seamen at every hazard." America's tars had proved themselves worthy in repeated naval battles, and American history "will hand down to posterity the names of Hull, Jones, Decatur, Bainbridge and the youthful and unfortunate Hero *Lawrence !* as the faithful supporters of '*Free Trade and Sailors' Rights*.'"[34] The *National Intelligencer*, the newspaper that was the mouthpiece for the Madison administration, claimed that at the beginning of the war, most of the naval officers were Federalists. However, after a little over a year of hostilities, "they have become so disgusted with the impolitic and iniquitous conduct of their party, in opposing and abusing the Government while it was doing all it could for the defence of 'Free Trade and Sailors' Rights,'" and while the officers and their crews were risking life and limb, "that we much doubt whether there is an officer in the Navy who will *now* avow himself a *Federalist*."[35] A short notice in the *Eastern Argus* declared "[m]odern federalism" hostile "to a navy and the powerful sentence '*Free Trade & Sailor's Rights*.'"[36] Hezekiah Niles dedicated an issue of his *Weekly Register* "to the Inestimable, the brave, high-minded, generous and humane AMERICAN SEAMEN," listing all the achievements of the navy. In the middle of the page Niles placed the following declaration: the seamen had "vindicated and maintain'd, by mighty deeds upon the sea" and with big bold capital letters that leap out at the reader "FREE TRADE & SAILOR'S RIGHTS."[37]

As in Clay's speech and in the Charleston toast, variants of the phrase were heard. At the New York dinner celebrating the victory of the *United States* over the *Macedonian* in early 1813, Captain Stephen Decatur offered the toast "Free trade and no impressment." Because of Decatur's status as a naval hero, this version became popular among Republicans in the spring of 1813. Politicians repeated the toast, and, as with "Free Trade and Sailors' Rights," advertised meetings, published election tickets, and reported speeches under its rubric.[38] Editors used "Free Trade and No Impressment" to headline articles describing specific cases of Americans forced into the British navy.[39] Most Republicans saw "*Decatur's toast*" and "*Porter's motto*" as "being synonimous," representing "[b]rief summaries of the inestimable things contended for."[40] However widespread Decatur's version became for a while, it lacked the larger appeal of Porter's, since it was limited to the issue of impressment, instead of making the broader claim of sailors' rights that emphasized Jack Tar as a citizen. Although at least three Republican newspapers relied upon "Free Trade and No Impressment" as a generic lead for their news stories for much of the rest of war, its overall popularity had decreased by the summer of 1813.[41] Decatur's iteration of the slogan did not have the staying power of the words Porter had stitched on the banner tacked to the mast of the *Essex*.[42]

As we have already seen, the phrase became so enshrined in the political rhetoric of the day that even members of the Federalist Party used free trade and sailors' rights, albeit usually to criticize the war. However, during the first part of the conflict some Federalists sought to appropriate the phrase for themselves and claimed that they advocated "'*the liberty of the seas*' and '*free trade and sailor's rights*' with as much pertinacity as the most squeamish admirer of the administration," reminding anyone who would listen that it was to establish the freedom of the seas "and protect sailors in their rights" that they had "earnestly laid the foundation of a navy." Moreover, the Federalists stated that "they have ever been the sailor's friend, as well as foremost in

# THE WEEKLY REGISTER.

No. 4 of vol. IV.]      BALTIMORE, SATURDAY, March 27, 1813.      [whole no. 82.

*Hæc olim meminisse juvabit.*—Virgil.

Printed and published by H. Niles, South-st. next door to the Merchants' Coffee House, at $ 5 per annum.

TO THE INESTIMABLE,
the brave, high-minded, generous and humane

# AMERICAN SEAMEN:

WHO HAVE BORNE COLUMBIA'S FLAG TRIUMPHANT

O'er the wide Atlantic deep;

And raised up to FAME, a monument, imperishable as

### Their Native Alleganies.

*Who have exalted their country to the pinnacle of Glory,*

And aveng'd their gallant brothers kidnapp'd by the unfeeling and remorseless foe;
WHO HAVE CARRIED TERROR
Into the cold heart of the MANSTEALER, and prostrate laid his haughty notions;

RODGERS, HULL, JONES, DECATUR & BAINBRIDGE;
*EVANS, PORTER, SMITH & LAWRENCE;*

With CHAUNCY, ELLIOTT, WOOLSEY, on the Lakes,
*MORRIS, BIDDLE & ALLEN—*

*And the much lamented dead, the untimely slain, the valiant BUSH and AYLWIN;*
With the unconquerable CHEEVES, whose latest breath was spent

### Shouting for Victory!

*And the nameless brave, of all conditions, that, unparallel'd, by*

### " COMMON LAW,"

black, bold and terrible—have vindicated and maintain'd, by mighty deeds upon the sea,

# FREE TRADE & SAILOR'S RIGHTS;'

And brought down the bloody cross, a grateful offering at the Eagle's feet—
SHEWING THE WONDERING WORLD
That first in *honest* peace, Columbia, also, is the first in *open* war:
Who have withdrawn the veil from British domination, and exhibited FATE's finger pointing to the time (not distant)
*When on the towering mast the bold Bald Eagle gloriously shall ride,*
AND THERE, BY HIGH COMMAND, DEFEND
The *pine-tree's* top [our banner bearing to earth's utmost verge]
WHERE ONCE,
*In forest deep, she built her nest, and rear'd her tender young, harmless and unoffending:*
Wielding the Trident to REDEEM mankind from pirates and robbers;
AND DEMANDING,
*IMPERATIVE AND LOUD AND IRRESISTABLE*

## Peace to a troubled World!

And to the desperate daring spirits that, in private armed vessels,
have swept the coasts of either hemisphere—certain as death, pouncing upon the foe;
*Returned with spoil RE-CLAIM'D : to their own profit, their country's benefit and enemy's distress,*
Leading to Justice through Suffering;

This number of the WEEKLY REGISTER,
the best tribute of respect that he knows how to offer,
IS DEDICATED—BY THE EDITOR.

VOL. IV.      D

ILLUSTRATION 17. When Hezekiah Niles published a special tribute to the sacrifices of American sailors fighting the war, he featured a proclamation that the navy had "vindicated and maintain'd, by mighty deeds upon the sea, FREE TRADE & SAILOR'S RIGHTS." Most Americans connected the victories won by the American navy with Porter's motto during the war. *Niles' Weekly Register*, March 27, 1813.

providing the means necessary to protect them against the marauders of the ocean."[43] In the fall of 1813 one Federalist wrote a series of essays under the title "FREE TRADE AND SAILOR'S RIGHTS" arguing for true neutrality and an abandonment of a policy that, as he saw it, befitted the French rather than American interests. This author insisted that if "the flag of a trading vessel should cover the cargo and crew," then the government should require "their cargo or crew to be of the country whose colors are displayed at mast head." Allowing foreigners among the crew and carrying cargo produced by other nations was doing little more than protecting the French at the expense of American interests. From this perspective "it is preposterous to talk of the American privileges, if they are to be shared in common by all sorts of foreigners indiscriminately." This Federalist believed that "[t]o mistake foreign traders and sailors with American masks for the real American traders and sailors, would be essentially erroneous in policy." Therefore, "It would be more for the public interest and of course more republican, in effect, to unmask the foreigners by patronizing our own countrymen directly." This policy "would render more real service to our commercial and maritime interests, than all the petitions, memorials, remonstrances, protests, electioneering harangues, or diplomatic flourishes for the last five years."[44]

Republicans challenged the Federalist use of free trade and sailors' rights as early as the spring of 1813. Under a headline with the motto, at least two Republican editors published an essay that explained the meaning of the slogan in the clearest of terms: "The present war is carried on principally for the protection of seamen; those who are opposed to the war, are, of course, not supporters of sailors rights." President Madison has insisted, the author explained, "as a preliminary condition of peace, that the impressment of seamen should be discontinued" and that all Americans on board British ships should be liberated. Anyone willing to seek peace on any other terms would be ignoring these men "and, therefore, are not in favour of sailors rights." Likewise, "The President of the United States is in support of the principle that the flag should protect the property on board neutrals, those who are favorable to an abandonment of this right, are not advocates of a free trade." The author asked: "Who are the friends of sailors rights and free trade?" It was not the friends of Great Britain. Rather, it was those who supported the Republicans. "Let those then, and those only who are the friends of the general government, as now administered by Mr. Madison, bear the motto of 'FREE TRADE AND SAILOR'S RIGHTS,' and let the spurious claim of others to that honorable distinction be ousted and denied."[45]

Before the war Federalists had contested the Republican rhetorical use of "free trade" with some success, but when they attempted to co-opt the linking of free trade with sailors' rights, they lost the war of words and soon gave up referring to the phrase in any positive light. Free trade and sailors' rights became so identified with the Republicans that for the Federalists, the very words became an anathema to be mocked and ridiculed. In November 1813, one short piece in the *New York Herald* complained that the Madison administration despite being "*advocates* of *Free Trade and Sailor's Rights*," really cared little about sailors, since the government did not help those seamen who had been prisoners of war when they returned in cartels. The article ended by venomously imploring, "let us no longer be insulted with the slang of *Free Trade and Sailor's Rights*."[46] As opposition to the war intensified, the language used to attack the slogan became even more severe. One editor stated that he had been asked "how far '*Sailors Rights and Free Trade*' extends." His snide answer, emphasizing the loss of even coastal trade in the face of the British blockade, was that it stretched all the way from Maine to Georgia on "about 4,000 carts and wagons drawn by about 16,000 oxen and horses." On most of "these vehicles" was the label "*Free Trade and Sailors' Rights*." Of course, the editor explained, "*no Sailors* are employed in this new mode of navigation," and he concluded that "[t]he fact is, that the *honest* sailor now has no rights. The 'land lubbers' have usurped them all."[47] This derision also appeared in an essay that chronicled the experience of one hapless tar who before the war, "whilst sailors were allowed to look out for themselves, and could come and go where they pleased," had made a decent living. Once the war broke out, "to fight for Sailors' Rights as they call it," he explained, "I've scarcely made shift to earn my biscuit." The down-on-luck seaman continued: "I used to be pretty well rigged . . . with plenty of shiners in my pockets" and without the patches that covered his clothes. "Since the war for free trade and sailors' rights, instead of a choice of voyages I've had only the choice to starve at home or rot in a prison ship." When poverty convinced him to sign on for a coastal voyage to South Carolina, he thought the ship was lucky to evade the British cruisers. As they entered Charleston, however, the captain and crew tempted the fates by raising a flag "with large capital letters FREE TRADE AND SAILORS' RIGHTS." Bad luck followed, but not in the form of capture by the British. Instead, he became trapped by Madison's embargo of December 1813. As the author had the Jack Tar explain, "*Free Trade* would not let us come home by water; and *Sailor's Rights* obliged us to travel about 1000 miles with nothing to bear our expenses."[48]

Federalist invective could also be more direct and bitter. A Washington Benevolent Society address in 1814 to commemorate the father of the country's birthday in St. Albans, Vermont, declared that using "Free Trade and Sailors Rights" as an explanation for the war was not only stupid and insulting, but also "hypocritically and treacherously false." The idea that "Free Trade was to be restored and protected" by "a war of anti-commercial Character and an Embargo prohibiting all commercial intercourse," which according to the provisions of the December 1813 measure would prevent ships from sailing even to ports in the same state, "was preposterous and paradoxical." "That 'Sailors' Rights' were to be vindicated and secured by fighting for, and protecting British deserters" who were stealing employment from Americans "is an attempt at popular imposition, equally ridiculous, humiliating and cruel." These Federalists thought that the war was an evil plot fomented by westerners and "Southern negro made nobility and plantation tyrants" at the expense of "the enterprising and persevering people of New England and the North." They argued that "the cowardly and imbecile operations of this plundering war" against Canada were never "intended by its authors for the benefit of 'Free Trade and Sailors Rights' or in vindication for national honor; but, for directly the reverse."[49]

By the fall of 1814, many Federalists saw the phrase "Free Trade and Sailors' Rights" as a "gross, insulting imposture" used by the Republicans to plunge the nation into untold calamities. After the burning of Washington, D.C., and after the British navy tightened its blockade to include New England, the Federalists of Massachusetts felt compelled to defend their seaports from the depredations of the royal navy. However threatened, New England Federalists refused to rally to "Free Trade and Sailors' Rights," which they called a "ridiculous imposition." Indeed, "What millions would the United States now pay with cheerfulness, for that free trade, which they enjoyed, when Bonaparte and Madison began the ruin of our commerce?" And: "What a sad reverse in the exercise of American sailors' rights, since their government has been fighting for the right of British sailors to abandon the flag of their native country, in her hour of peril?" Instead of defending "Bonaparte's maritime law" and "the cupidity of British deserters," the "worthy yeomanry of Massachusetts" had marched to defend their state "at the summons of our beloved governor" to repel an invasion caused by the policies of James Madison and the Republicans.[50]

Federalists even turned the motto against Captain David Porter in writing about the defeat of the *Essex* in the Battle of Valparaiso. Sarcastically admitting that "[t]he gallant PORTER," as well as the officers and crew of the *Essex*, had displayed "*Heroism*" in the "late inauspicious battle against *such* superior force, and under *so many* disadvantages," a Federalist editor asked, "who can look at the long and melancholy list of the killed, the wounded and the missing, without feeling the most heart-rendering anguish? – who can contemplate the idea of those unfortunate People thus sacrificing their lives, without feeling the sharpest resentment against those who plunged them into this wicked War, and infamously *deceived them*." Before the war, the "Honest American Yankee Tars" had been happy because "'They went where they wished and came when they would.' – No sailors upon the face of the earth or the waters ever enjoyed *a freer Trade* or more *unrestrained Rights* than they once did." Only "Mr. Madison's friend Bonaparte" threatened their livelihood, although "they were often protected by those our Rulers have declared our enemies [the British].... But the people of the South and West – men who did not know the stem from the stern of a ship, pretended to know more about these affairs than the Merchants and Sailors." These men – the Republicans – said "that France *loved* us and was our *Friend* – that Britain hated us, impress'd all our sailors, and wished to destroy our Commerce, &c. and that we must go to War against Great-Britain for *Free Trade and Sailors' Rights*." With the government destroying trade by fighting the British, sailors had no choice but to go "on board our ships of war." The article ended with a somber and bitter question: "What must be the situation of the families and friends of those who were killed or drowned or mangled in the horrible battle. Can Mr. Madison restore to them an Husband, a Brother or a Limb."[51]

Whether Federalist or Republican, much of the politics of war hinged on the rhetoric of free trade and sailors' rights. Republicans in the street, as well as in the halls of Congress, rallied to its cry. Sometimes Federalists sought to co-opt the phrase; more often they used it to attack their political opponents. This slogan, which had first appeared at the masthead of the frigate *Essex*, had gained a popularity and potency despite the poisonous political atmosphere of the war. A few short words seemed to ably summarize why Americans were fighting the war. The "GHOST OF MONTGOMERY" (the pseudonym referred to the Revolutionary hero Richard Montgomery, who died at the gates of Quebec in 1775) noted: "Free Trade and Sailors' Rights" was a "happily-conceived concise motto, conveying to future times a just idea of the contest in which the United States were compelled to engage."[52] During the war, the phrase spoke for itself. However, beneath the surface, we can see that free trade and sailors' rights went to the very core of American political culture. Free trade was shorthand for the defense of American maritime interests and called upon the ideals of the American Revolution. Sailors' rights not only protested impressment, but also harked back to the American fight for independence by proclaiming that sailors were citizens. As Henry Clay and others explained, seamen shared that citizenship with farmers and mechanics; however a man earned his living, as a citizen he had rights that had to be protected.[53] In short, free trade and sailors' rights gave political meaning to the War of 1812.

# 18

## Pursuit of Peace

No sooner had the United States declared war than President James Madison began his pursuit of peace. At first the conditions for ending hostilities were clear and linked to two simple demands that would soon be encapsulated in Porter's slogan of free trade and sailors' rights: protection of American neutral commerce and the end of impressment. With the British repeal of the orders in council, only one essential condition had to be dealt with – impressment. Although Jefferson had earlier sidestepped the issue, both the Americans and the British considered it vital to their national identity. The American support for "brother citizens" forced to serve in the British navy, combined with the British belief in their right to search American ships for British seamen, created an insurmountable barrier to peace in the first two years of the war. The British remained intractable on the issue, even as Madison began to show some flexibility and was willing to prohibit British subjects from serving on American merchant and naval vessels. Part of the problem with the argument over impressment was that it reflected two different definitions of citizenship: Americans believed that a seaman could choose his own allegiance, while the British thought that allegience to the British crown could never be lost. Those definitions came into bold relief in a conflict over the treatment of prisoners of war and the contrast between how the British perceived naturalized American citizens born in Great Britain and fighting for the United States, and impressed Americans serving in his majesty's navy. Only when impressment receded could peace be established. Eager for an honorable way out of the war, Madison quickly accepted a Russian offer to mediate in early 1813, but clung to the demand for an end of impressment. The British rejected the Russian intervention, but eventually agreed to direct negotiations. By the time the British and American commissioners met in Ghent in the summer of 1814 to discuss terms, the larger geopolitical situation had changed. In Europe,

Napoleon had been defeated, allowing the British to devote more men and resources to the American war. In North America, repeated American invasions of Canada had come to naught, and the British were preparing to launch an all-out assault on the United States that threatened to tear the nation apart. In the face of this adversity, and recognizing that with demobilization in Europe the impressment issue had become moot, Madison abandoned sailors' rights for the sake of peace. In the meantime, as the war dragged on, other questions had emerged to complicate matters. The British negotiators sought assurances for their Indian allies and even hoped to gain some American territory occupied by British troops. Within the United States political and regional divisions intensified, culminating in the Hartford Convention and discussion of secession in New England. Although, against all odds, a peace treaty emerged from the negotiations in Ghent, the final agreement ignored both free trade and sailors' rights. Bitter Federalists quickly and futilely pointed to this deficit as Republicans, and most Americans, celebrated the peace.

At the beginning of the war, both the American and British governments hoped that the conflict would end quickly and amicably. Receiving official notification of the war, the British minister to the United States, Augustus John Foster, made a courtesy call at the White House before leaving the country. Madison was quite gracious in this interview and said that if Britain repealed the orders in council and indicated that it was willing to negotiate impressment, then peace could be reestablished.[1] A few days later, Secretary of State James Monroe sent instructions to Jonathan Russell, the American representative in London, to seek an armistice as a preliminary to negotiations for a comprehensive agreement. "If the orders in council are repealed," Monroe wrote, "and no other illegal blockades are substituted for them, and orders are given to discontinue the impressment of seamen from our vessels, and to restore those already impressed, there is no reason why hostilities should not immediately cease." Monroe was willing to put off any discussion of British indemnity for violating American rights until after the armistice was established. In a shift from an earlier decision reached by Jefferson and Madison, Monroe informed Russell that to encourage the British to give up the practice of impressment, Russell could pledge that the United States would pass a law "to prohibit the employment of British seamen in the public or commercial service of the United States." Although Monroe tried to sugarcoat this proposal by insisting that the measure would be reciprocal – that is, the British would also have to agree not to hire or enlist any Americans – it marked an important retreat from protecting all men in their rights, since so many sailors on American ships were from Great Britain. Naturalized citizens, and those who had registered to become naturalized citizens, however, were to be protected as Americans. Although a similar proposal offered before the war might have made some headway, the British were uninterested now that war had already broken out. Lord Castlereagh, the

British foreign secretary, refused to negotiate with Russell, since Russell had been empowered only to present proposals decided in Washington and could not speak for his government. The result was that anything Russell agreed to could be overturned – as had happened in previous negotiations with other American representatives on some provisions of the Jay Treaty and the failed Monroe-Pinkney accord – while the British government would be committed to whatever Castlereagh said. Castlereagh went on to elaborate on the issue of impressment and declared that previous efforts to settle the question had not come as close to an agreement as Americans generally believed. He admitted that Rufus King had been well liked in London, but King was mistaken in thinking that he might have made an arrangement on impressment had he remained in England. Similarly, Castlereagh noted that Monroe and Pinkney had gained nothing more than an assurance that the British would promise to guard against abusing the system of impressment during their negotiations in 1806. If these earlier discussions, "under circumstances so highly favorable," had not settled the issue, it was unlikely that it could be settled with war already declared and in negotiation with Russell, who had "circumscribed and imperfect authority" to speak for his government. Castlereagh scolded Russell: "You are not aware of the great sensibility and jealousy of the people of England on this subject." Any government that ceded the right of impressment "without the certainty of an arrangement which should obviously be calculated most unequivocally to secure its object" would not remain in power for long.[2]

If the first American peace initiative stumbled over diplomatic formalities and impressment, the first British efforts failed only because of impressment. Castlereagh pursued peace along two fronts. On June 17, 1812, he sent instructions to his representative in Washington indicating that he would reinstitute the orders in council if the United States did not open its ports quickly, but within a week he backtracked and said that he would not do so without consulting American interests. As soon as Anthony Baker, who had become the British chargé d'affaires after Foster's departure, read the first set of instructions, and before he had received Castlereagh's second set, he went to the State Department to inform the American government that the orders had been repealed conditionally. Needless to say, this peace initiative got nowhere.[3] The second front was through Admiral Sir John Borlase Warren, who commanded the British squadron in North American waters. Castlereagh, believing that the repeal of the orders in council had removed the cause of the war, charged Warren with establishing a peace. Warren, however, could not make any additional concessions. Echoing Baker's earlier proposal, on September 30, 1812, Warren informed Monroe that he was authorized to establish an armistice with the United States on the basis of the repeal of the orders in council, but that if American ports were not opened to British warships and if the war continued, the orders would be reinstated. Almost a month later, Monroe responded by stating that an armistice could be established only based on the prospect of a lasting peace, which depended not only upon the repeal of the orders in council, but also on a guarantee against illegal blockades and the end of impressment. Reciting Russell's efforts to obtain an armistice, the secretary of state noted that the United States had offered a concession on the issue by promising a law to prohibit British subjects from serving on American ships. Moreover, the American government would include the British in determining effective procedures to enforce the law. Monroe stated that the president was willing to secure Great Britain "against the evils of which she complains" – the use of British subjects aboard American ships. Like his counterpart in Britain, who had lectured Russell on the significance of the issue of impressment to the English, Monroe felt compelled to emphasize the importance of impressment to the United States. He informed Warren that Madison sought to protect the citizens of the United States from "a practice [impressment], which, while it degrades the nation, deprives them [Americans] of their rights as freemen, takes them by force from their families and their country into a foreign service, to fight the battles of a foreign Power, perhaps against their own kindred and country." Madison may have tolerated impressment before the war broke out, but now that hostilities had begun, especially after his war message had rhetorically trumpeted the cause of the impressed Jack Tar, and after Americans had rallied to the banner of free trade and sailors' rights, he was not ready to surrender the issue.[4]

The conflict over impressment between the United States and Great Britain hinged on the definition of citizenship, a definition that led to controversy over the treatment of prisoners of war and that had the potential to make any peace treaty more difficult to achieve. Americans believed that immigrants could abandon any previous allegiance and, through the process of naturalization, become United States citizens with the same rights and protections as native-born citizens. The British also allowed for naturalization, and even considered men who married British women or sailed under the British flag for two years as regular subjects. Yet they rejected the notion that anyone born in Great Britain could ever renounce his or her allegiance to the crown. Ordinarily, two nations at war would exchange prisoners either on an ad hoc basis or through formal agreements. Following this international protocol, the United States and Great Britain exchanged prisoners informally and then established a provisional convention on November 28, 1812, to ensure proper treatment of prisoners of war and to set up exchange procedures. The two nations agreed to a second convention on May 12, 1813, but the British government refused to ratify it because it allowed for the paroling of prisoners of war at sea, a provision favorable to American privateers, which could extend their voyages by releasing captives instead of keeping them aboard ship and having to return to port.[5] Ad hoc exchanges as well as the formal conventions, however, became increasingly irrelevant when the British government threatened to treat captured sailors and soldiers born in Great Britain, regardless of American naturalization, as traitors and liable to execution.

The controversy began with a few seamen and soon extended to the land forces. On September 13, 1812, an American naval officer reported that the British had seized six sailors from the captured American warship *Nautilus*, claiming that they were really British subjects. Commodore John Rodgers took twelve British seamen from the *Guerrière* in retaliation, holding them in close confinement aboard the *President* and threatening to give them any punishment that might be given to the American sailors. In October the captain of the privateer *Sarah Ann* wrote that six of his captured crew had been taken by the British and sent to Jamaica, where they were "to be tried for their lives" as traitors. The Americans took twelve prisoners in Charleston, South Carolina, as hostages for the safekeeping of the American privateersmen. The British detained twelve additional men from the American sloop of war *Wasp* in December, "under the pretence of their being British subjects." Although in the spring of 1813 the British navy relented somewhat by transferring several of these so-called traitors to regular prisoner-of-war status, and although the Americans responded in kind by returning their hostages in like proportion to the general prisoner-of-war pool, the problem of the treatment of supposed British subjects captured fighting for the Americans not only continued but actually expanded.[6] Among the approximately 1,000 men taken at the Battle of Queenston Heights on October 13, 1812, the British claimed to have discovered twenty-three soldiers who had been born in the British Isles – mainly from Ireland. The British planned to ship these men to England to stand trial for treason, regardless of the fact that some of them had been naturalized and others had lived in the United States for some time. When officials in Washington, D.C., heard of this treatment in the spring of 1813, they retaliated by ordering twenty-three British soldiers held in close confinement and threatened them with execution if the British-Americans were hanged. Additional soldiers and sailors were added to the list of British traitors as well. This treatment of prisoners of war set off a round of retaliation – centered mainly on officers – in which each side threatened execution of more and more men. By early 1814 almost all of the captured officers on both sides were being held in close confinement with potential death sentences over their heads. Ignoring the fact that their government had started the spiral of prisoner-of-war mistreatment, many in Great Britain were outraged by the American reaction. "If Mr. Madison dare to retaliate by taking away of the life of one English prisoner," the London paper that most closely reflected the views of the British ministry declared, "America puts herself out of the protection of the law of nations, and must be treated as an outlaw."[7] For their part, the Americans thought that the British, in Madison's words, were "pursuing a course which threatens consequences most

afflicting to humanity" and, according to the secretary of state, were in violation of practices "countenanced by the proceedings of any European nation."[8]
Despite the apparent impasse on prisoners of war, in the spring and summer of
1814 the two governments managed to patch together an agreement. General
William Winder, a prisoner of war on parole in Canada, negotiated a settlement in April 1814 that did not include the twenty-three "traitors" captured
at Queenston or the first round of hostages. Because of these exclusions Madison refused to sign this accord, but when the Americans heard that the British
had gone ahead and released from close confinement most of their hostages,
and it was clear that the twenty-three "traitors" had been returned to regular
prisoner-of-war status and would not be prosecuted, a new convention was
signed on July 16, 1814. This document set up an exchange agreement and led
to the release of all hostages, except the original Queenston captives, who were
freed at the end of the war (only twenty-one were actually released, since two
had died in captivity). The prisoner-of-war agreement reached in the summer
of 1814 removed a potentially treaty-killing issue just as the British and the
Americans were beginning negotiations to end the war.[9]

Citizenship also became an issue concerning the treatment of the American
seamen who had already been pressed into the British navy. This controversy
helped to keep impressment in the minds of many Americans during the war
and also complicated any efforts to make peace. The British did allow some
native-born impressed Americans to leave the British navy once hostilities had
broken out. The British navy began transferring such men from the gundecks
of their ships to prisoner-of-war compounds as early as September 1812, and
continued to do so throughout the conflict. At the end of the war the State
Department compiled a list of 1,579 men who had been released from the
British navy and sent to prisons in England, the West Indies, and Halifax.[10]
This number does not include those who had been transferred to prisoner-of-
war status and exchanged during the war. The American government viewed
this release of some seamen as a half-measure. Monroe was outraged by the
fact that men who had been forced to serve in the British navy for years were
not "liberated and sent home at its [the British government's] own charge."
He also complained that the British had not released all of the Americans they
had impressed. Anyone pressed from a British merchant ship could be kept in
his majesty's navy, and those who could not provide proof of their nativity, or
who had married in England, or who had volunteered for the British navy –
many seamen had signed the ship's roster after impressment in order to collect
the enlistment bonus – were also retained. In addition, Monroe believed that
the British were keeping other Americans who should have been released even
by British standards. Commodore John Rodgers had captured a packet early in
the war and examined the muster books of two British ships, which indicated
that an eighth of their crews were American. As Rodgers explained, "if there

is only a quarter part of that proportion on board their other vessels," the British had "an infinitely greater number of Americans in their service than any *American* has yet an idea of." Monroe highlighted the contrast between the treatment of Americans captured by the British and the treatment of those sailors forced to remain on board British ships. Great Britain "impresses into its navy native citizens of the United States, and compels them to serve in it, and, in many instances, even to fight against their country; while it arrests as traitors, and menaces with death, persons suspected to be native British subjects, for having fought under our standard against British forces, although they had voluntarily entered into our army after having emigrated to the United States, and incorporated themselves into the American society." Impressment and citizenship remained indelibly connected and complicated any pursuit of peace.[11]

In an attempt to settle questions concerning the issues of both impressment and citizenship, early in 1813 Albert Gallatin and James Monroe wrote a special Seamen's Act that put into legal form the proposition Madison had offered to the British in the summer of 1812: that the United States would no longer allow British subjects to serve on American merchant and naval vessels if the British would renounce impressment from American ships and reciprocate by not permitting Americans to serve on British ships. The idea was to strengthen the government's hand in negotiating with the British by demonstrating American sincerity and removing the British complaint about American merchants luring British seamen with high wages. As Felix Grundy, who presented the bill to Congress, explained: "When it is known that not one British seamen could be found on board American vessels, it would be absurd to urge that fact as a motive for such impressment." Without impressment, Grundy asserted, there would be no war, since "the impressment of our seamen was that alone which prevented an armistice" during the Russell-Castlereagh exchange.[12] If the British responded positively to the law, the Seamen's Act would also ease the problem of having belligerent nationals in the service of their birth country's enemy by compelling the British to release all impressed Americans, while ensuring that there would be no British subjects on American warships. Madison also had a political agenda. Federalists had complained that the Republicans were fighting a war to defend British deserters who were stealing jobs from American sailors. The Seamen's Act erased that objection by proclaiming that the government wanted only to protect American seamen. Moreover, if the British refused to abandon impressment and continued hostilities, then the bill would place the blame for the war more squarely on the shoulders of the British. Some Republicans were against the bill because it posed the possibility of ending the war without addressing all of the offenses committed by the British against Americans. Congressmen Adam Seybert of Pennsylvania asked, "Have the wrongs been redressed for which the United States have contended?

Has atonement been made for our violated rights? Have our impressed sea-men been restored to their wives, their children, and their parents? Has Great Britain shown a disposition to meet us after we have advanced more than two-thirds of the way?" His response: "No! and *no* alone must be the uniform answer to all these questions." Republicans like Seybert also objected to the law because it would deny the right of naturalization to future British immi-grants and was thus a violation of the Constitution. "You cannot pass this bill," Seybert declared, "and thereafter naturalize foreigners with limited priv-ileges, unless the Constitution be amended, so as to establish different grades of citizenship," and such gradations would deny the equality of the American Revolution.[13] Although suspicious of the Republican motives behind the bill, Federalists voted for it in the hope that it would lead to peace. That support, along with the backing of administration stalwarts, led to its passage, writing into law the retreat from sailors' rights expressed by President Madison the previous summer. The law, however, did not advance the cause of peace.[14]

About the time of the passage of the Seamen's Act, Madison learned of a Russian peace initiative, which began for the United States a long process that stumbled over British intransigence concerning impressment and their opposition to free trade, but which eventually helped lead to direct negotiations with Great Britain. Russia had grown to depend on American trade and had recently rejoined the British as allies against Napoleon. An Anglo-American accord would therefore allow commerce with the United States to continue, while also freeing the British of any distractions from the war in Europe. The Russians had also long supported the notion of neutral rights and the idea that free ships make free goods. Andrei Dashkov, the Russian representative in the United States, explained to Monroe: "The Government of His Imperial Majesty will always be pleased to contribute to the maintenance of the esteem due to the rights of neutrals."[15] Moreover, the Russians would enhance their status in Europe if they could act as an intermediary in the Anglo-American war. The Russian chancellor, Count Nikolai Rumiantzev, approached both the British and American ministers in St. Petersburg in mid-September 1812 with a mediation proposal. John Quincy Adams, the American minister, encouraged the Russians, while the British minister responded more coolly. Rumiantzev then contacted the British and American governments directly. The British did not like the idea of mediation, since they believed that the Russian position on neutral rights favored the Americans. As Lord Liverpool later explained, "I fear the Emperor of Russia is half an American."[16] Any possibility that Russia might return to the free trade mantra of the armed neutrality days at the expense of the British had to be avoided. The British were also displeased that the Russians had proposed mediation to both nations without first discussing the idea with the British. This approach treated the two belligerents equally and thereby diminished the stature of the British in the international community.

In addition, victories along the Canadian border had made the war popular in Great Britain and seemed to promise a quick and positive outcome. Rather than simply rebuffing and alienating its new ally, the British government bided its time, claiming that the Americans were really fighting at the behest of the French and that the cabinet had already established its own channel for negotiations by authorizing Admiral Warren to seek an armistice. The British argued that they had attempted to avoid war by repealing the orders in council and that the United States had obstinately continued hostilities over the issue of impressment, and, as Castlereagh informed the Russians, "neither the English nation nor the English ministry would ever concede this point."[17]

Word of the Russian offer of mediation arrived in Washington in February 1813. Although Dashkov's efforts to arrange an immediate armistice with Admiral Warren and the American government failed as both sides refused to give ground over impressment, Madison responded positively to the official Russian proposal presented on March 8. News of the defeat of the French in Russia probably had some impact on this decision.[18] Like the British, Madison recognized that the Russians would be sympathetic to American commercial interests. "We are encouraged in this policy [Russian mediation]," Madison explained, "by the known friendship of the Emperor Alexander to this country; and by the probability that the greater affinity between the Baltic and American ideas of maritime law, than between those of the former and G.B. [Great Britain,] will render interposition as favorable as will be consistent with the character assumed by him."[19] Without waiting to hear the British response to the Russian proposal, the president quickly selected a three-man delegation for negotiations in St. Petersburg: John Quincy Adams, who was already there; James Bayard, a Federalist, which made the commission bipartisan; and Albert Gallatin, the treasury secretary and one of Madison's most trusted advisors. Their instructions, however, provided a recipe for failure. The secretary of state insisted that the British stop impressing seamen from American ships. Monroe wrote that "the great object which you have to secure, in regard to impressment, is, that our flag shall protect the crew." He also discussed at some length the new Seamen's Act, which he believed guaranteed the British that none of their subjects would serve in American crews, thereby making any search of American ships unnecessary. Although Monroe indicated that the commissioners should seek protection for neutral trade and a clear definition of blockades, everything depended on the one issue on which the British were not going to surrender – impressment. "If this encroachment of Great Britain is not provided against," Monroe explained, "the United States have appealed to arms in vain." And "[i]f your efforts to accomplish it should fail, all further negotiations will cease, and you will return home without delay."[20]

The instructions, as it turned out, were only one of the commission's problems. After his departure for Europe, Gallatin's political enemies in the Senate refused to confirm his nomination as a commissioner, since he had not resigned his position in the treasury. Gallatin, of course, would not find out about this difficulty until several months after his arrival in Russia. The British position on mediation created even more serious problems for the commissioners. When, in May 1813, the British heard of the American response to the Russians, they reiterated their opposition to mediation and informed the Russians that the nature of the conflict precluded the involvement of a third party, since the issues, particularly impressment, were so vital to national interests. To mollify Czar Alexander over this rejection, the British also suggested that they might consider direct negotiations. Castlereagh made it clear that this concession reflected the respect the British held for the czar: the British foreign minister was willing to open direct negotiations in order "to offer His Imperial Majesty a chance to realize his amicable intentions and at the same time to give him proof of England's desire to put an end to this struggle in which nobody is a winner."[21]

The American commissioners found themselves in a strange diplomatic bind. They knew about the British intransigence, since Rumiantzev had informed Adams of the British refusal of mediation in June 1813, and Alexander Baring, a British banker with ties to the United States, had written a letter on July 22 to Gallatin with the same information, adding that the British government might be willing to negotiate directly as long as the Americans relented on impressment.[22] But they still needed to wait for the Russians to renounce their peace initiative officially. And if the Russians did so, they could not themselves begin direct negotiations, since they did not have the appropriate portfolio. Compounding this odd situation was the byzantine nature of Russian court politics. The commissioners dealt directly with Rumiantzev, who was becoming increasingly isolated politically even though he was officially in charge of Russian diplomacy. Czar Alexander was not in St. Petersburg. Instead, the czar was in central Europe fighting Napoleon. During the summer of 1813 the French remained in the field, and Alexander needed British subsidies and support. Alexander thus began to speak at cross purposes, sending missives to Rumiantzev urging him to offer mediation again, while telling the British as early as August 22, 1813, that he could do "nothing more in the business."[23] Given Alexander's preoccupation with military affairs and vulnerability to British pressure, this waffling almost made sense. Back in St. Petersburg, Rumiantzev was left to entertain the Americans and to lead them on by telling them that he did not see the British rejection of mediation as final. European diplomacy was seldom open and direct. Stalling tactics, verbal refusals, even written notes might merely reflect an opening position in complex negotiations. We know now that the British never accepted the Russian mediation – and probably never seriously considered it. In St. Petersburg during the summer and fall of 1813 the situation was more in flux. If the war went badly in

North America, or if Napoleon's troops rebounded in Europe, or if war weariness in Great Britain threatened Lord Liverpool's government, the British might embrace an end to the American war with Russian help. Moreover, the United States had much to gain from Russian mediation, since Rumiantzev hoped to get the British to the bargaining table for his own purposes. As he explained to Czar Alexander, the negotiations would be a means "definitively to change the principle of England's policy, so despotic and so destructive for the well-being of neutral powers."[24] With this will-o'-the-wisp hope for a favorable Russian mediation, all the Americans could do was wait.

A strange sequence of events followed. On September 1, 1813, Lord Cathcart, Britain's military and diplomatic representative with the czar, again declined the Russian offer of mediation, and asked the Russians to inform the Americans that the British were willing to open direct negotiations in either London or Gothenburg, Sweden. But no one in the Russian government told Adams, Gallatin, and Bayard about the proposal. Rumiantzev wanted the Russian ambassador in London, Khristofor A. Lieven, to renew the offer of mediation, but knowing the British response, Lieven did not do so. Complicating matters further, in November the British informally told the American mission that they would not negotiate under Russian mediation, but did not do so in writing or through official channels. This awkward diplomatic stalemate, with notes passing between the Russians and the British and between the Americans and the Russians, with no official contact between the belligerents, continued into 1814. On January 17, 1814, Rumiantzev sent a note to Adams and Bayard (the Senate's refusal to confirm Gallatin as part to the commission meant that he had no official status in St. Petersburg) indicating that Lieven had taken no action, and had told Rumiantzev in a note (reflecting the convoluted workings of Russian diplomacy) that the czar would soon send Rumiantzev dispatches that would enable the chancellor to judge for himself "that it was no longer appropriate" for Lieven to present the note renewing the offer of mediation. Rumiantzev, however, would not provide a final written confirmation of his failure to help the Americans and British to end their war. Bayard and Gallatin therefore decided to leave Russia. After all, since the British had not responded positively to the Russians, and had even informally notified the Americans that there was no way that they would accept Russian mediation, there was no reason to prolong their stay. On January 25, still with no definitive word from the czar on whether he would continue to push for mediation with the British, and with only the verbal permission of Rumiantzev, Bayard and Gallatin departed on a six-week journey to Amsterdam.[25]

Although on the surface it might appear that the Russian offer to mediate a treaty between the United States and Great Britain wasted a year or more in the peace process, on a deeper level that may not have been the case. As indicated by comments made by Monroe, by Rumiantzev, and even by Lord

Liverpool, the Russian concern with neutral rights favored the United States. The Americans therefore believed that Russian mediation would be to their benefit. So determined were the Americans that Russia would support them that after Gallatin left St. Petersburg, and before the commencement of direct negotiations, he encouraged the Marquis de Lafayette to lobby Czar Alexander in Paris to make another offer of mediation and even sought an audience with the czar in London. In Paris Alexander promised Lafayette that he would renew his offer of mediation, but in London he told Gallatin that despite his friendship for the United States, there was not much he could do to help.[26] The czar was right. Not only were the British uninterested in resurrecting the issue of neutral rights with Russian involvement in the American peace treaty, but impressment remained a roadblock to peace. Throughout 1813 and well into 1814, neither Great Britain nor the United States had budged on the question of impressment. Any negotiations under Russian auspices, therefore, would probably have ended in failure.

The Russian interest in an Anglo-American peace, however, encouraged the British to seek direct talks with the Americans. On November 4, 1813, Castlereagh sent a formal letter to Monroe, and not to the commissioners in St. Petersburg, offering one-to-one negotiations and providing direct confirmation that he had rejected Russian mediation. However, this communication also acknowledged the Russian role in facilitating Castlereagh's peace overture: Castlereagh wrote that the Russians had informed him that the American commissioners were willing to come to London for peace talks (they had agreed to do so under Russian mediation months earlier), and that the Russians had also made it clear that the American commissioners could not undertake direct negotiations without a formal change in their portfolio. Castlereagh sent this note post haste and offered the protection of the British navy to ensure a swift and safe response and a conduit for new commissions. Further acknowledging the Russian contribution to the peace process, soon after Castlereagh sent his letter to Monroe, he notified Lieven of his contact with the Americans. In Washington, Madison reluctantly accepted the British proposal on January 5, 1814, and Monroe sent a new set of instructions and commissions to Bayard and Adams. Monroe named two new members to the negotiating team – Henry Clay, representing the War Hawks in Congress, and Jonathan Russell, an experienced diplomat. After replacing Gallatin at the treasury, Madison added him to the commission as well.[27]

There were more delays. The British took their time in picking their nego-tiators and in getting things started. After first selecting Gothenburg, Sweden, as the location for the negotiations, the British, with the connivance of two of the American commissioners (Gallatin and Bayard) decided to meet at the provincial city of Ghent in modern Belgium. The Americans arrived at that location in late June and early July; the British showed up a month later, and negotiations did not begin until August 8, 1814. The British appointed three commissioners to go to Ghent: Dr. William Adams, who was an admiralty lawyer; Vice-Admiral James Gambier, a navy veteran with forty-five years of service; and Henry Goulburn, an undersecretary in the colonial office. Historians often note that these three second-level bureaucrats were no match for the Americans, who were among the most experienced and talented diplomats and politicians in the United States. Certainly the British government had its first-team diplomats dealing with the larger foreign policy issues in Paris and Vienna, deciding the future of Europe. However, it really did not matter whom the British sent to Ghent. The British commissioners were given little real latitude, and almost every step taken during negotiations was guided by the British cabinet in London. Indeed, Britain's representatives at Ghent usually took tougher positions on issues than the British government, and the men in London pulling the strings repeatedly compelled their commissioners to give in to the Americans.[28]

The long wait to start the negotiations was just as well. Monroe's instructions in January 1814 had stated that Madison had not changed his mind on impressment and that it remained the one point upon which there could be no compromise. As far as Madison and Monroe were concerned, without an article preventing the British from impressing seamen from American ships, there could be no peace. However, the defeat of Napoleon compelled a change of policy in the United States.[29] On June 25 and 27, 1814, Monroe issued two letters with a new set of instructions that allowed the commissioners to drop impressment as a deal breaker. The first letter indicated that Madison would accept a commission to be appointed after the peace to settle the issue of impressment, if the British refused to include a provision in the treaty. "The United States," Monroe wrote, "having resisted by war the practice of impressment, and continued that war until that practice had ceased by a peace in Europe, their object has been essentially obtained for the present." If the British did not agree to stop impressing from American ships and another war broke out, "the United States will be again at liberty to repel it by war." In other words, since the British had halted impressing seamen after attaining a peace in Europe, the question had become moot as a cause of war – at least until a new European war broke out. The second letter retreated even further from a defense of sailors' rights and authorized the commissioners to "omit any stipulation on the subject of impressment" if necessary to end the war. However, even if the treaty were "silent on the subject of impressment," it should not "admit the British claim theron, or to relinquish that of the United States." These letters arrived in Ghent as the negotiations were beginning. The door was left open to sidestep the one question that had stymied previous peace initiatives. The American commissioners briefly mentioned impressment in the early phases of the talks, but did not follow through with any demands. Much later, Henry Clay included a provision on impressment in a draft of the treaty, which the British deleted. The Americans said nothing about it.[30]

With impressment off the negotiating table, an agreement should have been within easy reach. It was not. The British had changed their agenda. By 1814 resentment toward the Americans had grown in Great Britain. Many Britons believed that the United States had declared war at a particularly vulnerable moment and at a time when their government had sought conciliation by repealing the orders in council. As a result, there was a call for vengeance, or at least some thought of chastisement that would include territorial concessions. Newspapers in Britain listed a host of demands, including a new boundary for Canada, Indian independence, and the exclusion of Americans from the Newfoundland fisheries, the West Indies, the East Indies, and even the northwest coast in the Pacific. Some writers wanted to drive the Americans from Florida and New Orleans, and raised questions about the legitimacy of the Louisiana Purchase. They also asserted the right of search and insisted that the Americans adhere to "the international law as it is at present received in Europe," which from the British perspective meant that free ships did *not* make free goods. In short, there was a public outcry not only to deny free trade and sailors' rights, but also to punish the Americans for having the audacity to declare war over those issues.[31] The British instructions to the commissioners, however, took a position less extreme than that appearing in the public prints. The cabinet was prepared to make some small concession on impressment. Recognizing that the practice could be arbitrary, the British were willing to prevent such abuse, but would not give up impressment entirely. However, Castlereagh instructed the delegation that the best approach to this issue was not to include any word concerning impressment in the treaty. On questions relating to the Indians, Castlereagh's instructions provided guidelines rather than absolute demands. The British sought an assurance for the protection of Indian lands in the Northwest and an end to new American settlements in the region. Castlereagh even hoped to create an Indian buffer state in the Northwest, and during negotiations the British commissioners went so far as to suggest that American settlements be pulled back to the Greenville line of 1795 in Ohio. The British negotiators presented these ideas, but did not hold to them. Castlereagh also wanted an American demilitarization of the Great Lakes and a boundary revision for Canada, but made no specific demands. Likewise, if the American right to fish off the coast of Newfoundland was to be sustained, then the Americans had to make some equivalent concession. But, again, Castlereagh provided little specific direction.[32]

Once the issue of impressment had been set aside, there were three distinct phases in the negotiations. First came a discussion of the rights of Indians. The Americans vehemently resisted the idea that the British could interpose in "the relations between the acknowledged sovereign of the territory and the

Indians situated upon it" and viewed the suggestion that Native Americans be granted a buffer state as a violation of the practice of civilized nations.[33] With their positions so diametrically opposed, both the American and the British commissioners expected the negotiations to be broken off. The Americans had responded to the British terms in language that made the British position seem unreasonable. In early September, at the behest of their superiors in London (who were concerned with the domestic political ramifications of ending negotiations because of the insistence that the United States surrender a major portion of its nation to the Indians), the British commissioners abandoned the barrier state idea, but still sought guarantees for Indian lands. As the British shifted their position, the Americans remained immoveable on the Native American issue. They refused the proposition that there be a permanent boundary for Indian lands based on pre-war treaties and did not want to include in the treaty any mention of the Indians as allies to the British, since that would be admitting that Native American tribes were independent nations. The talks again stalled and appeared on the verge of breaking up. In late September word arrived that many of the Indians in the Northwest had agreed to a peace treaty with the United States: the Treaty of Greenville of July 22, 1814, not only ended hostilities, but also had the Indians pledge "to aid the United States, in prosecuting the war against Great Britain."[34] By early October, the British had had enough of the Indian question and, knowing that their forces had set fire to Washington, decided to concentrate on territorial concessions instead. The British commissioners, at the behest of the cabinet in London, agreed not to include the Indians as allies in the treaty, but insisted upon an article stating that both Great Britain and the United States would end hostilities with all Native Americans currently engaged in the war and would nullify any Indian land cessions made after 1811. Faced with what amounted to an ultimatum on conceding at least some weakened protection for Indians, the Americans grudgingly accepted this proposal, although the United States would ignore the land cession provision once the war was over.[35]

With the Indian question out of the way, negotiations moved on to the next phase to discuss territorial boundaries. The British, with their armies apparently triumphant in North America, hoped to begin this round of negotiations from a position of strength. On October 21, the British repeated the suggestion made in August that the frontier between Canada and the United States be drawn based upon *uti possidetis*, that is, each country should gain the land its armies had occupied at the end of war. After the burning of Washington, and regardless of the setbacks at Baltimore, Lake Champlain, and Fort Erie, the British believed they were winning the war. At the time, the British controlled Fort Niagara, Fort Mackinaw, and half the district of Maine, and they expected to occupy even more territory soon. From the British perspective the American situation looked desperate. The Americans had not been able to sustain invasions of

Canada; the British blockade was stifling their economy; and with the defeat of France and the failure of Russian mediation, they did not have any friends or supporters in Europe. Noting "that they had no authority to cede any part of the territory of the United States," the American commissioners rejected the British *uti possidetis* proposal on October 24. Negotiations once again almost collapsed, but were kept alive because the British administration did not want to be blamed for ending talks and did not want to open Parliament on November 8 having to explain a failure at Ghent.[36]

Although conditions on the battlefield had some impact on the negotiations, political developments in Europe and the United States had a greater effect, compelling the British government to give up *uti possidetis*. After decades of war, the British nation groaned under the burden of high taxation that could be relieved only by an end to all hostilities. The British cabinet feared the political cost of continuing the war with the United States and decided that the best way to ensure popular support for extending the conflict was to send their premier war hero, the duke of Wellington, to North America. Wellington reluctantly said he would go, but believed that the war was almost unwinnable. He said he could not launch an invasion from Canada without control of the lakes and that it would be impossible to stop continued American incursions across the border. Wellington thought that if he went to North America it would be to make a peace that might as well be negotiated at Ghent. Sending Wellington to the other side of the Atlantic posed additional problems as conditions in Europe became more volatile with the possibility of renewed war: there was a threat of revolution in France and, at the Vienna Congress, Great Britain and Russia were at loggerheads over Poland and the balance of power in Europe. In the meantime, the political situation in the United States shifted. Madison received dispatches on October 8 concerning the British demands in August for Indian land and territorial concessions. The president released this information two days later, and also published Monroe's instructions of June dropping the impressment issue. This maneuver changed the basis for fighting the war. No longer were Americans defending seamen from impressment – after all, the British navy was now dismissing men. Instead, it was fighting to protect its territorial integrity. Even many Federalists, including Alexander Contee Hanson, started to support the administration in the war, although there remained a core of diehards in New England who continued to oppose the conflict. A war fought in defense of the nation could generate additional soldiers and a flow of money that would make the British military task more difficult. Madison's action also strengthened the position of the critics of the war in Great Britain by exposing the Anglo-American conflict as a war of conquest instead of a war for maintaining British maritime rights. Based on Wellington's advice, the situation in Europe, and the political developments in Great Britain and the United States, on November 21 the

British cabinet decided to accept the status quo antebellum as suggested by the Americans.[37]

On November 26, the American commissioners learned of the British willingness to agree to all boundaries as they had existed at the beginning of the war. This British concession led to the last stage of negotiations, and the final details and wording of the peace treaty were ironed out by Christmas Eve. As had become clear from the beginning of the negotiations, the treaty did not say a word about free trade and sailors' rights. There was also no mention of Americans fishing off Newfoundland or of British navigation of the Mississippi (both had been allowed in the Treaty of Paris of 1783). Nor did it include any concessions of territory on either side. Instead, the treaty returned conditions to the status quo antebellum and provided for commissions to settle questions concerning disputed boundaries. The Great Lakes (except for Lake Michigan) remained divided and militarized. Without getting into specifics about the earlier controversy over prisoners and citizenship, the third article stated that "[a]ll prisoners of war taken on either side as well by land as by sea," were to "be restored as soon as practicable after the Ratifications of this treaty." The provision concerning peace with the Indians was included, and there was even an article in which both nations pledged to "use their best endeavours to" end the international slave trade. In all, neither nation won anything in the war, but both gained a peace.[38]

About the same time as the negotiators in Ghent were agreeing to their final terms, Federalists in New England met in a convention in Hartford to articulate their wartime grievances. Their aim was to protect the New England states against what they saw as impositions by the federal government. At a meeting held behind closed doors, a few extremists proposed secession from the Union, and others suggested a separate peace between New England and Great Britain. These proposals did not garner much support, and moderates dominated the proceedings. The report of the convention criticized President Madison and his war, while offering constitutional amendments to remedy the political problems of the New Englanders. Believing that the three-fifths clause gave the South disproportionate control over the federal government, the convention suggested that taxation and representation be proportionate to the free population of each state. Clinging to British ideas concerning citizenship, they wanted to exclude foreigners from holding office in the national government. Hoping to break the control of Virginia over the presidency, they wanted an amendment to limit the chief executive to one term and to prevent individuals from the same state from serving successively. Taken together, these measures would enhance the influence of New England in the national government and thereby limit future conflicts with Great Britain. To further protect against embargoes and wars for free trade and sailors' rights, the convention wanted an amendment preventing Congress from interfering with foreign commerce or declaring an offensive war except by a two-thirds vote. The timing of the Hartford Convention was terrible for the Federalists. Despite the bleak military outlook and the looming financial collapse of the government in December, reports of Jackson's victory and the Treaty of Ghent arrived in Washington at about the same time that the Federalists were bringing their proposed amendments to the nation's capital. Amid the jubilation of battlefield victory and the end of the war, Republicans portrayed the Federalists at the Hartford Convention as traitors to the United States.[39]

The path to the peace of Christmas Eve had been long and convoluted, with more than its share of dead ends. Madison had hoped for a quick war, but military victories proved hard to come by, and the questions of impressment and citizenship created what appeared to be insurmountable roadblocks to a treaty. Although the military situation did not improve dramatically, citizenship as it related to prisoners of war and concerns with impressed sailors receded into the background over time. The confused saga of Russian mediation may not have led to an immediate settlement, but at least it contributed to bringing British and American commissioners to the bargaining table in the summer of 1814. During the ensuing negotiations, the British at first set out to push the Americans for major concessions concerning Indians and territory. In the end, the British failure to make any significant headway during the campaigns of 1814 (putting aside the burning of Washington), the deteriorating diplomatic situation in Europe, and political conditions in the United States and Great Britain convinced the British to accept a treaty that abandoned the Indians (again) and left boundaries alone. For their part, the Americans heaved a sigh of relief and were eager to gain any peace, even if it ignored free trade and sailors' rights.

19

# Dartmoor

Regardless of the Federalist fulminations, and the truth of some of their accusations, free trade and sailors' rights carried special meaning for the sailors who fought in the War of 1812. Jack Tar seized upon the phrase and made it his own. Common seamen like Samuel Leech would look back decades later and use Porter's motto to explain the determination of the men who fought on the high seas. The slogan was plastered on tavern signs everywhere. Sailors shouted it in public demonstrations and referred to it in private conversations. And they could both revere and mock the phrase in Dartmoor, the great and dismal prisoner-of-war compound in southwestern England that stood atop the bleak moor of the same name. Dartmoor itself became a symbol of sailors' rights in the months after the signing of the Treaty of Ghent. Kept in confinement as diplomats wrangled over who would pay for their return passage, American sailors repeatedly expressed their own peculiar notions of liberty in defense of their rights, trying the patience of their captors until an explosion of violence by the prison guards left seven Americans dead and scores wounded. In the wake of the Dartmoor Massacre, as the tragic event quickly came to be known, there was a political uproar despite diplomatic efforts to sidestep the issue. Republicans were outraged by this brutal assault on American citizens and violation of sailors' rights. Some Republicans even called for revenge and a renewal of war. Federalists agreed about the importance of protecting their countrymen, but were more moderate in their approach and defended the Anglo-American report on the affair. They also charged the Republicans with using the massacre for political purposes and then chided the Republicans for their failure to protect sailors' rights and aid the returning prisoners of war. In the end, the hoopla over the massacre subsided. Dartmoor was added to the popular vocabulary as a byword for British brutality and as a symbol of the importance of sailors' rights. However much the Dartmoor Massacre lived on in popular memory, free trade and sailors' rights remained the central rhetorical phrase inherited from the War of 1812.

We can see how deeply Porter's motto became embedded in the common sailor's mind in the story of Samuel Leech. A young English sailor aboard the *Macedonian* when it fought the *United States*, Leech wrote a memoir of his thirty years at sea published in 1843. He had escaped from his prisoner-of-war status in New York after the British frigate's defeat in order to avoid being exchanged and returned to a berth in the British navy. Leech eagerly embraced his new identity and soon joined the American navy, wearing his hair long and letting it hang in ringlets rather than the queue typical of the British sailor. He dressed like an American seaman and sported an insignia "consisting of the stars of the American flag, with the British flag underneath." Leech remained an American the rest of his life. Looking back on the fateful battle of the *Macedonian*, Leech acknowledged that the American super frigate had an advantage in size, guns, and men. But he also believed that the seamen "in the two ships fought under the influence of different motives." The Americans on the *United States* were all volunteers, were better treated aboard ship, and knew what they were fighting for. Many of the British sailors had been impressed, and some of those were Americans who were "inwardly hoping for defeat." Both the American and British tars aboard the *Macedonian* were attracted to "the great principle for which the American nation so nobly contended in the war of 1812." After briefly explaining how the British "violated the American flag by insolently searching their vessels for her runaway seamen" and impressed Americans in the process, Leech concluded, "Free trade and sailors' rights, therefore, were the objects contended for by the Americans. With these objects *our men* could but sympathize, whatever our officers might do."[1]

For the common folk who went to sea during the War of 1812, free trade and sailors' rights not only summed up the aims of the war, it also became a shorthand to remind the rest of the world that sailors, too, were citizens who were central to the identity of the United States. Federalists unwittingly recognized the popularity of the slogan when they complained of the many taverns throughout the nation with signs sporting Porter's motto. Massachusetts newspapers lamented that "In the middle of the great road that leads through the Kentuckian Wilderness, a log tavern is kept by one of Mr. Madison's officers, having for a sign a coarse painting of Napoleon, with the motto, '*Free Trade and Sailors' Rights*.'" No doubt this sarcastic diatribe brought a cynical smile to many a New England Federalist merchant as he looked up from his counting-house desk and across an empty wharf into the salt sea. The historian reads the notice differently and sees unintended testimony of the deep popularity of the slogan.[2] Federalists provided additional evidence for the ubiquitous nature and popularity of the phrase in retelling the story of the poor tar who had been trapped in South Carolina by the 1813 embargo. As he wended his way on foot back to Boston, he passed "through many a town where Sailor's Rights" was "in every one's mouth," yet the wayward mariner complained, "I could not get a bit of bread to put in my own." According to the Federalist telling this story, this lack of charity for seamen displayed by people supposedly dedicated to their rights also occurred in seaports: "In one great city I saw more than a dozen signs with 'Free trade and Sailors' Rights;' and yet five of our ship's crew could get no lodging but in a stable." The "honest tar" stopped at one tavern kitchen looking for scraps and was told that there were some men in the bar celebrating a recent victory and toasting "Free trade and Sailors' rights." The proprietor urged him to go in, and "whilst they are drinking sailors' rights, they may give something to relieve his misfortunes." The sailor tried his luck and went into the bar. When he told the men where he was from, they replied that only "old tories" were from Boston and that since they were republicans, he was on "a wrong chase" and they would not assist him. After giving these supposed supporters of sailors' rights a verbal "broadside," and telling them that Bostonians "were better friends to their country & Sailors rights" than any Jeffersonian, the indignant tar left.[3]

Whatever the truth of this seaman's yarn concerning his sojourn from Charleston to Boston, most sailors rejected the Federalist view of the War of 1812. Although Federalists complained in March 1813 when the crew of the privateer *Alexander* marched boisterously to the Boston courthouse to vote at the annual town meeting – declaring that the tars had shouted "like the Cossacks when attacking the flying French" – Republicans claimed that the sailors had behaved peacefully and that "the only noise which proceeded from them was in giving three hearty cheers in support of '*Free Trade and Sailors' Rights*.'"[4] John Allen from Marblehead, Massachusetts, went to New York City in 1814 and signed on to a privateer. By that time Allen had already been captured once by the British, sent to Dartmoor Prison, and exchanged. Before going aboard the vessel, Allen visited with an old shipmate and met a number of other sailors. Allen noted that the men were all Jeffersonian democrats who believed thoroughly in "free trade and sailors' rights." He told them that his "early associations were with the Federalists and the ideas of Alexander Hamilton, but that now he believed that their position was better."[5] The maritime experience of Amos G. Babcock led to a similar conversion. He had at one time been a Federalist, but by the end of the war he viewed Governor Caleb Strong's dismissal of "Free Trade and Sailor's Rights" as wrong. Instead, he had sympathy only for the impressed tar, whom he saw as "Lacerated in his flesh, wounded in his honor, and debased by the slavish hand of a boatswain's mate."[6]

Both Allen and Babcock spent time at Dartmoor. The thousands of sailors held in Dartmoor believed that they had fought for free trade and sailors' rights. When news of the Treaty of Ghent arrived at Dartmoor Prison on December 29,

1814, the sailor prisoners of war were elated. Charles Andrews, a sailor who left an account of his experiences in Dartmoor, wrote that "[w]e were confident that the ground-work of the treaty must be free trade and sailors' rights; and made arrangements to celebrate it in a manner conformable to the rights of the ocean." The prisoners prepared a flag with a white background painted with the words "FREE TRADE AND SAILORS' RIGHTS." They displayed the banner at the focal point of their celebration atop Prison Number Three, "which was styled the Commodore." This political statement was more than the British commandant could bear. He entered the prison and requested that the banner be taken down, insisting that the British government would not appreciate the message of the slogan and that it might encourage mutiny. The American prisoners of war "were too full of spirits to comply with the request." That evening the commandant repeated his concerns, made some threats, but also offered a compromise. Believing that Porter's motto was more threatening than the stars and stripes, the British officer agreed to fly the American flag at one end of his house and the British flag on the other end. With this face-saving gesture, the American sailors took down the offensive standard, saying that they would wait to fly it until after the peace was ratified.[7]

Sailors understood the political meaning of Porter's motto, but they stretched the slogan in directions all their own. Despite the austere conditions in Dartmoor, Americans set up shops selling coffee, tobacco, potatoes, butter, and bread. They also produced hats, wooden shoes, gloves, clothing, model ships made of bone, and other articles that would be vended to customers outside the prison. By purchasing goods and necessaries at these "shops and stalls where every little article could be obtained," a prisoner who had "money in his pocket" could "live pretty well through the day in Dartmoor Prison."[8] Other sailors engaged in entrepreneurial activity by providing services, setting up schools to teach reading, writing, and arithmetic for six pence a month. It was even possible to study the principles of navigation in prison. Sailors could also learn to dance, fence, and box. Several prisons put on stage productions. Vice, too, became a commodity, with a beer house and many gambling establishments that featured card games, roulette, and a form of bingo. The various prizes included cash and more material items like bread.[9] Alcohol could be purchased all too easily, and one sailor later complained that young men who had fought for "free trade and sailors' rights" found themselves in prison "amid vice and roguery."[10] Prison Number Four gained a particularly rough reputation, since it was packed with African American sailors and outcasts from the other buildings. It also became the center of entertainment and entrepreneurial activity. One prisoner explained that he visited Prison Number Four "to see the Fashions and pass the time," and another wrote in his journal that he "spent considerable of my time" in the "Black's Prison" and concluded that "their [sic] is more amusement in this Prisson than all the rest of them."[11] Whether in

Number Four or any of the other prison buildings, sailors formed "joint stock companies" to run these businesses, which became so much a part of the life in prison that Andrews chortled, we had "free trade and sailors's rights."[12]

Sailors may have been amused by the free market in goods and services within the prison walls of Dartmoor, but they took Porter's motto seriously, especially when it came to sailors' rights. Seamen often asserted a sense of entitlement as prisoners that reflected their faith in their rights as men and their belief in their peculiar notions of liberty – a liberty that frequently expressed itself in unruly behavior that owed as much to a tradition of rowdiness as it did to the ideals of the American Revolution.[13] This attitude, "such a wild reckless, daring, enterprizing character," flummoxed British officials, who could only exclaim "that it would puzzle the d___l to keep them in good order."[14] Serving as a surgeon aboard a privateer, Babcock came to know and appreciate the common seamen, recognizing that sailors "are full of 'rights' and 'wrongs'; of 'justice and injustice'; and of defining crimes, and asserting 'the butts and bounds' of national and individual rights." Babcock later explained the "spirit of fun and frolic" that characterized American prisoners of war, and the "provoking" actions against their British captors, as one of "the luxuriant shoots of our *tree* of *liberty*" that revealed "the strength, depth, and extent of its roots, and the richness of the soil."[15] American sailor prisoners of war tried the patience of their captives repeatedly until tragedy struck in the Dartmoor Massacre of April 6, 1815 – a tragedy that only strengthened the appeal of the slogan free trade and sailors' rights among common men.

The months leading up to the massacre were fraught with tension in Dartmoor. American seamen had pushed and prodded their British captors in prisons throughout the Atlantic world before the peace. Once the ink was dry on the Treaty of Ghent, they tested the British even more. In the weeks and months after the peace of Christmas Eve of 1814, the British concentrated prisoners in Dartmoor, yet gave little indication that the men would soon be released. About six thousand Americans filled the prison; a third of them had served in his majesty's navy and been converted to prisoners of war. These men carried deep resentments, either because they had been impressed, or because as volunteers they believed their dismissal from the navy, only to be sent to Dartmoor during demobilization, reflected British ingratitude for their years of service. The four thousand other prisoners also held grudges against their jailors, complaining of mistreatment, poor food, and harsh conditions. Delay after delay kept the Americans in Dartmoor. The Treaty of Ghent stipulated that each nation had to release its prisoners of war "as soon as practicable" after ratification, but it did not make clear who was to pay for repatriation. The Americans could release their prisoners in Canada or ship them to nearby Halifax and Bermuda. The thousands held in Dartmoor, however, had to be transported over the Atlantic, a more expensive and complicated endeavor.

As the British and Americans dithered over the logistics of their release, the sailors in Dartmoor waited. The weather did not help. In the winter and early spring the moor was cold, damp, and often covered in mist and fog. All the markets and amusements noted in the private journals kept by prisoners could not compensate for the dreary and monotonous existence at Dartmoor Prison. Smallpox swept through the compound in March, leading to increased illness and death.

Under these circumstances "the luxuriant shoots" of the American "*tree of liberty*" repeatedly surfaced in scores of minor confrontations and in some larger demonstrations of pent-up emotion. One of the most dramatic expressions of this discontent erupted in late March, when Reuben Beasley, the agent in London responsible for protecting the interests of the American prisoners of war, sent a letter to Dartmoor indicating that there would be more delay in the release of the captive seamen because of the epidemic raging among the prisoners. A prisoners' court held a mock trial that convicted Beasley "of depriving many hundreds of your countrymen of their lives, by the most wanton and most cruel deaths, by nakedness, starvation, and exposure to pestilence." Before they hanged and burned his effigy, the court read a confession supposedly drawn up by Beasley that admitted that he "did most criminally neglect the American prisoners, who were dying daily for want of my assistance." Beasley's effigy also "confessed" to other crimes, including not sending the men home on exchange, not obtaining the release of men discharged from British men-of-war, and otherwise cheating the prisoners for personal profit.[16] On April 4, another major disturbance broke out in a controversy over the bread served in the prison. Ordinarily the British provided the American prisoners with recently baked soft bread. But the British kept a stock of hard bread in reserve in case there were any difficulties in delivery of the soft bread. Realizing that the prisoners would soon leave, the bread contractor decided to use up his storehouse of the hard bread so that it would not become a complete financial loss. The prisoners believed that being given hard bread violated their rights and refused to eat it. As the day wore on, and with empty stomachs, the prisoners became more surly. That evening, instead of returning to their prison buildings the men charged the gate, forced it open, and collected in front of the storehouse. The guards sounded the alarm, and soldiers with fixed bayonets confronted the mass of prisoners, who dared them to fire. The situation was precarious, since if the soldiers fired a volley they could easily be overwhelmed by the prisoners, who could then leave the compound en masse. The soldiers backed down, and the contractor promised to deliver soft bread if the seamen returned to the prison and order was restored.[17]

Calmer heads prevailed in the bread riot, but the situation remained tense. Two days later, on one of the first nice days of spring, some casual misbehavior by sailors led to a more tragic outcome. Two separate incidents precipitated the crisis. One group of prisoners were playing ball near a wall. When the ball went over the wall, they would ask a guard to retrieve it. This act of kindness was quickly abused and turned into a game of fetch, much to the annoyance of the soldier, who told the men that the next time the ball flew over the wall they could get it themselves. Soon enough the ball landed beyond the wall, and with the soldier no longer willing to return it, a couple of prisoners began digging a hole in the wall. The soldier asked the men to stop and even threatened them with his gun. But the men kept digging, attracting a loud and boisterous crowd urging them on. In another part of the compound, a handful of sailors had been given permission to rest on the grass between a rail and the wall. Others quickly joined them in this area, which was usually off limits. Rather than resting peacefully, however, the men began roughhousing, tossing turf and other odd items, like old shoes, at each other. With disorder breaking out at two separate locations in the prison, the British commander, Captain Thomas G. Shortland, who had reinforced the garrison with 200 British soldiers the day before, decided to ring the alarm and call out the garrison to compel the men to return to the prison buildings at the regular lockdown hour of 7:00 P.M. The alarm and all the hubbub, however, had the opposite effect. A large crowd of prisoners ran to the main gate and, as they had two days earlier, forced it open. Shortland and a file of soldiers quickly appeared, while other guards began to line the walls. The Americans were not easily cowed, especially after their recent triumphs. They called out to the soldiers, dared them to fire, and even tossed a few stones at the men. All was confusion. With some difficulty the British soldiers and their bayonets pressed the sailors back into the main prison yard. Then a shot rang out. As the stampede of Americans sought shelter in their prison buildings, other soldiers fired their guns. If the sailors had been frustrated by their prolonged captivity, the soldiers were also irritated and exasperated with their unruly charges. Many reloaded their weapons and kept on firing, even though their officers later claimed to have commanded them to stop. The shooting lasted twenty minutes.[18]

The Dartmoor Massacre created a diplomatic problem. Both the United States and Great Britain wanted peace, and neither government needed this incident to create complications. Immediately after April 6, the British military held an inquest that exonerated Shortland and blamed the violence on the prisoners for attempting to escape. At the same time the prisoners, who had developed a self-governing committee system in Dartmoor, held their own investigation, declaring that Shortland had ordered the soldiers to fire and professing their own blameless behavior. Castlereagh recognized that these contradictory reports would only exacerbate tensions between the two nations just as they had reestablished peace and were about to discuss a commercial agreement. He also had to worry about Napoleon returning to France from his brief exile on the island of Elba. On April 16 he proposed that either

Henry Clay or Albert Gallatin, who were in London to negotiate a commercial agreement, go to Dartmoor along with one of the British commissioners from Ghent to draw up an independent report. Clay and Gallatin agreed in principle to the joint investigation, but claimed that they could not, "with propriety, take such a duty upon themselves." They suggested giving the job to Reuben Beasley. However, he was too busy preparing cartels to ship the prisoners to the United States to go to Dartmoor. The American commissioners settled on Charles King, the son of the Federalist Rufus King, who was in England on business. King teamed up with the British appointee, Francis Seymour Larpent, a minor government official, and quickly traveled to Dartmoor to interview dozens of soldiers and prisoners. They issued a balanced report on April 26 that viewed the "incident" as the result of an unfortunate set of circumstances. Frustrations had been building on both sides: the prisoners were anxious to leave, while the soldiers were tired of American misbehavior. King and Larpent concluded that the sailors were not about to escape on that fateful day, but they also acknowledged that with a hole in the wall and the clamor at the gate, Shortland had reason to think so. Although King and Larpent did not come to a decision as to whether Shortland had given the order to fire, they admitted that from "a military point of view" the initial firing was justified "in order to intimidate the prisoners and compel them thereby to desist from all acts of violence, and to retire" to their prison buildings. That first fire, it appeared, was ineffective and may have been purposely aimed over the prisoners' heads. This empty show of force had only emboldened the crowd of prisoners, who, believing the soldiers had blank cartridges, renewed "their insults to the soldiery, which produced a repetition of the firing in a manner more destructive." If the sailors had brought bloodshed upon themselves by this behavior, the continued firing arose "from the state of individual irritation and exasperation on the part of the soldiers." In short, the report blamed both the prisoners and the guards for the "unfortunate occurrence ... at Dartmoor prison."[19]

The King-Larpent report provided a diplomatic solution to the problem posed by the Dartmoor Massacre, but its conclusions still rankled both governments. In forwarding the report to the new American minister to Great Britain, John Quincy Adams, King admitted that he thought that Shortland had probably given the order to fire, but felt that there was no conclusive evidence to support this. Adams, in turn, accepted the general outlines of the report, but told Castlereagh that, despite the contradictory testimony concerning Shortland's culpability, he wished that there had been a trial of the commandant. Castlereagh responded by saying that sometimes a trial was "the best remedy to be resorted to, but there were others in which it was the worst," and that if there were a trial and Shortland were acquitted, it "would place the whole affair in a more unpleasant situation than it would be without it." There was also an edginess to the prince regent's official apology. Even as he offered to compensate the victims of the "unhappy affair" and their families, he asserted that the first firing by the soldiers had been justified by the "turbulent conduct of the prisoners" and was not caused by malice or "animosity toward the prisoners." He attributed the continued shooting to the inexperience of the soldiers, who were only militia and thus poorly trained, improperly commanded, and had a "want of steadyness." In December Monroe accepted this apology with a certain lack of grace. He declined the offer of compensation, while explaining that the president "does full justice to the motives" of the prince regent "which dictated it." Monroe, however, could not allow the British the final word on the causes of "this unfortunate event," noting that both nations regretted the incident but that they did "not agree in sentiment respecting the conduct of the parties engaged in it." With that comment, agreeing to disagree over the absolute responsibility for the affair, the diplomats could drop the Dartmoor Massacre from their deliberations.[20]

The people of the United States saw things differently. News of the massacre began to drift into American ports in late May. The first reports merely repeated what was found in British newspapers, which provided garbled accounts of a prison riot put down by the military.[21] Returning prisoners soon arrived with their own versions of events. Republican newspapers pounced on these stories told by men eager to denounce British atrocities. On June 6 the New York *Columbian* carried a short account of the massacre as related by Charles Andrews and promised to publish abstracts of his journal, which was signed by sixty-nine officers attesting to its veracity. The editor, having read Andrews's account, concluded, in language that would be echoed by countless other Republican newspapers, "that a more wanton, unjustifiable, and malicious slaughter of human beings, has never disgraced the political history of any nation" and that "[i]t remained for Englishmen to cap the climax of savage barbarity, and by an act of cold-blooded butchery of their defenceless captives, to set national law at defiance, and place civilized humanity beneath their feet."[22] Andrews blamed the entire affair on Shortland and the British soldiers, and stated that Shortland had ordered the soldiers to fire and that "*[s]ixty three Americans bled to gratify the spleen of a British turnkey! Seven of them were relieved by death from the task of telling the degrading tale.*"[23] Within a week, the New York *Commercial Advertiser* printed the report drawn up by a committee of prisoners, which stated not only that Shortland had ordered the soldiers to fire, but that he had actually grabbed a gun from one reluctant guard and begun the shooting himself. The committee, claiming to be impartial, declared that the massacre had been "a premeditated scheme" to punish the sailors for their refusal to eat the hard bread a few days before and that Shortland had "determined on the diabolical plan of seizing the first slight pretext to turn the military to butcher the prisoners for the gratification of his malice and revenge." They also claimed that Shortland was intoxicated.[24] These accounts were reprinted in Republican newspapers and molded popular perceptions of the tragedy at Dartmoor. Moreover, the arrival of each cartel ship packed with returning prisoners seemed only to corroborate this version of events.[25] Republicans proclaimed the Dartmoor Massacre a "cowardly and malignant barbarity," a "cold blooded murder of our countrymen" that "surpasses in Savage ferocity, any deed that ever blackened the history of the most barbarous age," and called for revenge for our "slaughtered countrymen."[26] They even compared the massacre to the French reign of terror, calling it "one of the most foul, barbarous, unrelenting and unparalleled massacres that have ever disgraced the annals of any civilized age or country, not excepting the bloodiest and the foulest murders committed by the demon *Robspierre*, *Carriere*, *Marat*, and their diabolical associates, in the revolution of France." Before the end of June you could purchase an engraving of Dartmoor Prison, along with the committee account, for twenty-five cents.[27] Publishers rushed to print not only Andrews's story of Dartmoor, with its own illustrations, but also the committee report and other prisoner journals.[28]

Republicans were stunned by the appearance of the King-Larpent conclusions. Even before it appeared in print, Republicans voiced doubts concerning the report. The Dartmoor prisoners warned that they did not expect a fair report because they believed that King and Larpent were more interested in interviewing Shortland and the soldiers than the prisoners.[29] Many Republican editors agreed, and declared that there was no need for the report because there was plenty of public testimony sworn under oath by "men of as much worth and probity as Mr. LARPENT and Mr. KING," and to doubt the word of such testimony was "a blot upon the fame of men who have fought for their country, or suffered in her cause."[30] Once the final report was released in the United States in mid-July, Republicans denounced its failure to condemn Shortland and attacked it as pro-British and anti-American.[31] The prisoners issued a formal response detailing how they believed their evidence had been ignored.[32] The *Baltimore Patriot* pronounced the King-Larpent report "unsatisfactory" and expressed "indignation and contempt, at the cold, servile manner in which Mr. King treats the massacre of American citizens."[33] Other Republican editors denounced King as too conciliatory, and believed that had he acted in a "firm, manly, and independent manner" he would have insisted on Shortland's culpability.[34] "Under a guise of impartiality and candor," wrote one commentator, "this report is evidently nothing but a memoir justicative of the British side of the question."[35] Many Republicans wondered how a scion of the Federalist Rufus King had been given such a grave responsibility, noting that Charles King had been in London on private business and thus was not recognized in Europe as acting under any public authority. The inquiry was "of too high import to be settled between *young* Mr. King, and an unknown British lawyer;

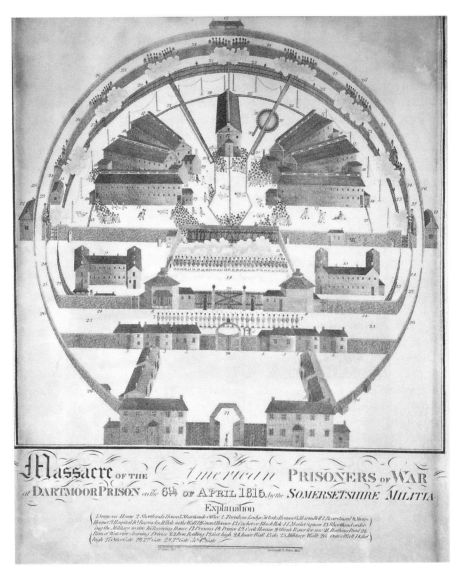

ILLUSTRATION 18. Dartmoor Massacre. For many Americans the Dartmoor Massacre was an atrocious action taken by the British and a denial of sailors' rights. Within days of the news of the massacre reaching the shores of the United States printers published engravings of the Dartmoor Prison, with its unique circular shape, and British soldiers firing upon unarmed prisoners. This illustration demonstrates that the Americans were not trying to escape as they ran for the safety of their prison buildings. Peabody Essex Museum, Salem, Massachusetts.

for if *sailors' rights* are worthy of the consideration of government, *sailors' blood* is a subject of equal magnitude."[36]

At first the Federalists moved cautiously in reacting to Dartmoor and urged Americans not to rush to judgment. They admitted that an atrocity had occurred, but they also believed that English justice would prevail and that all guilty parties would be punished. "The criminal laws of England never sleep over murder," the Baltimore *Federal Republican* asserted, "nor do they make distinctions between characters or persons." If the stories about Shortland were true, then he would be hanged "if there be but one rope or gallows in England."[37] Another Federalist admitted that "[t]he liberal minded American citizen, of whatever party, will sincerely regret the murder of his countrymen in Dartmoor prison," but reminded his readers that "he will suspend his judgement, and moderate his anger, till if possible, some mitigatory circumstances are known, which may lessen the apparent enormity, or account for the unparalleled atrocity of conduct."[38] The Federalists also charged the Republicans with using the Dartmoor Massacre for political purposes to drum up animosity against Great Britain. Some Federalists went so far as to claim that the War Hawks wanted a return to outright hostilities with Great Britain.[39]

Given the Federalist concerns, the King-Larpent report appeared as a godsend to defuse an explosive political and diplomatic situation. The report so fulfilled Federalist expectations that they could print it "just as we have received it, unbiased by a single remark," since "[w]e think it is more to be relied upon, than the multitude of inflammatory publications that have appeared in the different newspapers."[40] "We trust that a statement obviously so just and dispassionate," wrote another Federalist, "will . . . allay those hostile feelings it has been the study of so many to excite."[41] Much to the Federalists' chagrin, "those hostile feelings" were not immediately allayed; instead, the King-Larpent report drew fire as a pro-British and pro-Federalist document. Federalists responded by defending the fairness of the report and the honesty of Charles King. As far as the New York *Courier* was concerned, King had done the best job possible in a nearly impossible task when confronted with mounds of contradictory evidence. In turn, the paper attacked the Republican diplomats who had asked King to investigate the killing of American prisoners at Dartmoor. "Was an American Ambassador abroad too elevated a character to concern himself personally and directly in so trifling a matter as the murder and massacre of his imprisoned countrymen?" the *Courier* asked. Moreover, both Clay and Gallatin were better suited to the task. King was a well-educated young man, but he had no diplomatic or investigatory experience. Clay was a seasoned lawyer, "conversant by long and brilliant practice in all sorts of trials," while Gallatin was "an experienced disputant, a close investigator, and an able diplomat." Both were in the public employ of the United States and were not really doing anything at the time, other than "amusing and enjoying themselves" in

England at government expense. These wily arch-Republicans had selected the "frank, open, unsuspecting, generous" and Federalist King, a private citizen who refused compensation for his efforts at Dartmoor, so that he could be their "scapegoat" in an onerous task.⁴²

Federalists also lambasted the Republicans for their abandonment of the sailors they claimed to defend. The Federalists declared that had Madison speedily sent cartel ships to England, the prisoners would have left Dartmoor before the eruption of violence.⁴³ They also complained that after the treaty had been ratified, the Republican administration still had not acted fast enough to gain the release of all of the prisoners.⁴⁴ "*Nearly THREE MONTHS after the receipt of the ratified treaty in London,*" the *Federal Republican* reported, "*and TWO MONTHS after the massacre in Dartmoor prison* (the Commissioners Clay and Gallatin being still in England, but not in Dartmoor prison) *TWO THOUSAND FOUR HUNDRED of our unhappy captives remained at that detested spot!*" In addition, the Federalists charged, once the sailors had been returned to the United States, the government failed to help them. Beneath a headline with Porter's motto, a Federalist editor exclaimed that "[t]o the everlasting shame of the present administration be it spoken, that notwithstanding we have been at peace upwards of six months, yet no provision has been made to afford assistance to the American prisoners which are landing daily from Cartels, pennyless, from prisons in Europe." This failure to aid American seamen led the author to ask, "Is this the manner in which they [the Madison administration] manifest their tender regard for '*Free Trade and Sailor's Rights?*'"⁴⁵

Although by the fall of 1815 Dartmoor had receded as a political issue in the United States, it remained a part of the rhetoric created by the war. Charles King never quite shook the opprobrium attached to his name for having signed the report on the massacre. King's career, however, was not irreparably damaged. He later edited a newspaper and eventually became the ninth president of Columbia College. For the sailors at Dartmoor, the massacre remained deeply implanted in their consciousness. The wounded, including several amputees, could look at their scars, or the space where their limbs were supposed to be, and remember each day the injustice of the British attack. But even the men physically unscathed by the massacre could not forget the sixth of April. We will never know how many forecastle tales were repeated about the massacre, or how many sailors cursed Shortland while at sea or on liberty ashore. We can only get brief passing glimpses of the deep psychological mark left by Dartmoor. In 1839 the New York *Commercial Advertiser* carried an obituary for a Captain Samuel Morrison, who had "fought for his country in the struggle for independence, and was confined in Dartmoor prison by the British. As was the custom of seamen in those days, he had stamped on his arm 'Success to the United States of America' – with a full spread Eagle that he might not be impressed to fight against the Americans."[46] Etched into this old tar's skin were words reminding him of the fight against impressment, and, in this brief obituary, the only experiences worthy of notice in his life were that he had fought in the Revolution and that he had been a prisoner at Dartmoor.

If Dartmoor became a part of the rhetoric inherited from the War of 1812, it did so largely because it reflected the struggle for sailors' rights that helped to give meaning to that conflict. Free trade and sailors' rights may have first appeared on David Porter's *Essex* at the beginning of the war, but the words in the phrase had a long history that pulled on both the patrician and plebeian heritage of the American Revolution. During the War of 1812 sailors and soldiers, as well as politicians and common folk, relied upon the phrase. Other language emerged to rally support for the American cause, but none retained the resonance of Porter's motto. Republicans used the slogan to toast victories, and the Dartmoor prisoners rallied to its banner to celebrate the end of the war. When Republicans seemed to abandon the values expressed in the phrase with the Treaty of Ghent, Federalists vainly pointed to their opponents' hypocrisy. Regardless of the actions of politicians and diplomats, Americans maintained their faith in the values of free trade and sailors' rights and would carry those words and the memory of that conflict with them into the antebellum period.

# PART FIVE

# MEMORY

Republicans began to mold the memory of the War of 1812 as soon as the conflict ended. Regardless of all of the difficulties the United States had confronted in the war – the often pathetic performance of the military, the political paralysis that contributed to one disaster after another, and a peace treaty that settled none of the reputed causes of the war – by simply declaring victory, Americans were able to win the peace. Federalists were outraged by this approach and correctly pointed out that the Treaty of Ghent ignored Porter's motto.

Republicans, however, did not abandon either free trade or sailors' rights in their diplomacy after the War of 1812. Americans could not and would not forget the issue of impressment, even if without a major European war opposition to impressment was more a matter of abstract principle than opposition to an ongoing practice. Diplomats repeatedly brought the question before the British and decried even the hint of a return to the hated policy. The British navy, for its part, generally behaved itself and avoided this irritant to Anglo-American relations. However, Great Britain was as obstinate as the United States in refusing to concede officially its right to search neutral vessels for seamen. In the meantime, Americans sought to protect deserters from the British military in the Great Lakes region in a series of confrontations that asserted the territorial integrity of the United States. Americans may have established the sanctity of their borders as a refuge for British deserters, but on the high seas the flag did not provide absolute protection for the crews on their ships. The controversy over impressment lingered in the background of Anglo-American diplomacy, surfacing in the 1820s and even into the 1830s. However, by that time, and certainly by the 1840s, while never definitively settled, the issue of impressment became less important for both sides.

Free trade remained at the core of a persistent dream in the postwar years that Americans could be the vanguard of a new world diplomatic order. As we have seen, free trade was a complex concept. Before the War of 1812 Americans had at least five different and overlapping definitions of free trade, which they associated with their revolution. When he ran up his banner proclaiming free trade and sailors' rights at the beginning of the war, Porter never explained what he meant by free trade. No doubt, he was thinking about free trade as neutral trade, but his use of the words "free trade," whether consciously or not, conjured up all of the definitions as they pertained to the heritage of the American Revolution. After the War of 1812, the multiple meanings of free trade continued. But it also becomes possible to disentangle them a little more precisely. Without a major European war creating a crisis, free trade as neutral trade, like impressment, became an abstract principle. Free trade as reciprocal trade became more important as the desire to gain reciprocal treaties emerged as a driving force in American foreign policy in the late 1810s and 1820s. Part and parcel of this effort was a concern with free trade as the attempt to break mercantilist restrictions.

Politics dominated the discussion of free trade in relation to tariffs and the domestic economy. Oddly, just as diplomats were seeking to gain reciprocity and open colonial markets, the American government was pursuing protectionist policies. If in the years leading up to the War of 1812 most Americans used the words "free trade" in reference to neutral rights, in the years after the war those words were used most frequently, but not exclusively, in discussing tariffs. But, just as in the years leading up to the war, we need to keep in mind all the definitions of free trade in order to fully comprehend the rhetorical impact of the words. By the 1830s tariffs became a political football battered about by the emerging Democratic and Whig parties. Free trade as laissez-faire within the domestic arena also became a political issue. The Democrats, who sought to limit government interference in the economy, lower tariffs, and speak for the common man, should have inherited the motto of free trade and sailors' rights. Yet, whatever the policies pursued by the emerging Whig and Democratic politicians, Porter's slogan was important enough that both political parties used it.

Free trade and sailors' rights also remained deeply imbedded in American popular culture. Sailors, of course, continued to use the phrase, both in self-mocking terms and more seriously in the assertion of their right to strike for wages. It also appeared in their own iconography and in the material culture of the general society. At times Porter's motto, as it was in politics, was misused and even abused in all sorts of ways. Yet its more serious meaning persisted, particularly among African Americans, who were struggling against both slavery and racism. By the 1840s and 1850s Porter's motto had begun to lose its currency. It appeared at times, usually as a shorthand explanation for the War of 1812. But it was referred to as the "old motto" and now seemed to have as much relevance as slogans from the Revolutionary War. Reciting the words might be a way to assert patriotism, but it no longer seemed to address the issues at hand as the nation moved toward the Civil War.

# 20

# Winning the Peace

James Madison knew better. The closing months of 1814 and the first month of 1815 had been fraught with tension as the nation stood at the brink of disaster. Word from Ghent was not good. The British had made outrageous demands and seemed to be stalling until they gained more victories in North America. British veterans stood poised to overwhelm a hodgepodge army under Andrew Jackson at New Orleans. Federalists in New England seemed eager to break up the nation and had met in a special convention in Hartford. The banking system was a disaster. Congress, even though dominated by Republicans, appeared unable to do anything serious to bolster the war effort. Madison – the man who had masterminded the Constitution, created the Bill of Rights, led Republicans in Congress in opposition to the Federalists in the 1790s, and served ably as Jefferson's secretary of state – was inept and ineffectual as a war president. Then the miracles started to happen. All that the Federalists at Hartford came up with were some proposed amendments that had no chance of ever being ratified. No treason there. On February 4, a dispatch arrived in Washington reporting Jackson's astounding triumph at New Orleans. A British army had been annihilated, and the West was safe. Ten days later a courier arrived from New York with word of a peace treaty, already ratified in Great Britain. The treaty included no concessions of territory. Even if it did not address the causes of the war, commercial protection and impressment (which, with peace in Europe, had become moot anyway), it was a peace. The nation had been staring into a dark and threatening abyss. Now, with cheering crowds in the streets, illuminations that brightened every window, and celebrations sweeping across the country, Madison decided to declare victory regardless of the reality. Yes, Madison knew better, but he also must have heaved a sigh of relief as he began the great lie that the United States had won the war.[1]

On February 18, 1815, Madison sent the Treaty of Ghent to the Senate for ratification along with a message that included some of the most duplicitous words that had ever flowed from his pen. As he sat amid the charred ruins of Washington, he began by congratulating the Senate, and the people of the United States, "upon an event which is highly honorable to the nation, and terminates with peculiar felicity a campaign signalized by the most brilliant successes." In case the Senate missed his meaning, he expanded on this mischaracterization of the war by declaring that it "has been waged with a success which is the natural result of the wisdom of the legislative councils," councils that had stymied his initiatives to raise and fund armies to fight the British, "of the patriotism of the people," who were divided over the war and had supplied the enemy, and "of the public spirit of the militia," who had usually run at the first sign of trouble and often refused to leave their own state or to invade Canada. He also praised "the valor of the military and naval forces." By the end of the war the army had won some battles, but had lost many more. For its part, the navy had gained triumphs at the beginning of the war and on the lakes, but was largely bottled up and unable to sail on salt water by the time of the peace. In short, Madison's comments on the war bore no resemblance to the reality of the nation's pathetic performance. Truth did not seem to matter. Madison believed that "[p]eace at all times is a blessing," and therefore should be "peculiarly welcome,... at a period when the causes of the war have ceased to operate" and, in another burst of bombast, "when the Government has demonstrated the efficiency of its powers of defense, and when the nation can review its conduct without regret and without reproach."[2] The Senate, elated that the ordeal of war could be so easily ended, unanimously ratified the treaty within twenty-four hours.

The lie was perpetuated by the administration when, just as news of the peace arrived, it released a long pamphlet written by Alexander J. Dallas on the causes of the war. Dallas had prepared the pamphlet, which also appeared in newspapers, at the instigation of Madison and Monroe with the intent of building national and international support if the war continued. Peace precluded that necessity. Yet the pamphlet still had its domestic political usefulness. It began by reminding readers that the British had changed the nature of the war by making territorial demands for themselves and the Indians at the beginning of the negotiations at Ghent. That the treaty contained no concessions of territory implied that the Americans had successfully defended their nation. Most of the pamphlet, however, rehearsed the diplomatic history of the United States from 1793 to the outbreak of the war, portraying the Americans as pursuing a "neutral" and "pacific system," as opposed to the British, whose "pride of naval superiority, and the cravings of commercial monopoly, gave...the impulse and direction" to their councils. Dallas declared that the United States had defended its commercial rights and its sailors from impressment, although he never used the phrase "free trade and sailors' rights." Dallas also rehearsed the efforts of the United States to pursue peace during the war, including the early attempts at an armistice and the failure of Russian mediation. The last third of the pamphlet dwelt on the "desperate and barbarous character" of the British, whose "pride and passions...were artfully excited against the United States" at the same time as the causes of the war were being removed by peace in Europe. Unlike Madison, Dallas did not declare victory. But his trumpeting of the Americans as "good guys" fighting for justice and peace, and his depiction of the British as evil warmongers out for revenge and territory, painted a white-and-black portrait of the conflict that made it easy to believe that by holding the nation together and preventing the loss of territory, the good guys had won, and the bad guys had lost.[3]

Most Americans needed little convincing. Editor Hezekiah Niles spoke for many in early March when he asserted that "[t]he last six months is the proudest period in the history of the republic," which contained "a galaxy of glorious war deeds, terminating in an honorable peace, happily signed in the very arms of victory; a period without a blot or blemish." Gone was the humiliation of the burning of Washington or the years of frustration in failed invasions of Canada. Suddenly it appeared that "[s]uccess has crowned our arms in a wonderful manner" as "[t]he eagle banner, sustained by the hand of God, through hosts of heroes, triumphantly waved over *Champlain*, at *Plattsburgh*, at *Baltimore*, at *Mobile*, and *New Orleans*." There were even "signal victories" at sea. The war thus ended "in a blaze of glory, as though the Great Arbiter of all things had decreed that the wisdom and fortitude of our government" – here he was talking about the president and Congress, who had agreed on so little the previous three years – "and the desperately daring courage, invincible patience and ingenious qualities of our people, should be tried in a short contest, to *secure* future peace and *establish* our mild and benevolent institutions." Both the politicians and the people could swell with pride at such encomiums, however exaggerated or even falsified. The great lie of the American victory continued to grow, aided, if Niles is to be believed, by the Almighty. "Hail, holy freedom! – What though traitors within, and barbarians without, assailed thy banner – they have retired before the nervous arm of thy sons, and left thy *stars* unsullied!"[4]

Other Republican editors shared these sentiments and perpetuated the idea – the fabrication – that the United States was victorious. Reporting the "auspicious and happy news of an honorable PEACE," the *Boston Patriot* congratulated the nation on its success and heralded the "unparalleled victory at *New-Orleans*" as closing, in words similar to those used by Niles, "the war in a blaze of glory." The victory had "placed America on the very pinnacle of fame," and "[h]enceforward, neither England nor any other country will be anxious to seek a quarrel with America." After a quick survey of the other

ILLUSTRATION 19. "A Glorious tablau of the Peace of Ghent." This allegorical print, probably published in 1820, represents the great lie that many Americans came to believe: that the United States won the War of 1812. Depicted are a host of ancient gods, facing left, acting for the United States; Britannia is bowed and humbled on her knees in the bottom left-hand corner under an obelisk listing the names of American heroes, beginning with Captains Rodgers, Chauncey, Hull, and Lawrence. The base of the obelisk lists several American military victories. In the background is a reconstructed White House, thus erasing perhaps the greatest American humiliation of the war. Scrolled across the bottom of the print is an explanation of what each god represents for America, followed by the assertion that Minerva "dictates the conditions of peace" to Britannia, which Hercules forces her to accept on Minerva's shield. Library of Congress, Washington, D.C.


recent victories by the United States, completely ignoring the defeats and humiliations, the editor incredibly concluded, "In reviewing the events of this most glorious of all wars, a series of the most brilliant successes and exploits on the part of our own country, *presents* itself, almost unbroken even by the semblance of disaster." As if this reconstruction of reality had not pushed the edges of belief to its limits, the editor asked, "What *real victory* has Britain gained during the whole war?" His answer – none! "On what part of the *ocean*, the *lakes*, or the *land*, have the laurels of her heroes acquired additional verdure?" Again, the answer was none. "Exultingly" pointing to the American battlefield triumphs, the editor asked if the British scenes of pillage and massacre at

Washington, the River Raisin, and elsewhere were "evidences of their prowess, magnanimity and honor." Speaking for later generations of Americans, the editor pronounced his verdict: "The faithful historian will answer NO! in a voice of thunder, and tell to posterity, that in the *second* war forced upon America for her *Independence*, she lowered the arrogance of Britain to a greater degree than it had been lowered by twenty years of conflict in Europe."[5]

Strengthening the Republican claims of victory was the fact that many in Great Britain looked on the terms of the Treaty of Ghent as a surrender. Republican newspapers quickly took note of how the British Tory press viewed the peace. Indeed, the fact that the treaty had been decried in the *Times*, "a London paper which . . . has shewn a malignant spirit of enmity toward the U. States," was enough proof for some Republicans that the treaty was "highly honorable to our country."[6] As one British paper explained, in a passage excerpted by many American editors, the British government had "attempted to *force* our principles" concerning neutral trade and impressment on America and failed. Worse, the British government had "retired from the combat with the stripes yet bleeding on our backs – with the recent defeats at Plattsburg, and on Lake Champlain, unavenged." The author, of course, had not yet heard the news of the British disaster at New Orleans. Still, he believed that "[t]o make peace at such a moment, . . . betrays a deadness to the feelings of honor, and shews a timidity of disposition, inviting further insult."[7] After all of the great claims and public discussion of punishing the Americans in the summer of 1814, and the investment in money and manpower during that campaigning season, the Treaty of Ghent, with its status quo antebellum, was a letdown. It also entailed abandoning territory occupied by the British army in the upper Great Lakes, around Fort Niagara, and in Maine. This surrender left a bitter taste in the mouths of many Britons. News of American chest pounding only threw salt on these wounds, and publications like Dallas's pamphlet on the causes of the war were, in William Cobbett's words, "all *pith*; all *home blows*" that should not go unanswered.[8]

The British reaction to the peace only encouraged American braggadocio further. Republicans simply sidestepped the shortcomings of the treaty and the fact that it did not directly address the reputed causes of the war, protecting commerce and ensuring against impressment. Like Madison, Republicans could claim that the peace in Europe made those concerns moot. More important to these Americans as they declared victory regardless of reality, and thus crafted the future memory of the war, was a pride of place in the community of nations. "That the War has given the United States a proud and commanding station among the Nations of the earth is indispensable," explained one Republican editor. Asserting "'*I am an American Citizen*,'" Republicans now believed, would "be not only a passport of safety but a pledge of valor."[9] At the celebration of the peace in one upstate New York community, the seventeenth toast was to the war. The toast also rhetorically asked "What have we gained by it?" The answer was that Americans had obtained "[a] national character. A proud and exalted rank among the nations of the earth. The fears of our enemy and the respect and admiration of the rest of the world."[10] The *National Intelligencer* ran an article, repeated in newspapers across the country, under the heading "All the Points Gained," that outlined four reasons for the war:

1. To put an end to the unretaliated spoliations of our Commerce.
2. To resist the Orders in Council.
3. To oppose the practice of Impressment
4. To vindicate the Honor of the Nation.

The first was ended by the declaration of war and the seizure by the American navy and privateers of British shipping. The second reason was erased by the British government even before news of the war had crossed the Atlantic. The American government refused to cede ground on the third reason as long as impressment continued. Once the Anglo-French war was over, "the practice ceased," and with it the third reason disappeared. "As the cessation of the *practice* and not the cessation of the claim, was the object of the American Government... a written agreement was no longer indispensable." Finally, the honor of the nation had been vindicated by both the navy and the army. The essayist observed that "[t]his obvious view of the subject ought to convince every body that *American rights* have triumphed over *British wrongs*."[11] Perhaps Henry Clay put it best in a speech in January 1816: "Let any man look at the degraded condition of the country before the war. The scorn of the universe, the contempt of ourselves; and tell me we have gained nothing by the war?" Clay then went on to explain that the present situation was entirely different. The United States was now respected for its character abroad, and had "security and confidence at home." Admitting that the nation had experienced some "vicissitudes," Clay basked in "the glory acquired by our gallant tars – by our Jacksons and Browns on the land" and believed that in "the great account, when it came to be balanced, thank God," the military heroics "would be found vastly in our favor."[12]

   Asserting victory also allowed the Republicans to tar Federalists who opposed the war as traitors and not worthy of political support. Pennsylvania Congressmen Jonathan Roberts admitted that although "we have not got a stipulation about impressments & orders in council nor about indemnity," what was important – and here he echoed the great lie expressed by Madison and so many others – was that "victory perches on our banner & the talisman of invincibility no longer pertains to the tyrants of the Ocean." That victory had a domestic as well as a diplomatic meaning, and "the triumph over the Aristocrats & Monarchists is equally glorious with that over the enemy." As such, "It is the triumph of virtue over vice of republican men & republican principles over the advocates & doctrines of Tyranny."[13] Massachusetts Republicans were even more vehement in an election campaign. They labeled the Federalists "a desperate and wicked faction . . . , united in the most wanton exultations at British triumphs, and [who] encouraged our enemies to victory and conquest." Despite their aid to the British and their attack on the Constitution, "This war has ended, if possible, more gloriously than that of the revolution, and the opposition have been more active than the *tories*, and *with much less excuse*." Repeating the great lie – and by this time probably believing it themselves – the Massachusetts Republicans declared, "The original causes of the war being removed," the Madison administration had achieved its goal of "a PEACE consistent with our interest, honor, and future safety." Moreover, "By their justice and fortitude, by the wisdom and firmness of our ministers, the valor of our navy, army, and militia, the patriotism of the *republicans* and the interposition of HEAVEN, *this peace has been obtained*." After the war, the United States was "[c]onfident in her strength, strong in her government, and honored and respected by every nation in Europe." Great Britain, on the other hand, had been "humbled and disgraced! Distinguished only by savage cruelties, petty plunderings, and wanton conflagrations." The Federalists shared in this obloquy and were "Degraded, debased, despised!" As far as the Republicans were concerned, the Federalists were "entitled to the detestation of Britain, the contempt of America, and the derision of the world!"[14]

The Federalists were aghast at these attacks and the Republican claims of triumph in the war. "ANTI-BELLEGERENS" thought that if the war had been fought for the principle of neutral rights, then concluding the conflict because the peace in Europe had ended the grievance was a surrender of those rights. He explained that it was "ridiculous, when men are forced into a shameful peace, and a total abandonment of all their pretensions, to claim the merit of success and victory." Logically, "[i]f victorious and successful," as the Republicans had claimed, Madison's administration "ought to be impeached for surrendering what they had so often declared to be our rights; for not demanding stipulations for the *future*, and indemnity for the *past*." In other words, if the nation had ended the war in blaze of glory, then the United States should have been able to dictate terms to the British. On the other hand, "if the war was unfortunate and ill conducted," as the Federalists believed, "then the peace was *necessary*," and perhaps even honorable. The author advised Madison to thank the "Prince Regent, in granting you such a peace, though it was an abandonment of all your principles, and all the objects of the war" as "a mere act of grace, and by it he has fixed you for a short time on the American throne."[15]

Whatever the claims of the Republicans, the Federalists recognized a fundamental truth – in the peace treaty the Republicans had ignored the principles that had led them to fight the War of 1812. In a tacit recognition of how powerful the slogan free trade and sailors' rights had become, Federalists continued to refer to it as a way to expose this Republican hypocrisy. Even before the war ended, Alexander Contee Hanson ranted against Madison's abandonment of the issues that had caused the war. He harangued Congress that the protection of seamen from impressment "is abandoned by the very authors themselves of the cabalistic words 'free trade and sailors' rights.'" And he proclaimed that "[t]he question of 'free ships, free goods,' is also put at rest.' The right of visit and search is implicitly conceded, & flag is not to cover the crew."[16] Under the headline "Sailors' rights and Free Trade, ABANDONED BY ITS VOTARIES," one writer in March 1815 exclaimed that the "impatient eye looks for the redress of our grievances" in the treaty, "expecting every moment to find in *capitals* of *gold* 'FREE TRADE AND SAILOR'S RIGHTS' secured; but alas! They cannot be found."[17]

In this contest over public memory, being right did not matter. In the wake of the War of 1812, most Americans did not want to hear that blood and treasure had been spent for nothing. Nationally, the Federalists had been discredited. Madison's great lie took hold and became part and parcel of the history of the United States. Books written about the war quickly assumed this interpretation. *An Impartial and Correct History of the War* was anything but impartial. The preface explained that "[t]he military talents which sprang as if into miraculous existence during the late war; the patriotic courage which displayed itself on every occasion; their successful triumphs in almost every battle, are proud proofs, that where genius is free to act, and that influenced by an *amor patrie*, no dangers are too difficult to overcome, no difficulties too great to be subdued," and claimed that "[i]n giving details of these events, these imperishable monuments of American glory, a strict regard has been had to the truth."[18] Even more absurd was Gilbert J. Hunt's account of the war, "WRITTEN IN THE ANCIENT HISTORICAL STYLE." Relying on the cadences of the King James Bible, Hunt retold the story of the war as the struggle of God's chosen people against evil – Great Britain. Republican ministers had previously cast the war in religious terms and portrayed Americans as modern-day Israelites. Hunt provided a biblical history of the conflict that a more critical reader might consider sacrilege. Reprinted at least a half dozen times in the decade after the war, in Chapter LV, verses 25 through 30 (yes, that is how the book was organized), Hunt ended his history with a paean to Columbia, the symbol of the United States:

25. But, nevertheless, if this war, like all other wars, brought evil upon the sons of men, it demonstrated to the world, that the people of Columbia were able to defend themselves, single-handed, against one of the strongest powers of Europe.

26. And the mighty kings and potentates of the earth shall learn, from this example of Republican patriotism, that the PEOPLE are the only '*legitimate sovereigns*' of the land of Columbia.

27. Now the gladness of the hearts of the people of Columbia, at the sound of peace, was extravagant; inasmuch as it caused them to let loose their destroying engines, that were now become harmless, and set in motion their loud pealing bells, that sounded along the splendid arch of heaven.
28. Moreover, they made great fires and illuminations in the night time, and light was spread over the face of the land;
29. And the beauty thereof was as if, from the blue spangled vault of heaven, it had showered diamonds;
30. And all the nations of the earth beheld the glory of Columbia.[19]

Madison's lie had won.

# 21

# Remembering Impressment

Despite the failure to mention impressment in the Treaty of Ghent, Americans continued to seek an end to the British practice of taking men from American ships after the war. Unlike the situation in the years leading up to the War of 1812, diplomats who discussed impressment with the British after the war were not fighting to protect the lives and rights of sailors who were immediately imperiled. Instead, they were concerned with more abstract issues and viewed impressment as a matter of principle concerned with defending the honor of the American flag. In a sense, the efforts to settle the question had little to do with Jack Tar himself, and were more centered on resolving a lingering diplomatic grievance that was a legacy of the omissions in the Treaty of Ghent. As such, the memory of impressment became entangled in a series of other questions that preoccupied American foreign policy, including a more general commercial treaty, ending the international slave trade, and the Monroe Doctrine.

American diplomats sought to settle the controversy over impressment in the spring of 1815. Shortly after signing the Treaty of Ghent, Albert Gallatin and Henry Clay headed for London to conclude the second part of their commission and obtain a commercial agreement with Great Britain. Only three of the five American commissioners at Ghent would be involved in these negotiations. James Bayard, who was ill, sailed for the United States only to die within a week of his arrival in Delaware. Jonathan Russell went to Stockholm, where he took up his duties as minister to Sweden. John Quincy Adams joined Clay and Gallatin on May 25, 1815, having been appointed the new minister to Great Britain. By that time it was clear that the British were not interested in discussing what they considered their right to impress the king's subjects from neutral ships. During their preliminary negotiations with Henry Goulburn and William Adams, two of the British commissioners from Ghent, and Frederick John Robinson, a member of the British Board of Trade, Clay and Gallatin suggested that the "first and most important point" concerning neutral rights was impressment. Since both sides were convinced that they held the moral high ground, "[i]t would ... be unprofitable ... to go into a discussion of the right." Instead, they called for a practical solution based on the Seamen's Act passed by Congress in 1813, whereby the United States promised to exclude British seamen from their merchant service if the British renounced the right to take men from American ships. Clay and Gallatin claimed that the United States would be just as successful in enforcing this measure as it was in stopping smuggling (perhaps a weak analogy in the wake of the Embargo and the War of 1812, during which smuggling was rampant). They did argue, however, that "[t]his system [the non-employment of British seamen] would apply to and operate upon every American vessel; whilst that of impressment reached only the cases of those vessels with which it accidently came into contact." The British agreed that impressment remained "most difficult to arrange." They assured the commissioners that their government was seeking ways "to prevent the abuses of which" the Americans complained, and concluded that if the American law excluding foreign seamen proved to be effectual, then there would be no need to impress. However, they also noted that the Seamen's Act had not settled "the question" concerning "who were to be considered British subjects – a question on which the two countries might not be able to come to an understanding."[1] Recognizing the intractable nature of the problem of impressment, and interested in drawing up a commercial agreement, the negotiators dropped impressment and moved on to other issues.

But not for long. In his message to Congress on December 5, 1815, President James Madison called for a law to limit "the American navigation to American seamen" as a "conciliatory" gesture to the British and as a means "of increasing the independence of our navigation and the resources for our maritime defense."[2] John Quincy Adams used Madison's comments to reopen a discussion of impressment in January 1816 in conversations with Lord Castlereagh, the British foreign secretary. Each side went through the same round of arguments used a few months earlier, to the same effect – no settlement. Adams told Castlereagh that there was "great anxiety" over the subject in the United States because it had "the greatest danger of future dissensions" between the two nations, and that the best time "to prevent a recurrence of the same evils" was before a new war in Europe broke out. Castlereagh was pleased that the United States had shifted its position and might pass a law prohibiting foreign seamen from sailing on American ships, but he didn't see any reason for his government to renounce impressment (the 1813 law had promised to exclude British seamen only after the British stopped impressment). Reiterating the position of his commissioners in May, he said that if the proposed American law were effective, then "there would be no British seamen on board American vessels *to take*," ergo "the practice of ... [impressing seamen] would cease *of course.*" He also, in complete contrast to the American approach, said that there was little sense in settling the issue during peacetime, since the British navy was not currently impressing any men. Finally, and here was the nub of the British position, he admitted that "there was still in England a very strong and highly irritable feeling on the subject; that the Government *could not* incur the responsibility of a concession in relation to it." Therefore, it was better to let any new American law have its effect and prove that the British had no need for impressment. Adams temporarily dropped the issue, but vented his spleen in a letter to Secretary of State James Monroe by asserting that "the outrage of that practice can never be tolerated by a nation of the strength and resources to which the United States are rising" and that "the only means of protecting their seafaring citizens in the enjoyment of their rights will consist in the *energy* with which they are asserted."[3]

Although Adams remained somewhat prickly on impressment and personally did not want to give any ground on the question, later in 1816, at the behest of Monroe, he again sought an agreement concerning the forced recruitment of sailors from American ships. In one of his last major acts as minister to Great Britain, on September 17, 1816, Adams formally opened negotiations for a comprehensive agreement on the outstanding commercial issues. He repeated the offer, first developed in 1813 with the Seamen's Act, to mutually exclude each nation's seamen from the other's maritime service. Adams wrote that the United States did not "expect to derive any advantage, in itself," from this measure, but believed that it would be "the means to Great Britain of reserving to herself the services of all her native seamen, and of removing the necessity of resorting to means of force ... to take men from the vessels of the United States."[4] Although this suggestion led to an intense discussion in the British cabinet about the possibility of settling impressment, Castlereagh remained unresponsive to the proposal.[5]

Still, the Americans persisted, and President Monroe had Adams, as his secretary of state, instruct the new minister in England, Richard Rush, to continue to pursue an end to impressment. Rush, like Adams, met a wall of intransigence that led him to conclude the British were "rigid and inexorable" in their "indefinite continuance of a practice more afflicting to humanity, as far as the scale extends, than was ever the African slave trade, and in the highest degree insulting to the rights and dignity of an independent and powerful nation."[6] Two months after Rush wrote these bitter words, Castlereagh shifted his position. On August 13, 1818, Castlereagh told Rush that he would accept the American proposition whereby American ships would exclude British seamen and British ships would exclude American seamen. But he added some caveats. He stipulated that the agreement, which would end impressment, should last for a set period of time, either eight, ten, or twelve years, and that it should allow for termination with a three- or six-month notice. Castlereagh also wanted to ensure that British officers could ask for a crew list when they searched a ship "for a purpose justified under the law of nations." Rush thought Castlereagh had his eye on upcoming negotiations at Aix-le-Chapelle, where he hoped to gain the right to search the ships of other European nations in order to suppress the slave trade, and that the British foreign minister believed that ending the impressment controversy would prevent the United States from joining with European powers in objecting to such searches. Whatever the motives, the British proposal led to extended negotiations that came close to settling the problem. Ultimately, however, both sides balked at an agreement. The draft treaty on impressment called upon each nation to create a list of all naturalized seamen to be protected. The American negotiators – Rush and Albert Gallatin – believed that it would be almost impossible to draw up such a document given the varied naturalization procedures for granting immigrants citizenship before the passage of federal statutes, and given the complex and dispersed record keeping in the United States. They also argued that any list drawn up by the United States would be incomplete and that naturalized citizens excluded from the list would thereby not be protected by the government. The measure would create two classes of citizens, some protected in their rights and some unprotected, and would therefore be "an unconstitutional act," since it would deprive some Americans of a privilege not "merely political, but of the right of exercising the only profession they have for the support of themselves and their families." The negotiations over impressment ended when the British representatives, who may have suddenly become unwilling to make concessions affecting national honor in the wake of Andrew Jackson's execution of two British subjects in Florida, did not respond to these concerns.[7]

If in the immediate aftermath of the war American diplomats could not get the British to abandon the right of search and impressment on the high seas, the United States was able to establish the sanctity of its terrestrial borders and protect sailors on the Great Lakes. As the British military began to demobilize in 1815, hundreds of soldiers and sailors deserted before being shipped out of Canada. Crossing the Detroit, Niagara, and St. Lawrence Rivers, these men sought sanctuary in the United States. American officials refused to return the deserters, and many American citizens encouraged and assisted the runaways, much to the annoyance of the British. Some deserters, in a replay of events that had led to the *Chesapeake* affair, joined the American military. After eight deserters escaped across the Detroit River in early September 1815, a British lieutenant with twelve loyal seamen entered into American territory and recaptured one of them. Governor Lewis Cass of Michigan was not going to allow this violation of the American flag to go unpunished. Local officials arrested the lieutenant as he searched for the other deserters. The Michigan courts tried and convicted the British officer of riot for his actions. The incident led to a protest by the British and had the potential to escalate into a major crisis.

Madison eventually pardoned the British officer and remitted his fine. When Secretary of State Monroe informed the British of these actions, he included an admonition that "[n]o principle is better established that no government has a right to pursue offenders against its laws, or deserters from its service into the dominion of others" and warned that "[a] departure from this principle being a violation of sovereignty, seldom fails to produce disagreeable consequences."[8] During the same period the British navy on the Great Lakes stopped a number of American ships in search of deserters. The Americans approached these searches with equal firmness, while at the same time offering to demilitarize the lakes. The British, not wanting another North American war, hoping to avoid a costly arms race, and interested in profitable commercial relations with the United States, agreed to this proposal, signing the Rush-Baghot Treaty, which limited the naval forces of both nations on the lakes, in April 1817. In the process they stopped searching American ships on the Great Lakes and no longer pursued deserters across the border. From the American perspective this was not just a victory for sailors' rights, it was a victory for all men, even British deserters, who hoped to build a better life in the United States.[9]

Despite the lack of an official agreement on impressment, the British navy almost completely halted the practice of taking men from American ships on salt water as well. In 1826, Congress requested Secretary of State Henry Clay to report the number of recent impressments. His inquiry uncovered two instances, involving a total of five impressed seamen, since the end of the War of 1812, although there was some indication that there may have been some others. The removal of two men from a merchant ship in Sierra Leone in August 1825 had led to an exchange of testy notes between Clay and Charles R. Vaughan, the British minister to the United States. Vaughan, based on an informal interview held by the British consul in Boston with the merchant captain of the American ship whose men had been impressed, claimed that the two sailors had volunteered for service in the British navy, that one was a British subject and that the other, who had been born in Norway, had been returned because he had a protection issued by the United States. Clay questioned the British consul's procedures, insisting that the interview should have been conducted under an oath sworn by a local magistrate. He believed that such an interrogation would have provided more details, such as under what conditions the men had *"volunteered"* for the British navy and what degree of coercion had been used in their recruitment. Clay also wondered, even assuming that the British consul's report was accurate, about some of the details of the story. Although the British insisted that the men had left the American ship voluntarily, Clay believed that a boatload of armed men, with a ship of war in the distance, had made any resistance impossible. In short, Clay thought that this action represented a bad precedent that the British government needed to disavow. The second case was summarized in an extract from a letter from Condy Raguet, the American chargé d'affaires in Rio de Janario, written in 1826. Raguet reported that three Americans had recently been impressed by the British. Although he did not provide many details, Raguet also indicated that there were probably other impressed Americans in the British squadron stationed off Brazil and that these men were being mistreated. However egregious these two cases of impressment might have seemed, they are striking in their small number. Moreover, the incident in Sierra Leone revealed that even if the British still insisted on their right to a British subject who had "*volunteered*" for service in their navy, they were sensitive enough to American definitions of citizenship that they had released a sailor with a protection even though he had been born in another country.[10]

Whatever the actual practice of the British navy, impressment remained a concern of American diplomats and emerged as a contested issue as the British pursued an agreement on the right of search for their navy patrolling the seas to end the international slave trade. Stratford Canning, the British minister in Washington in the early 1820s, repeatedly brought up the slave trade in conversations with Secretary of State John Quincy Adams, who persisted in connecting the British right to search for slave traders with the supposed right to search for British subjects to impress. Although the American navy was involved in intercepting slave-trading ships, Adams refused to accept the idea that British ships should be allowed to search American vessels without a guarantee against impressment. In December 1821 he told Canning that "unless Britain would bind herself by an article, as strong and explicit as language can make it, never again in time of war to take a man from an American vessel, we never for a moment could listen to a proposal for allowing a right of search in time of peace."[11] Six months later Canning was again urging Adams to accept the right of search, more to convince France to allow the British navy to search its ships than in the expectation that the British would have to search American ships. During the conversation Canning asked Adams if he "could conceive of a greater and more atrocious evil than this slave-trade." Adams retorted, "Yes: admitting the right of search by foreign officers of our vessels upon the seas in time of peace; for that would be making slaves of ourselves."[12]

Having used these extreme terms, Adams soon found himself in an increasingly awkward position. As Canning reminded him, congressional committees had repeatedly supported the suppression of the international slave trade, and were even willing to allow a limited right of reciprocal search. The pressure increased after Congress passed a resolution calling for the suppression of the slave trade by an overwhelming majority on February 28, 1823. Undercut by this groundswell of opposition to the slave trade, and with the Congress and the British in apparent agreement, Adams knew he had to make some concession, but wanted to do so without surrendering entirely the right to search and thereby ceding ground on impressment. He found his way out of this dilemma by seizing upon the fact that Congress had also called the slave trade an act of piracy. If the United States could get other nations to agree to label the slave trade as piracy, then the question of search resolved itself: pirate ships were outlawed beyond the protection of any nation and therefore liable to search and seizure. By calling slavers pirates, then, Adams could sidestep the idea that the United States was giving the British the right to search legitimate American shipping. Admittedly this was drawing a fine legal distinction, but it enabled Adams to appear as if he were not backtracking on his earlier position and surrendering the right of search for impressment. Armed with this diplomatic cover, Adams sent instructions to Rush to negotiate a convention on the slave trade. But Adams remained firm in his belief that there had to be some safe-guards against impressment, and his proposal for the convention included a provision that prohibited search for any reason other than checking to see if the vessel was engaged in the slave trade.[13] He also indicated to Stratford Canning, shortly before the British minister returned to his home country, that if Great Britain went to war and once again began impressing men from American ships, the United States "should meet it by a war as long as this country could be kept afloat above the sea."[14] Adams, however, hoped to avoid conflict and believed that an agreement on a host of unresolved questions could be reached through negotiations conducted by Rush.[15]

Events in Europe seemed to provide an opportunity for an Anglo-American detente. Russia, Austria, and Prussia had formed the Holy Alliance and appeared ready to assist Spain in regaining its Latin American colonies. This move presented a serious challenge to both Great Britain and the United States as they were expanding trade in the area. George Canning, who had become the British foreign minister after Castlereagh's death in 1822, approached Rush to see if the United States and Great Britain could take some joint action that would warn off the Holy Alliance from establishing or reestablishing colonies in the Americas. Initially, with the United States and Britain seeming to agree on limiting the reach of the Holy Alliance into Latin America, the moment looked right to settle the outstanding maritime issues – impressment, neutral rights, and the slave trade. As late as December 8, 1823, Adams sent secret instructions to Rush in which he optimistically exclaimed "that the opening to a cordial harmony, in the policy of the United States and of Great Britain offered on this occasion, may be extended to the general relations between the two Countries."[16] But that cordiality only carried so far. Ultimately the two countries did not act in concert on Latin America. Within Europe, the British came to an understanding with France in the Polignac Memorandum of October 1823, in which both nations agreed not to assist Spain in recapturing its colonies. This effectively ended the threat of interference by the Holy Alliance in the Western Hemisphere. In turn, on December 2, 1823, the American government drew up its more forcefully worded Monroe Doctrine, declaring that any interference by European powers in the Western Hemisphere would be considered an act of aggression against the United States.[17]

Once the geopolitical dust had settled from the Holy Alliance crisis, Canning and Rush turned to negotiating both the slave trade and neutral rights in early 1824. Following his instructions from Adams, Rush was willing to separate the two questions. On March 13, 1824, the two diplomats agreed to a convention for the suppression of the slave trade that included a limited right of search. It stated that the citizens and subjects of both countries who were involved in the slave trade would be considered pirates, that both navies would join in the suppression of the slave trade, and that they had the right to search each other's merchant ships, unless a war ship from the other nation were present. To safeguard against impressment the convention also provided that no sailor would be taken out of his ship, and that the officers in each navy would not abuse the right of search. After all of this effort, however, the treaty ran into problems in the Senate. In part because Adams had political opponents in the Senate who wanted to embarrass him before the election of 1824, and in part because the memory of the insult to national honor of British ships stopping and searching American vessels before the War of 1812 remained so vivid, the Senate amended the convention to limit the right of search to African waters. The British rejected this change, and the convention was never ratified.[18]

In the meantime the negotiations over neutral rights came to naught. After Richard Rush presented the idea of a treaty dealing with maritime rights, the British asked him if he was willing to proceed without including impressment. Rush responded, "I was unwilling to enter at all upon other points of maritime law, unless the question of impressment was received by Great Britain as a part of the negotiation." When the British asked for new assurances about the use of British subjects on American ships, Rush could offer nothing beyond what had previously been put on the table. Rush's insistence on giving priority to impressment was on his own initiative, but he was also reiterating the position taken in earlier negotiations and that Adams had previously supported. Rush believed that impressment transcended "not only the importance of any other" question, "but the collective importance of them all." He explained further: "I knew of no other [issue] so closely linked in with the rights, the sovereignty, and the peace of the Republic." The British reaction was equally predictable. They considered searching neutral vessels for their subjects to impress as essential to Britain's highest interests, one that they deemed "as incontrovertible as it was ancient. It was a right interwoven with the frame" of their laws, and vital to the strength and protection of their nation. Although the British reaction reflected the fact that they no longer needed to be nice to the Americans in order to get a slave trade agreement that included the right of search, as well as their annoyance at the way the United States had proclaimed the Monroe Doctrine, this exchange stands as a testament to the memory of the impressment controversy on both sides. Even in the 1820s, even when the British were not taking men from American ships, and even when the British and the Americans seemed to be getting along, impressment could serve as a stumbling block in Anglo-American relations.[19]

Impressment, like Douglas MacArthur's old soldiers, did not die; it just faded away. As it declined as a controversy, however, American diplomats did not fully forget it. When Albert Gallatin served as minister to Great Britain in 1826 and 1827, he briefly discussed impressment with the British but did not pursue it. Instructions to subsequent American representatives in London frequently mentioned impressment and indicated a desire to negotiate the question if the British were willing to do so. By 1831 it was possible to say that impressment was "[a] question of no present importance" to the United States, but that it was also "of the most grave influence on our future peace." As Secretary of State Edward Livingston explained to Martin Van Buren, Andrew Jackson's new minister in London: "With the means now at our command of avenging insult and resisting aggression, the spirit of the people will no longer brook a practice consistent only with a state of actual vassalage." Livingston believed that "the first well authenticated act of aggression of this kind will be the signal for arraying the maritime force of the United States with that of the enemy with whom Great Britain may then be contending."[20] American officials, following the bellicose tack of John Quincy Adams, made it clear to the British that impressment from American ships meant war. As late as 1842, Daniel Webster recited the history of the subject for Lord Ashburton in a formal note attached to the treaty that they negotiated. Webster declared that "[t]he American Government, then, is prepared to say that the practice of impressing seamen from American vessels cannot be allowed to take place" and proclaimed that "[f]ifty years' experience, the utter failure of many negotiations, and a careful reconsideration of the whole subject" demonstrated the truth of Thomas Jefferson's statement in 1792 that "the simplest rule will be, that the vessel being American shall be evidence that the seamen on board are such."[21]

However much Webster and other diplomats decried impressment, they were more interested in defending national honor than in protecting sailors, as seen in their insistence on limiting the British right of search in the royal navy's efforts to stop the slave trade. Starting in 1815, American diplomats repeatedly sought a formal British promise to stop the practice of pressing men from American ships. The British were equally stubborn and refused to make any official concession. However, as Lord Ashburton informed Webster in 1842, the British had long since given up the practice.[22] Although the connection between the right of search, the slave trade, and the sanctity of the American flag persisted as an irritant in Anglo-American relations to the eve of the Civil War, impressment gradually disappeared as a point of contention.

# 22

# The Persistent Dream

American diplomats did not let free trade fade away, at least when it came to neutral rights, reciprocity, and the breaking up of mercantilist monopolies. These three overlapping notions of free trade became the centerpiece of American foreign policy in the years after the War of 1812. The United States gained limited international recognition for neutral rights, which, like impressment, was more a matter of principle in a world at peace than the real problem it had been during the Anglo-French conflicts before 1815. However, as far as reciprocity and opening trade with European colonies in the West Indies and elsewhere were concerned, what was not won on the battlefield was achieved through diplomacy and a shifting global context. The American triumph was not complete, but in pursuing the persistent dream of a new diplomatic order, the postwar generation proved to be far more successful than their revolutionary fathers.

After the Treaty of Ghent the United States sought a comprehensive agreement on neutral rights with Great Britain that would avoid the problems that had previously bedeviled Anglo-American relations. In the spring of 1815, Clay and Gallatin raised questions about trade with an enemy's colonies, the definition of what constituted a blockade, and the treatment of belligerent privateers and prizes, but they did not insist on including these issues in negotiations that led to a commercial convention in July.[1] This pattern reappeared almost every time American diplomats began serious discussions with the British. When John Quincy Adams sent his note to open negotiations on a new commercial accord in 1816, he suggested that "[i]t is equally desirable, in the view of the American Government, to arrange, at this time, every question relating to neutral rights, particularly those concerning blockade; contraband of war; visits at sea of merchant vessels by ships of war; the trade with the colonies of enemies; and between them and the parent country; and the trade from one port of an enemy to another." As Adams explained, "The tendency of discordant principles upon these points to embroil neutral and belligerent states with each other has been shown by the melancholy experience of the ages." Adams hoped for an agreement based on principles already accepted (so he claimed) by the British in order "to guard against collisions, which the recollection of the past so forcibly admonishes the rulers of both nations to obviate, if possible, for the future."[2] In the prolonged exchanges that followed, neutral rights got lost in the need to address other, more pressing matters.[3]

Regardless of these failures, Americans clung to their dream of establishing the neutral rights embraced during their revolution and proclaimed with such tenacity during the early years of the republic. In the parcel of instructions sent to Rush for negotiations in 1823 and 1824, Adams counseled against being discouraged by the failure of the Treaty of Ghent and the Convention of 1818 to protect neutral rights. Instead, Adams explained that because of the rift between Great Britain and the continental powers of the Holy Alliance, and the war between Spain and the rebellious colonies of Latin America, the international situation had changed in such a way that it was now in the best interests of the British to safeguard neutral rights. "The world in which we both moved is no longer the same," Adams wrote. Great Britain's "national interests are no longer the same. They were belligerent; they are now neutral. Maritime war itself, and all the questions connected with it, *must* be affected by the downfall of the colonial system."[4] Adams then suggested a truly radical notion – "the abolition of private war upon the sea." This idea would mean abandoning both privateering and the capture of merchant vessels by the regular navy and would thereby secure neutral rights. Adams directly linked his proposal to the American Revolution, citing Benjamin Franklin's desire in 1785 to do away with privateers and the guarantees concerning enemy property in the Prussian Treaty of that same year. He also saw this proposal as an extension of the protection of private property already practiced by European nations on land and connected it to the abolition of the slave trade. In other words, Adams wanted to take the liberalization of international relations to new heights. Adams, who after all was the most experienced American diplomat, was no Pollyana. He did not expect the British to sign on to such an agreement immediately. He believed that "the seed was then" – the 1770s and 1780s – "first sown, and had borne a single plant" – the Prussian Treaty – "which the fury of the revolutionary tempest" – the French Revolution – "had since swept away." For Adams the present moment was "eminently auspicious for sowing the same seed a second time." It might not "now take root in England," but Adams insisted that he had "the most cheering confidence that it would ultimately bear a harvest of happiness to mankind and of glory to this Union."[5] Ever pragmatic, despite such flights of fancy, Adams also suggested a variety of more standard protections for neutral rights. As we have already seen, when the British refused to include a discussion of impressment as part of the consideration of neutral rights, the talks ended before they had really even begun.[6]

The United States did not limit its concern for neutral rights to Great Britain. Adams was interested in convincing the reactionary regimes of the Holy Alliance of the righteousness of his cause. He prefaced his instructions to Rush by citing the Christian orientation of the Holy Alliance, believing that it reflected the commitment "to the principle that it is among the most indispensable duties of the rulers of mankind to combine their exertions for the general amelioration of the condition of man."[7] Adams wanted to propose his projected British treaty on commercial and neutral rights to France, Russia, "and all the maritime powers of Europe" in the belief that they, too, might eventually embrace a new world order of international relations that guaranteed the rights and property of everyone.[8]

Adams did not get to share his most idealistic vision with other nations. But that did not stop American diplomats from including some provisions for the protection of neutral trade in a number of treaties. As it had since American independence, "free ships make free goods" remained the goal. The 1815 Algerian Treaty, although the wording differed from the standard formula of earlier treaties, contained a comprehensive guarantee that declared, "If any goods belonging to any nation with which either of the parties are at war should be loaded on board of vessels belonging to the other party, they shall pass free and unmolested, and no attempt shall be made to take or detain them."[9] The 1816 and 1827 treaties with Sweden reaffirmed the "free ships shall make the merchandises free" provision (Article 7) of the 1783 Swedish treaty and also provided some definition of blockades.[10] The Prussian Treaty of 1828 confirmed the "free ships make free goods" article (Article 12) of the 1785 treaty with Prussia and the detailed protections of neutral rights spelled out in the 1799 treaty (Articles 12–24), including the agreement to act "in concert with other maritime Powers" in the future in order "to ensure just protection and freedom to neutral navigation and commerce" and to "advance the cause of civilization and humanity."[11] Some commercial treaties followed the 1799 Prussian treaty in other ways by recognizing that "free ships make free goods" might not work when one of the warring parties did not agree to the policy. The transcontinental treaty with Spain in 1819, best known for ceding Florida to the United States, followed this pattern: "if either of the two Contracting Parties shall be at War with a Third Party, and the other Neutral, the Flag of the Neutral shall cover the property of Enemies whose Government acknowledge this principle [free ships make free goods] and not of others."[12] Similar provisions were included in treaties with Colombia (1824), Brazil (1828), Mexico (1831), and Chile (1832 and 1833).[13] Although most commercial treaties with European powers excluded any "free ships make free goods" article, the protection of neutral rights in time of war remained an important goal of American foreign policy into the twentieth century.[14]

If diplomatic hopes to guarantee free trade in terms of neutral rights were only partially fulfilled, Americans were much more successful in gaining free trade through reciprocity – agreements that granted the merchants of both trading partners the same tariffs and tonnage duties as levied on their own citizens. In many ways reciprocity had been the Holy Grail of American foreign policy since the Revolution. As John Quincy Adams explained in a cabinet meeting in 1821, "Reciprocity is the law of freedom applied to intercourse between nations, as equal rights form the standard of freedom in civil society. The great principle was assumed at the very period of our Declaration of Independence, and has formed the basis of our commercial policy ever since."[15] Written into the Model Treaty of 1776, Americans had been unable to generate much international interest in the idea before 1815. Then the world of commerce changed. On March 3, 1815, Congress passed one of the most significant, and one of the least heralded, pieces of legislation of the nineteenth century. This law promised to remove all discriminatory tonnage duties on any nation that reciprocated and removed discriminatory duties on American merchants. Introduced by Senator Samuel Smith of Maryland, the measure was cast in the most pragmatic terms and was aimed mostly at Great Britain. Smith argued that the British countervailing duties in response to the discrimination practiced in American ports, now that peace had been restored, would quickly bring almost all trade into British ships. He also feared that other countries would follow a similar policy. "We are now at peace with the European nations," Smith explained, and "[i]t is in our interest that there should be no cause of future misunderstanding with them. If we continue our discriminating duties, and they continue their countervailing duties, the result must be, that our ships will be rendered useless." Increasing duties even more in reaction to the duties levied by other governments would only bring trade wars, which would increase prices and aggravate the situation. Smith asked if it would not be better "for us to agree to meet the nations of Europe on equal terms – the ships of each to be admitted into the ports of the other on the same terms with their own ships? Are we afraid of our want of enterprise, industry, or capital?" Smith answered his own questions: "For one, I am ready to agree" to establish reciprocal duties "and feel confident that the American merchant is equal in a fair competition to the merchant of any other nation."[16] The statute breezed through both houses of Congress and was quickly signed by President Madison.[17]

Of course, the law would have been a meaningless gesture had other nations refused to reciprocate. Fortunately for the United States, several European nations responded to the American overtures, beginning with the biggest prize, and surprise, of them all – Great Britain. The Convention of 1815 had many shortcomings as far as the United States was concerned. It did not address impressment or neutral rights, and it did not open the British West Indies to American ships. The agreement was also a temporary measure set to last only four years. Yet, along with the Reciprocity Act passed by Congress, it fulfilled a goal of American foreign policy established in the Model Treaty of 1776 by setting up reciprocity in a commercial arrangement between the United States and Great Britain. It also prevented discriminatory duties on imports and exports or on tonnage duties (but allowed drawbacks – government rebates – on re-export items from either country). In addition, the convention provided for Americans most-favored-nation status on trade between the United States and Calcutta, Madras, Bombay, and Penang. The Convention of 1818 renewed the reciprocity provisions for ten years, and a new agreement in 1827 extended reciprocity indefinitely. These treaties established a pattern for American commercial relations that has lasted to the present day.[18]

The British acceptance of reciprocity represented a reversal of earlier policies and marked the growing popularity of the free trade doctrine of Adam Smith. It also reflected the realization that an expanding American economy meant expanding markets for Great Britain. As the son of Lord Liverpool explained, "of all the powers on earth, America is the one whose increasing population and immense territory, furnish the best prospect for British produce and manufactures."[19] A contest over discriminatory duties, especially as their economy struggled to recover from decades of war, was not in the best interests of the British. Moreover, after the Treaty of Ghent, Lord Castlereagh pursued a policy of appeasement toward the United States. He worked to make sure that whatever his other diplomatic problems, his North American front was not only secure but also benign. At the same time that British and American negotiators were deciding on the Convention of 1815, Napoleon was marching from Paris toward Waterloo. During the negotiations for the Convention of 1818, Castlereagh was preparing to go to a European congress at Aix-le-Chapelle, where he would have to deal with the increasingly disgruntled continental powers forming the Holy Alliance. In these circumstances, good relations and profitable trade with the United States made sense.[20]

The French were not so ready to accept the new world order. They, too, were reeling from their wartime experiences and sought ways to revive their battered merchant marine and economy. In 1817 France claimed that according to the 1803 treaty with the United States, its merchants should enjoy most-favored-nation status in Louisiana and that they should pay the same low duties as the British. Adams rejected this interpretation, arguing that the British were granted lower tonnage duties because they had signed a reciprocal agreement with the United States and that to grant France the equivalent would mean that France would "enjoy as a free gift that which is conceded to other nations for a full equivalent." France not only would have most-favored-nation status, but would be placed "upon a footing more favored than any other nation."²¹ For the Americans the solution to this impasse was simple: signing a reciprocal treaty with the French. France, however, was not interested in this course and had set up discriminatory duties that would have meant that their ships would soon come to control trade between the two countries. In reaction, the United States enacted retaliatory duties on the French, to which the French responded with additional duties. This gave third-party nations, especially Great Britain, an advantage in the Franco-American trade. In 1822 an agreement was worked out whereby a measured reciprocity would divide American and French trade roughly in half between the two countries. Each nation was allowed to retain some discriminatory duties that would be reduced by one-fourth every two years until the duties all but disappeared or until either country renounced the treaty. Even if, as secretary of state, Adams saw this acceptance of limited discrimination "as surrendering the broad and liberal principle of reciprocity, upon which our whole commercial system from the first organization of our Government has been founded," it was successful: by 1827 Franco-American trade had come to be dominated by the United States, and, despite falling short of full reciprocity, the duties of both nations were roughly equal.²²

During the late 1810s and 1820s the United States sought reciprocity with several other European countries. Efforts to come to agreements with Spain and Portugal fell apart during negotiations.²³ Americans had better luck elsewhere. No deal was necessary with Russia, since that nation had no discriminatory duties to speak of and almost all of its trade with the United States was in American ships.²⁴ In 1815 the Dutch actually approached the Americans suggesting an end to mutual discrimination before passage of the Reciprocity Act. Because the United States exported to the Netherlands more than it imported, Madison did not think the deal worth pursuing. However, after reciprocity became official policy, the United States and the Netherlands entered into prolonged negotiations that ended with legislation passed by Congress on April 20, 1818, that established reciprocity with the Dutch not only for Dutch products, but also for those goods produced elsewhere in Europe that were usually shipped through ports in the Netherlands. In 1822 the Dutch, in an effort to revive their shrinking merchant marine, passed a discriminatory duty. The United States protested and threatened to retaliate, but in the end decided not to take any action; since so much of the trade was already in American hands, new discriminatory duties could only harm American commerce.²⁵ Jonathan Russell negotiated a treaty with the Kingdom of Sweden and Norway in 1816 that set up reciprocity in trade with the United States. Initially the agreement included produce from any Baltic country with a 10 percent premium added on, but the Senate insisted on deleting that provision and limiting reciprocity to Swedish and Norwegian goods in Swedish and Norwegian ships. An act passed on January 7, 1824, extended partial reciprocity to a host of countries, including Prussia, Sardinia, Russia, the Duchy of Oldenburg, and the Hanseatic cities of Hamburg and Bremen.[26]

The willingness to allow the Dutch to include goods from elsewhere in continental Europe marked a deviation from the standard American practice, codified in the Navigation Act of 1817 and reflected in Senate action in the treaty with Sweden, of exempting from discriminatory duties only goods produced in the signatory country. Because the ships from Great Britain and other European maritime powers often contained cargo from multiple countries, whereas American ships sailing from the United States generally had only American produce in their holds, this policy provided a competitive advantage to American shippers. The United States, however, began to move away from this policy toward an even freer trade in the 1820s. In his first annual address to Congress as president, Adams called for more liberal measures to open reciprocity to all goods, regardless of origin, carried by merchants from countries that promised not to levy discriminatory duties on Americans.[27] In other words, the exemption offered to the Dutch in the 1822 treaty was to become standard practice. This "broad principle of universal liberality," which, according to Henry Clay in 1828, provided "the most perfect freedom of navigation," would break and destroy "[a]ll the shackles which the selfishness or contracted policy of nations had contrived."[28] The new commercial treaty with Denmark of April 26, 1826, extended full reciprocity without restrictions, as did, with some minor exceptions, the July 4, 1827, accord with the Kingdom of Sweden and Norway. A treaty with the Hanseatic cities of Hamburg, Bremen, and Lubeck (December 20, 1827) did so as well, as did a new Prussian treaty enacted on May 1, 1828. The Papal States and Hanover were granted full reciprocity by presidential decree on July 7, 1827, and July 1, 1828, respectively. Congress wrote this policy into law in a statute on May 24, 1828, allowing the government to extend full reciprocity, regardless of the origins of the goods, to any nation that would do the same for the United States.[29]

Reciprocity was also the goal in commercial relations with the new Latin American nations, although the outcome of diplomatic efforts in this region was mixed. The first commercial treaty signed by the United States with any of the new republics was with Colombia on October 3, 1824, and included only a most-favored-nation clause. However, after Great Britain made its own reciprocal commercial agreement with Colombia in 1825, the United States claimed that its merchants should pay the same low duties with the South American republic as the British, under provisions of the most-favored-nation clause. The United States, which had denied France low duties under similar circumstances, was not as hypocritical as might first appear, since once the Colombians accepted the American demand, Congress passed a law on April 20, 1826, providing the Colombians with reciprocity. The commercial treaty with the Central American Federation (comprised of modern Honduras,

Guatemala, Nicaragua, Costa Rica, El Salvador, and parts of Mexican Chiapas) was the first American treaty to permit complete reciprocity with another country regardless of the origin of the cargoes. Adams was excited about this agreement and believed that it established an important precedent for international commercial relations. Unfortunately, it had little real impact; trade with Central America was limited, and the federation had a short and troubled history, ending its existence in 1838. The United States also agreed to a treaty with Brazil that established reciprocity, although the Brazilians insisted on including a provision allowing them to grant Portugal, because of strong historic and dynastic ties, some preference. Efforts to extend reciprocity to Mexico, Peru, and Argentina in the 1820s were unsuccessful.[30]

The impact of reciprocity on American trade was dramatic. Before 1793 the British dominated shipping to the United States. The Anglo-French wars from 1793 to 1815 provided a unique situation in which American shippers could expand operations while both Great Britain and France were preoccupied with their conflict. By 1800 American merchants controlled most imports and exports to and from the United States as well as the re-export trade. There were dangers inherent in this neutral trade, and those dangers led to the Embargo of 1807 and the War of 1812, which virtually wiped out American shipping. With peace in the Atlantic world after 1815, the advantages of neutral trade disappeared, and Samuel Smith was correctly concerned that the American merchant marine might not be able to compete in a discriminatory environment. Reciprocity offered an opportunity to level the playing field for Americans, and within a few years 90 percent of Anglo-American commerce, which was the largest single area of trade for both nations, was in the hands of American shippers.[31] American merchants also expanded and dominated their trade with other European nations, Latin America, the East Indies, China, and the Pacific. The level of exports and imports varied in the 1820s and 1830s depending upon economic conditions, but the total annual value of exports and imports usually hovered between 70 and 100 million dollars each.[32] There were good reasons for the American success in commerce. The population grew by leaps and bounds, as did overall economic activity. These developments meant the expansion of the production of export commodities, especially cotton from the South, and the growth of markets for imported goods. The American merchant marine also had advantages over many of its competitors, with access to capital through banking and financial services like insurance. An experienced maritime labor force also helped. American merchants paid higher wages than merchants from other countries, but their ships had smaller crews that worked harder and more efficiently than the crews of other nations. Moreover, Americans continued to build many ships of all sizes and became masters at design. Although American shipping did not dominate in every market – the British were highly competitive in Latin America, for example – merchant vessels flying the Stars and Stipes covered the globe in the years before 1860. Profits derived from these enterprises helped to fund American economic development in other areas, which led to more growth, which in turn increased the importance of commerce.[33]

Connected to reciprocity in commerce was the desire to break the monopoly of the European powers on trade with their colonies. Here, too, the new geo-political context of the post-1815 era, combined with spreading confidence in the ideal of free trade, led to new opportunities for American merchants. By the 1820s the independence of the Latin American states opened up a market that had previously been closed and promised to shatter the old colonial rules of trade. As Adams explained to Stratford Canning in 1822, "the independence of the South American provinces" made it "impossible that the old exclusive and excluding Colonial system should much longer endure anywhere."[34] A series of commercial agreements with these new states, many of them with some degree of reciprocity, broke the mercantilist stranglehold on this region. Spain even loosened its trade restrictions in its remaining colonies, including the islands of Cuba and Puerto Rico. Despite high tariffs, shipping to Cuba soon outpaced all of the trade with the British West Indies combined. The United States also worked to gain access to the rest of the Caribbean under European control.

The biggest problem for the United States was the British West Indies. Before 1776 the economies of the British West Indies and the British North American colonies had been intricately connected. Independence severed this tie and technically cut trade between the two regions. Smuggling, temporary openings due to emergencies (hurricanes and crop failures), and the Anglo-French wars permitted trade to continue at least until the Embargo of 1807. After the Treaty of Ghent, the new peacetime conditions allowed the British to reaffirm their mercantilist controls and exclude American shipping. Moreover, British merchants quickly gained an advantage by engaging in a triangular trade between Europe, the West Indies, and the United States. In reaction, Congress passed an act in 1817 adding an extra tonnage duty to ships sailing from ports closed to Americans. In 1818 Congress took stronger action by closing American ports to all such shipping and by making British merchants pay a special bond to ensure that they would not unload their cargos in the British West Indies after they left the United States. An additional measure passed in 1820 shut American ports to all ships from any British colony, even those from Bermuda, Nova Scotia, and New Brunswick, that had previously been opened. These efforts brought results; the British permitted American trade with the West Indies in 1822, but limited cargos to specific enumerated goods. In response, the United States allowed British ships arriving from the colonies that had been opened to the United States to enter its ports. To pressure the British further, the United States imposed additional duties on colonial produce imported in British ships until markets in all of the West Indies colonies became available to the Americans. This action triggered a trade war. The British retaliated by adding an additional duty on American ships arriving in West Indies ports. They also issued regulations in 1825, which took effect in 1826, closing their West Indies ports to American ships altogether until the United States removed its extra duties on British ships from the West Indies. Oddly, an American-controlled trade between the United States and the British West Indies continued, but now channeled through the West Indies colonies of other nations at added expense. The stalemate lasted until 1830, when President Andrew Jackson accepted the limited trade that had existed in 1825. Despite this opening, the British West Indies economy, in part because of the trade difficulties with the United States, had stagnated and, especially after British emancipation of slaves in 1834, never regained a prominent role in American commerce.[35]

The United States had more success in getting other European countries to permit American ships to trade with their colonies. In the 1827 treaty with the Kingdom of Sweden and Norway, the Swedes, who controlled the island of St. Bartholomew, not only permitted direct American trade, but also allowed American ships to carry goods between the island and Swedish ports. The 1826 commercial treaty with Denmark set up reciprocity between the two countries, including the Danish West Indies, but excluded trade between the islands and Denmark. Similar arrangements were worked out with the Dutch islands of St. Eustatia and Curacao. France relented from its limited mercantilist principles in 1826 by offering to remove discriminatory duties on trade with Martinique and Guadeloupe. Although the executive branch saw no real advantage in responding to the overture, since trade was limited to only the two islands and the French had not requested any action on the part of the United States, in 1828 Congress passed legislation to make the relationship reciprocal.[36]

Despite the failure to assert free trade in the Treaty of Ghent, Americans did not forget the dream of the Founding Fathers of a new commercial world order. Speaking for his generation, John Quincy Adams believed that "[a] liberal principle of commercial intercourse with foreign nations was, ... one of the ingredients of our national independence."[37] That ingredient was the essential element that bound together the major American foreign policy initiatives from the end of the War of 1812 until at least the 1840s, and was of even more immediate importance to national economic development than the expansion that has so preoccupied most historians of the period. After the Senate passed the Reciprocity Act of 1828, which allowed for nondiscriminatory trade regardless of the origin of the cargo, one newspaper editor proclaimed the measure "the largest stride towards the commercial millennium of free trade that the world ever witnessed."[38] Although party and partisan differences crept into some aspects of the concern for free trade, "free ships make free goods," ending discriminatory duties, and the overthrow of mercantilist restrictions transcended party during one of the most contentious political periods in American history. The willingness to use discrimination as a weapon to gain reciprocity represented the type of diplomatic muscle flexing that Alexander Hamilton had called for in *Federalist* Number 11 (which he later repudiated) and that James Madison and Thomas Jefferson had advocated in the 1790s. From the perspective of the foreign policy goals of the authors of the Constitution, the post–War of 1812 diplomacy of free trade, in terms of defending neutral rights, establishing reciprocity, and opening colonial markets, was a success.

# 23

## Politics

If politics played a minimal role in the application of free trade to neutral rights, reciprocity, and ending mercantilism, it was absolutely critical to free trade in relation to tariffs and the regulation of the domestic economy. Until questions concerning slavery engulfed the American political world in the 1840s and 1850s, free trade as the absence (or at least the reduction) of imposts and free trade as unfettered capitalism were the key political issues of the day. Although the actual words "free trade" were used most often in attacking higher tariffs, both anti-tariff free trade and free trade in domestic markets divided Republicans in the so-called Era of Good Feelings and contributed to the development of the two-party system. In the political debates that ensued, partisans articulated ideas centered on free trade with a new clarity. By the 1830s the Democratic Party of Andrew Jackson stood for low tariffs and minimal government interference in the economy, while the Whig Party of Henry Clay wanted higher tariffs and an activist government. As each side in this political debate scrambled for rhetorical tools with which to attract voters, they would sometimes return to Porter's slogan regardless of how applicable it was to their party platform, offering stark testimony to the potency of the words "free trade and sailors' rights" and the persistence of the memory of the War of 1812.[1]

The tariff became a critical issue only after 1815. In many ways the United States Constitution was written in order to collect a tariff and establish a reliable revenue stream for the federal government. The impost, as the tariff was then called, easily sailed through Congress during its first session, establishing a 5 percent tax on most imported items. Some luxury goods, like carriages, were charged an additional fee. A few Americans wanted higher duties to protect the production of iron and manufacturing, but before the War of 1812, there was no real effort to encourage any industry through a protective tariff. Because of the decline of trade during the embargo years and the War of 1812, there was an increase in manufacturing. These new businesses were threatened by the cheaper imported goods from Great Britain that were dumped on the market in 1815. In 1816, to protect this nascent industry, the Republican Congress passed a protective tariff that set a 25 percent tax on cotton and woolen goods as well as on other items. This action provoked a long debate over the costs and benefits of such a program, a debate that would continue for the rest of the century. As different political groups came to power the tariff was raised and lowered. In 1818, the 1816 tariff was extended until 1826. But protectionists increased the tariff in 1824 and again in 1828. After the Jacksonian Democrats gained power they lowered the tariff in 1832 and 1833, in part due to pressure from states like South Carolina. In 1842 the Whig Party was able to raise the tariff again, only to have the Democrats lower it in 1846.[2]

These gyrations generated arguments for and against free trade in a heated political atmosphere that had little relationship to the question of eliminating discriminatory duties. Reciprocity centered on whether or not all merchants, foreign and domestic, would pay the same tariff and tonnage fees, and not on how high such fees should be set. Therefore the debate over free trade as it related to the tariff did not challenge the multiparty support for the equality of fees regardless of nationality.

Those who wanted lower tariffs often did so based on personal interest, although they also developed more principled arguments in defense of that interest. Congressman Thomas Telfair of Georgia objected to the proposed tariff of 1816, claiming that it was a measure geared to the protection of northern manufacturing interests at the expense of southern agriculturalists. His most potent arguments, however, were rooted in a Jeffersonian faith in free trade. He warned Congress, "You are about to abjure that principle which was peculiarly your own, and the offspring of freedom, of leaving industry free to its own pursuit and regulation, and to assume to yourself the capacity and right of judging and dictating that labor which is the best for the people of this country." Telfair believed that the United States was an agrarian nation where "[t]he extent of territory, the genius of our people, the principles of our political institutions, have in their combination decreed, as by a law of nature, that for years to come, the citizens of America shall obtain their subsistence by agriculture and commerce." For agrarian free traders like Telfair, the tariff would "withdraw industry from its natural and accustomed channels" and prematurely make the United States a manufacturing nation, corrupt the country, and allow it to be dominated by monopolistic practices typical of Europe.[3]

Similar arguments emerged every time protectionists wanted to raise the tariff. In 1820 a memorial by the citizens of Charleston insisted that they had nothing against manufacturing, but they did object to giving manufacturers an advantage over southern agriculturalists. In a strange assertion by men from a slave society, the memorial insisted that it was "almost too self-evident for controversy, that, in every free or well regulated government, labor and capital should be permitted to seek and to find their own employment." These free market ideas led the Charlestonians to declare that "[a] government can never regulate to advantage the employment of capital, because success in the pursuit of wealth . . . depends upon local circumstances, on minute details, on personal exertions, which cannot be regulated." The memorial continued with an assertion of a free market ideology that Adam Smith would have been proud of: "It is equally obvious, that those employments of capital which are most profitable to the individual, must, on a general scale, prove the most advantageous to the state." The Charlestonians pushed this logic to its ultimate conclusion in relation to the tariff: "National [wealth] is but the aggregate of individual wealth; whenever, therefore, capital is diverted from one employment, in which it makes a certain profit," like agriculture, "to another, in which only a smaller profit can be obtained," like manufacturing, "the difference between these employments of capital is, exactly to the extent of that difference, an actual loss to the community." In other words, by adding a tariff to protect manufacturers, the government drained wealth from the nation.[4]

By the end of the 1820s, southerners had developed an elaborate argument against the tariff based largely on a belief in free trade. Writers like Thomas Cooper, an English radical émigré in 1793 who had first settled in Pennsylvania and later moved to South Carolina, where he became president of the state's college, helped to bring an intellectual respectability to the southern position. In 1824 Cooper published a short pamphlet on the tariff. On the first page of the tract Cooper conjured the memory of the War of 1812 by stating that "[d]uring the war the national motto was 'Free trade and Sailors' rights," and noted that these principles "are much more in danger from Mr. Baldwin's bill [to raise the tariff], than from the British navy." He then reiterated the arguments of Telfair, the Charleston citizens, and others. He even claimed that the measure was unconstitutional, since the tariff represented an unreasonable discretionary tax for the benefit of one group of citizens as opposed to another.[5] Two years later, Cooper published a more elaborate treatise on political economy that relied on the ideas of Adam Smith, Thomas Malthus, and David Ricardo to emphasize acting in one's own self-interest as the best way to encourage economic growth and to denounce the idea that one should sacrifice for the common good. Instead, he insisted that the collective result of each individual pursuing his own personal good would lead to greater wealth for everyone. He also reiterated ideas about commerce expressed by the revolutionary generation, that all trade was beneficial and "that human improvement, and national prosperity, are not promoted in any particular nation, by depressing every other, but by aiding, encouraging, and promoting the welfare of every nation around us."[6]

Although tariffs threatened the economic interests of the South most directly, anti-tariff and free trade ideas also appeared in other parts of the country. In 1828, "A FARMER" in Connecticut, echoing his southern cousins, claimed that the tariff protected the interests of manufacturing at the expense of agriculture and commerce. "Let it be remembered that it cannot be reconciled to the nature of man, or the spirit and general principles of our national constitution, that any tariff should long be willingly endured, of which all the advantages are for the manufacturer, and all the burdens on the merchant and farmer." Considering the protective tariff an "unjust *tribute*" paid "to the manufacturer," this author advocated a simpler and more equitable impost of across-the-board charges similar to the first impost established in 1789. Venerating the Founding Fathers, "A FARMER" declared that "This [level tariff] was the policy of an administration of the greatest patriots and statesmen that ever existed; of an administration that knew, and felt, and respected the rights of man." He continued, using a phrase that resonated with the rhythm and meaning – if not the exact words – of Porter's slogan, "Their [the Founding Fathers] motto was 'Free trade and equal rights.'"[7]

Whatever the support for free trade expressed by men like the Connecticut farmer and others in the North, in the late 1820s and early 1830s the words "free trade" became increasingly identified with the South. The 1828 tariff, labeled the Tariff of Abominations by its opponents, triggered massive opposition and a constitutional crisis as the state of South Carolina threatened to nullify the measure within its own borders. The debate that raged in the halls of Congress, state legislatures, conventions, political meetings, and newspapers lumped free trade together with nullification and the issue of state rights. Interestingly, most of the references to this controversy did not use the cadence of Porter's slogan, as in free trade and states rights, but instead reversed the order of words, proclaiming states rights and free trade. For example, in South Carolina proponents of free trade organized a "States Rights and Free Trade Association"; the *Winyah Intelligencer* ran the words "State Rights and Free Trade" across its masthead; and there was a short-lived newspaper published in Charleston with the name *State Rights and Free Trade Evening Post*.[8] The States Rights and Free Trade Association even proposed slates of candidates for elective office and held conventions in Columbia and Charleston rallying against the tariff.[9] Although there were times when free trade was listed before states rights, thus paralleling the structure of Porter's motto, the frequent appearance of states rights and free trade in the reverse order suggests that there was an effort, whether conscious or subconscious, to divorce this political slogan from the earlier one. In other words, by the 1830s southerners hoped to associate free trade more with lowering tariffs and states rights than with the other, earlier definitions of free trade.[10]

However much free trade became associated with the anti-tariff crusade, the other definitions – as we have already seen in the defense of neutral rights, the importance of reciprocity to diplomacy, and the efforts to end mercantilism – were not entirely erased from the collective memory. Free trade as it related to a free market economy also remained important. Indeed, there was a close relationship between the arguments for free trade in international commerce and for free trade in the domestic market. Repeatedly defenders of lower tariffs asserted the general principle that it was necessary to leave "industry free to its own pursuit and regulation" (in Telfair's words) and that "in every free and well regulated government, labor and capital should be permitted to seek and to find their own employment" (in the Charleston committee's words). This broad theoretical approach to defending free trade occasionally came back to haunt the opponents of the tariff. At the height of the nullification controversy, several newspapers reported the story of a southern merchant who was such "a great stickler for *Free Trade and State Rights*" that he plastered newspaper cuttings with those words all over his desk. Ordinarily, so the news item reported, "it is a custom, much honored in the strict observance" in the South that when a merchant bought a planter's cotton, the planter in turn purchased his regular supplies at the same store. When one planter went to a different grocery to obtain his supplies, "the merchant rated him for it very earnestly." The planter retorted, "'I saw *Free Trade* and States Right over your desk, and thought Free Trade was your political creed, I have only reduced your theory to practice.'" With obvious relish, the article concluded: "The next time the merchant's desk was observed, nothing but *State Rights* could be read on it."[11] This story may have mocked southern nullifiers, but it highlighted the fact that the concept of free trade as it related to domestic markets remained in use.

In fact, notions of laissez-faire in domestic markets became central to the Democratic Party. Andrew Jackson, after threatening military action, defused the nullification controversy by overseeing reductions in the tariff in 1832 and 1833. This action helped to buttress the emerging political coalition that made up the Democratic Party. Democrats identified themselves as producers and viewed the Whigs as part of a nonproducer elite. Drawn from a complex combination of southern and western agrarians, as well as urban working-men and immigrants, Democrats rejected an activist government whether it be involved in establishing higher tariffs, advocating internal improvements, or sustaining the national bank. Democrats were not against profit; they only wanted an "egalitarian commercialism" that would provide for "the personal accumulation of money."[12] The Democratic Party, as suggested in some of the language used to attack the tariff, espoused a strident individualism and a free market economy. Viewing any government intervention in the economy as wrongheaded, the Jacksonian Democrats were "opposed to all monopolies...believing that all men are not only born free and equal" but also that they "should have secured to them by law the same free and unrestricted right to acquire property."[13] These concerns can be seen in Jackson's attack on the Second Bank of the United States. Although Jackson did not explicitly refer to free trade in his veto message, the idea that markets should be open to all on an equitable basis lay behind his opposition to the monopoly privilege he saw in the bank charter. Admitting that distinctions were natural in society, Jackson insisted that "[i]n the full enjoyment of the gifts of Heaven and the fruits of superior industry, economy, and virtue, every man is equally entitled to protection by law." However, if government added "artificial distinctions, to grant titles, gratuities, and exclusive privileges" that made "the rich richer and the potent more powerful, the humble members of society – the farmers, mechanics, and laborers – who have neither the time nor the means of securing like favors to themselves, have a right to complain of the injustice to their Government." From this perspective, government should "confine itself to equal protection, and, as Heaven does its rains, shower its favors alike on the high and the low, the rich and the poor."[14]

Like their Democratic Party opponents, members of the Whig Party wanted to see economic development; but instead of relying only on individual enterprise, Whigs believed that government should play an active role in guiding the economy. Beginning immediately after the War of 1812, some Republicans decided that weak and indecisive government had left the nation floundering. The solution was to build upon an emerging nationalism and develop an "American System" that established a national bank (the Second Bank of the United States), advocated internal improvements, and raised tariffs to protect and encourage manufacturing. Led by Henry Clay in the 1820s, proponents of the American System became the nucleus of a National Republican Party. This political grouping, however, had disintegrated by the early 1830s, and in 1832 the Whig Party replaced it as the main opposition to Andrew Jackson and the Democrats.[15]

In response to the advocates of free trade, a group of writers, most notably Daniel Raymond, Matthew Carey, and Hezekiah Niles, provided an intellectual rationale for the idea that protective tariffs would foster manufacturing. In 1820 Raymond attacked the notion of free trade as short-sighted and denied "that the right of property was absolute in the individual." Instead, he insisted that it was "always relative and conditional," contingent on the general welfare of the nation. Raymond envisioned a paternalistic government that would act "like a good shepherd" and nourish "the feeble and weak ones in his flock."[16] He denounced Adam Smith and free trade, claiming that protective duties would ensure full employment and greater national wealth. Both he and Mathew Carey pointed out that a protective tariff also guaranteed higher wages for the workingman. As Carey explained: "One of two things must occur in this country. Our manufacturers must be protected by duties equivalent to the difference in the price of foreign labor, and to the rates of wool, &c. or wages must approximate to that of English labor, and the farmers must sell their wool as low as it is there."[17] Hezekiah Niles contended that the free trade position of the southerners reflected a minority view in the nation and that the majority of working people benefited from a tariff. Calling the "doctrine of 'free trade'... as idle *as the tale of an ideot twice told*," Niles argued that no nation practiced free trade and that "the population and power of Great Britain, France, Austria, Russia, Prussia, &c., &c., have been built up by liberally *encouraging* home production, and severely *restricting* foreign supplies." For Niles, the American system, especially the tariff, comforted "THE INDUSTRIOUS POOR" and cheered "THE WORKING MAN IN HIS MARCH TOWARD INDEPENDENCE."[18]

As stridently as the pro-tariff men denounced free trade, the protectionists and Whigs still embraced a belief in free markets in the realm of domestic policy. Nathan Appleton, who would later serve in Congress, defended the need for a protective tariff while at the same time pledging his faith in Adam Smith and agreed "fully in the general principle, that human industry is most productive when left free from restraint, unshackled by monopolies." He believed, however, that the British themselves did not practice free trade and that the first efforts of industrialization, which strengthened the nation, needed "inducements" to ensure success.[19] Niles went so far as to claim that the tariff debates had a negative impact on free trade on the domestic scene, writing that "[t]he incessant and ardent agitations of the tariff question has injuriously retarded the progress of the American System – and especially by preventing large investments in new establishments, *whereby the force of competition to lessen the price, has been materially lessened*."[20] An end to the debate over the tariff would unleash new capital investment and an expansion of industry within the United States. The Whigs believed that a secure higher tariff might initially raise prices. But they denied that there would be any monopolies, since all businessmen within the United States could invest in new manufacturing opportunities. The enticement of greater profits would bring more entrepreneurs into the production of goods, which would increase supply and drive down prices. Economies of scale would mean that manufacturers could afford to charge those lower prices, which, because of decreased shipping costs, would eventually lead to cheaper goods than imports. Thus, both the producer and the consumer would be better off, and the nation's wealth and strength would be enhanced.[21]

These basic laissez-faire ideas in the domestic sphere, shared by Democrat and Whig, anti-tariff and pro-tariff alike, permeated American society. During the long controversy challenging the monopoly of the Charles River Bridge between Boston and Cambridge in Massachusetts, advocates of the Warren Free Bridge dismissed the idea that their charter was unconstitutional.

They claimed their bridge protected the public welfare because it promoted "free trade which is interested in no small degree in cheapness of transportation."[22] Similar arguments against monopoly privilege appeared in New York City in the attack on the auction system, originally set up to facilitate the marketing of imports after the War of 1812. By the mid-1820s the auctioneers had gained so much control over credit that they were charged with being a "monied aristocracy" that influenced banks and stifled criticism. A public meeting against the auction system in 1828 resolved that "by monopolizing the sale of goods," the auctioneers had defeated "the industry" and rendered "nugatory the talents and enterprize of our own citizens." The "exclusive privileges to sell by auction," the meeting determined, "are at war with the principles of free trade."[23] Free trade was also an issue in labor relations. Early in the nineteenth century a series of court cases established the precedent that efforts by unions to set wages were conspiracies in restraint of trade. In 1806, Judge Moses Levy explained in the cordwainers case in Philadelphia: "The usual means by which the prices of work are regulated, are the demand for the article and the excellence of its fabric." Allowing the workers to join together and set wages was "the unnatural way of raising the price of goods or work."[24] These ideas persisted into the Jacksonian period. One newspaper commentator in 1835 objected to a recent turnout, or strike, by the tradesmen in New York, declaring that "Free Trade is the proper regulator in such matters, and any attempt to force prices by tariffs and combinations" was wrong.[25] Ironically, given the persistent resonance of Porter's motto, this attitude appeared in opposition to organizational efforts by seamen to defend their rights and raise wages. In 1834, New York sailors combined to increase wages from $13 to $15 a month and threatened physical harm to anyone who accepted a lower wage. Merchants viewed this action as a violation of the idea of free trade. After reporting one incident of violence, an editor urged the sailors to obey the law and advised "that Free Trade is better than combination." After another incident a few weeks later the same editor cautioned, "These combinations are dangerous things, particularly to the parties concerned." Not only would the strikers be punished for breaches of the peace, employers would find workers elsewhere, and the sailors would be paid less or left jobless. The editor concluded, "It will be just so with the sailors here, unless they return to the principles of FREE TRADE."[26]

Regardless of the prominence of free trade in the tariff debate and its application to the domestic economy, and regardless of the implicit dismissal of sailors' rights in discussing labor combinations, Americans remembered the rhetorical association between free trade and sailors' rights in politics. In the years immediately after the War of 1812 politicians continued to use free trade and sailors' rights to rally support. The remnants of the Federalist Party did not give up denouncing the Republicans for their abandonment of both free trade and sailors' rights in the treaty of peace. When nominating Rufus King for governor in 1816, New York Federalists lambasted the Republicans for "[w]aging a war... improvidently begun and feebly carried on, for 'free trade and sailors' rights'" and failing to guarantee either in the peace.[27] Such Federalist attacks disappeared as the party headed toward political oblivion. By the late 1810s the divisions among the Republicans became more important than the Federalist-Republican split. In the contests that ensued, support for the War of 1812 and free trade and sailors' rights became an acid test by which to measure political credentials. In 1817 the editor of the *Weekly Aurora* attacked fellow Republican William Findlay, who was campaigning for governor, by charging that "[h]e professed great zeal for free trade and sailors rights, and as much earnestness for war in support of them; but being a deep calculator, he found that it would cost him less to *profess* than to practice patriotism, hence he neither opened his purse, nor exposed his dear person in support of the war."[28] Similar challenges appeared in other states.[29] The slogan, however, could also be used in a more positive political context by Republicans in reporting electoral victories and as a toast during celebrations to highlight the memory of the War of 1812. In the spring of 1817 partisan newspapers described how after an election, "a victory recently has been obtained, not by force of arms, but by the powerful and irresistible *vox populi* over an enemy, as dangerous to the rights of free men, and the unalienable privileges of republicans, as ever the proud and haughty '*Bulwark*' [Great Britain] was to the *rights of sailors and free trade!*"[30] At a political celebration of an election in Pennsylvania that fall, Republicans toasted the navy and its accomplishments in the war by declaring, "'Rule Britannia' gave way to 'Free trade and Sailors' rights.'"[31] And in 1818, on the Fourth of July in Union, New Jersey, after toasting the United States, the memory of George Washington, and the president, the fourth toast was to the navy, "may it ever continue the scourge of tyrants and protectors of free trade and sailors rights."[32]

Free trade and sailors' rights also appeared in the tariff debates. Anti-tariff proponents, like Thomas Cooper, wielded Porter's motto to attack protectionists. In 1820, Congressmen James Johnson of Virginia claimed that a proposed increase in the tariff would destroy commerce and navigation only a few years after the nation had fought "a bloody but victorious war" to maintain "free trade and sailors' rights." "Having achieved at such a sacrifice these great objects," Johnson "deprecated their surrender."[33] As can be seen in Johnson's reference to the war, free trade and sailors' rights had gained a hallowed status as a patriotic shorthand to describe the causes of the war. This association with patriotism and the memory of the War of 1812 appeared in the *Salem Gazette* in 1828 when the editor proclaimed, "As to the people of Salem, we do not believe they are yet inclined to 'give up the ship.' They have fought for 'free trade and sailors' rights,' and they will not now suffer themselves to be wheedled out of them, by any dupe of a selfish aristocracy."[34] A southern free trader used a variant of Porter's motto to assert that the South had joined both the Revolutionary War and the War of 1812 not in defense of specific grievances, like the British imperial measures and restrictions on commerce that affected mostly the North, but "in support of the principle of taxation" only with representation in the Revolution, and "in defense of the principle of free trade and support of our brethren [sailors]" in the War of 1812.[35] The slogan was also associated with the will of the people. In 1828 the *Boston Gazette* proposed that the "mercantile interest" in the North convene an anti-tariff congress that would be "supported by every interest, and breathing the popular sentiment of *free trade* and sailor's rights!"[36]

If the anti-tariff forces might with some justification rally to Porter's motto, what is surprising is that at the same time politicians began to marshal the slogan in support of the tariff. In 1832, proponents of the tariff in Bangor, Maine, included among their Fourth of July toasts: "*The Tariff and American System* – We will not be gulled by fine terms, masking evil projects. Give us back the genuine old Democratic gathering cry of '*Free Trade and Sailors' Rights*'."[37] In an attack on Jackson's anti-tariff position, a broadside lambasted Jackson as being pro-British. As if the absurdity of labeling the Hero of New Orleans and murderer of British agents Alexander Arbuthnot and Robert Ambrister an Anglophile was not enough, the piece also included atop the sheet the phrase "Our Country . . . Our Industry" and three illustrations representing the alliance between industry (a man at the loom), commerce (a merchant ship), and agriculture (a farmer ploughing the field). Atop the ship were two pennants, one proclaiming "No Colonial Subjugation," the other "Free Trade & Sailor's Rights" – in apparent disregard for what the phrase "free trade" actually meant.[38] Similarly, during the debates over the tariff, one congressman, who was also an iron magnate, argued for protection of his industry, noting the near ruin of "those very manufacturers who had so willingly contributed, both by taxes and by loans, to a war in defense of 'free trade and sailor's rights.'"[39] This mixed message also appeared at a meeting of factory owners in Pawtucket, Rhode Island. With industrialist Samuel Slater presiding, the assembled gathering honored Henry Clay, whom they proclaimed as "the great champion and friend of domestic Manufactures." Surrounding a portrait of Clay were several banners, including one that declared that "Commerce and Manufactures are but kindred branches of the wealth of the nation. The one cannot exist without the other." This banner perhaps explains the truly incongruous standard nearby, which conjoined two seeming opposites without apparent contradiction: "Free Trade and Sailors' Rights and the Home Protecting Policy."[40]

These conflicting uses of the slogan also appeared in the politics of the emerging two-party system. Jacksonians embraced the motto as a means to

attack their political opponents and to trumpet their own democratic credentials. In 1828 they tagged followers of John Quincy Adams with the label
of Federalism and claimed that three-quarters of Adams's supporters were
"sheer, Hartford Convention federalists." Jacksonians, on the other hand, were
"the friends of freedom, civil liberty, free trade and sailor's rights."[41] Similar
distinctions appeared in the 1830s. In 1832 Jackson's opponents, according
to one Democratic editor, were willing to surrender "free trade and sailor's
rights."[42] Whereas, another editor explained in 1834, Jackson had defended
the ideals imbedded in the motto at the Battle of New Orleans and by advocating mercantile interests as president by recovering the claims from Denmark,
France, and Naples from ships seized during the Napoleonic era.[43] In 1835
Democrats repeatedly charged the Whig Party with giving "our enemies aid
and comfort in the last war," which was fought "for the support of 'free
trade and sailors' rights'."[44] Daniel Webster was particularly vulnerable to
these charges, since he had opposed the War of 1812. As the presidential
election of 1836 approached, one Democratic paper warned that "[t]he *old
tory, last war, Hartford Convention federalists* of New England" consistently
supported Webster's candidacy. This editor charged that "[w]hile his country was engaged in a holy *contest* for *free trade* and *sailors' rights*, and lie
bleeding at every pore, he *sneeringly exulted in the defeat* of her noble hearted
sons."[45]

Democrats also turned to Porter's motto simply for rhetorical flourish. Americans in 1776 "threw off their allegiance to Great Britain, and declared for
liberty," proclaimed one Democrat. In 1812, "the republic again buckled on
its armor, and declared for 'Free Trade and Sailor's Rights'." Now, in 1834,
Americans confronted "a Great Moneyed Corporation" – the Second Bank
of the United States – and once again had to do battle.[46] The Baptist John
Leland, known for his extravagant and emotional style of preaching, delivered
an address in western Massachusetts to celebrate the reelection of Andrew
Jackson to the presidency. The aged minister gave a rousing speech articu-
lating the main tenants of Jacksonian democracy. He informed his audience
that "[n]ext to the salvation of the soul, *the civil and religious rights of men*
have summoned my attention more than the acquisition of wealth or seals of
honor" and that in his career he had repeatedly spoken and written "pleading
*the rights of man against the claims of aristocrats*." Slipping into a nautical
metaphor, he told the crowd that having lived almost eighty years he was "like
an old weather worn sailor, yet on deck, in a boisterous sea, . . . before the mast,
sounding the deep with a short line; watching the winds and pirates; fearing
the rocks and looking for breakers; bearing at mast head '*Free trade and sailors
rights*.'" For Leland and his democratic listeners the nautical metaphors had a
certain rhetorical attractiveness, but the use of Porter's motto in the context of
a discussion of the rights of men demonstrated the persistence of the memory

of the War of 1812 and the salience of the ideals for which Americans believed they had fought the British.[47]

Jackson's opponents, too, were willing to use Porter's motto and the memory of the War of 1812 for political purposes. In 1832 one Whig paper called a few of Martin Van Buren's supporters "Hartford Convention democrats" and implied that Van Buren, who was running for vice president, and his followers did not believe in "free trade and sailors' rights."[48] A Maine editor took this approach a step further by claiming that Van Buren had been willing to negotiate away much of the state of Maine in exchange for British concessions on impressment. Such concessions (which were not made by Van Buren) were unnecessary, according to this editor, since if the British dared touch a single American seaman, "our Hulls and our Bainbridges, and our hardy seamen would all rush for the ocean together, with the broad pendant waving, with the ever memorable words, 'Free Trade and SAILORS' RIGHTS.'"[49] Whig papers also relied upon the phrase in a more positive, if somewhat contradictory, manner. One editor praised Henry Clay for being the "Father of the American System" and a staunch proponent of the tariff, while at the same time referring to him as "a distinguished champion of the war with Great Britain" whose speeches have resounded in "the vaulted dome of the Capitol" with "eloquent declamations in behalf of Free Trade and Sailors' Rights."[50]

Like their Democratic opponents, Whigs could bask in the reflected glory and memory of the War of 1812. In 1834, Philadelphia Whigs held a massive rally during local elections. Featured in a political procession that included thousands of participants was a scaled model of the USS *Constitution*, decorated with flags that read: "*Sustained by Freemen, we swear never to give up the Ship*" and "*Free Trade and Sailors' Rights – We are for the poor.*"[51] Whigs also turned to their heroes from the War of 1812 and used nautical metaphors. In 1835 Tom Bowline – a standard pseudonym for the common sailor – wrote an article praising William Henry Harrison as Old Tippecanoe (popular memory conflated Harrison's victory in northern Indiana with the War of 1812, even though the Battle of Tippecanoe took place in 1811). "Old Tippecanoe," wrote Tom, "is an American vessel every point of her, from the stern to the bowsprit, from keel to round top, from jib to main sheet, from marling-spike to anchors." And then, "Hark ye shipmates – I say Old Tippecanoe is as gallant a ship as ever fired a broadside in defence of free trade and sailors rights."[52]

The mixed approach to Porter's motto, with both political parties using the phrase and the memory of the War of 1812 for their own purposes, persisted into the 1840s. In the election of 1844, known mostly for the debate over expansionism, free trade and sailors' rights appeared as a political slogan. The Peabody Essex Museum in Salem has a banner that probably dates from this presidential election when Herman Melville watched a New York parade with flags displaying the slogan. Melville, as a sailor, took special note of the

ILLUSTRATION 20. Banner with Free Trade and Sailors Rights. Porter's motto appeared in political parades after the War of 1812. Melville noted one such banner in the 1844 election. The Peabody Essex Museum has another political banner probably from the same year. Peabody Essex Museum, Salem, Massachusetts.

phrase "free trade and sailors' rights," but there was probably no way for him to tell which political side was marching from the banner alone, since all parties claimed allegiance to the now much-abused and sacred phrase.[53] The Democratic Party had the surest title to the mantle of both "free trade" and "sailors' rights," since it opposed protectionism and claimed to speak for the common man. So it should not be surprising that Democrats like those in Charleston, South Carolina, would include in their parade celebrating James Polk's victory a pendant on a model ship with "We have met the enemy and they are ours" on one side and "Free Trade and Sailors Rights" on the other.[54] The Democratic claim to the slogan did not go uncontested. A Whig Party article headed "FREE TRADE AND SAILORS RIGHTS" lambasted the Democrats for allowing foreign ships to enter the coasting trade and declared, "What are Sailors Rights! That our Government should protect our own seamen against all and every foreign Power." The essay also claimed that the defenders of low tariffs were from the South, where slaves took many jobs away from sailors. The author pointed out that Henry Clay had always sought to protect seamen, citing specifically the Treaty of Ghent. Thus the best way to support "Free Trade and Sailors' Rights" was to vote for the pro-tariff Whigs.[55] It was even possible for Whigs to argue that the free trade of the southern anti-protectionists was not the same free trade that had served as a rallying cry during the War of 1812. As the editor of the *Boston Courier* explained, "In 1812, free trade was understood to mean freedom to navigate the ocean, 'the great highway of nations,' without annoyance from British and French men-of-war" and not the absence of tariffs. Given the complex of definitions of free trade current when Porter first raised his banner, this critique was only partially correct. The Whig editor missed the beauty of Porter's free trade – yes, it referred to neutral trade, but it also brought into play a host of other meanings that went to the very core of the American understanding of their revolution.[56]

The use of such political rhetoric did not stop with the Democrats and Whigs. From Nauvoo, Illinois, Joseph Smith hoped to marshal his legions of Mormons to lead the nation toward a *"theodemocracy."* In his political manifesto of April 15, 1844, Smith called for a nation "where God and the people hold power to conduct the affairs of men in righteousness; and where liberty, free trade, and sailor's rights, and the protection of life and property shall be maintained inviolate, for the benefit of ALL."[57] This message carried a special meaning for the Mormons, who had been driven out of Missouri in 1838 and would later seek refuge in Utah. Smith's followers did not forget his interest in Porter's motto after their leader's death and their arrival on the banks of the Great Salt Lake. In 1857, the *Deseret News* published a couple of articles recalling Smith's bid for the presidency in 1844, quoting a series of resolutions in support of his candidacy from a convention in Illinois, including the statement "that the better to carry out the principles of liberty and equal rights, Jeffersonian Democracy, free trade and sailors rights, and the protection of person and property, we will support General Joseph Smith of Illinois for the President of the United States at the ensuing election."[58]

During the late 1840s and into the 1850s and beyond, Porter's motto occasionally appeared in mainstream political rhetoric, but its resonance weakened as memories faded. One sign of this drift was the slogan's identification with Henry Clay rather than Captain David Porter.[59] Perhaps this is understandable given Clay's national prominence. Clay was more than willing to use the phrase for his own political purposes, and could even play upon its ideological content in his criticism of the Mexican War. But his use of the old rhetoric seemed to be out of tune with the era of Manifest Destiny. At a Whig rally in Lexington, Kentucky, on November 13, 1847, Clay contrasted the Mexican-American War of conquest with the "just war" fought in 1812 in which "the great object, announced at the time, was 'Free Trade and Sailors' Rights' against the intolerable and oppressive acts of British power on the ocean." Clay continued: "How totally variant is the present war! This is no war of defense, but one unnecessary and of offensive aggression. It is Mexico that is defending her fire-sides, her castles, and her altars, not we...."[60] However valid this criticism of the war might have been, few Americans wanted to view themselves as modern-day Britons acting the part of the bully and threatening the lives and homes of others.

Another indication of how out of place the slogan appeared in politics in the late 1840s was its occasional association with the Democratic candidate for president in 1848, Lewis Cass. In Detroit, local Democrats cheered him and pronounced, "Trusting in a glorious triumph, our motto is, 'free trade and sailors' rights!'" One popular campaign tune concluded:

> Our toast, 'Free Trade and Sailor's Rights'
>    Our banner to the breeze –
> Then here's success to LEWIS CASS,
>    And 'FREEDOM OF THE SEAS.'[61]

Cass had a modest military record during the War of 1812: the Democratic nominee had surrendered with General William Hull at the beginning of the conflict and had fought under William Henry Harrison at the Battle of the Thames. Most of his service during the war was as governor of Michigan. All of this experience was far from salt water and not easily associated with free trade and sailors' rights. However, Cass had also taken an outspoken stand in opposition to the British right of search while a diplomat in France in 1842, thus staking a more recent claim to defending sailors' rights. Perhaps the military and diplomatic experience combined to allow a few Democrats to rally to the old motto, but the slogan did not appear with great frequency and must have had a hollow ring when compared to the more recent triumphs of his Whig opponent, Zachary Taylor – "old rough and ready" – fresh from his triumphs at Monterey and Buena Vista.[62]

For the most part, as Americans began their grim march to the Civil War, Porter's slogan had lost much of its political punch. Before the Mexican War the phrase had been used with some frequency.[63] Free trade, after all, had emerged as a contentious issue in relation to the impost and in the domestic economy. It was therefore almost natural for the phrase to appear in the debates over the tariff and in the political wrangling between Democrats and Whigs. The fact that both political parties used Porter's motto for their own purposes, regardless of its ideological appropriateness, was a testimony to its continued resonance and its increasing hollowness. By 1848, except in the memory of an old War Hawk like Henry Clay or in its weak association with a Democrat like Lewis Cass, the motto had become less relevant to the major issues of the day.[64] More often than not, writers and speakers relied upon Porter's motto as a shorthand for explaining the War of 1812 or as a means to sound off on patriotic themes. In tracing the political history of the nation since 1788, the *Columbian Register* explained, using two of the standard labels for the conflict, "Times went on prosperously until the war of 1812, the second war of independence, which was waged for free trade and sailors' rights."[65] In 1852 a Michigan Democrat appealed to voters by reminding readers that when the British impressed American seamen before the War of 1812, the Federalists acquiesced, while the "Democracy ran up the stars and stripes, and a thousand republican cannon thundered in defence of 'free trade and sailors' rights.'"[66] As the nation became consumed with expansion and then with the conflict over slavery that followed, free trade and sailors' rights might surface briefly, but it also became disembodied and gradually lost its currency.

# 24

# Popular Culture

Free trade and sailors' rights remained embedded in American popular culture in the years between the War of 1812 and the Civil War. For the common seaman the phrase continued to have importance, although every sailor could as easily make fun of himself by misapplying the term in comic relief. For the rest of the public, the phrase may have resonated with the legacy of the Revolution and the memory of the War of 1812, but it could be also twisted and turned to a variety of uses. The phrase was plastered across a wide range of material objects, both for everyday use and also for special commemoration. As with politicians, common folk toasted free trade and sailors' rights on the Fourth of July and other special occasions. Americans also used and abused the phrase, spouting it to assert their patriotism and featuring it in business advertisements. Variations appeared, stretching its meaning to all kinds of purposes. African Americans confronting an intensifying racism could cite their participation in the War of 1812, along with the cry of free trade and sailors' rights, to assert their claim to citizenship. For many Americans, however, by the 1840s and 1850s, Porter's motto had begun to lose its appeal and meaning.

Seamen had a special claim to the legacy of free trade and sailors' rights, yet the ability to mock even what sailors held sacred, as was seen in Dartmoor prison, persisted in the years after the war. A group of sailors recruited for the United States Navy in 1845 objected to having the bar closed to them aboard a steamboat between Amboy and New York. The recruits democratically voted that this action was an outrage, or "as a wag of the party put it," this "aristocratic dram shop" had committed "an infringement on the ever-to-be-respected doctrine of Free Trade and Sailors Rights." With that declaration the sailors broke into the bar and drank without paying a cent.[1] One whaleman comically decorated a piece of scrimshaw with two rough-looking sailors leaning on an oval below an eagle holding a banner with free trade and sailors' rights above

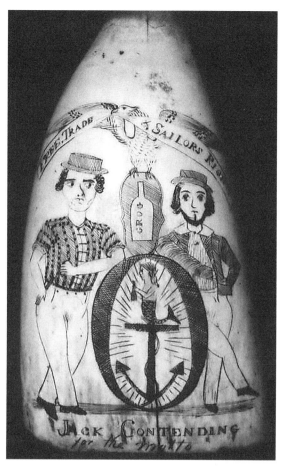

ILLUSTRATION 21. "Jack contending for the motto." Although all Americans could use Porter's motto, sailors had a special claim to it, even when they used it in self-mocking tones as appears in this piece of scrimshaw (etched whale bone or tooth, usually produced by whalemen on long voyages as mementos of their experience). New Bedford Whaling Museum, New Bedford, Massachusetts.

and a rum bottle between them. Inside the oval a topless mermaid held another bottle with the words "Jack contending for the motto" beneath.

Despite this trivialization of free trade and sailors' rights, the phrase retained its more serious meaning within the maritime community. At least one sailor felt the motto would make a wonderful decoration painted on his sea chest. If there is an example of scrimshaw that seems to make fun of the idea of free trade and sailors' rights, there are other examples of etched whalebone with the motto demonstrating pride, such as the *Ceres* piece dated from the mid-1830s that depicts an able seaman decked out in full naval regalia and emblems of nationality in the background.² Countless sailors, like Samuel Leech, looked back at the war and viewed it as a contest for sailors' rights. American seamen demonstrated their continued allegiance to the phrase well into the 1830s. During an officers' ball held aboard the USS *United States* in Trieste, 500 common sailors congregated on the forward decks for their own festivities. Among the decorations created by the "weather beaten" tars was "a rough picture of a frigate with the inscription '*Free trade and Sailor's rights*.'"³

Although newspaper editors might condemn strikes as combinations in violation of free trade, when sailors turned to labor action they often used Porter's motto as a rallying cry. In 1837 about one hundred New York "*Jacks*" paraded the streets to protest the dollar tax for a hospital fund exacted upon every seaman arriving from a foreign port. These men marched under banners proclaiming "free trade and sailors' rights – no dollar a voyage." Five years later a wage cut of 20 percent from the previous year led to a sailors' strike in New York and a procession of 400 seamen, with their own band providing music, marching under two banners: one proclaimed "$15 – Live and Let live," and on the other "was inscribed the old sailor's motto, under which he has shown himself ready to fight in days that are past, when the cause of his country demand it, Free Trade and Sailors Rights." A report of a meeting of Baltimore seamen, who were also protesting their low wages, appeared under the heading of free trade and sailors' rights. Two years later, and almost thirty years after the end of the War of 1812, sailors passed out a handbill with the heading "*Free Trade and Sailor's Rights*" calling for a meeting to demand an increase in wages.⁴

Recognizing the importance of the motto for the maritime community, religious reformers at times referred to free trade and sailors' rights in their attempt to preach to sailors in the decades after the War of 1812. One minister thanked God that "the happy day is very near when '*Holiness to the Lord*' shall be inscribed on every vessel, and the Bethel flag shall be the best protection of '*free trade and sailors' rights*.'"⁵ An issue of the reformist *Sailor's Magazine* used the phrase "Free Trade and Sailor's Rights" to argue that a sailor had the right to avoid strong drink, negotiate his own contracts, and "*to cease to do evil and learn to do well*." In short, a sailor's rights should be "guaranteed by Him who made the sea and the dry land."⁶ In 1849 an evangelical reformer hoping to convert the unregenerate along the waterfront sought to fit the slogan to his own purposes. Referring to the "free trade" in "sailor rights," the Reverend Azariah Eldridge viewed the sailor "as but a few removes above a slave." In a confused reading of the original phrase, Eldridge saw the method of contracting sailors, who were often inebriated and in debt when they signed on to their next voyage, as a "free trade" in human flesh that denied the sailor his

ILLUSTRATION 22. Smithsonian pottery. Pottery commemorating patriotic themes was very popular in the nineteenth century. The Smithsonian Institution has several examples of such pottery featuring the slogan "Free Trade and Sailors' Rights." Smithsonian Institution, Washington, D.C.

rights because crimps extorted "the maximum proceeds" of the sailor's wages for themselves and were "careful to secure the spoils by instruments under seal, whose drunken execution was a miserable farce" and "which made the poor sailor a willing and impotent victim upon the land."[7]

The popularity of free trade and sailors' rights reached beyond the waterfront. Iconography for both the maritime and the general American community featured the phrase. In landlocked Kentucky during the 1820s, "*Free Trade and Sailors' Rights*" was engraved on some change bills issued by a storekeeper.[8] Porter's motto also appeared on glassware and pottery. The Kensington Glass Works made a number of different flasks with patriotic designs, including one with Franklin on one side and Porter's motto on the other.[9] Pottery jugs were also adorned with the phrase. The Smithsonian Institution has several such items containing the words "Free Trade and Sailors' Rights." Some jugs featured the slogan on one side and a picture of Stephen Decatur on the other, commemorating his burning of the *Philadelphia* in Tripoli and his victory over the *Macedonian*. About 1858, Robert Lovett of Philadelphia cast a special coin with an engraving of a sea battle on one side, and on the other a statement that the picture was of the *Constitution*'s victory over the *Guerrière* in 1812, with free trade and sailors' rights etched along the top edge.[10] Obviously there remained enough interest in the War of 1812 and Porter's motto to create a market for this sort of paraphernalia. As we have already seen, the phrase appeared in the iconography of political meetings. It was also used in other public celebrations. When General Lafayette visited the Washington naval yard in 1824, the entrance "was very tastefully decorated with wreaths and festoons of evergreens and flowers"; over the door of one of the buildings was an eagle, "with a label in his beak, bearing the American motto, '*Free Trade and Sailor's Rights.*'"[11] The citizens of Baltimore planned their parade on the Fourth of July in 1828 around a model schooner twenty-seven feet in length and six feet in beam. Although the name of the ship – the *Union* – probably carried a political message connected to the tariff controversies swirling across the nation, the flags adorning each mast centered on the memory of the War of 1812 and local boosterism for a city that had constructed the nation's first railroad. Waving from the foremast was a banner with "DON'T GIVE UP THE SHIP," from the mainmast hung a standard with "FREE TRADE AND SAILORS RIGHTS," and from the mizzenmast was a flag with "SUCCESS TO THE RAILROAD."[12]

There were references to Porter's motto in a variety of public celebrations across the nation. At the "'*Raising*' of the New Bank of the United States" in June 1820, there were a series of toasts, including "The Navy of the United States – the nurse of gallantry, and protector of free trade and sailor's rights."[13] When the workers in a Connecticut comb factory gathered to commemorate the Fourth of July in 1824, they included among their toasts "*Captain Isaac Hull* – The Protector of 'Free Trade and Sailor's Rights.'"[14] Americans in Paris also gathered for a dinner on the Fourth that year, toasting "Commodore Porter; the friend of 'Free Trade and Sailors' Rights.'"[15] Lafayette attended the dinner that day. Later in the year he headed for his famous return visit to the United States. In New York City the Whitehall "boatmen took the great French and American patriot who fought beside George Washington in the Revolution for a short cruise on their racing boat '*American Star*.'" The watermen then presented their prized craft to Lafayette, urging him to take the boat with him back to France, "where it may occasionally remind you of the grateful friends you have left behind – of the ingenuity of the mechanics of a country which you assisted to liberate, and also of the great naval motto 'Free trade and Sailors' rights.'" Lafayette, obviously touched by this generosity, responded by assuring the boatmen that their gift would be "most carefully and fondly preserved" and offered them "the good wishes of a veteran heartily devoted to the great naval motto, 'Free trade and Sailors' rights.'"[16]

The slogan had other uses among the general population of the United States. The phrase popped up in a variety of situations, some patriotic and some not so patriotic. Reports of a supposed impressment in 1820 appeared under the heading "*Free Trade and Sailors*' Rights."[17] In a somewhat different vein, a New Hampshire newspaper used the phrase to headline a story about the efforts of some "canal proprietors" to detain boats on the Merrimac River, asserting that if they did "not put a stop to these high-handed measures, the people of New-Hampshire will put a stop to all trade upon the river."[18] After the Supreme Court decision in *Gibbon vs. Ogden*, which decreed that the steamboat monopoly granted by New York State could not regulate commerce with New Jersey, a lively competition for passengers broke out along the Hudson River wharfs. Runners for the new steamboat company called out to potential passengers on Courtlandt Street, "This way Sir, this way, to the Olive Branch, sir; no monopoly, free trade and sailors's rights; a fine boat, sir; low pressure; sails like the wind."[19] A number of advertisements connecting Porter's slogan to open competition and antimonopoly appeared. In the summer of 1839, Philip Martin began a newspaper advertisement for his Guilford, Vermont, "Cheap Cash Store" with the proclamation "NO MONOPOLY – NO COMBINA-TION!!!" followed by "Free Trade and Sailors' Rights is the old Republican doctrine."[20] Other businesses – including a tailor in Connecticut, a canal line in New York, and a dry goods store in Milwaukee – ran similar notices.[21] An extended advertisement for a book called *Songs for the People* highlighted the variety of national music published, including "the Songs of the War of 1812, in which the battles on the sea and land, for 'Free Trade and Sailors' Rights,' are celebrated by national poets."[22] When a Pennsylvania newspaper editor described one of the new official seals (there were two) designed for the state government in 1839, he felt compelled to wax eloquent about the female form of "America" patriotically defending the nation in 1776 and 1812. This icon for the United States, "with her liberty cap in the left hand, and her efficient sword of defiance in the right hand," exhibited "at once the character and spirit of this republican country." She had "her foot upon the neck and mane of the subdued British Lion, encircled by the motto '*Both cant survive.*'" The picture indicated "the prowess of American arms, both by land and sea, when forced to contend for Independence, or for 'free trade and sailors rights.'"[23]

So popular was the slogan that variations appeared, lumping free trade together with other working groups or concepts (suggesting again that when the nullifiers reversed the components of the phrase, their word order was probably intentional). Excited about the return to normal business, and perhaps mocking the Republican cause, Federalist shipbuilders declared for "*Free trade and carpenters rights*" in 1815.[24] The headline "PROSPECT OF PEACE, FREE TRADE AND FISHERMEN'S RIGHTS" prefaced a report on the availability of nets for sale in Hartford, Connecticut.[25] New York Democrats used

**Ithaca and Buffalo Line,**
**1837,**
DAY AND NIGHT.
*" Free Trade and Sailors' Rights !"*
**NO MONOPOLIES !**

THE proprietors of this Line will run th eir
Boats from the Store-House of *D. Hanmer &*
*Son,* in Ithaca, for Buffalo, during the season, on
the opening of navigation. One Boat will leave
Ithaca each week, on Tuesday evening, and one
Boat will leave Buffalo the same day for Ithaca.
After the first trips, the Boats will touch at Good-
win's Point, on their way down the Lake, wind
and weather permitting. For freight or passage
inquire of *Lewis Gregory,* at the Inlet, or at the
Store of D. Hanmer & Son in Ithaca, or at Swart-
wout & Miller's, Port Royal, or of Wilkeson, Big-
alow. & Swan, or Colson & Cook, Buffalo, or the
Captains on board.
                    **D. HANMER & SON,**
                    **SWARTWOUT & MILLER,**
                    **REUBEN COMPTON,**
                    **SMITH NORTON.**

ILLUSTRATION 23. Advertisement for the Ithaca and Buffalo Line. One of the many varied uses of the phrase "Free Trade and Sailors' Rights" for commercial purposes, this advertisement suggested how Porter's motto came to represent an attack on any monopoly in an era that touted laissez-faire economics and competitive capitalism. *Ithaca Herald*, June 14, 1837.

the same slogan in front of their thirteenth ward headquarters in 1834.[26] In 1818, another model ship, the *Constitution*, moved from one political meeting place to another in Boston to support *"Free trade and the Rights of Citizens & Sailors."*[27] Fourth of July celebrants in Kittery, Maine, toasted "Free Trade, Mutual Rights, & Equal Taxation" in 1828.[28] The New Jersey navigation lottery highlighted an advertisement with "'Free Trade' and Brokers Rights."[29] In Ohio, an advertisement for the *"Elyra Cash Store"* began, "Down with Combinations!!!" and then went on to assert that "'FREE TRADE AND EQUAL RIGHTS,' Are principals handed down by our immortal ancestors."[30] Free traders used a similar phrase to defend nullification.[31] Cloth workers in 1828 paraded with a banner proclaiming "FREE TRADE AND MECHANIC'S

RIGHTS" as a protest against merchants closing stores in the evening in Dover, New Hampshire. By exchanging the word "sailor" for the word "mechanic," these workers argued that if sailors were to have rights, so should skilled workmen. And, ignoring the meaning of "free trade" as it related to tariffs, the mechanics' standard seemed to be touting the notion of free trade in markets by urging the stores to stay open at times more convenient to working men.[32]

Free trade and sailors' rights also appeared in questions over race and slavery. Abolitionists referred to the motto when they attacked the Negro seamen's acts of the South. First passed in South Carolina in 1822 in response to the Denmark Vesey conspiracy, these state laws sought to limit contact between black seamen and slaves by imprisoning any black sailor who came ashore while in port. As early as 1824 a northern passenger complained of the South Carolina law and was shocked when the black cook from his ship was arrested in Charleston "on account of the horrible offense of having been *born black*." A circumstance, the writer sarcastically noted, which was "glorious proof of the devotion of the constituted authorities of *this* Commonwealth [South Carolina] to FREE TRADE AND SAILORS' RIGHTS."[33] By the 1840s similar laws had been passed in North Carolina, Georgia, Florida, Alabama, and Louisiana. John Quincy Adams raised objections to these statutes in Congress in 1842, and a group of Massachusetts merchants petitioned Congress to investigate the laws. Despite such outcries they remained in place.[34] Amid this discussion, the abolitionist newspaper *The Emancipator* raised the great clarion from thirty years before. In December 1842 the newspaper published a letter from Rufus Kinsman, a black seaman from Lisbon, Connecticut, who had been imprisoned and forced to work like a slave for having violated the Louisiana Negro's Seamen's Act by coming ashore when his ship arrived in New Orleans. The article went on to declare that "this outrage" had been "committed under the name of a slaveholding law, and at the direction of a slaveholding justice, among a people clamorous for free trade and sailor's rights!"[35]

Other African Americans relied upon the phrase to assert their citizenship in opposition to the Negro seamen's acts. A few months after the report of the incarceration of Rufus Kinsman, *The Emancipator* printed another article, written by William P. Powell, who ran the "house for colored seamen in New-York," that explored further the meaning of free trade and sailors' rights in relation to American history and the Negro seamen's acts. Powell created a fictional discussion between some sailors on watch at sea. Mr. Spunyarn began by saying: "Well, shipmates, I will give you a sentiment – 'Success to Free Trade and Sailors' rights.'" To which Jack Haulyards responded, in exaggerated sailor language, "Avast there, Matey; better belay that. 'Free Trade and Sailors' Rights!' what does that mean, Mr. Spunyarn?" The perplexed Mr. Spunyarn believed the slogan needed no explanation and could only retort,

"Why Jack, it means – it m-e-a-n–s 'Free Trade and Sailors' Rights,' to be sure." Haulyards was not satisfied with this nonanswer, and expanded on his own understanding of the slogan to his African American shipmates. Free trade and sailors' rights meant that in "the late war with Great Britain, the United States settled the question that her commerce should be *Free*, and her sailors protected in their rights, as American citizens." During that "great struggle . . . the whole nation looked up to our navy, and the hardy sons of the ocean, for protection." In the war, "when that beautiful motto 'Free trade and Sailor's rights,' was run up to the MAIN TRUCK of every ship of war, and flowing to the pure breeze of heaven," the "colored seamen . . . entered the service of their country" nobly fighting "by the side of Decatur, Perry, and others." Haulyards then added, with biting irony, that black sailors had "sacrificed their lives on their country's altar, and eventually secured to every American citizen, rights, privileges and immunities, which, alas, the colored sailors do not enjoy!" "Tom Handy," one of the other sailors, asked, "But Jack, you do not mean to say we are not American citizens?" Haulyards responded that they were "by no means" citizens, since the southern states had passed laws "imprisoning colored seamen when they go into their ports, and that too, when sailing under the Star-Spangled Banner" for "'no color of crime,' but for the 'crime of color!'" Haulyards condemned this injustice: "Shame! – Shame!! Shipmates I blush for my country, and am forced to exclaim, Oh Columbia! Columbia!! the pride of the world, the nation's glory. Dost not thou assume pre-eminence with all other nations for magnanimity and honor? . . . Does any high-minded nation imprison and enslave their benefactors – their own free fellow-citizens for no crime whatever?"[36]

Powell's memory, as revealed through the persona of Jack Haulyards, was selective. He focused on the active role African Americans had played in the War of 1812 fighting in the navy and aboard privateers. He ignored the prejudice faced by black sailors in the early nineteenth century, although it was a time when many black seamen served on American ships and shared berths on the same forecastle and gundeck with white sailors. That prejudice led to the segregation of African Americans, along with a handful of derelict others, in one prison building at Dartmoor. The conversation among black sailors on regular watch aboard a ship was also something of an imaginative creation in the 1840s. Although there remained some blacks working as able seamen in the 1840s, the proportion of African Americans serving as foremast hands had decreased by that decade, in part because of the Negro seamen's acts, and in part because of the intensifying racial prejudice in both the North and the South in the antebellum era. By the time of Powell's yarn of Haulyard's conversation, many African Americans in the merchant marine had been relegated to the kitchen as cooks. Powell, of course, knew all about this racism. After all, he ran the "Colored Sailors' Home" as a temperance boarding house in New York to provide Christian shelter for African Americans denied entry into the New York Sailor's Home run by the American Seamen's Friend Society.[37]

However reflective of reality Powell's story may have been, the memory of African American participation in the War of 1812, and the significance of free trade and sailors' rights, retained an important place within the black community. On August 1, 1842, African Americans in Philadelphia marched in a temperance parade, which also celebrated the anniversary of emancipation in the British West Indies, carrying what some whites believed were "Inflammatory Banners." An attack on the procession by whites led to a street battle followed by two days of rioting, marked by assaults on blacks and their property, in several wards of the city. A newspaper sympathetic to the plight of the African Americans later explained: "It seems that the inscriptions upon these banners were, 'Liberty or Death' and 'Free Trade and Sailors' Rights.'" Both sayings harked back to American struggles for freedom; the first "may be found in a speech of Patrick Henry" in 1775, while the second "was a favorite one with the people of the United States during the last war."[38]

Another measure of the identification of African Americans with the phrase can be found in the work of Frederick Douglass. Memory is not always a constant. Douglass's newspaper, the Rochester *North Star*, often lambasted the South. In 1848 the paper attacked the Negro seamen's acts by citing the War of 1812, when "this government contended with the most powerful nation on the globe for 'free trade and sailor's rights.'" This dedication to the ability of ships to sail to any port and have the rights of their sailors protected was challenged by the Negro seamen's acts "in several Southern States," where, "in violation of the Constitution, citizens, seamen from the North, are imprisoned, and if their captains, after being unjustly deprived of their services, will not pay the ransom of slavery, they are sold as chattels."[39] Many years later, when Douglass published the full story of his 1838 escape from slavery on a train from Baltimore to Philadelphia wearing sailor's clothing, he remembered the motto, but did not connect it to the War of 1812. Having spent years on the waterfront as a caulker, Douglass knew that there were plenty of black sailors who traveled by land from port to port. Perhaps focusing more on the opposition to the Negro seamen's acts than on earlier events, he claimed that the sympathy for Jack Tar at the time, especially in relationship to "free trade and sailors' rights," had helped to protect him in his journey to freedom.[40]

For many Americans the phrase seemed to have been pushed and pulled in all kinds of directions and lost some of its relevance. As memories dimmed, the motto was no longer attached to Porter and could as easily be associated with Henry Clay, Lewis Cass, Stephen Decatur, Isaac Hull, Joshua Barney, or even Benjamin Franklin. Likewise, as is clear from a number of advertisements, somehow the phrase became identified with the antimonopoly sentiments that were a part of the free market ideology that was so dominant in the nation.

For example, a newspaper attack on the New Orleans City Council for seeking to regulate the local oyster market included the call for giving the oystermen "free trade and sailors' rights," urging the city to let them "have a chance to get a fair price for their labor and peril."[41] Similarly, an author with the "cognomen" of "Free Trade and Sailors' Rights" argued against the Virginia legislature granting a steamboat monopoly between the James River and New York, only to have a defender of the charter, calling himself "ENTERPRISE," claim that the company was not seeking a monopoly and that "Competition is what is desired; that is what produces '*Free Trade and Sailors Rights*,' if I understand the term properly."[42] Another Virginian argued against a fencing law, calling it a form of English enclosure and asking, "does all of this look like free trade and sailors rights?"[43] It was even possible to misremember the origins of the phrase. In 1853 a Connecticut newspaper, under the heading "THE FIRST SHOT," retold the story of the murder of Pierce by the British in 1806, and then falsely reported that many among the huge crowd at the funeral "wore mournful badges with the motto, 'Free Trade and Sailors' Rights.'"[44]

Most Americans who remembered the phrase, however, continued to connect it to the second war with Great Britain. The victory fabricated by Madison and other Republicans as the war closed fit the triumphalist and exceptionalist history that dominated the nineteenth-century view of the American past. Americans had fought the British in defense of principles – free trade and sailors' rights – and won. Gone from the American saga was the abandonment of those principles in the Treaty of Ghent. This lapse of memory was just as well, since during the following decades the Americans gained several victories for free trade and sailors' rights that could not be won on the battlefield. In the years after the war, the British stopped impressing Americans, even if, despite the repeated entreaties of diplomats, they refused to concede that right officially. Free trade, too, won out – at least in some of its definitions. Americans pursued the defense of neutral rights, making some gains, if not obtaining the full protection of property on the high seas that had been the dream of the revolutionaries and men like John Quincy Adams. Free trade as reciprocal trade, another vision inherited from the Revolution, became more of a reality and today is standard practice in many international trade agreements. Decolonization, begun in the nineteenth century and continued in the twentieth century, has led to the end of mercantilism. Free trade as reduced tariffs and in the domestic economy has had a more troubled history. The tariff became a divisive issue in the Jacksonian era and continued to plague American politics into the twentieth century. Even if most Americans have long had faith in a free market, the role of the government in regulating the economy remains a contentious question in American politics. Exactly how long free trade and sailors' rights persisted in popular culture is unclear. Although the belief that ideas matter and that all men have equal rights has been a constant in American history, Porter's motto had a limited shelf life. American sailors and the public at large clung to the slogan for decades. By midcentury, with the generation who had fought in the War of 1812 passing on, and with the Civil War looming, free trade and sailors' rights continued to fade until it was all but forgotten.

# Conclusion

By the eve of the Civil War, free trade and sailors' rights had become a catchall that was almost divorced from its original meaning. At the beginning of the War of 1812 the phrase had represented a potent mixture of patrician ideas borrowed from the Enlightenment and plebeian ideas derived from the experience of the Age of Revolution. There were many reasons for the War of 1812, but for most Americans a few simple words encapsulated what they were fighting for and served as a powerful retort to any insult issued by an aristocratic Briton. Free trade highlighted the importance of new economic relations among people and nations. Sailors' rights brought the world of Jack Tar front and center to the American national consciousness and emphasized the ideal of equality. But once the war was over, the many uses of the words weakened their meaning even as they appeared and reappeared in a host of contexts.

The ideals behind each component of Porter's motto had a long lineage. Concern with free trade predated the Enlightenment. The Age of Reason, however, provided an intellectual context and rationale for free trade that swept across the Atlantic from Europe and inspired American revolutionaries who hoped to change the world. But free trade was a slippery concept that had different meanings in different contexts. Free trade could refer to openly trading in any market, the removal of mercantilist restrictions, the setting up of reciprocal agreements whereby merchants from the complying nations pay the same duties and fees in each other's ports, the reduction or removal of all tariffs, or the protection of neutral rights. The boundaries between these definitions were hazy and clouded with ambiguity. In the years before their revolution, the use of free trade by Americans reflected each of these overlapping definitions, and during the fight for independence the words "free trade" emerged as an ideal in both domestic and diplomatic arrangements. Indeed, the phrase gained such a hallowed status that it became associated with the meaning of the American Revolution. Although some Americans argued for price controls during the war, ultimately almost all Americans embraced the emerging market economy as the most sensible way to encourage growth. First the Articles of Confederation, and then, more forcefully, the Constitution created a free trade zone without tariffs and duties among what might have become the divided states instead of the United States. As the new nation declared itself independent, Americans hoped to establish "a free trade with all the world" by stripping away the mercantilist barriers of the European overseas empires, writing reciprocal agreements with other nations, and ensuring that "free ships make free goods." The Founding Fathers had limited success in fulfilling these goals. Europeans were not eager to open their colonies to American interlopers, and reciprocity remained a pipe dream in the face of hard-nosed Old World diplomats. However, a few European nations were willing to agree to some guarantees of neutral rights. The strongest naval power, Great Britain, remained uninterested in the free trade ideals of the United States. The Anglo-French wars that began in 1793 brought new challenges for the Americans. Over the next twenty years the United States stumbled from one crisis to another in its efforts to guarantee free trade.

Rhetorically, Americans may have stressed certain definitions of free trade with greater frequency at different times and in different circumstances from the mid eighteenth to the mid nineteenth century, yet the other definitions always hovered in the background. The story of free trade in the Age of Revolution (1750 to 1850) is not how the term changed meanings over time. Rather, it is how the phrase shifted its shape, amoebalike, depending on the needs of its protagonists while retaining the multiple meanings that had become so essential to the American national identity. When John Adams wrote the Model Treaty in 1776, the hope was to gain free trade as reciprocal trade. The French commercial treaty, with its most-favored-nation clause, and the refusal of the British to embrace reciprocity in a commercial treaty at the end of the war put that idealistic goal on hold. During the 1780s, American diplomats dropped their push for reciprocity, although it remained near and dear to their hearts, and centered their attention on loosening mercantilist restrictions, gaining access to markets, and seeking assurances for neutral rights. Once the British and the French went to war, the belligerents eased restrictions on trade with their colonies (even Great Britain granted temporary suspensions, allowing trade with its West Indies possessions during emergencies), and the issue of neutral rights became transcendent. After the passage of the Embargo of 1807, neutral rights remained important, but Federalists began to speak of free trade as any trade without American government restrictions. During the War of 1812, free trade as the protection of neutral rights became most important. After the war, the tariff was so divisive that when Americans used the language of free trade they were mainly discussing whether to raise or lower import duties. Despite these shifts in emphasis, every time Americans uttered the words "free trade" with one definition, they conjured up the heritage of the Revolution that included the other definitions as well.

American interest in sailors' rights also had a long history. Unlike free trade, the words "sailors' rights" came into vogue only at the beginning of War of 1812. Concern for sailors' rights reflected a grassroots development. It reached back to Anglo-American traditions and the faith that a community ought to protect its own. That faith was tested as the British sought to integrate the North American colonies into their regime more fully in the middle of the eighteenth century. Colonial Americans knew about the opposition to the impress in Great Britain and used similar tactics to resist the British navy in riots and by recitation of law. This experience, in turn, became vital in the resistance to imperial regulation in the 1760s. Jack Tar eagerly joined the riotous crowds as the Sons of Liberty and committeemen combined fear of the impress with opposition to taxation in an explosive formula that spawned a revolution. Impressment – a word coined by Americans in the mid 1790s – reemerged as a volatile issue after 1793 when the British navy sought manpower in its life-and-death struggle with the French. Impressment soon became a diplomatic problem with no easy solution as the United States and Great Britain competed for English-speaking sailors to man their ships. American merchants offered peaceful employment, high wages, and better living conditions; the British had press gangs and force of arms. Protests over impressment meant that Americans had to clarify their understanding of citizenship. An Act for the Relief and Protection of American Seamen, passed in 1796, offered a protective umbrella for all American seamen, regardless of color or place of birth, and asserted that the humble Jack Tar was equal in his rights as a citizen to any other American, including the legislator who had voted on the statute. Although the words were not yet reified and given the rhetorical resonance of free trade, there was little question that sailors' rights had become ingrained in the American consciousness. This belief that sailors were citizens was a direct outgrowth of the egalitarianism imbedded in the American Revolution. Sailors had served as the shock troops of the mobs that had resisted British imperial regulation. They had fought and suffered during the Revolutionary War – and here the image of the thousands of dead on the prison ship *Jersey* was especially important. After the war, seamen carried the produce of the nation overseas. They fought the French in the Quasi War and the bashaw of Tripoli in the Barbary wars. The image of Jack Tar as the purveyor and defender of commerce thus became a symbol for the entire nation. Allowing these citizens to be impressed was, regardless of the calculations of Jefferson and his cabinet, unacceptable. With the renewal of the Anglo-French War in 1803, and especially after the British attack on the *Chesapeake* in 1807, more and more Americans became convinced that impressment was an evil that had to be stopped.

ILLUSTRATION 24. "Columbia Teaching John Bull his new Lesson." Artist William Charles drew this caricature explanation for the War of 1812, with Columbia on the left holding a staff with liberty cap pointing to both France and Great Britain and declaring to her protagonists, "I tell you Johnny, you must learn to read Respect – Free Trade – Seamen's Rights &c." She then promises the uniformed figure in the middle, representing Napoleon and France, "As for you Mounseer Beau Napperty, when John gets his lesson by heart I'll teach you Respect – Retribution &.c &c." Library of Congress, Washington, D.C.

The two issues, free trade and sailors' rights, came together in the decade before 1812. There were other reasons for hostility between Great Britain and the United States. Americans coveted Canada and Florida and hoped to end the British support of Native Americans that prevented easy expansion to the Mississippi Valley. However important these reasons for war, ultimately the desire to ensure neutral trade and the need to protect sailors convinced many Americans that fighting a war was a matter of national honor.

As that war began, one hot-headed captain with a penchant for mischief ran up a flag on the foretopgallant mast of the *Essex* with a new motto – free trade and sailors' rights. Politicians quickly seized upon Captain David Porter's phrase as a short and meaningful way to explain the war. That the navy gained great triumphs, while the army struggled and staggered around the Canadian border, only enhanced the appeal of the slogan. Porter himself added to the luster of the phrase by undertaking a fabulous voyage to the South Seas, wreaking havoc on the British Pacific whaling fleet and then losing a desperate battle against overwhelming odds. Even in defeat, Porter and his crew remained committed to free trade and sailors' rights, with one seaman uttering the motto as he expired on the bloodstained deck. In the United States the phrase appeared in every village and town, adorning taverns, emblazoned on banners, repeated in toasts. Powerful words, indeed. Common sailors made it their own. But so did Americans high and low. In a nation with limited military successes, divisive politics, an inadequate government, and a crumbling economy, free trade and sailors' rights reflected a greater purpose that was supposed to bring Americans together. And yet, as the war raged on and one disaster followed another, politicians and diplomats decided to sidestep its principles in order to escape a conflict that was on the verge of tearing the nation apart.

Even as President Madison and the Republicans convinced Americans that they had won the war regardless of the failure to include guarantees to protect neutral rights or to prevent impressment, and despite the tragedy at Dartmoor that seemed to belie the American interest in seamen, the cry of free trade and sailors' rights was not forgotten. Within months of the end of the war, diplomats strove to obtain an agreement ending forced recruitment from American ships. They persisted in this effort for decades. At times the Americans came close to settling the question, only to fail in the face of British intransigence. Although the British refused to give up impressment officially, their navy all but abandoned the practice in regard to the United States. By the 1840s, the American flag came to protect a ship's crew without an official concession in a treaty. American diplomats were more successful in fulfilling many of the idealistic goals of free trade first articulated in the Revolution. Immediately after the end of the War of 1812, free trade as reciprocal trade reemerged as a goal of American diplomacy, as spelled out in the unsung reciprocity acts of 1815 and 1828 and written into conventions and treaties with Great Britain and a host of other nations. Simultaneously, a new geopolitical situation emerged when the Spanish-American empire collapsed, promising an end to mercantilist restrictions. Not only was Latin America opened to American merchants, those nations that still held onto colonies in the West Indies, one after another, permitted trade with the United States. Several nations also provided guarantees for neutral rights, although here the achievement of the goals established in the Revolution remained only partially fulfilled.

Porter's motto continued to be used by politicians of every stripe regardless of ideological affinity, following a path established in the political reliance on free trade rhetoric before the War of 1812. As early as the Revolutionary War, those who opposed price controls and those who supported them both claimed to be speaking for free trade. The same cross-party appeal of free trade appeared in the debates over commercial restrictions after the passage of the Embargo in 1807. Federalists used free trade in attacking Republican commercial restrictions, while Republicans asserted that they were merely seeking to defend free trade by imposing those same restrictions. Once free trade was combined with sailors' rights, the same contest over language appeared during the War of 1812. Federalists briefly attempted to claim the phrase as their own. After that effort failed, they mocked the Republicans by highlighting the hypocrisy of the Republican reliance on the phrase as empty cant. This charge had some validity by the end of the war, when both free trade and sailors' rights were excluded from the Treaty of Ghent. Republicans used the phrase repeatedly, placing it on political tickets, parading under its banner, and proclaiming their allegiance to free trade and sailors' rights. Politically, to turn to a naval metaphor, they raked the Federalists fore and aft with the phrase at every possible opportunity. Shattered by these blasts, and tainted by their own near-traitorous behavior and the Hartford Convention, the Federalists quickly faded from the national political scene. During the 1820s and 1830s, as a new set of political alignments emerged, both Democrats and Whigs supported free trade and sailors' rights. Even in the debate over the tariff, opponents and proponents of high import duties rallied to Porter's motto. In the process, although asserting free trade and sailors' rights remained important as a display of patriotism, the phrase began to have a hollow ring. By the 1840s free trade and sailors' rights might still be used, but it had lost some of its potency and was beginning to fade out of the political language.

Free trade and sailors' rights probably had greater longevity in the popular culture, despite the fact that common folk also used it in a variety of con-tradictory ways. Sailors, of course, adored the phrase, even if they sometimes applied it in self-mocking tones. At Dartmoor prison they quickly raised a banner with the motto when they heard of the end of the war, while joking that their small business enterprises, making and selling items in prison, repre-sented a special example of free trade and sailors' rights. For decades after the war, sailors would etch the motto on whalebone, paint it on trunks, celebrate holidays under its standard, and use it while striking for higher wages. The slogan reached beyond the maritime community and appeared in many public celebrations. It was plastered across a host of material goods, ranging from change bills to pottery. Small businessmen headed their advertisements with free trade and sailors' rights and its variants. African Americans also turned to the motto to protest racism and slavery, especially in relation to the Negro seamen's acts. The phrase lingered in the popular culture. Sometimes it had an ideological content, as it did when used in conjunction with cries against monopoly. But for the most part, by the 1850s it had simply become that "old motto" echoing with patriotic rhetoric and a quick and easy way to refer to a war that the next generation was beginning to forget.

American history is littered with political slogans. Some have been long remembered and others quickly forgotten. Each has addressed the generation that gave it birth, and many have been loaded with meaning. Free trade and sailors' rights was ubiquitous during the War of 1812. It so aptly explained the war while pulling on long strands of the American experience. Free trade had been bantered about throughout the Revolution and was tied to the high ideals of the Enlightenment. American identity was wrapped up in its complex and multiple meanings. In 1812, the phrase "sailors' rights" was of more recent coinage, but the ideas behind it, too, reached back to a Revolution that proclaimed that all men were created equal. Porter's motto continued in use after peace was restored between the United States and Great Britain in 1815. There was something in those words that attracted Americans – that spoke to who they were. Decades passed, and the phrase was used and abused by politicians and common folk alike. And still it persisted. By the 1850s it had faded in memory. The Civil War would all but erase both the slogan and the war it explained. Americans in the twenty-first century, however, should not forget the War of 1812 or Porter's motto. Our second war with Great Britain was not a mistaken or meaningless war. It was a contest for the ideals of the American Revolution, bringing together the high culture of the Enlightenment and the low culture of the common folk; it joined the effort to establish a new political economy on both the diplomatic and domestic fronts with an assertion of the equality of mankind. In short, understanding the War of 1812 and the motto that came to explain it – free trade and sailors' rights – allows us to better comprehend the origins of the American nation.

# Notes

## Introduction

1. The report of Porter's banner and motto first appeared in the Baltimore *Federal Gazette*, July 6, 1812. On Porter's first cruise see [Philadelphia], *Poulson's American Daily Advertiser*; September 11, 18, 1812; *New York Gazette*, September 12, 18, 1812.

2. For Yeo's challenge and Porter's response, see *New York Gazette*, September 21, 1812. Reports were repeated in newspapers across the country. For a sampling of these reports, see Exeter, New Hampshire, *Constitutionalist and Weekly Magazine*, July 7, 1812; Washington, D.C., *Courier*, July 9, 1812; Washington, D.C., *National Intellegencer*, July 8, 1812; Charleston *City Gazette*, October 1, 1812; *Boston Patriot*, September 23, 1812; Wilmington, Delaware, *American Watchman*, September 23, 1812; Walpole, New Hampshire, *Democratic Republican*, September 28, 1812; Raleigh *Register and North Carolina Gazette*, October 2, 1812; Charlestown, Virginia [West Virginia], *Farmer's Repository*, October 16, 1812.

3. Lawrence actually flew a banner with "Free Trade and Sailors' Rights" in his fatal encounter between the *Chesapeake* and the *Shannon*, while Perry named his flagship after the departed Lawrence and used a flag with "Don't give up the ship" during the Battle of Lake Erie.

4. Donald R. Hickey, *The War of 1812: A Forgotten Conflict* (Urbana: University of Illinois Press, 1989).

5. The building that houses the C. V. Starr Center for the Study of the American Experience was built as a residence in 1746, but a local customs inspector worked in an adjacent office. The library is in an addition erected in the 1770s, and the building is called the "Custom House."

6. The cruise on the *Sultana* was as the guest of President Baird Tipton of Washington College, while the sail on the *Pride of Baltimore II* was arranged by my hosts at C. V. Starr Center for the Study of the American Experience, Adam Goodheart and Jill Ogline Titus.

7. James D. Richardson, ed., *Compilation of Messages and Papers of the Presidents, 1789–1897* (Washington, D.C.: Government Printing Office, 1896), 1: 500–01.
8. On memory in American history, see Michael Kammen, *A Season of Youth: The American Revolution and the Historical Imagination* (New York: Oxford University Press, 1978). On the memory of the American Revolution, see Robert E. Cray, Jr., "Commemorating the Prison Ship Dead: Revolutionary Memory and the Politics of Sepulture in the Early Republic, 1776–1808," *William and Mary Quarterly*, 3rd ser., 55 (July 1999), 565–90. On the memory of the Civil War, see David W. Blight, *Race and Reunion: The Civil War in American Memory* (Cambridge, Mass.: Harvard University Press, 2001).

## 1. The Enlightenment and Defining Free Trade

1. For the literature on American Revolutionary diplomacy, see Samuel Flagg Bemis, *The Diplomacy of the American Revolution* (Bloomington: Indiana University Press, 1957); Thomas E. Chavez, *Spain and the Independence of the United States: An Intrinsic Gift* (Albuquerque: University of New Mexico Press, 2002); Alexander DeConde, "Historians, the War of American Independence and the Persistence of the Exceptionalist Ideal," *International History Review*, 5 (August 1983), 399–430; Jonathan R. Dull, *A Diplomatic History of the American Revolution* (New Haven: Yale University Press, 1985); Ronald Hoffman and Peter J. Albert, eds., *Diplomacy and the Revolution: The Franco-American Alliance of 1778* (Charlottesville: University Press of Virginia, 1981); Lawrence S. Kaplan, *Entangling Alliances with None: American Foreign Policy in the Age of Jefferson* (Kent, Ohio: Kent State University Press, 1987); Richard B. Morris, *The Peacemakers: The Great Powers and American Independence* (New York: Harper and Row, 1965); Bradford Perkins, *The Cambridge History of American Foreign Relations, Volume 1: The Creation of a Republican Empire, 1776–1865* (Cambridge: Cambridge University Press, 1993); Paul A. Varg, *Foreign Policies of the Founding Fathers* (East Lansing: Michigan State University Press, 1963).
2. Jean Lerond d'Alembert, *The Plan of the French Encyclopædia, or Universal Dictionary of Arts, Sciences, Trades and Manufactures. Being an Account of the Origin, Design,* . . . (London: Innys et al., 1752), 2; Denis Diderot, *Political Writings*, John Hope Mason and Robert Wokler, trans. and eds. (Cambridge: Cambridge University Press, 1992), 21.
3. For a sampling of the literature on the Enlightenment, see Peter Gay, *The Enlightenment, an Interpretation: The Rise of Modern Paganism*, 2 vols. (New York: Knopf, 1966–69); Alan Charles Kors, ed., *The Encyclopedia of the Enlightenment*, 4 vols. (New York: Oxford University Press, 2003); Roy Porter, *The Creation of the Modern World: The Untold Story of the British Enlightenment* (New York: Norton, 2000). For the Enlightenment in America, see Robert A. Ferguson, *The American Enlightenment, 1750–1820* (Cambridge, Mass.: Harvard University Press, 1994).
4. This analysis builds upon the work of Felix Gilbert, *To the Farewell Address: Ideas of Early American Foreign Policy* (Princeton: Princeton University Press, 1970; orig. pub. 1961). For a different approach, see James H. Hutson, "Intellectual

Foundations of Early American Diplomacy," *Diplomatic History*, 1 (Winter 1977), 1–19; John E. Crowley, *The Privileges of Independence: Neomercantilism and the American Revolution* (Baltimore: Johns Hopkins University Press, 1993). For a short general discussion of European diplomacy in the context of the Enlightenment, see Karl W. Schweizer, "Diplomacy," in Kors, ed. *Encyclopedia of the Enlightenment*, 1: 360–64.

5. Quoted in Gilbert, *To the Farewell Address*, 60–61.

6. Montesquieu, *Spirit of the Laws*, Anne M. Cohler et al., eds. (Cambridge: Cambridge University Press, 1989; orig. pub. 1748).

7. Thomas Paine, *Common Sense*, Isaac Kramnick, ed. (New York: Penguin Books, 1976; orig. pub. 1776), 80–81.

8. Thomas Paine, among others, articulated this vision. See Paine, *Common Sense*, 80–81. See also David M. Fitzsimons, "Tom Paine's New World Order: Idealistic Internationalism in the Ideology of Early American Foreign Relations," *Diplomatic History*, 19 (Fall 1995), 569–82; Lawrence S. Kaplan, *Colonies into Nation: American Diplomacy 1763–1801* (New York: Macmillan, 1972), 93.

9. Quoted in Anthony Pagden, *Lords of All the World: Ideologies of Empire in Spain, Britain and France, c. 1500–c. 1800* (New Haven: Yale University Press, 1995), 180–82.

10. Isaac Gervaise, *The System or Theory of the Trade of the World . . .* (London: H. Woodfall; and sold by J. Roberts, near the Oxford, 1720), 19.

11. Quoted in Pagden, *Lords of All the World*, 180–82.

12. David Hume, "Of the Jealousy of Trade," *Essays Moral, Political, and Literary*, Eugene F. Miller, rev. ed. (Indianapolis: Liberty Classics, 1985), 327–28. See also Pagden, *Lords of All the World*, 180–82.

13. Adam Smith, *An Inquiry into the Nature and Causes of the Wealth of Nations*, Edwin Cannan, ed. (New York: Modern Library, 1994; orig. pub. 1776), 526–27.

14. For the Mireabeau quotation, see Pagden, *Lords of All the World*, 181. On the idea of sentiment in the eighteenth century, see John Brewer, *The Pleasures of the Imagination: English Culture in the Eighteenth Century* (New York: Farrar Straus Giroux, 1997). See also Sarah Knott, *Sensibility and the American Revolution* (Chapel Hill: University of North Carolina Press, 2009).

15. Gilbert, *To the Farewell Address*, 57–66. See also Paul Cheney, "A False Dawn for Enlightenment Cosmopolitanism? Franco-American Trade during the American War of Independence," *William and Mary Quarterly*, 3$^{rd}$ ser., 63 (July 2006), 469–72.

16. Hugo Grotius, *The Free Sea*, David Armitage, ed. (Indianapolis: Liberty Fund, 2004; orig. pub. 1609).

17. Cathy Matson, *Merchants and Empire: Trading in Colonial New York* (Baltimore: Johns Hopkins University Press, 1998), 6–8, 128.

18. New London *Connecticut Gazette*, November 16, 1770; Salem *Essex Gazette*, October 16–23, 1770.

19. Rivington's *New York Gazetteer*, August 25, 1774.

20. Quoted in Pagden, *Lords of All the World*, 117.

21. The essay was published in the *English Review* and reprinted in the Charleston *South-Carolina Weekly Gazette*, August 23, 1783.

22. David Armitage, *The Ideological Origins of the British Empire* (Cambridge: Cambridge University Press, 2000); Eliga H. Gould, *The Persistence of Empire: British Political Culture in the Age of the American Revolution* (Chapel Hill: University of North Carolina Press, 2000); Pagden, *Lords of All the World*.

23. Quoted in Thomas M. Truxes, *Defying Empire: Trading with the Enemy in Colonial New York* (New Haven: Yale University Press, 2008), 154.

24. Leonard W. Labaree et al., eds, *The Papers of Benjamin Franklin* (New Haven: Yale University Press, 1959-), 13: 133.

25. For a discussion of the efforts at customs regulation, see Charles M. Andrews, *The Colonial Background of the American Revolution* (New Haven: Yale University Press, 1924); I. R. Christie, *Crisis of Empire: Great Britain and the American Colonies, 1754–1783* (New York: Norton, 1966).

26. Smith, *The Wealth of Nations*, 504, 951–70.

27. For the New York petitioners, see Truxes, *Defying Empire*, 154. For a general discussion of smuggling, especially as it related to free trade, see Matson, *Merchants and Empire*.

28. Cadwallader Colden, *The Interest of the Country in Laying Duties: or a Discourse, Shewing How Duties on Some Sorts of Merchandize May Make the Province of New-York Richer than it Would Be Without Them* (New York: J. P. Zenger, [1726]), 6.

29. Archibald Kennedy, *Observations on the Importance of the Northern Colonies under Proper Regulations* (New York: James Parker, 1750), 10.

30. Quoted in Bernard Friedman, "The Shaping of the Radical Consciousness in Provincial New York," *Journal of American History*, 56 (March 1970), 789. See also the discussion in Cathy D. Matson and Peter S. Onuf, *A Union of Interests: Political and Economic Thought in Revolutionary America* (Lawrence: University of Kansas Press, 1990), 21–26.

31. Stephen Hopkins, *An Essay on the Trade of the Northern Colonies of Great Britain in North America* (Philadelphia, London: reprinted for T. Becket & P. A. De Hondt, 1764), 21–22, 26.

32. *Observations on Several Acts of Parliament . . . Published by the Merchants of Boston* ([Boston]: Eddes & Gill, [1769]). Quotations from ibid., 7, 24.

33. Stamp Act Congress, *Proceedings of the Congress at New-York* (Annapolis: Jonas Green, 1766), 16.

34. John Morgan et al., *Four Dissertations, on the Reciprocal Advantages of a Perpetual Union Between Great-Britain and Her American Colonies. Written for Mr. Sargent's Prize-medal . . .* (London: T. Payne, [1766]), 17, 22; Gould, *The Persistence of Empire*, 123–24.

35. William Hicks, *The Nature and Extent of Parliamentary Power Considered, in Some Remarks upon Mr. Pitt's Speech in the House of Commons, Previous to the Repeal of the Stamp-act. With an Introduction. Applicable to the Present Situation of the Colonies* (New York: Re-printed from the Pennsylvania journal, by John Holt, 1768), 32, 13.

36. Pauline Maier, *From Resistance to Revolution: Colonial Radicals and the Development of American Opposition to Britain, 1765–1776* (New York: Random House, 1972); Arthur Meier Schlesinger, *The Colonial Merchants and the American Revolution* (New York: Columbia University Press, 1918); Edmund S. and Helen M. Morgan, *The Stamp Act Crisis: Prologue to Revolution* (Chapel Hill: University of North Carolina Press, 1953).

37. *Journals of the Continental Congress* 1: 76; David Ammerman, *In the Common Cause: American Response to the Coercive Acts of 1774* (Charlottesville: University Press of Virginia, 1974).

38. Salem *Essex Gazette*, January 7 to 14, 1772.

39. Ibid., January 28 to February 4, 1772.

40. Thomas Jefferson, A *Summary View of the Rights of British America. Set Forth in Some Resolutions Intended for the Inspection of the Present Delegates of the People of Virginia. Now in Convention. By a Native, and Member of the House of Burgesses* (Williamsburg, [Va.]: Clementina Rind, [1774]), 8.

41. Joseph Galloway, *Americanus Examined, and His Principles Compared with Those of the Approved Advocates for America, by a Pennsylvanian* (Philadelphia: no pub., 1774), 17.

42. Philadelphia *Pennsylvania Evening Post*, June 22, 1775.

43. Wilkes's speech was reported in American newspapers. See Cambridge, Massachusetts, *New England Chronicle*, January 18 to January 25, 1776. See also the discussion in Peter Onuf and Nicholas Onuf, *Federal Union, Modern World: The Law of Nations in an Age of Revolutions, 1776–1814* (Madison, Wis.; Madison House, 1993), 103–06.

44. Armitage, *The Ideological Origins of the British Empire*, 41.

45. Smith, *The Wealth of Nations*, 1014.

46. Maurice R. O'Connell, *Irish Politics and Social Conflict in the Age of the American Revolution* (Philadelphia, University of Pennsylvania Press, 1965); Vincent Morely, *Irish Opinion and the American Revolution, 1760–1783* (Cambridge: Cambridge University Press, 2002); R. B. McDowell, *Ireland in the Age of Imperialism and Revolution, 1760–1801* (New York: Oxford University Press, 1979).

47. Gervaise, *The System or Theory of the Trade of the World*, 23.

48. Montesquieu, *The Spirit of the Laws*, 338.

49. Hume, *Essays Moral, Political, and Literary*, Miller, ed., 253–67, 308–31.

50. Crowley, *The Privileges of Independence*, 2–8. James H. Hutson centers much of his criticism on Gilbert's *To the Farewell Address* by acknowledging only this definition of free trade. Hutson, "Intellectual Foundations of Early American Diplomacy," *Diplomatic History*, 1 (Winter 1977), 1–19.

51. Quotations found in Smith, *The Wealth of Nations*, 493–94, 521, 680.

52. Smith, *The Wealth of Nations*, 501.

53. Crowley, *The Privileges of Independence*, 93, 85.

54. George Chalmers, *Collection of Treaties Between Great Britain and Other Powers*, 2 vols. (London: John Stockdale, 1790), 1: 402–04; Francis Taylor Piggott, "The Freedom of the Seas, Historically Treated," *Peace Handbooks: International Affairs*, vol. 23, no. 148 (London: H. M. Stationery Office, 1920), 14–28.

55. Chalmers, *Collection of Treaties Between Great Britain and Other Powers*, 1: 402–04; Bemis, *The Diplomacy of the American Revolution*, 130–63; Piggott, "The Freedom of the Seas" *Peace Handbooks*, 23: 14–28.
56. Emer de Vattel, *The Law of Nations*, Béla Kapossy and Richard Whatmore, eds. (Indianapolis: Liberty Fund, 2008; orig. pub. 1758).
57. Gould, *The Persistence of Empire*, 56.
58. Alice Clare Carter, *The Dutch Republic in Europe in the Seven Years War* (Coral Gables, Fla.: University of Miami Press, 1971); Carl J. Kulsrud, *Maritime Neutrality to 1780: A History of the Main Principles Governing Neutrality and Belligerency to 1780* (Boston: Little, Brown, and Company, 1936), 61–106.
59. Quoted in Truxes, *Defying Empire*, 64–65.
60. Quoted in Gould, *The Persistence of Empire*, 57.

## 2. The Revolutionary Experience

1. *Journals of the Continental Congress*, 10: 323–24, ibid., 11: 569–70.
2. Kenneth Scott, "Price Control in New England during the Revolution," *New England Quarterly*, 19 (December 1946), 453–73.
3. Jonathan Trumbull, *Jonathan Trumbull, Governor of Connecticut, 1769–1784* (Boston: Little, Brown, and Company, 1919), 223.
4. For quotations see Scott, "Price Control," *New England Quarterly*, 19 (December 1946), 462, 470. Newburyport *Essex Journal*, November 8, 1776.
5. Paul A. Gilje, *Rioting in America* (Bloomington: Indiana University Press, 1996), 24, 58; Barbara Clark Smith, "Food Rioters and the American Revolution," *William and Mary Quarterly*, 3rd ser., 51 (1994), 3–38; quotations from Smith, ibid., 7, 22, 24.
6. Pelatiah Webster, *Political Essays on the Nature and Operation of Money, Public Finances, and Other Subjects . . .* (Philadelphia: Joseph Crukshank, 1791), 9, 24.
7. Philadelphia *Pennsylvania Packet*, September 10, 1779.
8. John K. Alexander, "The Fort Wilson Incident of 1778: A Case Study of the Revolutionary Crowd," *William and Mary Quarterly*, 3rd ser., 31 (1974), 589–612; Kristen A. Foster, *Moral Visions and Material Ambitions: Philadelphia Struggles to Define the Republic, 1776–1836* (Lanham, Md.: Lexington Books, 2004); Steven Rosswurm, *Arms, Country, and Class: The Philadelphia Militia and "Lower Sort" during the American Revolution, 1775–1783* (New Brunswick, N.J.: Rutgers University Press, 1987).
9. Philadelphia *Independent Gazetteer*, January 8, 1791. For another author arguing for free trade, but more for international commerce, who cites Adam Smith in particular, see *Baltimore Evening Post*, August 8, 1792.
10. For a sampling of this literature, see Joyce Oldham Appleby, *Capitalism and a New Social Order: Republican Visions of the 1790s* (New York: New York University Press, 1984); Appleby, *Inheriting the Revolution: The First Generation of Americans* (Cambridge, Mass.: Harvard University Press, 2000); Gordon S. Wood, *The Radicalism of the American Revolution* (New York: Knopf, 1992). See also Paul A. Gilje, ed., *Wages of Independence: Capitalism in the Early Republic* (Madison, Wis.: Madison House, 1997).

11. Philadelphia *Pennsylvania Evening Post*, June 9, 1783.

12. Providence *United States Chronicle*, August 5, 1790; Philadelphia *General Advertiser*, June 15, 1793; *Philadelphia Gazette*, May 18, 1796.

13. Thomas Paine, *Common Sense*, Isaac Kramnick, ed. (New York: Penguin Books, 1976; orig. pub. 1776), 87.

14. Anthony Pagden, *Lords of All the World: Ideologies of Empire in Spain, Britain and France, c. 1500–c. 1800* (New Haven: Yale University Press, 1995), 184.

15. Paine, *Common Sense*, 86–87; Pagden, *Lords of all the World*, 184. See also the discussion in Felix Gilbert, *To the Farewell Address: Ideas of Early American Foreign Policy* (Princeton: Princeton University Press, 1970; orig. pub. 1961), 44–75; Peter S. Onuf and Nicholas Onuf, *Federal Union, Modern World: The Law of Nations in an Age of Revolutions, 1776–1814* (Madison, Wis.: Madison House, 1993), 93–122.

16. Moses Mather, *America's Appeal to the Impartial World. Wherein the Rights of the Americans, as Men, British Subjects, and as Colonists; the Equity of the Demand, and of the Manner in Which it Is Made upon Them by Great-Britain, Are Stated and Considered. And, the Opposition Made by the Colonies to Acts of Parliament, Their Resorting to Arms in Their Necessary Defence, Against the Military Armaments, Employed to Enforce Them, Vindicated . . .* (Hartford: Printed by Ebenezer Watson, 1775), 70.

17. David Ramsay, *An Oration on the Advantages of American Independence: Spoken Before a Publick Assembly of the Inhabitants of Charlestown in South-Carolina, on the Second Anniversary of That Glorious Aera* (Charlestown [Charleston, S.C.]: John Wells, Jun., 1778), 8.

18. John E. Crowley even points out that Congress considered a proposal by Benjamin Franklin that would pledge support for the British navigation acts for 100 years if the British accepted the Olive Branch Petition. John E. Crowley, *The Privileges of Independence: Neomercantilism and the American Revolution* (Baltimore: Johns Hopkins University Press, 1993), 50–51. For an examination of the Declaration of Independence in its international context, see David Armitage, *The Declaration of Independence: A Global History* (Cambridge, Mass.: Harvard University Press, 2007); and Armitage, "The Declaration of Independence and International Law," *William and Mary Quarterly*, 3rd ser., 59 (January 2002), 39–64.

19. "Plan of Treaties," *Papers of John Adams*, Robert J. Taylor et al., eds. (Cambridge, Mass.: Harvard University Press), 4: 260–302, esp. 277–78.

20. Plan of Treaties (September 17, 1776), *Journals of the Continental Congress*, 5: 768–69. See discussion in Gilbert, *To the Farewell Address*, 44–54; James H. Hutson, *John Adams and the Diplomacy of the American Revolution* (Lexington: University Press of Kentucky, 1980), 26–31; William C. Stinchcombe, *The American Revolution and the French Alliance* (Syracuse: Syracuse University Press, 1969), 1–31.

21. Hunter Miller, ed., *Treaties and Other International Acts of the United States of America*, 8 vols. (Washington, D.C.: Government Printing Office, 1931), 2: 3–44; Paul Cheyney, "A False Dawn for Enlightenment Cosmopolitanism? Franco-American Trade during the American War of Independence," *William and Mary Quarterly*, 3rd ser., 63 (July 2006), 462–88.

22. John Holroyd, earl of Sheffield, *Observations on the Commerce of the American States with Europe and the West Indies...* (Philadelphia: Robert Bell, 1783), [3–4], 40–41; Samuel Flagg Bemis, *Jay's Treaty: A Study in Commerce and Diplomacy* (New York, 1924), 30; Lawrence S. Kaplan, *Colonies into Nation: American Diplomacy 1763–1801* (New York: Macmillan, 1972), 158–61. See also *Newport Mercury*, August 17, 1782; Worcester *Massachusetts Spy*, June 19, 1783; *New-York Gazette*, September 15, 1783; Philadelphia *Pennsylvania Packet*, August 27, 1782.

23. See the discussion in David C. Hendrickson, *Peace Pact: The Lost World of the American Founding* (Lawrence: University of Press of Kansas, 2003), 115–57; Onuf and Onuf, *Federal Union, Modern World*, 108–116; Peter S. Onuf, "A Declaration of Independence for Diplomatic Historians," *Diplomatic History*, 22 (Winter 1998), 71–83.

24. The exact words of the provision were: "No State shall lay any imposts or duties, which may interfere with any stipulations in treaties, entered into by the United States in Congress assembled, with any King, Prince or State, in pursuance of any treaties already proposed by Congress to the courts of France and Spain." Articles of Confederation, Article 6.

25. For the information on different state charges, see The Society of Ship-Owners of Great Britain, *Collection of Interesting and Important Reports and Papers on the Navigation and Trade of Great Britain, Ireland, and the British Colonies* ([London]: Printed by order of The Society of Ship-owners of Great Britain, 1807), 55–60; Providence *United States Chronicle*, August 11, 1785; Bemis, *Jay's Treaty*, 24–25; Frederick W. Marks III, *Independence on Trial: Foreign Affairs and the Making of the Constitution* (Lantham, Md.: SR Books, 1984; orig. pub. 1973), 52–95. Washington quoted in Bemis, *Jay's Treaty*, 25.

26. United States Constitution, Article 1, sections 8 and 10; ibid., Article 2, section 2.

27. Miller, ed., *Treaties and Other International Acts of the United States of America*, 2: 55–95, 123–50, 162–84. For the wording of the Treaty of Utrecht provision on neutral shipping, see George Chalmers, *Collection of Treaties Between Great Britain and Other Powers*, 2 vols. (London: John Stockdale, 1790), 1: 403–04.

28. Gregg L. Lint, "The American Revolution and the Law of Nations, 1776–1789," *Diplomatic History*, 1 (Winter 1977), 20–34.

29. Philadelphia *Pennsylvania Packet*, July 11, 1780.

30. Quoted in Francis Taylor Piggott, "The Freedom of the Seas, Historically Treated," *Peace Handbooks: International Affairs*, vol. 23, no. 148 (London: H. M. Stationery Office, 1920), 23: 54. See also Lint, "The American Revolution and the Law of Nations, 1776–1789," *Diplomatic History*, 1 (Winter 1977), 20–34; Nikolai N. Bolkhovitinov, *The Beginnings of Russian-American Relations, 1775–1815* (Cambridge, Mass.: Harvard University Press, 1975), 3–29.

31. Piggott, "The Freedom of the Seas," *Peace Handbooks*, 23: 50.

32. Isabel De Madariaga, *Britain, Russia, and the Armed Neutrality of 1780: Sir James Harris's Mission to St. Petersburg during the American Revolution* (New Haven: Yale University Press, 1962). See also Samuel Flagg Bemis, *The Diplomacy of the American Revolution* (Bloomington: Indiana University Press, 1957), 149–63;

Richard B. Morris, *The Peacemakers: The Great Powers and American Independence* (New York: Harper and Row, 1965), 164–68.

33. Philadelphia *Pennsylvania Packet*, April 27, 1779; Worcester, Massachusetts, *Massachusetts Spy*, December 27, 1781. See also Philadelphia *Pennsylvania Packet*, July 11, 1780; ibid., June 27, 1782; Philadelphia *Pennsylvania Evening Post*, July 28, 1780; Boston *Independent Ledger*, November 27, 1780; *New-York Gazette*, March 18, 1782.

34. *Boston Evening-Post*, September 20, 1783.

## 3. The New Diplomacy

1. Providence *American Journal*, August 1, 1781.

2. Philadelphia *Pennsylvania Packet*, December 7, 1785. See also Boston *New-England Chronicle*, September 27, 1781; and Philadelphia *Pennsylvania Evening Post*, April 16, 1782.

3. *Newport Mercury*, July 29, 1776.

4. Philadelphia *Freeman's Journal*, May 5, 1784.

5. New York *Independent Journal*, February 5, 1785.

6. Philadelphia *Federal Gazette*, July 4, 1790.

7. For other toasts before 1800, see New York *Royal American Gazette*, July 22, 1783; Philadelphia *Federal Gazette*, July 13, 1792; *Philadelphia Gazette*, July 6, 1795; Baltimore *Federal Gazette*, August 14, 1797; *Greenleaf's New York Journal*, November 22, 1797; New Haven *Connecticut Journal*, October 3, 1798; Portsmouth *New Hampshire Gazette*, February 28, 1798.

8. *Boston Evening-Post*, September 20, 1783.

9. Richard B. Morris, *The Peacemakers: The Great Powers and American Independence* (New York: Harper and Row, 1965), 317–19, 333, 350–63, 409, 431–32; Andrew Stockley, *Britain and France at the Birth of America: The European Powers and the Peace Negotiations of 1782–1783* (Exeter, UK: University of Exeter Press, 2001), 177–83; Dumas Malone, *Jefferson and the Rights of Man* (Volume 2 of *Jefferson and His Time*) (Charlottesville: University Press of Virginia, 1951), 221–49; William Howard Adams, *The Paris Years of Thomas Jefferson* (New Haven: Yale University Press, 1997), 159–206; Merrill D. Peterson, "Thomas Jefferson and Commercial Policy, 1783–1793," *William and Mary Quarterly*, 3rd ser., 22 (October 1965), 589–90, 594–601.

10. *Boston Evening-Post*, September 20, 1783.

11. Malone, *Jefferson and the Rights of Man*, 21–26; Francis Wharton, ed., *The Revolutionary Diplomatic Correspondence of the United States*, 6 vols. (Washington D.C.: U.S. Government, 1889), 6: 717–19, 801–04.

12. For the model treaty and relevant documents, see Julian P. Boyd et al., eds., *The Papers of Thomas Jefferson*, (Princeton: Princeton University Press, 1950–), 7: 463–90.

13. Boyd et al., eds., *The Papers of Thomas Jefferson*, 7: 466; Jefferson to Adams, July 28, 1785, Boyd et al., eds., *The Papers of Thomas Jefferson*, 8: 315–20.

14. Jefferson to Monroe, June 17, 1785, Boyd et al., eds., *The Papers of Thomas Jefferson*, 8: 231.

15. Peterson, "Thomas Jefferson and Commercial Policy, 1783–1793," *William and Mary Quarterly*, 3rd ser., 22 (October 1965), 591.

16. "Draft of a Model Treaty," Boyd et al., eds., *The Papers of Thomas Jefferson*, 7: 482–83, 85.

17. "Draft of a Model Treaty," Boyd et al., eds., *The Papers of Thomas Jefferson*, 7: 486; "American Commissioners to De Thulemeier," November 10, 1784, ibid., 7: 491–92. For similar views expressed by Benjamin Franklin, see Franklin to M. Dumas, June 5, 1780, Leonard W. Labaree et al., eds, *The Papers of Benjamin Franklin* (New Haven: Yale University Press, 1959–), 32: 476.

18. To compare the model treaty to the Prussian treaty, see "Draft of a Model Treaty," Boyd et al., eds., *The Papers of Thomas Jefferson*, 7: 479–93; and Hunter Miller, ed., *Treaties and Other International Acts of the United States of America*, 8 vols. (Washington, D.C.: Government Printing Office, 1931), 2: 162–84. For the articles altered in negotiations, see Boyd et al., eds., *The Papers of Thomas Jefferson*, 8: 26–33.

19. Quoted in Felix Gilbert, *To the Farewell Address: Ideas of Early American Foreign Policy* (Princeton: Princeton University Press, 1970; orig. pub. 1960), 71–72.

20. Paul Leicester Ford, ed., *The Autobiography of Thomas Jefferson, 1743–1790: Together with a Summary of the Chief Events in Jefferson's Life*, new intro. by Michael Zuckerman (Philadelphia: University of Pennsylvania Press, 2005), 92–96.

21. For post-1783 diplomacy, see Samuel Flagg Bemis, *Jay's Treaty: A Study in Commerce and Diplomacy* (New York: Macmillan, 1924); Stanley Elkins and Eric McKitrick, *The Age of Federalism: The Early American Republic, 1788–1800* (New York: Oxford University Press, 1993); John Lamberton Harper, *American Machiavelli: Alexander Hamilton and the Origins of U.S. Foreign Policy* (Cambridge: Cambridge University Press, 2004); Reginald Horsman, *The Diplomacy of the New Republic, 1776–1865* (Arlington Heights, Ill.: H. Davidson, 1985); Daniel George Lang, *Foreign Policy in the Early Republic: The Law of Nations and the Balance of Power* (Baton Rouge: Louisiana State University Press, 1985); Frank T. Reuter, *Trials and Triumphs: George Washington's Foreign Policy* (Fort Worth: Texas Christian University Press, 1983); Robert W. Smith, *Keeping the Republic: Ideology and Early American Diplomacy* (DeKalb, Ill.: Northern Illinois University Press, 2004).

22. *Annals of Congress*, House of Representatives, 1st Congress, 1st sess., 117.

23. Ibid., 214.

24. Ibid., 247.

25. Boyd et al., eds., *The Papers of Thomas Jefferson*, 27: 574.

26. Portsmouth *New-Hampshire Gazette*, April 7, 1790. See also *Newport Herald*, August 20, 1789; Philadelphia *Pennsylvania Packet*, December 22, 1789; *Philadelphia Gazette*, May 11, 1795; ibid., October 3, 1795; Greenleaf's *New York Gazette*, December 19, 1795.

27. Douglass C. North, *The Economic Growth of the United States, 1790–1860* (New York: Norton, 1966; orig. pub. 1961), 24–58. See especially Table B-III in Appendix I, ibid., 221.

28. *American State Papers: Foreign Relations*, 1: 140.

29. Quotation in Bemis, *Jay's Treaty*, 158. See also ibid., 138–202; Boyd et al., eds., *The Papers of Thomas Jefferson*, 27: 532–81; *Annals of Congress*, House of Representatives, 3rd Congress, 1st sess., 155–59, 174–248, 256–349, 352–410, 412–32.

30. Miller, ed., *Treaties and Other International Acts of the United States of America*, 2: 245–74; Francis Taylor Piggott, "The Freedom of the Seas, Historically Treated," *Peace Handbooks: International Affairs*, vol. 23, no. 148 (London: H. M. Stationery Office, 1920), 63; Bemis, *Jay's Treaty*, 218–31. Article 18 of the treaty defined contraband. See Miller, ed., *Treaties and Other International Acts of the United States of America*, 2: 258–59.

31. Philadelphia *Gazette of the United States*, July 29, 1795. For a discussion of the Jay Treaty opposition, see Todd Estes, *The Jay Treaty Debate, Public Opinion, and the Evolution of Early American Political Culture* (Amherst: University of Massachusetts Press, 2006), 71–126; James Roger Sharp, *American Politics in the Early Republic: The New Nation in Crisis* (New Haven: Yale University Press, 1993), 113–37.

32. Philadelphia *Gazette of the United States*, July 28, 1795.

33. Miller, ed., *Treaties and Other International Acts of the United States of America*, 2: 247; New York *American Minerva*, July 21, 1795.

34. *Philadelphia Gazette of the United States*. For other Federalist Party articles using free trade while defending Jay's Treaty, see Mount Pleasant, New Jersey, *Jersey Chronicle*, May 2, 1795; Providence *United States Chronicle*, July 23, 1795; Philadelphia *Gazette of the United States*, July 18, 1795; ibid., July 23, 1795; Concord, New Hampshire, *Mirrour*, July 31, 1795; Philadelphia *Gazette of the United States*, August 7, 1795; Boston *Columbian Centinel*, August 19, 1795; Concord *Courier of New Hampshire*, August 22, 1795; Boston *The Courier*, October 7, 1795; *Philadelphia Gazette*, April 28, 1796; Boston *Columbian Centinel*, May 4, 1796; New York *Minerva*, July 28, 1796; Bennington *Vermont Gazette*, August 19, 1796.

35. The quotations are from the speech as reported in newspapers. See *Greenleaf's New York Journal*, January 22, 1794. For the full text of the speech in the official record, see *Annals of Congress*, House of Representatives, 3rd Congress, 1st sess., 210–25.

36. Philadelphia *Independent Gazetteer*, March 15, 1794.

37. *Philadelphia Gazette*, July 6, 1795.

38. Georgetown *Centinel of Liberty*, June 17, 1796.

39. *Journals of the Continental Congress*, 31: 477.

40. Miller, ed., *Treaties and Other International Acts of the United States of America*, 2: 318–49. See also Arthur Preston Whitaker, *The Spanish American Frontier: 1783–1795: The Westward Movement and the Spanish Retreat in the Mississippi Valley* (Lincoln: University of Nebraska Press, 1927).

41. Quoted in Alexander DeConde, *The Quasi-War: The Politics and Diplomacy of the Undeclared War with France, 1797–1801* (New York: Charles Scribner's Sons, 1966), 10.

42. Allan Potofsky, "The Political Economy of the French-American Debt Debate: The Ideological Uses of Atlantic Commerce, 1787 to 1800," *William and Mary Quarterly*, 3ʳᵈ ser., 63 (July 2006), 489–516; Stephen G. Kurtz, *The Presidency of John Adams: The Collapse of Federalism* (Philadelphia: University of Pennsylvania Press, 1957), 284–85; Joel Barlow to Jefferson, March 12, 1798, Boyd et al., eds., *The Papers of Thomas Jefferson*, 30: 174.

43. *American State Papers: Foreign Relations*, 2: 12.

44. DeConde, *The Quasi-War*, 3–33. For quotation see ibid., 10. See also *American State Papers: Foreign Relations*, 2: 28–65.

45. James D. Richardson, ed., *Compilation of Messages and Papers of the Presidents, 1789–1897* (Washington, D.C.: Government Printing Office, 1896), 1: 233–39.

46. *American State Papers: Foreign Relations*, 2: 169–82. Quotations ibid., 172, 175.

47. *American State Papers: Foreign Relations*, 2: 153–57.

48. DeConde, *The Quasi-War*, 36–73; *American State Papers: Foreign Relations*, 2: 157–82.

49. Charles Francis Adams, ed., *The Works of John Adams, Second President of the United States*... (Boston: Little, Brown, and Company, 1854), 9: 180–236. For quotations see ibid., 182, 228, 204, 208, 217.

50. Philadelphia *Gazette of the United States*, June 25, 1798. See also Baltimore *Federal Gazette*, July 6, 1798; Albany *Gazette*, July 6, 1798.

51. Baltimore *Federal Gazette*, June 25, 1798.

52. Adams, ed., *The Works of John Adams*, 9: 185–86.

53. Boston *Independent Chronicle*, January 14, 1799.

54. See the correspondence in J. Franklin Jameson, ed., "Letters of Toussaint Louverture and of Edward Stevens, 1798–1800," *American Historical Review*, 16 (October 1910), 67–72. See also Laurent Dubois, *Avengers of the New World: The Story of the Haitian Revolution* (Cambridge, Mass.: Harvard University Press, 2004); C. L. R. James, *Black Jacobins: Toussaint L'Ouverture and the San Domingo Revolution* (New York: Random House, 1963).

55. Baltimore *Federal Gazette*, July 14, 1798.

56. *New York Gazette*, January 1, 1799.

57. *Annals of Congress*, House of Representatives, 5ᵗʰ Congress, 3ʳᵈ sess., 2740–92.

58. *American State Papers: Foreign Relations*, 2: 244–69. Quotations from ibid., 250, 246.

59. Ibid., 301–06. Quotation from ibid., 305. See also DeConde, *The Quasi-War*, 237.

60. Piggott, "The Freedom of the Seas," *Peace Handbooks*, 23: 75–80; DeConde, *The Quasi-War*, 232, 243–45, 251–53, 303–06, 310–11.

61. Bradford Perkins, "Sir William Scott and the *Essex*," *William and Mary Quarterly*, 3ʳᵈ ser., 13 (April 1956), 172–73.

## 4. Legacy

1. Adams to Hendrik Calkoen, October 5, 1780, Robert J. Taylor et al., eds., *Papers of John Adams* (Cambridge, Mass.: Belknap Press of Harvard University Press, 1977–), 10: 203.

2. James D. Richardson, ed., *Compilation of Messages and Papers of the Presidents, 1789–1897* (Washington, D.C.: Government Printing Office, 1896), 1: 321–24.

3. Springfield, Mass. *Hampshire Chronicle*, December 23, 1789; Worcester, Mass., *Massachusetts Spy*, December 14, 1796.

4. *Compilation of Messages and Papers of the Presidents*, 1: 321–24.


Part Two: Sailors' Rights

1. Paul A. Gilje, *Liberty on the Waterfront: American Maritime Culture in the Age of Revolution* (Philadelphia: University of Pennsylvania Press, 2004).


5. Anglo-American Traditions

1. *Oxford English Dictionary*; Daniel James Ennis, *Enter the Press-Gang: Naval Impressment in Eighteenth-Century British Literature* (Newark: University of Delaware Press, 2002), 27–28; Denver Alexander Brunsman, "The Evil Necessity: British Naval Impressment in the Eighteenth-Century Atlantic World" (Ph.D. dissertation, Princeton University, 2004), 25.

2. Peter Kemp, *The British Sailor: A Social History of the Lower Deck* (London: Dent, 1970), 99–103, 162–63; Christopher Lloyd, *The British Seaman 1200–1860: A Social Survey* (London: Collins, 1968), 112–93, 285–86.

3. *The Sailors Advocate. First Printed in 1727–8. To Which Is Now Prefixed, Some Strictures, Drawn from the Statutes and Records, Relating to the Pretended Right of Taking Away Men by Force, under the Name of Pressing Seamen.* 8th ed., with Additions (London: B. White, and E. and C. Dilly, 1777), 2, 4, 8. Ennis identifies the author of the pamphlet as James Ogelthorpe, the philanthropist and founder of Georgia. Ennis, *Enter the Press-Gang*, 29.

4. As quoted in Brunsman, "The Evil Necessity," 58–59.

5. Ennis, *Enter the Press-Gang*, 53–63.

6. Ibid., 17, 63–66, 97–101.

7. Paul A. Gilje, *Liberty on the Waterfront: American Maritime Culture in the Age of Revolution* (Philadelphia: University of Pennsylvania Press, 2004); Bradford Perkins, *Prologue to War: England and the United States, 1805–1812* (Berkeley: University of California Press, 1968); James Fulton Zimmerman, *Impressment of American Seamen* (Port Washington, N.Y.: Kennikat Press, 1966).

8. Nicholas Rogers, *The Press Gang: Naval Impressment and Its Opponents in Georgian Britain* (London: Continuum, 2007), 60.

9. Rogers, *The Press Gang*, 37–80.

10. Michael Foster, *A Report of Some Proceedings on the Commission of Oyer and Terminer and Goal Delivery for the Trial of the Rebels in the Year 1746 in the County of Surry, and of Other Crown Cases . . .* (Oxford: Clarendon Press, 1762), 154–79. Quotations from ibid., 159, 174, 155–56.

11. Henry Cowper, *Reports of Cases Adjudged in the Court of King's Bench from Hilary Term, the 14th of George III, 1774, to Trinity Term, the 18th of George III, 1778, Both Inclusive*, 1st American from the 2nd London ed. (Boston: John West and Co., 1809), 2: 512–22. Quotations from ibid., 2: 517–18.

12. Foster, A *Report of Some Proceedings*, 157.
13. Cowper, *Reports of Cases*, 2: 519.
14. For this colonial background on the impress, see Brunsman, "The Evil Necessity"; Dora Mae Clark, "The Impressment of Seamen in the American Colonies," in *Essays in Colonial American History Presented to C. M. Andrews by His Students* (New Haven: Yale University Press, 1931), 198–224; Jesse Lemisch, *Jack Tar vs. John Bull: The Role of New York's Seamen in Precipitating the Revolution* (New York: Garland Publishing, 1997), 13–49.
15. Boston *News-Letter*, May 16–23, 1734; and Boston *New-England Weekly Journal*, July 22, 1734.
16. Philadelphia *American Weekly Mercury*, July 20–27, 1738; *Boston Gazette*, August 13–20, 1739.
17. *Boston Gazette*, September 3–10, 1739.
18. *Boston Post-Boy*, September 8, 1740.
19. Boston *News-Letter*, March 18–25, 1742.
20. On colonial labor and sailors, see Richard B. Morris, *Government and Labor in Early America* (New York: Columbia University Press, 1946), 225–78; Lemisch, *Jack Tar vs. John Bull*, 3–49; Daniel Vickers, *Farmers and Fishermen: Two Centuries of Work in Essex County, Massachusetts, 1630–1850* (Chapel Hill: University of North Carolina Press, 1994), 85–259; Vickers with Vince Walsh, *Young Men and the Sea: Yankee Seafarers in the Age of Sail* (New Haven: Yale University Press, 2005).
21. Kemp, *The British Sailor*, 99–103, 162–63; Lloyd, *The British Seaman*, 112–93.
22. John J. McCusker and Russell R. Menard, *The Economy of British America, 1607–1789* (Chapel Hill: University of North Carolina Press, 1985), 35–88; see especially 40, 57.
23. Quoted in Brunsman, "The Evil Necessity," 193. The analysis in this paragraph builds on Brunsman, "The Evil Necessity." See also Rogers, *The Press Gang*, 96–101.
24. Rogers, *The Press Gang*, 82–87.
25. Brunsman, "The Evil Necessity," 89–92, 176–266.
26. Quoted in ibid., 240.
27. Boston *American Weekly Mercury*, November 28 to December 5, 1745; *Boston Gazette*, November 26, 1745; *Boston Evening Post*, November 25, 1745.
28. Brunsman, "The Evil Necessity," 246–52.
29. John Lax and William Pencak, "The Knowles Riot and the Crisis of the 1740s in Massachusetts," *Perspectives in American History*, 10 (1976), 167–214; Gary B. Nash, *The Urban Crucible: Social Change, Political Consciousness, and the Origins of the American Revolution* (Cambridge, Mass.: Harvard University Press, 1979), 221–24.
30. Lemisch, *Jack Tar vs. John Bull*, 23–24.
31. Thomas M. Truxes, *Defying Empire: Trading with the Enemy in Colonial New York* (New Haven: Yale University Press, 2008), 34–35.
32. *Boston Post-Boy*, April 17, 1758.
33. *New-York Gazette*, April 17, 1758.

34. *New-York Mercury*, May 12, 1760.

35. Brunsman, "The Evil Necessity," 261.

36. *Boston Evening Post*, December 6, 1756.

37. *Boston News-Letter*, May 11, 1758.

38. *New-York Mercury*, August, 11, 1760.

39. *New-York Gazette*, August 25, 1760.

40. Lax and Pencak, "The Knowles Riot," *Perspectives in American History*, 10 (1976), 167–214; Nash, *The Urban Crucible*, 221–24.

### 6. The Rise of Jack Tar

1. Gary B. Nash, *The Urban Crucible: Social Change, Political Consciousness, and the Origins of the American Revolution* (Cambridge, Mass.: Harvard University Press, 1979), 312–38.

2. Quoted in Denver Alexander Brunsman, "The Evil Necessity: British Naval Impressment in the Eighteenth-Century Atlantic World" (Ph.D. dissertation, Princeton University, 2004), 273–74, 275.

3. Thomas Nicolson, March 29, 1767, Logbook *Remembergrace*, Folder 3, Navigation and Logbooks, 1766–1813, Ms. N-590, Massachusetts Historical Society.

4. Brunsman, "The Evil Necessity," 278–80.

5. Ibid., 280–81; *Boston News-Letter*, July 19, 1764.

6. Quoted in Brunsman, "The Evil Necessity," 280; *Newport Mercury*, June 10, 1765.

7. Hartford *Connecticut Courant*, July 22, 1765; Philadelphia *Pennsylvania Gazette*, July 25, 1765.

8. Quoted in Brunsman, "The Evil Necessity," 282.

9. Norfolk *Virginia Gazette*, October 1, 1767; Portsmouth *New Hampshire Gazette*, October 30, 1767. Pauline Maier, *From Resistance to Revolution: Colonial Radicals and the Development of American Opposition to Britain, 1765–1776* (New York: Knopf, 1972), 7, 20.

10. Paul A. Gilje, *The Road to Mobocracy: Popular Disorder in New York City, 1763–1834* (Chapel Hill: University of North Carolina Press, 1987), 3–68. See also Gilje, *Liberty on the Waterfront: American Maritime Culture in the Age of Revolution* (Philadelphia: University of Pennsylvania Press, 2004), 99–106; Jesse Lemisch, *Jack Tar vs. John Bull: The Role of New York's Seamen in Precipitating the Revolution* (New York: Garland Publishing, 1997), 51–157; Lemisch, "Jack Tar in the Streets: Merchant Seamen in the Politics of Revolutionary America," *William and Mary Quarterly*, 3rd ser., 25 (July 1968), 371–407; Peter Linebaugh and Marcus Rediker, *The Many-Headed Hydra: Sailors, Slaves, Commoners, and the Hidden History of the Revolutionary Atlantic* (Boston: Beacon Press, 2000), 211–47.

11. *Boston Chronicle*, June 13, June 20, 1768. See also *Boston Post-Boy*, June 20, 1768; New Haven *Connecticut Journal*, June 24, 1764.

12. *New-York Gazette and Weekly Mercury*, July 4, 1768.

13. *Boston* Chronicle, April 27, 1769; New-York *Journal*, June 22, 1769; Salem *Essex Gazette*, May 23–30, June 13–20, 1769; *Boston News-Letter*, June 1, 22, 1769; *Boston Post-Boy*, June 19, 1769. For Adams's comments on the trial many years

later, see "Diary," Charles Francis Adams, ed., *The Works of John Adams, Second President of the United States . . .* 10 vols. (Boston: Little, Brown, and Company, 1854), 2: 224–26, 526–34; "The Inadmissable Principles of the King of England's Proclamation of October 16, 1807, Considered," ibid., 9: 317–19; Adams to Dr. J. Morse, January 20, 1816, ibid., 10: 204–10. For Hutchinson's comments on the case, see Thomas Hutchinson, *The History of the Province of Massachusetts Bay, from 1749 to 1774: Comprising a Detailed Narrative of the Origin and Early Stages of the American Revolution* (London: John Murray, 1828), note, 231–33. See also Brunsman, "The Evil Necessity," 288–99; William Pencak, "Thomas Hutchinson's Fight against Naval Impressment," *New England Historical and Genealogical Register*, 132 (1978): 33.

14. On revolutionary riots in ports, see Gilje, *The Road to Mobocracy*, 3–68; Lemisch, *Jack Tar vs. John Bull*; Maier, *From Resistance to Revolution*, 3–157; Nash, *The Urban Crucible*, 292–328.

15. *An Act for the Encouragement of the Fisheries Carried on from Great-Britain, Ireland, and the British Dominions in Europe; and for Securing the Return of the Fishermen, Sailors, and Others, Employed in the Said Fisheries, to the Ports Thereof, at the End of the Fishing Season* (London: Charles Eyre and William Strahan, 1775), 22, 30–31.

16. *The Statutes at Large, from the Thirteenth Year of the Reign of King George the Third to the Sixteenth Year of the Reign of King George the Third, Inclusive . . .* (London: Charles Eyre and William Strahan, 1776), 227–31, 257–60; Allan J. McCurry, "The North Administration and the Outbreak of the Revolution," *Huntington Library Quarterly*, 34 (February 1971), 141–57. See also Christopher P. Magra, *The Fisherman's Cause: Atlantic Commerce and Maritime Dimensions of the American Revolution* (Cambridge: Cambridge University Press, 2009), 142–58.

17. Gilje, *Liberty on the Waterfront*, 114–16.

18. Ibid., 97–129.

19. Quoted in Cathy Matson, *Merchants and Empire: Trading in Colonial New York* (Baltimore: Johns Hopkins University Press, 1998), 122.

20. David Armitage, *The Ideological Origins of the British Empire* (Cambridge: Cambridge University Press, 2000), 142–43.

21. James Thomson, *Alfred: A Masque Represented before Their Royal Highnesses the Prince and Princess of Wales, at Cliffden, on the first of August, 1740* (London: A. Millar, 1740); Armitage, *The Ideological Origins of the British Empire*, 173–74.

22. Daniel James Enis, *Enter the Press Gang: Naval Impressment in Eighteenth-Century British Literature* (Newark: University of Delaware Press, 2002), 92.

23. Adams to Thomas Jefferson, August 4, 1785, Julian P. Boyd et al., eds., *The Papers of Thomas Jefferson* (Princeton: Princeton University Press, 1950–), 8: 341–42.

24. For a fuller treatment of reasons for fighting in the Revolutionary War aboard ships, see Gilje, *Liberty on the Waterfront*, 97–129.

25. Thomas Andros, *The Old "Jersey" Captive or a Narrative of the Captivity of Thomas Andros . . .* (Boston: William Pierce, 1833).

26. John Foss, *A Journal of the Captivity and Sufferings of John Foss; Several Years a Prisoner at Algiers . . .*, 2nd ed. (Newburyport, [Mass.]: Angier March, [1798]), 120.

27. For the report on whaling, see Boyd et al., eds., *Papers of Thomas Jefferson*, 14: 217–72. For the report on fisheries, see ibid., 19: 139–236. For the report on commerce, see ibid., 27: 532–81. Quotations see ibid., 19: 219; ibid. 14: 243.

28. Elizabeth Maddock Dillon, "Slaves in Algiers: Race, Republican Genealogies, and the Global Stage," *American Literary History*, 16 (Fall 2004), 410, 416; Susan L. Rattiner, ed., *Great Poems by American Women* (Mineola, N.Y.: Dover Publications, 1998), 18–19.

29. The musical was written under the pseudonym Isaac Bickerstaff, which was used by several British authors. Peter A. Tasch, *The Dramatic Cobbler: The Life and Works of Isaac Bickerstaff* (Lewisburg: Bucknell University Press, 1971), 31–39. [Isaac Bickerstaff], *Thomas and Sally: Or, The Sailor's Return. A Musical Entertainment . . .* (Philadelphia: Henry Taylor, 1791).

30. For collections of songs, see *The Festival of Mirth and American Tar's Delight: A Fund of the Newest Patriotic, Hunting, and Sea Songs . . .* (New York: Thomas B. Jansen, 1800); *Patriotic Medley: Being a Choice Collection of Patriotic, Sentimental, Hunting, and Sea Songs . . .* (New York: Jacob Johnkin, 1800); *The Sailor's Medley: A Collection of the Most Admired Sea and Other Songs* (Philadelphia: Matthew Carey, 1800); *The Syren; A Choice Collection of Sea, Hunting, and Other Songs* (Philadelphia: Matthew Carey, 1800); and John C. Purse, *Songs in the Purse; or, Benevolent Tar . . .* (Philadelphia: Wrigley and Berriman, 1794). For individual songs, see James Cobb, *The Capture: A Favorite Song in the Pirates Composed by S. Storace* (Philadelphia, Carr, [1793]); [Cobb], *Lullaby* (Philadelphia, Carr, [1793]); [Cobb], *A Sailor Lov'd a Lass Composed for the Cherokee* (Philadelphia: B. Carr, [1796]); Charles Dibden, *The Lucky Escape* (Philadelphia: Carr & Rice, [1794]); Dibden, *Poor Tom Bowling* (Philadelphia: Carr, [1794]); Dibden, *The Taken* [Philadelphia]: Carr, [1794]; Dibden, *'Twas in the Good Ship Rover . . .* (Philadelphia: Carr, [1794]); Prince Hoare, *The Sailor Boy* ([Philadelphia: Carr, 1793]); William Reeve, *When Seated with Sal: A Favorite Sea Song . . .* (Philadelphia: Carr, [1795]); Susanna Rowson, *The Little Sailor Boy: A Ballad* (Philadelphia: Carr, [1798]); Rowson, *Truxton's Victory: A Naval Patriotic Song* ([Boston: Thomas and Andrews, 1799]); Rowson, *Huzza for the Constellation* (Philadelphia: B. Carr, [1799]); and Steven Storace, *The Shpwreck's Seamen's Ghost* (Philadelphia: Carr, 1793). For other British plays and musicals with nautical themes produced in the United States, see J. C. Cross, *The Purse; or, Benevolent Tar. A Musical Drama in One Act as Performed at the Boston Theatre, Federal Street* (Boston: W. Pelham, 1797); and Richard Cumberland, *The Sailor's Daughter: A Comedy in Five Acts* (New York: David Longworth, 1804).

31. Philadelphia *Aurora General Advertiser*, February 2, 1795.

32. Paul Baepler, "The Barbary Captivity Narrative in American Culture," *Early American Literature*, 39 (June 2004), 220.

33. Matthew Carey, *A Short Account of Algiers . . .* (Philadelphia: J. Parker for M. Carey, 1794), 16, 44.

34. *American State Papers: Foreign Relations*, 1: 419.
35. See also Robert J. Allison, *The Crescent Obscured: The United States and the Muslim World, 1776–1815* (Chicago: University of Chicago Press, 1995); Dillon, "Slaves in Algiers," *American Literary History*, 16 (2004), 407–34; James R. Lewis, "Savages of the Seas: Barbary Captivity: Tales and Images of Muslims in the Early Republic," *Journal of American Culture*, 13 (Summer 1990), 75–84; Lawrence A. Peskin, *Captives and Countrymen: Barbary Slavery and the American Public, 1785–1816* (Baltimore: Johns Hopkins University Press, 2009).
36. *American State Papers: Foreign Relations*, 1: 140, 151. See also Alexander DeConde, *Entangling Alliance: Politics and Diplomacy under George Washington* (Durham, N.C.: Duke University Press, 1958), 214–16; Stanley Elkins and Eric McKitrick, *The Age of Federalism: The Early American Republic, 1788–1800* (New York: Oxford University Press, 1993), 345–47.
37. *American State Papers: Foreign Relations*, 1: 429.
38. *Greenleaf's New York Journal*, July 29, 1795.
39. *American State Papers: Foreign Relations*, 2: 28–29; Alexander DeConde, *The Quasi-War: The Politics and Diplomacy of the Undeclared War with France, 1797–1801* (New York: Charles Scribner's Sons, 1966), 10–17.
40. Susannah Rowson, *Truxton's Victory; with Megen Oh–oh Megen-ee: and the Soldier's Farewell* ([United States: no pub., 1799?]); *Patriotic Medley*, 16; Gilje, *Liberty on the Waterfront*, 156–57.
41. Gilje, *Liberty on the Waterfront*, 130–62.

## 7. Impressment

1. Philadelphia *Gazette of the United States*, April 23, 1795.
2. Philadelphia *Aurora General Advertiser*, June 4, 1796.
3. *Greenleaf's New York Journal*, March 22, 1796.
4. Richard B. Morris, *The Peacemakers: The Great Powers and American Independence* (New York: Harper & Row, 1965), 349.
5. Charles Francis Adams, ed., *The Works of John Adams, Second President of the United States* . . . 10 vols. (Boston: Little, Brown, and Company, 1854), 8: 450–51, 455–56.
6. *American State Papers: Foreign Relations*, 1: 131–32.
7. Ibid., 123–24.
8. Philadelphia *Dunlap's American Daily Advertiser*, June 8, 1791.
9. Jefferson to Pinckney, June 11, 1792, Julian P. Boyd et al., eds., *The Papers of Thomas Jefferson* (Princeton: Princeton University Press, 1950–), 24: 59–64; Pinckney to Jefferson, August 29, 1792, December 13, 1792, ibid., 24: 329–31, 735–40; Pinckney to Jefferson, January 3, 1793, March 13, 1793, ibid., 25: 11–13, 373–78.
10. This proposal originated with Phineas Bond. Phineas Bond to Lord Grenville, February 1, 1793, J. Franklin Jameson, ed., "Letters of Phineas Bond, British Consul at Philadelphia, to the Foreign Office of Great Britain, 1790–1794," *Annual Report of the American Historical Association for the Year 1897* (Washington, D.C.: Government Printing Office, 1898), 524–27; James Fulton Zimmerman, *Impressment of American Seamen* (Port Washington, N.Y.: Kennikat Press, 1966), 44–45.

11. Samuel Flagg Bemis, "The London Mission of Thomas Pinckney, 1792–1796," *American Historical Review*, 28 (January 1923), 228–47; Charles R. Ritcheson, "Thomas Pinckney's London Mission, 1792–1796, and the Impressment Issue," *International History Review*, 2 (October 1980), 523–41; Zimmerman, *Impressment of American Seamen*, 44–55. Quotations in Bemis, "The London Mission of Thomas Pinckney, 1792–1796," *American Historical Review*, 28 (January 1923), 239–40; Zimmerman, *Impressment of American Seamen*, 51.

12. *American State Papers: Foreign Relations*, 1: 472–74.

13. Ibid., 481–82. For a discussion of the political use of impressment, see Gerard H. Clarfield, *Timothy Pickering and American Diplomacy, 1795–1800* (Columbia, Mo.: University of Missouri Press, 1969), 46.

14. *Greenleaf's New York Journal*, July 29, 1795.

15. Philadelphia *Gazette of the United States*, September 5, 1795.

16. Philadelphia *Aurora General Advertiser*, June 4, 1796.

17. Ibid., October 20, 1795.

18. New York *Argus*, April 16, 1796.

19. Philadelphia *Aurora General Advertiser*, June 4, 1796.

20. New York *Argus*, April 16, 1796.

21. *Salem Gazette*, March 14, 1796.

22. Newburyport, Massachusetts, *Political Gazette*, April 12, 1796.

23. Clarfield, *Timothy Pickering and American Diplomacy*, 72–75.

24. *Salem Gazette*, May 31, 1796.

25. Philadelphia *Gazette of the United States*, August 7, 1795.

26. Boston *Columbian Centinel*, March 23, 1796.

27. Newburyport, Massachusetts, *Impartial Herald*, March 15, 1796; Boston *Federal Orrery*, March 17, 1796; Concord *Courier of New Hampshire*, March 21, 1796; Zimmerman, *Impressment of American Seamen*, 39.

28. Paul A. Gilje, *Liberty on the Waterfront: American Maritime Culture in the Age of Revolution* (Philadelphia: University of Pennsylvania Press, 2004), 157–62.

29. Bond to Grenville, February 1, 1793, Jameson, ed., "Letters of Phineas Bond," *Annual Report of the American Historical Association for the Year 1797*, 524–27.

30. Stockbridge, Massachusetts, *Western Star*, May 17, 1796.

31. John Algeo, ed., *The Cambridge History of the English Language: Volume 6, English in North America* (Cambridge: Cambridge University Press, 2001); David Simpson, *The Politics of American English, 1776–1850* (New York: Oxford University Press, 1986).

32. Boston *Federal Orrery*, March 17, 1796.

33. Mount Pleasant, New Jersey, *Jersey Chronicle*, August 22, 1795.

## 8. Citizenship

1. James H. Kettner, *The Development of American Citizenship, 1608–1870* (Chapel Hill: University of North Carolina Press, 1978). See also Douglas Bradburn, *The Citizenship Revolution: Politics and the Creation of the American Union, 1774–1804* (Charlottesville: University of Virginia Press, 2009).

2. William T. Hutchinson, ed., *The Papers of James Madison*, 17 vols. (Chicago: University of Chicago Press, 1962–92), 14: 168, 244–46.

3. Paul A. Gilje, *Liberty on the Waterfront: American Maritime Culture in the Age of Revolution* (Philadelphia: University of Pennsylvania Press, 2004); W. Jeffrey Bolster, *Black Jacks: African American Seamen in the Age of Sail* (Cambridge, Mass.: Harvard University Press, 1997).

4. Tracy quotation from *Annals of Congress*, House of Representatives, 4th Congress, 1st sess., 384. For the debate see ibid., 381–93, 395–400, 802–820. For the Senate action see ibid., Senate, 62–66, 73, 78, 101, 105. See also Ira Dye, "The Philadelphia Seamen's Protection Certificate Applications," *Prologue: Journal of the National Archives*, 18 (1986), 46–55; James Fulton Zimmerman, *Impressment of American Seamen* (Port Washington, N.Y.: Kennikat Press, 1966), 56–57, 68. 80–81; Gerard H. Clarfield, *Timothy Pickering and American Diplomacy, 1795–1800* (Columbia: University of Missouri Press, 1969), 77–82.

5. *Annals of Congress*, House of Representatives, 4th Congress, 1st sess., 387.

6. Zimmerman, *Impressment of American Seamen*, 62–73; Clarfield, *Timothy Pickering and American Diplomacy*, 80–86.

7. Nicholas Rogers, *The Press Gang: Naval Impressment and Its Opponents in Georgian Britain* (London: Continuum, 2007), 30–32.

8. *American State Papers: Foreign Relations*, 1: 243; Zimmerman, *Impressment of American Seamen*, 33–35.

9. [Niles'] *Weekly Register*, February 27, 1813.

10. *American State Papers: Foreign Relations*, 1: 123–24, 761–66; *American State Papers: Foreign Relations*, 2: 126–50, 269–80, 292–94, 471–74, 593–95, 730–32, 737, 776–98; *American State Papers: Foreign Relations*, 3: 36–79, 166, 347–48, 405.

11. *Philadelphia Gazette*, January 9, 1799; Norwich, Connecticut, *Courier*, January 16, 1799.

12. *American State Papers: Foreign Relations*, 2: 203–04; *Naval Documents Related to the Quasi-War between the United States and France: Naval Operations from November 1793 to March 1799* (Washington, D.C.: Government Printing Office, 1935), 2: 26–34, 110, 227, 243. Phillips later claimed that he did surrender his ship by lowering its flag and raised the flag only when the British squadron sailed away. Isaac Phillips, *An Impartial Examination of the Case of Captain Isaac Phillips, Late of the Navy, and Commander of the United States Sloop of War Baltimore, in 1798 . . .* (Baltimore: Benjamin Edes, 1825). For the British reaction, see George W. Kyte, "Robert Liston and Anglo-American Cooperation, 1796–1800," *Proceedings of the American Philosophical Society*, 93 (June 10, 1949), 259–66.

13. For Federalist questions about the story, see the Boston *Columbian Centinel*, February 27, 1799.

14. *Philadelphia Gazette*, March 7, 1799. For a slightly different version of the same story, see ibid., February 15, 1799.

15. Hartford, Connecticut, *American Mercury*, March 21, 1799; Homer C. Votaw, "The Sloop-of-War Ganges," United States Naval Institute *Proceedings*, 98 (July 1972), 82–84.

16. *Greenleaf's New York Journal*, March 22, 1796.

### 9. The *Hermione* and the Rights of Man

1. James Dugan, *The Great Mutiny* (New York: New American Library, 1967; orig. pub. 1965); Dudley Pope, *The Black Ship* (New York: Henry Holt and Company, 1998; orig. pub. 1963); Joseph P. Moore III, "'The Greatest Enormity that Prevails': Direct Democracies and Workers' Self-Management in the British Naval Mutinies of 1797," in Colin Howell and Richard J. Twomey, eds., *Jack Tar in History: Essays in the History of Maritime Life and Labour* (Fredericton, New Brunswick: Acadiensis Press, 1991), 76–104; Niklas Frykman, "The Mutiny on the Hermione: Warfare, Revolution, and Treason in the Royal Navy," *Journal of Social History*, 44 (Fall 2010), 159–87.
2. Both reports appeared in New York *Diary*, June 26, 1797.
3. Springfield, Massachusetts, *American Intelligencer*, June 27, 1797.
4. Job Sibly, *The Trial of Richard Parker, Complete; President of the Delegates, for Mutiny, &c...* (Boston: Samuel Etheridge, 1797). To get a further sense of the extent of the newspaper coverage in the United States, see *Philadelphia Gazette*, June 3, 15, 16, 27, August 1, 2, 3, 10, 11,19, 21, 22, 26, 28, 30, 1797.
5. Newburyport, Massachusetts, *Political Gazette*, April 12, 1796; *Greenleaf's New York Journal*, July 5, 1796; James Fulton Zimmerman, *Impressment of American Seamen* (Port Washington, N.Y.: Kennikat Press, 1966), 40–41.
6. The best discussion of these cases and their legal implications is Ruth Wedgewood, "The Revolutionary Martyrdom of Jonathan Robbins," *Yale Law Journal*, 100 (November 1990), 268–86.
7. Wedgewood, "The Revolutionary Martyrdom of Jonathan Robbins," *Yale Law Review*, 100 (November 1990), 286–308; *American State Papers: Foreign Relations*, 2: 284–85.
8. *Annals of Congress*, House of Representatives, 6th Congress, 1st sess., 511–12, 515–18, 525–26, 531–32, 541–78, 583–620. Quotations ibid., 511, 575, 617.
9. Quoted in Pope, *The Black Ship*, 292.
10. For quotations and a discussion of "The Hermione Phobia," see Christopher Mckee, *A Gentlemanly and Honorable Profession: The Creation of the U.S. Naval Officer Corps, 1794–1815* (Annapolis, Md.: United Stats Naval Institute, 1991), 255–67.

### Part Three: Origins

1. For interpretations on the origin of the War of 1812, see Reginald Horsman, *The Causes of the War of 1812* (Philadelphia: University of Pennsylvania Press, 1962); Donald Hickey, *The War of 1812: A Forgotten Conflict* (Urbana: University of Illinois Press, 1989); Bradford Perkins, *Prologue to War: England and the United States, 1805–1812* (Berkeley: University of California Press, 1968); Richard Buel, Jr., *America on the Brink: How the Political Struggle over the War of 1812 Almost Destroyed the Young Republic* (New York: Palgrave Macmillan, 2005); Julius W. Pratt, *Expansionists of 1812* (New York: Macmillan, 1925); J. C. A. Stagg, *Mr. Madison's War: Politics, Diplomacy, and Warfare in the Early American Republic, 1783–1830* (Princeton: Princeton University Press, 1983);

Roger H. Brown, *The Republic in Peril: 1812* (New York: Columbia University Press, 1964). For regional examinations of the causes of the war, see Robert V. Haynes, "The Southwest and the War of 1812," *Louisiana History*, 5 (Winter 1964), 41–51; Reginald Horsman, "Western War Aims, 1811–1812," *Indiana Magazine of History*, 53 (March 1957), 1–18; Martin Kaufman, "War Sentiment in Western Pennsylvania: 1812," *Pennsylvania History*, 31 (October 1964), 436–48; Margaret Kinard Latimer, "South Carolina – Protagonist of the War of 1812," *American Historical Review*, 61 (July 1956), 914–29; Brian Schoen, "Calculating the Price of Union: Republican Economic Nationalism and the Origins of Southern Sectionalism, 1790–1828," *Journal of the Early Republic*, 23 (Summer 2003), 173–206. For historiographical summaries, see Clifford L. Egan, "The Origins of the War of 1812: Three Decades of Historical Writing," *Military Affairs*, 38 (April 1974), 72–75.

## 10. Empire of Liberty

1. See, for example, Bradford Perkins, *The Cambridge History of American Foreign Relations, Volume 1: The Creation of a Republican Empire, 1776–1865* (Cambridge: Cambridge University Press, 1993).

2. Jefferson to Monroe, November 24, 1801, Julian P. Boyd et al., eds., *The Papers of Thomas Jefferson* (Princeton: Princeton University Press, 1950–), 35: 719.

3. Jefferson to Archibald Stuart, January 25, 1786, Boyd et al., eds., *The Papers of Thomas Jefferson*, 9: 218.

4. Julian P. Boyd, "Thomas Jefferson's 'Empire of Liberty'," *Virginia Quarterly Review*, 24 (1948), 548. See also the discussion in Robert W. Tucker and David C. Hendrickson, *Empire of Liberty: The Statecraft of Thomas Jefferson* (New York: Oxford University Press, 1990), 159–62, 312–14.

5. Drew R. McCoy, *The Elusive Republic: Political Economy in Jeffersonian America* (Chapel Hill: University of North Carolina Press, 1980).

6. Boyd et al., eds., *The Papers of Thomas Jefferson*, 33: 150.

7. François Furstenberg suggests that this focus on the trans-Appalachian West was part of a longer contest for the region among Native Americans, Spain, France, Great Britain, and the United States in which the final outcome remained unclear until the end of the War of 1812. From this Atlantic perspective the War of 1812 was the last episode of the "Long War for the West" that lasted from 1754 to 1815. See Furstenberg, "The Significance of the Trans-Appalachian Frontier in Atlantic History," *American Historical Review*, 113 (June 2008), 647–77.

8. Douglas Adair, "Hamilton on the Louisiana Purchase: A Newly Identified Editorial from the New-York Evening Post," *William and Mary Quarterly*, 3rd ser., 12 (April 1955), 276.

9. Quoted in Henry Adams, *History of the United States of America: During the First Administration of Thomas Jefferson*, 9 vols. (New York: Charles Scribner's Sons, 1891–98), 2: 97, 100.

10. Benjamin Rush, "An Account of the Progress of Population. Agriculture, Manners, and Government in Pennsylvania, in a Letter to a Friend in England," in Rush, *Essays, Literary, Moral & Philosophical by Benjamin Rush, M. D. and Professor*

*of the Institutes of Medicine and Clinical Practice in the University of Pennsylvania* (Philadelphia: Thomas & Samuel F. Bradford, 1798), 213–15.

11. George Washington to Benjamin Harrison, Oct. 10, 1784, The George Washington Papers on line, 1741–1799, Library of Congress.

12. John Mack Faragher, *Daniel Boone: The Life and Legend of an American Pioneer* (New York: Henry Holt and Company, 1992), 274–79. Quotation in ibid., 274. See also Furstenberg, "The Significance of the Trans-Appalachian Frontier in Atlantic History," *American Historical Review*, 113 (June 2008), 655–67; Frederick W. Marks III, *Independence on Trial: Foreign Affairs and the Making of the Constitution* (Lantham, Md.: SR Books, 1984; orig. pub. 1973), 34–36; James Roger Sharp, *American Politics in the Early Republic: The New Nation in Crisis* (New Haven: Yale University Press, 1993), 92–112.

13. Arthur Preston Whitaker, *The Spanish American Frontier, 1783–1795: The Westward Movement and the Spanish Retreat in the Mississippi Valley* (Boston: Houghton Mifflin Company, 1927). For the connection between free trade and the right of deposit in New Orleans, see *Alexandria Expositor*, March 9, 1803; *Alexandria Advertiser*, March 28, 1803; Boston *Independent Chronicle*, July 4, 1803; Portsmouth *New-Hampshire Gazette*, December 20, 1803; Kingston, New York, *Plebeian*, June 20, 1804.

14. Jefferson to Robert R. Livingston, February 3, 1803, Paul Leicester Ford, ed., *The Works of Thomas Jefferson*, 12 vols. (New York: G. P. Putnam's Sons, 1904–05), 9: 441.

15. Report on Negotiations with Spain, March 18, 1792, Boyd et al., eds., *The Papers of Thomas Jefferson*, 23: 296–317; quote from ibid., 303.

16. Jefferson to Archibald Stuart, January 25, 1786, Boyd et al., eds., *The Papers of Thomas Jefferson*, 9: 218.

17. Jefferson to Livingston, April 18, 1802, Ford, ed., *The Works of Thomas Jefferson*, 9: 364.

18. Laurent Dubois, *Avengers of the New World: The Story of the Haitian Revolution* (Cambridge, Mass.: Harvard University Press, 2004); C. L. R. James, *Black Jacobins: Toussaint L'Ouverture and the San Domingo Revolution* (New York: Random House, 1963); Lester Langley, *The Americas in the Age of Revolution, 1750–1850* (New Haven: Yale University Press, 1996).

19. Alexander DeConde, *The Affair of Louisiana* (New York: Scribener's, 1976); Peter J. Kastor, *The Nation's Crucible: The Louisiana Purchase and the Creation of America* (New Haven: Yale University Press, 2004): Jon Kukla, *A Wilderness So Immense: The Louisiana Purchase and the Destiny of the America* (New York: Knopf, 2003).

20. Thomas D. Clark and John D. W. Guice, *Frontiers in Conflict: The Old Southwest, 1795–1830* (Albuquerque: University of New Mexico Press, 1989); Robert L. Gold, *Borderland Empires in Transition: The Triple-Nation Transfer of Florida* (Carbondale: Southern Illinois Press, 1969); Frank Lawrence Owsley, Jr., and Gene A. Smith, *Filibusters and Expansionists: Jeffersonian Manifest Destiny, 1800–1821* (Tuscaloosa: University of Alabama Press, 1997), 7–31; Tucker and Hendrickson, *Empire of Liberty*, 108–88; David J. Weber, *The Spanish Frontier in North America* (New Haven: Yale University Press, 1992).

21. Presidential Proclamation, [October 27, 1810], Robert E. Rutland et al., eds., *The Papers of James Madison: Presidential Series*, vols. 1– (Charlottesville: University Press of Virginia, 1984–), 2: 595.

22. James G. Cusick, *The Other War of 1812: The Patriot War and the American Invasion of Spanish East Florida* (Gainesville: University Press of Florida, 2003).

23. Karen Racine, *Francisco de Miranda: A Transatlantic Life in the Age of Revolution* (Wilmington, Del.: Scholarly Resources, 2003).

24. Owsley, Jr., and Smith, *Filibusters and Expansionists*, 32–60.

25. Alan Taylor, *The Divided Ground: Indians, Settlers, and the Northern Borderland of the American Revolution* (New York: Knopf, 2006).

26. Quotation in Julius W. Pratt, *Expansionists of 1812* (New York: Macmillan, 1925), 35.

27. *Annals of Congress*, House of Representatives, 12th Congress, 1st sess., 425–26.

28. Jefferson to Madison, April 27, 1809, J. Jefferson Looney et al., eds., *The Papers of Thomas Jefferson: Retirement Series*, vols. 1– (Princeton: Princeton University Press, 2004–), 1: 169.

## 11. Indians in the Way

1. Claudio Saunt, *A New Order of Things: Property, Power, and the Transformation of Creek Indians, 1733–1816* (Cambridge: Cambridge University Press, 1999); John Sugden, *Blue Jacket: Warrior of the Shawnees* (Lincoln: University of Nebraska Press, 2002).

2. Patrick Griffin, *American Leviathan: Empire, Nation, and Revolutionary Frontier* (New York: Hill & Wang, 2007).

3. Quoted in Colin G. Calloway, *Crown and Calumet: British-Indian Relations, 1783–1815* (Norman: University of Oklahoma Press, 1987), 10–11.

4. For a discussion of the Indian experience in the Revolutionary War and the years immediately after, see Colin G. Calloway, *The American Revolution in Indian Country: Crisis and Diversity on Native American Communities* (Cambridge: Cambridge University Press, 1995); Gregory Evans Dowd, *A Spirited Resistance: The North American Indian Struggle for Unity, 1745–1815* (Baltimore: Johns Hopkins University Press, 1992); Joseph T. Glatthaar and James Kirby Martin, *Forgotten Allies: The Oneida Indians and the American Revolution* (New York: Hill and Wang, 2006); Griffin, *American Leviathan*; Thomas M. Hatley, *The Dividing Paths: Cherokees and South Carolinians through the Era of Revolution* (New York: Oxford University Press, 1995); Eric Hinderaker, *Elusive Empires: Constructing Colonialism in the Ohio Valley, 1673–1800* (Cambridge: Cambridge University Press, 1997); William G. McLoughlin, *Cherokee Renascence in the New Republic* (Princeton: Princeton University Press, 1986); James H. Merrell, *The Indians' New World: Catawbas and Their Neighbors from European Contact through the Era of Removal* (Chapel Hill: University of North Carolina Press, 1989); Saunt, *A New Order of Things*; Alan Taylor, *The Divided Ground: Indians, Settlers, and the Northern Borderland of the American Revolution* (New York: Knopf, 2006); Richard White, *The Middle Ground: Indians, Empires, and the Republic in the Great Lakes Region, 1650–1815* (Cambridge: Cambridge University Press, 1991).

5. *Journals of the Continental Congress*, 25: 680–93.

6. Washington to James Duane, September 7, 1783, John C. Fitzpatrick, ed., *The Writings of George Washington from the Original Manuscript Sources 1745–1799* (1931–44), vol. 27, electronic edition, Preface to the Electronic Edition, Frank E. Grizzard, Jr., George Washington Resources at the University of Virginia Library.

7. Quoted in Reginald Horsman, *Expansion and American Indian Policy, 1783–1812* (Norman: University of Oklahoma Press, 1992; orig. pub. 1967), 36.

8. *American State Papers: Indian Affairs*, 1: 13, 61; Knox to Wayne, January 5, 1792[3], Richard C. Knopf, ed., *Anthony Wayne, A Name in Arms: Soldier, Diplomat, Defender of Expansion Westward of a Nation (The Wayne-Knox-Pickering-McHenry Correspondence)* (Pittsburgh: University of Pittsburgh Press, 1960), 165.

9. *Journals of the Continental Congress*, 33: 479–80.

10. Horsman, *Expansion and American Indian Policy, 1783–1812*, 32–52.

11. *American State Papers: Indian Affairs*, 1: 356.

12. For the diplomacy behind these developments, see Samuel Flagg Bemis, *Jay's Treaty: A Study in Commerce and Diplomacy* (New York: Macmillan, 1924), 109–33, 161–96. On the Treaty of Greenville, see Andrew R. L. Cayton, "'Noble Actors' upon 'the Theatre of Honour': Power and Civility in the Treaty of Greenville," in *Contact Points: American Frontiers from the Mohawk Valley to the Mississippi, 1750–1830*, Cayton and Fredrika J. Teute, eds. (Chapel Hill: University of North Carolina Press, 1998), 235–69.

13. Arthur Preston Whitaker, *The Spanish American Frontier, 1783–1795: The Westward Movement and the Spanish Retreat in the Mississippi Valley* (Boston: Houghton Mifflin Company, 1927).

14. *U.S. Statutes at Large* 1 (1790), 137–38; Francis Paul Prucha, *American Indian Policy in the Formative Years: The Indian Trade and Intercourse Acts, 1790–1834* (Cambridge, Mass.: Harvard University Press, 1962), 41–50.

15. For Washington's use of the phrase, see Washington to Duane, September 7, 1783, Fitzpatrick, ed., *Writings of George Washington* (1931–44), vol. 27, electronic edition, George Washington Resources at the University of Virginia Library. For recent discussion of the process of frontier settlement in the early republic, see Stephen Aron, *How the West Was Lost: The Transformation of Kentucky from Daniel Boone to Henry Clay* (Baltimore: Johns Hopkins University Press, 1996); Cayton and Teute, eds, *Contact Points*; Andrew R. L. Cayton, *The Frontier Republic: Ideology and Politics in the Ohio Country, 1780–1825* (Kent, Ohio: Kent State University Press, 1986); Cayton, *Frontier Indiana* (Bloomington: Indiana University Press, 1998); John Mack Faragher, *Daniel Boone: The Life and Legend of an American Pioneer* (New York: Henry Holt and Company, 1992); Christopher Morris, *Becoming Southern: The Evolution of a Way of Life, Warren County and Vicksburg, Mississippi, 1770–1860* (New York: Oxford University Press, 1995); Alan Taylor, *William Cooper's Town: Power and Persuasion on the Frontier of the Early American Republic* (New York: Knopf, 1995).

16. Horsman, *Expansion and American Indian Policy, 1783–1812*, 32–65.

17. James D. Richardson, ed., *Compilation of Messages and Papers of the Presidents, 1789–1897* (Washington, D.C.: Government Printing Office, 1896), 1: 380.

18. "To the Miamis, Powtewatamies, Delawares, and Chipeways," December 21, 1808, *The Writings of Thomas Jefferson*, 20 vols. (Washington, D.C.: Issued under the Auspices of the Thomas Jefferson Memorial Association of the United States, 1903–04), 16: 439.

19. Bernard W Sheehan, *Seeds of Extinction: Jeffersonian Philanthropy and the American Indian* (Chapel Hill: University of North Carolina Press, 1973); Anthony F. C. Wallace, *Jefferson and the Indians: The Tragic Fate of the First Americans* (Cambridge, Mass.: Harvard University Press, 1999).

20. Jefferson to Harrison, February 27, 1803, Logan Esary, ed., *Governors Messages and Letters: Messages and Letters of William Henry Harrison*, 2 vols. (Indianapolis: Indiana Historical Commission, 1922), 1: 71.

21. Saunt, *A New Order of Things*; Gregory Evans Dowd, "Spinning Wheel Revolution," in James Horn et al., eds., *The Revolution of 1800: Democracy, Race and the New Republic* (Charlottesville: University Press of Virginia, 2002), 267–87; Frank Lawrence Owsley, Jr., *Struggle for the Gulf Borderlands: The Creek War and the Battle of New Orleans, 1812–1815* (Gainesville: University Press of Florida, 1981); Michael D. Green, *The Politics of Indian Removal: Creek Government and Society in Crisis* (Lincoln: University of Nebraska Press, 1982); Benjamin W. Griffith, Jr., *McIntosh and Weatherford, Creek Indian Leaders* (Tuscaloosa: University of Alabama Press, 1988); Joel W. Martin, *Sacred Revolt: The Muskogees' Struggle for a New World* (Boston: Beacon Press, 1991).

22. Dowd, *A Spirited Resistance*; Anthony F. C. Wallace, *The Death and Rebirth of the Seneca* (New York: Knopf, 1969).

23. Quoted in R. David Edmunds, *Tecumseh and the Quest for Indian Leadership* (Boston: Little, Brown and Company, 1984), 131.

24. R. David Edmunds, *The Shawnee Prophet* (Lincoln: University of Nebraska Press, 1983); Edmunds, *Tecumseh and the Quest for Indian Leadership*.

25. Reginald Horsman, *The Causes of the War of 1812* (Philadelphia: University of Pennsylvania Press, 1962), 158–77, 204–16; Edmunds, *Tecumseh and the Quest for Indian Leadership*, 135–60. Quotation in ibid., 136.

26. *Annals of Congress*, House of Representatives, 12th Congress, 1st sess., 425–26.

27. Ibid., 484–90. Quotation in ibid., 490.

28. Ibid., 500.

29. Edmunds, *Tecumseh and the Quest for Indian Leadership*, 136.

## 12. Contested Commerce

1. Reginald Horsman, *The Causes of the War of 1812* (Philadelphia: University of Pennsylvania Press, 1962), 24–43, 63–82; James Stephens, *War in Disguise: or, the Frauds of the Neutral Flags* (London: C. Whittingham, 1805), 146, 185–86.

2. Bradford Perkins, *The First Rapprochement: England and the United States, 1795–1805* (Philadelphia: University of Pennsylvania Press, 1955), 129–38.

3. Madison to Monroe, July 1, 1804, Stanislaus Murray Hamilton, ed., *The Writings of James Monroe, Including a Collection of His Public and Private Papers and Correspondence Now for the First Time Printed*, 7 vols. (New York: G. P. Putnam's Sons, 1898–1903), 4: 218–23.

4. Horsman, *The Causes of the War of 1812*, 44–62.

5. New Haven *Connecticut Herald*, July 2, 1805.

6. James D. Richardson, ed., *Compilation of Messages and Papers of the Presidents, 1789–1897* (Washington, D.C.: Government Printing Office, 1896), 1: 384.

7. James Madison, *An Examination of the British Doctrine, Which Subjects to Capture a Neutral Trade, Not Open in Time of Peace* ([Philadelphia?]: no pub., [1806?]), 10, 203, 137, 139, 171. See also Irving Brant, *James Madison: Secretary of State, 1800–1809* (Indianapolis: Bobbs-Merrill, 1953), 297–304.

8. *Annals of Congress*, House of Representatives, 9th Congress, 1st sess., 412–13.

9. The Jay Treaty had a time limit set at either twelve years after it was ratified by both the United States and Great Britain or two years after the end of the British war with France. The Peace of Amiens ended the Anglo-French conflict, albeit temporarily, so the treaty expired in 1803 rather than 1807. Donald R. Hickey, "The Monroe-Pinckney Treaty of 1806: A Reappraisal," *William and Mary Quarterly*, 3rd ser., 44 (January 1987), 66, n. 4.

10. Quotation in Bradford Perkins, *Prologue to War, 1805–1812: England and the United States* (Berkeley: University of California Press, 1968), 113.

11. *U.S. Statutes at Large* 2 (1806), 379–81.

12. Quotation in Perkins, *Prologue to War*, 106.

13. Horsman, *The Causes of the War of 1812*, 63–82.

14. For the numbers and impact of British seizure of ships, see Hickey, "The Monroe-Pinckney Treaty," *William and Mary Quarterly*, 3rd ser., 44 (January 1987), 71–72.

15. New York *American Citizen*, April 28, 1806; Philadelphia *United States Gazette*, April 29, 1806.

16. *New York Evening Post*, April 28, 1806.

17. For a report of the incident, see *New York Daily Advertiser*, April 28, 1806. For additional examples of the political reaction to the incident, see *Trenton Federalist*, May 12, 1806; Easton, Maryland, *Republican Star*, May 27, 1806; Walpole, New Hampshire, *Political Observatory*, June 27, 1806.

18. *American State Papers: Foreign Relations*, 3: 119–58.

19. Jefferson to Madison, April 21, 1807, Paul Leicester Ford, ed., *The Works of Thomas Jefferson*, 12 vols. (New York: G. P. Putnam's Sons, 1904–05), 10: 388–90. For the list of provisions, almost all of them commercial in nature, that Jefferson and Madison believed needed to be renegotiated, see Madison's note to Monroe and Pinkney, May 20, 1807, *American State Papers: Foreign Relations*, 3: 166–75. For a fuller analysis of impressment and the Monroe-Pinkney Treaty, see the discussion in the next chapter.

20. *Salem Register* [Massachusetts], August 23, 1804.

21. Boston *Independent Chronicle*, October 3, 1805. See also Philadelphia *Aurora General Advertiser*, October 23, 1805.

22. Hickey, "The Monroe-Pinckney Treaty," *William and Mary Quarterly*, 3rd ser., 44 (January 1987), 65–88. Quotation in ibid., 86–87.

23. *American State Papers: Foreign Relations*, 3: 171–72.

24. Horsman, *The Causes of the War of 1812*, 101–39.

25. *American State Papers: Foreign Relations*, 3: 6–23; Washington, D.C., *National Intelligencer*, June 26, 1807; Baltimore *American and Commercial Daily Advertiser*, June 27, 1807; Philadelphia *United States Gazette*, June 29, 1807.

26. New York *Commercial Advertiser*, June 30, 1807; Hudson, New York, *Balance*, July 21, 1807.

27. *Alexandria Advertiser*, June 30, 1807.

28. Philadelphia, *The Democratic Press*, July 6, 1807.

29. Danville, Vermont, *North Star*, July 14, 1807.

30. New York *Commercial Advertiser*, July 7, 1807.

31. Lansingburgh, New York, *Farmer's Register*, July 7, 1807. For a sample of other resolutions and reactions, see *Alexandria Advertiser*, July 6, 1807; Richmond *Virginia Argus*, July 11, 1807; Easton, Maryland, *Republican Star*, July 28, 1807; New York *Public Advertiser*, August 18, 1807; Frankfort, Kentucky, *Western World*, September 24, 1807.

32. *Compilation of Messages and Papers of the Presidents*, 1: 422–24.

33. *American State Papers: Foreign Relations*, 3: 7–12.

34. Spencer C. Tucker and Frank T. Reuter, *Injured Honor: The Chesapeake-Leopard Affair, June 22, 1807* (Annapolis, Md.: Naval Institute Press, 1996), 99–139; Dumas Malone, *Jefferson the President: Second Term, 1805–1809* (Boston: Little, Brown, and Company, 1974), 451–68; Merrill D. Peterson, *Thomas Jefferson and the New Nation: A Biography* (New York: Oxford University Press, 1970), 877–78; James Duncan Phillips, "Jefferson's 'Wicked Tyrannical Embargo'," *New England Quarterly*, 18 (December 1945), 466–78; Thorp Lanier Wolford, "Democratic-Republican Reaction in Massachusetts to the Embargo of 1807," *New England Quarterly*, 15 (March 1942), 35–61.

35. Peterson, *Thomas Jefferson and the New Nation*, 876.

36. *Compilation of Messages and Papers of the Presidents*, 1: 433; *U.S. Statutes at Large* 2 (1807), 451–53.

37. Boston *Independent Chronicle*, November 25, 1805.

38. Walter W. Jennings, *The American Embargo, 1807–1809* (Iowa City: University of Iowa Studies in Social Science, 1929); Louis Martin Sears, *Jefferson and the Embargo* (Durham: Duke University Press, 1927); Burton Spivak, *Jefferson's English Crisis: Commerce, Embargo, and the Republican Revolution* (Charlottesville: University Press of Virginia, 1979).

39. Springfield, Massachusetts, *Hampshire Federalist*, June 23, 1808; Douglass C. North, *The Economic Growth of the United States, 1790–1860* (Englewood Cliffs: N.J.: Prentice Hall, 1961), 221, 229; Sears, *Jefferson and the Embargo*, 197–200. 229–31.

40. Paul A. Gilje, *Liberty on the Waterfront: American Maritime Culture in the Age of Revolution* (Philadelphia: University of Pennsylvania Press, 2004), 146–49; Spivak, *Jefferson's English Crisis*, 156–97. For an argument that the embargo could have been successful, see Jeffrey A. Frankel, "The 1807–1809 Embargo against Great Britain," *Journal of Economic History*, 42 (June 1982), 291–308.

41. New York *Public Advertiser*, February 1, 1808; *New-York Evening Post*, February 25, 1808; Boston *Columbian Centinel*, June 18, July 2, 1808; Portland *Gazette*,

June 20, 27, 1808; *Newburyport Herald*, June 28, August 2, 1808; Baltimore *North American*, August 27, 1808; Rutland *Vermont Courier*, December 26, 1808; *Providence Gazette*, January 21, 1809.

42. *Trenton Federalist*, February 29, 1808.

43. Boston *New England Palladium*, March 25, 1808.

44. Portland *Gazette*, March 28, 1808.

45. Boston *New England Palladium*, March 29, 1808.

46. Hartford *Connecticut Courant*, March 30, 1808.

47. *Albany Gazette*, April 4, 1808.

48. *Salem Gazette*, April 1, 1808. See also Portland *Gazette*, April 4, 1808; Worcester *Massachusetts Spy*, April 6, 1808.

49. *Litchfield Gazette*, April 27, 1808.

50. Portland *Gazette*, September 19, 1808.

51. Boston *Repertory*, August 30, 1808.

52. Brattleboro, Vermont, *The Reporter*, April 2, 1808. See also Boston *Democrat*, May 11, 1808; Northampton, Massachusetts, *Republican Spy*, September 28, 1808; Newburyport, Massachusetts, *The Statesman*, October 20, 1808.

53. Charleston *City Gazette*, May 7, 1808. See also *Rutland Herald*, September 24, 1808.

54. Easton, Maryland, *Republican Star*, October 4, 1808.

55. Boston *Independent Chronicle*, July 14, 1808; Washington, D.C., *Monitor*, June 4, 1808.

56. *Boston Courier*, July 21, 1808.

57. Portland *Eastern Argus*, September 1, 1808.

58. Norwalk, Connecticut, *Courier*, September 7, 1808.

59. New Haven *Connecticut Herald*, September 27, 1808.

60. Horsman, *The Causes of the War of 1812*, 137–40.

61. *American State Papers: Foreign Relations*, 3: 213–20.

62. Perkins, *Prologue to War*, 148–49; Horsman, *The Causes of the War of 1812*, 121.

63. Horsman, *The Causes of the War of 1812*, 141–43; Clifford L. Egan, *Neither Peace nor War: Franco-American Relations, 1803–1812* (Baton Rouge: Louisiana State University Press, 1983), 97–98.

64. *U.S. Statutes at Large* 2 (1811), 528–33.

65. *American State Papers: Foreign Relations*, 3: 295–97, 299–308. See also the discussion in Horsman, *The Causes of the War of 1812*, 144–57.

66. North, *The Economic Growth of the United States*, 221, 229.

67. Perkins, *Prologue to War*, 239–43; *U.S. Statutes at Large* 2 (1810), 605–06.

68. *American State Papers: Foreign Relations*, 3: 323–26, 386–88.

69. *Compilation of Messages and Papers of the Presidents*, 1: 481–82.

70. *American State Papers: Foreign Relations*, 3: 388–93, 400–403, 500–21; see also Egan, *Neither Peace nor War*, 67–124.

71. Perkins, *Prologue to War*, 223–60; Horsman, *The Causes of the War of 1812*, 178–203. For the 1811 law, see *U.S. Statutes at Large* 2 (1811), 651–52.

72. Easton *Pennsylvania Herald*, October 8, 1808.

73. Haverhill, Massachusetts, *Merrimack Intelligencer*, March 11, 1809.

74. Boston *Columbian Centinel*, March 29, 1809.
75. Catskill, New York, *American Eagle*, April 5, 1809.
76. Ballston Spa, New York, *Independent American*, April 24, 1809.
77. New York *Commercial Advertiser*, April 24, 25, 1809. See also Albany *Balance*, April 25. 1809; Baltimore *Federal Republican*, May 2, 1809; and Catskill, New York, *American Eagle*, May 24, 1809.
78. New York *Public Advertiser*, March 22, 1809.
79. Trenton *True American*, April 3, 1809.
80. Brattleboro, Vermont, *The Reporter*, June 17, 1809.
81. Trenton *True American*, July 3, 1809.
82. New Bedford, Massachusetts, *Old Colony Gazette*, September 8, 1809.
83. Ibid., August 25, 1808.
84. Boston *Independent Chronicle*, August 8, 1809.
85. *Saratoga Advertiser*, August 28, 1809.
86. Portland *Eastern Argus*, March 29, 1810. For other attacks on "Gore and Free Trade," see Boston *Independent Chronicle*, August 17, 21, October 2, 1809; Portland *Eastern Argus*, August 24, September 21, 1809; Worcester, Massachusetts, *National Aegis*, September 13, 1809; Warren, Rhode Island, *Bristol County Register*, October 7, 1809; *Rutland Herald*, October 18, 1809; Philadelphia *Democratic Press*, December 30, 1809; Windsor *Vermont Republican*, January 15, 1810; Hallowell, Massachusetts [Maine], *American Advocate*, February 6, March 20, 1810; Charleston, Virginia [West Virginia], *Farmer's Repository*, June 8, 1810; *New York Journal*, July 14, 1810.
87. Wilmington, Delaware, *American Watchman*, September 9, 1810. See also Poughkeepsie, New York, *Political Barometer*, July 18, 1810.
88. Wilmington, Delaware, *American Watchman*, August 1, 1810.
89. Trenton *True American*, August 20, 1810.
90. Richmond *Virginia Patriot*, August 24, 1810.
91. *New-York Evening Post*, November 11, 1810. See also *Alexandria Gazette*, November 15, 1810; Concord, New Hampshire, *Concord Gazette*, February 5, 1811.
92. Portland *Gazette*, March 4, 18, 1811. See also Greenfield, Massachusetts, *Traveller*, March 19, 1811; Boston *Repertory*, March 29, 1811.
93. Greenfield, Massachusetts, *Traveller*, March 30, 1811. For additional political uses of free trade, see Boston *Columbian Centinel*, March 16, 1811; Pittsfield, Massachusetts, *Berkshire Reporter*, March 30, 1811; Providence *Rhode-Island American*, July 26, 1811; Baltimore *Federal Gazette*, August 19, 1811; *Trenton Federalist*, September 23, 1811; Philadelphia *Poulson's American Daily Advertiser*, September 27, 1811.
94. Baltimore *Federal Gazette*, June 13, 1811.
95. *New York Gazette*, July 16, 1811. For another use of the slogan "free trade" on the Fourth of July, see *Philadelphia Tickler*, July 24, 1811.
96. Greenfield, Massachusetts, *Traveller*, March 30, 1811; *Boston Gazette*, April 4, 1811; *Trenton Federalist*, April 8, 1811; New Haven *Connecticut Herald*, May 7, 1811; *Providence Gazette*, August 31, 1811; Philadelphia *Poulson's American Daily Advertiser*, September 5, 13, 1811.

97. New York *Commercial Advertiser*, September 28, 1811.

98. Hartford *American Mercury*, May 16, 1811.

99. New York *Commercial Advertiser*, November 1, 1811.

100. Boston *Independent Chronicle*, March 25, 1811; Easton, Maryland, *Republican Star*, April 30, 1811. See also Hudson, New York, *Bee*, March 29, 1811.

101. Newport *Rhode-Island Republican*, April 10, 1811. See also Boston *Independent Chronicle*, April 29, 1811.

102. *Alexandria Herald*, June 17, 1811.

103. Salem *Essex Register*, April 10, 1811.

104. Hudson, New York, *Bee*, February 22, 1811.

105. Wilmington, Delaware, *American Watchman*, June 19, 1811; New York *Public Advertiser*, July 24, 1811; Salem *Essex Register*, August 21, 1811; Boston *Independent Chronicle*, September 16, 1811.

106. Hartford *American Mercury*, August 22, 1811. See also Washington, D.C., *National Intelligencer*, September 5, 1811.

107. Portland *Eastern Argus*, May 9, 1811.

108. *American State Papers: Foreign Relations*, 3: 537–38.

109. *Annals of Congress*, House of Representatives, 12th Congress, 1st sess., 424.

110. *Carlisle Gazette*, July 26, 1811.

## 13. The Ordeal of Jack Tar

1. Easton, Maryland, *Republican Star*, January 10, 1809.

2. Philadelphia *Weekly Aurora*, May 21, 1811.

3. Hudson, New York, *Bee*, August 2, 1803.

4. Robert J. Allison, *The Crescent Obscured: The United States and the Muslim World, 1776–1815* (New York: Oxford University Press, 1995), 187–206.

5. Worcester, Massachusetts, *National Aegis*, October 2, 1805; Baltimore *Federal Gazette*, October 10, 1805; Philadelphia *Aurora General Advertiser*, October 19, 1805; Allison, *The Crescent Obscured*, 31–34; Paul A. Gilje, *Liberty on the Waterfront: American Maritime Culture in the Age of Revolution* (Philadelphia: University of Pennsylvania Press, 2004) 153–54.

6. In 1810, for example, one newspaper reported that estimates for the number of impressed sailors varied from 5,000 to 15,000. *New-York Journal*, March 17, 1810. Early in 1812 Republicans seized upon a government report indicating that there were 6,257 Americans impressed into the British navy. Federalists contested this number as merely reflecting the number of men who claimed to be Americans and argued that there were many fewer native Americans impressed. For Federalist statements on numbers, see Boston *New-England Palladium*, January 17, February 28, 1812; *Boston Gazette*, March 2, 1812; *Portland Gazette*, March 9, 1812. For Republican statements on numbers, see Newport *Rhode-Island Republican*, February 5, 1812; Salem *Essex Register*, March 4, 1812; Providence *Columbian Phenix*, March 7, 1812; Plattsburgh, New York, *Republican*, March 13, 1812; *Albany Register*, March 20, 1812; Hartford *American Mercury*, April 1, 1812; Philadelphia *Weekly Aurora*, May 5, 1812. Zimmerman provides an appendix that counts the number of men who claimed to be Americans and who petitioned

for release before 1812. Following his calculations, this number is about 10,000. However, it should be noted that there were many Americans who were impressed and who never had the opportunity to apply for release. During the War of 1812, the British navy allowed 1,421 men who claimed to be Americans to be transferred to Dartmoor as prisoners of war. Several hundred more men were also allowed to become prisoners of war in Halifax and the West Indies. Based on these numbers, I can use with confidence the 10,000 number, although the total number of Americans impressed was probably larger. James Fulton Zimmerman, *Impressment of American Seamen* (New York: Columbia University Press, 1925), 259–75; Gilje, *Liberty on the Waterfront*, 157–58.

7. Elizabethtown, New Jersey, *Federal Republican*, May 3, 1803; New York *Commercial Advertiser*, April 15, 1803; Worcester *Massachusetts Spy*, April 27, 1803; Philadelphia *Poulson's American Daily Advertiser*, May 17, 1803; Wilmington, Delaware, *Mirror of the Times*, June 22, 1803; Philadelphia *Gazette of the United States*, June 30, 1803.

8. Trenton *True American*, August 8, 1803; Richmond *Virginia Argus*, August 20, 1803; Portland *Eastern Argus*, September 15, 1803; Philadelphia *Aurora*, December 13, 1803.

9. Hudson, New York, *Bee*, August 2, 1803.

10. Philadelphia *Aurora*, September 21, 1803.

11. Ibid., September 14, 1803.

12. Hudson, New York, *Bee*, September 6, 1803.

13. Ibid., October 1, 1805.

14. Boston *Independent Chronicle*, September 26, 1803; Philadelphia *Aurora*, February 2, 4, 1805.

15. Philadelphia *Aurora*, August 22, 1803. See also New York *Commercial Advertiser*, June 26, 27, 1804; Albany *Gazette*, September 13, 1804; Philadelphia *Democratic Press*, March 27, April 1, 8, July 20, 1807; Philadelphia *Aurora*, July 20, 1807; New York *Columbian*, October 9, 1810, August 17, 1811; Washington, D.C., *National Intelligencer*, October 12, 1810; New York *Public Advertiser*, July 2, 1811.

16. *A Bill to Provide for the Further Protection of American Seamen* (Washington, D.C.: Government Printing Office, 1804). See also Fredericktown, Maryland, *Republican Advocate*, February 3, 1804; Philadelphia *Aurora*, February 7, 29, 1804; Pittsfield, Massachusetts, *Sun*, February 20, 1804. For the Federalist view of the bill, see Philadelphia *Poulson's American Daily Advertiser*, February 14, 1804.

17. *Charleston Courier*, August 24, 1803. See also Baltimore *Republican or Anti-Democrat*, September 2, 1803; Boston *New-England Palladium*, December 23, 1803; Boston *Independent Chronicle*, December 22, 1803; Philadelphia *Poulson's American Daily Advertiser*, February 14, 1804; *New-York Evening Post*, June 28, 1804; New Haven *Connecticut Herald*, February 12, 1805.

18. Baltimore *Republican or Anti-Democrat*, September 21, 1803.

19. *Trenton Federalist*, August 12, 1805. See also Hudson, New York, *Balance*, February 10, 1807; Philadelphia *United States' Gazette*, March 9, July 22, December

28, 1807; New York *People's Friend*, March 11, June 17, 1807; Springfield, Massachusetts, *Hampshire Federalist*, August 6, 1807; New York *Bee*, October 20, 26, 1807.

20. *American State Papers: Foreign Relations*, 3: 83–87; James Fulton Zimmerman, *Impressment of American Seamen* (New York: Columbia University Press, 1925), 96–99.

21. *American State Papers: Foreign Relations*, 3: 100. See also Anthony Steel, "Anthony Merry and the Anglo-American Dispute about Impressment, 1803–6," *Cambridge Historical Journal*, 9 (1949), 331–51.

22. Zimmerman, *Impressment*, 94–117.

23. *American State Papers: Foreign Relations*, 3: 139–40.

24. Ibid., 166–73; Zimmerman, *Impressment*, 120–34; Anthony Steel, "Impressment in the Monroe-Pinkney Negotiation, 1806–1807," *American Historical Review*, 57 (January 1952), 352–69.

25. Albert Gallatin to Thomas Jefferson, April 13, 1807, Thomas Jefferson Papers Series 1, General Correspondence, 1651–1827, Library of Congress. Interestingly, some Federalists came to the same conclusion. See Boston *Repertory*, August 21, 1807.

26. Jefferson to Gallatin, April 21, 1807, *The Writings of Thomas Jefferson*, 20 vols. (Washington, D.C., Issued under the Auspices of the Thomas Jefferson Memorial Association of the United States, 1903–04), 11: 195; Madison used almost the same words in a letter to Jefferson: "Mr. Gallatin's estimate of the number of foreign seamen in our employ renders it prudent to suspend all propositions respecting our nonemploiment of them." Quoted in Burton Spivak, *Jefferson's English Crisis: Commerce, Embargo, and the Republican Revolution* (Charlottesville: University Press of Virginia, 1979), 66.

27. Gilje, *Liberty on the Waterfront*, 69–74; Spivak, *Jefferson's English Crisis*, 64–7.

28. Philadelphia *Aurora*, January 29, 1805.

29. New York *Mercantile Advertiser*, January 25, 1806; *Alexandria Advertiser*, February 21, May 5, 1806; Philadelphia *United States Gazette*, March 6, 1806.

30. For popular support of the rejection of the treaty because of the impressment issue, see Philadelphia *Democratic Press*, April 1, July 21, 1807; Easton, Maryland, *Republican Star*, May 12, 1807. Even as late as 1812 some Republicans defended this position. See Hallowell, Massachusetts [Maine], *American Advocate*, June 2, 1812.

31. Washington, D.C., *National Intelligencer*, March 26, 1806; Northampton Massachusetts, *Republican Spy*, April 22, 1806; Brattleboro, Vermont, *Reporter*, April 26, 1806.

32. Boston *New England Paladium*, July 18, 1806.

33. Philadelphia *Aurora*, March 7, April 23, 1805.

34. Charleston *City Gazette*, October 4, 1805.

35. New Haven *Connecticut Herald*, February 11, 1806.

36. Philadelphia *Aurora*, July 16, 1806.

37. For the previous activities of the *Leander*, see Philadelphia *Aurora*, August 9, 1804; New York *Republican Watch-Tower*, August 15, 1804; New York *American*

*Citizen*, August 24, 1804. For discussion of the *Leander* in conjunction with
impressment, see Sag Harbor, New York, *Suffolk Gazette*, May 19, 1805. For
a sampling of articles mentioning the *Leander* incident, impressment, and other
grievances, see Frankfort, Kentucky, *Western World*, August 6, 1807; Danville,
Vermont, *North Star*, February 1, 1808; New York *Public Advertiser*, February 3,
July 7, 1808; Trenton *True American*, May 30, 1808; Walpole, New Hampshire,
*Political Observatory*, June 13, 1808; Washington, D.C., *Spirit of Seventy-Six*,
September 20, 1808; Richmond *Enquirer*, November 25, 1808; *Rutland Herald*,
July 22, 1809; *New York Journal*, August 30, 1809; Plattsburgh, New York, *American Monitor*, February 17, 1810; Poughkeepsie, New York, *Political Barometer*,
February 21, 1810; New York *Columbian*, June 15, 1810; Newark *Centinel of Freedom*, September 4, 1810; Concord *New-Hampshire Patriot*, February 26, 1811;
Hartford *American Mercury*, February 28, 1811; Morristown, New Jersey, *Palladium of Liberty*, March 26, 1811.

38. *The Trial of John Wilson, Alias Jenkin Ratford for Mutiny, Desertion and Contempt to Which Are Subjoined a Few Cursory Remarks* (Boston: Snelling and
Simons, 1807), 6; Spencer C. Tucker and Frank T. Reuter, *Injured Honor: The
Chesapeake-Leopard Affair, June 22, 1807* (Annapolis, Md.: Naval Institute Press,
1996), 69–79; Robert E. Cray, Jr., "Remembering the USS Chesapeake: The Politics of Maritime Death and Impressment," *Journal of the Early Republic*, 25
(Fall 2005), 445–74. It should also be noted that only a few months before the
*Chesapeake-Leopard* incident a British navy officer had allowed an American officer to search his ship for men who had deserted the United States army. See *The
Trial of John Wilson*, 14.

39. Boston *Democrat*, February 27, 1808.

40. *Frankfurt Argus*, May 26, 1808.

41. Washington, D.C., *Monitor*, September 13, 1808.

42. New York *American Citizen*, February 27, 1809. See also *Albany Register*, January
19, 1808; *Portland Gazette*, June 20, 1808; Washington, D.C., *Monitor*, November 11, 1808; Brattleboro, Vermont, *Reporter*, November 11, 1809; *Washington
Reporter* [Pennsylvania], September 17, 1810.

43. New York *American Citizen*, January 16, 1808. See also Easton, Maryland, *Republican Star*, August 11, 1807. For arguments against impressment after the *Chesapeake* affair, see New York *Watch-Tower*, July 31, 1807; Philadelphia *Aurora*,
August 8, 15, 29, 1807; *Alexandria Advertiser*, August 11, 1807; Salem *Essex
Register*, August 17, 24, 1807, January 13, 1808; Trenton *True American*, August
31, October 12, 19, 1807; Lansingurgh, New York, *Farmer's Register*, September
8, 1807; Charleston *City Gazette*, September 9, 1807; Boston *Democrat*, September 19, 1807; Philadelphia *Democratic Press*, December 14, 22, 1807; Richmond
*Enquirer*, December 22, 1807.

44. The database of *America's Historical Newspapers* allows word searches. These
numbers include repeat articles. Whether the articles were reprinted or not is irrelevant to this crude instrument for measuring public interest. The point remains that
public interest grew after 1805 and then expanded rapidly after 1807 and again
in 1812. The database of *America's Historical Newspapers* adds titles over time.

The count used in the text was accessed on January 18, 2010. Additional newspaper titles should not alter the statistical trend reported here. *America's Historical Newspapers*, Archive of Americana, published by Readex, a division of NewsBank.

45. Robert Cray argues that race and class did matter in the public outlook toward the sailors taken from the *Chesapeake*. But he also suggests that the lack of interest in their identities at the time reflected a certain embarrassment over their being a reminder of the inability of the United States to stop impressment. By contrast, the men killed in the action against the *Chesapeake* were lionized. Cray, Jr., "Remembering the USS Chesapeake" *Journal of the Early Republic*, 25 (Fall 2005), 463–67.

46. Walpole, New Hampshire, *Political Observatory*, December 22, 1807.

47. [John Adams], *The Inadmissible Principles, of the King of England's Proclamation, of October 16, 1807 – considered*. By the late President Adams. (Originally published in the *Boston Patriot*.) (Boston: Everett & Munroe, 1809), 9.

48. Paul A. Gilje, *The Road to Mobocracy: Popular Disorder in New York City, 1763–1834* (Chapel Hill: University of North Carolina Press, 1987), 178–79; Gilje, *Liberty on the Waterfront*, 150; *New York Evening Post*, September 22, 1809, September 15, 21, 1810.

49. *American State Papers: Foreign Relations*, 3: 183–93.

50. Ibid., 213–20.

51. Ibid., 183–200. Zimmerman, *Impressment*, 138–58; see also the newspaper citation in note 87.

52. Baltimore *Federal Republican*, March 24, 1809. See also Baltimore *North American*, April 14, 1808.

53. *Boston Gazette*, May 19, 1808.

54. Pittsfield, Massachusetts, *Berkshire Reporter*, January 7, 1809.

55. Gilje, *Liberty on the Waterfront*, 148–49.

56. Baltimore *Federal Republican*, March 24, 1809. See also *Boston Repertory*, April 1, 1808, June 29, 1810; Boston *New England Palladium*, April 15, 19, 1808; *Portland Gazette*, May 23, 1808, January 8, 1810; Baltimore *Federal Republican*, November 9, 1808, May 2, 1809, September 27, 1810; Ballston Spa, New York, *Independent American*, January 17, 1809; New York *Commercial Advertiser*, March 9, 1809; Portland *Freeman's Friend*, March 25, 1809; New York *American Citizen*, April 25, June 20, 1809; *Portsmouth Oracle*, May 27, 1809; Wilmington, Delaware, *American Watchman*, November 29, 1809; Worcester *Massachusetts Spy*, January 3, 1810; *Boston Gazette*, January 8, 1810; *Alexandria Gazette*, March 7, 1810, October 3, 1811, January 9, 1812; *New-York Evening Post*, June 22, 1810; *Boston Patriot*, December 19, 1810; *New-Bedford Mercury*, December 21, 1810.

57. Salem *Essex Register*, February 10, 1808. See also New York *American Citizen*, March 11, 1808.

58. *New-York Evening Post*, February 13, 1808.

59. Ibid., June 22, 1810. See also Georgetown *Independent American*, April 24, 1810.

60. Boston *New-England Palladium*, January 17, 1812. See also *New-York Evening Post*, January 28, 1812; Providence *Rhode-Island American*, May 5, 1812.

61. Hudson, New York, *Balance*, April 12, 1808; Windsor, Vermont, *Washingtonian*, May 20, 1811; New York *Commercial Advertiser*, July 11, 1811; *Portland Gazette*, August 5, 1811. See also *New-York Herald*, January 20, 1808; Baltimore *North American*, July 21, 1808; *New-York Evening Post*, October 17, 1808, May 9, August 7, 1810; Worcester *Massachusetts Spy*, October 19, November 29, 1808; Hudson, New York, *Balance*, December 13, 1808; New Haven *Connecticut Journal*, October 26, 1809; *Boston Gazette*, January 15, 1810, June 8, 1811; Baltimore *Federal Republican*, July 4, 7, 10, 1810; New Haven *Connecticut Journal*, July 12, 1810; *New-Bedford Mercury*, April 25, 1811; Providence *Rhode Island American*, May 31, 1811; *Boston Repertory*, July 9, 1811.

62. *Cooperstown Federalist*, May 25, 1811; Hudson, New York, *Northen Whig*, May 31, 1811, June 1, 1812; New York *Commercial Advertiser*, July 11, 27, August 17, 1811; Washington, D.C., *Universal Gazette*, August 2, 1811; Philadelphia *Poulson's American Daily Advertiser*, August 8, 1811, May 20, 1812; *Boston Gazette*, September 9, 1811; *New-York Evening Post*, November 2, 1811, January 17, 1812; *Concord Gazette*, September 17, November 19, 1811; *Geneva Gazette* [New York], December 25, 1811; Boston *New-England Palladium*, March 13, 1812; Boston *Repertory*, March 13, 1812; New Bern *Carolina Federal Republican*, April 4, 1812.

63. Portland *Gazette*, March 23, 1812. See also Boston *Repertory*, March 13, 1812.

64. Providence *Rhode-Island American*, March 31, 1812.

65. *Newburyport Herald*, May 1, 1812.

66. Portland *Gazette*, May 11, 1812.

67. Providence *Rhode Island American*, October 25, 1811.

68. Philadelphia *Aurora*, February 25, 1805. See also New York *Public Advertiser*, July 20, 1807; Hudson, New York, *Bee*, July 28, 1807; New London *True Republican*, August 12, 1807; Portland *Eastern Argus*, August 4, 1808; Walpole, New Hampshire, *Political Observatory*, December 26, 1808.

69. Richmond *Enquirer*, July 18, 1809. Like many other articles from this era, this article was reprinted by other editors. See Charleston, Virginia [West Virginia], *Farmer's Repository*, July 28, 1809; Charleston *City Gazette*, August 25, 1809; Washington, D.C., *National Intelligencer*, September 6, 1809.

70. Newport *Rhode-Island Republican*, April 4, 1810.

71. Salem *Essex Register*, April 28, 1810. For other first-person and emotional accounts, see Charleston *Carolina Gazette*, October 6, 1809; Boston *Independent Chronicle*, March 22, 29, 1810, March 14, May 13, 23, 1811, January 23, 1812; *Albany Register*, April 20, 1810, March 20, 1812; *New-York Journal*, April 28, 1810; New York *Columbian*, October 9, 1810; Salem *Essex Register*, September 5, 1810, November 24, 25, 1811, February 29, June 13, 1812; Concord *New-Hampshire Patriot*, May 15, 1810; Providence *Columbian Phenix*, May 26, 1810; Newark *Centinel of Freedom*, July 3, 1810, March 24, 1812; Easton, Maryland, *Republican Star*, July 3, 1810, December 24, 1811; Charlestown, Virginia [West Virginia], *Farmer's Repository*, February 15, 1811; *Boston Patriot*, March 27, August 28, 1811; Richmond *Enquirer*, March 29, May 31, 1811; Portsmouth *New Hampshire Gazette*, April 30, 1811; Bridgeport, Connecticut, *Republican*

*Farmer*, May 15, 1811; *Alexandria Herald*, August 12, 1811; Washington, D.C., *National Intelligencer*, September 3, 1811; Portland *Eastern Argus*, January 2, 1812; New-Bedford, Massachusetts, *Gazette*, February 21, March 20, 1812; *Washington Reporter* [Pennsylvania], March 9, 1812; Boston *Yankee*, March 13, 1812; Windsor *Vermont Republican*, April 4, 1812; New York *Public Advertiser*, May 18, 1812; Hallowell, Massachusetts [Maine], *American Advocate*, May 26, 1812; Charleston *City Gazette*, June 3, 13, 1812; Brooklyn, *Long-Island Star*, May 6, 1812.

72. In addition to the examples cited above referring to slavery, see New York *Public Advertiser*, January 12, 1807; Salem *Essex Register*, August 3, 1807, October 14, 1809, April 28, 1810; New York *American Citizen*, January 16, 1808; New York *Public Advertiser*, September 16, 1808; Washington, D.C., *Spirit of Seventy-Six*, September 20, 1808; New York *Republican Watch-Tower*, March 7, 1809; Lexington, Kentucky, *Reporter*, September 9, 1809; Pittsfield, Massachusetts, *Sun*, September 29, 1809; New Bedford, Massachusetts, *Old Colony Gazette*, April 6, 1810; New York *Columbian*, June 19, 1810; Charlestown, Virginia [West Virginia], *Farmer's Repository*, February 1, 1811; Washington, D.C., *National Intelligencer*, September 3, 1811. For flogging see Richmond *Enquirer*, March 29, 1811.

73. Charleston, Virginia [West Virginia], *Farmer's Repository*, May 10, 1811. See also New Bern, North Carolina, *True Republican*, July 17, 1811.

74. Boston *Democrat*, January 9, 1808.

75. New York *Columbian*, June 19, 1810. See also Boston *Columbian Detector*, February 24, 1809; New Bern, North Carolina, *True Republican*, July 17, 1811.

76. *Annals of Congress*, House of Representatives, 10th Congress, 2nd sess., 1382.

77. Gilje, *Liberty on the Waterfront*, 148.

78. Robert E. Cray, Jr., "Commemorating the Prison Ship Dead: Revolutionary Memoir and the Politics of Sepulture in the Early Republic, 1776–1808," *William and Mary Quarterly*, 3rd ser., 56 (July 1999), 581–86. Quotations in ibid., 581, 583, 585.

79. *New York Public Advertiser*, October 7, 1808. See also Gilje, *Liberty on the Waterfront*, 146–47.

80. Boston *Democrat*, February 27, 1808. See also Morristown, New Jersey, *Palladium of Liberty*, May 30, 1808.

81. *Rutland Herald*, August 5, 1809. See also Wilmington, Delaware, *American Watchman*, August 5, 1809.

82. Halowell, Massachusetts [Maine], *American Advocate*, March 13, 1810.

83. Poughkeepsie, New York, *Political Barometer*, May 22, 1811.

84. Philadelphia *Weekly Aurora*, May 21, 1811.

85. *Alexandria Gazette*, May 21, 1811.

86. *Annals of Congress*, House of Representatives, 12th Congress, 1st sess., 477, 458.

87. Concord *New-Hampshire Patriot*, December 31, 1811. See also Lexington, Kentucky, *Reporter*, January 30, 1809; Philadelphia *Poulson's American Daily Advertiser*, February 23, 1809; *Boston Patriot*, March 3, 1809, January 24, 1810, July 27, 1811; Walpole, New Hampshire, *Political Observatory*, March 6, 1809; New Haven *Connecticut Herald*, May 2, 1809; Wilmington, Delaware, *American*

*Watchman*, August 26, 1809, December 14, 1811, April 25, 1812; New York *Republican Watch-Tower*, September 12, 1809; Sag Harbor, New York, *Suffolk Gazette*, March 18, May 6, 1809, October 6, 1810; New York *American Citizen*, March 20, 1809; Concord *New-Hampshire Patriot*, April 18, 1809, February 23, May 1, November 13, 1810, February 19, 1811; *Albany Register*, January 16, 1810; Hartford *American Mercury*, February 1, 1810, February 28, 1811; Wilmington *Delaware Gazette*, February 14, 1810; Plattsburgh, New York, *American Monitor*, February 17, 1810, May 1, 1812; New York *Columbian*, February 21, June 15, September 8, 1810, September 16, November 13, 1811; Poughkeepsie, New York, *Political Barometer*, February 21, 1810, June 5, 1811: Charleston *City Gazette*, March 20, May 31, December 12, 1810, March 18, 1812; *New-York Journal*, April 24, 1810; Easton, Maryland, *Republican Star*, May 15, 1810, June 16, August 27, 1811; Morristown, New Jersey, *Palladium of Liberty*, July 10, 1810, March 26, 1811; Philadelphia *Weekly Aurora*, July 3, August 28, 1810, February 19, September 3, 1811; Newark *Centinel of Freedom*, September 4, 1810; New York *Public Advertiser*, October 27, 1810, May 25, 1812; Salem *Essex Register*, March 13, 27, 1811; Washington, D.C., *National Intelligencer*, May 23, 1811, June 9, 1812; Richmond *Enquirer*, July 12, October 4, 1811; Washington, D.C., *Universal Gazette*, August 9, 1811, May 1, 1812; Hudson, New York, *Bee*, October 15, 1811; New-Bedford, Massachusetts, *Gazette*, January 17, March 27, April 3, May 1, 1812; Windsor *Vermont Republican*, January 27, March 30, 1812; Providence *Columbian Phenix*, April 4, 1812; Brattleboro, Vermont, *Reporter*, April 18, 1812; Hallowell, Massachusetts [Maine], *American Advocate*, May 19, 1812; Windsor *Vermont Republican*, May 25, 1812; Milledgeville *Georgia Journal*, June 10, 1812.

## 14. Honor

1. Charles Royster, *The Revolutionary People at War: The Continental Army and the American Character, 1775–1783* (Chapel Hill: University of North Carolina Press, 1979), 210.
2. Joanne B. Freeman, *Affairs of Honor: National Politics in the New Republic* (New Haven: Yale University Press, 2001); Bruce C. Baird, "The Social Origins of Dueling in Virginia," in Michael A. Bellesiles, ed., *Lethal Imagination: Violence and Brutality in American History* (New York: New York University Press, 1999), 87–112; Bertram Wyatt-Brown, *Southern Honor: Ethics and Behavior in the Old South* (New York: Oxford University Press, 1982).
3. Baltimore *Federal Gazette*, June 29, 1807.
4. *Frankfort Argus* [Kentucky], May 26, 1808.
5. Ballston Spa, New York, *Saratoga Advertiser*, February 27, 1810.
6. Providence *Columbian Phenix*, April 14, 1810.
7. New Bedford, Massachusetts, *Old Colony Gazette*, April 6, 1810.
8. Hartford *American Mercury*, June 13, 1811.
9. Charleston *City Gazette*, September 12, 1808.
10. Wilmington, Delaware, *American Watchman*, August 26, 1809.
11. New York *Public Advertiser*, January 9, 1810.

12. Newport *Rhode-Island Republican*, September 25, 1811.

13. *Annals of Congress*, House of Representatives, 12ᵗʰ Congress, 1ˢᵗ sess., 484.

14. *American State Papers: Foreign Relations*, 3: 317, 319. For the Smith-Jackson correspondence see ibid., 3: 307–23. See also Richard Buel, Jr., *America on the Brink: How the Political Struggle over the War of 1812 Almost Destroyed the Young Republic* (New York: Palgrave Macmillan, 2005), 90–96.

15. Robert A. Rutland et al., eds., *The Papers of James Madison: Presidential Series*, vols. 1– (Charlottesville: University Press of Virginia, 1984–), 4: 17.

16. *American State Papers: Foreign Relations*, 3: 497–98. For both British and American testimony, see ibid., 477–99; William M. Fowler, Jr., *Jack Tars and Commodores: The American Navy, 1783–1815* (Boston: Hougthon Mifflin, 1984), 158–60; Bradford Perkins, *Prologue to War, 1805–1812: England and the United States* (Berkeley: University of California Press, 1968), 272–73.

17. *American State Papers: Foreign Relations*, 3: 545–57; Buel, *America on the Brink*, 139–41.

18. Brooklyn *Long-Island Star*, November 20, 1811.

19. Brattleboro, Vermont, *Reporter*, April 18, 1812.

20. Quoted in Roger H. Brown, *The Republic in Peril: 1812* (New York: Columbia University Press, 1964), 77.

## 15. The Odyssey of the *Essex*

1. David F. Long, *Nothing Too Daring: A Biography of Commodore David Porter, 1780–1843* (Annapolis: United States Naval Institute, 1970). Long could not verify all of the details about Porter's early experiences at sea described in David Dixon Porter, *Memoir of Commodore David Porter, of the United States Navy* (Albany, N.Y.: J. Munsell, 1875).

2. Frances Diane Robotti and James Vescovi, *The USS Essex and the Birth of the American Navy* (Avon, Mass.: Adams Media, 1999), 41, 149–53.

3. *Dictionary of American Naval Fighting Ships*, Naval History Center, Naval History and Heritage Command, http://www.history.navy.mil/danfs/index.html; Philip Chadwick Foster Smith, *The Frigate Essex Papers: Building the Salem Frigate 1798–1799* (Salem: Peabody Museum, 1974); Robotti and Vescovi, *The USS Essex and the Birth of the American Navy*.

4. Long, *Nothing Too Daring*, 33.

5. Ervin's name is variously spelled Erving and Irving. Newspapers reported the incident with partisan slants. For the Republican approach, which denied that Porter had anything to do with the incident, see New York *Public Advertiser*, June 30, 1812; Trenton *True American*, July 6, 1812. For the Federalist criticism of Porter, see *New-York Evening Post*, June 27, 1812. See also Long, *Nothing Too Daring*, 63–66.

6. Porter published two versions of his journal. There are some differences in the material in each version. All citations here will be from the second edition. David Porter, *Journal of a Cruise Made to the Pacific Ocean by Captain David Porter, in the United States Frigate Essex, in the Years 1812, 1813, and 1814 . . .*, 2nd ed.,

2 vols. (New York: Wiley & Halsted, 1822), 1: 221–22. For the first edition, see David Porter, *Journal of a Cruise Made to the Pacific Ocean by Captain David Porter, in the United States Frigate Essex, in the Years 1812, 1813, and 1814 . . .*, 2 vols. (Philadelphia Bradford and Inskeep, New-York Abraham H. Inskeep, and for sale by O. C. Greenleaf, Boston, 1815).

7. Long, *Nothing Too Daring*, 65.

8. Jefferson to Thaddeus Kosciuszko, June 28, 1812, Paul Leicester Ford, ed., *The Works of Thomas Jefferson*, 12 vols. (New York: G. P. Putnam's Sons, 1904–05), 11: 258–62; Long, *Nothing Too Daring*, 62–63.

9. Every book on the War of 1812 devotes some space to the war at sea. For books that focus more exclusively on naval developments, see the three classic accounts of the American naval war: James Fenimore Cooper, *The History of the Navy of the United States: A Facsimile Reproduction of the 1841 Edition with an Historical Introduction and Notes by R. D. Madison* (Delmar, N.Y.: Scholar's Facsimiles & Reprints, 1988; orig. pub. 1841); Theodore Roosevelt, *The Naval War of 1812: Or, the History of the United States Navy During the Last War with Great Britain, to Which Is Appended an Account of the Battle of New Orleans* (New York: G. P. Putnam's Sons, 1902); A. T. Mahan, *Sea Power in Its Relations to the War of 1812* (Boston: Little, Brown, and Company, 1919; orig. pub. 1903). For more recent studies, see George C. Daughan, *If by Sea: the Forging of the American Navy – from the American Revolution to the War of 1812* (New York: Basic Books, 2008); William M. Fowler, Jr., *Jack Tars and Commodores: The American Navy, 1783–1815* (Boston: Hougthon Mifflin, 1984); Ian W. Toll, *Six Frigates: The Epic History of the Founding of the U.S. Navy* (New York: Norton, 2006); Kevin D. McCranie, *Utmost Gallantry: The U.S. and Royal Navies at Sea in the War of 1812* (Annapolis: Naval Institute Press, 2011).

10. Donald Hickey, *The War of 1812: A Forgotten Conflict* (Urbana: University of Illinois Press, 1989), 34, 113, 165, 245–46.

11. Fowler, Jr., *Jack Tars and Commodores*, 185–209, 241–60; *Richmond Enquirer*, August 31, 1813; *Niles' Weekly Register*, February 26, 1814.

12. Porter, *Journal of a Cruise*, 1: 1–85. For the Pacific cruise, see also the accounts in Robotti and Vescovi, *The USS Essex*; Long, *Nothing Too Daring*; and Frank Donovan, *The Odyssey of the Essex* (New York: David Mckay Company, 1969).

13. For reports in the press on the *Essex*, see *Salem Gazette*, July 23, 1813; *Niles' Weekly Register*, September 11, October 2, December 11, 18, 1813, May 7, 1814. These reports were reprinted in newspapers across the nation, from the biggest cities to the smallest villages.

14. Porter, *Journal of a Cruise*, 2: 59–60.

15. Ibid., 2: 1–142.

16. Long, *Nothing Too Daring*, 148. For the Chilean perspective on the *Essex*, see Captain A. S. Merrill, translator, "First Contacts – The Glorious Cruise of the *Essex*," *United States Naval Institute Proceedings*, 66 (February 1940), 218–23.

17. My interpretation of this war of words and the subsequent battle is heavily influenced by Greg Dening, "The Face of Battle: Valparaiso, 1814," *War and Society*, 1 (1983), 25–42.

18. Porter, *Journal a Cruise*, 2: 147–56; *Niles' Weekly Register*, August 20, 1814.

19. Porter, *Journal of a Cruise*, 2: 155–56; *Niles' Weekly Register*, August 20, 1814.
20. Dening, "The Face of Battle: Valparaiso, 1814," *War and Society*, 1 (1983), 25–42. See also Paul A. Gilje, *Liberty on the Waterfront: American Maritime Culture in the Age of Revolution* (Philadelphia: University of Pennsylvania Press, 2004), 106–29, 163–91. For ambiguous loyalties on the frontier, see Alan Taylor, *The Civil War of 1812: American Citizens, British Subjects, Irish Rebels, and Indian Allies* (New York: Knopf, 2010).
21. Porter, *Journal of a Cruise*, 2: 148–53.
22. Ibid., 2: 147, 154–58, 162–63.
23. Ibid., 2: 164–70; *Niles' Weekly Register*, August 20, 1814.
24. Porter, *Journal of a Cruise*, 2: 171.
25. Ibid., 2: 159–64.
26. Ibid., 2: 175–77.
27. *Niles' Weekly Register*, July 23, 1814; New York *Mercantile Advertiser*, July 27, 1814; Baltimore *Patriot*, August 2, 1812; *Providence Patriot*, August 6, 1814.
28. *Niles' Weekly Register*, July 23, 1814; Baltimore *American and Commercial Daily Advertiser*, July 12, 1814.
29. *Niles' Weekly Register*, August 20, 1814.
30. *Alexandria Gazette*, July 12, 1814.
31. Worcester, Massachusetts, *National Aegis*, July 13, 1814.
32. Philadelphia *Democratic Press*, July 9, 1814.
33. Baltimore *American and Commercial Daily Advertiser*, July 18, 1814. See also *Boston Gazette*, July 18, 1814; Richmond *Enquirer*, July 27, 1814.
34. Baltimore *American and Commercial Daily Advertiser*, July 12, 1814.
35. New Haven *Columbian Register*, July 12, 1814.
36. New York *Columbian*, July 8, 1814; *Niles' Weekly Register*, July 23, 1814. See also New York *Columbian*, July 15, 1814. The British public, on the other hand, painted Porter as a villain for his depredations on whalers, his treatment of Ervin, and his violation of his parole. After the publication of the first edition of Porter's journal, one British review was so hostile that Porter felt compelled to respond in detail to the British charges of dishonorable behavior in the second edition of the journal. Long, *Nothing Too Daring*, 71–72.
37. Philadelphia *Democratic Press*, July 9, 1814.

## 16. The Language of Combat

1. "CONQUER OR DIE" quoted in Donald Hickey, *The War of 1812: A Forgotten Conflict* (Urbana: University of Illinois Press, 1989), 81. For Hull's surrender of Detroit, see ibid., 80–84.
2. The narrative of the campaigns in this section relies heavily on two general surveys of the war and several more specific secondary accounts. Hickey, *The War of 1812* provides an American perspective; and Jon Latimer, *1812: War with America* (Cambridge, Mass.: Harvard University Press, 2007) offers the British and Canadian view. Also of great use is Alan Taylor, *The Civil War of 1812: American Citizens, British Subjects, Irish Rebels, and Indian Allies* (New York: Knopf,

2010). For the Niagara campaign in 1812, see *Hickey, The War of 1812,* 86–88; Latimer, *1812,* 73–83; Taylor, *The Civil War of 1812,* 175–201; and Pierre Berton, *The Invasion of Canada, 1812–1813* (Toronto: McClelland and Stewart, 1980), 79–198.

3. Quoted in Hickey, *The War of 1812,* 88.
4. Ibid., 88–90; Latimer, *1812,* 111.
5. Gallatin to Thomas Jefferson, December 18, 1812, Thomas Jefferson Papers, Library of Congress.
6. Hickey, *The War of 1812,* 85–86; Latimer, *1812,* 117–20.
7. Hickey, *The War of 1812,* 135–36; Latimer, *1812,* 134–39.
8. David Curtis Skaggs and Gerard T. Altoff, *A Signal Victory: The Lake Erie Campaign, 1812–1813* (Annapolis: Naval Institute Press, 1997). See also Hickey, *The War of 1812,* 132–35; Latimer, *1812,* 181–84.
9. [Worcester, Mass.], *National Aegis,* Oct. 6, 1813; [Concord] *New Hampshire Patriot,* Oct. 5, 1813; *National Songster; Or, a Collection of the Most Admired Patriotic Songs, on the Brilliant Victories, Achieved by the Naval and Military Heroes of the United States of America, over Equal and Superior Forces of the British. From the Best American Authors* (Hagers-town [Md.]: Printed by John Gruber and Daniel May, 1814), 9, 17, 20.
10. John Sugden, *Tecumseh's Last Stand* (Norman: University of Oklahoma Press, 1985); Pierre Berton, *Flames Across the Border: The Canadian-American Tragedy, 1813–1814* (Boston: Little, Brown, and Company, 1981), 175–208. See also Hickey, *The War of 1812,* 137–39; Latimer, *1812,* 186–92.
11. Robert Malcomson, *Lords of the Lake: The Naval War on Lake Ontario, 1812–1814* (Annapolis: Naval Institute Press, 1998). See also Hickey, *The War of 1812,* 127–31, 183–85; Latimer, *1812,* 176–77, 192–94, 231–32, 278–81, 340–43.
12. Berton, *Flames Across the Border,* 245–68. See also Hickey, *The War of 1812,* 140–43; Latimer, *1812,* 223–28.
13. Berton, *Flames Across the Border,* 209–43; Latimer, *1812,* 194–216. See also Hickey, *The War of 1812,* 124–30, 144–46.
14. James G. Cusick, *The Other War of 1812: The Patriot War and the American Invasion of West Florida* (Gainsville: University Press of Florida, 2003).
15. Benjamin W. Griffith, Jr., *McIntosh and Weatherford, Creek Indian Leaders* (Tuscaloosa: University of Alabama Press, 1988); Frank Lawrence Owsley, Jr., *Struggle for the Gulf Borderlands: The Creek War and the Battle of New Orleans, 1812–1815* (Gainsville: University Press of Florida, 1981). See also Hickey, *The War of 1812,* 146–51; Latimer, *1812,* 219–21.
16. Quoted in Latimer, *1812,* 237.
17. Hickey, *The War of 1812,* 146; Latimer, *1812,* 234–35.
18. Latimer, *1812,* 268–76.
19. Don Hickey notes that this story appeared in Winfield Scott's memoirs and that there is no contemporary information to substantiate it. Whatever the origins and veracity of Scott's claims, the army has officially embraced them. Donald R. Hickey, *Don't Give Up the Ship: Myths of the War of 1812* (Urbana: University of Illinois Press, 2006), 72–73.

20. Richard V. Barbuto, *Niagara 1814: America Invades Canada* (Lawrence: University Press of Kansas, 2000), 170–83; Berton, *Flames Across the Border*, 319–26. See also Hickey, *The War of 1812*, 185–87; Latimer, *1812*, 283–87.

21. Barbuto, *Niagara 1814*, 206–33; Berton, *Flames Across the Border*, 332–42. See also Hickey, *The War of 1812*, 187–88; Latimer, *1812*, 289–99.

22. Latimer, *1812*, 345–48.

23. David G. Fitz-Enz, *The Final Invasion: Plattsburgh, the War of 1812's Most Decisive Battle* (New York: Cooper Square Press, 2001). See also Hickey, *The War of 1812*, 189–94; Latimer, *1812*, 345–68.

24. Christopher T. George, *Terror on the Chesapeake: The War of 1812 on the Bay* (Shippensburg, Pa.: White Mane Books, 2000), 65–125; Charles G. Muller, *The Darkest Day: 1814: The Washington-Baltimore Campaign* (Philadelphia: J. B. Lippincott, 1963), 42–172. See also Hickey, *The War of 1812*, 195–202; Latimer, *1812*, 301–22.

25. *The Bladensburg Races. Written Shortly after the Capture of Washington City, August 24, 1814* (Washington, D.C.: no pub., 1816).

26. Hickey, *The War of 1812*, 221–54; J. C. A. Stagg, *Mr. Madison's War: Politics, Diplomacy, and Warfare in the Early American Republic, 1783–1830* (Princeton: Princeton University Press, 1983), 423–24, 429–33, 464–65.

27. George, *Terror on the Chesapeake*, 126–56; Muller, *The Darkest Day: 1814*, 177–205. See also Hickey, *The War of 1812*, 202–04; Latimer, *1812*, 323–33.

28. *National Songster*, 30–31.

29. Wilburt S. Brown, *The Amphibious Campaign for West Florida and Louisiana, 1814–1815: A Critical Review of Strategy and Tactics at New Orleans* (Tuscaloosa: University of Alabama Press, 1969); Benton Rain Patterson, *The Generals: Andrew Jackson, Sir Edward Pakenham, and the Road to the Battle of New Orleans* (New York: New York University Press, 2005); Robert V. Remini, *The Battle of New Orleans: Andrew Jackson and America's First Military Victory* (New York: Viking, 1999). See also Hickey, *The War of 1812*, 206–14; Latimer, *1812*, 369–88.

30. Worcester, Massachusetts, *National Aegis*, August 31, 1814. The White House and English Channel reference appeared in a speech by Alexander Contee Hanson in which he attacked the Treaty of Ghent. *Niles' Weekly Register*, Feb. 25, 1815. See also Washington, D.C., *Daily National Intelligencer*, September 26, 1814.

### 17. Politics of War

1. The two best studies that cover the politics of the War of 1812 are Donald Hickey, *The War of 1812: A Forgotten Conflict* (Urbana: University of Illinois Press, 1989), and J. C. A. Stagg, *Mr. Madison's War: Politics, Diplomacy, and Warfare in the Early American Republic, 1783–1830* (Princeton: Princeton University Press, 1983). The most comprehensive history of the period remains Henry Adams, *History of the United States of America*, 9 vols. (New York: A. and C. Boni, 1930). For other studies of politics leading up to the War of 1812, see Andrew Burstein and Nancy Isenberg, *Madison and Jefferson* (New York: Random House, 2010); Claude G. Bowers, *Jefferson in Power: The Death Struggle of the Federalists*

(Boston: Houghton Mifflin, 1936); Richard Buel, Jr., *America on the Brink: How the Political Struggle over the War of 1812 Almost Destroyed the Young Republic* (New York: Palgrave Macmillan, 2005); Noble E. Cuningham, Jr., *The Jeffersonian Republicans in Power, 1801–1809* (Chapel Hill: University of North Carolina Press, 1963); David Hackett Fischer, *The Revolution of American Conservatism: The Federalist Party in the Era of Jeffersonian Democracy* (New York: Harper & Row, 1965); Reginald Horsman, *The New Republic: The United States of America, 1789–1815* (Harlow, England: Longman, 2000); Linda K. Kerber, *Federalists in Dissent: Imagery and Ideology in Jeffersonian America* (Ithaca: Cornell University Press, 1970); Marshall Smelser, *The Democratic Republic, 1801–1815* (New York: Harper & Row, 1968); Steven Watts, *The Republic Reborn: War and the Making of Liberal America, 1790–1820* (Baltimore: Johns Hopkins University Press, 1987). For state and regional studies, see James M. Banner, Jr., *To the Hartford Convention: The Federalists and the Origins of Party Politics in Massachusetts, 1789–1815* (New York: Knopf, 1970); Dixon Ryan Fox, *The Decline of Aristocracy in the Politics of New York, 1801–1840* (New York: Columbia University Press, 1919); John S. Pancake, *Samuel Smith and the Politics of Business, 1752–1839* (Tuscaloosa: University of Alabama Press, 1972); Norman K. Risjord, *The Old Republicans: Southern Conservatism in the Age of Jefferson* (New York: Columbia University Press, 1965); Andrew Shankman, *Crucible of American Democracy: The Struggle to Fuse Egalitarianism and Capitalism in Jeffersonian Pennsylvania* (Lawrence: University of Kansas Press, 2004).

2. Stagg, *Mr. Madison's War*, 56–68.
3. Parts of the address originally appeared in newspapers. Robert Smith, *Robert Smith's Address to the People of the United States* (Baltimore: no pub., 1811), 11, 38. For the Madisonian response, see Joel Barlow, *A Review of Robert Smith's Address to the People of the United States. Originally Published in the National Intelligencer* (Philadelphia: John Binns, 1811).
4. Stagg, *Mr. Madison's War*, 71–78.
5. Hickey, *The War of 1812*, 29–51; Stagg, *Mr. Madison's War*, 84–88, 120–76.
6. Norman K. Risjord, "Election of 1812," in Arthur M. Schlesinger, Jr., *History of American Presidential Elections, 1789–1968* (New York: McGraw Hill, 1971), 249–96; Evan Cornog, *The Birth of Empire: DeWitt Clinton and the American Experience, 1769–1828* (New York: Oxford University Press, 1998).
7. Hickey, *The War of 1812*, 100–25, 159–81, 221–54; Stagg, *Mr. Madison's War*, 289–94, 314–19, 383–86.
8. *Annals of Congress*, House of Representatives, 12th Congress, 2nd sess., 512.
9. *Annals of Congress*, House of Representatives, 13th Congress, 1st sess., 149–52; Stagg, *Mr. Madison's War*, 304–08.
10. *Annals of Congress*, House of Representatives, 13th Congress, 2nd sess., 512.
11. *Annals of Congress*, House of Representatives, 13th Congress, 1st sess., 249.
12. Ibid., 199.
13. Ibid., 212.
14. Ibid., 181–82.
15. Ibid., 212.

16. *Annals of Congress*, House of Representatives, 12ᵗʰ Congress, 2nd sess. 573, 576–77.
17. Ibid., 601.
18. Ibid., 613.
19. Ibid., 669–76.
20. Ibid., 176.
21. Charleston *The Carolina Gazette*, December 5, 1812; New York *Spectator*, Dec. 5, 1812; *Annals of Congress*, House of Representatives, 12ᵗʰ Congress, 2nd sess., 676; *Annals of Congress*, House of Representatives, 13th Congress, 2nd sess., 1005–06; Washington, D.C., *Daily National Intelligencer*, January 20, 1814; *Annals of Congress*, House of Representatives, 13th Congress, 2nd sess., 1962; *Niles' Weekly Register*, April 23, 1814.
22. Philadelphia *Weekly Aurora*, January 26, 1813.
23. *Baltimore Patriot*, January 16, 1813; *Raleigh Register*, March 12, 1813.
24. Charleston *City Gazette*, March 10, 1813.
25. Washington, D.C., *Universal Gazette*, March 26, 1813; Howell, Massachusetts (Maine), *American Advocate*, April 1, 1813.
26. Salem *Essex Register*, March 13, 1813.
27. New York *Columbian*, April 17, 21, 26, 1813; New York *National Advocate*, April 26, 1816. For political meetings elsewhere, see New York *Columbian*, April 19, 1813.
28. New York *National Advocate*, March 10, 1813.
29. For political tickets with free trade and sailors' rights, see New York *National Advocate*, April 26, 1816; Newark *Centennial of Freedom*, September 11, 26, 1813; Elizabethtown *New Jersey Journal*, September 14, 1813; Philadelphia *Tickler*, September 29, 1813. For political articles with this headline, see Newark *Centennial of Freedom*, August 31, 1813; Salem *Gazette*, June 14, 1814. For a sample of articles that referred to free trade and sailors' rights, see New York *Gazette*, March 17, 1813; Providence *Columbian Phoenix*, April 17, 1813.
30. New York *The War*, November 21, 1812.
31. *Baltimore Patriot*, March 18, 1813.
32. Washington, D.C., *Daily National Intelligencer*, April 19, 1813. For other election reports using the phrase, see Salem *Essex Register*, March 13, 1813; and Washington, D.C., *Universal Gazette*, March 26, 1813.
33. New York *Columbian*, April 21, 1813.
34. Washington, D.C., *Daily National Intelligencer*, July 8, 1813.
35. Ibid., October 8, 1813.
36. Portland *Eastern Argus*, October 14, 1813.
37. *Niles' Weekly Register*, March 27, 1813.
38. Providence *Columbian Phoenix*, March 6, 1813; Portland *Eastern Argus*, April 1, 1813; Boston *The Yankee*, April 2, 1813; *Boston Patriot*, April 3, 1814; Baltimore *American and Commercial Daily Advertiser*, April 14, 1813; Hudson, New York, *Bee*, April 27, 1813.
39. Concord *New Hampshire Patriot*, January 26, 1813.
40. *Albany Argus*, April 27, 1813.

41. For the headings, see the following dates: *Boston Patriot*, March 10, 1813; *Baltimore Patriot*, April 27, 1813; Providence *Columbian Phoenix*, May 8, 1813.

42. New York *Spectator*, January 9, 1813; *Boston Patriot*, January 16, February 17, 1813; Providence *Columbian Phoenix*, January 16, 1813; Richmond *Enquirer*, January 16, 1813; Boston *Independent Chronicle*, March 1, 1813; *American Mercury*, March 10, 1813.

43. Annapolis *Maryland Gazette and Political Intelligencer*, September 16, 1813.

44. Philadelphia *Poulson's Daily Advertiser*, September 17, 20, 21, 1813.

45. New York *Military Monitor*, April 26, 1813; Easton, Maryland, *Republican Star or Eastern Shore General Advertiser*, May 11, 1813.

46. *New York Herald*, November 10, 1813.

47. Philadelphia *Tickler*, November 10, 1813.

48. New York *Evening Post*, April 27, 1814; *New York Herald*, April 30, 1814. For additional Federalist articles attacking the slogan, see Philadelphia *Poulson's Daily Advertiser*, July 9, 1813; *Salem Gazette*, September 3, 1813.

49. Windsor, Vermont, *Washingtonian*, March 21, 1814.

50. *Boston Spectator*, September 17, 1814

51. Boston *New England Palladium*, July 12, 1814.

52. Washington, D.C., *Daily National Intelligencer*, December 9, 1814.

53. *Annals of Congress*, House of Representatives, 12th Congress, 2nd sess., 669–76; Utica *Columbian Gazette*, April 6, 1813.

## 18. Pursuit of Peace

1. Bradford Perkins, *Castlereagh and Adams: England and the United States, 1812–1823* (Berkeley: University of California Press, 1964), 4.

2. *American State Papers: Foreign Relations*, 3: 585–94.

3. Perkins, *Castlereagh and Adams*, 12.

4. *American State Papers: Foreign Relations*, 3: 595–97; Perkins, *Castlereagh and Adams*, 12–14.

5. Hunter Miller, ed., *Treaties and Other International Acts of the United States of America*, 8 vols. (Washington, D.C.: Government Printing Office, 1931), 2: 557–73.

6. *American State Papers: Foreign Relations*, 3: 597–99, 633–34. See also John Mason to [Bayard], January 6, 1814, "Papers of James A. Bayard, 1796–1815," Elizabeth Donan, ed., *American Historical Association Annual Report*, 1913, 2: 249–51.

7. Quoted in Donald Hickey, *The War of 1812: A Forgotten Conflict* (Urbana: University of Illinois Press, 1989), 178.

8. James D. Richardson, ed., *Compilation of Messages and Papers of the Presidents, 1789–1897* (Washington, D.C.: Government Printing Office, 1896), 1: 536; *American State Papers: Foreign Relations*, 3: 632.

9. *American State Papers: Foreign Relations*, 3: 630–84; *Compilation of Messages and Papers of the Presidents*, 1: 536–37; Hickey, *The War of 1812*, 177–80.

10. *American State Papers: Foreign Relations*, 4: 56–90.

11. *American State Papers: Foreign Relations*, 3: 600–02, 630–32.

12. *Annals of Congress*, House of Representatives, 12th Congress, 2nd sess., 933–36.

13. Ibid., 972–74.
14. James Fulton Zimmerman, *Impressment of American Seamen* (New York: Columbia University Press, 1925), 195–200; *Annals of Congress*, House of Representatives, 12ᵗʰ Congress, 2ⁿᵈ sess., 932–1011, 1015, 1017–19, 1022–55.
15. Dashkov to Monroe, August 2, 1812, Nina N. Bashkina et al., eds., *The United States and Russia: The Beginnings of Relations, 1765–1815* ([Washington, D.C.: U.S. Govt. Print. Off., 1980]), 872.
16. Quoted in Perkins, *Castlereagh and Adams*, 65.
17. Quoted in Nikolai N. Bolkhovitinov, *The Beginnings of Russian-American Relations, 1775–1815*, Elena Levin, trans. (Cambridge, Mass.: Harvard University Press, 1980), 316.
18. Frank A. Golder, "The Russian Offer of Mediation in the War of 1812," *Political Science Quarterly*, 31 (September 1916), 380–91; David W. McFadden, "John Quincy Adams, American Commercial Diplomacy, and Russia, 1809–1825," *New England Quarterly*, 66 (December 1993), 613–29. See also Fred L. Engelman, *The Peace of Christmas Eve* (New York: Harcourt, Brace & World, 1960), 3–67.
19. Madison to John Nicholas, April 2, 1813, Gaillard Hunt, ed., *The Writings of James Madison Comprising His Public Papers and His Private Correspondence . . .*, 9 vols. (New York : G. P. Putnam's Sons, 1900–10), 8: 243–44.
20. *American State Papers: Foreign Relations*, 3: 623–27.
21. Quoted in Bolkhovitinov, *The Beginnings of Russian-American Relations*, 317.
22. From the Diary of John Quincy Adams, June 15, 22, 1813, Bashkina et al., eds., *The United States and Russia*, 971–75; *The Writings of Albert Gallatin*, Henry Adams, ed., 3 vols. (Philadelphia: J. B. Lippincott, 1879), 1: 546–52.
23. November 3, 1813, The Diaries of John Quincy Adams, Digital Collection, Massachusetts Historical Society.
24. Quoted in Bolkhovitinov, *The Beginnings of Russian-American Relations*, 318–19.
25. For the key diplomatic correspondence on this turn of events, see Bashkina et al., eds., *The United States and Russia*, 878–1047. See also Bayard to Andrew Bayard, August 27, September 11, 1813, Commissioners to Monroe, November 19, 1813, "Papers of James A. Bayard, 1796–1815," Donan, ed., *American Historical Association Annual Report*, 1913, 2: 242–43, 244–45, 246–47; John Quincy Adams to the Secretary of State, February 5, 1814, Worthington Chauncey Ford, ed., *The Writings of John Quincy Adams*, 7 vols. (New York: Macmilan, 1913–17), 4: 12–22. For secondary accounts see Bolhovitinov, *The Beginnings of Russian-American Relations*, 304–33; Golder, "The Russian Offer of Mediation," *Political Science Quarterly*, 31 (September 1916), 380–91; McFadden, "John Quincy Adams, American Commercial Diplomacy, and Russia, 1809–1825," *New England Quarterly*, 66 (December 1993), 613–29; Samuel Flagg Bemis, *John Quincy Adams and the Foundations of American Foreign Policy* (New York: Knopf, 1949), 180–220; Engelman, *The Peace of Christmas Eve*, 43–67.
26. W. H. Crawford to the American Commissioners, May 24, 28, 1814, LaFayette to Gallatin, June 3, 1814, La Fayette to W. H. Crawford, May 26, 1814, Gallatin to Monroe, June 3, 8, 20, 1814, Gallatin to Emperor Alexander, June 19, 1814, Adams, ed., *Writings of Albert Gallatin*, 1: 619–27, 632–33.

27. *American State Papers: Foreign Relations*, 3: 621–23; Bashkina et al., eds., *The United States and Russia*, 1029–32.

28. Perkins, *Castlereagh and Adams*, 58–80.

29. *American State Papers: Foreign Relations*, 3: 701–02; Bayard and Gallatin to Monroe, May 23, 1814, Adams, ed., *Writings of Albert Gallatin*, 1: 618–19.

30. Quotation in *American State Papers: Foreign Relations*, 3: 711. See also ibid., 3: 708–24; Perkins, *Castlereagh and Adams*, 81–101.

31. Perkins, *Castlereagh and Adams*, 62–64.

32. Ibid., 68–69.

33. *American State Papers: Foreign Relations*, 3: 711.

34. *American State Papers: Indian Affairs*, 1: 826; September 29, 1814, The Diaries of John Quincy Adams, Digital Collection, Massachusetts Historical Society.

35. *American State Papers: Foreign Relations*, 3: 703–04; Perkins, *Castlereagh and Adams*, 69–71; Engelman, *The Peace of Christmas Eve*, 131–56, 175–208.

36. Quotation in *American State Papers: Foreign Relations*, 3: 725. See also ibid., 3: 724–26; Perkins, *Castlereagh and Adams*, 98–107.

37. *American State Papers: Foreign Relations*, 3: 724–26; Perkins, *Castlereagh and Adams*, 102–15; Engelman, *The Peace of Christmas Eve*, 229–65.

38. Miller, ed., *Treaties and Other International Acts of the United States*, 2: 574–84.

39. James M. Banner, *To the Hartford Convention: The Federalists and the Origins of Party Politics in Massachusetts, 1789–1815* (New York: Knopf, 1970).

### 19. Dartmoor

1. Samuel Leech, *Thirty Years from Home, or a Voice from the Main Deck* . . . (Boston: Tappan & Dennet, 1843), 193–94, 149–51.

2. *Salem Gazette*, September 3, 1813; *Newburyport Herald*, September 7, 1813.

3. The article appeared originally in the *Boston Spectator* and was reprinted in the *New-York Evening Post*, April 27, 1814; *New-York Herald*, April 30, 1814.

4. *Salem Gazette*, March 16, 1813; Salem *Essex Register*, March 17, 1813.

5. John Allen, "NY and departure of *General Armstrong*," [1814], Jacob Reeves Papers, 1809–1835, Massachusetts Historical Society.

6. Benjamin Waterhouse, *A Journal of a Young Man of Massachusetts* . . . (Lexington, Ky.: Worsley & Smith, 1816), 70–71. The real author of this book is Amos G. Babcock. The book appeared under the name Benjamin Waterhouse. Waterhouse, a noted scientist and medical doctor, agreed to edit Babcock's journal. For some reason the book was then published under Waterhouse's name, even though Waterhouse was born in 1754 and did not serve on a privateer during the War of 1812. See Henry R. Viets, "A Journal of a Young Man of Massachusetts . . . Written By Himself, Boston: 1816 and a Note on the Author," *Yale Journal of Biology and Science*, 12 (1940), 605–22.

7. Charles Andrews, *The Prisoners' Memoirs, or Dartmoor Prison* . . . (New York: For the Author, 1815), 136–37; Nathaniel Pierce, "Journal of Nathaniel Pierce of Newburyport, Kept at Dartmoor Prison, 1814–1815," *Essex Institute Historical Collections*, 73 (1937), 26.

8. Josiah Cobb, *A Green Hand's First Cruise: Roughed Out From the Log-Book of Memory, of Twenty Five Years Standing* . . . , 2 vols. (Boston: Otis, Broaders, and

Company, 1841), 2: 40, 132–36; Nathaniel Hawthorne, ed., *The Yarn of A Yankee Privateer* (New York: Funk and Wagnalls, 1926), 208; Waterhouse, *A Journal of a Young Man*, 157.

9. Pierce, "Journal," *Essex Institute Historical Collections*, 73 (1937), 27; ibid., 53–55; Cobb, *A Green Hand's First Cruise*, 2: 172–73.

10. Waterhouse, *A Journal of a Young Man*, 105, 135–36.

11. Joseph Valpey, Jr., *Journal of Joseph Valpey, Jr. of Salem, November 1813–April 1815: With Other Papers Relating to His Experience in Dartmoor Prison* (n.p.: Michigan Society of Colonial Wars, 1922), 16–20; Pierce, "Journal," *Essex Institute Historical Collections*, 73 (1937), 33–34.

12. Cobb, *A Green Hand's First Cruise*, 2: 40; Andrews, *The Prisoners' Memoirs*, 73–74.

13. For a fuller exploration of this point, see Paul A. Gilje, *Liberty on the Waterfront: American Maritime Culture in the Age of Revolution* (Philadelphia: University of Pennsylvania Press, 2004).

14. Hawthorne, ed., *The Yarn of a Yankee Privateer*, 82.

15. Waterhouse, *A Journal of a Young Man*, 58, 239.

16. Andrews, *The Prisoners' Memoirs*, 156–61; Cobb, *A Green Hand's First Cruise*, 2: 187–91; L. P. C., "Reminiscences," *Knickerbocker*, 24 (1844), 459–60; Waterhouse, *A Journal of a Young Man*, 192–93.

17. Andrews, *The Prisoners' Memoirs*, 165–70; Cobb, *A Green Hand's First Cruise*, 2: 210–11; Hawthorne, ed., *The Yarn of A Yankee Privateer*, 264–68; Pierce, "Journal," *Essex Institute Historical Collections*, 73 (1937), 39; Waterhouse, *A Journal of a Young Man*, 195–97.

18. For descriptions by American sailors, see Andrews, *The Prisoners' Memoirs*, 172–82; Cobb, *A Green Hand's First Cruise*, 2: 214–21; Hawthorne, ed., *The Yarn of A Yankee Privateer*, 271–79; L. P. C., "Reminiscences," *Knickerbocker*, 24 (1844), 459–60, 460–63; Pierce, "Journal," *Essex Institute Historical Collections*, 73 (1937), 40–41; Valpey, *Journal*, 27; and *Niles' Weekly Register*, June 17, 1815, 267–71, 283; ibid., July 8, 1815, 321–28; ibid., Aug. 5, 1815, 389–92. See also Box 605, RG 45, National Archives; United States, *Annals of Congress*, House of Representatives, 14th Congress, 1st sess., 1506–81; *American State Papers: Foreign Relations*, 4: 19–56; *Dartmoor Massacre* [Pittsfield: Phineas Allev, 1815].

19. *American State Papers: Foreign Relations*, 4: 22–23.

20. Ibid., 23–24. In early 1816 Congress considered investigating the massacre and the King-Larpent report, but did not pursue the matter. Boston *Independent Chronicle*, January 18, 1816; Cooperstown, New York, *Otsego Herald*, January 18, 1815.

21. New York *Commercial Advertiser*, May 24, 1815.

22. New York *Columbian*, June 6, 1815.

23. Ibid., June 7, 1815.

24. New York *Commercial Advertiser*, June 12, 1815.

25. Salem *Essex Register*, June 10, 1815; New York *Columbian*, June 10, 1815; New York *National Advocate*, June 29, 1815; *Albany Register*, June 30, 1815.

26. Washington, D.C., *Daily National Intelligencer*, June 13, 1815; Hartford *American Mercury*, June 14, 1815; Concord *New-Hampshire Patriot*, June 20, 1815.

27. *Albany Register*, June 23, 1815. See also *Baltimore Patriot*, June 16, July 7, 1815; Hartford *American Mercury*, June 28, 1815; Wilmington, Delaware, *American Watchman*, June 28, July 8, 1815; Hallowell, Massachusetts [Maine], *American Advocate*, July 1, 1815; *Albany Register*, July 11, 1815; Carthage, Tennessee, *Carthage Gazette*, August 22, 1815; *Albany Argus*, August 25, 1815; New York *Columbian*, September 26, 1815.

28. New York *Columbian*, June 6, 19, September 26, 1815; Bridgeport, Connecticut, *Republican Farmer*, June 28, 1815; *Baltimore Patriot*, January 13, 1816.

29. New York *National Advocate*, June 27, 1815.

30. *Albany Register*, June 23, 27, 1815.

31. Washington, D.C., *Daily National Intelligencer*, July 14, 1815; New York *National Advocate*, July 18, 1815.

32. New York *National Advocate*, July 25, 1815.

33. *Baltimore Patriot*, July 15, 1815.

34. Richmond *Enquirer*, July 22, 1815; *Baltimore Patriot*, July 24, 1815.

35. Hartford *American Mercury*, July 24, 1815.

36. Boston *Independent Chronicle*, July 26, 1815. See also Philadelphia *Weekly Aurora*, July 25, August 15, 1815; *Baltimore Patriot*, July 26, 1815; Boston *Independent Chronicle*, July 27, 1815; Hudson, New York, *Bee*, August 22, 1815; Trenton *True American*, September 11, 1815.

37. Baltimore *Federal Republican*, June 16, 1815. See also ibid., June 20, 1815; Hudson, New York, *Northern Whig*, June 20, 1815.

38. *Newburyport Herald*, June 20, 1815.

39. New York *Courier*, July 1, 1815; *Salem Gazette*, July 4, 1815.

40. *New-York Evening Post*, July 17, 1815.

41. Providence *Rhode-Island American*, July 21, 1817.

42. New York *Courier*, July 24, 1815. See also *Salem Gazette*, July 11, 1815. To Clay's credit he stood by King and sent a letter to King's brother explaining his choice and stating that he had "entire confidence in the purity of motives and conduct of your brother on this occasion." Clay to John A. King, April 9, 1816, James F. Hopkins et al., eds., *The Papers of Henry Clay*, 11 vols. (Lexington: University of Kentucky Press, 1959–92), 2: 191–93. See also *New-York Evening Post*, March 21, April 25, 1816; Hudson, New York, *Bee*, March 26, 1816; *Albany Register*, April 25, 1820.

43. For a Republican defense against this charge, see New York *National Advocate*, July 26, 1815.

44. Georgetown, Washington, D.C., *Federal Republican*, July 28, 1815.

45. *New-York Herald*, Aug. 2, 1815; Georgetown, Washington, D.C., *Federal Republican*, Aug. 8, 1815.

46. New York *Commercial Advertiser*, August 30, 1839.

## 20. Winning the Peace

1. Most biographies of Madison have bought into Madison's triumphalism. See Ralph Ketchum, *James Madison: A Biography* (London: Macmillan, 1971), 594–99; Jack N. Rakove, *James Madison: And the Creation of the American Republic*, 3rd ed.

(New York: Pearson, 2007), 200–03; Robert Allen Rutland, *The Presidency of James Madison* (Lawrence: University Press of Kansas, 1990), 183–89; Garry Wills, *James Madison* (New York: Henry Holt, 2002), 150–59.

2. James D. Richardson, ed., *Compilation of Messages and Papers of the Presidents, 1789–1897* (Washington, D.C.: Government Printing Office, 1896), 1: 552–54.
3. *An Exposition of the Causes and Character of the Late War with Great Britain. Published by the Authority of the American Government* (London: W. I. Clement, 1815). Quotations, ibid., 37, 44, 72. Madison had a strong hand in composing the pamphlet. See J. C. A. Stagg, *Mr. Madison's War: Politics, Diplomacy, and Warfare in the Early American Republic, 1783–1830* (Princeton: Princeton University Press, 1983), 452n.
4. *Niles' Weekly Register*, March 4, 1815.
5. *Boston Patriot*, February 15, 1815.
6. Bridgeport, Connecticut, *Republican Farmer*, February 15, 1815.
7. New York *Commercial Advertiser*, February 12, 1815.
8. *An Exposition of the Causes and Character of the Late War*, title page. See also Bradford Perkins, *Castlereagh and Adams: England and the United States, 1812–1823* (Berkeley: University of California Press, 1964), 132–38.
9. Baltimore *American Commercial and Daily Advertiser*, February 17, 1815.
10. *Albany Argus*, March 7, 1815.
11. Newark *Centinel of Freedom*, March 7, 1815.
12. James F. Hopkins et al., eds., *The Papers of Henry Clay*, 11 vols. (Lexington: University of Kentucky Press, 1959–92), 2: 148.
13. Quoted in Roger H. Brown, *The Republic in Peril: 1812* (New York: Columbia University Press, 1964), 190–91.
14. Boston *Independent Chronicle*, February 27, 1815.
15. *Salem Gazette*, March 10, 1815.
16. *Annals of Congress*, House of Representatives, 13th Congress, 3rd sess., 662; *Niles' Weekly Register*, February 15, 1815.
17. Balston Spa, New York, *Independent American*, March 8, 1815.
18. *An Impartial and Correct History of the War Between the United States of America and Great Britain . . .* (New York: John Low, 1815), 6.
19. Gilbert J. Hunt, *The Late War Between the United States and Great Britain: From June 1812 to February 1815, Written in the Ancient Historical Style . . .* (New York: David Longworth, 1816), 305–06. For religious leaders and the War of 1812, see Steven Watts, *The Republic Reborn: War and the Making of Liberal America, 1790–1820* (Baltimore: Johns Hopkins University Press, 1987), 283–89; William Gribbin, *The Churches Militant: The War of 1812 and American Religion* (New Haven: Yale University Press, 1973), 61–77.

## 21. Remembering Impressment

1. *American State Papers: Foreign Relations*, 4: 9–10.
2. The 1813 law was contingent on British action. Madison suggested in 1815 that Congress pass a law that would prohibit hiring British seamen before the British

government took any action. James D. Richardson, ed., *Compilation of Messages and Papers of the Presidents, 1789–1897* (Washington, D.C.: Government Printing Office, 1896), 1: 563.

3. *American State Papers: Foreign Relations*, 4: 360.

4. Ibid., 363.

5. Bradford Perkins, *Castlereagh and Adams: England and the United States, 1812–1823* (Berkeley: University of California Press, 1964), 253–58; Samuel Flagg Bemis, *John Quincy Adams and the Foundations of American Foreign Policy* (New York: Knopf, 1949), 235–36.

6. *American State Papers: Foreign Relations*, 4: 373–74.

7. Ibid., 379, 389–90, 394, 395–96, 399–400; Charles Francis Adams, ed., *Memoirs of John Quincy Adams, Comprising Portions of His Diary from 1795 to 1848*, 11 vols. (Philadelphia: J. B. Lippincott, 1875), 4: 147–50; Bemis, *John Quincy Adams*, 295–98; Perkins, *Castlereagh and Adams*, 261–72; James Fulton Zimmerman, *Impressment of American Seamen* (New York: Columbia University Press, 1925), 227–34.

8. William R. Manning, ed., *Diplomatic Correspondence of the United States: Canadian Relations, 1784–1860*, 3 vols. (Washington, D.C.: Carnegie Endowment for International Peace, 1940) 1: 236.

9. Alan Taylor, *The Civil War of 1812: American Citizens, British Subjects, Irish Rebels, and Indian Allies* (New York: Knopf, 2010), 430–35; Manning, ed., *Diplomatic Correspondence of the United States*, 1: 233–37, 246–55, 783–86, 790–91, 808; Perkins, *Castlereagh and Adams*, 240–44.

10. *American State Papers: Foreign Relations*, 6: 368–72.

11. Adams, ed., *Memoirs of John Quincy Adams*, 5: 448.

12. Ibid., 6: 37.

13. *American State Papers: Foreign Relations*, 5: 335–37.

14. Adams, ed., *Memoirs of John Quincy Adams*, 6: 154.

15. Bemis, *John Quincy Adams*, 423–32.

16. Ibid., Appendix 2, 578.

17. Ibid., 363–408.

18. Ibid., 432–35; James E. Lewis, Jr., *John Quincy Adams: Policymaker for the Union* (Wilmington, Del.: Scholarly Resources, 2001), 81–83.

19. Bemis, *John Quincy Adams*, 442–44; *American State Papers: Foreign Relations*, 5: 550–51; Richard Rush, *A Residence at the Court of London, Comprising Incidents, Official and Personal, from 1819 to 1825 . . .*, 2 vols. (Philadelphia: Lea & Blanchard, 1845), 2: 119–323 (esp. 225–48).

20. Quoted in Zimmerman, *Impressment of American Seamen*, 239–40.

21. Hunter Miller, ed., *Treaties and Other International Acts of the United States of America*, 8 vols. (Washington, D.C.: Government Printing Office, 1931), 3: 472–77. Quotations ibid., 475. See also Zimmerman, *Impressment*, 239–47; John Belohlavek, *George Mifflin Dallas: Jacksonian Patrician* (University Park: Pennsylvania State University Press, 1977), 168–74.

22. Miller, ed., *Treaties and Other International Acts*, 4: 472–77.

## 22. The Persistent Dream

1. *American State Papers: Foreign Relations*, 4:9–10.
2. Ibid., 363.
3. Hunter Miller, ed., *Treaties and Other International Acts of the United States of America*, 8 vols. (Washington, D.C.: Government Printing Office, 1931), 2: 658–62.
4. *American State Papers: Foreign Relations*, 5: 529–33.
5. Charles Francis Adams, ed., *Memoirs of John Quincy Adams, Comprising Portions of His Diary from 1795 to 1848*, 11 vols. (Philadelphia: J. B. Lippincott, 1874–76), 6: 164.
6. Samuel Flagg Bemis, *John Quincy Adams and the Foundations of American Foreign Policy* (New York: Knopf, 1949), 436–47, Appendix, 579–85; James E. Lewis, Jr., *John Quincy Adams: Policymaker for the Union* (Wilmington, Delaware: Scholarly Resources, 2001), 81–84.
7. *American State Papers: Foreign Relations*, 5: 529.
8. Adams, ed., *Memoirs of John Quincy Adams*, 6:164.
9. Miller, ed., *Treaties and Other International Acts*, 2: 586.
10. Ibid., 128–29, 611; ibid., 3: 296–97.
11. Ibid., 170–71, 442–53; ibid., 3: 435–36.
12. Ibid., 3: 338.
13. Ibid., 170–72, 460–62, 609–11, 679–81.
14. Francis Taylor Piggott, "The Freedom of the Seas, Historically Treated," *Peace Handbooks: International Affairs*, vol. 23, no. 148 (London: H. M. Stationery Office, 1920).
15. Adams, ed., *Memoirs of John Quincy Adams*, 5: 353.
16. *Annals of Congress*, Senate, 13th Congress, 3rd sess., 265–66.
17. Vernon G. Setser, *The Commercial Reciprocity Policy of the United States, 1774–1829* (Philadelphia: University of Pennsylvania Press, 1937), 184–85.
18. *American State Papers: Foreign Relations*, 4: 17–18, 348–402; ibid., 6: 639–706; Miller, ed., *Treaties and Other International Acts*, 2: 595–600, 658–62; ibid., 3: 314–85; Setser, *The Commercial Reciprocity*, 185–88; Perkins, *Castlereagh and Adams*, 224–25.
19. Bradford Perkins, *Castlereagh and Adams: England and the United States, 1812–1823* (Berkeley: University of California Press, 1964), quoted on 222.
20. Ibid., 196–282; Bemis, *John Quincy Adams*, 220–43, 278–99.
21. *American State Papers: Foreign Relations*, 5: 152.
22. Ibid., 149–213; Adams, ed., *Memoirs of John Quincy Adams*, 5: 353; Miller, ed., *Treaties and Other International Acts*, 3: 77–83; Setser, *The Commercial Reciprocity*, 195–208; Bemis, *John Quincy Adams*, 450–54.
23. Setser, *The Commercial Reciprocity*, 208–14.
24. Ibid., 220–21.
25. *American State Papers: Foreign Relations*, 4: 172–73; ibid., 5: 590–96; Setser, *The Commercial Reciprocity*, 188–94.

26. *American State Papers: Foreign Relations*, 4: 213, 419–22; Miller, ed., *Treaties and Other International Acts*, 2: 602–05; Setser, *The Commercial Reciprocity*, 183–222.

27. James D. Richardson, ed., *Compilation of Messages and Papers of the Presidents, 1789–1897* (Washington, D.C.: Government Printing Office, 1896), 2: 300–01.

28. Quoted in Setser, *The Commercial Reciprocity*, 247.

29. *American State Papers: Foreign Relations*, 6: 707–43, 945–46; Setser, *The Commercial Reciprocity*, 214–20; Miller, ed., *Treaties and Other International Acts*, 3: 239–41, 286, 389–91, 429–31. By treaty the United States extended full reciprocity to Russia in 1832, Greece in 1837, and Sardinia in 1838. Miller, ed., *Treaties and Other International Acts*, 3: 725–28; ibid., 4: 109–11, 146–48.

30. Setser, *The Commercial Reciprocity*, 243–51; *American State Papers: Foreign Relations*, 5: 696–735, 760–82.

31. Perkins, *Castlereagh and Adams*, 222–24.

32. Douglass C. North, *The Economic Growth of the United States, 1790–1860* (New York: Norton, 1967; orig. pub. 1961), 233–34.

33. Robert Greenhalgh Albion, *The Rise of the Port of New York, 1815–1860* (Hamden, Conn.: Archon Books, 1961; orig. pub. 1939); Stuart Bruchey, *Enterprise: The Dynamic Economy of a Free People* (Cambridge: Cambridge University Press, 1991); Howard L. Chapelle, *The Search for Speed under Sail, 1700–1853* (New York: Norton, 1967); Carl C. Cutler, *Greyhounds of the Sea: The Story of the American Clipper Ship*, 3rd ed. (Annapolis: Naval Institute Press, 1984); William H. Goetzmann, *New Lands, New Men: America and the Second Great Age of Discovery* (New York: Viking, 1986); Diane Lindstrom, *Economic Development in the Philadelphia Region, 1810–1850* (New York: Columbia University Press, 1978); Samuel Eliot Morison, *The Maritime History of Massachusetts, 1783–1860* (Boston: Houghton Mifflin, 1941); North, *The Economic Growth of the United States*; Ralph D. Payne, *The Old Merchant Marine: A Chronicle of American Ships and Sailors* (New Haven: Yale University Press, 1919); Charles Sellers, *The Market Revolution: Jacksonian America, 1815–1846* (New York: Oxford University Press, 1991); George Rogers Taylor, *The Transportation Revolution* (New York: Harper & Row, 1951).

34. Adams, ed., *Memoirs of John Quincy Adams*, 6: 104.

35. *American State Papers: Foreign Relations*, 4: 409–12; ibid., 5: 1–13, 81–90, 224–40; ibid., 6: 213–66, 294–356, 638, 963–85; Setser, *The Commercial Reciprocity*, 224–42; Bemis, *John Quincy Adams*, 457–61; John M. Belohlavek, *"Let the Eagle Soar!": The Foreign Policy of Andrew Jackson* (Lincoln: University of Nebraska Press, 1985), 53–60.

36. Miller, ed., *Treaties and Other International Acts*, 3: 241, 289; Setser, *The Commercial Reciprocity*, 242–43; *American State Papers: Foreign Relations*, 6: 825–29.

37. Adams, ed., *Memoirs of John Quincy Adams*, 5: 427.

38. New York *Commercial Advertiser*, February 11, 1828.

## 23. Politics

1. For the politics of this period, see George Dangerfield, *The Era of Good Feelings* (New York Harcourt, Brace and World, 1952); Daniel Walker Howe, *What Hath*

*God Wrought: The Transformation of America, 1815–1848* (New York: Oxford University Press, 2007); Lawrence Frederick Kohl, *The Politics of Individualism: Parties and the American Character in the Jacksonian Era* (New York: Oxford University Press, 1989); Harry L. Watson, *Liberty and Power: The Politics of Jacksonian America* (New York: Hill and Wang, 1999); Sean Wilentz, *The Rise of American Democracy: Jefferson to Lincoln* (New York: Norton, 2005). For surveys that focus on the market as well as politics, see John Lauritz Larson, *The Market Revolution in America: Liberty, Ambition, and the Eclipse of the Common Good* (Cambridge: Cambridge University Press, 2010); Charles Sellers, *The Market Revolution: Jacksonian America, 1815–1846* (New York: Oxford University Press, 1991).

2. F. W. Taussig, *The Tariff History of the United States* (New York: G. P. Putnum's Sons, 1892).

3. *Annals of Congress*, Senate, 14th Congress, 1st sess., 1316–20.

4. *Memorial of the Sundry Citizens of Charleston, S. C. Against the Tariff* (Washington, D.C.: Gales and Seaton, 1820), 3.

5. Thomas Cooper, *A Tract on the Proposed Alteration of the Tariff . . .* (Philadelphia: Joseph R. A. Skerrett, 1824; orig. pub. Charleston: no pub., 1823), 3.

6. Thomas Cooper, *Lectures of the Elements of Political Economy* (Columbia [South Carolina]: D. E. Sweeny at the Telescope Press, 1826), 9, 279. See also James L. Huston, "Virtue Beseiged: Virtue, Equality, and the General Welfare in the Tariff Debates of the 1820s," *Journal of the Early Republic*, 14 (Winter 1994), 523–47; James L. Huston, *Securing the Fruits of Labor: The American Concept of Wealth Distribution, 1765–1900* (Baton Rouge: Louisiana State University Press, 1999), 164–70, 239–43; Brian Schoen, "Calculating the Price of Union: Republican Economic Nationalism and the Origins of Southern Sectionalism, 1790–1828," *Journal of the Early Republic*, 23 (Summer 2003), 173–206.

7. New Haven *Connecticut Herald*, February 12, 1828.

8. Georgetown, South Carolina, *Winyaw Intelligencer*, April 21, 1832. Note: both the singular and the plural of "state" were used at this time, as in "state rights" and "states rights."

9. Richmond *Enquirer*, March 6, 1832.

10. For the nullification controversy see William W. Freehling, *Prelude to Civil War: The Nullification Controversy in South Carolina, 1816–1836* (New York: Harper & Row, 1965).

11. Washington, D.C., *Daily National Intelligencer*, April 25, 1832.

12. These terms are from Wilentz, *The Rise of American Democracy*, 511.

13. Hartford *Times*, February 2, 1835.

14. James D. Richardson, ed., *Compilation of Messages and Papers of the Presidents 1798–1897* (Washington, D.C.: Government Printing Office, 1896), 2: 590.

15. On these political developments see Howe, *What Hath God Wrought*; Michael F. Holt, *The Rise and Fall of the American Whig Party: Jacksonian Politics and the Onset of the Civil War* (New York: Oxford University Press, 1999).

16. Daniel Raymond, *Thoughts on Political Economy: In Two Parts* (Baltimore: Fielding Lucas, Jun'r., 1820), 348–49, 231.

17. Mathew Carey, *Thirteen Essays on the Policy of Protecting Manufacturing in this Country* (Philadelphia: Clark and Raser, 1830), 13.

18. *Niles' Weekly Register*, March 24, 1832.

19. *Boston Weekly Advertiser*, January 17, 1828.

20. *Niles' Weekly Register*, March 24, 1832.

21. Huston, *Securing the Fruits of Labor*, 247–48.

22. *Salem Gazette*, February 26, 1828. See also Stanley I. Kutler, *Privilege and Creative Destruction: The Charles River Bridge Case* (New York: Norton, 1978; orig. pub. 1971).

23. Ira Cohen, "The Auction System in the Port of New York, 1817–1837," *Business History Review*, 45 (Winter 1971), 488–510. First quotation ibid., 502. Resolution quotations from New York *Commercial Advertiser*, May 3, 1828.

24. John R. Commons et al., eds., *A Documentary History of American Industrial Society*, 10 vols. (Cleveland: Arthur H. Clark, 1910), 3: 228.

25. Philadelphia *National Gazette*, April 4, 1835.

26. Both examples were reported in the New York *Journal of Commerce* and were reprinted elsewhere. See Charleston *Southern Patriot*, July 10, 1834; *Salem Gazette*, July 29, 1834.

27. Salem, New York, *Northern Post*, March 28, 1816.

28. Philadelphia *Weekly Aurora*, July 7, 1817.

29. *New-York Evening Post*, September 8, 1817; New York *National Advocate*, November 7, 1817.

30. Hartford *American Mercury*, April 22, 1817.

31. Washington, Pennsylvania, *Washington Examiner*, December 1, 1817.

32. Elizabethtown *New-Jersey Journal*, July 14, 1818. See also New York *Columbian*, July 12, 1817; Milledgeville, Georgia, *Reflector*, July 7, 1818; Philadelphia *Franklin Gazette*, July 10, 1818; Hartford *Connecticut Herald*, July 11, 1820.

33. *Alexandria Gazette*, May 6, 1820.

34. *Salem Gazette*, September 23, 1828.

35. *Augusta Chronicle* [Georgia], August 20, 1828.

36. Ibid., August 13, 1828. For other anti-tariff references to free trade and sailors' rights, see Washington D.C., *Daily National Intelligencer*, June 9, 1824; *Baltimore City Gazette and Daily Advertiser*, August 25, 1829; *New York Herald*, February 19, 1830; Portland *Eastern Argus*, August 30, 1831; *Richmond Enquirer*, January 15, February 23, 1833.

37. Portland *Eastern Argus*, July 7, 1830.

38. *Our Country . . . Our Industry*, Broadside Collection, portfolio 117, no 13 c – Rare Book Collection, Library of Congress.

39. Middletown, Connecticut, *American Sentinel*, March 10, 1824.

40. Baltimore *Patriot*, January 28, 1828. For other pro-tariff references to free trade and sailors' rights, see *Alexandria Gazette*, March 14, 1833.

41. Portland *Eastern Argus*, August 19, 1828.

42. Philadelphia *National Gazette*, March 8, 1832.

43. Portland *Eastern Argus*, August 15, 1834.

44. Hartford *Times*, February 2, 1835. See also Hartford *Patriot and Eagle*, March 21, 1835.

45. Concord *New-Hampshire Patriot*, May 18, 1835.

46. Saratoga Springs *Saratoga Sentinel*, March 25, 1834. See also *Richmond Enquirer*, January 1, 1834.

47. Pittsfield, Massachusetts, *Sun*, March 21, 1833.

48. *Alexandria Gazette*, June 2, 1832.

49. *Portland Advertiser*, March 20, 1832.

50. New London *Connecticut Gazette*, October 10, 1832.

51. *Philadelphia Inquirer*, April 23, 1834; *Baltimore Patriot*, April 25, 1834.

52. Brattleboro *Vermont Phoenix*, August 14, 1835. See also *Jamestown Journal* [New York], September 23, 1840.

53. Hershel Parker, *Herman Melville: A Biography, Volume I, 1819–1851* (Baltimore: Johns Hopkins University Press, 1996), 334.

54. Charleston *Southern Patriot*, November 19, 1844.

55. Albany *Evening Journal*, November 1, 1844.

56. *Boston Courier*, July 29, 1844.

57. *Milwaukee Sentinel*, June 8, 1844. See also Salem *Register*, June 6, 1844.

58. Salt Lake City *Deseret News*, September 2, 1857. See also ibid., August 26, 1858.

59. New London *Connecticut Gazette*, October 10, 1832; Washington, D.C., *Daily National Intelligencer*, August 26, 1839; *Salem Register*, February 19, 1844; New London *People's Advocate*, March 20, 1844; Albany *Evening Journal*, November 1, 1844.

60. Philadelphia *North American*, November 23, 1847; speech in Lexington, Kentucky, November 13, 1847, *The Papers of Henry Clay*, James F. Hopkins, ed., 10 vols. (Lexington: University Press of Kentucky, 1959–91), 10: 361–77. There were a few other criticisms of the war that referred to free trade and sailors' rights. See *Salem Register*, December 18, 1845, for an article repeated in many newspapers that implied that once a war broke out, peace was what really counted. For other references during the Mexican War, see *Augusta Chronicle* [Georgia], September 14, 1846; *Alexandria Gazette*, November 3, 1846; *New London Democrat*, February 7, 1847; Bridgeport *Republican Farmer*, August 24, 1847; Natchez *Mississippi Free Trader*, February 23, 1848.

61. Pittsfield, Massachusetts *Sun*, June 29, 1848; *Litchfield Republican* [Connecticut], September 7, 1848.

62. For other references to Cass and free trade and sailors' rights in 1848, see Pittsfield, Massachusetts, *Sun*, June 29, 1848; Columbus *Daily Ohio Statesman*, July 7, August 18, 1848; *Plattsburgh Republican*, July 8, 1848; Bennington *Vermont Gazette*, October 17, 1848. For Cass on the right of search, see Lewis Cass, *An Examination of the Question now in Discussion between the American and British Governments Concerning the Right of Search* (Paris: H. Fournier, 1842). For Cass's position in relation to free trade and sailors' rights, see Keene *New Hampshire Sentinel*, April 19, 1843.

63. For additional political use of free trade and sailors' rights in the decade before the Mexican-American War, see New Bern *North Carolina Sentinel*, June 8, 1836; *Richmond Enquirer*, July 12, 1836; Hartford *Times*, July 23, 1836; New Haven *Columbian Register*, May 6, 1837; *Gloucester Democrat*, August 11, 1837; *Kalamazoo Gazette*, March 16, 1839; *Richmond Enquirer*, May 17, 1839; *Albany*

*Evening Journal,* November 4, 1839; New York *The Emancipator,* November 5, 1840, November 3, 1842; Concord *New Hampshire Patriot,* July 23, 1841; August 22, 1844; Baltimore *Sun,* January 27, 1842; Portsmouth *New-Hampshire Gazette,* March 29, 1842, July, 16, 1844, May 6, 1845; Madison *Wisconsin Democrat,* March 28, 1843; *Boston Evening Transcript,* March 7, 1844; Concord *New Hampshire Patriot,* August 22, 1844.

64. For later political uses see San Francisco *Daily Placer Times and Transcript,* August 20, 29, 1855; New York *Weekly Herald,* June 21, 1856; *New York Herald,* July 21, 1856, April 2, 1860.

65. New Haven *Columbian Register,* January 15, 1851.

66. *Kalamazoo Gazette,* October 29, 1852. For similar references see *Augusta Chronicle* [Georgia], September 20, 1847; *New York Herald,* February 2, 1848; Columbus *Daily Ohio Statesman,* March 8, 1851; Washington, D.C., *Daily Globe,* February 27, 1853; Little Rock *Arkansas Gazette,* March 19, 1854.

## 24. Popular Culture

1. Charles Nordhoff, *Man-of-War Life: A Boy's Experience in the United States Navy, During a Voyage around the World in a Ship-of-the-line,* John B. Hattendorf, ed. (Annapolis: Naval Institute Press, 1985; orig. pub. 1855), 33–34.

2. The scrimshaw is owned by the Nantucket Historical Association. Martha Lawrence, *Scrimshaw: The Whaler's Legacy* (Atglen, Pa.: Schiffer Publishing, 1993), 30. Mystic Seaport owns a similar piece of scrimshaw. See ID/Accession number 1996.160.5, Mystic Seaport Museum, Inc. The Mystic information was provided by Paul O'Pecko of the G. W. Blunt White Library, Mystic Seaport, Connecticut.

3. Concord *New-Hampshire Patriot,* February 25, 1834.

4. Philadelphia *Enquirer,* June 9, 1837; New York *Spectator,* October 26, 1842; *New Hampshire Gazette* [Portsmouth], November 8, 1842; *Baltimore Sun,* December 27, 1842; *Sheet Anchor* [Boston], 2 [March 16, 1844], 41–42.

5. *Christian Herald and Sailors Magazine* 9 (January 18, 1823), 535.

6. *Sailors Magazine,* 19 (December 1846), 120–21.

7. New Bedford Port Society Records, *Annual Reports,* 1849, New Bedford Whaling Museum, Temp. #8, 19.

8. *Saturday Evening Post,* January 25, 1828.

9. See The Great Antique Bottles website of Ed and Kathy Gray. Accessed August 17, 2011. http://www.greatantiquebottles.com/flaskpage.html.

10. See http://forums.collectors.com/messageview.cfm?catid=7&threadid=816477. Accessed August 17, 2011.

11. Fincastle, Virginia, *Fincastle Mirror,* October 22, 1824.

12. *Baltimore Gazette and Daily Advertiser,* July 3, 1828.

13. Philadelphia *Franklin Gazette,* June 6, 1820.

14. New Haven *Connecticut Herald,* July 13, 1824.

15. Washington, D.C., *Daily National Intelligencer,* September 13, 1824. For other toasts see *Baltimore Patriot,* July 13, 1826; *Richmond Enquirer,* July 10, 1835.

16. *Alexandria Gazette*, July 14, 1825.

17. Amherst, New Hampshire, *Hillsboro Telegraph*, March 18, 1820; Portland *Eastern Argus*, March 21, 1820.

18. Concord *New-Hampshire Patriot*, May 9, 1820.

19. *Baltimore Patriot*, July 21, 1824.

20. Brattleboro *Vermont Phoenix*, July 26, August 2, 9, 1839.

21. *Hartford Times*, May 15, 1838; *Ithaca Herald*, April 5, 1837; *Milwaukee Sentinel*, May 28, 1842.

22. *Litchfield Republican* [Connecticut], February 17, 1848.

23. Philadelphia *North American*, September 3, 1839.

24. Georgetown, D.C., *Federal Republican for the Country*, April 14, 1815.

25. Hartford *American Mercury*, February 28, 1815.

26. New York *Commercial Advertiser*, October 23, 1834.

27. *Boston Intelligencer*, September 5, 1818.

28. Portland *Eastern Argus*, July 11, 1828.

29. Philadelphia *Franklin Gazette*, October 20, 1819.

30. *Elyra Republican* [Ohio], February 19, 1835.

31. Philadelphia *National Gazette*, April 4, 1833.

32. Laurel Thatcher Ulrich, *The Age of Homespun: Objects and Stories in the Creation of an American Myth* (New York: Knopf, 2001), 391, 476, n. 42.

33. Concord *New Hampshire Observer*, February 9, 1824.

34. Philip M. Hamer, "Great Britain, the United States and the Negro Seamen Acts, 1822–1848, *Journal of Southern History*, 1 (1935), 3–28. See the petition and accompanying correspondence with Rufus Choate and Robert C. Winthrop in Jonathan Ingersoll Bowditch Papers II, 1842–43, Ms. S-468, Massachusetts Historical Society. See also W. Jeffrey Bolster, *Black Jacks: African American Seamen in the Age of Sail* (Cambridge, Mass.: Harvard University Press, 1997), 190–214.

35. New York *Emancipator*, December 1, 1842.

36. Ibid., March 9, 1843.

37. W. Jeffrey Bolster has compiled several tables indicating the percentage of black sailors in crews in different ports. In some ports, such as Philadelphia, the percentage of blacks in crews was nearly constant from the early 1800s to the 1840s. In other ports, like New York, the percentage was halved. Bolster, *Black Jacks*, 234–39. See also the discussion in ibid., 190–232; Paul A. Gilje, *Liberty on the Waterfront: American Maritime Culture in the Age of Revolution* (Philadelphia: University of Pennsylvania Press, 2004), 181–82, 208–11.

38. Keene *New Hampshire Sentinel*, August 24, 1842. The exact nature of these banners was controversial. See *New-York Spectator*, August 3, 1842; Washington, D.C., *Daily National Intelligencer*, August 3, 1842; Baltimore *Sun*, August 3, 1842; Boston *Daily Atlas*, August 4, 1842; *Philadelphia Inquirer*, August 5, 1842; Philadelphia *North American*, August 11, 1842; Boston *The Liberator*, August 12, 1844.

39. Rochester *North Star*, May 12, 1848.

40. Frederick Douglass, *Life and Times of Frederick Douglass...*, rev. ed. (Boston: DeWolfe, Fiske & Co., 1892), 246–47.
41. New Orleans *Picayune*, October 4, 1837.
42. *Richmond Enquirer*, January 12, 1847.
43. Ibid., June 1, 1847.
44. Middletown *The Constitution*, June 8, 1853.

# Index